Journal of Semitic Studies Supplement 32

THE EGYPTIAN HISTORIAN ʿABD AL-RAḤMĀN AL-JABARTĪ

HIS LIFE, WORKS, AUTOGRAPHS, MANUSCRIPTS AND THE HISTORICAL SOURCES OF *ʿAJĀʾIB AL-ĀTHĀR*

By

Shmuel Moreh

Published by Oxford University Press
on behalf of the University of Manchester
2014

OXFORD
UNIVERSITY PRESS
Great Clarendon Street, Oxford OX2 6DP

Oxford University Press is a department of the University of Oxford.
It furthers the University's objective of excellence in research, scholarship,
and education by publishing worldwide in
Oxford New York
Athens Auckland Bangkok Bogotá Buenos Aires Cape Town
Chennai Dar es Salaam Delhi Florence Hong Kong Istanbul Karachi
Kolkata Kuala Lumpur Madrid Melbourne Mexico City Mumbai Nairobi
Paris São Paulo Shanghai Singapore Taipei Tokyo Toronto Warsaw
with associated companies in Berlin Ibadan
Oxford is a registered trade mark of Oxford University Press
in the UK and in certain other countries
Published in the United Kingdom
by Oxford University Press, Oxford

First published 2014

A catalogue for this book is available from the British Library

Library of Congress Cataloguing in Publication Data
(Data available)

ISSN 0022-4480
ISBN 978-0-19-872224-3

Subscription information for the *Journal of Semitic Studies* is available at the journal website:
jss.oxfordjournals.org

Printed in Great Britain by Bell & Bain Ltd, Glasgow

In memory of my dear friend and mentor, the late

Professor David Ayalon (1914–1998), with gratitude.

Contents

List of Plates vi

Abbreviations vii

Scheme of Transliteration x

Preface xi

Chapter One: Al-Jabartī, His Life and Works 1

Chapter Two: A Survey of al-Jabartī's Autographs and Manuscripts and their Significance. Stemma of al-Jabartī's Manuscripts 55

Chapter Three: Al-Jabartī's Method of Composing his Chronicle *'Ajā'ib al-Āthār fi 'l-Tarājim wa 'l-Akhbār* 171

Chapter Four: The Egyptian Scholar Ḥasan al-ʿAṭṭār and his Contribution to al-Jabartī's Works 195

Chapter Five: The Islamic Moon-like Cycle of Civilization in Arabic Poetry; Arabic Poetics from the 18th Century to the Beginning of the 19th Century 223

Chapter Six: Theatrical Performances in Egypt According to *'Ajā'ib al-Āthār* 261

Chapter Seven: The Role of the *'Ulamā'* in Egypt in the Years 1688–1821 291

Conclusion 323

Appendix I 337

Appendix II 345

Bibliography 354

Index 367

Plates 385

List of Plates

Plate I. Map
Plate II. Mudda Leiden 1b-2a
Plate III. Mudda Leiden 26b
Plate IV. Mazhar Cambridge Title
Plate V. Mazhar Cambridge 1b-2a
Plate VI. Mazhar Cambridge colophon
Plate VII. Mazhar Rampur title la
Plate VIII. Mazhar Rampur title lb-2a
Plate IX. Mazhar Rampur title colophon
Plate X. ʿAja'ib Cambridge vol. I 1b-2a
Plate XI. ʿAja'ib Cambridge vol. I, 295b
Plate XII. ʿAja'ib Cambridge vol. II, 1b-2a
Plate XIII. ʿAja'ib Cambridge vol. II, 179a
Plate XIV. ʿAja'ib Cambridge vol. III, 1b-2a
Plate XV. ʿAja'ib Cambridge vol. III, 300b
Plate XVI. ʿAja'ib Selly Oak vol. IV, 1b-2a
Plate XVII. ʿAja'ib Selly Oak vol. IV, colophon
Plate XVIII. ʿAja'ib Cambridge vol. III, Magh, 1a
Plate XIX. ʿAja'ib Berlin vol. I , 1b-2a
Plate XX. ʿAja'ib Berlin vol. I, 299a
Plate XXI. ʿAja'ib Berlin vol. I, missing folios
Plate XXII. ʿAja'ib Berlin vol. IV, 1a
Plate XXIII. ʿAja'ib Berlin vol. IV, 1b-2a
Plate XXIV. ʿAja'ib Selly Oak vol. III, 1b-2a
Plate XXV. ʿAja'ib Selly Oak vol. III, colophon
Plate XXVI. ʿAja'ib Selly Oak vol. IV, 1b-2a
Plate XXVII. ʿAja'ib Selly Oak vol. IV, colophon
Plate XXVIII. ʿAja'ib Khuda Bakhsh vol. IV, 1a
Plate XXIX. ʿAja'ib Khuda Bakhsh vol. IV, 1b-2a
Plate XXX. ʿAja'ib Khuda Bakhsh vol. IV, 139b-140a
Plate XXXI. ʿAja'ib Khuda Bakhsh vol. IV, colophon

Abbreviations

Add. = addition

A.H. = Hijran era.

'Aj. = The new companion Arabic edition of ʿAbd al-Raḥmān al-Jabartī's *'Ajā'ib al-Āthār fi 'l-Tarājim wa 'l-Akhbār*, based upon the Cambridge autograph of al-Jabartī, edited by Shmuel Moreh and published by The Max Schloessinger Memorial Foundation, The Institute of Asian and African Studies, The Faculty of Humanities, The Hebrew University of Jerusalem.

'Aj. = *'Ajā'ib al-Āthār fi 'l-Tarājim wa 'l-Akhbār*, as the title of the book without referring to editions.

'Aj. Būlāq = Būlāq edition of *'Ajā'ib al-Āthār fi 'l-Tarājim wa 'l-Akhbār*, 1297 /1879–1880.

'Ajā'ib al-Āthār = *'Ajā'ib al-Āthār fi 'l-Tarājim wa 'l-Akhbār.*

Biographical Dictionary = Murtaḍā al-Zabīdī's *Mu'jam mukhtaṣṣ bi-dhikr man akhadhtu 'anhu al-'ulūm wa 'l-ma'ārif min shuyūkhī wa-ābā'ī.*

BM = British Library (former British Museum), London, England.

BN = Bibliothèque Nationale, Paris, France.

BSOAS = *Bulletin of the School of Oriental and African Studies*, SOAS, University of London.

Cambridge autograph = Volumes 1–3 autograph manuscripts of *'Ajā'ib al-Āthār* (MS *'Aj.* Cam., Qq. 169, 170, 171), composed in 1806 by ʿAbd al-Raḥmān al-Jabartī.

Cambridge group = Six manuscripts of *'Ajā'ib al-Āthār* (MS *'Aj.* Cam. 2nd., Qq. 166, 167, 168 and MS *'Aj.* Cam., Qq. 169, 170, 171), collated by ʿAbd al-Raḥmān al-Jabartī.

Cambridge MS = Six manuscripts of *'Ajā'ib al-Āthār* (MS *'Aj.* Cam. 2nd., Qq. 166, 167, 168 and MS *'Aj.* Cam., Qq. 169, 170, 171), collated by ʿAbd al-Raḥmān al-Jabartī.

CE = Christian era.

cf. = compare.

cm. = centimetres.

d. = died.

DKQ = Dār al-Kutub al-Qawmiyya, now called Dār al-Kutub wa'l-Wathā'iq al-Qawmiyya/The National Library and Archives of Egypt, Cairo, Egypt.

ed. = editor.

eds = editors.

EI = *Encyclopedia of Islam.*

enl. = enlarged

f. = folio; f. 1a = folio 1 recto, f. 1b = folio 1, verso, etc.

ff. = following pages, folios.

Fihris al-A'lam = A general index of proper names and books compiled by Jans Bakker.

fn. = footnote.

fols = folios.

GAL. = Carl Brockelmann, *Geschichte derarabischen Litteratur* (Leiden 1943–9).

GAL., Suppl. = Supplement to Carl Brockelmann, *Geschichte der arabischen Litteratur* (Leiden 1937–42).

The Great History of the People of the Twelfth Century = *al-Tārīkh al-Kabīr li-Ahl al-Qarn al-Thānī 'Ashar*, a lost work of Murtaḍā al-Zabīdī.

H. = Hijrī date.

History = *'Ajā'ib al-Āthār.*

in. = inch.

JSAI = *Jerusalem Studies in Arabic and Islam.*

l. = line.

ll. = lines.

loc. cit. = loco citato, reference to the same page in the work immediately preceding.

Maz. = *Maẓhar al-Taqdīs bi-Zawāl Dawlat al-Faransīs/Maẓhar al-Taqdīs bi-Dhahāb Dawlat al-Faransīs.*

Maẓhar al-Taqdīs = *Maẓhar al-Taqdīs bi-Zawāl Dawlat al-Faransīs.*

MIDEO = *Mélanges de l'Institut dominicain d'études orientales.*

mm. = millimetres.

MS = manuscript.

MS *'Aj.* Bankipore = *'Ajā'ib al-Āthār* manuscript in the Khuda Bakhsh Bankipore Oriental Public Library at Patna, India.

MS *'Aj.* Ber. = *'Ajā'ib al-Āthār* manuscript in the Staatsbibliothek, Berlin, Germany.

MS عجب [Berlin] = *'Ajā'ib al-Āthār* manuscript in the Staatsbibliothek, Berlin, Germany.

MS *'Aj.* Birmingham = *'Ajā'ib al-Āthār* manuscript in the Main Library, University of Birmingham, Birmingham, England.

MS *'Aj.* BM = *'Ajā'ib al-Āthār* manuscript in the British Library, London.

MS *'Aj.* BN = *'Ajā'ib al-Āthār* manuscript in the Bibliothèque Nationale, Paris.

MS *'Aj.* Cam. = Three manuscript volumes of *'Ajā'ib al-Āthār*, Qq. 169, 170, 171, in Cambridge University Library, Cambridge, England.

MS *'Aj.* Cam. 2nd. = Three manuscript volumes of *'Ajā'ib al-Āthār*, Qq. 166, 167, 168, in Cambridge University Library.

MS *'Aj.* DKQ. = *'Ajā'ib al-Āthār* manuscript in Dār al-Kutub al-Qawmiyya, Cairo.

MS *'Aj.* Tārīkh = *'Ajā'ib al-Āthār* manuscripts in Dār al-Kutub al-Qawmiyya, Cairo.

MS *'Aj.* Iraq = *'Ajā'ib al-Āthār* manuscript in the Iraq Museum, Baghdad.

MS *'Aj.* Leeds = *'Ajā'ib al-Āthār* manuscript in the University Library, University of Leeds, Leeds, England.

MS *'Aj.* Len. = *'Ajā'ib al-Āthār* manuscript in the Institute of Oriental Studies, St Petersburg (Leningrad), Russia.

MS *'Aj.* MA = *'Ajā'ib al-Āthār* manuscripts in al-Maktaba al-Azhariyya, Cairo.

MS *'Aj.* Manchester = *'Ajā'ib al-Āthār* manuscript in the John Rylands University Library, University of Manchester.

MS *'Aj.* ML = *'Ajā'ib al-Āthār* manuscript in the Bayerische Staatsbibliothek, Munich, Germany

MS*Maz.* Bay. = MS Cevdet Pāshā 76 of *Maẓhar al-Taqdīs bi-Zawāl Dawlat al-Faransīs* in the *Defter-i Kutubkhāne-i Weli el-Dīn*, Istanbul, 1304/1886–7, 280, now in the Bayezid Library, Istanbul.

MS*Maz.* Cam. = Manuscript of *Maẓhar al-Taqdīs bi-Zawāl Dawlat al-Faransīs* in Cambridge University Library, 1058 (Qq 214).

MS*Maz.* DKQ. = Tārīkh M 101/microfilm 29362 of *Maẓhar al-Taqdīs bi-Zawāl Dawlat al-Faransīs* in Dār al-Kutub al-Qawmiyya, Cairo.

MS*Maz.* Ram. = *Maẓhar al-Taqdīs* manuscript in the Khuda Bakhsh Library, Rampur, India.

MS *Mudda* = *Mudda*

MS Princeton = Manuscript of *Mu'jam Mukhtaṣṣ*, 126–7 in Princeton University Library, Princeton, USA.

MSS = manuscripts.

Mudda = MS *Mudda* = *Hādhā Tārīkh Dukhūl Muddat al-Faransīs bi-Miṣr*; this MS is kept at the Leiden University Library, Netherlands.

Mu'jam Mukhtaṣṣ = Murtaḍā al-Zabīdī's *Mu'jam mukhtaṣṣ bi-dhikr man akhadhtu 'anhu al-'ulūm wa 'l-ma'ārif min shuyūkhī wa-ābā'ī.*

n. = note.

no. = number.

nos. = numbers.

p. = page.

pp. = pages.

Pt. = part.

StaBi = Staatsbibliothek, Berlin.

Tāj al-'Arūs = Murtaḍā al-Zabīdī's lexicon *Tāj al-'Arūs min Jawāhir al-Qāmūs.*

UCLA = University of California, Los Angeles.

vol.= volume.

vols = volumes.

Scheme of Transliteration

ṭ	ط	a/'a, 'u, 'i	أ , ؤ , ئـ
ẓ	ظ	'	أ
'	ع	ā	ى or آ ، ـا
gh	غ	b	ب
f	ف	t	ت
q	ق	th	ث
k	ك	t	In construct ـة
l	ل	j	ج
m	م	ḥ	ح
n	ن	kh	خ
h	هـ	d	د
-	long وُ	dh	ذ
aw	in diphthong وَ	r	ر
ī	long يِ	z	ز
ay	in diphthong يَ	s	س
u	ـُ	sh	ش
a	ـَ	·	ص
i	ـِ	ḍ	ض

Notes:

1. The definite article *al-* is used before solar and lunar letters.
2. ـة at the end of words and names is not transliterated, e.g. مدينة (*madīna*).
3. A *shadda* is represented by doubling the relevant letter.
4. Arabic words or letters transcribed into Latin characters are shown in italics.

Preface

Encouraged by what my mentor and colleague the late Professor David Ayalon (1914–98) wrote in his foreword to my edition of al-Jabartī's *Chronicle of the First Seven Months of the French Occupation*,[1] I undertook the task of editing the same author's imposing *'Ajā'ib al-Āthār fī 'l-Tarājim wa 'l-Akhbār*[2] (The Marvellous Compositions of Biographies and Chronicles) (henceforth *'Aj.*) with his guidance and support. This work presents the main chronicles and biographical sources dealing with the history of Egypt between 1688 and 1821, edited and re-written in a clear style by ʿAbd al-Raḥmān al-Jabartī. The later part of this chronicle, written and compiled by our author, constitutes the main historical source and biographies for the years 1777–1821. They are written from the point of view of someone who was aware of the drastic changes in Islamic culture and the world order in his days. Ayalon's pioneering study 'The Historian al-Jabartī and his Background', first published in *BSOAS* (1960), is now reprinted as an English preface to volume one of our Arabic edition of *'Ajā'ib al-Āthār fī 'l-Tarājim wa 'l-Akhbār* published by The Max Schloessinger Memorial Foundation, The Institute of Asian and African Studies, The Faculty of Humanities, The Hebrew University of Jerusalem. This article is the first comprehensive, and still the most frequently cited, biography to date. In it, Ayalon emphasizes the need for a critical edition of this work, based upon its manuscripts: 'A thorough check and comparison of the numerous copies of *'Ajā'ib al-Āthār*, scattered all over the world, will undoubtedly yield important results'.[3] This introductory volume is based upon the result of our research undertaken to compile the new Arabic edition published separately, using all of our author's manuscripts of his historical

1 *'Abd al-Raḥmān al-Jabartī, al-Jabartī's Chronicle of the First Seven Months of the French Occupation of Egypt, Muḥarram-Rajab 1213/15 June-December, 1798, Tārīkh Muddat al-Faransīs bi-Miṣr*, S. Moreh ed. and trans. (Leiden 1975).

2 ʿAbd al-Raḥmān al-Jabartī, *'Ajā'ib al-Āthār fī 'l-Tarājim wa 'l-Akhbār*, The Institute of Asian and African Studies, The Max Schloessinger Memorial Foundation, The Faculty of Humanities, The Hebrew University of Jerusalem, 2013. On the different orientations of al-Jabartī in writing these chronicles, see Dr Lars Bjørneboe in his pioneering research, entitled *In Search of the True Political Position of the 'Ulama: An Analysis of the Aims and Perspectives of the Chronicles of Abd al-Rahman al-Jabarti (1753–1825)* (Aarhus 2007).

3 See David Ayalon, 'The Historian al-Jabartī and his Background', *BSOAS* 23:2 (1960), 229, n. 3.

works that we were able to examine. To allow readers to see for themselves the additions and deletions of both the author and the copyists, mainly in that of the Būlāq edition of 1297/1879–80, we used a new method of collation developed jointly by the two of us. We based the main text on the author's autographs of the first three volumes kept at the Cambridge University Library (henceforth MS *'Aj.*, Cam.) and on the fourth volume kept at the Berlin Staatbibliothek, copied from al-Jabartī's lost autograph. These were then collated with manuscripts copied by copyists on the author's orders and later revised by him, as well as with manuscripts copied by various copyists and with the Būlāq edition of 1297/1879–80. We give the volume number and page numbers of the Būlāq edition and the folio numbers of the important manuscripts collated with the Cambridge autographs and the Berlin MS.

During both the Baḥriyya (1250–1382), and Burjiyya (1382–1517) Mamluk rule in Egypt, local historians close to the rulers produced an abundance of rich and well-documented chronicles in literary Arabic (such as al-ʿAynī [1360–1451], al-Maqrīzī [1364–1441], Ibn Taghrī Birdī [1411–69], Ibn Iyās [1448–1524]) and others, and in semi-literary Arabic (as, for example, the senior official Ibn Zunbul al-Rammāl [d. 1572]), supported by the Mamluk sultans. In contrast, many chronicles written during the Ottoman rule were of rather inferior quality. *'Ulamā'* such as Yūsuf al-Malwānī, al-Qīnālī, and Aḥmad Shalabī Ibn ʿAbd al-Ghanī (d. 1737) wrote their chronicles in semi-literary Arabic with no universal historical, religious, cultural, and literary outlook. On the other hand, soldiers such as al-Damurdāshī (d. after 1755) and other writers with superficial historical insight wrote chronicles in colloquial Arabic, relating in brief the conflicts of the rival factions of the corrupt Mamluk society.

The latter wrote their chronicles for their fellow soldiers, for information and entertainment. They used the narrative method of colloquial storytelling, and described the sequence of events with no attempt to analyse or to understand their political, economical, psychological, cultural, religious, social, and other causes and implications. Blind chance and predestination were the only causes, which they seemed to understand. Until quite recently, this type of chronicle received little attention from Arab scholars and orientalists. Modern Arab scholars have looked with disdain at any text written in colloquial Arabic, imperfectly understood even by Egyptian scholars. Few orientalists have been willing to undertake the difficult task of deciphering such difficult manuscripts with the help of outstanding Arab scholars.

ʿAbd al-Raḥmān al-Jabartī (1753–1825) was a historian, best known for his three accounts of the history of Egypt. The first two are short, *Tārīkh Muddat al-Faransīs bi-Miṣr* (hereafter *Mudda*) (Muḥarram-Rajab 1213/15 June–December 1798), dealing with the first seven months of the French occupation by Napoleon and *Maẓhar al-Taqdīs bi-Zawāl Dawlat al-Faransīs* (hereafter *Maẓ.*), dealing with the French occupation of Egypt (1798–1801). After recording the events of the year 1805–6, our author wrote a comprehensive Egyptian history (1688–1806) entitled *'Ajā'ib al-Āthār fi 'l-Tarājim wa 'l-Akhbār* in three volumes. He went on to write a fourth volume till 1821 and edited copies of his first three volumes, until his eyesight failed in 1821. The last copy that he edited copied by Aḥmad Ḥasan al-Rashīdī al-Shāfiʿī known as Ṣawbaʿ and read in his presence in 1240/1824–5 is MS *'Ajā'ib*, Dār al-Kutub al-Qawmiyya, Cairo, al-Zakiyya, 859/microfilm 54236 (positive) and microfilm 17952 (negative) (VII 32. c. in Chapter Two)(hereafter, MS *'Aj.*, DKQ) kept at the National Library (Dār al-Kutub al-Qawmiyya) (hereafter, DKQ) in Cairo.[4]

Al-Jabartī's magnum opus, *'Ajā'ib al-Āthār fi 'l-Tarājim wa 'l-Akhbār* may be regarded as the swan song of medieval Arab-Muslim history and culture, witnessed and recorded by a talented historian possessing unusual insight, a devoted Khalwatī *Ṣūfī* with strong orientation towards *ḥadith* studies and the *sunna*. In this capacity, he symbolizes the endeavours of both the religious scholars and the *Ṣūfī* orders to revive the glorious past of Islam to challenge European imperialism. He was aware of being the last eyewitness of what he considered as the decline of medieval Islamic civilization and military might. He perceived that the causes of this decline were Ottoman tyranny and corruption and the Mamluks, or rather Egypt's officers, beys and soldiers with their cruelty, greed, factional conflicts and lack of leadership. According to our author, the elements of decline were the deterioration of the status of the *'ulamā'*, whom he accused of shirking their duty as guardians of the *sharī'a*, as advisers to rulers and as mediators between rulers and subjects for the welfare of the Muslim community. To all these he adds their greed and servility to the

4 The full title of the library is Dār al-Kutub wa'l-Wathā'iq al-Qawmiyya/ The National Library and Archives of Egypt.

ruling class, and Muḥammad ʿAlī's oppressive reforms, which abolished the old feudal and *waqf* systems,[5] introduced the employment of indigenous Christans and Jews and European non-Muslims, and replaced the *'ulamā'* with secular administrators and officials some of whom had received their education in France.

As a historian al-Jabartī is known for his accounts of the French occupation of Egypt from 1798 and 1801, and especially for his third and main work, a comprehensive history of Egypt in the years 1688 to 1806 (and his fourth volume, in which he continues on until 1821). His reaction to the French presence, science and philosophy is revealing and very likely stirred in him a quest for knowledge. Because of the great importance of this last chronicle it was published in several editions, the latest of which was edited by ʿAbd al-ʿAzīz Jamāl al-Dīn (Cairo 1997), followed by the edition of ʿAbd al-Raḥīm ʿAbd al-RaḥmānʿAbd al-Raḥīm (Cairo 1998), based upon the Būlāq edition only.[6]

The first edition mentioned above (ʿAbd al-ʿAzīz Jamāl al-Dīn's) is based on a manuscript kept at the University of Cairo, which does not mention the name of the copyist or the date of the copy's completion, and does not seem to be an autograph. ʿAbd al-ʿAzīz Jamāl al-Dīn thought that there was no autograph of *'Ajā'ib al-Āthār* extant in any public library in the world. However, we were able to gain access to the microfilm of the autograph of *'Ajā'ib al-Āthār* at Cambridge University Library. We were also able to acquire the microfilms of other *'Ajā'ib al-Āthār* MSS kept there, as well as those at the Bibliothèque Nationale in Paris, Leeds University Library, Birmingham University Library and Bankipore Library, and undertook the task of collating them with the manuscripts kept at the British Museum, at the National Library of Cairo as well as with all the printed editions. Besides the

5 On the economic crisis of the *waqfs* which supported the *madrasa* system, see A. Ben-Zaken, 'Political Economy and Scientific Activity in the Ottoman Empire', in Hasan Celâl Güzel, Cem Oğuz, and Osman Karatay (eds), *The Turks, vol. 3 (The Ottomans)* (Ankara 2002), 776–94.

6 ʿAbd al-ʿAẓīm Ramaḍān, Chairman of the Scientific Committee of this edition, justified this reprinting of the Būlāq edition by ʿAbd al-Raḥīm, on Moreh's statement that this edition contains more details than the MSS of *'Ajā'ib al-Āthār* at Cambridge, the Bibliothèque Nationale and the British Library. See ʿAbd al-Raḥmān al-Jabartī, *Maẓhar al-Taqdīs*, ʿAbd al-Raḥīm ʿAbd al-Raḥmān ʿAbd al-Raḥīm (ed.)(Cairo 1998), z (=7).

Cambridge autographs, we were able to identify three copies of the first three volumes of *'Ajā'ib al-Āthār*, which have title pages and colophons, and the last lines at the end of the three volumes, written in al-Jabartī's handwriting with no colophon, and the text of which was edited and corrected in the margin by himself. These manuscripts are kept at the Cambridge University Library, the Bibliothèque Nationale in Paris, and the National Library in Cairo (see Chapter Two of this book). The second manuscript of *'Ajā'ib al-Āthār* in the Cambridge University Library is in *Maghribī* handwriting and was edited by al-Jabartī; on its margin are comments by Ḥasan al-ʿAṭṭār (1166–1250 [/1766–1835]), al-Jabartī's friend, who added many corrections and remarks concerning the historical events and the biographies in the MS, as well as notes on his journeys throughout the Ottoman Empire.

In order to verify the contents of the various versions of the chronicle we also compared al-Jabartī's work with that of earlier historians such as al-Isḥāqī, al-Damurdāshī, Aḥmad Shalabī Ibn ʿAbd al-Ghanī, al-Qīnālī, and also with other historical material and related manuscripts. Al-Jabartī's biographies were compared with those of al-Murādī, and consequently different versions of both the data and the biographies are given in the margin of the Arabic text. However important the publication of al-Damurdāshī's and Ibn ʿAbd al-Ghanī's *Chronicles* may be, it is obvious that these in no way affect the considerable value of al-Jabartī's data dealing with the years 1100–50/1688–1738, even if one limits oneself to the military and political conflicts and intrigues between the Ottoman authorities and the Mamluk factions in Egypt. Certainly one cannot ignore the fact that volumes I–II contain valuable biographical information, long quotations of poetry and prose, documents, historical data from oral and written sources and from interviews with old people, as well as religious and cultural information on Egyptian society of the time.[7]

Al-Jabartī's great merit is that he copied, and in some cases rewrote, his information from existing historical and biographical works, giving those Islamic values philosophical, social and historical significance. He quotes discussions and debates which he heard from the learned and members of the

7 See ʿAbd al-Ḥayy b. ʿAbd al-Kabīr al-Kattānī, *Fihris al-Fahāris wa 'l-Athbāt wa-Mu'jam al-Ma'ājim wa 'l-Mashyahāt wa 'l-Musalsalāt*, Iḥsān ʿAbbās (ed.), (Beirut 1402/1982), in which he discusses al-Jabartī's studies with Aḥmad al-Dūqāṭī al-Ṭahṭāwī, and also his studies on *fiqh* with Ḥasan al-Jabartī, through works such as *Matn Nūr al-Īḍāḥ* (*'Aj.*, IV, 260).

ruling classes, and adds the negative aspects of events and personalities that others were careful not to mention. He used sources which were written in colloquial Arabic and provides information and criticism lacking in works written in canonical Arabic such as *al-Mu'jam al-Mukhtaṣṣ* by Murtaḍā al-Zabīdī (1145–1205 [/1732–91]), who quoted scholars praising his *Tāj al-'Arūs min Sharḥ Jawāhir al-Qāmūs*[8] and his commentary on al-Ghazālī's *Iḥyā' 'Ulūm al-Dīn*. Many of these works were either unknown or only recently discovered. Al-Jabartī integrated this material into his own work, written in a style which the present day reader can still comprehend, and arranged them in chronological order. The biographies which he himself wrote are original and insightful. He judges the *'ulamā'* as well as the rulers according to the sublime principles of justice, piety, mercy, and integrity, as they are given in the Qur'ān and the *sunna*. He also gives his own personal opinions and adds sarcastic remarks on the events he records, interpreting them from the point of view of a pious Muslim who regards history as predestination determined by Allāh, according to the principle of reward and punishment. Although some information was copied from other historical works, one cannot overlook the originality and the wealth of details in al-Jabartī's descriptions. In fact, for a long time his book was the only reliable historical, political, religious, cultural, literary and economic source for the period in question available to scholars, and although some of his sources have recently been published in scholarly editions, others are lost and it is doubtful whether they will ever be found. If the only merits of al-Jabartī were that he saved these lost sources from oblivion, it would by itself be enough to make his work a valuable historical and literary source.

Three objections might be raised against the publication of a new Arabic edition of *'Ajā'ib al-Āthār*: one possible objection is that this book has already been so widely used that the planned edition is not going to have a great impact in the field; secondly, there already exist printed editions with historical remarks and explanations, especially those of ʿAbd al-ʿAzīz Jamāl al-Dīn and ʿAbd al-Raḥīm, and there may thus be no need for another edition; and thirdly, a good English translation has recently been published by T. Philipp and M.

8 On al-Zabīdī and his works, see Stefan Reichmuth, *The World of Murtada al-Zabidi (1732–91). Life, Networks and Writing* (Exeter 2009) and 'Notes on Murtaḍā al-Zabīdī's *Mu'jam* as a Source for al-Jabartī's History', *Jerusalem Studies in Arabic and Islam*, 25 (2001), 374–83 (hereafter *JSAI*).

Perlmann (1994).[9] Such criticism which has been or may still be made ignores the fact that these editions both ignored al-Jabartī's autographs and do not provide a critical edition of the Arabic text as do the footnotes of our new edition.

None of the printed editions so far has been based on al-Jabartī's autographs, or on copies edited by him. We made an effort to reconstruct al-Jabartī's text by correcting copyists' misreadings, lacunae and other distortions of the original text, that have come down to us in many different manuscripts with a great number of variant readings. This issue was discussed by the present author in a review article published in *Die Welt des Islams* 37:2 (1997), where by means of a comparison of the Būlāq edition with al-Jabartī's autograph it was demonstrated that 'no translation, even if it is precise and elaborate, can be considered as a substitute to the original Arabic work'.[10]

For the present Arabic edition which is published separately from this English introductory volumeby The Max Schloessinger Memorial Foundation, a thorough comparison was made of the entire text as found in the most important manuscripts and in the printed editions. This enabled us to demonstrate that it took many years to compose his chronicle, and that he wrote it in several stages. After a thorough examination of the remarks which he made in the margins of the Cambridge autographs, it became clear that he composed his chronicle by continuously adding new information and new material which he found over the course of time.[11] As for the importance of comparing the various manuscripts and the consequent publication of a critical text edition, it is vital not to lose sight of the fact that the majority of Arabic readers do not need an English translation to study this work, but still deserve to have access to a sound, scholarly and critical edition of this important chronicle which provides such a wealth of information on a diversity of

9 The English translations from al-Jabartī's Arabic text quoted hereare based upon 'Abd al-Raḥmān al-Jabartī, *'Abd al-Raḥmān al-Jabartī's History of Egypt*, Thomas Philipp and Moshe Perlmann (eds) (Stuttgart 1994), except when otherwise stated with my initials, S.M. Suggestions for the translation of some terms and words are given after the Arabic transliteration in brackets.

10 See the review of Shmuel Moreh of the English translation, ''Abd ar-Raḥmān al-Gabartī: *'Abd al-Raḥmān al-Jabartī's History of Egypt,'Ajā'ib al-Āthār fī 'l-Tarājim wa 'l-Akhbār.* (Stuttgart 1994). Edited by Thomas Philipp and Moshe Perlmann, vols I…IV, with *A Guide to 'Abd al-Raḥmān al-Jabartī's History of Egypt: 'Ajā'ib al-Āthār fī 'l-Tarājim wa 'l-Akhbār*, by Thomas Philipp and Guido Schwald…', in *Die Welt des Islams* 37:2 (1997), 235–42.

11 See Lars Bjørneboe's work in note 2 above and Chapter One, notes 2 and 10 below.

subjects, not just on the political and military aspects of Egyptian history. This is because al-Jabartī's interests were not limited to Mamluk *amīr*s and Ottoman rulers, but covered all aspects of life, including religious, social, economic, financial, and cultural issues, literature, poetry, the status of women, morals and Muslim customs, *Ṣūfī* sects and popular practices such as the worship of saints, the urban, agrarian and Bedouin populace, Azhari students and scholars and other religious functionaries, the various religious and secular sciences in Egypt, Muslim and non-Muslim festivals, the merchant classes, markets, financial and numismatic matters, educational institutions, guilds, religious minorities such as Syrians, Copts, Greeks and other European minorities and their customs, slave markets, as well as disasters such as storms, floods, locusts, famine and plague, popular medicine, the weather, astronomical and astrological phenomena, the flooding of the Nile. All these topics are discussed from the point of view of an Azhari scholar, well versed in both religious and secular Islamic sciences and a member of the Khalwatī order, who not only belonged to the Egyptian elite but also had good relations with people from many backgrounds, including rulers, merchants and commoners.

The project of editing the first three volumes of *'Ajā'ib al-Āthār* began in 1991 and lasted until 1995. It was made possible by a grant of the Israel Science Foundation (ISF), run by the Israeli Academy for Science and Humanities, and preceded under the guidance of an Editorial Committee headed by Professor D. Ayalon and S. Moreh. Other members of the committee were Professor Irene Bierman (UCLA), Professor P. Lyons (Cambridge), Professor Svetlana Kirillina (Moscow), Professor Fu'ād Ayman Sayyid (former Executive Director of the National Library, Cairo, and of Ein Shams University), Dr Philip Sadgrove and Professor Rex Smith (Manchester), Professor Stephan Wild (Bonn), and Professor M. Winter (Tel-Aviv). After a break the project was continued in 1997 by a grant from the Deutscher Akademischer Austauschdienst e.V (DAAD), and in 1998, through the generous grant of The German Israeli Foundation (GIF), with Professor S. Wild (Bonn) as supervisor for the general index in Arabic of proper names and books, compiled by Mr. Jans Bakker of the Orientalisches Seminar at Bonn University and finally by a grant from the the Israel Science Foundation (ISF).

Unfortunately, my colleague and friend Professor David Ayalon passed away before the completion of this edition, on June 2 1998. Until the end of his life he continued to follow the process of the preparation of the Arabic edition with great interest and advised me on many editorial problems. I would like to take this opportunity to thank Professor David Ayalon for the devotion andinterest he took in the project and for kindly having agreed to republish his important study 'The Historian al-Jabartī' and his Background', which originally appeared in *BSOAS* 23:2 (1960), and is reprinted in the Preface of volume one of our Arabic edition of *'Ajā'ib al-Āthār*. Moreover, I am grateful for his cooperation and help as consultant-editor to the Arabic text of all the four volumes of *'Ajā'ib al-Āthār* and for his continuous advice and encouragement. I would also like to thank my friend Professor Dr Stefan Wild of Bonn University who joined this project in 1998 and supervised the general index of Proper Names (*Fihris al-A'lām*) and Books in al-Jabartī's four volumes of *'Ajā'ib al-Āthār* compiled by Mr Jans Bakker. Thanks are due to Dr Philip Sadgrove of the Department of Middle Eastern Studies, The University of Manchester, who has accompanied this project since 1992; to Philipp Thomas for giving permission to consult his excellent translation and his *Guide* compiled with Dr Guido Schwald and to Professor Ralph Elgar of Munich University for allowing me to use his manuscript copy of Ibn Shamma's work *Muntahā al-'Ibārāt*. I am indebted also to the member of our Board of Editors, Professor Fu'ād Ayman Sayyid formerly of the National Library of Cairo for his kind and sincere help, assistance and advice during my work in the Microfilm Section of Dār al-Kutub al-Qawmiyya in Cairo, to the section staff, as well as to the writer Mr Anīs Manṣūr whose recommendation made my visits to this important Library more pleasant. I would like to offer my special thanks to Professor Dr Gudrun Krämer of Freie Universität Berlin, to Professor Irene A. Bierman and the staff of the Gustav E. von Grunebaum Center for NES, UCLA, to Professor S. Wild, Dr Jans Bakar (Bonn University) and Dr Philip Sadgrove and their staff who were always helpful, generous and hospitable during my several working visits to their universities, to Professor Jane Hathaway (Ohio University) and Professor Stefan Reichmuth (Bochum University) for reading some parts of this book. Without their valuable help this work would not have been completed in its present form.

Our thanks are also due to all the Directors of the Libraries who supplied us with microfilms and photos of their manuscripts, especially to the directors and staff of the following libraries: British Library, London; Bibliothèque Nationale, Paris; Birmingham University Library, Selly Oak College's

Library; Cambridge University Library, especially the Syndics of the Library who permitted me to use their al-Jabartī autograph for my Arabic edition; the Chester Beatty Library, Ireland; the John Rylands University Library, University of Manchester; Leeds University Library; Leiden University Library; the Staatsbibliothek zu Berlin that permitted me to use the fourth volume of their manuscript for my new edition; the K. Hof- und Staatsbibliothek, Munich; the National Library of Cairo; the Iraq Museum Library in Baghdad; Dr Md. Atiqur Rahman, of the Khuda Bakhsh Oriental Public Library in Patna, Bankipore, India; the Library of Congress, Washington; UCLA Library, as well as the Hebrew University National Library and the Faculty of Humanities at the Hebrew University for supporting this important project. Finally, a word of sincere thanks to the team which helped to carry out this work with diligence and kindness: to Mrs Lucille Cohen, Manchester, to Dr Clara Brakel from Leiden University, who helped in the project in 1998, to Ms Shireen Twaiti who undertook the hard task of word processing and revising the work of former typists and for her devoted work on the various Indices, to Dr Fu'ād Kanʿānī for his help in the Literary Index and proofreading, to Dr Julia Rovanovitch and to Dr Olga Bramson for helping Mrs B. Nammar' in collating the manuscripts with the Būlāq edition, and to Mr Jans Bakker for his devoted work on the Index and all the students who have helped me over the years. The considerable task of the final editing of this study for publication was carried out by my good friend, Philip Sadgrove, with the help of Andrew Patrick.

I would like to end this preface with a word of thanks for the generous grants of The German Academic Exchange Service (DAAD); The Israel Science Foundation (ISF), run by the Israeli Academy for Science and Humanities; the German Israeli Foundation (GIF) and the support of my late friends Mr Saleh R. Masri (New York) and Mr George Elias (Manchester), without whom this project could not have been carried out.

Shmuel Moreh

The Hebrew University, Jerusalem
September, 2011

Chapter One

Al-Jabartī: His Life and Work[1]

Unlike many other historians, we know very little about the details of the life of ʿAbd al-Raḥmān al-Jabartī (1167–1240/1753–1825)[2]; we are in the dark about even the crucial events of his life. Although he copied and wrote hundreds of detailed biographies of others, not one of his contemporaries, not even the copyists of his works including those who were employed by his own son Maḥfūẓ, took the trouble of doing the same for him; they did not even mention the date of his death. This is quite surprising, in the light of the admiration enjoyed later on by his monumental history of Egypt. He was aware that writing history in his time was discarded, overlooked, abandoned and neglected 'considering it the work of idle men, calling it the legends of lore'.[3] In what follows we shall attempt to trace his intellectual biography from the few hints which he left in his historical writings.

There are few Muslim historians who wrote their works based on a well-defined theory of history. One outstanding exception is ʿAbd al-Raḥmān Ibn Khaldūn (1332–1406), a true giant of Muslim historiography, who wrote his *Muqaddima* long after the death of the theologian and philosopher Ibn Rushd (Averroes, 1126–98), when Greek logic and philosophy had gone into a rapid decline and ceased to have any real influence in the Muslim world. Averroes asserted that reason is compatible with Islam, and that training in mysticism could help in the attainment of rational knowledge, but that it could not replace it. Using such a logical approach, Ibn Khaldūn was able to develop his social

1 My thanks are due to Professor Stefan Reichmuth of Bochum University, Germany and to Professor Jane Hathaway, for reading this chapter and for their valuable comments and references.

2 On ʿAbd al-Raḥmān al-Jabartī, see Ayalon, 'The Historian', 222; S. Moreh, *al-Jabartī's Chronicle of the First Seven Months of the French Occupation of Egypt, Muḥarram-Rajab 1213/15 June–December, 1798* (Leiden 1975); see Dr Lars Bjørneboe in his pioneering study *In Search of the True Political Position of the 'Ulama, An Analysis of the Aims and Perspectives of the Chronicles of Abd al-Rahman al-Jabarti (1753–1825)* (Aarhus 2007). See also M.W. Daly (ed.), *The Cambridge History of Egypt. Vol. 2, Modern Egypt, from 1517 to the End of the Twentieth Century* (Cambridge 1998).

3 See *'Aj.*, I, 5. Al-Zabīdī confirmed that some *'ulamā'*, who became interested in secular sciences lost the respect of the authorities and the common people.

theory of the dynamics of history and civilization. He defended his rational approach against the fantasy and exaggerations of medieval Muslim historians, and wrote a study of the human past, social, economic and cultural aspects and the reasons for the decline of civilizations.

On the other hand, ʿAbd al-Raḥmān al-Jabartī lived in times when al-Ghazālī's mystical dogma was in vogue. Sufism was also very important to al-Jabartī, especially the *Khalwatiyya*,[4] based upon the Qur'ān and the *sunna*, and he paid great attention to esoteric sciences and practices. In his time, Sufism dominated Muslim life in the Ottoman Empire and there was a general belief in the ability of the human soul to perform miracles and achieve eternal happiness. Al-Jabartī therefore placed divine revelation and spiritual *Ṣūfī* sensitivity above reason. This made him critical of the Wahhābīs in spite of his sympathy for their strict observance of Islamic principles (*arkān*) and their zeal, which was such that a woman leader among them was able to defeat the Ottomans in defending her city.[5] He was a historian of the Muslim East (*Mashriq*) who wrote his work with a defined worldview and a value system based upon Islamic religious concepts of predestination and God's determination of the path of world history. This worldview was based upon the concept that God revealed His divine laws to a series of prophets whose mission was finally achieved and accomplished by his last messenger Muḥammad, through the revelation of the Qur'ān, a blueprint for maintaining justice and equality in this world and the afterlife. In Islam, God's judgment was accomplished through a hierarchical system (consisting of God, the prophets, saints, rulers, *'ulamā'*, and the common people) and a policy of rewards and punishments (*thawāb wa-'iqāb*). Because of the corrupt and tyrannical rulers of his time, al-Jabartī placed the *'ulamā'* above the rulers, because the latter are entrusted to keep the divine laws and to serve as advisers to the rulers. Thus the *'ulamā'* became the *ūlū al-amr* (leaders [of the Muslim community]) (see Qur'ān 4:59), who were to be obeyed above everyone except God and His Prophet.

---

4 On the Khalwatī *Ṣūfī* order, also known as Qarabāshliyya, which follows the Qur'ān and the *sunna*, see *'Aj.*, I, 289–304. Their Shaykh, Muḥammad b. Sālim al-Hifnāwī or al-Ḥifnī (1689–1767), was a scholar of *fiqh* (jurisprudence), *manṭiq* (logic), *uṣūl* (foundations of law), *ḥadīth* (traditions), and *kalām* (dogmatic theology), as well as of al-Ghazālī's *Iḥyā'* (see *'Aj.*, I, 289). See also F. de Jong, 'Khalwatiyya', *EI*², IV, 991–3, and Ernst Bannerth, 'La Khalwatiyya en Egypte', *MIDEO* 8 (1964–6), 1–74.

5 See *'Aj.*, IV, 206, about the rebel Wahhābī woman called Ghāliyā.

The history of Egypt was al-Jabartī's main concern. He lived in a period which he, along with his friend Ḥasan al-ʿAṭṭār and other Arab scholars, considered one of the low points of Arab and Islamic culture. They argued so, in spite of the rich chronicles it possessed and the rise of the Riḍwān Katkhudā's literary circle of poets and writers of *maqāmāt*, in which they criticized popular Sufism, social vices and hypocrisy in society, in both canonical and colloquial Arabic, and which dominated both historical and literary writing. Al-Jabartī's *Chronicle* reflects the collective consciousness of the *'ulamā'* in Egypt and their ambivalent attitude towards the Ottomans, the Mamluk *amīr*s, the French invaders, the Albanian mercenary ruler Muḥammad ʿAlī and the non-Muslim minorities. Al-Jabartī may be said to represent the historical memory of intellectual Egyptians and others in the Arabic-speaking world during the eighteenth and the first two decades of the nineteenth century. In writing his chronicle he made use of his knowledge of Islamic traditional (*naqliyya*) and intellectual (*'aqliyya*) sciences, mainly astronomy, astrology and the Islamic calendar (*taqwīm*), as well as of the available chronicles and biographies of his time. The fate of the Muslim people, their religion and science, as well as the *'ulamā'*, were the main concerns reflected in his historical writings.

Al-Jabartī was one of the last great Muslim scholars and historians able to echo in a traditional method of history writing the swan song of conventional Muslim traditional culture, administration, and military lore, and the social worldview of his time and society. Unlike al-Zabīdī who admired the Ottomans and was 'convinced that their rule will last even beyond the coming of the Mahdī',[6] his student considered it as tyrannical rule and the French occupation as 'successive sufferings and turning times', since 'Thy Lord would never destroy the cities unjustly'.[7] Al-Jabartī expressed nostalgia for the lost cultural and moral heights, which he had witnessed among the generation of his father and his mentors. His chronicle attests to a certain dynamic within Muslim culture, which was limited to few eminent scholars such as Ḥasan al-ʿAṭṭār, al-Zabīdī, al-Murādī, and a period of considerable wealth and cultural efflorescence, which both he and al-ʿAṭṭār considered as a period of stagnation compared to the glorious past of the golden age of the ʿAbbasid period. His

6 See S. Reichmuth, *The World of Murtaḍā al-Zabīdī (1732–91), Life, Networks and Writings*, The Gibb Memorial Trust, 2009, Chapter 3, and *'Aj.*, IV, 47.

7 *'Aj.*, I, 2, quoting Qur'ān, 11:117.

incredible precision and his art of critical biography (for example, the biographies of Shaykh Abu 'l-Anwār ibn Wafā, Shaykh al-Sādāt and al-Zabīdī), represent a step beyond mere traditional writing. Most probably, this was due to his strong ties with European travellers whom he met before E.W. Lane's visit to Cairo during 1825–6, such as Burckhardt, Belzoni and some of the French scholars during the French occupation.[8]

Al-Jabartī's writing provides insights into a Muslim historical memory and the collective consciousness of a pious Muslim with an Azhari education and the status of the *'ulamā'* of his time. In this capacity, he might be the first Arab-Muslim historian in the Ottoman period to have revived the connection between Islamic historiography writing, religion, culture, and science. He was willing to change his mind about people and events in accordance with his experience in life and a re-examination of the facts. He may be regarded as the first herald of the Arab renaissance, opposing popular Sufism and superstitions, and also the first Muslim Arab thinker who was aware of the spirit of the French Revolution which had such a profound effect on European thought and society.

The method applied in the present work is one that may be termed 'manuscript archaeology'. By this we mean that we shall first of all try to establish the text which the author himself left (his 'autograph') in manuscript form, since in the period in question only very few religious and official printing presses had been established in the Arab world. The second stage will be to collate the autograph or autographs with other manuscripts copied by various copyists. The autograph(s) enable us to use a detective-like method of 'interrogating' the text of the manuscript,[9] and the deletions and additions of the author in the text and in the margins, and later on to detect the sources from which the author collected his biographical and other information. This

8 Professor Reichmuth is inclined to think that 'it certainly depends on the chosen focus. Muḥammad b. ʿAlī al-Shawkānī's *al-Badr al-Ṭāli' bi-Maḥāsin mā ba'd al-Qarn al-Sābi'* (Cairo 1332/1914) is a similar biographical collection, and much more optimistic at that, also very much in tune with his own time. There are many other scholarly chronicles from other parts of the Muslim world, the Maghrib and elsewhere, also Muḥammad b. ʿAlī al-Sanūsī's, *al-Salsabīl al-Ma'ān fi 'l-Ṭuruq al-Arba'īn*, Muḥammad Ibn Ghalbūn (ed.), (Manchester 1990), with undeniable merits, to say nothing of the vigorous Arabic writing in provincial and more peripheral regions like the Caucasus or West Africa. In the Ḥijāz, Aḥmad Zaynī Daḥlān achieved a great deal.

9 Cf. André Raymond, *Le Caire des Janissaires: l'apogée de la ville ottomane sous 'Abd al-Rahmân Katkhudâ* (Paris 1995) and *The Cambridge History of Egypt*, vol. 2.

method, although time-consuming, has proven to be the best for arriving at valid conclusions and theories, in a way, which the printed edition of al-Jabartī's *Chronicle* cannot offer. By interrogating the autographs and collating them with previous sources it is possible to understand the religious, political and economic factors and trends behind his writings. In particular we have focused on the additions, deletions and corrections of words and sentences in the margins, as well as within the text of both autographs and printed editions. This method has given us the opportunity to discover the historical and biographical sources which our author used. Moreover, it will enable us not only to see the changes in his attitude towards the rulers of Egypt, but also to reveal the actual religious, political and social trends which influenced the author. We are indebted to Dr Lars Bjørneboe for having taken the trouble of applying this method to my edition of al-Jabartī, *Tārīkh Muddat al-Faransīs bi-Miṣr*, which enabled him to arrive at important new conclusions.

In the case of al-Jabartī's autographs, this method has enabled us to reveal the sequence and the dates of composition of his three chronicles of the history of Egypt, viz. *Tārīkh Muddat al-Faransīs bi-Miṣr, Maẓhar al-Taqdīs bi-Zawāl Dawlat al-Faransīs* and *'Ajā'ib al-Āthār fi 'l-Tarājim wa 'l-Akhbār*. It may perhaps also help us solve the enigma of our author, whether he was a 'giant among dwarfs' as the late David Ayalon asserted, or a 'plagiarist' as Daniel Crecelius claimed.

In his textual method, Dr Lars Bjørneboe was able in his Ph.D. thesis, published under the title, *In Search of the True Political Position of the 'Ulama: An Analysis of the Aims and Perspectives of the Chronicles of Abd al-Rahman al-Jabartī (1753–1825)*, to arrive at the following conclusion: 'the outcome of this analysis will determine the point of focus, the purpose of the author and create the basis on which his stated comments should be evaluated'. Dr Bjørneboe, using his meticulous method of textual research, was able to examine the real currents of political ideology, and the religious and intellectual principles which were debated by the *'ulamā'* in Cairo concerning how they should deal with the French invasion.[10]

10 Lars Bjørneboe's aim in this book is to deal with 'compositional structure of the text, i.e. how and, if possible, why the material is divided into volumes and sections (preface, introductions, necrologies, epilogue, divisions by the years, months and dates, or, as in the MS*Mudda*, just lines left in the text. Moreover, he dealt with important textual traits such as (pp. 112–22): 1. the position of the narrator, 2. the use of letters and documents, 3. the use of direct speech and

ʿAbd al-Raḥmān and his Father, Ḥasan al-Jabartī's Scientific Works

The Egyptian scholar ʿAbd al-Raḥmān al-Jabartī was well-known not only as a historian and biographer, but also as an expert in astronomy and mathematics and a student of literature and medicine. ʿAbd al-Raḥmān was the son of the wealthy businessman and eminent scholar Ḥasan Afandī b. Ibrāhīm b. Ḥasan[11] (1110–88/1698–1775), whose *kunya* (honorific name) was Abu 'l-Tadānī and his *laqab* (nickname) Badr al-Dīn. Ḥasan, was the *Shaykh Riwāq al-Jabart* (head of the Jabart students' residence) at al-Azhar. He excelled in mathematics, geometry, algebra, astronomy, engineering, Islamic philosophy and jurisprudence (*fiqh*) of the rational Ḥanafī School.[12] Al-Shaykh ʿAlī al-ʿAdawī commented that 'Never have I seen or heard of a man delving into rationale and philosophical studies (*ʿilm al-ḥikma wa 'l-falsafa*) and increasing in faith, except for him',[13] revealing the schism between religious studies and philosophy among the *ʿulamāʾ* of his time.

He excelled in many different fields; he was a draftsman of sundials, scales, and measures and a versifier of scientific rules and morals, in addition

---

dialogue, 4. the use of description. His analysis enabled him to 'determine the point of focus, the purpose of the author, and create the basis on which his stated comments should be evaluated' and to develop our knowledge of al-Jabartī's chronicles and the influence of the *ʿulamāʾ* and rulers of Egypt upon his works.

11 On Ḥasan al-Jabartī, see *ʿAj.*, I, 385–408 and *Fihris al-Aʿlām* in the indices of our Arabic edition under Ḥasan b. Burhān al-Dīn Ibrāhim... There are several autographs and MSS by Ḥasan al-Jabartī in the Chester Beatty Library, Dublin, Ireland. My thanks go to Mr Zvi Gabbay, former ambassador of Israel to Ireland, for his help in arranging my visit to the library. Leiden University Library also obtained some of his MSS (see below, notes 14 and 17). The Egyptian scholar Muḥammad Anīs in his article 'Ḥaqā'iq ʿan ʿAbd al-Raḥmān Mustamadda min Wathā'iq al-Maḥkama al-Sharʿiyya', *al-Majalla al-Tārīkhiyya al-Miṣriyya*, vols IX–X, 1960–2, 80, says that the title *afandī* means that he had been appointed by the Ottomans as a judge or *muftī*. On the title *afandī*, see Aḥmad al-Saʿīd Sulaymān, *Taʾṣīl Mā Warad fi Tārīkh al-Jabartī min al-Dakhīl* (Cairo 1979), 20–3. This title is actually broader than that and does not necessarily connote a position in the Ottoman judicial hierarchy or bureaucracy. See Gustav Bayerle, *Pashas, Begs, and Effendis: A Historical Dictionary of Titles and Terms in the Ottoman Empire* (Istanbul 1997), 44: 'a title for educated people, especially for scribes...Particularly, it signified traditional *medrese* education...'. On Ḥasan al-Jabartī, see C. Brockelmann, *Geschichte der arabischen Litteratur* (Leiden 1938), II, 472 (hereafter *GAL*) and *GAL, Suppl.*, II, 487. (My thanks are due to Jane Hathaway for drawing my attention to this definition.)

12 See *ʿAj.*, II, 181. Our author calls his father *faylasūf al-Islām* (philosopher of Islam), ibid., I, 385.

13 See ibid., I, 396.

to having achieved fluency in Turkish and Persian, according to the testimony of his son. Some of his works, extant in manuscript form, have also been published in Cairo and Beirut.[14] According to his son ʿAbd al-Raḥmān, Ḥasan al-Jabartī was of a perfect Muslim character; he was a hospitable, generous, modest, pious, and zealous Muslim, who respected and helped Muslim students and scholars and had friendly relations with the Ottoman rulers. He was well versed in the ways (*ṭarīqa*) of the *Khalwatiyya* and *Naqshbandiyya Ṣūfī* orders. Besides being an erudite, multi-professional scholar, he was a *muftī*, lecturer at al-Azhar, the Shaykh of *riwāq al-Jabart*, and an influential *'ālim*for whom religious obligations of collective religious duties (*farḍ kifāya*) were no less important than Muslim individual duties (*farḍ 'ayn*). He believed that it was his duty to maintain the welfare of Islamic society, and reinstated proper weights and measures in Egypt when this was urgently needed.[15] On the title-page of the printed edition of his *al-Aqwāl al-Mu'riba 'an Aḥwāl al-Ashriba* (a treatise on beverages and drinks) he is mentioned as a *mujtahid* (a *sharī'a* jurist who sets new theological precedents) and *muftī al-diyār al-Miṣriyya* (Grand Muftī of Egypt)[16] an honorific title which may have been an anachronistic addition of the printer. His zeal as a pious Muslim is demonstrated in the highly rhetorical introduction to his work *Ḥaqāyiq al-Daqāyiq 'alā Daqāyiq al-Ḥaqāyiq* (a commentary on a work of arithmetic and astronomical calculations),[17] in which he used arithmetical terminology

---

14 The MSS of works by Ḥasan b. Ibrāhīm b. Ḥasan b. ʿAlī al-Zaylaʿī al-ʿAqīlī al-Ḥanafī Badr al-Dīn Abu 'l-Tadānī are to be found in the Microfilm Department of Dār al-Kutub al-Qawmiyya in Cairo. Cf. David A. King, *A Survey of the Scientific Manuscripts in the Egyptian National Library* (Cairo 1981–4) and *Islamic Mathematical Astronomy* (London 1986). For more details on the father's works, see *GAL*, II, 477, *GAL, Suppl.*, II, 487, 731, and the Arabic translation of Brockelmann, *Ta'rīkh al-Adab al-'Arabī* (Cairo 1959–62), pt. 8, 337–8. See also notes 17 and 19.

15 See his biography in *'Aj.*, I, 398–9 and Ayalon, 'The Historian', 238–41. Cf. also *The Turkish Letters of Ogier Ghiselin de Busbecq, Imperial Ambassador at Constantinople, 1554–1562: Translated from the Latin of the Elzevir Edition of 1663* (quoted in B. Lewis, *What Went Wrong? Western Impact and Middle Eastern Response* [London 2003], 132).

16 Some of his shorter treatises and books were copied by his friend Muḥammad b. Mūsā al-Janājī al-Shāfiʿī, who taught ʿAbd al-Raḥmān the Qur'ān by heart in 1176/1762–3. See *'Aj.*, II, 126.

17 See Ḥasan al-Jabartī, *Majmū'a Mushtamila 'alā Thalāth Rasā'il* (Cairo 1327/1909). Cf. also Anīs, 'Ḥaqā'iq', 75; on p. 86, fn. 7 he is called: *Shaykh mashāyikh ahl al-wa'ẓ wa 'l-iftā' wa 'l-ijtihād bi 'l-Jāmi' al-Azhar*. See also Petrus Voorhoeve ed., *Handlist of Arabic Manuscripts in the Library of the University of Leiden and the Collections in the Netherlands* (Leiden 1980); a MS of Ḥasan al-Jabartī is listed: *Kitāb Ḥaqā'iq al-Daqā'iq 'alā Daqā'iq al-Ḥaqā'iq,*

metaphorically to express the importance of calculation in dividing booty during a Holy War (*jihād*). He wrote about calculating booties, despite successive defeats suffered by the Ottomans after the Treaty of Carlowitz in 1699, and especially after the defeat of 1769, as well as those in Crimea, Vidin, Ismail (on the Danube in Moldavia) and others. These defeats were known to the Mamluks, as expressed in 1787 by their *amīr*s in the Ṣaʿīd advising ʿĀbidī Pasha to fight the 'infidels' who defeated the Ottoman armies in Europe instead of the Egyptian Muslim army.[18] Ḥasan al-Jabartī's *Introduction* is as follows:

> 'We pray [to God] and ask peace for our most noble Lord Muḥammad, who gathered armies to exalt the powerful position (*kalima*) of religion, he subtracted (*ṭaraḥa*) [i.e. exterminated] every harmful person from the multitudes of infidels through those [Muslim heroes] who struck them [with swords]. He divided (*qassama*) the spoils in the most perfect and approved percentage. He divided [the booty] into equal portions after cutting the throats of the polytheists'...[19]

---

li-Mawlānā wa-Ustādhinā Farīd 'Aṣrih Mawlānā al-Shaykh Ḥasan b. Ibrāhīm al-Jabartī al-Ḥanafī Raḥimahu Allāh Ta'ālā, Āmān (MS. Ar. 2167). This is a commentary on *Daqā'iq al-Ḥaqā'iq fī Ḥisāb al-Daraj wa 'l-Daqā'iq* by Badr al-Dīn Muḥammad Sibṭ al-Mārdānī (d. after 891/1486) (Leiden, MS 2591, see *GAL*, II, 168). The book by Sibṭ al-Mārdānī is mentioned by al-Jabartī in *'Aj.*, II, 252. A unique book, which belonged to Ḥasan al-Jabartī, is in the possession of the al-Ḥusayniyya Library in Rabat. It is entitled *Sharḥ al-Mawāqif* by ʿAḍud al-Dīn al-Ījī, copied by ʿAlī b. Muḥammad b. ʿAlī al-Ḥusaynī al-Ḥanafī (d. 816/1413), vol. II, in Shawwāl 807/1–30 April 1405 in Samarqand. It has the name Ḥasan al-Jabartī on it, together with his signature and seal with the year 1145/1732–3 (See Muḥammad b. ʿAbd al-Hādī al-Manūfī, *Fahāris Makhṭūṭāṭ al-Khizāna al-Ḥasaniyya Ḥasab Arqāmihā 'ala'l-Rufūf* [Rabat al-Maṭba'a al-Malakiyya, 1403/1983], 147–8). Other works by Ḥasan al-Jabartī at the Chester Beatty Library in Dublin are: 1) *Raf 'al-Ishkāl bi-Ẓuhūr al-'Ashr fī 'Ashr fī Ghālib al-Ashkāl*, by Ḥasan Ibrāhīm b. Ḥasan al-Zaylaʿī al-Jabartī al-Ḥanafī [A tract on geometry], fols 12, 12.2 x 15.7 cm. Clear scholar's *naskh*, undated, 12/18th century. *GAL*, II, 359; *GAL, Suppl.*, II, 487. (See Arthur J. Arberry, *The Chester Beatty Library: A Handlist of the Arabic Manuscripts*, vol. V, MSS 4001–4500 (Dublin 1962), 23, no. 4069); 2) *Al-'Iqd al-Thamīn fīmā Yata'allaq bi 'l-Mawāzīn*, by Ḥasan b. Ibrāhīm b. Ḥasan al-Zaylaʿī al-Jabartī al-Ḥanafī [A treatise on balances and weights], Foll. 28. 18.2 x 14.4 cm. A clear scholar's *ta'līq*. Copyist: Abū Saʿīd Muḥammad al-Wannī (*The Chester Beatty Library. A Handlist*, no. 4367).

18 See *'Aj.*, II, 125, cf. necrologies of the year 1200/1785–6 and the death of ʿAlī b. Muḥammad al-Jazā'irlī as a prisoner of war in the land of Muscovy, *'Aj.*, I, 369–70, in the early years of the Ottoman-Russian war in 1185 (/1771–2).

19 See Leiden University Library, MS Ar. 2167, f. 1b. In the Bayerische Staatsbibliothek, München, Cod. Arab. 860 there is a booklet by Ḥasan al-Jabartī entitled *Akhṣar al-Mukhtaṣarāt 'alā Rub' al-Muqanṭarāt*, Cod. Or. 319, 5 fols 17 lines in 8^0. In his Introduction

This method of using professional terminology in literary writing is typical of the *khuṭba* (sermon), a well-known genre that developed into an embellished and rhetorical form in medieval Arabic literature. Ḥasan al-Jabartī used this style in many of his introductions to treatises on different sciences using the special terminology of the particular science in question. Other writers used it in *maqāmāt* dealing with professional craftsmen. The significance of this Introduction lies in the fact that it reflects the rise and gradual military defeats of the Ottoman Empire expressed by our author. In *'Ajā'ib al-Āthār* he gives detailed accounts concerning the return of the Ottomans to Egypt in 1801 which was achieved only with the help of the British to deliver Egypt from the French.[20] The Ottoman economy, political and religious power were based upon *jihād* (holy war) and *ghazw* (military conquest), and its main revenue was the farming of taxes (*iltizām*) and the yearly revenue (*māl al-khazna / khazīna*) imposed on salyane provinces. This revenue was sent to the Sultan's treasury in Constantinople, while the poll-tax (*jizya*) on free non-Muslims in the Empire was marginal. Abolishing the *tīmārs* and replacing them with the *iltizām* system brought wealth to the coffers of the state. It also led to the emergence of local elites in many provinces. All these revenues began to decrease after the Treaty of Carlowitz (1699) with the Habsburg Empire;[21] this was reflected by the chronicle of Ḥasan al-Jabartī's

to *Akhṣar al-Mukhtaṣarāt* he used astronomical terminology in his praise of God (see MS Dār al-Kutub, Cairo of *Akhṣar al-Mukhtaṣarāt*, shelf mark: *Falak* 462).

20 See *'Aj.*, III, 221; IV, 22–3, and the comments of Ḥasan al-'Aṭṭār in the margin of *'Aj.*, III, 92–3 in our Arabic edition and Appendix I. However, recent historians reject the notion of Ottoman 'decline' in favour of a paradigm of crisis and adaptation. See e.g., Suraiya Faroqhi, part II of vol. 2 of Halil Inalcik and Donald Quataert (eds), *An Economic and Social History of the Ottoman Empire, 1300–1914* (Cambridge 1994). By the early eighteenth century, as Şevket Pamuk has pointed out in *A Monetary History of the Ottoman Empire* (Cambridge 2004), as well as his appendix to *An Economic and Social History*, the Ottoman economy had recovered, and even its military fortunes were improving. However, the *jizya* was no more than about 2% of total revenues of the Ottoman Empire. My thanks are due to Jane Hathaway for this remark.

21 See *'Aj.*, IV, 106. One should add to these factor which led to the decline of the Ottoman Empire, the 'economic crisis of the *waqfs*, which supported the *Madrasa* system', see Avner Ben-Zaken, 'Recent Currents in the Study of Ottoman-Egypt Historiography, with Remarks about the Role of the History of Natural Philosophy and Science', *JSS* 49:2 (2004), 303–28 and his article, 'Political Economy', 776–94. The pattern of decline of the Ottomans under discussion has been much challenged in more recent Ottoman scholarship. Economic development was very uneven for many provinces, Egypt even experiencing a period of considerable wealth *c.* 1650–1750. The decline really sets in only around 1775. Karl K.

son ʿAbd al-Raḥmān *'Ajā'ib al-Āthār* in which he criticized the tyranny of the Ottoman rulers, their cruelty in collecting taxes, corruption, and their bribery. He argued that these were the main reasons for their successive defeats in wars with European armies, and especially that of Russia.[22]

The above-mentioned *Introduction*, can explain the strict attitude of ʿAbd al-Raḥmān, mainly during the eighteenth century, towards the *ahl al-dhimma* (non-Muslim subjects), and his insistence upon maintaining Muslim superiority over them. This superiority was based upon depriving them of any privilege, even that of the pilgrimage to Jerusalem, or of holding an official post which would give a non-Muslim the possibility of acquiring power and authority over Muslims.

In his comprehensive biography of his father, ʿAbd al-Raḥmān enumerates those sciences that served to maintain Islamic law (*sharī'a*), in which his father excelled: 'he worked on the mathematical sciences… He learned about azimuth and altitude, [instruments for] divisions, i.e. dividers and quadrants, [the basic concepts of spherical knowledge known as) second and first declination, and the [two auxiliary functions of astronomical timekeeping known as] 'the true' and 'the adjusted' fundamental principle. He associated with the leading men of science...using astronomical handbook[s] and tables of planetary equations and [he dealt with] epicyclic motions and planetary sector'. At al-Azhar he taught Ḥanafī jurisprudence, philosophy, astronomy and geometry and the art of computing the times of prayer (*'ilm al-ḥikma wa 'l-hay'a wa 'l-handasa wa-fann al-tawqīt*).[23]

In order to devote himself to his religious and scientific studies, Ḥasan al-Jabartī depended upon slaves and servants to maintain his household. He owned three houses where his wives and concubines (*sarārīy*, sing. *surriyya*),[24]

Barbir, *Ottoman Rule in Damascus, 1708–1758* (Princeton 1980), 3–4, 8, 13 also describes the early eighteenth century as a period of considerable prosperity. Cf. on this discussion Inalcik and Quataert (eds), *An Economic and Social History of the Ottoman Empire*; D. Crecelius, 'Egypt in the Eighteenth Century', in M.W. Daly (ed.), *The Cambridge History of Egypt*,vol. 2, *Modern Egypt, from 1517 to the End of the Twentieth Century* (Cambridge 1998), 59–86 where he discusses the issue of Egypt and Karl K. Barbir, 'From Pasha to Efendi: The Assimilation of Ottomans into Damascene Society, 1516–1783', *International Journal of Turkish Studies*, 2 (1979–80), 61–93.

22 See Leiden University Library, MS Ar. 2167, f. 1b.

23 *'Aj.*, I, 392 and IV, 231.

24 Ibid., I, 392 and IV, 231. The English translation is taken from *'Abd al-Raḥmān al-Jabartī's History*.

female and male servants, mamluks and visiting scholars lived. Slavery in those days enabled well-to-do scholars to concentrate upon their religious, scientific, and literary work. Fortunately, for Egyptian historiography, out of Ḥasan's forty sons and daughters by his wives and concubines, ʿAbd al-Raḥmān, born in 1167/1753–4 to a white slave (*surriyya*),[25] was the only one to survive and to follow his father's example. He too pursued research in the sciences, especially medicine and astronomy, *tawqīt* (defining prayer times), and the *qibla* (direction of praying towards the *Ka'ba*) of the *miḥrāb* (prayer niche) in mosques,[26] made calculations for eclipses of the sun and the moon, etc. Ḥasan al-Jabartī's interest in Islamic sciences and culture had a great influence upon his only surviving son, ʿAbd al-Raḥmān.

ʿAbd al-Raḥmān al-Jabartī's Studies

ʿAbd al-Raḥmān's *kunya* was Abu 'l-ʿAzm (the determined person), given to him by Shaykh al-Sajjāda al-Wafā'iyya Abu 'l-Imdād Aḥmad b. Ismāʿīl al-

25 Maḥmūd al-Sharqāwī says in his *Dirāsāt fī Tārīkh al-Jabartī: Miṣr fi 'l-Qarn al-Thāmin 'Ashara* (Cairo 1957, I, 12) that he believes his mother was a white slave girl. From al-Jabartī's own writing, it cannot be ascertained whether his mother was black or white. See *'Aj.*, I, 396, cf. *'Aj.*, II, 50: *wa-kāna yad'ūnā bi-ibn khālatī li-anna ummahu wa-ummī min al-sarārīy*, cf. *'Aj.*, II, 274, where al-Jabartī distinguishes between a white slave (*surriyya bayḍā'*) and Ethiopian and Negro slaves (*jāriya*: *jāriya Ḥabashiyya wa-jāriyatayn sūd li 'l-khidma*, but in *'Aj.*, III, 63, he writes *wa 'shtarā 'l-sarārīy al-bīḍ wa 'l-ḥubūsh wa 'l-sūd* (he bought white, Abyssinian and black concubines). The son of a *surriya Rūmiyya* was called Ibn al-Sitt, see *'Aj.*, II, 100. Dr Fu'ād Kanʿānī, in his unpublished Ph.D. thesis at the Hebrew University, states in his work 'al-Ḥayāt al-Adabiyya fī Miṣr' (*Literary and Cultural Life during 1688–1821 in Egypt According to 'Ajā'ib al-Āthār*... [Jerusalem 2007], 23–5), that his mother was the white slave girl whom his father's wife, the daughter of Ramaḍān Chalabī, who was barren, asked to keep for herself. As a sign of her love to her husband Ḥasan al-Jabartī, she presented her as a bride to him on 1165/1751–2 (*'Aj.*, I, 391–2). The fact that ʿAbd al-Raḥmān was born less than two years after this marriage (1753), and that he chose to speak about her several times and in detail, induced Kanʿanī to suggest that this 'white slave girl' was his mother. Such an act of presenting the husband with a young bride as a pious act in imitation of Sarah's act of presenting her slave Hagar to the Patriarch Abraham as his second wife may be called 'Sarah's law'. This law, based on the Qur'ān and the Bible, is equivalent to the law of Joseph in Egypt, where God decreed that a white slave should rule Egypt for its own welfare (Qur'ān, 12:21), al-Jabartī, *Maẓhar al-Taqdīs*, ʿAbd al-Raḥīm (ed.), 7, *'Ajā'ib al-Āthār*, ʿAbd al-ʿAzīz Jamāl al-Dīn (ed.), I, 505, and Ḥusayn Afandī al-Ruznāmjī, 'Tartīb al-Diyār al-Miṣriyya fi 'l-ʿAṣr al-ʿUthmānī', Muḥammad Shafīq Ghurbāl (ed.), *Majallat Kulliyyat al-Ādāb*, IV, pt. 1 (Cairo May 1936).

26 See *'Aj.*,II, 222. On our author, see *Fihris al-A'lām* in the indices of our Arabic edition under Ḥasan b. Burhān al-Dīn Ibrāhīm.

Ḥusaynī, and his *laqab* Zayn al-Dīn.[27] He studied religious subjects at al-Azhar. He also studied at home with his father and with a private teacher, ʿUthmān b. Salīm al-Wardānī,[28] who taught him mathematics, astronomy, and other secular sciences necessary for religious matters, such as dividing inheritances and shares and fixing prayer times. His father taught him Arabic grammer and other secular sciences useful for religious studies. He studied *fiqh* (jurisprudence) under the guidance of both his father and his father's student in *fiqh Ḥanafī*, ʿAbd al-Raḥmān b. ʿUmar al-ʿArīshī (d. 1208/1793–4),[29] chief of the Syrian residents in al-Azhar (*Shaykh Riwāq al-Shawām*). He also studied books on *fiqh* such as *al-Durr al-Mukhtār* and *Matn Nūr al-Īḍāḥ*, in the company of a fellow student named Sayyid Aḥmad, the progeny of Muḥammad al-Dūqāṭī al-Taḥṭāwī and Sayyid Aḥmad used to help him in his studies. Other teachers with whom he studied were the Shafiʿī scholars Aḥmad al-Damanhūrī, Aḥmad al-ʿArūsī, who both served as Shaykh al-Azhar, and with Muḥammad b. Mūsā al-Janājī al-Shāfiʿī (d. 1785) who instructed him in religious subjects and mathematics. In 1230 [/1814–15] al-Jabartī, who was a supervisor of the al-Qarāfa cemetery, gave permission to Sayyid Aḥmad to build a tomb there for his eventual burial.[30]

In the biography of Shaykh Abū ʿAbd Allāh Muḥammad al-Murrī al-Fāsī al-Tāwūdī Ibn Sūda (d. 1210/1795–6), our author ʿAbd al-Raḥmān described how he learned mathematics from his father Ḥasan and astronomy from the scholars Sālim al-Qayrawānī and Aḥmad al-Sūsī. In this biography, the author related how he studied astronomy together with the sons of Muḥammad al-

27 Anīs, 'Ḥaqā'iq', 79–80. Cf. *GAL*, II, 632; *GAL, Suppl.*, II, 730–1.

28 Cf. Murtaḍā al-Zabīdī, *Muʿjam Mukhtaṣṣ bi-Dhikr Man Akhadhtu ʿanhu al-ʿUlūm wa 'l-Maʿārif min Shuyūkhī wa-Ābāʾī*, Maktabat Aḥmad ʿĀrif Ḥikmat, al-Jāmiʿa al-Islāmiyya, al-Madīna al-Munawwara, ṭalab 52, microfilm no. 6238, where he is described as a student of Ḥasan and as a fellow student with ʿAbd al-Raḥmān attending al-Zabīdī's lectures. Some personal papers of his can be found in StaBi (Staatsbibliothek, Berlin), Carlo von Landberg, *Catalogue de manuscrits arabes provenant d'une bibliothèque privée à El-Medîna, et appartenant à la maison E.J. Brill ... rédigé par C. Landberg* (Leiden 1883), 526, among other things his notes of al-Zabīdī's *Amālī* in the Shaykhūniyya and Ḥanafī mosques.

29 On al-ʿArīshī, see *ʿAj.*, II, 51–4. See *ʿAj.*, II, 52, 181, 244. Although he studied with his father who was a versifier of Arabic sciences and Arabic literature, ʿAbd al-Raḥmān al-Jabartī was not good in Arabic prosody (*ʿarūḍ*) and many verses, which he quoted, were not according to the rules of Arabic meters. The only verses, which were possible to trace, are his verses to Shaykh Ṭāhir al-Ḥusaynī from Jerusalem concerning selling some books to the latter. See his letter in Appendix II.

30 Ibid., IV, 261.

Fāsīal-Tāwūdī. They used to 'stay up most of the night on the roofs observing the rising, setting, and movements of the stars in the twilight'. Their teacher was with them on the other side of the roof, and they would consult him about anything that was not clear to them. 'Abd al-Raḥmān, who was better instructed in mathematics, taught Sidī Abū Bakr the method of drawing a quarter of an arched sphere and its sine.[31] In 1185 [/1771–2], at the age of 19, he wrote a commentary on his father's work on the instrument that indicated the hour according to the altitude of the sun, *Risāla bi-Khaṭṭ al-Jabartī fī 'l-'Amal bi 'l-Rub'* (On the Use of the Quadrant).[32] Later on, he attached great importance not only to *tawqīt*, but also to astronomy. In his chronicle, he complained from time to time of the chaos involved in fixing the beginning of the fast of Ramaḍān according to the lunar calendar. He also believed that God revealed his historical plans according to conjunctions of the stars and planets,[33] basing his belief on the Quranic verse (16/16) '*wa-'alāmāt wa-bi 'l-najmi hum yahtadūn*' (cf. also 6/97, 7/54, 16/12). In his various introductions to the events of a number of years, especially at the beginning of volumes III and IV, he describes the location of the planets, their influence on coming events, and their significance to what God had decreed regarding the fate of the rulers and subjects.

After the death of his father, he studied the *Awwaliyya* (i.e. *ḥadīth al-raḥma*) and attended the classes of his mentor Murtaḍā al-Zabīdī[34] on the *Ṣaḥīḥ al-Bukhārī* in 1189 (/1775–6). He joined the *Ṣūfī* Khalwatiyya order through Yūsuf al-Ḥifnī and his master and guide in the Khalwatiyya brotherhood (*ṭarīq* or *ṭarīqa*) was Shaykh Maḥmūd al-Kurdī (d. 1780). He was

---

31 See *'Aj.*, II, 77 and 243. On the subject of astronomy and the institutions of the *mu'adhdhin* and the *muwaqqit* in the Mamluk period, see E.W. Lane, *The Manners and Customs of the Modern Egyptians* (London 1963), 74, 84–5, and King, *Islamic Mathematical Astronomy*² (London 1993), D 88. 4.5.30, and the bibliography in his article 'Mamluk Astronomy and the Institution of the *Muwaqqit*', in Thomas Philipp and Urlich Haarmann (eds), *The Mamluks in Egyptian Politics and Society* (Cambridge 1998), 153–62.

32 See *'Aj.*, II, 243, *'Abd al-Raḥmān al-Jabartī's History*, II, 404. On this *Risāla*, see *al-Jabartī's Chronicle*, 8, n. 29. Its colophon reads: 'The end of its composition by the humble 'Abd al-Raḥmān was on the eve of Tuesday, the morning of which start the 1st of Jumādā II 1185 [/10 September 1771] ...'. See also al-Zabīdī's *Mu'jam Mukhtaṣṣ*, f. 60a (see note 48 below).

33 See also *Rasā'il Ikhwān al-Ṣafā*, Khayr al-Dīn al-Ziriklī (ed.) (Cairo 1347/1928–9), I, 135.

34 Al-Jabartī's *Sanad al-Ḥadīth al-Musalsal bi 'l-Awwaliyya* which he obtained from al-Zabīdī in 1190/1776–7 has been preserved with others in MS StaBi 526, f. 310ff., copied by al-Wardānī, with a special license (*ijāza*) note by al-Zabīdī himself at the end.

also associated with the Wafā'iyya order and was attached to his teachers Sayyid ʿAbd al-Raḥmān al-ʿAydarūs, ʿAlī al-Ṣaʿīdī and Aḥmad Ibn Wafī Abū al-Imdād.[35] ʿAbd al-Raḥmān was, unlike his father, not well versed in Turkish, and was hardly able to understand the content of a decree read in audience.[36] He studied with his father's student in mathematics, Shaykh Aḥmad al-ʿArūsī.[37] Later, he taught with great success at al-Azhar mosque and until the end of his life many students attended his classes.[38] He succeeded his father at the post of *shaykh riwāq al-Jabart*. One of his close friends among the Mamluk ruling class was the Amīr Riḍwān Katkhudā Ibrāhīm with whom he traveled extensively. The Amīr was very likely among those influential friends of his who supplied him with information concerning the Mamluk ruling classes and their intrigues.[39] It seems that our author used to accompany al-Zabīdī during his visits to scholars such as ʿAlī al-Qināwī to get information about their travels and about other scholars they met.[40] The fact that we could not find anycopy of *'Ajā'ib al-Āthār* in the libraries of Istanbul or other cities in Turkey indicates that the Ottomans did not view the book with favour. Moreover, no elegy in his memory by his friends, especially not by Ḥasan al-ʿAṭṭār has been found, indicating that the people around Muḥammad ʿAlī did not dare to express their feelings of appreciation towards him.

Al-Jabartī as Book-dealer

In al-Jabartī's *Introduction* to *'Ajā'ib al-Āthār*, written in 1221 (/1806–7) after the turmoil of the French occupation, and his employment as a member of their third *Dīwān* with a respectable salary, al-Jabartī said:

35 See *'Aj.*, I, 287, 301, 339, 364, 375, 404 and II, 88, 97, 169, 181, 262. On Shaykh Maḥmūd al-Kurdī see *'Aj.*, II, 61-8. On the Khalwatiyya *Ṣūfī* order, see *'Aj.*, III, 355–6, and F. de Jong, 'Khalwatiyya', *EI*², IV, 991–3.

36 See his comment on a letter read in public in Turkish, *'Aj.*, II, 125, where he says: 'In short, what I have understood of this letter in Turkish is…' (وحاصل ما فهمته من المكتوب بالتركية).

37 See *'Aj.*, II, 52–3. Shaykh Aḥmad b. Muḥammad al-Ḥaḍrāwī al-Makkī al-Hāshimī, *Nuzhat al-Fikar fīmā Maḍā min al-Ḥawādith wa 'l-'Ibar min Awā'il al-Mawj-dāt ilā Ākhir al-Qarn al-Thālith 'Ashar*, Dār al-Kutub al-Qawmiyya, Cairo, MS Tārīkh Taymūr 1970/microfilm 29516, vol. IV, 400, copied word for word from *'Aj.*, II, 52–3. On Aḥmad al-ʿArūsī, see *'Aj.*, II, 252–5.

38 See al-Ḥaḍrāwī, *Nuzhat al-Fikar*, IV, 401–2 and Anīs, 'Ḥaqā'iq', 80.

39 *'Aj.*, III, 290–1.

40 Ibid., II, 90.

> 'It is only a person like myself- secluded as I am in the corner of obscurity, neglected and retired from employment unlike other people- who would keep himself busy in his solitude and would alleviate his loneliness by enumerating the Good and Evil of Time'.

However, only after he inherited his father's rich library and bought al-Zabīdī's books and papers from the latter's widow, was he able to start writing his first three volumes of *'Ajā'ib al-Āthār*. It seems that the French occupation of Egypt was the main incitement for al-Jabartī to resume his interest in recording the history of Egypt. Beside the single copy of a MS of *Muddat al-Faransīs* found in Leiden, the autograph of *'Ajā'ib al-Āthār* kept at Cambridge University Library reveals that the author composed first the three first volumes dealing with the years 1688–1805/6. According to the additions in the margins of this autograph, the author revised it twice. The first revision was made to the original text, while in the second revision he added in the margindozens of biographies copied from the autograph of his mentor al-Zabīdī, *Mu'jam Mukhtaṣṣ*, and other biographies, such as the one he composed on al-Murādī as well as others copied from other sources. From the first three volumes MSS kept at the Bibliothèque Nationale in Paris, it is possible to presume that the author employed copyists who copied *'Ajā'ib al-Āthār* from his autograph. These copyists copied the autograph first and later on the author wrote the title pages of the three volumes, revised them and wrote the last lines of the MSS. However, our author never mentioned his name as author, the name of the copyists or the date in the colophons. This MS seems to have been ordered by the authorities of the Bibliothèque Nationale in Paris, while another was copied at the request of some European consuls in Cairo. He did the same in the second autograph of volume III of *'Ajā'ib al-Āthār* kept at Dār al-Kutub al-Qawmiyya in Cairo.[41] Moreover, Ḥasan al-ʿAṭṭār's letter dated 3 Rajab 1229 (/21 June 1814) to the Muftī of Jerusalem Muḥammad Ṭāhir Afandī after his arrival in Cairo, mentioned the financial difficulties of our author during the reign of Muḥammad ʿAlī. He added that he suffered like everyone else from the calamities of the time ('*ghawā'il al-waqt*') and appalling hardships ('*khuṭūb mudlahimma*') that forced him to delay sending the books he had promised. These hard economic conditions were the result of high prices,

41 See the next chapter dealing with al-Jabartī's MSS where more facts can be detected from these MSS.

especially of food, because of taxes and customs duties imposed by Muḥammad ʿAlī.[42]

It seems that there was a delay in sending two books to Muḥammad Ṭāhir Afandī in Jerusalem, *al-Baḥr al-Rā'iq fī Sharḥ Kanz al-Daqā'iq* on Ḥanafī law, and a commentary on al-Nasafī by Ibn Nujaym (d. 970/1562–3), which had been in the possession of his father. The letter reveals the hardship and poor economic conditions endured by al-Jabartī which forced him to usebargaining tactics with the involvement of al-ʿAṭṭār who refused the price offered by Shaykh Ṭāhir and the 700 *qirsh* which al-ʿAṭṭār offered to settle the bargain. Our author insisted on 1000 *qirsh*, as he wrote in his letter to the Muftī of Jerusalem dated 21 Rabīʿ I 1229 (/13/14 March 1814). The manuscript of *al-Baḥr* consisted of three volumes in folio format (*muḥayyar al-kāmil*) of 40 fascicles each, without its *Supplement* (*takmila*). He added that this was a manuscript that had been in the possession of the great Ḥanafī jurist al-Dalajī and that it had later been acquired by his father Ḥasan al-Jabartī. He also added that if the Muftī needed its *Supplement*, he could ask a copyist to copy it and send it to him.[43]

However, a long time before he compiled his *'Ajā'ib al-Āthār* he started dealing in books, selling his own and his father's books, and copying and perchasing others for sale. His interest in books, copyists, calligraphy and bookbinding, reveals his activities as a book dealer. The fact that he sold in 1232 (/1816–17) his autographs of *Maẓhar al-Taqdīs*, *'Ajā'ib al-Āthār* and other manuscripts to J.L. Burckhardt (or, to use his Muslim name, al-Shaykh Ibrāhīm),[44] as well as the fact that he traded a copy of *Zīj al-Rāṣid Ulugh Beg al-Samarqandī* in 1196 (/1781–2), and bought books from al-Zabīdī's widow. All these transactions indicated that he had been a book dealer at least since 1816.[45] His bargain with the Muftī of Jerusalem Muḥammad Ṭāhir Afandī

42 See al-ʿAṭṭār's letter dated 3 Rajab 1229 (/21 June 1814) in the Appendix, and its English translation by Butrus Abu-Manneh, 'Four Letters of Šayḫ Ḥasan al-ʿAṭṭār to Šayḫ Ṭāhir al-Ḥusaynī of Jerusalem', *Arabica* 1:I (2002), 91. Cf. *'Aj.*, IV, 156–7, 230–1.

43 See al-Jabartī's letter to Shaykh Ṭāhir in the Appendix of this book. One might even ask whether the Princeton copy of the *Mu'jam Mukhtaṣṣ* with its clear connections to Jerusalem was not related to that contact with the Muftī Ṭāhir al-Ḥusaynī.

44 In *'Aj.*, IV, 284, our author called him Sīdī al-Shaykh Ibrāhīm al-Mahdī al-Inkilīzī. '*Sīdī*' is an honorific given to close friends and sons of sultans, while the title Mahdī is given to male converts to Islam.

45 See *al-Jabartī's Chronicle*,8 and plate VI and *'Aj.*, II, 70. See also Nelly Hanna, 'Cultural Life in Mamluk Households (Late Ottoman Period)', in T. Philipp and U. Haarmann (eds), *The*

concerning one of his father's books, and later on offering its *Supplement* to be copied by a certain copyist, is a clear indication that al-Jabartī was an efficient dealer who preferred business and science over politics and employed copyists to copy his own and his father's books.[46] The fact that there are at least three copies of *'Ajā'ib al-Āthār* copied by different copyists revised in al-Jabartī's hand and that many manuscripts of Ḥasan al-Jabartī's works are kept at the Chester Beatty Library in Dublin, Ireland, while manuscripts of his son's works are kept at Leiden University Library, confirm this suggestion. The copy of volumes II–III of *'Ajā'ib al-Āthār* kept at DKQ (al-Zakiyya nos. 858 and 859) states that it was read to the author, so that he could revise it. This is the best evidence that he employed copyists to copy his bookat the request of wealthy men and consuls of European countries for payment until the end of his life when he became blind. The fact that the autograph of the *Mu'jam Mukhtaṣṣ* and some other autographs of al-Zabīdī were purchased by the Ottoman Shaykh al-Islam Aḥmad ʿĀrif Ḥikmet (1786–1859), and kept in his *waqf* library in Medina, may also be explained in a sale of these MSS by al-Jabartī. Ḥikmet was *molla* (*qāḍī*) of Cairo in 1236 (/1820–1) and Medina (1239 [/1823–4]) when al-Jabartī was still alive.[47]

Al-Jabartī's Biography

As far as we know, no copyist of his books and no contemporary scholar recorded any biography of ʿAbd al-Raḥmān al-Jabartī during his lifetime except his mentor and friend Murtaḍā al-Zabīdī (d. 1205/1790–1) in his *Mu'jam Mukhtaṣṣ*. We are indepted to Professor Stefan Reichmuth who was able to get for the first time a microfilm of this important autograph of the *Biographical Dictionary*, kept at a library in Medina, and brought to our

---

Mamluks in Egyptian Politics and Society (Cambridge 1998), 196–204. On al-Jabartī's relationship with Burckhardt, see *'Aj.*, IV, 284.

46 See ʿAdel Manna, 'Cultural Relations between Egyptian and Jerusalem *'Ulamā'* in the Early Nineteenth Century', *Asian and African Studies, Journal of the Israel Oriental Society* 17: 1–3 (November 1983), 139–52. See the original Arabic letter of al-Jabartī to Shaykh Ṭāhir Afandī al-Ḥusaynī (p. 151, Appendix II, of Manna's article and its English translation (ibid., 142–4). For an English translation of the letters of Ḥasan al-ʿAṭṭār, see Butrus Abu-Manneh, 'Four Letters', 79–95. The Arabic text of these letters is reprinted in Appendix II of this book. My thanks are due to Mrs Lubnā Ṣafadī-ʿAbbāsī, Mr Ṣāliḥ ʿAbbāsī and Buṭrus Abū Manneh for presenting me with a copy of these letters.

47 Cf. 'ʿĀrif Ḥikmet Bey', *EI²*, I, 432 and Mustafa L. Bilge, 'Ârif Hikmet Bey, Sheyhülislâm', *Islâm Ansiklopedesi* 3 (Istanbul 1991), 365–6.

knowledge the existence of another copy kept at Princeton University Library. The *Mu'jam Mukhtaṣṣ* contains important information on 629 Muslim scholars from all over the Muslim world. Al-Jabartī copied 196 biographies from this *Mu'jam Mukhtaṣṣ* and other works by his mentor, especially from *al-Murabbā al-Kābulī*. Murtaḍā al-Zabīdī confirmed in his biography recorded in his manuscript of the *Mu'jam Mukhtaṣṣ* that his student ʿAbd al-Raḥmān al-Jabartī 'compiled a history of his epoch in which he mentioned excellent things, may God help him to finish it. He [al-Jabartī] has helped me in [collecting] some biographies which I needed for my *Great History of the People of the Twelfth Century*' (*al-Tārīkh al-Kabīr li-Ahl al-Qarn al-Thānī'Ashar*). (وقد جمع تاريخا لعصره ذكر فيه اشياء مستجادة اعانه الله على اتمامه وأعانني على بعض تراجم احتجت اليها في كتابي التاريخ الكبير لأهل القرن الثاني عشر)

Stefan Reichmuth suggests that there is evidencein the *Mu'jam Mukhtaṣṣ*to 'confirm the existence of a separate collection of biographies' i.e. *al-Tārīkh al-Kabīr* as distinct from the *Mu'jam Mukhtaṣṣ*, adding that 'this would account for al-Jabartī's disappointment with the highly personal material which he finally managed to acquire'.[48]

In the unique untitled autograph of Murtaḍā al-Zabīdī's *Biographical Dictionary*many biographies give an impression of having been written due to the author's personal interest in the personalities involved, especially friends of his who praised his lexicon *Tāj al-'Arūs* in prose and verse. In the

48 The MS of al-Zabīdī's *Biographical Dictionary* has no title page, but in the introduction the author calls it *Mu'jam Mukhtaṣṣ bi-Dhikri Man Akhadhtu 'anhu al-'Ulūm wa 'l-Ma'ārif min Shuyūkhī wa-Ābā'ī*. This *Dictionary*, which is kept at the Medina Islamic University in the Library of the Ottoman scholar Aḥmad ʿĀrif Ḥikmat (Maktabat Aḥmad ʿĀrif Ḥikmat, al-Jāmiʿa al-Islāmiyya bi 'l-Madīna al-Munawwara) under *ṭalab* 52, microfilm 6238, in 177 fols, was brought to my attention by Professor Stefan Reichmuth's article entitled 'Murtaḍā az-Zabīdī (d. 1791) in Biographical and Autobiographical Accounts. Glimpses of Islamic Scholarship in the 18th Century', *Die Welt des Islams* 39:1 (1999), 64–102. Professor Reichmuth was kind enough to present me also with his other scholarly papers dealing with this manuscript, such as his unpublished draft 'Annotated Index of Murtaḍī al-Zabīdī, *Mu'jam al-Mashā'ikh*, al-Jāmiʿa al-Islāmiyya bi 'l-Madīna al-Munawwara, Ṭalab: 52, Film raqam: 6238, 'adad al-awrāq: 177 (Min Maktabat Aḥmad ʿĀrif Ḥikmat)'. See also Reichmuth, 'Notes', 374–83, where he deals with the possibility that al-Zabīdī's *al-Tārīkh al-Kabīr li-Ahl al-Qarn al-Thānī 'Ashar* is a separate work which 'included scholars and other personalities with whom he had not been in personal contact but had gathered information about and he was assisted in this by al-Jabartī'. (See 'Notes', p. 378). Professor Muḥammad ʿAdnān al-Bakhīt, University of Amman, History of Bilād al-Shām Committee, is in the process of editing al-Zabīdī's *Mu'jam Mukhtaṣṣ*.

*Introduction*to the *Biographical Dictionary*, al-Zabīdī assured the reader that he had recorded the biographies of his teachers, forefathers and friends and in his *Introduction* he described his work as: *Mu'jam Mukhtaṣṣ bi-dhikr man akhadhtu 'anhu al-'ulūm wa 'l-ma'ārif min shuyūkhī wa-ābā'ī* ([A Biographical] Dictionary Pertaining to Those from Whom I Have Learned Science and Knowledge among My Teachers and Forefathers.). One might understand this sentence to imply that he also wrote another biographical *Dictionary* which might be his *Kitāb al-Tārīkh al-Kabīr* mentioned above. However, al-Zabīdī admitted in his biography of ʿAbd al-Raḥmān al-Jabartī that the latter assisted him in collecting biographies and that al-Jabartī at the same time also collected materials for writing a historical book on Egypt.

Another book by al-Zabīdī from which al-Jabartī copied at least 24 biographies is *al-Murabbā al-Kābulī fīman Rawā 'an al-Shams al-Bābilī* (Leiden University Library, MS Or. 2448). Possible confirmation of this may be seen in al-Jabartī's admission that he used *al-Ḍaw' al-Lāmi' li-Ahl al-Qarn al-Tāsi'*, by Shams al-Dīn Muḥammad b. ʿAbd al-Raḥmān al-Sakhāwī (1427–97), with his mentor Murtaḍā al-Zabīdī, his patron Muḥammad Abu 'l-Iqbāl b. Wafī Shaykh al-Sādāt, and his friend Ḥasan al-ʿAṭṭār. At the end of al-Sakhāwī's manuscript of volume X,[49] the scholars al-Zabīdī and al-ʿAṭṭār wrote that they have read this volume (*anhāhu muṭāla'atan*), while al-Jabartī with his sense of history recorded his reading in detail: 'I am the humble (*faqīr*) ʿAbd al-Raḥmān b. Ḥasan al-Jabartī, also finished reading it as well as the former two volumes, except the first. This is because [the first volume] is absent and was borrowed by the eminent mentor al-Sayyid Muḥammad Abu 'l-Iqbāl the *khalīfa* of the House of al-Sādāt al-Wafā'iyya, may God bestow him with long life and make him happy. I have gained by reading it some interesting facts, may God reward its author, the person who lent it and those who borrowed it with blessings…'. According to the year of al-Zabīdī's death (1791), this happened when al-Jabartī helped his mentor in collecting biographies and during the time in which he was busy writing the history of Egypt during the twelfth/eighteenth century.

Scholars who have dealt with ʿAbd al-Raḥmān al-Jabartī's life generally give the year of his death as 1237 (/1821–2), basing their conclusion on a colophon at the end of the Būlāq edition, which states that he wrote his

49 See *'Ajā'ib al-Āthār*, Beirut edition, Dār al-Jīl, 1422/1992, X, 66.

chronicle up to the year 1236 (/1820–1) and that he died after he had written the fourth volume.[50] However, David Ayalon came to the conclusion that al-Jabartī died in 1241 [/1825-26].[51] A similar date is found in the historical work by Shaykh Aḥmad b. Muḥammad al-Ḥaḍrāwī al-Makkī al-Hāshimī (1252–1327 [/1836–1909]), entitled: *Nuzhat al-Fikar fīmā Maḍā min al-Ḥawādith wa 'l-'Ibar min Awā'il al-Mawjūdāt ilā Ākhir al-Qarn al-Thālith 'Ashar*, which gives the following information about al-Jabartī. Quoting al-Bannānī, al-Ḥaḍrāwī said about ʻAbd al-Raḥmān that he was:

> ... [T]he honorable, distinguished scholar, the perfect ideal, the spiritual head of Islam (*Shaykh al-Islām*) and of the Muslims, and the pillar of investigators. His father was a *Muftī* in Cairo and many eminent scholars and other people benefited from him. When ʻAbd al-Raḥmān reached the age of maturity he attended the classes on Islamic jurisprudence (*fiqh*) taught by his father's pupil Shaykh ʻAbd al-Raḥmān b. ʻUmar al-ʻArīshī, chief of the Syrian residents in al-Azhar (*Shaykh Riwāq al-Shawām*), who was impressed by his student's excellent memory. His first lessons dealt with the religious works *Matn Nūr al-Īḍāḥ* (a treatise on prayer) by al-Shurunbulālī, then with *Matn al-Kanz* (a work on Ḥanafī jurisprudence) and its commentary by Mullā Miskīn. He studied half of the *Durar* (a work on Ḥanafī jurisprudence) and thereafter the *Commentary* of al-Sayyid [al-Sharīf ʻAlī b. Muḥammad al-Jurjānī] on the *Sirājiyya fi 'l-Farā'iḍ* (a treatise on inheritance law). His father taught him Arabic language and grammar and other sciences. Later he studied with al-Sayyid Murtaḍā al-Zabīdī al-Ḥanafī, the above-mentioned author of *Sharḥ al-Qāmūs*, and with some distinguished scholars such as Shaykh ʻAlī al-Ṣaʻīdī and others. He studied with al-Shaykh Sulaymān al-Jamal, the author of *al-Tafsīr* and *al-Hidāya* [a legal work] with al-Shaykh Muṣṭafā al-Ṭā'ī and also with his father, and he progressed in many arts. Then he wrote some works such as his history of Egypt, its *amīr*s and annals. He wrote the biographies of the elders of his epoch in his [historical] work entitled *'Ajā'ib al-Āthār fi 'l-Tarājim wa 'l-Akhbār* in four volumes from the beginning of the year 1100 (/1688–9) until 1237 (/1821–2).[52]

---

50 ʻAbd al-Raḥmān al-Jabartī al-Ḥanafī, *al-Ta'rīkh al-Musammā 'Ajā'ib al-Āthār fi'l-Tarājim wa 'l-Akhbār* (Būlāq 1297/1879–80) (hereafter *'Aj.* Būlāq), IV, 320.

51 Ayalon, 'The Historian', 247, n. 3. Ismāʻīl Bāshā al-Baghdādī in his *Hadiyyat al-'Ārifīn bi-Asmā' al-Mu'allifīn wa-Āthār al-Muṣannifīn* (Istanbul 1951), I, 556 also says that al-Jabartī was strangled in Shubrā in 1237 (/1821–2).

52 See al-Ḥaḍrāwī, *Nuzhat al-Fikar*, IV, 400; Ayalon, 'The Historian', 247, n. 3. (Cf. Anīs, 'Ḥaqā'iq', 86–7; 90–1, 100.) Al-Ḥaḍrāwī, *Nuzhat al-Fikar*, IV, 401–2 says, quoting al-Jabartī's biography on his teacher of *fiqh*, ʻAbd al-Raḥmān al-ʻArīshī. (See Appendix II at the end of this book). On Shaykh Amīn al-Madanī as owner of the MS *Mudda* see Moreh, *al-Jabartī's Chronicle*, 12, n. 40. See Anīs, 'Ḥaqā'iq', 75, where Anīs quotes Ḥasan ʻAbd al-

The Date of al-Jabartī's Death

Unlike Cardin, the Egyptian translators of *'Ajā'ib al-Āthār* into French and Khalīl Shaybūb who copied his information from Cardin, none of the copyists and contemporary biographers of our author, including al-Bannānī and al-Ḥaḍrāwī and not even his son Maḥfūẓ, mentioned the tragic death of al-Jabartī's son Khalīl. One of the reasons that might explain this conspiracy of silence, revealed only by the Frenchman Cardin, is that they were afraid of being punished by Muḥammad ʿAlī and his successors. Al-Ḥaḍrāwī continued his narrative as follows:

> Then the above-mentioned Shaykh [ʿAbd al-Raḥmān al-Jabartī] lost his sight and abandoned writing his History [*'Ajā'ib al-Āthār*] for three years until 1240 [/1824–5]. Amīn Afandī al-Ḥulwānī al-Madanī informed me of this. He [al-Jabartī] was wealthy and held a superior position because of his teaching at al-Azhar. Many people benefited [from his knowledge]. His students became numerous, and he was famous until his death in 1241 [sic] [/16 August 1825–5 August 1826] in Cairo, where he was buried in al-Mujāwirīn [cemetery].[53]

As stated in the above fragment, al-Ḥaḍrāwī received this information from Amīn Afandī b. Ḥasan al-Ḥulwānī al-Madanī (d. 1316/1898), who owned al-Jabartī's autograph of his short work on the first seven months of the French occupation giving it the title *Tārīkh Muddat al-Faransīs bi-Miṣr*, which will be discussed in the following chapter.

According to Cardin, al-Jabartī lost his sight as a result of his grief and perhaps of cataracts also, over the assassination of his son Khalīl, who is said to have been killed by Muḥammad ʿAlī's agents on the 28 Ramaḍān 1237 (/19 June 1822).[54] We will deal with these erroneous dates at the end of this chapter.

Wahhāb's article in *al-Ahrām* (14 July 1944) describing the site of al-Jabartī's grave. The photographs of the grave are on pp. 116–18.

53 See al-Ḥaḍrāwī, *Nuzhat al-Fikar*, IV, 400. In fact, Amīn al-Madanī's large collection included many manuscripts from Cairo and Medina, and also several autographs of al-Zabīdī and the above-mentioned collection von Landberg, 526, with material from al-Wardānī and others. The collection was split up and sold to Berlin, Leiden, and Princeton (Garrett Collection). The library is quite impressive, and invaluable as a sample of an Egyptian scholar's library of the nineteenth century, if taken as a whole.

54 See Khalīl Shaybūb,*'Abd al-Raḥmān al-Jabartī*, Iqra', no. 70 (Cairo 1948), 113–15 and Abdurrahman Gabarti, *Journal d'Abdurrahman Gabarti pendant l'occupation française en Egypte: suivi d'un précis de la même campagne, par Mou'allem Nicolas el-Turki*, trans. A. Cardin, T.X. Bianchi (ed.)(Paris 1838), 2.

The documents from the *Awqāf* Archives in Cairo dealing with ʿAbd al-Raḥmān al-Jabartī's inheritance, which Muḥammad Anīs published in 1960–2, give more information on al-Jabartī's private life.[55] Apparently, he married three wives and had three children. His marriage to the first wife took place in 1182 (/1768–9). His second wife, who was the stepdaughter of ʿAbd Allah Darwīsh al-Rūmī, might have been the mother of his son Khalīl, but not of his daughter Amīn. In the *Muʿjam Mukhtaṣṣ* there is a detailed biography of ʿAbd Allāh Darwīsh al-Rūmī, whose details were most probably supplied by al-Jabartī himself; in the margin of this *Muʿjam Mukhtaṣṣ* he added in his own handwriting some important information about his second wife, shedding new light on her and on the education received by a young girl in a learned family. This is a significant addition in which, as far as we can tell, a Muslim scholar discusses in detail and without reservation a proposal for marriage. This is what al-Jabartī writes:[56]

> The humble (*al-ḥaqīr*) ʿAbd al-Raḥmān al-Jabartī says, 'I have become a son-in-law of the above-mentioned person [al-Rūmī], the subject of this biography, and married his stepdaughter (*wa-tazawwajtu bi-ibnat zawjatih*) in 1196 [/1781–2]. It was in the same year in which the woman who was with me during the lifetime of my late father died. When he [al-Rūmī] was informed of her death, he came to me and told me, "I have come to propose to you and am willing to be your friend and relative. Do you accept me?" I asked him "and what do you offer?" He replied, "I have a stepdaughter whom I have looked after since she was three years old. I have educated her and taught her the Qur'ān and prayer and whatever it is necessary to learn. Many people have asked for her hand and offered great dowry. I have refused to agree to anyone until what God has decreed happens and He knew before that she would be yours and that she is your luck". I told him my conditions, and he agreed, adding details, which I did not reveal out of shyness of him. I sent a [woman] whom I could trust who saw her and she informed me of things that made me happy. So I brought them all to my house … He died on the 12 Jumādā I 1199 [/22/23 March 1785]'.

55 See Anīs, 'Ḥaqā'iq', 72–3, where he mentions the following documents: سجل مبايعات الباب سنة 1240 – سلسلة 375 – مادة 443، ص147. and سجل تقارير النظر (1239–1244) سلسلة 73 المادة-9:1 ص 29. See also al-Zabīdī, *Muʿjam Mukhtaṣṣ*, f. 109b.

56 In the margin of al-Zabīdī's *Muʿjam Mukhtaṣṣ* (f. 109b) al-Jabartī added in his own handwriting the story of the way in which ʿAbd Alāh Darwīsh al-Rūmī proposed to ʿAbd al-Raḥmān that he marry al-Rūmī's step-daughter. The same narrative is to be found in the Princeton MS of *Muʿjam Mukhtaṣṣ*. My thanks are due to Professor S. Reichmuth for the copy of f. 109b of the manuscript.

According to Anīs' article mentioned above, 'His third wife was Shawq, who gave birth to his son Maḥfūẓ and survived her husband until 1260 (/1844–5). After al-Jabartī's death she married Ḥammāda Rajab and had two sons by him named Ḥasan and Ḥusayn. His first-born child Khalīl was employed by Muḥammad ʿAlī as *muwaqqit li 'l-ṣalāt wa-hilālay Ramaḍān wa-Shawwāl*, (he who fixes the time of the prayers and decides the appearance of the crescent in the months of Ramaḍān and Shawwāl [to fix the beginning of the fast of Ramaḍān and its end.] [S.M.]. Muḥammad ʿAlī is blamed for the latter's death and some have confused the identity of the victim with his father'.[57]

His son from his third wife, Maḥfūẓ possessed two MSS of his father's works, *Maẓhar al-Taqdīs*, now kept at the British Library (see below, Chapter Two, section II, 5) and *'Ajā'ib al-Āthār*, copied for him and now kept at the Institute of Oriental Studies (St Petersburg C 732, catalogue 9420; see below Chapter Two, section III, 10. a 1.) In these two MSS there is not one word about the death of his stepbrother Khalīl or the year of his father's death. Maḥfūẓ was accused of wasting his father's fortune.

Al-Jabartī's Scientific Works

ʿAbd al-Raḥmān al-Jabartī had an interest in diverse aspects of science and was able to incorporate his vast knowledge of both scientific (*'ulūm 'aqliyya*) and religious (*naqliyya*) studies into his chronicles. He relied on al-Maqrīzī for detailed descriptions of the different quarters and streets of Cairo and villages of Egypt and on al-Zabīdī for his copious biographies. Only a few of his scientific works are extant in MSS. In the Egyptian National Library (DKQ) in Cairo, there are two scientific works by al-Jabartī. The first is al-Jabartī's abridged version of Dāwūd b. ʿUmar al-Anṭākī's (d. 1008/1599–1600) *Mukhtaṣar Tadhkirat Ūlī al-Albāb wa 'l-Jāmi' li 'l-'Ajab al-'Ujāb, al-Ma'rūfa bi-Tadhkirat Dāwūd* in three manuscripts possessing varying numbers of folios: MS 1, in 246 ff. was written in 1236 (/1820–1) (shelf-mark: *Ṭibb* 136); MS 2 is in 89 ff. (shelf-mark 1627) and MS 3 is in 129 ff. (shelf-mark *Ṭibb, Ṭal'at* 532). Al-Anṭākī's work on medicine became a major source for numerous works on pharmacology and maladies, not only by al-Jabartī but also by al-Zabīdī in *Tāj al-'Arūs*. Moreover, in his *'Ajā'ib al-Āthār* he showed

57 See note 11 above on Anīs,'Ḥaqā'iq', reprinted in the margin of *'Aj.*, ʿAbd al-ʿAzīz Jamāl al-Dīn ed., II, 37, 779–87.

a special interest in plagues and diseases, and described their symptoms, their medical treatment and consequences. He was interested in the medical activities of the French, especially their pamphlet on smallpox (*judarī*), dismissed their precautionary quarantine (*karantīla*) on the pretext that it was against divine fate, and ridiculed European doctors and their method of treatment during Muḥammad ʿAlī's reign (see the Medical Index of the Arabic text of *'Ajā'ib al-Āthār* in our Arabic edition.) Many, if not all of the medical, spiritual and magical terms used by al-Jabartī are based upon al-Anṭākī's book.

A second scientific work which reflects the broad knowledge that the author brought to bear in his chronicle is a short treatise entitled *Dustūr Taqwīm al-Kawākib al-Sab'a wa 'l-Jawāhir wa 'l-Ahilla wa 'l-Tawārīkh al-Thalātha wa-Mawāsimihā wa-Tawāqītihā fī Sanat 1209 H. (Ḥisāb) al-Shaykh 'Abd al-Raḥmān al-Jabartī.* It contains seven folios under the shelf-mark *Mīqāt* M 86 (Egyptian National Library in Cairo).[58] This short treatise dealt with various seasonal phenomena, providing their Muslim, Coptic and Rūmī dates. In this treatise on the 'The Rule for the Calibration of the Seven Stars', al-Jabartī describes the seasonal cycle of the Nile floods, the kinds of vegetables and fruits that grew and ripen in every season, the constellation of the moon and the sun, the breeding of cattle, local fauna and flora, bees, the mating season of mosquitoes, as well as many other subjects. All of these items of information reflect the author's wide and diverse knowledge of climate, agriculture, geography, astronomy, seasons and nature in Egypt. He thus mentioned the flooding of the Nile, the reading of the Nilometer, the changing of the weather, gales, rain, solar and lunar eclipses and every aspect of life that affected Egypt's economy and religious life.

His first scientific work was a commentary on his father's treatise on astronomy, about which al-Zabīdī wrote:[59] 'He excelled in astronomy so that he wrote a commentary on his father's treatise dealing with this science. His father approved of it, which is an indication of his profound knowledge of this science' (*wa-mahara fī'ilm al-falak ḥattā annahu sharaḥa risālat fī hādhā al-fann ta'līf wālidihi fa 'staḥsanahu wa-dalla 'alā rusūkhihi fīhi.*) This may well

58 See *Fihrist al-Kutub al-'Arabiyya al-Maḥfūẓa bi'l-Kutubkhāna al-Khidiwiyya al-Miṣriyya*, (Cairo 1301–10 [/1883–92]), vol. V, 246. See King, *A Survey*, 114, no. D 92, 2.2.3; 2.3.12, Solar Longitude Tables. On the origins of such calendars see Huda Lutfi, 'Coptic Festivals of the Nile: Aberrations of the Past', in Philipp and Haarmann, *The Mamluks*, 258–9.

59 Al-Zabīdī, *Mu'jam Mukhtaṣṣ*, f. 60a. See note 28 above.

be a reference to the manuscript in 4 folios on astronomy entitled *Risāla bi-Khaṣṣ al-Jabartī fī 'l-'Amal bi 'l-Rub'* (A Treatise Written in the Handwriting of al-Jabartī on Work with the Quadrant) kept at the Leiden University Library.[60]

Al-Jabartī's Historical Works

Besides these scientific works, al-Jabartī wrote three chronicles of varying lengths on the history of Egypt, elaborating successfully his theories on history and society. He was an admirer of Ibn Khaldūn and his *Muqaddima*, in which he employed the Greek method of logic in writing the history of the Maghrib. This was at a time when the Muslim world faced the double challenge of fighting with the Spanish Catholic armies in al-Andalus and defending against the Mongol armies in the Mashriq. Al-Jabartī wrote his chronicle during a period when the Muslim countries were in great danger in their conflict with Christian Europe. He employed his own religious studies, moral views and values when writing his history of Egypt during what he seems to have regarded as the decline of the Ottoman Empire and of the traditional Mamluk system of military training. In this epoch the threat posed by the European imperialist powers culminated in the French invasion of Egypt. In these chronicles, the Islamic *sharī'a* and the *sunna* are the main criteria for evaluating events, and as a result he supported his judgments with Quranic verses (*āyāt Qur'āniyya*) and *ḥadīth* in order to assert his view of God's reward and punishment as admonitions to Muslim rulers and scholars. On the other hand, he used proverbs and poetry for moral purposes to back his reformist ideas. He tried to prove that prosperity could prevail only through the strict application of the *sharī'a* by Muslim rulers and subjects guided by the advice of the *'ulamā'*. Only then would Muslims be able to reform their administrative, social and economic systems, restore their military power, unite the Muslim world in general and Egypt in particular in order to restore the glorious past of the rightly guided caliphs and of the early Ottoman sultans. Only those two, were according to al-Jabartī, 'among the best to rule the (Islamic) community since the rightly-guided caliphs... They upheld the performance of Islamic rites and the *sunna* of Muḥammad. They honoured the

60 See *al-Jabartī's Chronicle*, 1, n. 3, 8–9, n. 29, 11, n. 38 and King, *A Survey*, 114. See also Voorhoeve, *Handlist*, 3 (Or. 2437); von Landberg, 61 (autograph).

'ulamā' and religious leaders…, and upheld the rules and principles of justice by observing Islamic laws and practices'.[61]

The important precept, that the *'ulamā'* are keepers, guardians, and interpreters of the *sharī'a* and also guides to both Muslim rulers and their subjects, was applied in all his chronicles.[62] In fact, these chronicles reflect the exertion of the leading *'ulamā'* to find a safe way to deal with the changing political situation in Egypt. His first extant chronicle was written during the traumatic French invasion with the purpose of understanding the real intentions of the enemy, advising how the *'ulamā'* should handle this unexpected new Crusade, and deciding to what degree Muslims should collaborate with the invader orhinder his incursions.[63] In his *Introduction* to *'Ajā'ib al-Āthār* he developed his theory of the role of the *'ulamā'*, describing the *'ulamā'* as the heirs of the prophets, who are the '*khulafā' al-Raḥmān*' (the deputies of God, the merciful), even if forced to live in obscurity.

Moreover, he decided to write his *'Ajā'ib al-Āthār* guided byhis own experience, although his new orientation put him in opposition to the authorities and infuriated them. However, he dared to reconsider some of his basic religious and historical approaches and to develop political opinions of his own. This eventually led to his isolation under Muḥammad ʿAlī and to the banning of the publication of his history until the reign of Khedive Tawfīq (1879–92). He also supported the Mamluk leader al-Alfī, his alliance with the British and the liberal ideas he espoused after visiting England, as his account of him clearly shows. His relations with the French were also quite ambiguous. He was fascinated by their quest for learning, their libraries, laboratories, tools, scientific equipments and their justice, especially with the trial of Sulaymān al-Ḥalabī, Kléber's assassin. His experience with the French convinced him that justice could be achieved even by infidels.

Al-Jabartī lived in a period that many Arab scholars, among them al-Jabartī himself and his friend Ḥasan al-ʿAṭṭār, considered a time of cultural stagnation

61 See *'Aj.*, I, 20–1. It is not the place here to deal with al-Jabartī's ethical approach, which has a remarkably individualistic touch as he upholds the individual caliphate of every believer who is responsible for his religious and ethical purity. This position, i.e. the individual caliphate has quite complex roots, mainly in mysticism and philosophical ethic (Miskawayh, Rāghib al-Iṣfahānī, and others). A version of it can also be found in al-Zabīdī's *Itḥāf.*

62 See Chapter Seven below on the status of the *'ulamā'*.

63 On the attitude of the *'ulamā'* as reflected in al-Jabartī's chronicles, see Bjørneboe, *In Search*, 287–330.

and decline, with the exception of the glorious days of Cairo under the Janissaries, especially for the circle of Riḍwān Katkhudā al-Jalfī. He observed that the standard of contemporary historical works provided an excellent example for the deterioration of Ottoman Egyptian historiography. In a comparative study of al-Jabartī's historical works, Jane Hathaway concluded that his chronicle 'is not an anomalous throwback to the glory days of Mamluk historiography but, on the contrary, is entirely consistent with the Ottoman Egyptian historical school exemplified by *Akhbār al-Nuwwāb* and the chronicles of al-Ḥallāq and Aḥmad Chelebi'.[64]

Al-Jabartī's historical works were written from the point of view of a pious Sunni *'ālim* concerned with maintaining and enhancing the status of his fellow *'ulamā'* as advisers to rulers whom they expected to rule according to the *sharī'a* for the welfare of the Muslim community, keeping away from political and administrative affairs and influence.[65] In this capacity, he expressed his religious ideas on justice and corruption under the rule of the Ottomans, Egypt's regimental officers and beys, the French and Muḥammad 'Alī, and the role of the *'ulamā'*, the military class, the ordinary Muslim subjects, and the religious minorities in Egypt.

By the eighteenth century the *Ṣūfī* movement in Egypt was headed by the *ashrāf*, descendants of Muḥammad, the Bakriyya (those who claim descendance from Abū Bakr the father of 'Ā'isha, Muḥammad's wife), and the *sādāt* who trace their descent from 'Alī. Their spiritual function as religious guides forbade them from joining the ranks of the political and military authorities of the Ottomans and Egypt's officers and beys, they preferred to become heads of the *Ṣūfī*s, to enjoy respect and religious authority amongst the people. According to al-Jabartī, the palaces of the two heads of the Bakriyya and al-Sādāt were like the courts of kings. Those religious scholars and *Ṣūfī* orders were reluctant to serve secular authorities, since that would lead to *ẓulm* (oppression) and God's punishment. Even during the French occupation, when the French asked the members of the *Dīwān* why they did not control the mobs, they affirmed that the 'Cairo mob did not fear anybody except the Turks, and that nobody else could control the people'.[66]

64 See Jane Hathaway, 'Sultans, Pashas, *Taqwīms*, and *Mühimmes*', in Daniel Crecelius, *Eighteenth Century Egypt: the Arabic Manuscript Sources* (Claremont, CA, 1990), 77.

65 See *'Aj.* Būlāq, III, 142, 287, IV, 32, and Bjørneboe, note 10 above.

66 *'Aj.*, III, 11.

His interest in recording the history of Egypt, according to his testimony in *'Ajā'ib al-Āthār*, first arose in 1190 (/1776–7). Although it may have been even earlier when al-Jabartī was 22 years of age, following the death of his father (1 Ṣafar, 1188 [/13 April 1774]), since the first time he speaks of an informant (*nāqil*) was on the event of the death of Muḥammad Bek Abu 'l-Dhahab in 1189 (/1775–6). However, his mentor Murtaḍā al-Zabīdī (d. 1791) in his *Mu'jam Mukhtaṣṣ* related that his student had already begun writing a chronicle of Egypt.[67] Al-Jabartī confirmed this fact, but later on he tells us that these papers were lost.

The first chronicle that he recorded and has survived was given an erroneous title by the scholar mentioned above, Amīn al-Madanī: *Hādhā Tārīkh Muddat al-Faransīs bi-Miṣr min Sanat 1213 ilā Sanat 1216, ta'līf al-'Allāma 'Abd al-Raḥmān al-Miṣrī bi-Khaṭṭihi Raḥimahu Allāh.*[68] In fact, it dealt with the first seven months of the French occupation of Egypt, from Muḥarram to Rajab 1213 (15 June 1798–December 1798). It seems that it was written in 1798 under the immediate impact of the French invasion, which crushed the legendary Mamluk military forces. (In our Arabic edition it is indicated by the letters مدة *mudda*).

It seems that MS*Mudda* is a fair copy of the first seven months of the French occupation written by al-Jabartī when he decided to resume his historical recording of events in Egypt after neglecting his undertaking following the death of al-Murādī (1791). There is no clear indication of the real motive for resuming his recording except for the unusual events of the ear; was it the shock of the unexpected invasion which he considered to be a new wave of Crusaders with renewed religious zeal, or was it a matter of political solidarity with his co-religionists the Ottomans? Was he inspired by the remarkable events that occurred during and after the French invasion, or was he invited by the Ottomans to join forces in their religious, military, and psychological war against the French? In his plentiful documentation of the period of the French invasion, al-Jabartī reports on the attitudes of the

67 Al-Zabīdī, *Mu'jam Mukhtaṣṣ*, MS Princeton 126–7, ff. 60a–60b.

68 See *al-Jabartī's Chronicle*, 1, n. 3, 7–12 (English part), and 11, n. 38. See also Voorhoeve, *Handlist*, 3 (Or. 2437). It appears under the incorrect title of *'Agā'ib al-Āthār fī 't-Tarāgim wa'l-Akhbār* (*GAL*, II, 480; *GAL*, *Suppl.*, II, 730); von Landberg, 61 (autograph). On al-Jabartī's chronicles, see Lars Bjørneboe, *In Search of the True Political Position of the 'Ulamā, An Analysis of the Aims and Perspectives of the Chronicles of Abd al-Rahman al-Jabarti (1753–1825)*(Aarhus 2007).

*'ulamā'*and gives information about the Ottomans; this along with the documents on the reaction of and news from Constantinople towards the events, may support the theory that he was recruited by the Ottomans.[69]

An Ottoman *firmān* written in Arabic and sent by the Sultan to various Arab port cities had many points in common with the comments of al-Jabartī on the first French proclamation. Both documents refute the principles of the French Revolution and its materialistic views on religion, and its secular ideology and materialistic philosophical outlook. Al-Jabartī's repetition of all these principles in his vehement criticism of the content and style of the first French proclamation is the best evidence that he received copies of the Firman and of the French proclamation. There is no indication how our author received them. Did he receive them together or separately? He mentions only three types of information:

(1) The *mukātabāt* (sing. *mukātaba*) and *awrāq* (letters, written correspondences, or printed proclamations) which were carried by messengers (*su'āt*). These correspondences were also read in public.

(2) *Akhbār* (sing. *khabar*) (oral news, or rumours spreading among people).

(3) *Munādāt* (official announcement, order or information issued by local authorities proclaimed in public).

It is clear that officials who were eyewitnesses or had first-hand information and could give a detailed and precise indication of times, places and events that happened in Alexandria and elsewhere during the French occupation, and formulate their accounts of them in a professional and official manner wrote the *mukātabāt*. On the other hand, the term *akhbār* might be synonymous with *qīla* (rumours). No single person could collect all these pieces of information; rather the authorities needed the cooperation of people involved and interested in supplying these reports to historians. Most probably, al-Jabartī was already known to the Ottomans for his attempt to write the history of Egypt and his collaboration with al-Zabīdī and al-Murādī. This fact can be inferred from al-Murādī's description, in a letter dated 1200/1785–86 directed to al-Zabīdī describing a *majlis* in Istanbul in which the neglect of recording history was discussed. Al-Murādī was present at this meeting along

69 I hope that some scholar will take the trouble to check the Ottoman archives for any related records on al-Jabartī.

with other scholars, among whom was a person who was 'avidly for hunting for news' (*iqtināṣ al-akhbār*). This informant (*rajul ikhbārī*) spoke about al-Zabīdī and his cooperation with al-Murādī[70] in writing 'a great history' of eminent men of the period. We may presume that after the death of al-Zabīdī the Ottomans found no better historian and scholar, who could join them in their efforts to unite the Muslims against the French *kuffār* (infidels) and be their agent. Moreover, the fact is that a member of the entourage of the Ottoman general and grand vizier Yūsuf Ḍiyā Pasha asked our author, whose father was a close friend of the Ottomans, and ʿAbd Allāh al-Sharqāwī, both members of the *Dīwān* established by the French, to write an account of the French occupation. All these facts show that the Ottomans considered them as their loyal friends, and probably that they had knowledge of al-Jabartī's recording of events. There is no indication the *Muddat al-Faransīs* was an intelligence report, although the *Maẓhar al-Taqdīs* was translated into Turkish in 1222 (/1807–8) or 1225 (/1810–11).

Al-Jabartī's second work, a book entitled *Maẓhar al-Taqdīs bi-Zawāl Dawlat al-Faransīs* (The Manifestation of Blessing in the Demise of French Authority), deals with the French occupation between 15 June 1798 and the end of December 1801 (Muḥarram 1213 to Shaʿbān 1216) (In our Arabic edition it is indicated by the letters مَظْهر *maẓhar* according to MS*Maẓhar al-Taqdīs*, Rampur, and not *Muẓhir*). In the Introduction al-Jabartī mentions the contribution of his friend Ḥasan al-ʿAṭṭār to this work. The higher stylistic standard of *Maẓhar al-Taqdīs*, compared to that of *Muddat al-Faransīs* convince us that al-ʿAṭṭār, who was famous for his excellence in grammar, style and poetry, polished al-Jabartī's text in the hope that the author and his friends would be cleared of any charge of having collaborated with the enemies of Islam. This work was written at the request of a member of Grand Vizier Yūsuf Pāshā Ḍiyā's entourage and was dedicated to him. Therefore the author flattered the general, added al-ʿAṭṭār's panegyric poetry, and expressed his belief that only a man named Yūsuf was destined by God to deliver Egypt from calamities, as in the case of Joseph, the son of Jacob, and Yūsuf Ṣalāḥ al-Dīn before Yūsuf Ḍiyā Pāshā. The author praises the Ottoman officials, and criticizes the 'infidel French', who tried to lure the Muslims from their *sharīʿa* and from their heritage and moral values, attempting to incite them against

70 *ʿAj.*, II, 235–6.

their legitimate Muslimrulers, the Ottomans.[71] The book was translated into Turkish by the Chief Physician Muṣṭafā Bahjat Afandī under the title تاريخ مصر ترجمهء بهجت افندي, *Tārīkhī Miṣr, Tarjama-'i Bahjat Afandī Ra'īs al-Aṭibbā'*, who on page 5 said about the author: أعلام علماء مصريه دن شيخ حسن جبرتي مرحومك نجل نجيبي عبد الرحمن أفندي ... مظهر التقديس بخروج طائفة الفرنسيس. The book was translated by the order of the Serdar Yūsuf Ḍiyā Pāshā:[72] سعادتلو يوسف ضيا باشا حضرتلري سردار اكرم.

It seems that al-Jabartī continued to record events without biographies until 1806, changing his attitude towards the French and the Ottomans and adding vehement criticism of the vicious behaviour of the Ottoman soldiers and officials. It seems that this change came out of his conviction as to the importance of the duty of the *'ulamā'* to 'enjoin good and forbid evil' (*al-amr bi 'l-ma'rūf wa 'l-nahy 'an al-munkar*); this conviction pushed him to criticize Ottoman rule in Egypt. When Muḥammad ʿAlī felt himself strong enough in Egypt, he started to restrain the *'ulamā'*, who brought him to power and expelled the *sharīf* ʿUmar Makram. He preferred to replace them with obedient secular western-educated officials who would implement his reforms.

The fact that, as far as we know, no manuscript of *'Ajā'ib al-Āthār* is kept in any Turkish library is of considerable significance and indicates that the Ottomans eventually became hostile towards al-Jabartī. We know that al-ʿAṭṭār carried with him a copy of the first 3 volumes of *'Ajā'ib al-Āthār* written in *Maghribī* script during his travels in the Ottoman central lands and Syria in the expectation of being able to circulate them as he had done with al-Zabīdī's books. Nonetheless, he returned to Egypt with them and sold them to Burckhardt. This fact might indicate that al-ʿAṭṭār was not able to sell his copy of *'Ajā'ib al-Āthār* in Turkey and Syria because of its contents, while he was able to sell other books which he took with him or copied to sustain himself at a time when he was in great need of money. This raises further questions: was the manuscript, which was copied in Syrian script and is kept at the Iraq Museum, covering the first half of *'Ajā'ib al-Āthār*, volume I, an attempt to copy the chronicle for circulation in Syria? Can we presume that the Ottomans

---

71 *al-Jabartī's Chronicle*, 18. Cf. Afaf Lutfi al-Sayyid Marsot, 'A Comparative Study of Abd al-Rahman al-Jabarti and Niqula Turk', in Crecelius, *Eighteenth Century Egypt*, 116–17. See also Ayalon, 'The Historian', 238–41, which is reprinted as a Preface to volume I, *'Ajā'ib al-Āthār*, of our Arabic Edition.

72 See UCLA Library, shelf mark: PJ8190. I8/M66 1997.

had banned al-Jabartī because he criticized them in volume III of *'Ajā'ib al-Āthār*, and aso they refused to buy or to copy the book in contrast to their attitude to *Maẓhar al-Taqdīs* a few years previously? Could al-Jabartī have suffered from his association with Sultan Salīm III, or at least with one of his grand viziers, namely Yūsuf Ḍiyā? In any case, it is possible to presume that MS *'Aj.* Tārīkh 1426/microfilm 35532 (VI. 19. c.) kept at DKQ in Cairo, is the enlarged version of *Maẓhar al-Taqdīs* and was converted by the author as the draft of volume III of his first three volumes of *'Ajā'ib al-Āthār*, which will be discussed below.

His third and final work on Egyptian history is the voluminous and comprehensive chronicleof *'Ajā'ib al-Āthār fi 'l-Tarājim wa 'l-Akhbār* (The Marvellous Compositions of Biographies and Chronicles), first written in three volumes to which he later added a fourth which he ended with the year 1821, with the intention of writing a fifth. In his long *Introduction*, he abstained from praising and flattering rulers. Instead, he discussed in detail his Islamic historical philosophy and value system, including the importance of the *sharī'a*, the role of the *'ulamā'* as its guardians and as guides who should show rulers how to adhere to their religious rules, and how to apply the Islamic rules of justice, equality, and unity. Al-Jabartī's ability to change his judgments and views after his experience with the rule of the Ottomans, the Mamluks and the French, and to criticize Muḥammad ʿAlī's Western reforms, reveal his greatness as an objective historian who was able to follow his new convictions and adhere to his own truth.

In fact, this comprehensive chronicle reflects two main periods in the religious, political, and intellectual history of Egyptian society. The first two volumes of *'Ajā'ib al-Āthār* (1688–1797) reflect the period in which *Ṣūfī* orders, both those headed by the Sunni oriented branches of the Khalwatis, the Wafā'iyya and al-Bakriyya and the popular branches with their orientation towards magic, superstition and saint worship, dominated religion, politics and the economic realms of Egyptian society. The first branch not only encouraged the study of *ḥadīth*, but also formed religious and literary salons, which encouraged literary and historical studies and attracted poets and men of letters under the patronage of wealthy and noble *Ṣūfī* families descended from the Prophet, his relatives and his companions. To his chronicle al-Jabartī added to his data short biographies of popular *Ṣūfī* saints, who had become famous for their miracles. Popular poets composed panegyric and elegiac poems and songs, accompanied by music and dancing to celebrate the deeds and miracles of these saints on their birthdays (*mawlid*s) and festivals. These festivals were not merely religious gatherings in which poems in praise of the Prophet Muḥammad and the saints were recited in the *dhikr* sessions, but were also literary, social and trading occasions frequented by serious and popular poets who offered their compositions to the *Ṣūfī* leaders and *'ulamā'*. Poets and scholars of *ḥadith* were engaged in public affairs and voiced social, religious, and political criticism. Their biographies comprise most of the necrologies in al-Jabartī's first two volumes, which were mostly copied from al-Zabīdī's works. The poems of the *Ṣūfī* poet Ḥasan al-Badrī al-Ḥijāzī,[73] a scholar of *kalām*, are quoted as part of coverage of historical events. On the other hand, moral advice dealing with proper conduct and warnings against evil people are also quoted by al-Jabartī in these necrologies. These quotations form a considerable part of his anthology, mirroring the period. On the other hand, volumes III–IV consist of annals dealing mainly with the unusual events of the French invasion and the military, economic, and social reforms of Muḥammad ʻAlī, while the necrologies in volume IV are short and confined to a few religious scholars and secular officials.[74]

This last chronicle has come down to us in a large number of manuscripts, at least 38, but, as far as we know, not one from Turkey. Some are in al-Jabartī's own handwriting and others are copied by various copyists; some are edited by the author with his corrections in the margins. These MSS either contain the three volumes as did al-Jabartī's autograph written in 1220 (/1805–6) or include the fourth volume as well, completed by al-Jabartī in 1237 (/1821–2). Some of the MSS only contain one of these volumes.

The third stage of his history is represented by an autograph of al-Jabartī, now kept at the Cambridge University Library, covering the years 1100 (/1688–9) to 1220 (/1805–6). It was acquired by the orientalist and traveller Johann Ludwig Burckhardt (1784–1817) [al-Shaykh Ibrāhīm], probably in 1232 (/1816–17). Presumably, he bought it in the same year in which he

73 *'Aj.*, I, 75–83.

74 M.W. Daly (ed.), *The Cambridge History of Egypt, Vol. 2, Modern Egypt, from 1517 to the End of the Twentieth Century* (Cambridge 1998); R.J.A. McGregor, *Sanctity and Mysticism in Medieval Egypt, The Wafa' Sufi Order and the Legacy of Ibn 'Arabi* (New York 2004); see Fu'ād Kanʻānī, 'al-Ḥayāt al-Adabiyya fī Miṣr', unpublished Ph.D. thesis (Hebrew University, Jerusalem 2007).

bought the manuscript of *Maẓhar al-Taqdīs*, as he recorded on the title page of his copy.[75] The autograph was completed in 1220 (/1805–6) and comprises three volumes, MS *'Aj.* Cam., Qq. 169, 170, 171 (see Chapter Two, section III, 1 a–c below)(henceforth MS *'Aj.* Cam.) It covers the period between 1100 (/1688–9) and 1220 (/1805–6). In our Arabic edition it is indicated by the letters عك *'k*, with the sign // ..... // to mark passages specific to this version. In volume I of this manuscript there is a note in the margin that the biography of Amīr Riḍwān Aghā al-Faqārī should be moved from the years 1106–42 (/1694–1730) to the year 1143 (/1730–1). The biographies in MS *'Aj.* Cam., Qq. 169, vol. I, f. 48b are given in a different order from p. 66 of the Būlāq edition. (In our Arabic edition it is indicated by the letters عج *'j* with the sign *[...]*). In volume II, there are also some differences in the biographies, e.g. the order of some sentences in the biography of Shaykh Muḥammad al-Halbāwī, MS *'Aj.* Cam., Qq. 169, vol. I, f. 48a, was changed in the Būlāq edition of volume II, 55. Volume III of the Cambridge autograph ends with the events of 25 Dhu 'l-Ḥijja of the year 1216 (/28 April 1802), without the necrologies of that year. The events between 1213 (/1798) and the end of Shaʿbān 1216 (/5 January1802) are based on *Maẓhar al-Taqdīs*. To the data contained in *Maẓhar al-Taqdīs* the author adds biographies mainly in the margin, which indicate that they were added later on, after he had managed to buy al-Zabīdī's biographical dictionary from the latter's widow.[46] He also adds a number of events which are not mentioned in *Maẓhar al-Taqdīs*, such as the trial of Sulaymān al-Ḥalabī, and changes the accounts of others, such as a summary of the Wahhābī proclamation of Muḥarram 1218 (/23 April–22 May 1803), the full version of which is given in a later copy, edited by himself. All these additions and corrections indicate that the three parts were in fact a draft or preliminary version of *'Ajā'ib al-Āthār*.

Besides the Cambridge autograph in three volumes, there exist at least three other manuscripts of the first three volumes of *'Ajā'ib al-Āthār* that were inspected and collated by al-Jabartī personally. The title pages, the last lines of the volumes and the corrections in the margins are in al-Jabartī's handwriting, copied according to the Cambridge autograph. These are MS *'Aj.* Cam. 2nd., Qq. 168,written in a *Maghribī* script; MS *'Aj.* BN 6, both in three volumes, and volume III only of MS *'Aj.* DKQ., Tārīkh 174 in Cairo.

75 See MS *Maẓhar al-Taqdīs* in *al-Jabartī's Chronicle*, 7–9 and plate VI.

It is possible to understand from the words in the autograph 'it was read...in the presence' that the collation was done in the last days of the author's life, when he was already blind and that he continued employing copyists in response to various orders for copies of the book. This colophon was written by Aḥmad b. Ḥasan al-Rashīdī known as Ṣawbaʿ on 14 Rabīʿ I 1240 (/6 November 1824). The explanation for this remark could be that al-Jabartī, as a rich book dealer with broad connections with Muslim scholars, European consuls and travellers such as Belzoni, Burckhardt and Asselin, was still engaged at the time in employing copyists, collating their copies with his autographs and correcting them according to his memory and his new world view of the past. This fact indicates that al-Jabartī could employ several copyists to deal with selling and buying books,[76] mainly those that he inherited from his father or those that he wrote.

During his journey in the Arabic speaking countries in the service of the Company for Discovering the Sources of the Nile, Burckhardt was presented by many Muslim *'ulamā'* with letters of recommendation as a bibliophile looking for rare books and interested in antiquaries. It seems that by means of this cover identity with which he tried to hide his main mission of discovering the sources of the Nile, he met al-Jabartī and bought many of his books, befriended him and with him went to see the statues that Belzoni brought from Upper Egypt on their way to the British Museum in London.[77]

The success of al-Jabartī's works, *Maẓhar al-Taqdīs*, and the first three volumes of *'Ajā'ib al-Āthār* brought him fame, especially after the translation of his book into Turkish by the chief physician of the Sultan Salīm III, Muṣṭafā

76 See the colophon in *'Aj.*, IV, 320. No autograph of the fourth volume of *'Ajā'ib al-Āthār* has yet been discovered. According to Jūrjī Zaydān there was a manuscript in the Muḥammad Bek Āṣaf Library in Cairo, copied by Aḥmad b. Ḥasan al-Rashīdī in 1237/1821–2, and authorized by al-Jabartī on 6 November 1824 (see Jurjī Zaydān, *Tārīkh Ādāb al-Lugha al-'Arabiyya* [Cairo 1911–22], 1st edn., IV, 283, cf. Ayalon, 'The Historian', 229, n. 3). Another manuscript in which al-Jabartī wrote a colophon and added many passages and annotations in the margins, is in Dār al-Kutub al-Qawmiyya, *Amānat al-Makhṭūṭāt*, Cairo, MS *'Aj.* Tārīkh 174, vol. III only (VI. 14. c. below), which is catalogued as volume I of *'Ajā'ib al-Āthār*. A third copy is also in Dār al-Kutub in a collection called 'al-Zakiyya', which was in the possession of Aḥmad Zakī Pāshā, containing of *'Ajā'ib al-Āthār*, volumes II–III, said to have been copied in 1237 (/1821–2) (see Chapter Two, VII. 31. b. and 32. c.). I was not able to examine these two volumes during my visits to Dār al-Kutub al-Qawmiyya in September 1993 and in February 1995, because they were in the photographic department at the time.

77 See Stanley Mayes, *The Great Belzoni, The Circus Strongman Who Discovered Egypt's Treasures* (New York 1959 and 2003).

Bahjat Afandī in 1222 (/1807–8). The MSS of *'Ajā'ib al-Āthār* held in some major European capitals seem to have been ordered either to be copied or purchased by their consuls in Cairo a long time before al-Jabartī sold his draft autographs of *Maẓhar al-Taqdīs* and *'Ajā'ib al-Āthār* to Johann Ludwig Burckhardt. This is the reason why our author was able to revise and collate these MSS prepared by some of his copyists from the draft of his first three parts of *'Ajā'ib al-Āthār*, now kept in Cambridge.

The first of these three copies, which were revised by al-Jabartī and represent the second stage in the composition of his book *'Ajā'ib al-Āthār*, was copied in *Maghribī* script from his autograph draft, acquired first by Ḥasan al-ʿAṭṭār and then by Burckhardt, and eventually sent to Cambridge University Library, (Cambridge University Library, in three volumes Qq. 166, 167, 168) (henceforth MS *'Aj.* Cam. 2nd.)(See Chapter Two, III. 2. a–c below). There are only a few corrections and additions added in the margin in al-Jabartī's handwriting, with no colophon. However, all three volumes contain copious marginal comments and remarks by al-Jabartī's friend Ḥasan al-ʿAṭṭār with his signature, added during his journey to Istanbul, Izmir, Damascus, Jaffa and Jerusalem.[78]

This copy of *'Ajā'ib al-Āthār*in *Maghribī* scripts raises some questions. Was it meant to be sent to one of the sultans of Morocco? It was after all customary to do so with important works by famous authors, as in the case of the copies made of the *Sharḥ Iḥyā' 'Ulūm al-Dīn* which al-Zabīdī copied and sent to Istanbul, Syria and the Maghreb[79] and his *Tāj al-'Arūs*,[80] which he sent to a number of rulers in the hope of being rewarded and gaining a reputation in the Muslim world? Why was this particular copy carried with al-ʿAṭṭār, who was of *Maghribī* origin, to Turkey and Greater Syria but not to the Maghreb? Why did al-ʿAṭṭār bring it back to Egypt with his comments and corrections, with additions, reports of his experiences and impressions of the places that he had visited, in a style utterly incongruent with the style of his friend al-Jabartī? Why did al-Jabartī sell it to Burckhardt and not allow al-ʿAṭṭār to sell it for him when he was in need as al-ʿAṭṭār had done with other books that he took with

78 See the margins of MS *'Aj.* Cam. 2nd., Qq. 166–8 where al-ʿAṭṭār describes the itinerary of his voyage to Turkey and Syria, and S. Moreh, 'al-Jabartī's Method of Composing his Chronicle', *JSAI* 25 (2001), 368–9, plates 1–2.

79 *'Aj.*, II, 201.

80 Ibid., II, 197–9.

him, as we have mentioned above? Was it because al-Jabartī could not find anyone who would agree to take the chronicle to the Maghreb as a result of his critical attitude towards *Maghribī* belief in the supposed supernatural powers of al-Zabīdī[81] and therefore sent it with his friend with the intention to publishing his book in Istanbul? Was it because of his severe criticism of the Ottomans in *'Ajā'ib al-Āthār* that the book did not meet with a favourable reception and was returned to the author, as against the case of *Maẓhar al-Taqdīs*, which was received favourably by Sultan Salīm III?

Whatever the truth of the matter, this is an important copy because of its lengthy marginal comments and remarks added in all the first three volumes in a different hand signed by al-Jabartī's friend 'Ḥasan b. Muḥammad *al-shahīr* (well-known as) *bi* 'l-ʿAṭṭār', or '*al-faqīr* (humble) al-ʿAṭṭār'. Many of these comments contain the latter's impressions of his journey to Istanbul, Izmir, Damascus, Jaffa and Jerusalem, as well as versified elegies, comments on events and corrections of al-Jabartī's grammar and usage of Arabic.

There are two other copies of importance, which were also edited by the author and contain, in addition to the title page, many marginal corrections in the author's hand, noting the copyist's omissions due to homoeoteleuton (missing sentences with similar endings) or misreading. These are MS *'Ajā'ib al-Āthār* in the Bibliothèque Nationale, Paris (see Chapter Two, III. 7. a–c below) and MS *'Ajā'ib al-Āthār* in the DKQ, Cairo, shelf mark Tārīkh 174/microfilm 10730 (see Chapter Two, VI. 14. c. volume III only). The latter has a passage within the text, as well as the final lines of the manuscript, written in the hand of al-Jabartī himself. Most of these corrections are also found in MS *'Aj.* Cam., and there are only a very few additions to the second version. This fact indicates that al-Jabartī collated it by himself with his draft copy of MS *'Aj.* Cam.

Besides these three revised copies, there are a number of MSS which contain, in addition to the first three volumes including the emendations of the second stage in which the author or the copyist incorporated al-Jabartī's corrections and additions, a fourth volume which covers the events of the years 1221 to 1236 (/22 March 1806–7 September 1821). This third stage in the compilation of *'Ajā'ib al-Āthār* is represented by MSS kept at DKQ, shelf-mark MS *'Aj.* Tārīkh 466/microfilm 35088 (VI. 15. d. below), MS *'Aj.* Tārīkh

81 Ibid., II, 200–1.

1425 (VI. 18. d.), MS *'Aj.* Tārīkh 1427 (VI. 20), MS *'Aj.* Tārīkh 1872 (III. 21), MS *'Aj.* Tārīkh Taymūr 1562 (VI. 21. d.). At the end of this fourth volume of MS *'Aj.* Tārīkh 1425/microfilm 12749 (negative) and microfilm 54400 (positive), the colophon reads that coverage of events will be in the following volume (i.e. the fifth), and that the task of copying the manuscript ended on 7 Rabīʿ II 1289 (/13/14 June 1872), as follows:[82] أما حادثة الأروام التي هي باقية حتى الآن ... فسيتلى عليك ان شاء الله تعالى بكماله في الجزء الآتي بعد ذلك والله الموفق للصواب ... وكان الفراغ من كتابة هذا الجزء يوم الخميس المبارك سبعة أيام خلت من شهر ربيع الثاني سنة 1289 من الهجرة النبوية... ('God willing, we shall relate to you all their subsequent doings in the forthcoming part'). So far nothing has been found of such a 'forthcoming part' or any autograph of volume IV in any library or manuscript collection to which we have had access. It seems that these parts were burnt in the fire, which destroyed al-Jabartī's house in al-Ṣanādiqiyya.

In the fourth stage when all four volumes of *'Ajā'ib al-Āthār* were being copied, perhaps after the author's death, each one of the four volumes was divided into two parts and the copyist took the liberty in many cases of changing the author's style from *lectio difficilior* (difficult reading) into *lectio facilior* (easy reading), as in the following examples:

1. وكاونوهم الى الليل (they fought with them until nightfall) (MS *'Aj.* Cam., Qq. 169, vol. I, f. 104b), while in *'Aj.* Būlāq, I, 142, the verb, which denotes mutual action, is distorted to an intransitive verb: وكامنوهم الى الليل (they lay in wait for them [i.e. ambushed them] until nightfall);

2. والهجن والبغال وارباب العيط (racing camels, mules and the owners of prime camels) (MS *'Aj.* Cam., Qq. 170, vol. II, f. 162a), while in *'Aj.* Būlāq, II, 224, it is distorted to the senseless words: ...وأرباب الصيت (the prestigious people);

3. فخرست المزروعات (the cultivated fields were spoiled (MS *'Aj.* Cam., Qq. 170, vol. II, f. 164b), while in *'Aj.* Būlāq, II, 226, it is distorted to فحرثوا المزروعات (they ploughed some of the fields);

4. MS *'Aj.* Cam., Qq. 171, vol. III, f. 33a: مناور القناديل والمجامع العظيمة (oil lamps and huge chandeliers of four lamps [*majāmi'*] which men carry), while *'Aj.* Būlāq, III, 140 has the completely different meaning: ...والجوامع العظيمة مناور القناديل [sic] (lamps of minarets and large mosques [!], such as men would carry [!]);

82 See the colophon in *'Aj.*, IV, 320.

5. والرج والشك... والناس بين ناف ومثبت ('people were in turmoil and suspicious, ... variously rejecting and affirming'), while in *'Aj*. Būlāq, III, 306 it is distorted into a phrase carrying the opposite meaning in favour of the Ottomans: ...الفرح والشنك ('Rejoicing and celebrating with fireworks and shooting of cannons continued');

6. تطوّست (the wool of the texture of the kiswa [the black, brocaded carpet covering the walls of the Ka'ba] has been buffed) (MS *'Aj*. Ber., IV, f. 164b). This *lectio difficilior* became in the Būlāq edition. توسّخت (soiled, became dirty) a *lectio facilior* version of erroneous meaning (*'Aj*. Būlāq, IV, 179).

7. Muḥammad 'Alī is mentioned in the Būlāq edition as Pasha and the Mamluks are cursed, while in the autograph MS *'Aj*. Cam., he is mentioned without the title of Pasha and with no curses against the Mamluks who were massacred (*'Aj*. Būlāq, III, 343). It seems that the copyist or the editor of the MS., an official editor at the government press at Būlāq, took the liberty of changing the author's version.

8. Some officials with the title of Afandī or Bek (Bey) in the Cambridge group of MSS (our Arabic edition, vol. III, n. 68) are given higher ranks in the Būlāq group of MSS, e.g. Aghā and Bāshā (Pasha) (*'Aj*. Būlāq, III, 344). This is another clear indication that the editor of the MS on which the Būlāq edition was based was an official who was aware that these officials had been promoted in his time and he changed their ranks accordingly.

In this fourth stage, each of the four volumes was divided into two parts. This is represented by MS Bankipore 1076–83 MS H. L. 2324 in the Khuda Bakhsh Library, Patna (Chapter Two, section IV. 11. a1–d2, below), and by the edition of 'Abd al-'Azīz Jamāl al-Dīn printed by Madbūlī Publications (Cairo 1997), which is based on a single microfilmed MS, owned by Cairo University. This MS seems to be copied after the death of our author; therefore, it is similar to the Būlāq edition.

In fact, the *'Ajā'ib al-Āthār* MSS, scattered in various libraries, may be classified into two main types according to the number of volumes they contain: those MSS that contain volumes I–III and those, which contain volumes I–IV. The two types can be distinguished according to the following criteria:

1) A change in a phrase in the opening sentences of volume I of *'Ajā'ib al-Āthār*, p. 2, which appears in the Cambridge autograph in three volumes and in all the MSS copied from it, as: الحمد لله القديم الأول ... خالق الخلايق ومنزه عن العلايق . In all the MSS that contain four volumes

including some MSS of the Būlāq group, this opening phrase was changed to الحمد لله القديم الأول خالق الخلايق وعالم الذرّات بالحقايق ...

2) The absence of blessings following the names of God (الله), prophets and caliphs in the Cambridge autograph and in all the MSS copied from it. In later copies, blessings were added, as for example: ...الله تعالى، سيدنا إبراهيم عليه الصلاة والسلام، عمر رضي الله عنه

3) A case of homoeoteleuton in *'Ajā'ib al-Āthār*, I, 6 وتواريخ المسعودي أخبار الزمان والأوسط ومروج الذهب. ومن أجلّ التواريخ تواريخ الذهبي الكبير والأوسط المسمى بالعبر ... The sentence between the two words الأوسط was dropped due to homoeoteleuton in the Būlāq edition only.

The printed Būlāq edition is based upon the manuscripts in the Library of the Būlāq Press which were presented to al-Kutubkhāna al-Miṣriyya (nowadays Dār al-Kutub al-Qawmiyya), hereafter termed 'the Būlāq group of MSS' on 6 January, 1895, as recorded on MSS nos. 16, 17, 19 (Chapter Two, VI. 17. a. 1.–21. a. 1. below). The first two volumes in the Būlāq group of MSS, from which the edition was prepared, are more or less identical to the Cambridge autograph. The differences consist mainly of variations in sentences due to scribal errors and misreading, especially in volume I. Several sentences were changed or deleted due to homoeoteleuton. Beside the MSS of the Būlāq group, there is a MS in the K. Hof- und Staatsbibliothek in Munich, MS Or. Prunneri 259, which corresponds to the first volume of the Būlāq edition (see Chapter Two, III. 8. a. below). Moreover, there are two MSS corresponding to the first volume of the Būlāq edition kept at the Khuda Bakhsh Library, Patna: MS Bankipore, 1076–7 (Chapter Two, IV. 11. a1–a2 below).

Whereas the first two volumes of the printed Būlāq edition run largely parallel to the Cambridge autograph, the production of volume III seems to have been more complex, as it contains many passages that are not found in the autograph or in any of the *'Ajā'ib al-Āthār* manuscripts kept at DKQ in Cairo, which we were able to examine. There may be several reasons for this divergence. On the one hand, there are indications that volume III of *'Ajā'ib al-Āthār* was composed by al-Jabartī in various phases. The first phase ends with the last events of 25 Dhu 'l-Ḥijja 1216 (/28 April 1802), when a woman was hanged for stealing clothes from a public bath, and without the necrologies of the year 1216 (/1801–2); the Cambridge autograph (MSS nos. 169, 170, 171) represents it. Here, al-Jabartī gives the Wahhābī proclamation of

Muḥarram 1218 (/23 April–22 May 1803) in summarized form, while the quotation from al-ʿAṭṭār describing the beauty of the al-Azbakiyya quarter, is modified. The second phase has the additional events of the year 1216 (/1801–2) and its necrologies, as well as a long poem in praise of Ismāʿīl Bey which al-Jabartī was able to find among some discarded papers in the handwriting of Shaykh Muḥammad al-Ghamrī (MS *'Aj.* Cam., Qq. 169, vol. I, f. 86a, *'Aj.* Būlāq, I, 121–2). The third phase has the hypercorrection in the French proclamation, made by a copyist. In addition, it has the full text of the Wahhābī proclamation while changes have been made in the passage of al-ʿAṭṭār describing the al-Azbakiyya quarter.

Although it is at present rather difficult to ascertain which MSS were used by the editors of the Būlāq edition, especially for the third volume, careful scrutiny, and comparison of all extant MSS may provide some clues. For example, in volume III of the Būlāq edition there is a hyper-corrected sentence in the text of Bonaparte's first proclamation to the Egyptians. In al-Jabartī's autograph and the other three MSS which he personally edited (i.e. MS *'Aj.* Cam. 2nd., Qq. 166–8, the Paris MS and MS *'Aj.* Tārīkh 174), the end of paragraph four and paragraph five follow the original proclamation by the French: وبيّن المماليك [!] ما العقل والفضائل والمعرفة التي تميّزهم عن الآخرين وتستوجب أنهم يتملّكوا وحدهم كلما يحلوا به حيات [!] الدنيا * حيثما يوجد ارض مخصبه فهي مختصّة للمماليك والجواري الاجمل والخيل الاحسن والمساكن الاشهى فهذا كله لهم خاصا, which corresponds with the original French proclamation: 'Or, quelle sagesse, quelles talents, quelles vertus, distinguent les Mamlouks, pour qu'ils aient exclusive, ont tout ce qui rendre la vie aimable et douce?'[83] This passage was changed, most probably by one of the copyists of volume III of *'Ajā'ib al-Āthār*, into what he considered a more idiomatic and clear style, as follows:[84] بَيْن المماليك والعقل والفضائل تضارب فماذا يميزهم عن غيرهم حتى يستوجبوا أن يتملكوا مصر وحدهم ويختصوا بكل شئ أحسن فيها من الجواري الحسان والخيل العتاق والمساكن المفرحة This hyper-corrected passage might have been accepted by the editor of the Būlāq edition, and adopted by all the printed editions of *'Ajā'ib al-Āthār.* As such, it should be taken as a criterion for deciding which MSS were copied directly from the autograph of al-Jabartī and thus can help us identify the manuscripts from which volume III of the Būlāq edition was prepared.

---

83 See ʿAbd al-Raḥmānal-Jabartī, *Journal d'un notable du Caire; durant l'expédition française 1798–1801*, traduit et annoté par Joseph Cuoq, préface de Jean Taulard (Paris 1979).

84 See *Mudda*, 8 (Arabic Text), cf. *'Aj.*, III, 5, ll. 1–3.

One of the MSS which was copied in 1237 (/1821–2) and read to al-Jabartī in 1240 (/1824–5), is MS *'Aj.* al-Zakiyya, 859/microfilm 54236 (Chapter Two, VII. 32. C.). This MS was not in the possession of the Būlāq Press, and may therefore, be presumed not to have been used for volume III of the Būlāq edition. Jurjī Zaydān states that in the library of Muḥammad Bey Āṣaf he found a manuscript of *'Ajā'ib al-Āthār* which was read to al-Jabartī and collated with another copy of *'Ajā'ib al-Āthār* in the presence of the author in 1240 (/1824–5). Muḥammad Bey Āṣaf intended to donate his library to an Egyptian institute, but it seems he was not able to do so. Examination of the stamps on the title page show that it was donated first to the Ministry of Endowments (*Wizārat al-Awqāf*) and then to the National Library in Cairo from the al-Zakiyya Library of Aḥmad Zakī Pāshā.

Of the Dār al-Kutub al-Qawmiyya manuscripts which we examined, only one corresponds closely to volume III of the Būlāq edition. This is MS *'Aj.* Tārīkh 1426/microfilm 35532 (VI. 19. c.) of Dār al-Kutub in Cairo, donated by the Library of the Būlāq Press on 6 January 1895 to the Khedivial Library (later on Dār al-Kutub al-Qawmiyya). However, this is one of the most problematic MSS. Although it deals with the years 1798–1806, it is registered as volume I in the Dār al-Kutub catalogue. This is either a mistake or is likely due to its being copied from a draft which was meant to be a continuation of *Maẓhar al-Taqdīs*, prior to the first version of the Cambridge *'Ajā'ib al-Āthār* autograph. This MS does not have a title page and, in many instances, shows an affinity with *Maẓhar al-Taqdīs*. Its description of the assassination of Kléber is short and crude and seems to be based on rumours rather than on the French protocol of the affair, as is also the case in Nīqūla al-Turk's version of the incident. The MS is full of mistakes and omissions, especially at the end of the manuscript, where events, which occurred in the middle of each month, are omitted. Besides, like *Maẓhar al-Taqdīs*, it does not contain any biographies and does not include the trial of Sulaymān al-Ḥalabī, Kléber's assassin. About this trial al-Jabartī says in the third volume of *'Ajā'ib al-Āthār*[85] that 'Formerly, I refrained from quoting the (transcripts of the trial) because of their length and poor style …, but then I observed that many people were eager to read them…'; therefore he recorded the court proceedings in the other

85 See *'Aj.*, III, 116–17: وقد كنت أعرضت عن ذكرها لطولها وركاكة تركيبها لصورهم في اللغة… (*al-Jabartī's Chronicle*, 2, n. 7.)

version of his book *'Ajā'ib al-Āthār*.[86] From the author's statement, we can understand that he added the proceedings only when he decided to write *'Ajā'ib al-Āthār* and that MS *'Aj.* Tārīkh 1426 is the draft of the expanded version of *Maẓhar al-Taqdīs* which al-Jabartī later enlarged and turned into the third volume of his book. Thus, there is a possibility that this MS is in fact the first draft of volume III, although some events, which are mentioned in the MS, occur neither in *Maẓhar al-Taqdīs* nor in the Cambridge autograph, but only in the Būlāq edition. Thus, the editor of the Būlāq edition presumably made use of the MS and corroborated these events, which were overlooked by al-Jabartī when composing his first version of *'Ajā'ib al-Āthār*, now kept in the Cambridge University Library.

To conclude this discussion of the text's development, one copyist shortened this work by deleting all poems and literary quotations, and managed to condense it into three volumes. This version is represented by MS *'Aj.* Tārīkh 2287 *badal*/microfilm 35946, vol. I; microfilm 35959, vol. II; microfilm 35385, vol. III, pt. 1; microfilm 35547, vol. III, pt. 2 (see Chapter Two, VI. 24. a.–c. 2) which was in the possession of the poet, soldier and politician Maḥmūd Sāmī al-Bārūdī in 1285 [/1868–9]).

Sources of al-Jabartī's Information

In *'Ajā'ib al-Āthār*, al-Jabartī notes that he included three types of information that could be verified by old people who witnessed the events, that which he recorded, and that from literary and political salons (*majālis*), registers, tombstones and existing chronicles. Among these chronicles he mentions *Kitāb* or *Laṭā'if Akhbār al-Uwal fī-man Taṣarraf fī Miṣr min Arbāb al-Duwal* (Cairo, 1311 [/1893–4]), by al-Isḥāqī (d. 1060/1650). To these we may add information from travellers, merchants, pilgrims, financial and tax-farming officials, and visitors who came especially to inform him of important events. However, he denied that he made use of *Awḍaḥ al-Ishārāt fī-man Tawallā Miṣr al-Qāhira min al-Wuzarā' wa 'l-Bāshāt* by Aḥmad Shalabī b. ʿAbd al-Ghanī (d. 1150 [/1737–8]) (ʿAbd al-Raḥīm ʿAbd al-RaḥmānʿAbd al-Raḥīm ed., 1st edition Cairo 1978) which he describes as being lost,[87] and spurned the use of pamphlets written by common soldiers, represented mainly by the al-

86 See *'Aj.* Būlāq, III, 116, l. 30–117, l. 2.

87 2nd edn., 1994; see also the edition by Fu'ād Muḥammad al-Māwī (Cairo 1977).

Damurdāshī group of manuscripts. He also denied having copied biographies from his mentor al-Zabīdī's *Mu'jam Mukhtaṣṣ* and *al-Murabbā al-Kābulī*, or from Ḥasan b. ʿAlī Shamma al-Fuwwī, *Kitāb Muntahā al-'Ibārāt fī Ba'ḍ Mā li-Mashāyikhinā min al-Manāqib wa 'l-Karāmāt*, and others.[88]

In the margin of MS *'Aj.* Cam., Qq. 170, II, ff. 169a–170a (cf. *'Aj.* Būlāq, II, 233–4), al-Jabartī notes in an apparently sudden flash of memory, in connection with his biography of the Damascene historian al-Murādī (1760–91), that the initial motive to write a history of Egypt in which 'Biographies and Chronicles' were combined came to him. He relates that al-Murādī invited his master Murtaḍā al-Zabīdī (1732–91) to help him in collecting biographical data. The latter asked his student al-Jabartī to join him in this task.[89] A further incentive no doubt came from the unique events that took place during the French occupation of Egypt, which al-Jabartī recorded in his *Tārīkh Muddat al-Faransīs* in 1798. He wrote *Maẓhar al-Taqdīs* in 1801 at the request of the grand vizier Yūsuf Pāshā Ḍiyā whom he received with a group of religious scholars, among them ʿAbd Allāh al-Sharqāwī in Bilbays on 12 May 1801. Our author wrote *Maẓhar al-Taqdīs* in six months, hoping that Yūsuf Pāshā could restore justice, security, and prosperity after the atrocities of the French and their cruel extortion of taxes. However, according to al-Shaykh Ibrāhīm (the Muslim name of Burckhardt), al-Jabartī wrote *Maẓhar al-Taqdīs* in order to clear himself of the accusation of collaboration with the French, because he had been a member of the third Dīwān formed by the French to govern Egypt. This fact is noted on the title page of the *Maẓhar al-Taqdīs* MS kept in Cambridge, which was bought by Burckhardt in 1816–17, and is written in Arabic in Burckhardt's handwriting. The success of *Maẓhar al-Taqdīs* and its translation into Turkish on the order of Yūsuf Pasha gave him the final impulse to write his major work *'Ajā'ib al-Āthār* in 1220–1 (/1805–6).

Another reason which al-Jabartī mentions for composing his books was that it was in order to enable people to know the dates of their birth. He says that he found that many people remembered their birthdays through association with special events or extraordinary phenomena such as celestial

88 See MS *'Aj.* Tārīkh 1008. My thanks are due to Professor Ralf Elger of Munich University for allowing me to use his copy of this MS.

89 See Moreh, 'al-Jabartī's Method', 372–3, plates V–VI.

happenings or mishaps such as plagues, fires, wars, or else by the date of a ruler ascending to the throne or of his death.[90]

Although some attempts have been made to belittle the importance of al-Jabartī's work, his third chronicle is still considered the best account of Egyptian history from the seventeenth to the nineteenth centuries. Both D. Ayalon and André Raymond describe al-Jabartī's chronicle *'Ajā'ib al-Āthār* as an irreplaceable and often almost unique source. The latter makes extensive use of this chronicle for his work *Egyptiens et Français au Caire, 1798–1801*.[91]

As far as we know, the first scholar to have accused al-Jabartī of plagiarism (*saṭw*) was al-Ḥājj Muḥammad al-Kattānī (1858–1927), who in a fanatical and unjustified attack claimed that al-Jabartī had copied all his biographies of the *'ulamā'* of the twelfth/eighteenth century from his master Murtaḍā al-Zabīdī. He added that al-Jabartī himself did not add anything but a few biographies of Jews, Copts and some Muslims.[92]

Daniel Crecelius has recently made an even sharper attack on al-Jabartī's work. He suggests that: 'al-Jabartī is not the primary source for the greater part of the twelfth *hijrī* century of Egyptian history, but the transmitter of earlier sources', and also that 'he could not have obtained the detailed information as to dates and the events of the late seventeenth, and early eighteenth centuries by the methods he himself described'. He even accuses him of 'deliberately trying to obscure his true sources'.[93] Crecelius, in his attempt to defend al-Damurdāshī's colloquial style in reporting clashes among Mamluk factions (1099–1169 [/1687–1756]), and in his translation of it into English together with Dr 'Abd al-Wahhāb Bakr, classifies al-Jabartī as a 'transmitter' of other

90 See *'Aj.*, IV, 276.

91 Le Caire, Institut français d'archéologie orientale, 1998. See also al-Kattānī, *Fihris al-Fahāris*, IV, 260, where he deals with al-Jabartī's studies with Aḥmad al-Dūqāṭī al-Ṭaḥṭāwī and with Ḥasan al-Jabartī on *fiqh* books such as *Matn Nūr al-Īḍāḥ*, mentioned in the Preface, note 7 above.

92 On Jews in Egypt cf. Jacob M. Landau, 'The Decline of the Jewish Community in Eighteenth-Century Cairo: A New Interpretation in the Light of Two Iberian Chronicles', in Shimon Shamir (ed.), *The Jews of Egypt, A Mediterranean Society in Modern Times* (Boulder and London 1987), 15–29; see also Jacob M. Landau, *Toldot Yehudei Mitsrayim be-Tkufa ha-Ottomanit (1517–1914)* (in Hebrew)(Jerusalem 1988), 471–509.

93 Daniel Crecelius, 'Aḥmad Shalabī Ibn 'Abd al-Ghanī and Aḥmad Katkhudā 'Azabān al-Damurdāshī: Two Sources for al-Jabartī's *'Ajā'ib al-Āthār fī 'l-Tarājim wa 'l-Akhbār*', in Crecelius, *Eighteenth Century Egypt*, 100.

historians in his first two volumes. Yet such an evaluation overlooks al-Jabartī's connotative and emotional style, his universal view of history, his sound evaluation of events and of the causes of the rise and decline of rival factions, dynasties and states, his utility of his vast knowledge of Islamic religious and of the *Ṣūfī* orders, and his use of secular sciences in judging events and personalities. In fact, all these traits put him in a place of honour among historians in general, besides his insight, his verification and evaluation of events, his desire to reform the Muslim world according to Islamic ethics and the justice, truth and absolute divine rules which he believed in. Adding to all these his courage in criticizing vicious and unjust rulers and corrupted scholars of his time fearlessly, and his ability to reflect the collective historical memory of his class of Muslim scholars, all of which make him one of the most important historians in the Arab world. Thus, for example we may compare his discussion of the reasons for the Mamluks' defeat with those of European scholars who discuss the reasons for the successive defeats of the Christian European states during the peak of Ottoman power. To understand the insight of our author one can compare the reasons for the critical defeat of the Egyptian army at Imbāba; al-Jabartī gives approximately the same reasons which were given by the sixteenth-century Habsburg ambassador to the Ottoman court Ogier Ghislain de Busbecq in Constantinople for the defeat of the European armies by the Ottomans.[94] Both speak of the broken spirit of their soldiers, and their lack of endurance and training. The soldiers are insubordinate, the commanders avaricious, the army is lacking in discipline, while the enemies are united and courageous and ready to sacrifice themselves.

Al-Jabartī, who opposed popular Sufism, superstition and the sorcery attributed to common shaykhs, with an ambivalent attitude towards the French, was indeed the first herald of the Arab renaissance, and can be ranked together with seventeenth and eighteenth century authors in this respect, beginning with ʿAbd al-Laṭīf al-Baghdadī, Ḥasan al-Yūsī, Muḥammad al-Muḥibbī, al-Murādī, Ghulām ʿAlī Azad, al-Zabīdī, and others. At first, in shock at the French occupation of Egypt, he reiterated the Ottoman accusations that the French were 'materialists who deny all God's attributes, the hereafter and the

94 Compare *Mudda*, p. 20, (f. 6a–b), and its English translation, 49–50, *Yawmiyyāt al-Jabartī: Maẓhar al-Taqdīs*, Muḥammad ʿAṭā (ed.) (Cairo 1958), 2 vols (Ikhtārnā Laka, nos. 59–60), 50, *ʿAj.*, III, 8, with the description by de Busbecq quoted by Lewis, 'What Went Wrong?', 10.

resurrection, and who reject prophethood and messengership'.[95] As far as we know, al-Jabartī is the first Egyptian Muslim, and even the first Arab thinker, with the exception of the Syrian Christian Nīqūla al-Turk, who was entirely aware of the modern spirit of the French Revolution and recorded in writing his reaction to the French and the Napoleonic era with its slogans of liberty, equality, and fraternity.

After the expulsion of the French from Egypt and the consequent return of the Ottomans, al-Jabartī expressed his appreciation for European scientific, technical and moral achievements in his chronicle *'Ajā'ib al-Āthār*. Impressed by the chemical and physical experiments of French scientists that he witnessed, he states, 'These are things that the minds of people like us cannot grasp'.[96] Although there are many aspects of French behaviour, which he condemns, such as the liberal attitude towards women and the cruel manner of collecting taxes, he appreciates the French quest for knowledge comprising science, art, languages, and literature. His unique biography of Muḥammad Bey al-Alfī describes how his attitude towards the treatment of the peasants and common people, his character and morals were changed to the better during his stay in England.[97] He also remarks that, in contrast to the Mamluk *amīr*s who 'used to wake up their Muslim workers at the earliest prayer at dawn (*fī ṣalāt al-Shāfi'ī*) by beating them', the French treated their workers well as 'they did not coerce them to perform forced labour and paid them generously...'.[98] As an expression of his admiration, he also gives a meticulous description of the tools, which the French used for carrying loads with carts on wheels, making the work of the labourers easier to perform. Al-Jabartī records his admiration for French justice and for the fair trial given to Sulaymān al-Ḥalabī, Kléber's killer, despite his having been caught with the knife in his hand. On the other hand, he accuses the Ottoman soldiers of being

---

95 See *al-Jabartī's Chronicle*, 11 and 47 of the Arabic text, which reiterates the Ottoman *firmān* of 1798 quoted in Arabic by Ḥaydar Aḥmad al-Shihābī, *Tārīkh Aḥmad Bāshā al-Jazzār* (Beirut 1955), 125–8. See the translation of this *firmān* in P.D. Martin, *Histoire scientifique de l'expédition française en Egypte pendant les années 1798–1801* (Paris 1815), IV, 142–53; J. Kabrda, *Quelques firmans, concernant les relations franco-turques lors de l'expedition de Bonaparte en Egyptem (1798–1799)* (Paris 1947); Stanford J. Shaw, *Between Old and New, The Ottoman Empire under Sultan Selim III, 1789–1807* (Harvard Middle Eastern Studies, Cambridge, MA 1971), 263; Lars Bjøerneboe, *In Search*, 163–5.

96 See *'Aj.*, III, 36, ll. 6–7.

97 See ibid., IV, 26–42, especially pp. 40–1 where he mentioned al-Alfī's visit to England.

98 See ibid., III, 33 and IV, 315.

vicious, cruel, greedy, thieves, rapists and of having no respect for human life.[99]

His awareness of the shortcomings of the Muslim nations of his time predates the call of later generations of reformers for a return to the original, sublime, Islamic religious laws, morals, customs, and beliefs in order to achieve God's promised rewards, which would lead to a scientific revival in the Arab world. Al-Jabartī's comments confirm that the renaissance of the Arab intelligentsia cannot be attributed, only to the internal dynamics of the Arab world and did not commence only with the Ottoman reforms of the nineteenth century. It really began with the French occupation of Egypt, despite the short time it lasted. G. Delanoue and others concluded that, by and large, the French occupation remained an interlude without much consequence for Egyptian culture before the times of Saʿīd and Ismāʿīl, *ghalā min al-zaman* (a mistake of fate), as al-Jabartī calls it at some point. There is a good deal of mythology around about this harsh French flirtation with Egypt.[100]

He was well aware of the merits of French society and its superiority over pre-industrial Muslim society,[101] but had his reservations about French attitudes towards revealed religion and women's rights. Both al-Jabartī and his friend Ḥasan al-ʿAṭṭār expressed their astonishment at how a small group of well-equipped and well-trained 'infidel' French soldiers was able to defeat the whole Ottoman army in Egypt.[102] Similarly, Nīqūla al-Turk said with some exaggeration that 'a small, disciplined and devoted group of soldiers was able to defeat some millions [!] [of Muslim soldiers]'.[103] Al-Jabartī, al-ʿAṭṭār and al-Turk attributed this decline of military force, which was a new phenomenon in the history of Islam, to the power of modern firearms and strict military discipline, as well as to the general weakening of Muslim religious zeal.

---

99 See ibid., III, 117, ll. 1–10.

100 See Gilbert Delanoue, *Moralistes et politiques musulmans dans l'Egypte du XIXème siècle (1798–1882)*(Le Caire 1982).

101 See P. Crone, *Pre-Industrial Societies: Anatomy of the Pre-modern World* (Oxford 1995). On the decline of states in Arabic civilization see the English introduction to our Arabic edition, n. 5; cf. *Rasā'il Ikhwān al-Ṣafā*, 130.

102 See Ḥasan al-ʿAṭṭār's comment recorded in his hand in the margin of MS *'Aj*. Cam. Qq. 171, vol. III, MS no. Or. 4630, p. 105, note (a in our Arabic edition, events of 20–4 Shawwāl 1314 (/16–20 March 1800), cf. *'Aj*. Būlāq, III, 92–4. See also Chapter Four, note 4.

103 See Nakoula el-Turk, *Histoire de l'expédition des français en Égypte*, trad. M. Desgranges ainé (Paris 1839), 186.

The irony of destiny is that although al-Jabartī wrote the biographies and recorded the dates of death of his friends, scholars and rulers, we do not know much of his life or the exact date of his death or its cause. Moreover, no Egyptian copyist or historian of his time dared speak about the death of his son Khalīl, perhaps due to the fact, that al-Jabartī was considered *persona non grata* by Muḥammad ʿAlī and his entourage. The fact that there is no manuscript of *'Ajā'ib al-Āthār*, as far as we know, kept in any library in Istanbul, Damascus or Jerusalem, might confirm our suggestion that he became *persona non grata* in the Ottoman Empire. This might be a result of his harsh criticism of the Ottoman rulers, although his friend Ḥasan al-ʿAṭṭār carried his copy with him during his journey to these cities in the hope that scholars would be interested in copying it. Another question, which is difficult to solve is, why despite the friendly ties between al-ʿAṭṭār and al-Jabartī, did the latter not compose an elegiac poem to lament his friend's death? Did he also fear Muḥammad ʿAlī's revenge? The discovery of such a poem might help solve the enigma of the exact year of al-Jabartī's death, since in the last verse it would perhaps contain a numerical hemistich indicating the date of death.

Moreover, the collation between the MSS of *'Ajā'ib al-Āthār* shows that there is no indication that the Būlāq edition deleted al-Jabartī's criticism of Muḥammad ʿAlī, as stated by Jurjī Zaydān,[104] and by Anastase-Marie al-Kirmili on the MS *'Ajā'ib al-Āthār* of the Iraq Museum.[105]

The date of ʿAbd al-Raḥmān al-Jabartī's death is not mentioned on his tombstone either. Even the copyist of his chronicle *'Ajā'ib al-Āthār*, MS *'Aj.* Tārīkh 466/microfilm 35088 (VI. 15. d. below), does not mention al-Jabartī's name and the date of his death in his list of 271 Muslim scholars belonging to the Shāfiʿī, Ḥanafī and Mālikī schools, arranged according to the year of their deaths. Thus, we do not have any definite information about his fate, nor that of his son Khalīl who was murdered in 1237 (/1821–2). In volume I of the same MS (see Chapter Two, II, VI. 15. a. below) the name of the copyist is mentioned as al-Ḥājj Muḥammad Ḥusayn Aḥmad Miṣbāḥ al-Shāfiʿī al-Azharī, the Egyptian scholar who probably copied all four volumes of *'Ajā'ib al-Āthār* in 1272 (/1855–6). At the end of the fourth volume there is a brief account of

104 See Jurjī Zaydān, *Tārīkh Ādāb al-Lugha al-'Arabiyya*, Shawqī Ḍayf (ed.)(Cairo 1957), IV, 256 and 1st edn., IV, 284.

105 See *al-Jabartī's Chronicle*, 3, n. 11.

the works and the dates of death of famous Egyptian scholars who died between 1235 (/1819) and 1272 (/1855–6), yet for some reason this list does not give the years in which al-Jabartī and his son Khalīl died, although it includes among others al-Jabartī's friends Ismāʿīl al-Khashshāb (d. 1229 [/1813–14]) and Ḥasan al-ʿAṭṭār (d. 1250 [/1835]).[106] The list of deceased scholars ends by saying: '*wa-baqiyat nās min awā'il al-qarn wa-nās fī wasaṭih wa-nās fī awākhir tilka al-sinīn yujhal tārīkhuhum wa-nasab ba'ḍihim wa-bilād ba'ḍihim, min 'uẓamā'ihim al-Shaykh Sulaymān b. 'Umar min Bajīyram, Shāfi'ī lahu ta'ālīf ka-*Ḥāshiyat al-Manhaj'. (Moreover, there remained some people from the beginning of the century (thirteenth/nineteenth), and others in the middle, and at the end of that century, whose date of death or whose pedigree or birthplace, are unknown. One of the greatest of these is Shaykh Sulaymān b. ʿUmar of Bujayram; he was a Shāfiʿī and among his works is a commentary on *al-Manhaj* [by Zakariyyā al-Anṣārī])'.

According to the Egyptian writer Maḥmūd al-Sharqāwī, because of al-Jabartī's criticism in the fourth volume of *'Ajā'ib al-Āthār*, of Muḥammad ʿAlī, the new ruler of Egypt, the volume was confiscated, and al-Jabartī's son was assassinated in 1238 (/1822–3).[107] After this tragedy, al-Jabartī, blind and grieving, stopped writing his chronicle,[108] confined himself to his house, and died of sorrow in 1241 (/1825–6).

The Syrian poet Khalīl Shaybūb[109] accepted at face value the information on al-Jabartī's death as given in the 'Notice sur la vie et l'œuvre de l'auteur' which was published in the *Introduction* to the French translation of *'Ajā'ib al-Āthār*, entitled *Merveilles biographiques et historiques ou chroniques du Cheikh Abd-el-Rahman el Djabartī*. Providing no direct evidence it states that al-Jabartī was strangled on 27 Ramadan 1237/18 June 1822 when he returned from Muḥammad ʿAlī's palace near Shubrā: 'Dans la nuit du 27 Ramadan 1237 (18 juin 1822), comme El Djabartī revenait du château de Mohammed Aly, situé a Choubrah, et qu'il rentrait au Caire, il fut étranglé sur l'avenue de Choubrah et attaché, avec une corde, à un des pieds de son âne. Le lendemain

106 MS *'Aj.* Tārīkh 466/microfilm 35088, see Chapter Two, VI, 15. d.

107 See al-Sharqāwī, *Miṣr fī 'l-Qarn al-Tāsi''Ashar, Dirāsāt fī Tārīkh al-Jabartī*, I, 15–16, and Ayalon, 'The Historian', 247–8. See also the colophon of MS *'Aj.* Bankipore (Chapter Two, IV.11. d2).

108 The colophon of MS *'Aj.* Bankipore; Cardin, *Journal d'Abdarrahman Gabarti*, 3.

109 See Shaybūb, *'Abd al-Raḥmān al-Jabartī*, 113–15.

seulement, les passants trouvèrent sur leur chemin un cadavre et reconnurent en lui celui d'Abd-el-Rahman el Djabartī. Il avait sur lui un astrolabe, un rapporteur et quelques cahiers manuscript'.[110] The translators added that there were several different explanations for this [alleged] murder, such as that Mohammed Bey el Defterdar [sic], because of an old grudge, informed Muḥammad ʿAlī that al-Jabartī had bitterly criticized his conduct in his chronicle. However, they add that, 'There is no precise evidence to support this. In fact, they state that, 'At that moment in time, when Mohammad Ali was at the height of his power, he had absolutely no reason to carry out this deed on al-Jabartī in the darkness of the night'. Moreover, they rightly say, 'if Muḥammad ʿAlī would have caused the death of our author, nothing would have stopped him from destroying his work as well'. Furthermore, the fact that no copyist mentioned this murder in the colophon supports Cardin's testimony, i.e. that al-Jabartī lost his eyesight because of his grief over the murder of his son.[111]

The Egyptian scholar Muḥammad Anīs made a serious attempt to verify the date of al-Jabartī's death using the archives of the *sharīʿa* (religious) court in Cairo, where he examined the document of a *waqf* managed by al-Jabartī while he was still alive, and another document dealing with the sale of al-Jabartī's house by his heirs. None of these documents specified the exact date of al-Jabartī's death. However, as the first document of the *waqf* managed by al-Jabartī is dated 1 Rabīʿ II 1240 (/23 November 1824), and the second document dealing with his inheritance is dated Saturday, 27 Ramaḍān 1240 (/17 May 1825), Anīs came to the conclusion that al-Jabartī died between 23 November 1824 and 14 May 1825. According to Anīs, these documents should put an end to speculations regarding the date of al-Jabartī's death, in particular the date 1241 (/1825–6), previously given by al-Bannānī and al-Ḥaḍrāwī.[112]Another document which confirms the findings of Anīs is the colophon statement of Aḥmad b. Ḥasan al-Rashīdī al-Shāfiʿī known as Ṣawbaʿ that he finished reading and redacted the whole of volume III of *'Ajā'ib al-*

110 Abd El-Rahman el-Djabarti, *Merveilles biographiques et historiques ou chroniques du Cheikh Abd-el-Rahman el Djabarti*, trans. Chefik Mansour Bey, Abdulaziz Kahil Bey, Gebriel Nicolas Kahil Bey and Iskender Ammoun Effendi (Cairo 1888), I, IX, and see Ayalon, 'The Historian', 247.

111 See A. Cardin, *Journal d'Abdurrahman Gabarti, pendant l'occupation française en Egypte*, T.X. Bianchi (ed.)(Paris 1838).

112 See Anīs, 'Ḥaqā'iq', 72–3 in note 11 above. Ayalon, 'The Historian', 247.

Āthār (MS *'Aj.* al-Zakiyya 859/microfilm 54236, vol. III, p. 1373) in the presence of its author on 14 Rabīʿ I 1240 (/6 November 1824). It may be this MS, which Jurjī Zaydān in his *Tārīkh Ādāb al-Lugha al-'Arabiyya* claimed that he found in the library of Muḥammad Bey Āṣaf. It seems, therefore, that al-Jabartī died between 1 Rabīʿ II and 27 Ramaḍān 1240 (/23 November 1824–17 May 1825). However, it is a known fact that inheritances according to bequests, are recorded in the Religious Court a short time after the death of a Muslim, immediately after the burial, and that debts should then, be returned and inheritors receive their shares by the decision of the Religious Court (*maḥkama shar'iyya*). This should all happen within no more than two to three days of the death. If this is the case, one can conclude that al-Jabartī died between Wednesday, 24 and Friday, 26 Ramadan 1240 (/14–16 May 1825). In any case no more than forty days (*al-arba'īn*) after death all bequests should be settled.[113] This finding does not confirm the statements of E.W. Lane who said that, 'he died in 1825 or 1826, soon after my first arrival to Cairo';[114] Stanley Lane-Poole says that Lane arrived in Cairo on 2 October 1825.

Anīs adds some information about the site where al-Jabartī is buried. He confirms that he was buried in the main cemetery of Turbat al-Ṣaḥrā' (the burial ground of the desert) in the section called the Bustān al-Mujāwirīn (orchard of the Azhar students), in the compound of the Jabartī family and probably above his father's grave. On this site, there are two family graves of the Jabartīs, one of which used to have a large tombstone with a poem in praise of Ḥasan al-Jabartī ending with a numerical hemistich indicating the date of his death in 1188 (/1774–5). This stone was transported to the entrance gate of the Jabartī family graveyard in 1958, but apparently there is no separate tombstone to specify the name and date of his son's death. Anīs quotes the poem and gives some photographs of the tomb and the stone with its epitaph.[115]

---

113 My thanks go to Dr Muḥammad al-Ḥashshīsh of the Orientalisches Seminar at the University of Bonn, who serves as the *imām* of the mosque in Bonn for this information.

114 Lane, *Manners*, 222 and Stanley Lane-Poole, *The Life of Edward William Lane* (London 1877).

115 See note52 above. During my visit to Cairo in February 2000 to work at the National Library, I asked my friend the Egyptian senator and writer Anīs Manṣūr to accompany me to the graveyard of the Jabartīs. He kindly agreed, but the Ministry of Awqāf informed us that there is no exact registration of the al-Jabartī's graveyard and they do not know exactly where they are buried. The Department of Antiquities (*Qism al-Āthār*) in Cairo, informed the writer of

The irony of fate is that the date of the death of al-Jabartī, who was careful to record the date of the death of hundreds of rulers, officials and scholars of the period he covered, remains unrecorded, even on his grave in his own family's graveyard. As none of the MSS or documents, which were examined, gives any definite information, one can attempt to infer the date of his death from information contained in al-Jabartī's work. In his description of the plague in the year 1205 (/1790–1), he notes that an inheritance passed three times within one week to different relatives.[116]

Members of the Dīwān which the French had set up to rule Egypt were engraved or painted with their names by painters of the French expedition and published in the *Description de l'Egypte*, a monumental work which is indebted to al-Jabartī's *'Ajā'ib al-Āthār* yet in which, al-Jabartī's picture with his name do not appear. However, Professor André Raymond has suggested that the engraving of the astronomer in the *Description* might be that of ʿAbd al-Raḥmān al-Jabartī and of the poet might be of his friend Ḥasan al-ʿAṭṭār.[117]

Al-Jabartī was a pious Muslim who judged others according to their adherence to Islamic *sharī'a*, rituals, practices and Khalwatī value system based upon *al-amr bi 'l-ma'rūf*, and criticized other Muslim sects, mainly those of the Maghreb and the Wahhābīs, whose members observed only cult practices and rejected *Ṣūfī* spiritual esoteric aspects. He opposed any relaxation of Islamic laws pertaining to the superiority of Muslims over non-Muslims and to the inferior and submissive status of the *dhimmi*s. He also attacked any perceived laxity in these matters shown by rulers or scholars. In spite of his religious awareness, he allowed himself to copy ample biographies and data without acknowledgment and to ascribe the work of other authors to himself, especially parts of the work of his mentor al-Zabīdī. We may thus conclude this chapter by saying that a true believer would ascribe the neglect by other scholars to record the exact date of his death as perhaps constituting a just punishment for such behaviour. However, his achievement was great, and the depth and exactness of his critical biographical writing certainly had no peers.

---

these lines that no record exists of al-Jabartī's family plot in either the al-Basātīn or the al-Mujāwirīn cemetery (S.M.).

116 See *'Aj.*, II, 191: واتفق أن الميراث انتقل ثلاث مرّات في جمعة واحدة (It happened thatthe succession to the was transferred three times in one week). Cf. Muḥammad Anīs in note 52 above.

117 See André Raymond, 'A propos de deux portraits dans la *Description de l'Egypte*, "l'astronome" et "le poète"', *Annales islamologiques* (Cairo 2001), 35, 385–92 and his *Egyptiens et Français*, 2.

The biographies of his father, of al-Zabīdī and also of those of the Shaykh Abu 'l-Anwār al-Sādāt and of Muḥammad al-Alfī, provide ample evidence of this. In fact, they go far beyond what al-Murādī and others had to offer.[118]

118 *'Aj.*, I, 385–408 (Ḥasan); II, 196–214 (Murtaḍā al-Zabīdī); IV, 26–44 (Muḥammad al-Alfī); IV, 185–96 (Abu 'l-Anwār).

Chapter Two

A Survey of Al-Jabartī's Autographs and Manuscripts and their Significance

In this chapter, a description of all extant MSS written by al-Jabartī, copied during his lifetime, or copied after his death will be given and their significance will be analysed with the resulting stemma. The attempt to collate al-Jabartī's autographs of his three chronicles on Egypt, examine the various changes which he made in his autographs and those made by his copyist in these MSS, analyse the additions in the margins and the way the author arranged his data,helps us to arrive at new conclusions. It will supply us with evidence of the direct religious, political, economic and moral influences which he confronted and his purpose for writing different versions. Moreover, it sheds new light on his attitude towards Ottoman officials, Mamluk rulers, French invaders, Muḥammad ʿAlī's rule, leading *'ulamā'*, religious and ethnic minorities, the common people, and the dynamics of the events.In any culture, great writers, poets, artists, and historians represent, consciously or unconsciously, the collective consciousness, religious and moral values, and the historic memory of their group, society, or nation in a particular time and under certain rulers. They derive their ideals and admonition from their past and their religious values. They criticize the evil of their present and they indicate the way that they think proper to lead their group or nation to deliver their people from their contemporary evils and their tyrannical rulers.

Dr Lars Bjørneboe, in his Ph.D. thesis,[1] noticed these important factors. He used the method of comparison between the MSS of al-Jabartī's three chronicles to understand the 'developments in Egypt in the years around 1800 by means of an analysis of the opinions, values, and outlook expressed in al-Jabartī's chronicles, the way he expressed them and changed them in his

1 Lars Bjøerneboe, 'In Search of the True Political Position of the 'Ulama, An Analysis of the Aims and Perspectives of the Chronicles of Abd al-Rahman al-Jabarti (1753–1825)', in his Ph.D. thesis, Odense (Centre for Middle Eastern Studies, University of Southern Denmark 2002), 8, published by Aarhus University Press, The Danish Institute in Damascus, 2007; he compares al-Jabartī's attitude towards the French invasion and that of the historians of Western European countries which were occupied by Nazi Germany, see 94–8, and notes 25–33.

writings. It intends to supply some empirical evidence of the opinions and discussions current among high-ranking *'ulamā'*. He argues that al-Jabartī's historical works *Muddat al-Faransīs*, *Maẓhar al-Taqdīs* and *'Ajā'ib al-Āthār* form at least three (or more) texts, and they 'were written by the same author at different dates and obviously rely on each other. As such they constitute parts of a more or less continuous working process'.[2] He suggests that they:

> 'represent as evidence of, or comments on, or may be even contributions towards a debate in Cairene society in the decades around 1800 and to investigate them for clues as to whether al-Jabartī represents more than himself, and if that is the case, who?'[3]

Bjørneboe concludes that, 'the MS*Mudda* seems to be a contribution to a debate in which al-Sādāt, the leader of the Wafā'iyya order is being promoted as the proponent of a stand which warns against cooperating too closely with the rulers, while al-Sharqāwī, the Shaykh of al-Azhar, is presented as a leader who by his ready cooperation all but ruins the Muslim community... This would suggest that the issue was primarily ideological and religious in nature and was fought out between a group centred around the Shaykh al-Sādāt, the Wafā'iyya order and the Ḥusaynī shrine and mosque on one hand, and the Shaykh al-Sharqāwī and the Shaykh of al-Azhar in alliance with the Shaykh al-Bakrī on the other'.[4]

However, the final conclusion of Dr Bjørneboe that, 'the additions in this second draft of the MS*Mudda* show a clear and obvious pattern: they are nearly all taken up with corroborating and enlarging the critical line taken in the rough draft of the MS*Mudda* towards the *amīr*s, al-Sharqāwī and the leading shaykhs, and its correlation, the vindication of the position of the Shaykh al-Sādāt, as sketched out above'.[5] In our opinion, the obvious implication of this conclusion is that in these additions we are, 'presented with al-Sādāt's comments on the rough draft and that the *ṣaḥḥa* at the end of the additions constitute al-Sādāt's approval'.[6] Bjørneboe's conclusion that, the additions in the margin are 'al-Sādāt's comments on the rough draft' and his 'approval', would be correct if these additions in the margin were written in a

---

2 Bjørneboe, *In Search*, 83.

3 Ibid., 84–159.

4 Ibid., 153–4.

5 Ibid., 159.

6 Ibid., 163–5.

different handwriting and different ink or width of pen, and would be endorsed by al-Sādāt himself. The best evidence for our argument is that when Ḥasan al-ʿAṭṭar, corrected, commented, and added some of his poems in the margin of his own copy of *'Ajā'ib al-Āthār* in *Maghribī* hand, he never wrote *ṣaḥḥa* but signed his name after adding the word *kātibuhu* ('the writer of these lines'). Further evidence is to be found in MS *'Aj.* Cam., Qq. 170, vol. II, in which the comment of a reader is ended with the abbreviation أ.هـ. (= الى هنا or إنتهي) (See below III. 1. b.) in addition, not with the word *ṣaḥḥa*. The additions, which end with the word صح, as in the case of all the autographs of the first three volumes of *'Ajā'ib al-Āthār*, *Muddat al-Faransīs* and *Maẓhar al-Taqdīs* were in all likelihood made by the author during his final revision without the interference of others. Most probably, the editions in the margin ended with صح, were added by the author after verification with informants,[7] such as al-Sādāt and others, or after he received new information or having changed his mind after rethinking the matter.

As discussed in the previous chapter, al-Jabartī states in his *Introduction* to *'Ajā'ib al-Āthār*, volume I, that he started recording historical events between 1778 and 1792. This fact is confirmed by his mentor Murtaḍā al-Zabīdī in his biography of our author included in his *Biographical Dictionary Mu'jam Mukhtaṣṣ*. After the death of his mentor, al-Jabartī was asked by al-Murādī to send to him all the biographies which al-Zabīdī had collected for al-Murādī and to add to them those which al-Jabartī had collected. The news of al-Murādī's death reached al-Jabartī before he sent the biographies collected by al-Zabīdī. After these two tragic events, al-Jabartī lost interest and left his papers aside until a sudden motivation induced him to resume his data recordings. The motivation in question might have been the humiliating French proclamation in Arabic backed bythe firman of Sultan Salīm inciting the Muslim populace of the Mediterranean ports against the French invasion of Egypt. There is no evidence that al-Jabartī was requested by the Ottomans to be their agent and to report to them, or that as a pious *'ālim* interested in history he thought that it was his duty to record these unusual events in the Muslim world. In fact, this invasion, as was confirmed by Nikūlā al-Turk as well, was a religious, cultural, and emotional earthquake for Muslim Egyptians and for the Ottomans as a whole. Six months after the invasion our author

7 See above, Chapter One, note 68; cf. Bjørneboe, *In Search*, 104.

recorded the events in a pamphlet, without giving it a title or writing the *basmala* to the *Introduction* or a colophon at the end of the MS. After the death of al-Jabartī, it was in the possession of the owner of the library in 'El-Medina', Shaykh 'Emin el-Madanī' who gave the manuscript the title *Hādhā Tārīkh Muddat al-Faransīs bi-Miṣr.*[8] Later on, al-Sayyid Muḥammad al-Amīr al-Ḥanafī al-Rashīdī bought this MS in Jumādā 1281 (/2–29 October 1864) for 9 *qirsh.*

Al-Jabartī recorded his second chronicle at the request of a high official in the entourage of the Ottoman general Yūsuf Ḍiyā Pasha who expelled the French with the help of the British navy. In this book, which was written out of fear of being considered a collaborator with the French, al-Jabartī expressed his hope that the Ottomans would treat Egyptian Muslims with mercy after a long period of suffering. He expressed his joy at the departure of the French 'infidels' and the return of the 'delivering' Ottomans. The book, which was well received by the Vizier, was translated into Turkish. Our author, who was faithful to his friend al-ʿAṭṭār and tried to protect him from the accusation of collaboration with the French, added some of al-ʿAṭṭār's praise poems to the Ottomans and their commander. They both revealed their belief that the expulsion of the French by a Muslim general named Yūsuf, as in the case of Yūsuf, the son of the Patriarch Jacob, and Yūsuf Ṣalāḥ al-Dīn, was a divine decree, since the three of them had delivered Egypt from disasters. They both formulated its flattering title with the religious wording *Maẓhar al-Taqdīs* (The Manifestation of Blessing) which he ended in Shaʿbān 1216/December 1801–January 1802.

In 1805–6 al-Jabartī decided to write the history of Egypt from 1100 (/1688–9) to 1806 which he entitled *'Ajā'ib al-Āthār fi 'l-Tarājim wa 'l-Akhbār* (The Marvellous Compositions of Biographies and Chronicles), a title part of which had been mentioned in the *Introduction* of *Maẓhar al-Taqdīs*. In his *Introduction*, he stated the Islamic moral values by which he judged the religious scholars, the rulers and events, which he discussed in his history by omitting his former flattery of the rulers. Because of the atrocities brutally committed against the Egyptian population by the returning armies of the

8 It seems that the owner of the MS Amīn al-Madanī gave it this title. In *GAL*, *Suppl.*, II, 731, this MS is mentioned among al-Jabartī's works as *Muddat Dukhūl al-Faransīs bi Miṣr*, and in von Landberg, 21, 61, it is listed under the title *Muddat Dukhūl al-Faransīs bi-Miṣr*; but other scholars do not mention it as a separate work. See also Chapter One, notes 52–3 above.

Ottomans, our author revised his opinion towards the latter and the French. He compared French justice, their quest for knowledge and science, law and order with the brutality and ignorance of the Ottomans. In his sincere approach in criticizing the evil of his time according to the sublime religious Islamic value system, he was able to write one of the unique histories with a universal outlook.

There are at least forty-three MSS of al-Jabartī's most comprehensive work, *'Ajā'ib al-Āthār*, kept in different libraries all over the world, some comprising one of the first three volumes, the three first volumes, and a few the complete four volumes. In order to determine which of these manuscripts are the author's autographs, it is necessary to collate them with the autographs of the two other historical works of al-Jabartī, the first is MS*Mudda* kept at Leiden University Library, and the second, the two autographs of *Maẓhar al-Taqdīs*kept at Cambridge University Library and the Dār al-Kutub al-Qawmiyya in Cairo. By examining these autographs, it is possible to study the specific qualities of al-Jabartī's handwriting, the significance, and reason for his changes or omissions. Moreover, it will be possible to decide if the author made these changes deliberately, and what was the reason for such changes in his three works. Moreover, it will be possible to recognise the changes that the redactors, editors, copyists, and printers of his works made. Moreover, by collating al-Jabartī's Cambridge autograph of *'Ajā'ib al-Āthār* with manuscripts copied by scribes it may well be possible to solve many problems caused by mistakes made during the copying process, such as homoeoteleuton, homoeoarchy, homoeotopy, dittography, the wrong placing of diacritical dots (*taṣḥīf*) and similar errors, and hence to establish the author's authentic statements and style.

As far as it was possible to examine our author's MSS, there is only one autograph of the first three volumes written and re-edited by al-Jabartī himself (MS *'Aj.* Cam., Qq. 169, 170, 171, [III. 1. a–c. below]). John Ludwig Burckhardt, who after his conversion to Islam in Aleppo called himself al-Shaykh Ibrāhīm, bought them. Other copies of the first three volumes edited by the author are MS *'Aj.* Cam., 2 Qq. 166, 167, 168 (III. 2. a.–c. below), MS *'Aj.* BN (III. 7. a.–c. below), and volume III, MS *'Aj.* Tārīkh 174 (VI. 14. c.), in the National Library in Cairo. It seems that foreign consuls and book dealers, ordered these copies from the author for European libraries. These copies were probably copied by copyists employed by the author, who sold them to libraries and dealers. On these copies made by his copyists, al-Jabartī wrote himself first the title page and later on the last lines of the last page without adding the date or name of the copyist in the colophon. Then he revised, corrected, and added a few sentences in the margin of the MS. The fact is that the last copy of *'Ajā'ib al-Āthār*, which was revised in 1240 (/1824–5), in the author's presence, is identical with the Cambridge autograph and with all other copies collated by al-Jabartī (hereafter the Cambridge group of MSS). This fact proves that all the changes in style, grammatical usage, passages quoted, etc., made in all the MSS copied after the author's death, were copied later by other copyists who took the liberty of adding passages, changing the grammatical usage and the names of places and persons as well as passages and documents quoted by al-Jabartī. It also indicates that after two or three decades copyists were unable to understand the author's terms and style and that some even tried to add in the margin the meaning of certain terms to help the readers. The comparison of the identified Cambridge autograph of *'Ajā'ib al-Āthār*, as well as the copies edited by al-Jabartī himself, may give us a clearer insight to the manner in which al-Jabartī composed his chronicle. It will clarify the rationale behind these changes, and finally, will enable us to determine how and in which sequence he compiled his data, as well as the writing and copying sequences of the MSS.

Due to his modesty as a Khalwatī *ṣūfī*, the task of identifying al-Jabartī's autographs is complicated because he did not write his name or the date in which he finished writing his particular book in the colophon (*khātima*) of each autograph. He also did not take the trouble to indicate the date he edited any of the MSS that are examined here. He never even mentioned any of his earlier works in the four volumes of his major work *'Ajā'ib al-Āthār fī 'l-Tarājim wa 'l-Akhbār*. He does not refer to the short composition dealing in full detail with the events of the first seven months of the French occupation of Egypt; this autograph was entitledlater on by the book dealer Amīn al-Madanī, *Hādhā Tārīkh Muddat al-Faransīs bi-Miṣr min Sanat 1213 ilā Sanat 1216* ('This is the history of the period of the French [occupation] in Egypt from the year 1213 [/1798] to the year 1216 [/1801]'). He also did not mention his abridged version of Dā'ūd al-Anṭākī's *Tadhkirat Ūlī al-Albāb*;[9] although its

9 *GAL*, II, 364; cf. Ayalon 'The Historian', 247, n. 1.

great influence is reflected not only by our author's giving detailed descriptions of maladies, herbal medicine, magic, and the effects of the stars upon persons, but also in his usage of medical, astronomical and astrological vocabulary. Our author did not mention his own expurgated edition of *Alf Layla wa-Layla*, from which he deleted the erotic descriptions.[10] However, his *Maẓhar al-Taqdīs bi-Zawāl Dawlat al-Faransīs*,[11] is mentioned only in an esoteric way, which most readers would hardly notice.[12]

There are various printed editions of *'Ajā'ib al-Āthār*, in four volumes, which are probably all copied from the Būlāq edition (1297/1879–80). Only the recent printed editions in three volumes published in Beirut by Dār al-Fāris (no date of printing) and by Dār al-Kutub al-ʿIlmiyya, Beirut, 1997 from which poems and literary passages were deleted, were based on a different manuscript. There is no indication on which MSS the editors based their new version. These two editions are abbreviated versions in which most of the poems and *maqāmāt* quoted by al-Jabartī mainly in his first two volumes, and copied from al-Zabīdī's *Mu'jam Mukhtaṣṣ*, are deleted. However, they are identical with MSS kept at DKQ in Cairo in the possession of General Maḥmūd Sāmī al-Bārūdī (1839–1904) (VI. 24 a.–c. below), the poet and

10 Edward William Lane and Stanley Lane-Poole, *The Thousand and One Nights: Commonly Called in England, The Arabian Nights Entertainments; a New Tr. from the Arabic with Copious Notes* (London 1883). Cf. Ayalon, 'The Historian', 246, n. 1.

11 The vowelling of the title is according to the Rampur MS. The same vowelling was applied by E.G. Browne, *A Hand-list of the Muhammadan Manuscripts Including All Those Written in the Arabic Character, Preserved in the Library of the University of Cambridge* (Cambridge 1980), I, 207, no. 1058 (Qq 214), while *GAL, Suppl.*, II, 730–1), Franz Babinger (*Die Geschichtsschreiber der Osmanen und ihre Werke* [Leipzig 1927], 340), D.B. Macdonald ('al-Djabartī', *EI*[1], ii, 986), and others, transcribed it as *Muẓhir al-Taqdīs*.

12 *'Aj*. Būlāq, III, 116, l. 30–117, l. 2. Al-Jabartī, speaking about the protocol of the trial of Sulaymān al-Ḥalabī, the assassin of General Kléber, said: وانقضت الحكومة على ذلك وألفوا في شأن ذلك أوراقا وذكروا فيها صورة الواقعة وكيفيتها وطبعوا منها نسخا كثيرة...وقد كنت أعرضت عن ذكرها لطولها وركاكة تركيبها لقصورهم في اللغة ثم رأيت كثيرا من الناس تتشوق نفسه الى الاطلاع عليها لتضمنها خبر الواقعة وكيفية الحكومة ولما فيها من الاعتبار وضبط الأحكام ... We suggest that al-Jabartī is referring to *Maẓhar al-Taqdīs*. This protocol is missing in the MSS of *Maẓhar al-Taqdīs* as well as in its printed editions. It is also possible to presume that the author is referring also to an autograph from which MS *'Aj*. Tārīkh 1426/microfilm 35532, vol. III (VI. 19. c. below) was copied in which this protocol is also missing, having the same version of *Maẓhar al-Taqdīs* on this assassination. However, if we know that in the catalogue of DKQ, Cairo, this particular MS is indicated as volume I. and not volume III, then it is obvious that this particular MS was copied from al-Jabartī's version *Maẓhar al-Taqdīs* in which he continued to add his data, before he decided to write his first three volumes of *'Ajā'ib al-Āthār*.

Minister of War who joined the ʿUrābī revolution, and the second is MS *ʿAj.* Tārīkh 2287. The four volume edition of Būlāq is based on a MS that the Būlāq editor prepared after comparing several MSS of *ʿAjā'ib al-Āthār* and choosing the one, which he approved of for its grammatical and stylistic 'corrections'. Unfortunately, it is full of errors and omissions of sentences with similar endings (homoeoteleuton). Besides, some villages which al-Jabartī mentioned by their old names, were given the new administrative names during Muḥammad ʿAlī's rule. The same is true of the ranks of some officials who in our author's time bore the title of Afandi and Bey while in the Būlāq edition their ranks are mentioned as higher ranks of Aghā and Pāshā.

In our attempt to prepare a scholarly edition based on the autographs written by al-Jabartī, we tried, first, to identify the original autographs. In this stage, one can easily be misled by contradictions and misconceptions on the part of scholars who described these MSS and by errors in the catalogues listing these manuscripts. It has proved impossible to trace the original manuscript which al-Jabartī wrote on the history of Egypt between 1786–95 as he stated in his *Introduction* and was confirmed by al-Zabīdī in his *Muʿjam Mukhtaṣṣ*. However, most of the following MSS were collated with the Būlāq edition. In addition, the different versions of the Cambridge autographs are given in special brackets (//...//), if they are not found in the Būlāq group of MSS. Wherever these versions in the Būlāq edition can add special significance to the text, they are added in a footnote even when erroneous:

I. Manuscripts of *Hādhā Tārīkh Muddat al-Faransīs bi-Miṣr min Sanat 1213 ʾilā Sanat 1216* (This is the history of [the ruling] period of the French [occupation] in Egypt between the years 1213–1216 [/1798–1801], by the scholar ʿAbd al-Raḥmān al-Jabartī, written in his own hand writing, may God has mercy upon him).[13]

I. 1. MS Mudda kept at the Leiden University Library.

Von Landberg, in his *Catalogue de manuscripts arabes*,[14] lists this manuscript under the title *Muddat Dukhūl al-Faransīs bi-Miṣr* and adds that it deals with

13 See *al-Jabartī's Chronicle*, 11–12 and plate X. Voorhoeve, *Handlist*, 3, lists this under the title *'Ajā'ib al-Āthār* (following M.J. de Goeje and Th.W. Juynboll, *Catalogus codicum arabicorum bibliothecae academiae Lugduno-Batavae* [Leiden 1907], II, pt. 1, 100, no. 988). See GAL, *Suppl.*, II, 731.

14 Von Landberg, 21, no. 61. Cf. also *GAL, Suppl.*, II, 731.

the events of the year 1217 (/1802–3), although the title states clearly, 'the years 1213 [/1798] to 1216 [/1801]'. In fact the manuscript deals with the events of the French occupation from 10 Muḥarram 1213 (/15 June 1798) to the end of Rajab of the same year (/7 January 1799).[15] It is clear that the title, which is written in a different hand was given after the author's death by one of the owners of the manuscript, most probably Amīn Afandī b. Ḥasan al-Ḥulwānī al-Madanī. It seems that this book dealer was acquainted with al-Jabartī's handwriting, but was unaware of the manuscript's exact content, which covers the years 1213–16 (/1798–1801), so he gave it the erroneously dated title in his own hand-writing: هذا تاريخ مدة الفرنسيس بمصر من سنة 1213 السنة 1216 تاليف العلامة عبد الرحمن الجبرتي المصري بخطه رحمه الله ('This is the history of [the ruling] period of the French [occupation] of Egypt from the year 1213 [/1798] to the year 1216 [/1801] by the most erudite 'Abd al-Raḥmān al-Jabartī the Egyptian, in his own handwriting, may God have mercy upon him'.)[16] Yet the work deals only with the second half of the year 1213 (/1798–9); the owner of the MS probably tried to sell it as if it were an autograph of *Maẓhar al-Taqdīs* by writing that it was written 'by the most erudite...al-Jabartī... in his own handwriting, may God has mercy upon him'. On the title-page, the name of the owner (or one of the owners) is added to the left of the title: ʿal-Sayyid Muḥammad al-Amīr al-Ḥanafī al-Rashīdīʿ', who is also the owner of the *Risāla fī 'l-'Amal bi 'l-Rub'*, with the date and price (fī 6 J[umādā?] sanat 81 [sic 1181][/29 September 1764], 9 [qirsh]), composed by al-Jabartī in his own hand.

The manuscript of *Muddat al-Faransīs* does not have an introduction and the usual invocation, the *basmala*, is missing.[17] This is a peculiarity of all al-Jabartī's autographs which might be out of modesty as a Khalwatī, although it has been erronousely suggested that his omission of the *basmala* and the

15 See *al-Jabartī's Chronicle*, 1, n. 3, 11, n. 38. On Amīn al-Ḥulwānī al-Madanī see Khayr al-Dīn al-Ziriklī, *al-A'lām* (Beirut 1984), II, 15–16. The specimen of the handwriting of al-Madanī given by al-Ziriklī resembles that on the title page of *Mudda*.

16 *al-Jabartī's Chronicle*, 11–12 and plates X–XI. On the importance of MS *Mudda*, see Bjørneboe, *In Search*, 84–116. Professor P. van Koningsveld of Leiden informed me that the owner of the library in Medina, Shaykh 'Emin el-Madanī', wrote the title to MS *Mudda*.

17 The fact that this text lacks the *basmala* suggests that the author considered it as part of other material in his possession, as he stated in his various versions. Cf. *'Aj*. Būlāq, I, 2, ll. 6–15, 6, ll. 16–30; II, 233, ll. 15–236, or as a pious Muslim he abstains from using it in a profane subject.

invocations to the prophets were out of a desire to save paper. The text starts directly with the year 1213 (/1798) and lists the names of the Sultan and the rulers of the Ottoman Empire, the Grand Vizier and the Mamlūk *amīr*s of Egypt and the Pāshās of Syria and Acre. The handwriting is a clear *nasta'līq*, similar to that of MS*'Aj.* Cam. and MS*Maẓ.* Cam. and *Risāla fī 'l-'Amal bi 'l-Rub'* as well as the addition of al-Jabartī in the margin of al-Zabīdī's *Mu'jam Mukhtaṣṣ* and his letter to Shaykh Ṭāhir al-Ḥusaynī the Muftī of Jerusalem. It contains 26 folios with an irregular number of lines of between 22 and 32 per page. There are copious marginal emendations and additions, and it ends with the words: الحمد لله الواحد القهار ('Judgment is by the one Omnipotent God'), without a colophon. The few additions in the margin of MS*Mudda* are written in al-Jabartī's hand and are indicated by an arrow pointing to the additions and ending them with the Arabic abbreviation, صح. This abbreviation denotes that the addition is corrected, and added by the author himself.

Professor P.Sj. van Koningsveld of Leiden University has pointed out to the writer of this study that the collation of MS*Mudda* is as follows: one *kurrāsa* (fascicle) is of 12 leaves (i.e. 24 folios) bound with one *kurrāsa* of one leaf (i.e. 2 folios). This fact implies that al-Jabartī was not fully aware of the final length of his work when he began to write it; otherwise, he would certainly have made a *kurrāsa* of 13 leaves. This again indicates that it is the rough draft of an autograph. On the other hand, Lars Bjørneboe, argues 'The arrangement of the text on the leaves shows that he had 26 folios at his disposal when he set out to write and that this is what he needed. The fact that the text uses all the pages minus one show that he had a fairly accurate idea of the length of his text'.[18] However, while the writer of this study used a photocopy of the MS, Bjørneboe was able to examine more thoroughly the original MS. He described it as follows: 'It consists of a text of 26 folios held together with a string, creating a small book, consisting of 52 pages. The outer leaf (f. 1ab, 26ab) is somewhat stiffer than the rest. The inner leaf (f. 12ab, 13ab) is slightly smaller than the rest and has a double frame in red ink, but the text on these pages does not follow the frame. One of the folios (f. 6ab, 19ab) has a more glazed surface and the area on which the text is written is discoloured, perhaps indicating that the paper of this leaf has been reused. These features indicate that we are dealing with [a] draft, written on cheap,

18 Bjørneboe, *In Search*,103, l. 3.

second-hand paper'.[19] He suggests that 'the finishing date of the rough draft [was] somewhere in January 1799'.[20]

II. Manuscripts of Maẓhar al-Taqdīs bi-Zawāl Dawlat al-Faransīs (The Manifestation of Blessing in the Demise of French Authority).

II. 2.The Cambridge University Library Manuscript (henceforth **MS*Maẓ.* Cam.**). E.G. Browne describes this manuscript as 'an autograph copy, bought from the author'.[21] The title of the manuscript is *Kitāb Maẓhar al-Taqdīs bi-Zawāl Dawlat al-Faransīs li-Jāmi'ih al-Faqīr 'Abd al-Raḥmān al-Jabartī al-Ḥanafī 'Afā Allāh 'anhu*, while in the preface the title is given as *Maẓhar al-Taqdīs bi-Dhahāb Dawlat al-Faransīs.* In the upper left-hand corner of the title page, in a 'Syrian' script, the owner wrote: *Bi-khaṭṭ al-Shaykh al-Jabartī, ishtarāhu min al-mu'allif al-Shaykh Ibrāhīm fī 1232* ('An autograph of al-Shaykh al-Jabartī; it was bought from the author by al-Shaykh Ibrāhīm in 1232 [/1816–17]'). If we know that al-Shaykh Ibrāhīm is Burckhardt, who continued his studies of Arabic in Aleppo, then it is obvious that his handwriting would be Syrian.

On the left-hand side of the title page, in a hand resembling that of Shaykh Ibrāhīm (Burkhardt), there is an important annotation, which might explain why al-Jabartī wrote his book:

وكان الشيخ الجبرتي أحد من [!] علماء الديوان الذي نصبوه [!] الفرنسيس في مصر فهو رجل ماهر في علوم الادب وعلم الفلك والميقات فحيثما كان يعاشر علماء الفرنسيس وقت قيامهم في القاهرة خاف على نفسه من بعد ذهابهم وألف هذا الكتاب ليبرى ذمته وليظهر محبته الى الدولة العاليه. الشيخ حسن العطار المشار عليه عند تسمية الكتاب هو أعالم [!] علماء مصر في وقتنا هذي في علم النحو والبديع والعروض ومخصوص في علم اللغة. ('Al-Shaykh al-Jabartī was one of the savants [*'ulamā'*] of the council [*dīwān*] which the French established in Egypt. He is an expert in literature and in the arts of astronomy and the calendar. As he used to associate with the French scientists during their stay in Cairo, he was worried about his safety after their evacuation, so he compiled this book in order to relieve his conscience and to demonstrate his allegiance to the Ottoman Empire. Al-Shaykh Ḥasan al-'Aṭṭār, who is mentioned [in the

---

19 Ibid., 103, l. 32.

20 Ibid., 105, and that 'the author [was] starting with an even rougher draft than the one we know as the MS *Mudda* '

21 Browne, *A Hand-list*, I, 207, no. 1058 (Qq 214). Cf. also Clément Huart, *Littérature arabe* (Paris 1902), 415. Cf. *al-Jabartī's Chronicle*, 7–9, and plate VI.

preface] where the name of the book is given, is the most prominent scholar of Egypt of our times in grammar, the art of metaphor, prosody, and is especially gifted in philology'.)

In order to understand the full importance of these remarks on the title-page of the manuscript, one has to remember, as previously stated, that 'Shaykh Ibrāhīm', was the well-known Swiss traveller and orientalist Johann Ludwig (John Lewis, Jean Louis) Burckhardt (b. Lausanne, 24 or 25 November, 1784–d. Cairo, 15 or 17 October, 1817). The latter bought this autograph from al-Jabartī himself and wrote the above note concerning al-Jabartī and al-ʿAṭṭār, Burckhardt, after his conversion to Islam in Aleppo, called himself 'Shaykh Ibrāhīm b. ʿAbd Allāh'. As a young man who adopted the cosmopolitan spirit of the European enlightenment with the aim of exchanging scientific knowledge, Burckhardt accepted a commission from the Association for Promoting the Discovery of the Interior Parts of Africa to cross the continent from Cairo to the Niger and to record his discoveries. For this purpose, he was sent to Cambridge to study Arabic and attended lectures on chemistry, astronomy, mineralogy, and medicine. In February 1808, Burckhardt travelled to Malta and in July reached Aleppo, where he studied Arabic for three years. Later he converted to Islam, studied the Qur'ān, and translated the novel *Robinson Crusoe* into Arabic. He was among the first orientalist converts and made the pilgrimage to Mecca and Medina (1814–15), when Muḥammad ʿAlī sent his army to fight the Wahhābīs. He recorded his pilgrimage and travels in the book *Travels in Arabia.*[22] Burckhardt first arrived in Cairo in September 1812, a year after Muḥammad ʿAlī became the autocratic ruler of Egypt, and again went there in the middle of 1815 after Muḥammad ʿAlī's reoccupation of the Ḥijāz. During this stay Burckhardt recovered from a violent fever that seriously weakened him. After his travels in the Sinai Peninsula (1816), Burckhardt returned to Cairo and, with the British Consul, commissioned the Italian traveller Giovanni Belzoni to transport the granite head of Ramses II to Alexandria,and from there to the British Museum in London (1818). During his stay in Cairo, Burckhardt visited Muḥammad ʿAlī, and according to the date which he recorded on the title page of *Maẓhar al-Taqdīs*, i.e. 1232 (/1816–17), he met ʿAbd al-Raḥmān al-Jabartī. Burckhardt visited our author at his home and bought two of his autographs, the *Maẓhar al-Taqdīs* and the

22 See John Lewis Burckhardt, *Travels in Arabia, Comprehending an Account of Those Territories in Hedjaz, Which the Mohammadans Regard as Sacred* (London 1829), vols I–II.

first three volumes of *'Ajā'ib al-Āthār* with the copious additions in the margin. Apparently, at the time, the author was still expanding this text, collecting and recording material for his fourth volume, and most probably, employing copyists to copy the first three volumes. This would explain, why some other manuscripts, of which the title page and the corrections in the margin which were made by al-Jabartī himself, contain some additions missing in the autograph sold to Burckhardt, and kept at Cambridge University Library. It also shed light on the question why the manuscripts of the first three volumes of the *'Ajā'ib al-Āthār* autograph and its copies differ from the MSS that contain four volumes, including the printed Būlāq edition.

It is not clear whether al-Jabartī ordered the copy of *'Ajā'ib al-Āthār* in *Maghribī* script, kept now in Cambridge University Library (MS *'Aj.* Cam. 2nd.), in order to be sold in the Maghreb. In consequence of his failure to sell it, he gave it to al-ʿAṭṭār to try to interest scholars in Istanbul and in Arab speaking cities which he intended to visit. During this journey, al-ʿAṭṭār took the liberty of correcting al-Jabartī in some grammatical and historical facts, adding some of his elegies, but still he failed to convince scholars to copy al-Jabartī's *'Ajā'ib* or to buy his copy. In this case, we can presume then that Burckhardt met Shaykh Ḥasan al-ʿAṭṭār, most probably in 1816 after his return from his journey to Turkey and Syria in 1815 and bought from him this copy of *'Ajā'ib al-Āthār* in *Maghribī* script with the title pages of volumes II and III written by al-Jabartī's hand (MS *'Aj.* Cam. 2nd.). It seems to us that the main reason for sending MS *'Aj.* Cam. 2nd. with al-ʿAṭṭār on his journey, might be the desire of al-Jabartī to make his book known and copied in the main Islamic cities, which he was supposed to visit. The success of his *Maẓhar al-Taqdīs* in Istanbul and its translation into Turkish, printed under the title *Tārīkhī Miṣr, Tarjama-'i Bahjat Afandī Ra'īs al-Aṭibbā'*, by the order of the Serdar Yūsuf Ḍiyā Pāshā, might have encouraged him to do so. Apparently, al-ʿAṭṭār kept this copy with him during his journey to Istanbul, Izmir, Damascus, Jerusalem, Jaffa and back to Cairo between 1222–9 (/1807–14).[23] This is evident from al-ʿAṭṭār's letters and his recordings on the margins of his MS of *'Ajā'ib al-Āthār*, which include not only his comments on what al-Jabartī recorded about some scholars and events but also his own impressions of the Ottoman

23 See below Chapter Four on Ḥasan al-ʿAṭṭār, and the Appendices on the comments of al-ʿAṭṭār on the margin of his copy of *'Ajā'ib al-Āthār*.

officials and cities, which he visited, and his longing for Egypt, calling it '*waṭanī*' (homeland). As far as we know, this is one of the earliest expressions of Egyptian patriotic identity, as against pan-Islamic Ottoman orientation.

These facts indicate that al-Jabartī was in contact with European travellers such as the Swiss Burckhardt, the Italians Belzoni and Giambatista Brocchi, the Frenchman Asselin and the Briton Lane, who visited him and probably supplied him with information about their travels and experiences. Burckhardt recorded his reminiscences of the massacre of the Mamluks in the Citadel in 1811, published in 1819 in *New Voyages and Travels*.[24] In December 1822 al-Jabartī was already blind.[25] Earlier he had daily contacts with the French authorities during his membership of the Dīwān formed by them, and frequent encounters with the French savants whom he visited and whose institutes, libraries and experiments he described with great admiration.

Burckhardt fell ill: 'on the 5th of October 1817, he was suddenly seized with dysentery which, in spite of the attendance of an English physician, hurried him to an untimely end on the 15th of that month'.[26] On his deathbed in Cairo, Burckhardt left instructions that his library of three hundred Arabic manuscripts was to go to the University of Cambridge. The *Library Donations* book 1800–65 records their arrival in 1819; they stand at Qq. 1–300 and still constitute the Library's most important single collection of Arabic manuscripts.[27]

MS*Maẓ*. Cam., contains 128 folios of 21 x 15.5 cm. averaging 25 lines per page. The handwriting is a clear Egyptian *nastaʿlīq* similar to that of MS *ʿAj*. Cam. There are many emendations and additions in the margins with the subscript *ṣaḥḥ* and a few lines are deleted. The colophon does not mention the date or the name of the scribe: وصلى الله على سيدنا محمد وآله وسلم والحمد لله رب العالمين.

24 Introduction to John Lewis Burckhardt, 'Travels in Egypt and Nubia', from the Calcutta Journal, in Sir Richard Phillips (ed.), *New Voyages and Travels: Consisting of Originals, Translations and Abridgements* (London 1819), II, 6.

25 G. Brocchi, *Giornale delle osservazioni fatte ne' viaggi in Egitto, nella Siria e nella Nubia*, 5 vols (Basano 1841–3), I, 151.

26 Burckhardt, introduction in *New Voyages and Travels*, II, 6.

27 See T. Preston, *Catalogus Bibliothecae Burckhardtianae* (Cambridge 1853); Andrew Dalby, *ADictionary of Oriental Collections in Cambridge University Library, in Transactions of the Cambridge Bibliographical Society*, IX (1988), 248ff, and D.J. McKitterick, *Cambridge University Library, a History* (Cambridge 1986), II, 388–92.

('May God bless our Master Muḥammad, grant him salvation and his family and thanks be to God, Lord of the Universe'.)

II. 3. The *Maẓhar al-Taqdīs* manuscript in the Dār al-Kutub al-Qawmiyya, Cairo (henceforth **MS*Maẓ.* DKQ**), Tārīkh M 101/microfilm 29362 is written in a neat *naskhī*script identical to the handwriting of the autograph MS*Maẓ.* Cam. It contains 146 rubricated folios of 23 lines each. Some words left unfinished at the ends of lines are completed in the margins. There are copious marginal additions concerning dates of important events and names and titles of important personalities. The title page indicates that this MS is part of the legacy of Khalīl Rifʿat Pāshā and that in 1250 (/1834–5) it belonged to ʿAbd al-Ḥaqq, the head of the Sultan's physicians. In 1272 (/1855–6), it passed into the possession of Muḥammad ʿĀrif Ḥilmī the *qāḍī* in Istanbul:

٨٥ قرش. ورثة تركة خليل رفعت باشا مصطفى خسرو باشا وحضرت سلطانم محمود خان عبد الحميد رحمه الله. جـ ٨٣٩٦ [!] استكتب هذا الكتاب الموسوم بمظهر التقديس بخروج دولة الفرنسيس وانا الفقير مصطفى بهجت العاصي في الماضي الحمد لله امين، من كتب الفقير عبد الحق رئيس الأطباء السلطاني في سنة ١٢٥٠. نمره ١٠١ تاريخ م. من ودائع الدهر لدى الفقير محمد عارف حلمي المتشرف رتبة القاضي بدار الخلافة العلية عفي عنه امين. في سنة ١٢٧٢، ق غ فيه مع تحفة الغزاة.شوالصالي [!]٢٨

F. 1b starts with the *basmala* and the *Introduction* of *Maẓhar al-Taqdīs*: بسم الله الرحمن الرحيم. وبه ثقتي ورجائي، حمدا لمن جعل كلمة الذين كفروا السفلى وكلمة الله هي العليا وجعل دولة العثمانية والمملكة الخاقانية بهجة الدين والدنيا ... F. 146a ends with the colophon stating that the book was compiled in 1216 (/1801–2) and copied once more by the author (*wa-ayḍan ḥarrartu hādhihi 'l-nuskha al-mubāraka*) in Muḥarram 1224 (/16 February–17 March 1809). The additions in the margins of MS*Maẓhar al-Taqdīs*, Cam., are copied inside the text of MS *Maẓhar al-Taqdīs*, DKQ. This fact indicates that this MS was copied by the author including his additions in the margins of MS *Maẓhar al-Taqdīs*, Cam. in the text of his new copy eight years later:

فلهذا يقول بشرى أرخ   باجتناء السرور جاء[sic= جاد]الوزير

وصلى الله على سيدنا محمد ... ووافق التمام سلخ شهر شعبان سنة ١٢١٦ من الهجرة النبوية ... وايضا حَرّرتُ هذه النسخة المباركة وكان الفراغ منها سنة ١٢٢٤ في غرة محرم الحرام افتتاح سنة اربعة وعشرين ومائتين والف، تم بعون الله وحسن توفيقه امين م.

Under this colophon, there is a stamp reading:al-Maktaba al-Khudaywiyya al-Miṣriyya.

Another manuscript of *Maẓhar al-Taqdīs* in Dār al-Kutub al-Qawmiyya, Cairo is MS*Maẓ.* Tārīkh 330 in 28 pages, copied in 1293 (/1876–7).

II. 4. The *Maẓhar al-Taqdīs* manuscript of the Bayezid Library, Istanbul (henceforth **MS*Maẓ.* Bay**). *GAL*, II, 731, stated that there was an autograph of *'Muẓhir'* [sic] in the Bayezid Library. The manuscript is not 'Bayezid 76' (as Brockelmann said), but MS Cevdet Pāshā 76 as listed in the catalogue *Defter-i Kutubkhāne-i Weli el-Dīn* (Istanbul 1304/1886–7), 280. However, this catalogue does not state whether the manuscript is an autograph or a copy, and there is no statement or mark to confirm Brockelmann's information. The handwriting does not resemble that of any of the other manuscripts, which were examined for this purpose including the Cambridge MSS. The script is a clear *naskhī*, with golden illumination at the beginning of the preface. The manuscript is rubricated with a few marginal annotations and corrections between the lines. It contains 420 pages of 23 lines each.

The title page bestows the honorific title *afandī* on the author and uses the word 'Zādeh' instead of the Arabic 'Ibn' which indicate that the MS was copied in Istanbul by an efficient copyist on the orders of a rich patron. The MS title reads: كتاب مظهرالتقديس بزوال دولة الفرنسيس جمع عبد الرحمن افندي جبرتي زاده الحنفي غفر الله له ولو الديه آمين

The colophon says that the book was compiled in Shaʿbān 1216 (/7 December 1801–4 January 1802), not mentioning a date of copying: ...وصلى الله على سيّدنا محمد وعلى آله وصحبه وسلم ووافق التمام سلخ شهر شعبان سنة ١٢١٦ من الهجرة النبوية على صاحبها افضل الصلاة والسلام امين م.

II. 5.The *Maẓhar al-Taqdīs* manuscript of the Rampur Raza Library, Rampur, India (henceforth **MS*Maẓ.* Ram.**). Fu'ād Sayyid[28] states that this manuscript was copied in 1216 (/1801–2). Maḥmūd al-Sharqāwī initiated the assumption that it is an autograph,quoting the opinion of an expert at the Institute of Arabic Manuscripts in Cairo (Maʿhad Iḥyā' al-Makhṭūṭāt al-ʿArabiyya) that it 'might be an autograph'.[29]

The manuscript contains 175 folios of 22 x 16 cm., averaging 23 lines per page. The script is a clear *nasta'līq,* but it does not resemble the hand of any of

28 See Fu'ād Sayyid et al, *Fihris al-Makhṭūṭāt al-Muṣawwara* (Cairo 1959), II, pt. 3, 281, no. 1232. Cf. *Fihrist-i Kutub-i 'Arabī Mawjūda-i Kutubkhāna-i Riyāsat-i Rampūr* (Rampūr 1928), II, I, no. 3634–F. 3302.

29 Al-Sharqāwī, *Dirāsāt fī Tārīkh al-Jabartī*, I, 44, n. 1.

the manuscripts already described. The names of months and the beginnings of chapters are rubricated in large characters, and there is slight moth damage.

The title reads: مَظهر التقديس بزوال دولة الفرنسيس جمع الشيخ عبد الرحمن افندي جبرتي زاده الحنفي عامله الله بلطفه الخفي آمين. The letter *mīm* in the word *Maẓhar al-Taqdīs* has a *fatḥa*. There are very few emendations or remarks in the margins. The most important marginal note is on f. 37, remarking on an error: كذا كتبوا و التلاوة خاينة ('Thus they wrote and the reading is treacherous'.) This comment shows that the owner of the manuscript thought that the copyist made this error out of 'traitorous' '*tilāwa*' ('reading' or 'dictating [the text to a copyist] out loud'), which definitely indicates that it was not the author's fault. Some of the words are fully vowelled. The similarity between the colophon of MS*Maẓ*. Ram. to that of MS*Maẓ*. Bay., as well as the date of copying both MSS, indicates that it was copied from the MS*Maẓ*. Bay: ... وصلى الله على سيّدنا محمد وعلى آله وصحبه وسلم والحمد لله أولا وآخرا، ووافق التمام سلخ شهر شعبان المعظم سنة ١٢١٦ [/1801] من الهجرة النبوية على صاحبها أفضل الصلاة والسلام امين م.

In our opinion, this date (as in the case of MS*Maẓ*. Bay.) denotes the time at which al-Jabartī finished compiling the book and not the date of copying the manuscript by the transcriber. This is because al-Jabartī himself says at the end of the book: ناسب أن يجعل ختام هذا التاريخ شهر رمضان المعظم ('it is suitable to end this history with the [events of the] glorious month of Ramaḍān').[30] Moreover, Maḥmūd al-Sharqāwī said that the colophon of a manuscript copied in 1224 (/1809–10) states that 'the compilation [of the book] was finished at the end of

---

30 See 'Abd al-Raḥmān al-Jabartī, *Yawmiyyāt al-Jabartī, Maẓhar al-Taqdīs bi-Zawāl Dawlat al-Faransīs*, Muḥammad 'Aṭā (ed.) (Cairo 1958, Ikhtarnā Laka, nos. 59–60), 2 vols. The title of the second volume is *Maẓhar al-Taqdīs bi-Dhahāb Dawlat al-Faransīs, Yawmiyyāt al-Jabartī*. See *Maẓhar al-Taqdīs bi-Dhahāb Dawlat al-Faransīs, 'Yawmiyyāt al-Jabartī'*,II, 198, ll. 7–9. Another important edition, entitled as in the case of MS*Maẓ*. Cam., *Maẓhar al-Taqdīs bi-Zawāl Dawlat al-Faransīs*, was published in Cairo (1961), in two volumes, edited by M.F. 'Abd al-Laṭīf, 'A.M. 'Āmir, and A.Z. 'Aṭiyya. The editors allowed themselves to simplify the style of al-Jabartī. It is based upon the second autograph of al-Jabartī kept at DKQ in Cairo (MS*Maẓ*. Tārīkh M 101/microfilm 29362), copied in 1224 (/1809–10) and upon two other MSS with footnotes and maps. Another edition was published by Ḥasan Muḥammad Jawhar and 'Umar al-Dasūqī in Cairo, 1969. The latest edition is by Aḥmad 'Abduh 'Alī, entitled, *Maẓhar al-Taqdīs bi-Dhahāb Dawlat al-Faransīs bi 'l-Ishtirāk ma'a Ṣadīqih ... Ḥasan al-'Aṭṭār* (Cairo 1419/1998) attributing it also to Ḥasan al-'Aṭṭār as co-author. It is based upon the former edition of 1961. Another scholarly edition is by 'Abd al-Raḥīm (Cairo 1998), based upon MS*Maẓ*. Tārīkh 330 and copied in Rajab 1293 (/August 1878) by Aḥmad Rizq. The editor gave definitions of places, streets, tribes, etc. with comprehensive indexes.

the month of Shaʿbān of the year 1216 [/5 January 1802]'.[31] That means, that, in fact, the author recorded the events of Shaʿbān in Ramaḍān, hoping to receive the blessings of the holy month. Therefore, the latter date is not the date of the completion of the transcription[32] and both Brockelmann and Sharqāwī were misled by the date of al-Jabartī's colophon, which was copied in both MSS.

II. 5. The *Maẓhar al-Taqdīs* manuscript of the British Library (henceforth MS*Maẓ*. BM.).[33] This manuscript contains 171 folios of 23 x 15.5 cm., 27 lines per page, 'written in cursive and rather indistinct *Neskhī*'. The title is similar to that of MS*Maẓ*. Ram. It reads: مظهر التقديس بزوال دولة الفرنسيس جمع الشيخ عبد الرحمن افندي جبرتي زاده الحنفي عامله الله بلطفه الخفي آمين. The manuscript is rubricated and each page has a frame traced in red ink. On f. 6b, ll. 5–6 the title is given in red ink as *Maẓhar al-Taqdīs bi-Dhahāb Dawlat al-Faransīs*, where the words '*bi-zawāl*' (demise) are changed into '*bi-dhahāb*' (departure). The beginnings of the paragraphs in the last folios are in green ink. The colophon states that Aḥmad Rizq completed the transcription in 14 Rabīʿ I 1263 (/1846–7) and that it was in the possession of al-Jabartī's son, Maḥfūẓ. The last lines are written in red and green ink alternately. In the following two verses the copyist asks the readers to invoke God's blessings upon him to escape the fire of hell:[34]

... وصلى الله على سيّدنا محمد وعلى آله وسلم والحمد لله أولا وآخرا، ووافق التمام ١٤ شهر ربيع أول سنة ١٢٦٣ [/1847] على يد كاتبه الفقير الى الله تعالى الراجي عفو الله تعالى أحمد رزق غفر له ولوالديه ولمن دعا له بخير آمين.

سألتك بالله الذي خضعت	له السموات وهو الواحد الباري
إذا تأملت فاستغفر لكاتبه	لعلّه ينجوا [!] من النار

ملك نجل المؤلف الفقير محفوظ ابن الشيخ عبد الرحمن الجبرتي الحنفي غفر الله له ولوالديه آمين.

---

31 Shaʿbān is the eighth month while Ramaḍān is the ninth. *Yawmiyyāt al-Jabartī*, ʿAṭā (ed.), I, 36, 43.

32 See al-Sharqāwī, *Dirāsāt fī Tārīkh al-Jabartī*, I, 44. n. 1. Al-Sharqāwī thought that this was the date of transcription.

33 Charles Rieu, *Supplement to the Catalogue of the Arabic Manuscripts in the British Museum*, (London 1894), 359–60, no. 561. It is worth mentioning here that the most accurate details about al-Jabartī's manuscripts are to be found in this catalogue. On the last page of the manuscript are the words 'BT [= bought?] of Baron von Kremer 9 Jan. 1886'.

34 For other *Maẓhar al-Taqdīs* manuscripts see *GAL*, *Suppl.*, II, 730–1, and Ayalon, 'The Historian', 245, n. 1.

III. *'Ajā'ib al-Āthār* manuscripts in European libraries. There are several MSS of *'Ajā'ib al-Āthār* written by the author's hand or corrected by him or those which were copied during his lifetime. The most important ones are two manuscripts of *'Ajā'ib al-Āthār* in the Cambridge University Library, acquired by J.L. Burckhardt, which are part of the three hundred manuscripts he asked to be sent to Cambridge University after his death (1817) and a copy amongst the MSS of the Bibliothèque Nationale.

III. 1. The first copy of *'Ajā'ib al-Āthār* at the Cambridge University Library. This MS consists of three volumes, Qq. 169, 170, 171 (MS *'Aj.* Cam.). According to E.G. Browne's description,[35] the manuscript includes the first three volumes of *'Ajā'ib al-Āthār*; it is marked 'Autograph Copy', and 'contains copious marginal annotations and corrections'.

None of the three volumes has a title page; each folio is 21.2 x 16 cm. containing 27 lines. With the exception of a few words, both the text and the marginal annotations and corrections are written in the same hand in Egyptian *nasta'līq*, as are the passages and annotations added in the margins, with the conventional subscript word *ṣaḥḥ* ('correct') added,[36] as well as two small square slips of paper (*ṭayyārāt*) written upon both sides. These annotations seem to have been introduced after a general revision of the text by al-Jabartī, and later as he came across more information. It is important to note here that in this MS and those which were copied from it (Cambridge group of MSS), some personalities who have titles such as Afandī or Bek were given a different title indicating a higher rank such as Aghā and Bāshā in the MS of DKQ in Cairo, which resembles the Būlāq edition.[37] This is a clear indication that these people had been promoted in rank at the time when the MSS on which the Būlāq edition was based (some of which are now kept at DKQ, Cairo) were copied, probably because many years had passed since al-Jabartī's autograph had first been copied. This anachronism escaped the attention of the copyists of the *'Ajā'ib al-Āthār* autograph.

35 Browne, *A Hand-list*, I, 118, nos. 669–71.

36 Ibid.

37 See *'Aj.* Būlāq, III, 344, and our new Arabic edition of *'Aj.*, III, 344, n. 68.

In our New Edition of the Arabic text, the MS *'Aj.* Cam. volumes I–III are indicated by the letters 'عك' (*'k*) and two perpendicular lines indicate its variants // ... //. Only volume I, f. 1a starts with the *basmala.* بسم الله الرحمن الرحيم

III. 1. a. MS *'Aj.* Cam., Qq. 169, vol. I, has 295 folios, of 21 lines each. It contains the events of the years 1100–89 (/1688–1776). F. 1b starts with the *basmala*and... وبه نستعين. Al-Jabartī's introduction begins on line 2: الحمد لله القديم الأول الذي لا يزول ملكه ولا يتحول خالق الخلايق ومنزه عن العلايق... Copious marginal annotations, additions in the margin and on pieces of paper, corrections, and crossed lines, all in the same handwriting, start to appear with f. 2a. Folios 91a, ll. 8–27 and 91b–92a are blank. Folio 235b is half-blank, and folios 236a–237b are also blank. The lacunae in this volume are: f. 81a, one line; f. 81b, ll. 11–27–f. 82a; f. 91a, ll. 8–27, ff. 91b–92a; f. 139a, one line; f. 235b, half blank; ff. 236a–237b; f. 255b, ll. 16–27; f. 256b, f. 257a–b; f. 268b, l. 17–f. 269a are blank. The blank parts indicate that the author intended to complete the missing information after he revised them.

In this volume the order of the biographies, under the title ذكر من مات في هذه السنين ('the necrology of these years'), is very confused. They are not arranged according to dates of death, which were added in red ink in the margins to enable the copyists and readers to see the right sequence. There are many corrections and lines to indicate the correct order of the paragraphs and biographies. In some places, words are added between the lines, while numerous lines are deleted. Moreover, there are large blank spaces in many places, occupying between half a page and two pages.[38] Small pieces of paper were added to some pages to continue the marginal notes.[39] The manuscript, which ends with f. 295a (= *'Aj.* Būlāq, I, 420), does not have a colophon and

38 MS *'Aj.*Cam., Qq. 169, I, ff. 6a, 81a–82a, 91b, 242b, 255b, 268b–269a, and immediately after the year 1188/1774, in II, ff. 46b, 47a.

39 See for instance MS *'Aj.* Cam., Qq. 169, I, f. 151a; II, f. 159a. The biography of Muḥammad Khalīl al-Murādī (d. 1206/1791–2) was written in this way (II, ff. 158a–159a, cf. *'Aj.* Būlāq, II, 233, l. 15–236, l. 24). This fact suggests that the author wrote it in a sudden flash of recollection while editing once more his autograph MS; thus he was not thinking of the other two versions in the Introduction of his book in which he stated his methods and motives for compiling it (ibid., I, 2, ll. 6–30). See also Ayalon 'The Historian', 222–7. Beside those versions of al-Jabartī's motives for recording his Chronicles, one should not overlook the fact that he was very much impressed by French scientific and cultural activities, their recording and chronicling of events and their description of every aspect of Egyptian life (*'Aj.*, III, 34–6, IV, 192, ll. 10–11). This may well have given him another incentive to undertake his enterprise.

concludes with the sentence: وسيتلى عليك من ذلك أنباء واخبار ما حل بالاقليم بسببهم من الخراب والدمار وبه ختم هذا الجزء من عجايب الآثار في التراجم والأخبار والله سبحانه وتعالى اعلم. ('The narration of these events and of the ruin and destruction that befell the country on their [the Mamluk] account will be related to you. God is most knowledgeable'.)

III. 1. b. MS *'Aj*.Cam., Qq. 170, vol. II, has 179 folios of 27 lines each. It contains the events of the years 1190–1212 (/1776–98), and starts on f. 1b without the *basmala*: سنة تسعين ومائة والف / وكان سلطان العصر فيها السلطان عبد الحميد بن احمد خان العثماني...

Many biographies in the text or added in the margin provide the year of death. This may have been an indication written by the author to the copyist, telling him how to arrange the biographies in chronological order. Some biographies added in the margins were deleted and the words سهو ('inadvertence')[40] or مكرر ('repeated'), or ('ditto'), or محله بعد هذا التاريخ ('the location [of this biography] is after this date' [1123/1711–12]), were inscribed beside them.[41] The biography of Muḥammad Khalīl al-Murādī (d. 1206 [/1791–2]) is written in the margin.[42] There is also a critical note in a thick, ugly hand (II, f. 60b, equivalent to *'Aj*. Būlāq, II, 84): ومحصل هذه الأفاعيل ... إنها حيل على سلب الأموال والبلاد... This remark might indicate that al-Jabartī gave this MS for copying or revision, or lent it in 1221 (/1806–7), a year after its compilation, to another scholar:

> وواقع الآن نظير ذلك بين محمد باشا علي وبين محمد بيك الالفي مع خشداشينه من جهة مراسلاتهم للعثملي [!] وذلك في سنة ١٢٢١ فالله يحسن العواقب فان اهل القرى قد اشتد بهم الضنك والسلب واظن الشيخ حفظه الله المولف قد بيّن ذلك بأتم بيان فيما سيأتي. أ.هـ ('A similar [affair] to this one is happening now in the year 1221 [/1806–1807] between Muḥammad Bāshā 'Alī and Muḥammad Bey al-Alfī with his *khushdāsh*s (comrades) regarding their correspondence with the Ottomans. May God cause it to have a good outcome,because distress and plunder are harassing the villagers and I presume that the Shaykh, may God save him, [I mean] the author, has elucidated this in the clearest way in the following [pages]'). This note indicates that

---

40 MS *'Aj*. Cam., Qq. 170, II, f. 120.

41 Ibid., II, ff. 51a–52a. On other abbreviations of words used in manuscripts, see W. Wright, *A Grammar of the Arabic Language* (Cambridge 1955), I, 25–6.

42 MS *'Aj*. Cam., Qq. 170, II, ff. 169a–170a equivalent to *'Aj*. Būlāq, II, 233, l. 15–236, l. 24. See also Moreh, 'al-Jabartī's Method', 372–3, plates V–VI.

according to the person who wrote it, al-Jabartī was busy preparing the fourth volume of his chronicle.

The lacunae in this volume are f. 46b, ll. 11–27 and f. 110a, ll. 6–16. This volume does not have a colophon, and the last folio (f. 179a) ends in the same way as volume II of the Būlāq edition, as follows: ومات... السيد حسن بن عبد الرحمن... المنزلاوي الشافعي في منتصف شهر شعبان من السنة غفر الله لنا وله بمنه وكرمه.

III. 1. c. MS *'Aj.* Cam., Qq. 171, vol. III, in 300 folios of 21 lines each. F. 1b starts... سنة ثلاثة عشر [sic] ومايتين والف / وهي سني الملاحم العظيمة والحوادث الجسيمة ('The Year 1213 [/15 June 1798–4 June 1799]. This was the year of the fierce fights and important incidents'). It ends on f. 300b with the biography of Muḥammad b. Ḥubaysh al-Maqdisī with the words: حسن به ختم هذا الجزء من عجائب الآثار في التراجم والأخبار والله سبحانه وتعالى أعلم.

Line 10 has been scratched out in f. 225b. At the end of the third volume (f. 300b) there is an illegible line in another hand, resembling that of Burckhardt (al-Shaykh Ibrāhīm), which has been almost completely obliterated. However, with the aid of a ultra-violet lamp one can read the following words written in handwriting similar to that on the title page of MS Cambridge of *Maẓhar al-Taqdīs*:[43]... وهذه النسخة بخط المألف [!] الشيخ حسن [!] الجبرتي وهي مبياض الكتاب ('This copy is an autograph by al-Shaykh Ḥasan [sic] al-Jabartī and it is a fair copy of the book'). The manuscript is undated. MS *'Aj.* Cam. does not belong to the group of MSS in which each volume has been divided into two parts, like the Khuda Bakhsh MS IV. 11 below. Similarly in the Beirut, Dār al-Fāris (n.d.) and Dār al-Kutub al-ʿIlmiyya (1997) editions,[44] the poems and the literary parts have been omitted.

The collation between MS *'Aj.* Cam. and the printed editions shows that the Cambridge MSS and the MSS copied from them ('the Cambridge group') differ from the printed editions. All the following editions contain many homoeoteleuton, reading mistakes, grammatical 'corrections', and printing

43 See MS *'Aj.* Cam., Qq. 171, III, f. 300b and *al-Jabartī's Chronicle*, 5 and plate V.

44 This is the case of MS *'Aj.* Tārīkh 2287 *badal*/microfilm 35959 (VI. 24. b.) in Cairo, which omits all the poems and the literary material quoted by al-Jabartī in the biographical sections. It is interesting to note here that it was in the possession of Maḥmūd Sāmī al-Bārūdī. The editions of Dār al-Fāris in Beirut (n.d. with no name of the editor), and Dār al-Kutub al-ʿIlmiyya, Ibrāhīm Shams al-Dīn (ed.), (1997) seem to be copied from MS *'Aj.* Tārīkh 2287 *badal*/microfilm 35959 or from a copy of it.

errors: the Būlāq edition of 1297 (/1879–80), al-Maṭbaʿa al-ʿĀmira al-Sharafiyya edition of 1322–3 (/1904–5), the *'Ajā'ib al-Āthār* edition in the margin of *al-Kāmil* by Ibn al-Athīr, and the edition of Ḥasan Muḥammad Jawhar, ʿAbd al-Fattāḥ al-Siranjāwī and al-Sayyid Ibrāhīm Sālim in seven volumes (1958–67), vols 3–7 edited by Ḥasan Muḥammad Jawhar, ʿUmar al-Dasūqī, and al-Sayyid Ibrāhīm Sālim. The same is true of the first new edition of ʿAbd al-ʿAzīz Jamāl al-Dīn (Cairo 1997), Ṣafaḥāt min Tārīkh Miṣr, 5/37, pts 1–5), based upon a microfilm of a MS kept at Cairo University, which belongs to the group of MSS which were copied after the death of al-Jabartī. This MS was compared with the Būlāq edition and has very few different readings. The merits of this edition are that it contains many significant documents, articles and works by various contemporary Egyptian historians, as important supplements to the original text. The second new edition of ʿAbd al-Raḥīm ʿAbd al-Raḥmān ʿAbd al-Raḥīm, published by the Egyptian National Library, Center of Documents and Contemporary History of Egypt (*al-Hay'a al-'Āmma li-Dār al-Kutub wa 'l-Wathā'iq al-Qawmiyya-Markaz Wathā'iq wa-Tārīkh Miṣr al-Mu'āṣir*) (Cairo 1997–8) is also based upon the Būlāq edition. It contains several important indices of personal names, geographical, tribal, and administrative terms with important comments.

All these printed editions, except the one in the margin of *al-Kāmil* by Ibn al-Athīr, so strongly resemble the Būlāq edition that it may be assumed that they are all based on the final MS *'Aj.* Birmingham, nos. 908–11 (1361–4) (IX, 37 below) copied in 1296 (/1878–9) from an autograph dated 1236 (/1820–1). According to H.L. Gottschalk, it was copied on the order of the manager of al-Maṭbaʿa al-Kubrā (Būlāq Press). The printed editions not only have numerous major printing errors and homoeoteleuton, but also are full of grammatical and stylistic 'corrections'. Religious expressions have been added, such as the word *ta'ālā* (exalted) whenever the word Allāh occurs. A few copyists of the manuscript, which the editor of the Būlāq edition took as his main manuscript, most probably made these changes and the editors of the other printed editions later copied these. The main differences appear in volume III of the Būlāq edition, where many annotations and passages were added or changed. For instance, at the end of the record of the month of Dhu 'l-Ḥijja 1216, concluding after the 25th (/28 April 1802) with the sentence (*'Aj.* Būlāq, III, 211, ll. 26–7): وفي خامس عشرينه قبضوا على امرأة سرقت أمتعة من حمام فشنقوها عند باب

.زويلة ('on the 25th a woman was caught stealing clothes at a bath and was hanged near Bāb Zuwayla'), ('the events and the biographies of the men who died'), which follow in the Būlāq edition are lacking in MS *'Aj.* Cam., Qq. 171, III, f. 168a.

In effect, in all these printed editions and manuscripts nos. III. 2. 1. c.; 3. 2. c.; 5. c.; 7. c.; 14. c.; 16. c.; 21. c. lengthy biographical additions follow after the events of 25 Dhu 'l-Ḥijja 1216 (/28 April 1802) (*'Aj. Būlāq*, III, 211, l. 26–220, l. 10): وانقضت هذه السنة وما تجدد بها من الحوادث التي من جملتها ان شريف افندي الدفتردار احدث ... وقتل مع من قتل ودفن بالاسكندرية. \ محرم الحرام ابتداء سنة ١٢١٧هـ. These events and biographies are not mentioned in the *'Aj.* Cambridge group of MSS: MS *'Aj.* Cam., Qq. 171, III, f. 168a; MS *'Aj.* BN, Suppl. arabe 1863 (III. 7. c.), MS *'Aj.*. Tārīkh 466, microfilm 34682 (VI. 15. c. below); MS *'Aj.* Tārīkh 1424/microfilm 14198 (VI. 17. c. below); MS *'Aj.*. Tārīkh 1425/microfilm 19286 (VI. 18. c. below).[45]

Volume III contains the original of Napoleon's proclamation, but no record of the events of 22 Ṣafar 1216 (/4 July 1801), which deals with ʿAbd al-ʿAzīz bin Saʿūd al-Wahhābī who entered Mecca and destroyed tombs surrounding the Kaʿba. In MS *'Aj.* Cam., Qq. 171, III, f. 213b, and *'Aj.* Būlāq, III, 255, dealing with the events of Saturday, 29 Ṣafar 1218 (/19–20 June 1803), the proclamation of Muḥammad b. ʿAbd al-Wahhāb is given in a summarized form, as in the case of manuscript MS *'Aj.* Tārīkh 174/microfilm 10730 (VI. 14. c. below). In *'Aj.* Būlāq, III, 255–7; the Beirut edition of Dār al-Fāris; MS *'Aj.* Ber., III (III. 9. c.), MS *'Aj.* Tārīkh 466/microfilm 34682, 235 (VI. 15. c. below); MS *'Aj.* Tārīkh 1424/microfilm 14198 (VI. 17. c. below); MS *'Aj.* Tārīkh 1425/microfilm 19286 (VI. 18. c. below); MS *'Aj.* Tārīkh 2129/microfilm 36545 (VI. 23. c. below) this proclamation is not summarized but given in full. Only in the Būlāq edition (*'Aj.* Būlāq, III, 257, ll. 1–4, the Beirut, Dār al-Fāris edition, and the Beirut Dār al-Kutub al-ʿIlmiyya edition, vol. II, 412–13), MS *'Aj.* Cam. and MS *'Aj.* Ber., are the following four lines of this proclamation mentioned: وقد بسط الكلام في ذلك ابن القّيم في كتابه إغاثة اللهفان وكتاب مصائد الشيطان وغير ذلك. انتهى. ('Ibn al-Qayyim has written profusely on the subject in his book *Ighāthat al-Lahfān* and in the book *Maṣā'id al-Shayṭān*,

45 These biographies are mentioned in full in *'Aj.* Būlāq, III, 211, l. 27–220, l. 10, MS *'Aj.* Ber., III, f. 315a, l. 3–f. 327a, MS *'Aj.* Tārīkh 174/microfilm 10730, ff. 140a–150a; MS *'Aj.* Tārīkh 2287/microfilm 35385, fascicle 22.

etc'.) This indicates that the Būlāq edition was based on a comparison of MSS, one of which was a copy of the Berlin MS (III. 9. c. below).

These facts are of great importance, because they show that MS *'Aj.* Cam., Qq. 171, III, which is an autograph, differs from MS *'Aj.* Ber., III (III. 9. c. below), and from MS *'Aj.* Tārīkh 174, in that it gives the biographies of the year 1216 (/1801–2) in full. Apparently, MS *'Aj.* Tārīkh 174 forms the link between MS *'Aj.* Cam., Qq. 171, III and the Būlāq edition. No manuscript has yet been found which is completely identical to the edited text of Būlāq, which confirms our conclusion that it is in fact a conglomerate of *'Ajā'ib al-Āthār* MSS, which were in the possession of the Būlāq Press. This proves that the Būlāq edition was produced according to a manuscript transcribed based on a comparison of a number of different copies of al-Jabartī's manuscripts.

The handwriting of all three volumes of MS *'Aj.* Cam. resemble al-Jabartī's *Maẓhar al-Taqdīs* manuscript at the Cambridge University Library (Qq. 214)[46] where, as we have seen above, the owner al-Shaykh Ibrāhīm (Burckhardt) wrote:[47] بخط الشيخ الجبرتي. اشتراه من المؤلف الشيخ ابراهيم في ١٢٣٢ ('an autograph of al-Shaykh al-Jabartī; it was bought from the author by al-Shaykh Ibrāhīm in 1232 [/1816–17]'. To recapitulate briefly: al-Shaykh Ibrāhīm was the orientalist Johann Ludwig Burckhardt, who bought two of al-Jabartī's autographs, including the *Maẓhar al-Taqdīs*, where he noted the date of purchase: 1232 (/1816–17). Burckhardt's handwriting is Syrian in style, because he studied Arabic in Aleppo in 1811. It appears again at the end of MS *'Aj.* Cam., Qq. 171, vol. III, where he wrote: بخط المائلف [!] الشيخ حسن الجبرتي ('by the handwriting of the author, al-Shaykh Ḥasan [sic] al-Jabartī'). It may be presumed that when Burckhardt realized that he had attributed it to the father and probably because he misspelled the word المائلف (the author) he scratched out the sentence because he understood that he had wrongly attributed the work to Ḥasan al-Jabartī.

Moreover, the handwriting also resembles that of the manuscript marked 'autograph' entitled *Tārīkh Muddat al-Faransīs bi-Miṣr* (MS*Mudda*) which deals with the first seven months of the French occupation of Egypt from Muḥarram-Rajab 1213 (15 June 1798–December 1798). The fact that there is an unmistakable resemblance among the handwritings of all these manuscripts

46 Browne, *A Hand-list*, I, 207. See also *al-Jabartī's Chronicle*, 5 and plates IV–VII and XI–XII.

47 Browne, *A Hand-list*, I, 207, no. 1058 (Qq. 214) and *al-Jabartī's Chronicle*, 8 and plate VI.

and of a short manuscript on astronomy in four folios, which was copied by al-Jabartī and is entitled: رسالة بخط الجبرتي في العمل بالرُبع. (‘A Treatise on the Use of the Quadrant, from the Hand of al-Jabartī’)[48] and of the letter sent by al-Jabartī on 21 Rabīʿ II 1229 (/12 April 1814) to the *muftī* of Jerusalem, Ṭāhir Afandī al-Ḥusaynī, as well as al-Jabartī’s commentary on the biography of Darwīsh al-Rūmī in Murtaḍā al-Zabīdī’s *Muʿjam Mukhtaṣṣ*, all prove beyond doubt that MS *ʿAj.* Cam. is indeed an autograph.[49]

III. 2. a–c. The second copy of *ʿAjāʾib al-Āthār* at the Cambridge University Library,is also in three volumes MS *ʿAj.* Cam. 2nd., Qq. 166, 167, 168, of 15 x 21.2 cm. written in *Maghribī* handwriting. Each folio contains 21 lines. These three volumes contain 27 passages in the margins in the hand of al-Jabartī’s friend Ḥasan al-ʿAṭṭār, containing comments, corrections, and additions to the biographies and data as well as impressions of the Ottoman cities, noted during al-ʿAṭṭār’s journey to Turkey and Greater Syria. (See the margins of the Arabic text of our new edition of *ʿAjāʾib al-Āthār*, marked a, b, c, etc. III. 2. b). MS *ʿAj.* Cam. 2nd., Qq. 167, I, 384 folios, 21.2 x 15 cm., 22 ll. ff. 384 dealing with the events of the years 1100–90 (/1688–1777). There is no title page on f. 1a and no *tamlīk* (notes on the names of the owners or copyists.) The manuscript is in *Maghribī* script rubricated with red ink with a few corrections in the margins in the same *Maghribī* hand. On f. 2a, the title of the book is given in green ink. Only the fascicles are numbered. The *basmala* on f. 1b differs from that found in the other manuscripts بسم الله الرحمن الرحيم صلّى الله علي سيدنا محمد وعلى آله وأصحابه وسلم. الحمد لله القديم الأول / الذي لا يزول ملكه ولا يتحول خالق الخلايق ومنزّه عن العلايق...

48 See von Landberg, 21, no. 61. Cf. also *GAL*, *Suppl.*, II, 731, *al-Jabartī’s Chronicle*, 8, n. 29 and note 8, above. In R. Dozy, *Supplément aux dictionnaires arabes* (Leiden 1927), under *al-mīqāt:* ‘L’art de dresser les calendriers servant à indiquer les heures de la prière’. Among the manuscripts in Leiden University, MS Ar. 1794 (see von Landberg, n. 3), there is a short manuscript in 4 folios on astronomy copied by ʿAbd al-Raḥmān al-Jabartī. The owner of the library in Medina, Shaykh ‘Emin al-Madanī’, gave the erroneous title on f. 1a. The handwriting of the title is identical to the title on f. 1a of MS *Mudda*. The colophon on f. 4b states that the annotation by ʿAbd al-Raḥmān al-Jabartī ended on 1 Jumādā II 1185 (/10 September 1771).

49 See Manna, ‘Cultural Relations’, 142–4, 151, and Reichmuth, ‘Notes’, 374 and al-Zabīdī, *Muʿjam Mukhtaṣṣ*,f. 62a. Cf. also Moreh, ‘al-Jabartī’s Method’, 356–7, n. 39.

This manuscript is unique. Not only are the title pages of volumes I–II in an Egyptian script identical to al-Jabartī's hand, but it also contains copious marginal remarks concerning the contents, comments and corrections by al-Jabartī's friend Shaykh Ḥasan al-ʿAṭṭār.[50] Al-ʿAṭṭār sometimes added the date and the name of the cities outside Egypt about which he made these remarks, such as Istanbul, Izmir, Jaffa (1225–6 [/1810–12]) and Damascus (1227 [/1812–13]) see ff. 11a, 14b, 15a, 238b–239a, 240b, 259b, 260a, 262b, 263a, 263b, 282a, 320a, 322a, 353b. In some cases, al-ʿAṭṭār ended his remarks with the phrase: كاتبه الفقير حسن محمد العطار ('by its scribe, the humble Ḥasan b. Muḥammad al-ʿAṭṭār').[51] Again, there is no colophon, as is the case with all other manuscripts that have a title page written by al-Jabartī.[52]

III. 3. The 'Ajā'ib al-Āthār manuscripts in the British Library.

There are two copies of *'Ajā'ib al-Āthār* in the British Library, the first, is BM.Add. 26,042-4 (shelf mark Or. 4628-30)(henceforth **MS'*Aj.* BM1**), and the second one is Or. 4628-30 (henceforth MS'*Aj.* BM2). According to the description in *Catalogus codicum manuscriptorum orientalium qui in Museo Britannico asservantur*,[53] the manuscript contains the first three volumes of *'Ajā'ib al-Āthār*. However, all the title pages of the 3 volumes have the following blessing of the author: *ghafara Allāh lahu* ('May God grant him pardon'), which indicates that the author had already died by 17 Rabīʿ I 1242 (/19 October 1826) according to the colophon of MS'*Aj.* BM1, vol. III and that MS'*Aj.* BM2 was copied from it in 1245 (/1829).

---

50 See Browne, *A Hand-list*, 118. See these remarks by al-ʿAṭṭār in plates I–II in Moreh, 'al-Jabartī's Method', 368–9. See also the footnotes of our new Arabic edition of *'Ajā'ib al-Āthār*, volumes I–III, indicated by the letters: a. b. c. etc., and in the Indexes at the end of this book.

51 See these remarks by al-ʿAṭṭār in Moreh, 'al-Jabartī's Method', 368–9, plates I–II. The copyist of MS'*Aj.* Tārīkh 466, IV, f. 225a, gives the year of al-'Aṭṭār's death as 1250/1835: سنة الف ومايتين وخمسين، توفي الشيخ حسن بن محمد العطار من مصر القاهرة، شافعي تولى مشيخة الأزهر بعد الدمنهوجي، له مؤلفات كثيرة.

52 See the title pages and the last pages of MSS'*Aj.* BN, Suppl. arabe, nos.1861, 1862, 1863, volumes I–III (III. 7. a.–c below), and MS'*Aj.* Tārīkh 1426, III (VI. 19. c. below), in which the author writes all the title pages and the last lines.

53 British Museum. Department of Oriental Printed Books and Manuscripts, *Catalogus codicum manuscriptorum orientalium qui in Museo Britannico asservantur. Pars secunda, Codices Arabicos amplectens. Appendix*, William Cureton and Charles Rieu, Sir Frederic Madden (eds) (London 1871), no. 1497, 682, col. b.

III. 3. 1 a. MS *'Aj.* BM1, vol. I, Add. 26,042, is in 371 rubricated folios, 27 lines in 37 fascicles. It contains the events of the years 1101–89 (/1689–1776).The title page reads: الجزؤ الاول من عجايب الاثار في التراجم والأخبار تأليف العلامة الشيخ عبد الرحمن حسن الجبرتي غفر الله له وعفى [!] عنه امين. كراس عدد ٣٧. In addition, under it there is a stamp, which reads: توكلي على خالقي عبده يعقوب ('I put my trust in my Creator, his servant Yaʿqūb') followed by the numbers 1243 and 842.

F. 1b starts after the *basmala*: بسم الله ... خالق الخلايق وعالم الذرات بالحقايق ومنزه عن العلايق. مفني الامم ومحيي الرمم...., indicating that it belongs to the MS *'Aj.* Cam. group, as it is the same as the first sentence of MS *'Aj.* Cam., I. It differs from the Būlāq edition which is based upon a MS in which the copyist took the liberty of making corrections and pious invocations, and which reads: بسم الله...خالق الخلايق وعالم الذرات بالحقايق Important events are mentioned in red ink in the margin.

This manuscript ends with the year 1189 (/1775–6) and the colophon on f. 742, which contains no information on the copyist or on the date when the copying was finished, reads: والى هنا انتهى الجزؤ الاول ويليه الجزؤ الثاني وصلى الله على سيدنا محمد وعلى آله وصحبه وسلم تسليما كثيرا والحمد لله رب العالمين. ثم وكمل بحمد الله وعونه وحسن توعيد. م ('This ends volume I, and volume II will follow…'.), ending with prayers (*ṣalāt*) on the Prophet Muḥammad and his family.

III. 3. 1 b. MS *'Aj.* BM1, vol. II, Add. 26,043, has 244 folios, 27 lines in 37 fascicles. The title page reads: الجزء الثاني من عجايب الاثار في التراجم والأخبار تأليف العلامة الشيخ عبد الرحمن حسن الجبرتي الحنفي غفر الله له امين. ('Volume two of *'Ajā'ib al-Āthār* ... by the most erudite scholar ... al-Jabartī, may God forgive him'.) It contains the events of the years 1190–1212 (/1776–98). To the left of the title there is a stamp reading:توكلي على خالقي عبده يعقوب ('I put my trust in my Creator, his servant Yaʿqūb'). Summaries of important events are indicated in red ink in the margins; there are very few corrections in the margins.

The colophon, with no the name of the copyist, nor the date in which the copying was finished, ends with the *ṣalāt* (blessing on the prophet Muḥammad), and with the remark that the following volume will be volume III that commences with the year 1213 (/1798) (f. 244a):

والله سبحانه وتعالى اعلم بالصواب واليه المرجع والمآب وصلى الله علي سيدنا محمد وعلى آله وصحبه وسلم تسليما كثيرا والحمد لله رب العالمين امين. ويتلوه الجزؤ الثالث ومبتداءه[!] [ ] سنة ثلاثه عشر ومايتين والف.

III. 3. 1 c. MS *'Aj.* BM1, Add. 26,044, vol. III, has 335 folios, 27 lines in 34 fascicles. The title page, which also has *ghafara* ('May God grant him pardon'), not *raḥima* ('May God have mercy'), reads: الجزء الثالث من تاريخ العلامة الشيخ عبد الرحمن الجبرتي الحنفي غفر الله له امين. On the left upper side of the title page is written: ك [= كراس] 1 الجزء الثالث للشيخ الجبرتي (k [Fascicle] 1 of volume III, by Shaykh al-Jabartī), with the stamp of the owner of the MS Ya'qūb. This manuscript contains the events of the year 1216 (/1801–2) in full, including the biographies of those who died during that year (ff. 399b–415b). It resembles the Būlāq edition with the exception of the Wahhābī proclamation, which it mentions in summarized form (ff. 483b–484a).

The colophon on ff. 335a–b gives the name of the copyist as Ṣāliḥ 'Azab al-Jabalāwī and states the date on which the copying was finished as 17 Rabī' I 1242 (/19 October 1826). The year 1242 started on 5 August 1826, which is more than a year after al-Jabartī died, and by using *ghafara Allāh lahu*, the copyist indicated that he knew about al-Jabartī's death, yet he did not add a word on the author nor did he mention the exact date of his death. The last verse in the colophon asks the reader to forgive the copyist for any mistake because only God the Exalted has no fault:

> وحسن به ختم هذا الجزء من عجايب الآثار في التراجم والأخبار والله تعالى أعلم....وكان الفراغ من كابته [=كتابة] هذا الجزؤ والذي قبله في يوم الخميس الموافق لسبعة عشر يوم [!] خلت من شهر ربيع الأول من شهور سنة ١٢٤٢ اثنين واربعين ومايتين وألف على يد الفقير صالح عزب الجبلاوي:
>
> وإن تجد به عيبًا فسد الخللا جلّ من لا عيب فيه وعلا

The text is rubricated and surrounded by a frame in red ink on each page. There are a few marginal corrections, such as f. 209a. Some of the corrections are sentences which had been overlooked by the copyist and are added in the margin in a different handwriting.

III. 4. 2. MS *'Aj.* BM2. This MS in three volumes was in the possession of the famous orientalist E.W. Lane. According to the description of the manuscript by Charles Rieu in *Supplement to the Catalogue of the Arabic Manuscripts in* *the British Museum*, vol. II, 872, nos. 1280–2 (shelf mark Or: 4628–30): 'it has three uniform volumes, consisting respectively of fols 365a, 244b, 337, in 9 1/2 in. by 6 1/2; 27 lines, 4 1/8 in. long; written in fair *Neskhī*, dated Friday, 11 Jumādā I, A.H. 1245 [CE 1829]. In these three volumes no additions, corrections, or remarks have been added in the margin. The first volume extends from the beginning of the work to the end of 1189 [/1776]. The second volume comprises 1190–1212 [/1776–98], and the third one 1213–20 [/1798–1806]. Their contents correspond respectively with those of the first three volumes of the edition printed in four volumes, Cairo, 1297 [/1879–80]'.[54]

III. 4. 2 a. MS *'Aj.* BM2, Or. 4628, vol. I,in 365 folios in 37 fascicles. The copyist is 'Alī Maṭar al-Ghiryānī. All the volumes are rubricated, with a title reading as in 3.1 a. MS *'Aj.* BM1, vol. I: الجزء الاول من عجايب الاثار في التراجم والأخبار تأليف العلامة الشيخ عبد الرحمن حسن الجبرتي غفر الله له وعفى [!] عنه امين. كراس عدد ٣٧. with the addition of a stamp: توكلي على خالقي عبده يعقوب . F. 1b starts as in the case of MS *'Aj.* Cam. with the *basmala* as follows: بسم الله ... خالق الخلايق وعالم الذرات بالحقايق ومنزه عن العلايق. مفني الامم ومحيي الرمم... The colophon on f. 365a does not give the name of the copyist or the date of copying; it reads: والى هنا انتهى الجزؤ الاول ويليه الجزؤ الثاني وصلى الله على سيدنا محمد وعلى آله وصحبه وسلم تسليما كثيرا والحمد لله رب العالمين. ثم وكمل بحمد الله وعونه آمن . On f. 365b is written in pencil: '365 folios nar. 1893'. On f. 366b: 'bought from Dr. N.J.C. Tisrud HBP [representing the heirs of Mr. E.W. Lane]'.

III. 4. 2 b. MS *'Aj.* BM2 Or. 4629, vol. II, in 25 fascicles, with a title page and the colophon on f. 244b reading as 3.1 b. MS *'Aj.* BM1, vol. II, except for the word 'al-Ḥanafī' which was dropped from the title: الجزء الثاني من عجايب الاثار في التراجم والأخبار تأليف العلامة الشيخ عبد الرحمن حسن الجبرتي غفر الله له امين. كراس عدد ٢٥. F. 1b starts after the *basmala* with the events of the year 1213 (/1798–9). There is a slight change in the middle of the sentence in the colophon compared with the MS given in III. 3. 1b above (f. 244b):

> سامحه الله. توفي في منتصف شعبان من السنة غفر الله لنا وله بمنه وكرمه والله تعالى اعلم بالصواب واليه المرجع والمآب. وصلّى الله على سيدنا محمد وعلى آله وصحبه وسلم آمين م ويتلوه الجزؤ الثالث ومبداه سنة والف ومايتين ثلاثة عشر

54 See Rieu, *Supplement*, II, 827, no. 1280–82.

This colophon is followed by a sentence written in pencil: '244 folios Mar. 1893 HBP f. 246b. Bought of Dr. N. I. L. Tisrud [Representing the heirs of Mr. E.W. Lane]'.

III. 4. 2 c. MS *'Aj.* BM2, Or. 4630, vol. III, in 34 fascicles, with a title page reading: الجزؤ الثالث من عجايب الاثار في التراجم والأخبار تأليف العلامة الشيخ عبد الرحمن حسن الجبرتي عفي عنه آمين، كراس عدد ٣٤. F. 1b reads after the *basmala*: وبه الاعانة. سنة ثلاثه عشر ومايتين والف. وهي اول سني الملاحم العظيمة... This volume contains the events of the years 1213–20 (/1798–1806). Ff. 200b–208b cover the events of the year 1216 (/1801–2) in full, including the obituaries of those who died during that year (ff. 200b–208b). From f. 200b onward it resembles the Būlāq edition except that the Wahhābī proclamation is summarized ff. 242b–243a). The colophon on ff. 337b reads:

وحسن به ختم هذا الجز[ء] من عجايب الآثار. وكان الفراغ من كتابة هذا الجزؤ في يوم الجمعة المبارك أحدى عشر يوما خلت من شهر جمادى الأول سنة ١٢٤٥ على يد الفقير المعترف بالذنب والتقصير علي مطر الغرياني والله اعلم بالصواب واليه المرجع والمآب وصلى الله على سيدنا محمد وعلى آله وصحبه وسلم.

This is followed by the same sentence written in pencil on the former volumes, giving the number of folios as 337 and stating that it was bought from the heirs of E.W. Lane. The MS was copied by ʿAlī Maṭar al-Ghiryānī on Friday 11 Jumādā I 1245 (/8 November 1829).

III. 5. The *'Ajā'ib al-Āthār* manuscript at the Leeds University Library[55] (henceforth **MS *'Aj.* Leeds**). In our Arabic edition, it is indicated by the symbol and its variant versions are indicated between brackets < … > in the Arabic text.

III. 5. a. MS *'Aj.* Leeds, 9, vol. I,has 372 rubricated folios in 37 fascicles. It contains the events of the years 1101–89 (/1689–1776). The title is vowelled and written in a triangle:

55 See John Macdonald, *Catalogue of Oriental Manuscripts* (Leeds 1958), III, Arabic MSS 101–50, 29–32; cf. *GAL*, II, 632, 4 and *GAL, Suppl.*, II, 730, 4. My thanks are due to Leeds Library for supplying me with photos of samples of pages of this MS.

كِتَابُ عجائب الآثار \ في التراجم والأخبار \ تأليف العالم العلامة والبحر الفهامة الشيخ عبد الرحمن حسن الجبرتي الحنفي \غفر الله له ولوالديه\ولجميع المسلمين\ امين\ امين امين

Under this title is another triangle with the name of Maḥmūd b. Muṣṭafā Qāsim, the person who ordered the manuscript: كُتِبَ برسم العمدة الفاضل الشيخ الكامل، السيد محمود بن العمدة السيد مصطفى قاسم عفى [!] الله عنهم اجمعين بمنه وكرمه/ امين. There are no corrections or additions in the margin. To the right and left side of the triangle it is written that the MS became the property of its copyist, i.e. Muḥammad Ḥasan al-Fākihānī. It might indicate that Maḥmūd Qāsim did not pay the copyist the sum, which they agreed upon: وصار ملك كاتبه محمد حسن الفاكهاني غفر الله له ، ('it became the property of its writer Muḥammad Ḥasan al-Fākihānī'). The MS is rubricated, the top of f. 1b has a multicoloured qubba (decoration in the form of a cupola) and starts with the *basmala*. The text begins: ... ألحمد لله القديم الاول الذي لا يزول ملكه ولا يتحول

Like MS *ʿAj.* Cam. and the Būlāq edition, it contains the events of the years 1101–89 (/1689–1776). However, the colophon wrongly states that it is Pt. 1 of 'this History' and that the manuscript was copied on 25 Rajab 1266 (/5–6 June 1850), by ʿUmar b. Khaṭṭāb: وتأمر اتباعه من بعده وتقاسموا البلاد فيما بينهم والفوا المظالم وظنوها مغانم وتمادوا في الجور... وما حل بالاقليم بسببهم من الخراب والدمار. تم النصف الاول من هذا التاريخ بمنه وكرمه م. وكان الفراغ من نسخه يوم الخميس المبارك ٢٥ من شهر رجب الفرد من شهور سنة ١٢٦٦ ستة وستين ومائتين والف من الهجرة النبوية على صاحبها افضل الصلاة واتم السلام وذلك على يد كاتبه الفقير راجي عفو الوهاب ، عمر بن خطاب غفر الله له ولوالديه ولمن طالعه وقال اللهم امين امين وصلى الله على سيدنا محمدوآله وصحبه اجمعين آمين م

III. 5. b. MS *ʿAj.* Leeds, 129 (History), vol. II, has 26 fascicles in 251 unpaginated folios, 9 x 6¼ in. 25 lines each, written in thin, Egyptian *naskhī* handwriting does not have a title page and starts with the events of the year 1190 (/1776–7):

سنة ١١٩٠ تسعين وماية والف ، كان سلطان العصر فيها السلطان عبد الحميد ابن احمد خان العثماني ووالي مصر الوزير محمد باشا عزت الكبير...

The handwriting is the same as in MS *ʿAj.* Leeds 9, vol. I and has the same brown leather cover. There are no additions or corrections in the margin. It contains the events of the years 1190–1212 (/1776–98). The volume ends with the colophon on f. 251, stating that the copyist is ʿUmar b. Khaṭṭāb who copied on 12 Dhu 'l-Qaʿda 1266 (/18–19 September 1850), as follows:

توفي في منتصف شهر شعبان من السنة غفر الله لنا وله بمنه وكرمه امين وكان الفراغ من نسخ هذا التاريخ يوم الخميس المبارك اثني عشر يوما خلت من شهر القعدة الذي هو من شهور سنة ١٢٦٦ سنة سته وستين ومائتين والف من الهجرة النبوية على صاحبها الصلاة والسلام وذلك على يد أفقر العباد الى رحمة ربه الوهاب عمر بن خطاب. اللهم اغفر له ولوالديه ولجميع المسلمين والمسلمات ولمن نظر فيه وقال اللهم امين امين امين.

III. 5. c. (1) MS *'Aj.* Leeds, 130 (History), vol. III, has 31 fascicles in 295 un-paginated folios of 9 x 6¼ in. 25 lines each, written in the same thin *naskhī* handwriting as Leeds manuscripts 9 and 129. There is no title page. F. 1a does not have the *basmala* just like MS *'Aj.* Cam. and starts with the events of the year 1213 (/1798): سنة ١٢١٣ ثلاثه عشر ومايتين والف. وهي اول سني الملاحم العظيمة والحوادث الجسيمة ... In this MS, Napoleon's proclamation in Arabic of 1213 (/1798) (ff. 3a–b) has the paragraph dealing with the Mamluks, saying: وبين المماليك ما العقل والفضائل والمعرفة التي تميزهم عن الاخرين... which is the same as the original French proclamation in Arabic and the proclamation given in the Cambridge MS. There are some corrections in the margins of fascicle 2, f. 5a, fasc. 10, f. 4b. In fasc. 11, f. 9a onwards the events of 25 Dhu 'l-Ḥijja 1216 (/28 April 1802) are given in full with the obituaries of the same year, as in the Būlāq edition. In fasc. 19, f. 7a, dealing with the year 1217 (/1802–3), the Wahhābī proclamation is summarized as in the case of Cambridge MS.

The end of this MS reads as in MS *'Aj.* Cam., Qq. 171, III: وسنقيد ان شاء الله تعالى ما يتجدد بعدها من الحوادث من ابتدا سنة احدى وعشرين التي نحن بها الان ان امتد الاجل واسعف الامل ونرجو من الكريم المتعال صلاح الأحوال وانقشاع الهموم وصلاح العموم انه على كل شيء قدير وبالاجابة جدير والله اعلم. The colophon on f. 458 (fascicle 31, f. 7a) states that the manuscript was copied on 28 Dhu 'l-Qaʿda 1267 (/23–4 September 1851) by ʿUmar b. Khaṭṭāb:

وكان الفراغ من كتابته يوم الاربع المبارك ثمان وعشرين خلت من شهر القعدة الذي هو من شهور سنة ١٢٦٧ سبع وستين ومائتين والف من الهجرة النبوية على صاحبها الف سلام والف تحية وذلك على يد الراجي عفو ربه الوهاب الفقير عمر بن خطاب غفر الله له ولوالديه ولمن كان سببا في كتابته ولجميع المسلمين والمسلمات الاحيا منهم والاوموات وصلى الله على سيدنا محمد وآله وسلم آمين.

III. 5. c. (2) MS *'Aj.* Leeds, Arab MS. 131 (History) is a second copy of volume III. It has 458 un-paginated and rubricated folios of 7 x 4 in. in 21 lines; the fascicles are paginated. The manuscript is written in a thick Egyptian *naskhī* handwriting different from Leeds manuscripts 9 and 129. F. 1a has in small

Arabic letters on the left upper part of the page:فيه خرم ثلاث كراريس جزو ثالث ('There are gaps in three fascicles of volume three'.) On f. 2a is the title in a rectangle of double red lines: هذا ابتداء الجزء الثالث من تاريخ العلامة الشيخ عبد الرحمن الجبرتي المسمى عجايب الاثار في التراجم والاخبار. F. 1b starts with a decorated multi-coloured *qubba* (copula) with the *basmala* and the year 1213 (/1798): بسم الله الرحمن الرحيم ثلاثة عشر ومائتين والف وهي اول سني الملاحم العظيمة... In fascicle 6, f. 6b, the Arabic proclamation of Napoleon reads as in the Būlāq edition, volume III: وبين المماليك والعقل والفضايل تضارب... The events of the end of the year 1216 (/1802) are missing after 25 Dhu 'l-Ḥijja (/28 April 1802) (fascicle 34, f. 3a) and there are no obituaries as in the MS *'Aj.* Cam. As in the case of the Būlāq edition; the Wahhābī proclamation (fascicle 39, ff. 4a–7b.) in the events of the year 1217 (/1802–3) is given in a summarized form.

There is no colophon at the end of this volume:

> وسنقيد ان شاء الله تعالى ما يتجدد بعدها من الحوادث من ابتدى [!] سنة احدى وعشرين التي نحن بها الان ان امتد الاجل واسعف الامل ونرجوا [!] من الكريم المتعال صلاح الاحوال وانقشاع الهموم وصلاح العموم انه على كل شيء قدير ولاجابة جدير والله اعلم وصلى الله على سيدنا محمد.

III. 5. d. MS *'Aj.* Leeds, Arab MS. 132 (History), vol. IV, has 61 fascicles in 594 un-paginated and rubricated folios of 7 x 4 in. in 21 lines; the fascicles are paginated. The manuscript is written in thick Egyptian *naskhī* handwriting resembling MS *'Aj.* Leeds, 131. (5.c. [2]) F. 1a has on the upper part written in a thin, red pen: الجزء الرابع من تاريخ الجبرتي F. 1b under a multi-coloured *qubba*, the text starts as follows: سنة ١٢٢١ استهل شهر المحرم بيوم الخميس حسابا ويوم السبت هلالا... This manuscript does have a colophon stating that it was copied from an autograph of the historian al-Jabartī, and that 'this is the end of this part (vol. IV). Thereafter, the Shaykh died, without having written more'. Moreover, it states that the copying was completed on Wednesday, 23 Shaʿbān 1290 (/15 October 1873) by the copyist Aḥmad, the son of al-Ḥājj Muḥammad known as al-Shāhid:

> وهي حادثة الأروام. وذلك الى هنا انتهى ما نقل من خط العلامة الشيخ عبد الرحمن بن الشيخ حسن الجبرتي مؤرخ هذه المدة وما قبلها لغاية هذا التأريخ وهذا أخر الجزء الرابع وبعده توفي الشيخ ولم يكتب شي [!]. نجز نساخة في يوم الاربع ثلاثة وعشرين شعبان سنة تسعين ومايتين والف على يد كاتبه أحمد ابن الحاج محمد الشهير بالشاهد غفر الله له ولوالديه والمسلمين والمسلمات الى يوم الدين وصلى الله على اشرف المرسلين محمد صلى الله عليه وعلى آله الطاهرين...

This is one of the latest manuscripts copied just before the printing of the Būlāq edition; it belongs to the Būlāq group of MSS, which were copied and 'corrected' after the death of the author.

III. 6. The *'Ajā'ib al-Āthār* manuscript in the John Rylands University Library, University of Manchester[56] (henceforth **MS *'Aj.* Manchester**). The manuscript is rubricated in three volumes (vols I–III) with corrections in the margins. Some pages, which were stuck to one another, suffered some damage when they were separated. Some lines are crossed out and corrected in the margins. Damaged words are copied in the margin in a very thin handwriting. According to A. Mingana, 'The three volumes which compose the work are a transcript made for M. Asselin about A.D. 1830. They came first into the possession of Silvestre de Sacy and, at the sale of his books were bought by Ferrao de Castelbranco, at the sale of whose books in Lisbon (1888) they were acquired by Lord Crawford. A printed slip of paper pasted within the cover of the first volume describes in French the manuscript and its contents'. Asselin de Cherville was a French employee at the French Consulate in Cairo and collected some 1,515 manuscripts.[57]

III. 6. a. MS *'Aj.* Manchester, 278 [699], vol. I. contains 430b folios, of 21 x 14.8 cm. of 25 lines to the page, written in clear Egyptian *naskhī* script. Rubricated: كتاب عجايب الآثار في التراجم والأخبار In the *Catalogue of the John Ryland's Library* the title *'Ajā'ib al-Āthār fi 'l-Tarājim wa 'l-Akhbār* is translated as 'Wonders of Monuments in Lives and Information' and it is described as 'The first volume of the history of Egypt from 1100/1688 to

56 See A. Mingana, *Catalogue of the Arabic Manuscripts in the John Ryland's Library Manchester* (Manchester 1934), col. 444, MS no. 278 [699]–col. 446, MS no. 447, MS. no. 280 [701]. My thanks are due to Philip Sadgrove for his kind help in examining al-Jabartī's MS in the John Rylands University Library in the University of Manchester.

57 On Asselin de Cherville (1772–1822), see Georges Vajda and Yvette Sauvan, Bibliothèque Nationale, Département des manuscrits, *Catalogue des manuscrits arabes*, deuxième partie (Paris 1978), tome II, XXV, and Annie Berthier (ed.), *Manuscrits, xylographes, estampages: les collections orientales du Département des manuscrits: guide* (Paris 2002), 12, 23. My thanks are due to Professor J. Sadan for pointing out these books to me. In 1825, a list of these manuscripts, which were sent to the Bibliothèque Nationale in Paris, was made. The importance of this collection is that it contains *Histoire de l'Égypte* (MSS arabe 1861–3), dealing with the years 1100–1220 (1688–1806) by 'Abd al-Raḥmān b. Ḥasan al-Jabartī.

1220/1805, by: عبد الرحمن بن حسن بن علي بن محمد بن عبد الرحمن الجبرتي الزيلعي العقيلي who died in 1240/1825'.

F. 1b, which has been damaged by water, starts with a *basmala*, indicating that it belongs to the Būlāq group. As in the Būlāq edition, this volume begins as follows: بسم الله الرحمن الرحيم الحمد لله القديم الاول الذي لا يزول ملكه ولا يتحول خالق الخلايق وعالم الذرات بالحقايق ... changing the sentence of the Cambridge MSS group: ومنزّه عن العلايق ('he is without any cause') into the Būlāq MSS group version: وعالم الذرات بالحقايق ('who knows even the atoms of reality'.)It contains the events of the years 1100–89 (/1688–1776), like MS *'Aj.* Cam., and ends without colophon or date of copying with the words: وتأمر أتباعه من بعده وتقاسموا البلاد فيما بينهم... وما حل بالاقليم بسببهم من الخراب والدمار.

There are four types of marginal marks and corrections: (1) corrections to the text itself in Arabic in the same handwriting as the text; (2) important events and names of personalities; (3) corrections in the handwriting of an unknown orientalist; (4) remarks written in pencil (such as *manque* and *delendan*).

The manuscript is full of copying mistakes, such as: اهل الخونة اللئام في قولهم سعد وحرام ('the wicked treacherous people') instead of: اهل الحوف اللئام في قولهم سعد وحرام (MS *'Aj.* Cam., III, f. 20a, l. 20) (... in this respect, they came to resemble the wicked inhabitants of the Ḥawf region who backed [the rival factions] of Saʿd and Ḥarām).

III. 6. b. MS *'Aj.* Manchester, 279 [700], vol. II, has 28 fascicles of 279 folios of 25 lines each, written in a different, clear, Egyptian *naskhī* script. It contains the events of the years 1190–1212 (/1776–98), as in MS *'Aj.* Cam. and the Būlāq edition. F. 1a reads: الجزؤ الثاني من كتاب عجايب الاثار في التراجم والأخبار جمع الفقير عبد الرحمن الجبرتي عفي عنه امين. ('Volume II of *'Ajā'ib al-Āthār*... compiled by the humble ʿAbd al-Raḥmān al-Jabartī, may his sins be forgiven') which indicates that the title page of the MS from which it was copied was an autograph of al-Jabartī or that it was written when he was still alive (*'ufiya 'anhu*, may his sins be forgiven). Ff. 1b–2a are also damaged.

The manuscript ends with the biography of Ḥasan b. ʿAbd al-Rahmān... al-Manzalāwī al-Shāfiʿī and the date of his death in mid-Shaʿbān (/1 February 1798), as follows (ff. 278a–279a): ومات ... السيد حسن بن عبد الرحمن... المنزلاوي الشافعي ... الى آخرها وهي طويلة وله غير ذلك سامحه الله. توفي في منتصف شهر شعبان من السنة

غفر الله لنا وله بمنه وكرمه. without colophon or the date of copying, and no mention is made of the name of the copyist.

III. 6. c. MS *'Aj.* Manchester, 280 [701], vol. III, has 64 fascicles in 619 folios of 19 lines each, written in a careless Egyptian *naskhī* hand. It is not damaged and there are no corrections in the margin. It contains the events of the years 1213–20 (/1798–1806) and belongs to the MSS of the Būlāq edition. The title-page reads: الجزؤ الثالث من عجايب الاثار في التراجم والأخبار تأليف العلامة الشيخ عبد الرحمن حسن الجبرتي عفي عنه ('Volume III of *'Ajā'ib al-Āthār*, by the learned scholar ʿAbd al-Raḥmān al-Jabartī, may God give us benefit from this book') indicating that this MS was written or copied in al-Jabartī's lifetime. The text begins with the year 1213 (/1798–9) and its unusual events: سنة ثلاثة والف\ وهي عشر [sic] اول سني الملاحم العظيمة والحوادث الجسيمة مائتين والف.ومايتين...This manuscript is a copy of the second stage of al-Jabartī's compilation of *'Ajā'ib al-Āthār*, i.e. it does not resemble the Būlāq edition. As in the case of MS *'Aj.* Cam. it has the original version of Napoleon's first proclamation: وبين المماليك ما العقل والفضايل والمعرفة التي تميزهم عن الآخرين وتستوجب انهم يتملكوا وحدهم كلما يحلوا به حياة الدنيا. فحيثما يوجد ارض مخصبة فهي مختصة للمماليك والجواري الاجمل والخيل الاحسن والمساكن الاشهى... ('But among the Mamluks, what is there of reason, virtue and knowledge, which would distinguish them from others and qualify them alone to possess everything which sweetens life in this world…'.). This is yet another indication that this MS was copied while al-Jabartī was still alive.

From the fact that this MS contains the events and biographies of those who died in 1216 (/1801–2) (ff. 359a–372a), but (unlike the Būlāq edition), gives the Wahhābī proclamation (f. 441b) in a summarized form, we conclude that it represents the second stage of *'Ajā'ib al-Āthār*. The MS ends without colophon and date of copying, as in MSS *'Aj.* Cam.: وسنقيد ان شاء الله تعالى ما يتجدد بعدها من الحوادث من ابتدا سنة احدى وعشرين التي نحن بها الان ان امتد الاجل واسعف الامل ونرجو من الكريم المتعال صلاح الحوال وانقشاع الهموم وصلاح العموم انه على كل شيء قدير وبالاجابة جدير والله اعلم. انتهى.

III. 7. The *'Ajā'ib al-Āthār* manuscript at the Bibliothèque Nationale, Paris, Suppl. arabe, 840, nos. 1861, 1862, 1863 (henceforth **MS *'Aj.* BN**). According to the description in *Catalogue des manuscrits arabes de la*

Bibliothèque Nationale, par le baron de Slane,[58] this manuscript includes the first three volumes of the book in 473, 269, and 426 folios 22x 15.5 cm., 25 lines per page. It is unique and resembles MS *'Aj.* Cam. and MS *'Aj.* Tārīkh 174/microfilm 10730 (VI. 14. c.). The title pages and the last lines of the volumes I–III are written by al-Jabartī's hand. There are some corrections in the margin, in the handwriting of al-Jabartī. These are mainly homoeoteleuton. These facts might indicate that the MS had been ordered by somebody from al-Jabartī. The author ordered his copyists to copy it from his draft, which he sold later on to Burckhardt. He edited it with his handwriting, wrote the title pages and the last lines, and added his corrections in the margins. One might suggest that this is the copy, which was bought by J.-L. Asselin de Cherville and sent to the Bibliothèque Nationale for the use of the scholars of the French expedition writing their *Description de l'Égypte*.

III. 7. a. MS *'Aj.* BN, Suppl. arabe, 1861, vol. I. Before the title page, there is a page with the indication: 'Djeberty Adjayb-Al-Atsar, volume de 473 feuillets 27 juin 1874'. One leaf before the title page has a seal with 'Bibliothèque Royale', under which is written: 'Suppl. ar. no. 840. 1'. The title page (f. 1a) is written in the hand of al-Jabartī, different from the rest of the text. It contains the events of the years 1100–89 (/1688–1776). The handwriting is clear and well set out. Each folio has a red frame of two lines.

The title page gives first the title of the book and the name of the author with the blessing of *ghufira lahu* ('may he be granted pardon'), indicating that the author is still alive, as in MS *'Aj.* Cam. then reads: كتاب عجايب الآثار في التراجم والإخبار جمع الفقير عبد الرحمن بن حسن الجبرتي العقيلي الزيلعي الحنفي غفر له. The folios are rubricated and the heads of paragraphs, names, and commas are in thick red ink and bold letters, especially the poetry. In f. 1b the *basmala* is hard to read even by ultra-violet lamp, and begins as in the case of the Būlāq edition: بسم الله الرحمن الرحيم وبه نستعين، الحمد لله القديم الاول، الذي لا يزول ملكه ولا يتحول، خالق الخلايق وعالم بذرات الحقايق، مفني الامم، ومحيي الرمم، ومعيد النعم، ومبيد النقم، وكاشف، ومبيد النقم، وكاشف الغمم، وصاحب الجود والكرم، لا إلـه إلا هو، كل شـئ هالك الا وجهه له الحكم واليه ترجعون ...

There are a few additions and corrections in the margins (for instance, ff. 10b, 11a, 13a, 14a, 24a, 26a, 28b, 31a, 36a, 36b, 37a, 53a, 55b, 58a, 59b, 64b,

58 W.M. le Baron de Slane, *Catalogue des manuscrits arabes de la Bibliothèque National* (Paris 1883–95), I, 336, MS nos. 1861–3.

65a, 80a, 98b, 111b, 124a, 140b, 171a, 171b, 182a, 188b, 204b, 210a, 215b, 245b, 246b, 250a) in a hand similar to al-Jabartī's, as in the case of MS *'Aj.* Tārīkh 174 (VI. 14. c.). One may note here that on f. 31a the double line of the frame has a space in which the addition in al-Jabartī's handwriting is inserted, written through the lines of the frame without erasure. This might indicate that al-Jabartī was present at the time of dictation. Presumably he may have been dictating his history from an autograph (which he later sold to Burckhardt), i.e. the Cambridge manuscript, to several copyists at the same time, and he corrected eventual mistakes in the text, which were either the copyists' mistakes or his own. This is also the case with MS *'Aj.* Tārīkh 174/microfilm 10730.

On f. 118a at the end of the biography of al-Amīr Ibrāhīm Afandī Katkhudā al-ʿAzab, after the sentence: واستمر هناك الي أن مات there is a blank space of three lines, which have not been filled in any of the copies.

The volume ends (f. 473b) unlike all the MS copies of volume I: وتأمر اتباعه من بعده وتقاسموا البلاد فيما بينهم والفوا المظالم وظنوها مغانم وتمادوا في الجور...وما حل بالاقليم بسببهم من الخراب والدمار. تم (written in the form of a triangle, but without colophon.) To the left side of the triangle which ends the rubricated page is written the year 1190 (/1776–7), indicating that the following volume II will start with the year 1190 (/1776–7).

III. 7. b. MS *'Aj.* BN, Suppl. Arabe, 1862, vol. II. The folio before the title-page is inscribed: 'Volume de 269 feuillets 27 juin 1874'. The following page (f. 1a) has a seal with 'Bibliothèque Royale', above which is written: 'Suppl. ar. no. 840. II'. As the title page (f. 1a) is written in the hand of al-Jabartī it reads without the usual blessing to the author:

الجزء الثاني من عجائب الآثار في التراجم والاخبار جمع الفقير عبد الرحمن الجبرتي.

Only the heads of paragraphs, names, and commas are in thick red ink and bold letters, while the poetic verses are generally vowelled.

The colophon of the second volume indicates that it is the end of volume II, f. 269b قد تم الجزء الثاني من التراجم والاخبار، تاليف الاستاذ قدوة العارفين وملجأ الوافدين الشيخ: عبد الرحمن حسن الجبرتي الحنفي الخلوتي، نفعنا الله به آمين. ('This is the end of volume II of *al-Tarājim wa 'l-Akhbār* composed by the master, the example for the knowledgeable and the refuge for visiting foreigners … al-Jabartī al-Ḥanafī al-

Khalwatī, may God make us benefit (from his knowledge). There are no additional remarks'.)

The last line indicates clearly that the MS was written during the lifetime of the author. It ends with two verses in which the copyist asks the reader not to blame him if he finds copying mistakes:

تم

يا قارئ خطي　　　　اذا وجدت العيب غطي

تم

ولا تقل فيه عيب　　　　فالعبد ما زال يخطي

تم

III. 7. c. MS *'Aj.* BN, Suppl. Arabe, 1863, vol. III. The folio before the title-page is inscribed: 'Djaberty/*Adjayb-Al-Atsar*, arabe 1863. Volume de 426 feuillets 27 juin 1874'. The following page (f. 1a) has a seal with 'Bibliothèque Royale'. On the preceding page is written: 'Suppl. ar. no. 840. III'. The title of the third volume is in the same hand, similar to al-Jabartī's, as in MS *'Aj.* DKQ., Tārikh 174. There are a few additions in the margins (ff. 227b, 245a, 424a), also in a hand similar to al-Jabartī's. Only the title page is written by the hand of al-Jabartī. The title page gives the blessing to the author '*satara Allah 'uyūbah*' (may God conceal his faults), confirms the fact that it was written during the lifetime of the author: الجلد الثالث من عجايب الاثار في التراجم والاخبار جمع الفقير عبد الرحمن بن حسن الجبرتي العقيلي ستر الله عيوبه م.

There are a few corrections in the margins of the three volumes. The French proclamation f. 5a–b is identical to the printed proclamation and the MS *'Aj.* Cam.: وبين المماليك ما العقل والفضايل والمعرفة/ التي تميزهم عن الآخرين وتستوجب انهم يتملكوا وحدهمكلما يحلوا به حياة الدنيا، حيثما يوجد ارض مخصبة فهي مختصة للمماليك In f. 142a (the year 1215 [/1800–1]), the description of the assassination of General Kléber and trialof the assassin Sulaymān al-Ḥalabī is given in full.

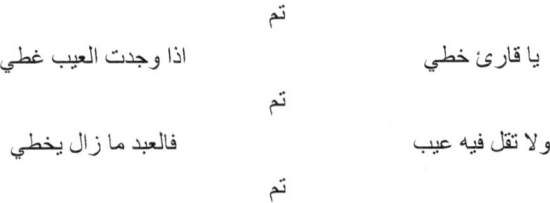

Neither the name of the transcribers nor the dates of copying are mentioned. However, the handwriting does not resemble that of any of the other manuscripts. Only the title pages and the two colophons of this volume are in al-Jabartī's handwriting; moreover, the titles of the three volumes as well as the marginal corrections and additions are in a hand similar to al-Jabartī's. We can infer that the copying was done by a copyist employed by al-Jabartī during his lifetime. This is clear from the phrase in the title of volume I, 'May God bestow on us his welfare': (نفعنا الله به) occurring in the colophons. As in the case of the Cambridge autograph of *'Ajā'ib al-Āthār*, this year (1216 [/1801–2]) concludes with the events of the 25 Dhu 'l-Ḥijja of the year 1216 (/28 April 1802) without the biographies with the sentence: وفي خامس عشرينه قبضوا على امراه سرقت أمتعة من حمام فشنقوها عند باب زويلة. ('On the 25 Dhu 'l-Ḥijja [/28 April 1802], a woman was caught stealing clothes at a bath and was hanged near Bāb Zuwayla'.)

The volume does not have a colophon, ending abruptly without indicating that volume IV will follow, or that the author will continue to deal with the events of the year 1221 (/1806–7) and the following years (cf. MS *'Aj.* Cam., III. 1. c. and III. 5. c. [2]): ورجال السادة الصوفية بالديار الشامية وحسن به ختم هذا الجزء من عجائب الآثار في التراجم والأخبار والله تعالى اعلم آمين . تم.

III. 7A. The *'Ajā'ib al-Āthār* manuscript at the Bibliothèque Nationale, Paris, Suppl. arabe, 1864, 1865, 1866 (henceforth **MS *'Aj.* BNII**). According to the description in *Catalogue des manuscrits arabes de la Bibliothèque Nationale, par le baron de Slane*, this manuscript includes the first three volumes of the book in 593, 423, and 402 folios in 23 x 15.5 cm., 25 lines per page.

III. 7A. a. MS *'Aj.* BNII, Suppl. arabe, 1864, vol. I. The title of the book on the leather cover is given: *Djeberti, Histoire de l'Egypte, Fonds Asselin, 42. Tom. I. Arabe 1864.*On f. 1a: 'Suppl. ar. no. 841/I, volume de 593 Feuillets 27 juin 1874'. One leaf before the title page has a seal with 'Bibliothèque Royale', under which is written: 'Suppl. ar. no. 841. 1'. On the title page (f. 1a), the lines are written in red and black ink alternately: كتاب / عجايب الاثار في التراجم والاخبار/ جمع الفقير عبد الرحمن/ ابن حسن الجبرتي/ الحنفي عفي/ الله عنه / بمنه / امين.On the left hand of this triangular title, the copyist wrote in a reversed triangle that the manuscript was copied from a fair autograph of the author: هذه النسخة نقلت من نسخة المولف المصححة عنده ('This manuscript was copied from the corrected autograph of the author which is in his possession'). It is not clear whether the copyist refers to the author's autograph of MS *'Aj.* Cam. The beginning of sentences and the commas are rubricated. The title page (f. 1a) is written in the hand of al-Jabartī. In f. 1b, unlike the MS *'Aj.* Cam. the *basmala* is added, beginning, as in the case of the Būlāq edition: بسم الله الرحمن الرحيم، وبه نستعين، الحمد لله القديم الاول، الذي لا يزول ملكه ولا يتحول، خالق الخلايق وعالم [كذا] بالحقايق، مفني الامم،

ومحيي الرمم، ... where the word *ʿālim* is omitted. The colophon on f. 539a reads: وما حل بالاقليم بسببهم من الخراب والدمار. والله رؤف بالعباد، انه كريم حليم جواد، ويليه الجزؤ الثاني من اول سنة تسعين ومااية والف. This is different from the first MS MS *ʿAj.* BN, Suppl. arabe, 1861, volume I mentioned above.

III. 7A. b. MS *ʿAj.* BNII, Suppl. arabe, 1865, vol. I. On the leather cover, the title of the book is given as *Djeberty, Histoire de l'Egypte, Tom. II. Arabe 1865.* On f. 1a: Fonds Asselin, no. 42. Volume de 423 feuillets 27 juin 1874'. On f. 2a: 'Suppl. ar. no. 841'. II. The title page (f. 2a), reads: الجزؤ الثاني من كتاب / عجايب الاثار في التراجم/ والاخبار جمع/ الفقير عبد الرحمن/ الجبرتي/ عفي/ عنه. In different handwriting, the title of the book is given on the middle of f. 2a.: تاريخ مصر للشيخ عبد الرحمان للجبرتي ('*The History of Egypt* by Shaykh ʿAbd al-Raḥmān al-Jabartī').The volume starts with the events of the year 1190 (/1776–7) with the names of the rulers of Egypt. There is no colophon at the end of the book, f. 423a: الى اخرها، وهي طويلة وله غير ذلك سامحه الله توفي في منتصف شهر شعبان من السنة غفر الله لنا وله بمنه وكرمه / امين/ ويتلوه الجزؤ الثالث من ابتدا سنة ثلاثة عشر ومايتين والف. without the two verses cited by the copyist of III. 7. b. MS *ʿAj.* BN, Suppl. arabe n. 1862 mentioned above.

III. 7A. c. MS *ʿAj.* BNII, Suppl. arabe, 1866, vol. III.The title of the book on the leather cover is: *Djeberti, Histoire de l'Egypte, Tom. I. Arabe 1864. On f. 1a: Fonds Asselin, no. 42. Volume de 402 feuillets 27 juin 1874.*The handwriting of this volume is different from the previous volumes I–II. There is no title page and the text starts with the events of the year 1213 (/1798), with no *basmala*: سنة ثلاثة عشر ومايتين والف وهي اول سني الملاحم العظيمة والحوادث الجسيمة والوقايع النازلة...

The text is similar to the MS *ʿAj.* Cam., Qq. 171,III, especially the wording of the French proclamation (f. 4b), which is similar to the Arabic text of the proclamation printed by the French. In f. 130b (the year 1215 [/1800–1]) the description and the trial protocol of the assassination of General Kléber (ff. 130b–153b) is given in full according to the MS *ʿAj.* Cam., and the Būlāq edition.

The colophon on ff. 482a–b reads:

> وحسن به ختم هذا الجزء الثالث من كتاب عجايب الآثار في التراجم والأخبار لغاية سنة عشرين ومايتين والف. وسنقيد ان شاء الله تعالى ما يتجدد بعدها من الحوادث من ابتدا سنة احدى وعشرين

التي نحن بها الان ان امتد الاجل واسعف الامل ونرجو من الكريم المتعال صلاح الأحوال وانقشاع الهموم وصلاح العموم انه على كل شي قدير والله اعلم / اصملى [!] / ا

III. 8. a. The *'Ajā'ib al-Āthār* manuscript at the Bayerische Staatsbibliothek in Munich,[59] cod. Or. Prunneri 259 (henceforth MS *'Aj.* ML), has volume I. only. It contains 310b folios of 19 lines each, written in a tiny, fine, and clear *naskhī* in a double spacing of 24.5 x 17.5 cm. in each folio. There is no title page and like *'Aj.* Būlāq, I, f. 1b starts with the *basmala* and the following phrase: بسم الله الرحمن الرحيم وبه نستعين. الحمد لله القديم الاول ... خالق الخلايق وعالم الذرات بالحقايق... ('who knows even the atoms of reality'). In the Cambridge group of MSS the underlined phrase is missing and the sentence reads instead: خالق الخلايق ومنزه عن العلايق ('he is without any cause').

On a slip of paper it is written: 'Geschichte von Egypten von letzten Viertel des 17 bis zur Mitte des 18 Jahrhunderts. Defekt. 31 Quinternen. 310 Blaetter'('History of Egypt from the last quarter of the 17th to the middle of the 18th century. Defect. 31 fascicles in 310 pages').

III. 9. The *'Ajā'ib al-Āthār* manuscript at the Staatsbibliothek zu Berlin,[60] **Pruessischer Kulturbesitz Orientabteilung (SBB) (MS Or. Qu. 658, 659, 673, 660)** (henceforth **MS *'Aj.* Ber.**), is indicated in our Arabic edition by the initials: عجب and its variants are indicated between brackets /.../). It contains four volumes eachvolume is copied in different handwritings, paper quality is different, and the numbers of lines is uneven. On f. 1a of volumes I, II and IV under the title of the book it is written: مشترى من كتبي في مصر المحروسة في ١٦ شعبان ١٢٩٢. ('Bought from the owner of a bookshop in Cairo, [the city] protected [by God], on 16 Sha'bān 1292 [/16 September 1875]').

III. 9. a. MS *'Aj.* Ber., 9487, Or. Qu. 658, vol. I, in 659 folios of 21 lines each, in thick, clear handwriting with red ink at the beginning of the description of events. This volume was copied in *c.* 1260 (/1844–5) (see also the catalogue, p.

59 Joseph Aumer, *Die arabischen Handschriften der K. Hof- und Staatsbibliothek in München* (Munich 1866), 155–6, Cod. Arab. 400/pos. (Cod. Or. Prunneri 259).

60 Staatsbibliothek zu Berlin. Preuss. Kulturbesitz Orientalabteilung (numbers 9487–90, Mq. 658, 659, 673, 660, see Wilhelm Ahlwart, *Verzeichniss der arabischen Handschriften der Königlichen Bibliothek zu Berlin* (Berlin 1897), 9, 93–5. My thanks to the authorities of the Staatsbibliothek zu Berlin for their kind help during my work at their library.

95, col. 2. The volume contains the events of the years 1101–89 (/1689–1776). The title on f. 1a reads: الجزء الاول من تاريخ الجبرتي and the first lines are the same as the Būlāq edition, beginning with the *basmala*: بسم الله الرحمن الرحيم. الحمد لله القديم الأول الذي لا يزول ملكه ولا يتحول، خالق الخلايق وعالم بذرات الحقايق. The MS ends on f. 659a without a colophon, so the name of the copyist and the date is missing. It ends with the words: إلى أن حصل ما حصل ونزل بهم وبالناس ما نزل وسيتلى عليك من ذلك أنبا وأخبار وما حلّ بالإقليم بسببهم من الخراب والدمار والله اعلم بالصواب واليه المرجع والمآب، وصلى الله على سيدنا محمد وآله وسلم.م. There are a few corrections in the margins and between the lines in the same handwriting, as well as the remark بياض (blank), which indicates blank spaces in the MS from which it was copied. In the margin of f. 605a, there are 5 blank lines left, which are indicated by the words: بياض في الأصل (blank in the original manuscript). In f. 564b, dealing with the year 1184 (/1770–1) (*ʿAj. Būlāq*, I, 352), in the margin of the biography of ʿAbd Allāh al-Idkāwī have been added the following few lines of an elegy praising the poetic talent of al-Idkāwī in a different handwriting: وقد رثاه الشيخ علي إلشرنفاشي بقوله

[الرمل]

إن الادكاوي أو[فـ]ـا   بفنون الشعر حدّه

كان في الفن إماما   منجزًا في الفضل وعده

ولقد مات فأرّخ   مات أس الشعر بعده

أ.هـ. [= إلى هنا]

In f. 485a, there is a remark in the margin concerning Ibrāhīm b. ʿĪsā al-Ḥasan that says that the vowelling of the word *ʿl-ḥ-y-a* is with a *ḍamma* on the letter ʻl': اللحية بضم اللام .أ.هـ. مولف. In f. 123a in the margin of the biography of Muḥammad al-Nashartī (*ʿAj. Būlāq*, I, 70), there is a remark on the words: وأخّر دفنه إلى يوم الأحد = كذا بالأصل ولعله الاثنين كما يفهم بالتأمل. كاتبه ('His burial was delayed until Sunday = sic. in the original [MS]. It might have been Monday, as is understood after contemplation. The copyist').

III. 9. b. MS *ʿAj.* Ber., 9488, Or. Qu. 659, vol. II, of 272 folios, in a different handwriting, in 25–6 lines. Years, personal names and the beginning of the description of important events and of paragraphs are rubricated with red ink. The title in f. 1a reads: الجزء الثاني من تاريخ الجبرتي . بمنه ('Volume II of al-Jabartī's *Chronicle*. By [God's] favour'). The volume contains the events of the years 1190–1212 (/1776–98) and begins: السنة ١١٩٠ تسعين وماية وألف كان سلطان

It العصر فيها السلطان عبد الحميد ابن احمد خان العثماني ووالي مصر الوزير محمد باشا عزت... ends on f. 272a with the biography of Ḥusayn b. ʿAbd al-Raḥmān al-Manzalāwī: توفي في منتصف شعبان من السنة غفر الله لنا وله بمنه وكرمه امين امين.

The colophon on f. 272a states that ʿUmar al-Khaṭṭāb copied it on the 5th Jumādā I (1264 [/9 April 1848]): وكان الفراغ من نسخه في يوم الجمعة المبارك خمسة أيام خلت من شهر جمادى الأولى الذي هو من شهور سنة ١٢٦٤ أربع وستين ومايتين والف من الهجرة النبوية على صاحبها أفضل الصلاة وأزكى السلام. وذلك على يد الراجي عفو ربه الوهاب الفقير عمر الخطاب. It is important to note here that ʿUmar al-Khaṭṭāb the copyist of this manuscript in 1264 (/1848) is also copyist of MS *'Aj.* Leeds in 1266 (/1849–50) (Leeds Arab MSS, nos. 9, 129 and 130 [History]), vols I–III, (while volume IV at Leeds is copied by Aḥmad Muḥammad al-Shāhid) (III. 5. above).

III. 9. c. MS *'Aj.* Ber., 9489, Or. Qu. 673, vol. III, is in 500 folios of 17–19 lines each. Inside the back of the cover it is written that it was copied 'in 1878 in Cairo for the Koen. Bibliothek'. The MS is written in a clear and neat *ruq'a* script with red ink at the beginning of paragraphs. There are several corrections in the margins in a different ink and hand. The MS is full of copying mistakes and homoeoteleuton. It does not have a title page, but on the outer cover of the leather box that contains the MS the following is written: تاريخ مصر للجبرتي وهو الجزؤ الثالث ('*The History of Egypt* by al-Jabartī, it is volume III'). The copyist states that it was copied from the autograph of the author and that for this reason he abstained from correcting the sentences which did not fit the context.

It contains the events of 1213–20 [/1798–1806] beginning with the year 1213 [/1798]: سنة ثلاثة عشر ومايتين وألف وهي أول سني الملاحم العظيمة. The colophon on f. 500b states that it was copied in 17 Dhu 'l-Ḥijja 1295 [/11–12 December 1878] by Muṣṭafā al-Shalshamūnī b. Muḥammad al-Shalshamūnī:

> السادة الصوفية وحسن به ختم هذا الجزؤ الثالث من كتاب عجايب الآثار في التراجم والأخبار ولغاية سنة عشرين ومائتين وألف من الهجرة النبوية على صاحبها أفضل السلام. وسنقيد إن شاء الله سبحانه وتعالى ما يتجدد بعدها من الحوادث من ابتدا سنة إحدى وعشرين التي نحن بها الان ان امتد الاجل واسعف الامل ونرجوا [!] من الكريم المتعال صلاح الاحوال وانقشاع الهموم وصلاح العموم انه على كل شيء قدير وبالإجابة جدير والله اعلم. م. م. كتبه الفقير إلى ربه القدير مصطفى الشلشموني ابن محمد الشلشموني غفر الله له ولوالديه وللمسلمين امين. وكان الفراغ من نسخه يوم الخميس المبارك الموافق لسابع عشره شهر ذي الحجة الحرام سنة الف ومايتين وخمسة وتسعين من الهجرة النبوية م.

The proclamation of Muḥammad b. ʿAbd al-Wahhāb is given in a summarized version (f. 373a, l. 2–f. 374a, l. 16) as it appears in MS *'Aj.* Cam.

Only the MSS MS *'Aj.* Cam., MS *'Aj.* Ber. III (ff. 374, ll. 12–16) and the Beirut, Dār al-Fāris edition give the following lines added in the Būlāq edition, demonstrating that this edition is a conglomerate of various MSS (III, 257, ll. 1–4): وقد بسط الكلام في ذلك ابن القيّم في كتابه إغاثة اللهفان وكتاب مصائد الشيطان وغير ذلك. انتهى. The chapter on the events of Rajab 1219 (/6 October–2 November 1804) (MS *'Aj.* Ber., III, f. 446b) the story of the incident in which Muḥammad ʿAlī killed a soldier who insulted him is toned down, as in the case of MS *'Aj.* al-Zakiyya, 859, p. 1178 (VII. 32. C.): وفي حادي عشره نزل الباشا في التبديل ومر من سوق السمكرية فرأى عسكريا يشتري كوز صفيح ... فقل له: أما تخف من الباشا، فقال: الباشا على كين وكيب [!][= كَيْت وكيت؟] فضربه الباشا وقتله ومضى. ('On the 11th the Pasha passed incognito through the tinkers' market. He saw a soldier buying a tin cup and offered the tinker five paras. The tinker held out for ten. The soldier refused and paid only five. Seeing this, the Pasha said: "Give him its price." The soldier, not knowing who it was, said, "What business is it of yours?" [The Pasha] said, "Aren't you afraid of the pasha?" He replied, "The Pasha is a so and so," at which point the Pasha knocked him down, killing him, and continued on his way'.)[61] This version is the same as the one in MS *'Aj.* Tārīkh 1872/microfilm 35107, III (VI. 22. c.). The other MSS and printed books give the following realistic version of the soldier's answer: ...فقال الباشا على زبي... ('He said: "The Pasha is on my penis"').

Unlike MS *'Aj.* Cam., Qq. 171, III (III. 1. c. above), f. 213b, this MS contains the events and biographies of the end of the year 1216 (1801–2) after the 25 Dhu 'l-Ḥijja 1216 (/28 April 1802), starting with the sentence: وفي خامس عشرينه قبضوا على امرأة سرقت أمتعة من حمام فشنقوها عند باب زويلة. ('on the 25th a woman was caught stealing clothes at a bath and was hanged near Bāb Zuwayla'), as is cited in the Būlāq edition (III, 211–20) on ff. 314a–326b (as in the case of MS *'Aj.* Tārīkh 174) (VI. 14. c.). In f. 290a there is vowelling of the Turkish rank of 'al-uchṭukhilliyya' (Three Horse Tails): أمامه العساكر الشامية والأمرا المصرية والمغاربة والغيلونجية والباشوات الأجطُخْلِيّة.

III. 9. d. MS *'Aj.* Ber., 9490, Or. Qu. 660, vol. IV, has 299 folios of 27 lines each, written in a clear and thick *ruq'a* script. The names of the months and

61 *'Aj.* Būlāq, III, 312, cf. *'Abd al-Raḥmān al-Jabartī's History*, III, 479–80.

years are left blank inside the text and are added in the margins. They are written in red ink until f. 10a. There are several corrections in the margins and between the lines in a different ink and hand. In our edition of the Arabic text, this MS is indicated by the initials عجب There is no title on f. 1a but the words: مشترى من كتبي في مصر المحروسة في ١٦ شعبان ١٢٩٢ have been inscribed. On the upper left hand margin the name: 'Spitta' is written. The volume contains the events of 1221–36 (/1806–21). It starts on f. 1b as in all other MSS with the events of the year 1221 (/1806–7): سنة احدي وعشرين ومايتين والف. استهل شهر المحرم الحرام بيوم الخميس حسابا.

In f. 14a in a scratched word in the margin under a correction of يوم الجمعة سابعه ('Friday the seventh of the month'), it is written that 'it is in accordance with the autograph of al-Jabartī' (في نسخة المؤلف. صح). In f. 67b describing the events of the month Dhu 'l-Ḥijja 1222 (/30 January–26 February 1808), dealing with the death of Sulaymān Bey al-Alfī *'Aj.*,IV, 75), the copyist misread the word اغتم ('to fill with grief'), and copied it as ختم ('to seal off'): وكانت الواقعة يوم الاربع سادس الشهر فما ورد الخبر بذلك على الباشا اظهر أنه ختم على[!] [=اغتمّ لـ] سليمان بيك وتأسف على موته. ('The battle took place on Wednesday, the sixth of the month. When news of it reached the Pasha, he pretended to seal off [the property of] (*khatama 'alā* [sic]) [*ightamma* =[to be grief-stricken over] Sulaymān, and was sorry for his death'.) A comment in the margin attempts to explain the incongruity, which was caused by the misreading, as follows: لعل الناهب هنا ياسين بيك والمنهوب سليمان بيك فليحرر من خص [!] الواقعة لان هذه النسخة منقولة من خط الجبرتي مؤرخ زمن تلك الوقائع ولا ينبغي لنا أن نصححها بالقياس. أ. هـ. ('It might be that the looter here is Yāsīn Bey and the looted is Sulaymān. Those who are interested in this battle should take note of it. Because the manuscript was copied from the autograph of al-Jabartī, the historian of these events, we should certainly not correct his words by analogy').

This MS ends on f. 299a, with the following colophon denoting that the copying of this MS ended in 1264 (/1847–8) from an autograph by al-Jabartī written in 1236 (/1820–1): أما حادثة الاروام ... وما وقع معهم من الحوادث وما ينتهي حالهم اليه فسيتلى عليك ان شاء الله بكماله في الجزء الآتي بعد ذلك والله الموفق للصواب واليه المرجع والمآب. تم لسنة ٣٦ ونقل هذا من نسخة بخط العلامة الفاضل عبد الرحمن ابن الشيخ الفاضل حسن الجبرتي المؤرخ سنة ٣٦ في ذي الحجة تمام ١٢٦٤ من الهجرة النبوية والله اعلم. صح ('The copying was ended in [12]36 [/1820–1]. This [manuscript] was copied from a manuscript written by the righteous scholar, the historian ʿAbd al-Raḥmān, the son of the righteous Shaykh Ḥasan al-Jabartī, in the year [12]36 [/1820–1]. [The copying was ended] in the month of Dhu 'l-Ḥijja the end of 1264 [/28 October–5 November 1848] of the Hijra, and God knows best. Corrected'.)[62]

III. 10. The *'Ajā'ib al-Āthār* manuscript of the Institute of Oriental Studies, St Petersburg (Leningrad) (C 732, 9420) (henceforth **MS *'Aj.* Len.**), in three volumes. According to the description in *Arabic Manuscripts of the Institute of Oriental Studies*, USSR Academy of Science,[63] the manuscript contains the first three volumes of *'Ajā'ib al-Āthār* 'from different complete sets'. All three bear the stamp of the Imperial Institute of Oriental Languages at the end of the volume.

III. 10. a. 1. MS *'Aj.* Len., C 732, vol. 1has 486 folios. It covers the years 1100–89 (/1688–1776). The Leningrad catalogue states 'autograph of the son of the author Maḥfūẓ' [!] (copied in 1259 [/1843–4]). It seems that the compilers of the catalogue understood the word '*rasama*' (ordered [to be copied]) as 'copied by Maḥfūẓ'. The title page indicates that al-Jabartī is considered as one of the 'pillars of those who are close to divine reality and certitude' ('*'Umdat ahl al-ḥaqq wa 'l-yaqīn*'), i.e. the *Ṣūfī*s, probably hinting that he was an important member of the Khalwatiyya order: كتاب عجائب الآثار في التراجم والأخبار للامام العلامه مفيد الطالبين وعمدة اهل الحق واليقين ، الشيخ عبد الرحمن بن حسن الجبرتي الحنفي عامله الله بلطفه الخفي وبره الوفي يا رب العالمين. ('This is the book, "The Marvellous Compositions of Biographies and Chronicles", by the learned scholar who is of benefit to [his] students, a pillar of the *Ṣūfī*s, Shaykh ʿAbd al-Raḥmān al-Jabartī al-Ḥanafī, may God treat him with His subtle mercy and His true kindness, O, Lord of the Universe)'. The colophon contains spelling mistakes and states that the MS was copied on the order of al-Jabartī's son Maḥfūẓ in the year 1259 (/1843–4), as follows: من جملت [!] ما رسم محفوظ نجل الفقير الجبرتي جامع هذه الشوارد سنت [!] الف ومائـتين وتسع وخمسين وسيتلى عليك من ذلك انبا واخبار ما حلّ بالاقليم بسببهم من الخراب والدمار والله اعلم والحمد لله وحده والصلاة والسلام على من لا نبي بعده، تم. ('This is part of what Maḥfūẓ has ordered [to be copied]. He is the son

---

62 The German orientalist Ahlwardt also gives the date of the copying of this volume as 1264/1848.

63 See *Arabic Manuscripts of the Institute of Oriental Studies, USSR Academy of Science*, Moscow, C 732, catalogue no. 9420. My thanks are due to Professor Svetlana Kirilina, Moscow State University, for this information.

of the humble al-Jabartī, the compiler of these passing events, in the year 1259 (/1843–4). The news of the ruin and destruction which befell the country, because of their (evil) deeds, and God knows best. Thanks be to God alone and prayer to the Prophet; there will be no prophet after him. End'.). A round stamp with the name of Maḥfūẓ occurs at the end of the volume; the *Catalogue* thus considers the manuscript as the autograph of Maḥfūẓ, ʿAbd al-Raḥmān al-Jabartī's son. This however cannot be, because the word '*bi-rasm*' means '[copied] by the order of' and the colophon of volume II gives the name of the copyist as 'Sulaymān Salāma al-Sunbulāwī'. It seems therefore that Maḥfūẓ tried to follow in his father's steps by employing copyists to sell his father's chronicle, probably through the agents of a foreign consul, in this case the consul of Russia. If it is true that Maḥfūẓ wasted his father's fortune, one can add that he did not succeed as a book dealer like his father. However, it is possible to presume that the 'order' or request of Maḥfūẓ to copy the chronicle of his father was a result of the request of the Russian consul to purchase a copy of it for the Russian Library in St Petersburg, and that the son continued to deal with copying and selling the works of his father.

III. 10. b. 2. MS *'Aj.* Len., C 732, 9420, vol. II, has 333 folios. It covers the years 1190–1212 (/1776–98) and begins with the same title as in volume I above. The colophon states that the copying of this volume ended on 26 Ṣafar 1262 (/22–3 February 1846), by the copyist Sulaymān Salāma al-Sunbulāwī and that this copy belongs to the Khawāja Timaviov (?), the dragoman of the Russian Consul: الى آخرها وهي طويلة وله غير ذلك سامحه الله ، توفي في منتصف شهر شعبان من السنة غفر الله لنا وله ولوالدينا وللمسلمين بمنه وكرمه وكان الفراغ من كتابة هذا الجزء ظهر يوم الاثنين المباركه سادس عشرين شهر صفر الخير سنة ١٢٦٢ من الهجرة على صاحبها الصلاة والسلام على يد الفقير الى الله تعالى راجي غفر المساوي سليمان سلامه السنبلاوي غفر الله ذنوبه وستر بالعفو عيوبه امين وقد صار هذا الجزء المذكور ملكا طلقا الى حضرة المحب الأكرم الخواجا تيمافيوف ترجمان بيك تابع حضرة قنصل الروسيه.

III. 10. c. MS *'Aj.* Len., C 732, 9420, vol. III, has 334 folios in 34 fascicles (*kurrāsīs*). It covers the years 1213–20 (/1798–1806). It begins: الجزء الثالث من كتاب عجائب الآثار في التراجم والأخبار جمع الشيخ عبد الرحمن الجبرتي الحنفي عامله مولاه بلطفه الخفي امين.

The colophon is dated 1262 (/1846) as is stated in the Leningrad catalogue. The volume ends as follows:

السادة الصوفية وحسن به ختم هذا الجزء الثالث من كتاب عجايب الآثار في التراجم والأخبار لغاية سنة عشرين ومايتين والف من الهجرة النبوية. وسنقيد ان شاء الله سبحانه وتعالى ما يتجدد بعدها من الحوادث من ابتدا سنة احدى وعشرين ان امتد الاجل واسعف الامل ونرجوا [!] من الله الاعانه امين.

IV. 11. The *'Ajā'ib al-Āthār* manuscript of the Oriental Public Library at Bankipore[64] **(Patna), Bahr, India** (henceforth **MS *'Aj.* Bankipore**), (Khuda Bakhsh O.P. Library, Patna, Prof. 2528 (old series), dated 21 June 1955, Section Manuscript). It contains four volumes, each divided into two parts, 55 as is the case in MS *'Aj.* Tārīkh 1424/microfilm 14586 and 36392, vol. I, pt. 1 (VI. 17. a. 1).

IV. 11. a1. MS *'Aj.* Bankipore, 1076 (H. L. 2324–bat. 1076), vol. I, pt. 1, has 45 fascicles in 229 folios 9 x 6¼ in., and 7½ x 4½ in., of 23 lines each written in *naskhī*, within double red-ruled borders. It covers the years 1100–90 (/1688–1777), and begins on the cover as follows: هذا الجزؤ الاول من التاريخ الكبير للعلامة عبد الرحمن الجبرتي وبدء هذا الجزء سنة ١١٠٠ ومنتهاه سنة ١١٩٠. The title page reads: جلد اول، قسم اول. كتاب عجايب الآثار في التراجم والأخبار للجبرتي. and the title is written inside a triangle: هذا الجزؤ الاول من تاريخ العلامة عبد الرحمن الجبرتي الحنفي رحمه اللهتعالى F. 1. starts:...الحمد لله القديم الاول الذي لايزول ملكه ولا يتحول

The manuscript is not dated (it is apparently a modern copy). It ends with the first half of volume I, without a colophon: فصل. عود وانعطاف في ذكر حوادث مصر وتراجم اعيانها وولاتها من ابتداء سنة اثنين وستين ومائة والف [1162] الى اواخر سنة ثلاثة وسبعين [1173].

IV. 11. a2. MS *'Aj.* Bankipore, 1077, vol. I, pt. 2, has 217 folios, 9 x 6¼ in. and 7½ x 4½ in, of 23 lines each, written in *naskhī* in double red-ruled borders. It covers the years 1162–80 (/1748–67), and begins: ... والآفاق فيندر فيهم القابلية The MS is not dated (apparently a modern copy) and there is no colophon.

64 See Mawlavi Muinuddin Nadwi, J.A. Chapman, Khuda Bakhsh Oriental Public Library (Patna, Inde), *Catalogue of the Arabic and Persian Manuscripts in the Oriental Public Library at Bankipore, Vol. XV, Arabic Mss., History* (Calcutta Patna, Superintendent of Bihar and Orissa 1929), 160–4, nos. 1076–83. Thanks are due to the authorities of the Khuda Bakhsh Library for supplying me with a microfilm of all the 4 volumes in 8 parts.

IV. 11. b1. MS *'Aj.* Bankipore, 1078, vol. II, pt. 1, has 178 folios, 9 x 6¼ in. and 7½ x 4½ in., of 23 lines each written in *naskhī*, in double, red-ruled borders. It covers the years 1190–1201 (/1776–87), and begins: سنة تسعين ومائة والف كان سلطان العصر فيها السلطان عبد الحميد خان العثماني ووالي مصر الوزير محمد باشا عزت الكبير ... The MS is not dated and there is no colophon.

IV. 11. b2. MS *'Aj.* Bankipore, 1079, vol. II, pt. 2, has 205 folios 9 x 6¼ in. and 7½ x 4½ in., of 23 lines each, written in *naskhī*, within double, red-ruled borders. It covers the years 1201–12 (/1786–98), and begins: واخلع على ثلثة اشخاص من امراء حسن بيك الجداوي وقلدهم صناجق وهم جاهين وعلى وعثمان...

The manuscript is dated Thursday (*yawm al-khamīs*), 15 Ramaḍān 1274 (28–9 April 1858), copied by Ḥusayn Ḥasan Idrīs al-Shāfi'ī al-Damanhūrī al-Khalwatī.

IV. 11. c1. MS *'Aj.* Bankipore, 1080, vol. III, pt. 1, has 227 folios, 9 x 6¼ in., and 7½ x 4½ in, of 23 lines each, written in fair *naskhī*, within double red-ruled borders. It covers the years 1213–15 (/1798–1801), and begins: سنة ثلاثة عشر ومائتين والف وهي اول سني الملاحم العظيمة والحوادث الجسيمة... The manuscript is not dated and there is no colophon.

IV. 11. c2. MS *'Aj.* Bankipore, 1081, vol. III, pt. 2, has 235 folios 9 x 6¼ in, and 7½ x 4½ in., of 23 lines each, written in *naskhī*, in double red-ruled borders. It covers the years 1215–20 (/1800–6), and begins: وكان مفوّها لسنا مشاركا قد حنكته الايام والتجارب فجعله كتخداه ووزيره... The manuscript is not dated, but according to the colophon it was collated by Muḥammad al-Ṣabbāgh al-Dimyāṭī with the aid of some scholars of the Azhar Mosque in 1276 (/1859–60), for a certain 'Abd al-Ḥamīd Bek:

قابله محمد الصباغ الدمياطي مع بعض اهل العلم المجاورين بالجامع الازهر لسعادة صاحب الاحسان عبد الحميد بيك حفظه الله تعالى في سنة ست وسبعين ومائتين بعد الالف.

IV. 11. d1. MS *'Aj.* Bankipore, 1082, vol. IV, pt. 1, has 160 folios 9 x 6¼ in., and 7½ x 4½ in., of 25 lines each, written in *naskhī*, in double red-ruled borders. The manuscript covers the years 1221–7 (/1806–13), and begins:

ثم دخلت سنة احدى وعشرين ومائتين والف. استهل شهر المحرم الحرام بيوم الخميس حسابا ويوم السبت هلالا ووافق ذلك انتقال الشمس لبرج الحمل فاتحدت السنة القمرية والشمسية.

As in the case of volume II, part 2 above, the manuscript is not dated and there is no colophon.

IV. 11. d2. MS *'Aj.* Bankipore, 1083, vol. IV, pt. 2, has 165 folios, 9 x 6¼ in., and 7½ x 4½ in., of 25 lines each, written in *naskhī*, in double, red-ruled borders. The headings are in red. It covers the years 1228–35 (/1813–20), and begins:

والكشميري والهندي ونحو ذلك فتندرج معها في قلة الكمرك وفي هذه الاوان يحلون رباط المحزوم ويفتحون الصندوق وينبشون المتاع ويهتكون ستره ويحصون عدده وياخذون عشره ...

This MS ends with the year 1235 (/1819–20) and not 1236 (/1820–1), unlike the other MSS of volume IV discussed above. However, the colophon is unique because it contains important biographical information, namely that al-Jabartī, owing to his blindness, could not continue to work any longer. However, the copyist, who seems to have known the author, does not attribute his blindness to grief at the assassination of his son Khalīl: وذلك الى هنا انتهى ما نقل من خط العلامة الشيخ عبد الرحمن بن الشيخ حسن الجبرتي مؤرخ هذه المدة وما قبلها لغاية هذا التاريخ وهذا آخر الجزء الرابع وبعده تأخر الشيخ عن الكتابة بسبب انكفافه الى ان توفى ولم يكتب. ('This is the end of what has been copied from theautograph of the scholar al-Jabartī, the historian of the recent period and the previous one. This is the end of volume IV. After this he stopped writing until he died without writing anything more due to his blindness'.)

The manuscript is dated 1301 (/1883–4). Of all the manuscripts of *'Ajā'ib al-Āthār* examined it is the only one copied after the publication of the Būlāq edition in 1297 (/1879–80).

V. 12. a. The *'Ajā'ib al-Āthār* manuscript in the Iraq Museum, Baghdad (henceforth **MS *'Aj.* Iraq**). It starts with the *basmala*, and the version of the fourth sentence of the introduction, is different from the MS *'Aj.* Cam. (III. 1. a.) which reads: ومنزه عن العلايق ('he is without any cause'), while in the Būlāq edition the fourth sentence is changed into: وعالم الذرّات بالحقايق ('who knows even the atoms of reality') and is slightly different: الحمد لله القديم الاول، الذي لا يزول ملكه ولا يتحول، خالق الخلايق، وعالم بذرات الحقايق، مفني الأمم، ومحي الرمم... In the

Cambridge group of MSS the underlined phrase is missing and the sentence reads instead: خالق الخلايق ومنزه عن العلايق. It is mentioned as an autograph in the catalogue of historical manuscripts in the Iraq Museum Library in Baghdad edited by Kūrkīs ʿAwwād.[65] Page 63 of the catalogue reads: عجائب الآثار في التراجم والأخبار ... وهذه النسخة بخط المؤلف على ما تحققه الاب انستاس ماري الكرملي ودونه على المخطوط وهي غير مؤرخة. ('This copy is an autograph, according to the verification of Père Anastase-Marie al-Kirmilī and he recorded it on the manuscript. It is undated'.)

The colophon (p. 405 on the MS) states that the manuscript was written by al-Jabartī himself: وهذا اخر ما يسره الله لي من تدوينه في هذه السنة نسأ[ل] الله جل جلاله حسن الخاتمة والحمد لله تبارك وتعالى في البدء والختام والصلاة والسلام على سيدنا محمد من هو للانبياء ختام وعلى اله واصحابه الأئمة الأعلام. قاله بفمه وحرّره بقلمه الفقير الحقير راجي رحمة ربه الغنى عبد الرحمن بن حسن الجبرتي الحنفى غفر الله له وعامله بلطفه م [= آمين].

The following words are written at the end of the manuscript stating that it differs from the Būlāq edition, because it did not suit the rulers in Egypt. It is in a different hand, which might be that of Père Anastase-Marie al-Kirmilī (1866–1947), as noted in the catalogue by Kūrkīs ʿAwwād:[66] هذا المخطوط بخط مؤلفه الجبرتي وهو يختلف كثيرا عن المطبوع لانه لما طبع حذف منه اشياء كثيرة ماكانت توافق آراء أهل الحل والربط فتصرفوا فيه. أما هذا المخطوط فهو المعوّل عليه إذ هو الأصل. ('This MS is the autograph of its author al-Jabartī. It differs much from the printed one because, when it was printed, many things were omitted which did not suit the opinions of the authorities so they took liberties with it. This MS, however, is reliable because it is the original').

The script is a *ruq'a* typical of the Syrian style. It is clear and well set out. The beginnings of chapters and months are rubricated. It has 405 pages, 28 x 20 cm. with 25 lines per page.

Although the colophon clearly states that it is an autograph, this is doubtful because it is written in a Syrian style *ruq'a* resembling the handwriting of Burckhardt, and differs from al-Jabartī's handwriting as known from other autographs. Moreover, in examining this 'autograph' carefully one can easily see that it is not the full text of *'Ajā'ib al-Āthār*, ending as it does in the middle of volume I. Up to the sentence before the colophon the manuscript is identical

65 Kūrkīs ʿAwwād, 'al-Makhṭūṭāt Maktabat al-Mathaf al-ʿIrāqī bi-Baghdād', *Revue de l'Institut des Manuscrits Arabes* I (1955), 45. See *al-Jabartī's Chronicle*, 2–3 and plates I–II.

66 It seems that al-Kirmilī was influenced by Jurjī Zaydān's remark in his *Tārīkh*, IV, 284.

with the Būlāq edition of *'Ajā'ib al-Āthār*. As for the middle of the first volume, i.e. up to p. 211, l. 31, where al-Jabartī said: ومن أهل الحجاز ابراهيم المنوفي وهذا تقريض الشبراوي... was interrupted and made into a colophon by the copyist of MS *'Aj.* Iraq as follows: ومن أهل الحجاز ابراهيم المنوفي وهذا آخر ما يسره الله لي من تدوينه في هذه السنة ...

There are two reasons why al-Kirmilī's remark in this manuscript arouses suspicion. The first is that the handwriting and style of the colophon are typical of Syrian scholars. The second is that al-Kirmilī's testimony is not reliable, since he lived in Iraq and died more than a century after al-Jabartī; he was thus not acquainted with the author nor was he his contemporary. From the remarks of the owners of other manuscripts it is clear that they either knew the author personally or at least were his contemporaries. Furthermore, the interesting similarity of the handwriting between the other manuscripts which are in cursive Egyptian *nasta'līq* (see above MSS nos. I. 1., II. 2., III. 1. c.), the evidence of their owners, and the dates mentioned on two of them (above nos. I. 1., and II. 2.) that lie within the author's lifetime, have convinced us that the statement in the colophon of MS *'Aj.* Iraq cannot be trusted.

VI. 13. The *'Ajā'ib al-Āthār* manuscripts in Dār al-Kutub al-Qawmiyya (The National Library in Cairo) (henceforth **DKQ**).[67]

VI. 13. a. MS *'Aj. Tārīkh* 173/microfilm 10728.This manuscript, consisting of one fascicle of only eleven folios, contains part of volume I of *'Ajā'ib al-Āthār*. F. 1a has two stamps, the first is: كتبخانه مصرية Kutubkhāna Miṣriyya and the second is: الكتبخانه الخديوية al-Kutubkhāna al-Khudaywiyya. F. 1b reads: كتاب عجائب الآثار في التراجم والأخبار. *Kitāb 'Ajā'ib al-Āthār fī 'l-Tarājim wa 'l-Akhbār*. In the DKQ catalogue,[68] the handwriting is called 'ordinary' (قلم معتاد); the fascicle 'ends with the discussion on the Ikhshīdī dynasty'. At least we know that it was in the possession of Rifāʿa Bek al-Ṭahṭāwī's family and that his son ʿAlī Fahmī read the book in 1870.

---

67 See Dār al-Kutub al-Miṣriyya, Qism al-Fahāris al-ʿArabiyya, *Fihris al-Kutub al-'Arabiyya al-Mawjūda bi 'l-Dār li-Ghāyat Shahr Dīsimbir 1928 m. al-Juz' al-Khāmis wa-Yashtamil 'alā Fihris al-Ta'rīkh* (Cairo 1348/1930), 262–3.

68 Ibid., 262.

VI. 13. b. MS *'Aj. Tārīkh* 173/microfilm 10729 (vol. II of *'Ajā'ib al-Āthār*), includes 233 paginated and rubricated folios of 27 lines each in *naskhī* script. It covers the events of the years 1190–1212 (/1776–98). F. 1a has two stamps: the first is: كتبخانه مصرية Kutubkhāna Miṣriyya and the second is الكتبخانه الخديوية al-Kutubkhāna al-Khudaywiyya. F. 1b begins كتاب عجائب التراجم والأخبار جمع الفقير: عبد الرحمن بن حسن الجبرتي الحنفي عفا الله عنه.

This heading is followed by a sentence stating that the manuscript was in the possession of Yaḥyā Ḥakam in 1263 (/1846–7) and that ʿAlī Fahmī the son of Rifāʿa Bey Rāfiʿ al-Ṭahṭāwī read it in Rabīʿ II 1287 (/30 June–28 July 1870): ملك الفقير يحيى حكم سنة ١٢٦٣. طالع هذا الجزء من أوله الى آخره المحتاج الى عفو ربه الكريم علي فهمي نجل رفاعة بك رافع في شهر ربيع الاخر من سنة ١٢٨٧. There is an unclear stamp next to these sentences. Under it are the words: محافظة تاريخ نمره ٢، ونمره ٢٨٧٢ تاريخ, then a stamp reading: كتبخانه مصرية Kutubkhāna Miṣriyya and on the left of the folio: نمره ١٧٣ تاريخ. F. 1b starts with the events of the year 1190 (/1776–7): سنة تسعين وماية والف. كان سلطان العصر فيها السلطان عبد الحميد ابن احمد خان العثماني ووالي مصر الوزير محمد باشا عزت... The colophon on f. 238a does not give the copyist's name, but states that the volume was copied in 1262 (/1845–6):

رعى الله ما قد راق منها وما حلا	والملا[!] سما برقعها متألق
حمى الله مرقاها ومعراج قدسها	بكوكبها السامي الذي ليس يلحق

VI. 14. c. MS *'Aj. Tārīkh* 174/microfilm 10730 (vol. III of *'Ajā'ib al-Āthār*), in 294b folios, each of 27 lines, written in a *ruq'a* script, covering the years 1212–20 (/1797–1806). The title page on f. 1a, is in al-Jabartī's handwriting, as in the case of MS *'Aj.* Cam. 2nd., Qq. 168 (III. 2. c.), MS *'Aj.* BN (III. 7. c.), which reads:

جمع العلامة الجبرتي.الجزء الثالث من كتاب عجائب الاثار في التراجم والاخبار

Under the title are the words: نمرة 3 تاريخ محافظة. The sentence is followed by a stamp reading:الكتبخانة الخديوية المصرية al-Kutubkhāna al-Khudaywiyya al-Miṣriyya. The number of the manuscript is noted to the left of the stamp: نمره 2873 نمره ١٧٤ تاريخ. F. 1b also gives the number of the volume: تاريخ نمره 3 ثلاثة, and starts with the events of the year 1213 (/1798): سنة ثلاثة عشر ومايتين والف وهي اول سني الملاحم العظيمة...

The names of important personalities and events mentioned in the text are written in red ink in the margins. The trial of Sulaymān al-Ḥalabī is given in full but folio 66b–67a is missing. The Wahhābī proclamation is summarized (ff. 187a–187b). The biographies of the year 1216 (/1801–2) are missing as in the case of the MSS of the first version of MS *'Aj.* Cam.

This manuscript is unique because the colophon on f. 294b is written in *nasta'līq* in a different hand, very similar to al-Jabartī's in the autographs of MS*Mudda*, MS*Maẓ.* Cam. and MS *'Aj.* Cam. (see above nos. I. 1., II. 2., and III. 1. a–c). The end of the volume, written in *ruq'a* (f. 264b), reads: وازدحمت على سدته زواره الى ان اجاب الداعي ونعته النواعي وذلك في سابع عشرين شهر شعبان من السنة. ولم يخلف بعده مثله. وبه ختمت دائرة المسلكين في الخلوتية ورجال السادة الصوفية. It is followed by the colophon in a *nasta'līq* identical with al-Jabartī's (f. 294b) in which the *ṣalāt* on the Prophet is dropped using the verb '*tajaddada*' in the past whereas in MS *'Aj.* Cam. the verb is in the present: وحسن به ختم هذا الجزء الثالث من كتاب عجايب الآثار في التراجم والأخبار لغاية سنة عشرين ومائتين والف من الهجرة النبوية. وسنقيد ان شاء الله سبحانه وتعالى ما تجدد بعدها من الحوادث من ابتدا سنة احدى وعشرين التي نحن بها الان ان امتد الاجل واسعف الامل ونرجوا [!] من الكريم المتعال صلاح الحوال وانقشاع الهموم وصلاح العموم انه على كل شيء قدير وبالاجابة جدير والله تعالى اعلم. انتهى. م.

In fact, this MS belongs to the group of the *'Ajā'ib al-Āthār* which was copied from the complete four volumes. This is because the group of MSS copied from the Cambridge autograph is based on the first three volumes and does not mention that it will be completed with a fourth volume.

The library stamp is followed by the words: حافظة. تاريخ عدد ٣٠ عدد ٢٩٤ ورقة DKQ catalogue, p. 262, states that the manuscript was 'written in 1220 (/1805–6)'. There are various marginal additions on many folios in the same handwriting as the colophon, especially on folios 1b–2b, 13b–14a, 44a, 51a, 73a, 98a–100a,113b–114a, 140b–153b, 211b–212a, 284a–294b.

VI. 15. a. MS *'Aj. Tārīkh* 466/microfilm 36339, vol. I, in 333 folios, written in a clear thin *nasta'līq*. The folios are paginated, and the title-page reads: كتاب عجائب الاثار في التراجم والاخبار تأليف العالم العلامة والبحر الفهامة الشيخ عبد الرحمن بن حسن الجبرتي الحنفي غفر الله له ولوالديه ولجميع المسلمين، امين.

There is an unclear oval stamp under this title. The first page is rubricated with decorations. The pages have a two-line frame. F. 1b begins with the *basmala*: الحمد لله القديم الاول... The colophon in f. 333a ends with a reversed triangle and states that the manuscript was embellished (*nammaqahu*) in an elegant style by al-Ḥājj Muḥammad Ḥusayn Aḥmad Miṣbāḥ al-Shāfiʿī al-Azharī on Friday 20 Rabīʿ I 1272 (/29–30 November 1855), and that this is the first half of volume I, but, in fact, it is the whole of volume I: وتأمر اتباعه من بعده وتقاسموا البلاد فيما بينهم والفوا المظالم وظنوها مغانم وتمادوا في الجور وتلاحقوا في البغي على القوم الى أن حصل ما حصل... وما حل بالاقليم بسببهم من الخراب والدمار. تم النصف الاول من هذا التاريخ بمنه وكرمه. نمّقه بيده الدنية الفقير الى رحمة الله تعالى الحاج محمد حسين مصباح الشافعي الازهري. وكان الفراغ من نمقه [!] يوم الجمعة في عشرين ربيع الاول سنة ١٢٧٢ اثنين وسبعين ومائتين والف، اللّهم اغفر لكاتبه وقاريه ولمن كان السبب فيه آمين آمين آمين يا رب العالمين. It is important to note here that this is the first time that a copyist admits that he has '*nammaqa*' (embellished [the style]), of the authors work in an elegant style. Therefore, one can presume that the Būlāq edition, with its corrected style, was based upon it, and that he is the copyist whose homoeoteleuton at the end of volume IV mixed the event of the last months of the year, as we will see below.

VI. 15. b. MS *'Aj. Tārīkh* 466, vol. II. There is no microfilm of it in Dār al-Kutub al-Qawmiyya in Cairo. According to the DKQ catalogue, volume II contains 240 folios written in ordinary handwriting and copied by al-Ḥājj Muḥammad Ḥusayn b. Aḥmad Miṣbāḥ in 1272 [/1855–6], who copied volume I (15. a.) above.

VI. 15. c. MS *'Aj.* Tārīkh 466/microfilm 34682, vol. III, in 328 paginated folios, of 25 lines each, written in ordinary handwriting. The titles and the first words of paragraphs are rubricated. F. 1a reads: نمره ١٥٤٩٢ نمره ٤٦٦ تاريخ. There is an unclear oval stamp under this line. There is no title-page. F. 1b starts: بسم الله الرحمن الرحيم. سنة ثلاثة عشر ومايتين والف وهي اول سني الملاحم العظيمة...

This manuscript resembles MS *'Aj.* Cam., Qq. 171, III (f. 168a) in that it does not contain (f. 199a) any of the biographies found in the Būlāq edition (III, 210, l. 27–220,l. 10): انقضت هذه السنة [1216] ... ودفن بالاسكندرية.... The Wahhābīs' proclamation of 29 Ṣafar 1218 (/19–20 June 1803) is cited in full (f. 234b) as in *'Aj.* Būlāq, III, 255, l. 5–275, l. 1: بسم الله ... المارقين المتعصبين..., but lines 1–4 in *'Aj.* Būlāq, III, 257: وقد بسط الكلام ... وغير ذلك are lacking (as in the case of MS *'Aj.* Ber., 9489 above).

328a states that the third volume ends with the year 1220 (/1805–6) and that new events would be recorded from the beginning of 1221 (/1806), in which the recording took place, if the span of life permitted. The MS has no colophon and ends with the biography of a *Ṣūfī* of the Khalwatiyya order named Muḥammad b. Sīrīn al-Maqdisī: ... السادة الصوفية وحسن به ختم هذا الجزء الثالث من كتاب عجايب الآثار في التراجم والأخبار ولغاية سنة عشرين ومائتين والف من الهجرة النبوية على صاحبها افضل الصلاة والسلام. وسنقيد ان شاء الله ما يتجدد بعدها من الحوادث من ابتدا سنة احدى وعشرين التي نحن بها الان ان امتد الاجل واسعف الامل ونرجوا [!] من الكريم المتعال صلاح الأحوال وانقشاع الهموم وصلاح العموم انه على كل شيء قدير وبلاجابة جدير والله اعلم. تم.

This MS also belongs to the group of the *'Ajā'ib al-Āthār* which was copied from the complete four volumes.

VI. 15. d. MS *'Aj.* Tārīkh 466/microfilm 35088 (positive), vol. IV, in 228 paginated folios of 25–7 lines each. The script is a clear thin *naskhī*, the spaces between the lines are wide, and the pages have a three-line frame. This MS might be an early version of volume IV since there are many missing sentences which are supplied in other MSS.The MS starts with squares giving the names and the years of the death of 721 *'ālim*, and the number of the page where they are mentioned in all the four volumes: هذه فهرست الجزء الرابع من كتاب الجبرتي. There are only a few corrections in the margins. It starts with the year 1221 (/1806–7); the first page reads: بسم الله الرحمن الرحيم. سنة ١٢٢١ احدى وعشرين ومائتين والف. استهل شهر المحرم الحرام بيوم الخميس حسابا ويوم السبت هلالا ووافق ذلك انتقال الشمس لبرج الحمل فاتحدت السنة القمرية والشمسية.

This MS of *'Ajā'ib al-Āthār*, MS *'Aj.* Tārīkh 466/microfilm 35088, vol. IV is identical to MS *'Aj.* Birmingham, vol. IV. In f. 221a, the events dealing with the month of Ṣafar 1236 (/7 November–7 December 1820) are different from the version of the Būlāq edition. The changes are in the names of the months in which certain events happened. Sometimes the events are given in summarized form. This change in the events of the months might be attributed to a copyist error, homoeoteleuton, when he skipped copying the events of the two months Ṣafar and Rabīʿ al-Awwal 1236 (/7 November–6 January 1821) and continued to copy the events of the month Rabīʿ II (/6 January–4 February 1821), as follows:

1. Part of the events of Ṣafar and all the events of Rabīʿ I 1236 which appear in *'Aj.* Būlāq, IV, 317 are missing in MS *'Aj.* Tārīkh 466/microfilm 35088, vol. IV, f. 221a and are given as the events of Rabīʿ II 1236, f. 221a:

واستهل صفر بيوم الخميس وفي اوايله حضر ابراهيم باشا من جهة [!] القبلية بعدما طاف الفيوم ايضا. وفيه اخرج الباشا عبد الله بيك الرندلي منفيا...

2. The events of Jumādā I (/4 February–6 March 1821), as are given in the Būlāq edition are attributed to Rabīʿ I 1236 (/7 December 1820–5 January 1821) in MS *'Aj.* Tārīkh 466/microfilm 35088, vol. IV, f. 221a.

3. The events of Jumādā II (/6 March–4 April 1821), as are given in the Būlāq edition are attributed to Rabīʿ II 1236 in MS *'Aj.* Tārīkh 466/microfilm 35088, vol. IV, f. 221a.

4. The events of Rajab 1236 (/4 April–3 May 1821) as are given in the Būlāq edition are attributed to the continuation of Rabīʿ II 1236 in MS *'Aj.* Tārīkh 466/microfilm 35088, vol. IV, f. 221a.

5. The events of Shaʿbān (/3 May–2 June 1821) which appear in the Būlāq edition are attributed to Jumādā I 1236 in MS *'Aj.* Tārīkh 466/microfilm 35088, vol. IV, f. 221a.

6. The events of Dhu 'l-Qaʿda (/30 July–29 August 1821) which appear in the Būlāq edition are attributed to Ramaḍān 1236 (/2 June–1 July 1821) in MS *'Aj.* DKQ,Tārīkh 466/microfilm 35088, vol. IV, f. 221b.

7. The events of Dhu 'l-Ḥijja (/29 August–28 September 1821) which appear in the Būlāq edition are attributed to Shawwāl 1236 (/1 July–30 July 1821) in MS *'Aj.*,Tārīkh 466/microfilm 35088, vol. IV, f. 221b, with which volume IV ends:

شـــهر شـوّال

واستهل شهر شوال. فيه خرجت عساكر كثيرة وفيهم محو بيك ومعهم آلآت الحرب وجميع اللوازم قاصدين بلاد النوبة وما جاورها وسافر ايضا محمد أغا لاظ المنفصل عن الكتخدائية الى اسنا ليتلقى القادمين. وفيه وصلت بشائر باستيلاء اسماعيل باشا على سنار بغير حرب فضربت مدافع لذلك.
وانقضت هذه السنة وما فيها من الحوادث التي انقضى بعضها والبعض باق الى الآن وهي حادثة الاروام. الى هنا تم الكتاب وصلى الله على سيدنا محمد النبي الأمي وعلى آله وصحبه وسلم ورضي الله عن آل بيت رسول الله وأصحابه وغفر لنا وللمسلمين آمين . تم.

This manuscript is unique and of special importance, because it continues al-Jabartī's *Chronicle* which ended with the year 1236 (/1820–1). On f. 222b the copyist gives in brief the names of important Egyptian scholars and some of their works arranged according to the year of their death from the year 1201 (/1786–7), among them Aḥmad al-Dardīr and Aḥmad al-Saḥīmī, up to the year 1271 (/1854–5): بسم الله الرحمن الرحيم. هذا تاريخ العلما المتوفين من القرن الثالث عشر مرتبين على ترتيب السنين . سنة الف ومايتين وواحد. توفي العلامة الشيخ احمد بن محمد بن احمد الدردير من بني عدي، صعيدي مالكي له تآليف مفيدة في ستة عشر خلت من شهر ربيع الاول. توفي الشيخ احمد بن محمد السحيمي من سحيم حنفي له تآليف جسيمة لستة عشر خلت من شوال...

F. 223a mentions that Shaykh Muḥammad b. Muḥammad ʿAbd al-Razzāq known as Murtaḍā al-Ḥusaynī [al-Zabīdī], author of *Sharḥ al-Qāmūs* and *Sharḥ Iḥyā' al-'Ulūm*, etc. died in 1205 (/1790–1): سنة الف ومائتين وخمس. توفي الشيخ محمد بن محمد بن عبد الرزاق الشهير بمرتضى الحسيني من زبيد اليمن، حنفي له تآليف عظيمة شرح القاموس وشرح احياء العلوم وغيرها.

F. 224b states that ʿAbd Allāh al-Sharqāwī from the village of al-Ṭawīla died in 1225 (/1810–11); he was the rector of al-Azhar and wrote important works such as *Ḥāshiyat al-Taḥrīr, Sharḥ al-Ḥikam* and *Wird Saḥar*, etc. He belonged to the Shāfiʿī school.

On f. 225a Ismāʿīl al-Khashshāb's death is reported in the year 1229 [/1813–14], (f. 225a) a Shāfiʿī, who composed good poetry (وله شعر جيّد). F. 225b reads: توفي الشيخ محمد قش الغرقي الزكي من منية الغرقا ، شافعي له تآليف كثيرة كحاشية الهدهدي. F. 226a the copyist indicates that no outstanding scholar died in the year 1243 (/1827–8) (سنة ١٢٤٣ خالية). The same is true of 1249 (/1833–4) (f. 226b), while in the year 1250 (/1834–5) (f. 226b) Ḥasan b. Muḥammad al-ʿAṭṭār's death is given on 19 Shawwāl 1250 (/18 February 1835): سنة الف ومايتين وخمسين. توفي الشيخ حسن ابن محمد العطار من مصر القاهرة، شافعي. تولى مشيخة الأزهر بعد الدمنهوجي، له مؤلفات كثيرة.

It is surprising that among the names of scholars who died between 1237 (/1821–2) and 1242 (/1826–7) (ff. 225b–226a), years in which al-Jabartī is said to have died, he is not mentioned at all. It is a mystery why the copyist mentioned the names and dates of death of so many eminent *'ulamā'*, among them al-Jabartī's close friends, such as Muḥammad Murtaḍā al-Zabīdī, al-Khashshāb and al-ʿAṭṭār, while he ignored al-Jabartī.

The following may give the reader an idea as to the scope of the list of the scholars who died during these years: in 1237 (/1821–2) al-Shaykh Muḥammad b. Sālim b. Nāṣir known as Thuʿaylib al-Ṣaghīr; in 1238 (/1822–3) Shaykh Shāfiʿī b. Yūnis al-Fayyūmī from Manāshī al-Khaṭīb in Fayyūm, a Mālikī; in the same year Shaykh ʿIwaḍ Sanbāwī from Sanbū in the Ṣaʿīd, the village of al-Shaykh al-Amīr, a Mālikī (f. 226a); Muḥammad b. Muḥammad al-Bāsāṭī from Bāsāṭ, a Mālikī; in 1239 (/1823–4) Muṣṭafā b. Muḥammad al-Dasūqī; in 1240 (/1824–5) Aḥmad b. ʿAbd Allāh, a Shāfiʿī; in 1241 (/1825–6) Aḥmad b. Muḥammad al-Ṣāwī from Ṣā al-Ḥajar and Muḥammad al-Busṭī b. Ibrāhīm b. Khalīl Afandī; the year 1242 (/1826–7) is 'void' (*khāliya*) [i.e. no person of importance died]; in the year 1243 (/1827–8) Thuʿaylib b. Sālim b.

Tāmir. There is no obvious reason why the year in which al-Jabartī died is not mentioned, although he is the author of the chronicle to which the copyist added the dates of the death of other scholars.

Among the 271 names of Egyptian scholars given by the copyist there are Shāfiʿīs, Mālikīs, and some Ḥanafī scholars to which al-Jabartī also belonged. The copyist continues to say that the dates of the death of others who died are not known, and here also the name of al-Jabartī is absent. Among the latter scholars the copyist mentions that one of them was the great Sulaymān b. ʿUmar al-Bajīrmī, a Shāfiʿī who composed the *Ḥāshiyat al-Manhaj*. In f. 228a the copyist gives a list of those who died during the year 1271 (/1854–5). The copyist adds that there are 'other famous people who died during the thirteenth century whose year of death he could verify, as well as their extraction and their place of origin'. (وبقيت ناس من أوايل القرن وناس في وسطه وناس في أواخر تلك السنين يجهل تاريخهم ونسب بعضهم وبلاد بعضهم من عظمايهم الشيخ سليمان بن عمر من بجيرم شافعي له تآليف كحاشية المنهج). At the end of this long list of names and the years of death the copyist concludes: 'The blessed names are completed' (تمت الأسماء المباركة). However, one can suggest that the copyist, who knew that al-Jabartī was *persona non-grata* with the authorities in Egypt, did not want to get in trouble and so he refrained from mentioning his name as one of the great scholars of his time.

VI. 16. c. MS *'Aj.* Tārīkh 1226/microfilm 365545, vol. III. It starts with the *basmala* and the events of the year 1213 (/1798–9). This manuscript resembles MS *'Aj.* Cam., Qq. 171, III (f. 168a) in that the year 1216 (/1801–2) ends without obituaries, and the manuscript moves directly to the events of 1217 (/1802–3) (f. 212), as in MS *'Aj.* Tārīkh 1425/microfilm 19286, vol. III. However, unlike MS *'Aj.* Cam. Qq. 171, III, f. 213b, it contains on ff. 250–3 the Wahhābī proclamation of 29 Ṣafar 1218 (/19/20 June 1803), cited in *'Aj.* Būlāq, III, 255, l. 5–275, l. 1, as in the case of MS *'Aj.* Tārīkh 1425/microfilm 19286, 18. c. below.

VI. 17. a. 1. MS *'Aj.* Tārīkh 1424/microfilm 14586 and 36392 (positive), vol. I, pt. 1, consists of 449 unpaginated folios of 21 lines each, written in a clear *ruq'a* script, only the fascicles are numbered. The DKQ catalogue, p. 262, states that the first volume, in two parts, was copied by Aḥmad b. Mūsā al-

Shāhid on Wednesday 24 Shawwāl 1289 (/24/25 December 1872). It covers the events of the years 1101–89 (/1689–1776). There are no corrections in the margins. The title page on f. 1a reads: هذا الجزء الأول من تاريخ العلامة الشيخ عبد الرحمن بن حسن الجبرتي رحمه الله تعالى ورحم أسلافه.

Under the title, the date 6 January 1895 refers to the day on which the manuscript was donated by the Library (*Kutubkhāna*) of the Būlāq Press to the al-Kutubkhāna al-Khudaywiyya al-Miṣriyya: وارد من كتبخانة مطبعة بولاق مجانا ومضاف في ٦ يناير سنة ١٨٩٥ نمره ١ يومية ، خصوصية ١٤٢٤ تاريخ. عمومية ٢٨١٥٩. Under these lines there is a stamp reading: الكتبخانة الخديوية المصرية al-Kutubkhāna al-Khudaywiyya al-Miṣriyya. On f. 1b there is a stamp reading: حسن ظني بالله ('my good trust in God') and the text starts with the beginning of volume I: بسم الله الرحمن الرحيم. الحمد لله القديم الاول الذي لا يزول ملكه ولا يتحول، خالق الخلايق وعالم الذرات بالحقايق.

The colophon on f. 449a states that this manuscript is the first half of volume I (which ends with the events of 1161 [/1748]), and that the second half starts with the year 1162 (/1748–9): فأمر الوالي بقتله فقتله والله تعالى أعلم بالحقايق. والى هنا انتهي نصف الجزء الاول من تاريخ الجبرتي ويليه النصف الثاني وابتاؤه فصل وعود وانعطاف في ذكر حوادث مصر وتراجم اعيانها وولاتها من ابتداء سنة ١١٦٢ الى سياق الحديث والله اعلم وصلى الله على اشرف المرسلين سيدنا محمد خاتم النبيين وعلى آله وصحبه اجمعين.

This manuscript resembles those described under 10 above as well as MS *'Aj.* Tārīkh 1872, 21. a. 1. below which ends with the first half of volume I. The events coincide with the *'Aj.* Būlāq, I, 186, l. 2, and the Beirut Dār al-Fāris edition, vol. I, 274.

VI. 17. a. 2. MS *'Aj.* Tārīkh 1424/microfilm 14674 (negative), vol. I, pt. II, in 310 folios. There is no title and f. 1a reads: النصف الثاني من الجزؤ الأول. Under this there is a sentence stating that this manuscript was in the possession of the Library (*Kutubkhāna*) of the Būlāq Press and was donated to the al-Kutubkhāna al-Khudaywiyya al-Miṣriyya on 6 January 1895: وارد من كتبخانة مطبعة بولاق مجانا ومضاف في ٦ يناير سنة ١٨٩٥ نمره 1 يومية ، خصوصية ١٤٢٤ تاريخ.

F. 1a starts with the *basmala* and states that it will cover the years 1162–73 (/1748–60): بسم الله الرحمن الرحيم الحمد لله رب العالمين والصلاة على اشرف المرسلين سيدنا محمد وعلى آله وصحبه اجمعين. فصل وعود وانعطاف في ذكر حوادث مصر وتراجم أعيانها وولاتها ابتداء سنة ١١٦٢ ... إلى أواخر سنة ١١٧٣... وذلك حسب التيسير والإمكان وما لا يدرك كله لا

يترك كله. فنقول لما عزل المكرم حضرة محمد باشا... وسبب تلقبه بذلك الاسم لأنه كان بعينه بعض حول ... وكان الكاشف بالبحيرة إذ ذاك حسن أغا كتخدا...

On the left side of f. 1b are the following words بياض بأصله ('blank place in the original [manuscript]'), and in a new line the sentence: بيك تابع عمر بيك توفي هناك.

This manuscript resembles those described in no. 10 above as well as nos. 21 and 22 below, which end with the first half of volume I. The end coincides with *'Aj.* Būlāq (I, 186, l. 2), where on the right-hand side of the page the editor notes that there are 'blank spaces in all the manuscripts in his possession'. In the Beirut Dār al-Fāris edition, I, 274, l. 16, this paragraph is similar, but without mentioning a 'blank space'. The manuscript concludes with the same lines as volume I of the Būlāq edition. The colophon on f. 310a states that it was copied in 1289 (/1872–3) without mentioning the name of the copyist: إلى إن حصل ما حصل ونزل بهم وبالناس ما نزل وسيتلى عليك من ذلك أنبا وأخبار وما حلّ بالإقليم

VI. 17. b. MS *'Aj.* Tārīkh 1424/microfilm 14673 (negative), vol. II, in 346 folios in ordinary handwriting. The title page reads: الجزء الثاني من / تاريخ الجبرتي After the title there is a sentence stating that the manuscript was in the possession of the Library (*Kutubkhāna*) of the Būlāq Press and was donated to al-Kutubkhāna al-Khudaywiyya al-Miṣriyya on 6 January 1895: من كتبخانة مطبعة بولاق مجانا ومضاف في ٦ يناير سنة ١٨٩٥ نمره ١ يوميه. خصوصية ١٤٢٤ تاريخ. عمومية ٢٨١٥٩. Under this line there is a stamp reading: الكتبخانة المصرية الخديوية al-Kutubkhāna al-Khudaywiyya al-Miṣriyya. The manuscript covers the events of the year 1190–1212 (/1776–98). On f. 1b a stamp reading: حسن ظني بالله ('my good trust in God') and under it, the text starts with the year 1190 (/1776–7) without the *basmala* والف كان سلطان العصر فيها السلطان عبد الحميد ابن احمد خان العثماني...سنة تسعين وماية

On the last page, f. 346, the colophon states that the manuscript was copied by Aḥmad b. Muḥammad b. Mūsā al-Shāhid (MS *'Aj.* Tārīkh, 1424, III, 262) on Saturday 29 Ṣafar 1290 (/27 April 1873) as in the case of VI. 17. c. below:

حمى الله مرقاها ومعراج قدسها　　　بكوكبها السامي الذي ليس يلحق

الى آخرها وهى طويلة، وله غير ذلك سامحه الله. توفي في منتصف شعبان من السنة غفر الله لنا وله ولوالدينا وللمسلمين بمنه وكرمه. كان الفراغ من كتابة هذا الجزء / اواخر يوم السبت المبارك

تاسع عشرين صفر الخير ١٢٩٠ من الهجرة / على صاحبها الصلاة والسلام على يد الفقير احمد بن محمد الشاهد / عفا عنهما بحق طه ويس، تم.

This colophon, up to the words *bi-mannih wa-karamih* is similar to the colophon in MS *'Aj.* Tārīkh 1428 (VI. 21. a.) below and MS *'Aj.* Tārīkh 173 (VI. 13. b.) above and states this part was copied on Wednesday 24 Shawwāl 1289 [/25 December 1872]: بسببهم من الخراب والدمار والله تعالى اعلم. الحمد لله على التمام والحمد لله على الاحسان والامتنان وصلى الله على سيدنا محمد ابن عدنان وعلى آله وأصحابه في كل وقت وأوان. قد تم نسخ هذا الجزء يوم الأربعاء الموافق ٢٤ من شهر شوال سنة ١٢٨٩.

VI. 17. c. MS *'Aj.* Tārīkh 1424/microfilm 14198 (negative), vol. III. The manuscript is written in clear *ruq'a* script in 541a folios of 21 lines each in 43 fascicles. F. 1a starts with the title page: هذا الجزء الثالث من تاريخ الجبرتي المسمى عجائب الآثار في التراجم والأخبار وصلى الله على سيدنا محمد وعلى آله آمين. After this title, there is a sentence stating that the manuscript was donated to the Būlāq Press on 6 January 1895 with the shelf number: نمره ١ يومية ، خصوصية ١٤٢٤ تاريخ. عمومية ٢٨١٥٩ and under it the stamp of the Bibliothèque Khédiviale (al-Kutubkhāna al-Khudaywiyya al-Miṣriyya), as in the case of volumes I–II, above.

F. 1b starts with the *basmala* and the events of 1213 (/1798–9): بسم الله الرحمن الرحيم. سنة ثلاثة عشر ومايتين والف وهي اول سني الملاحم العظيمة... This manuscript (fascicle 49, f. 7b–cont. 50, f. 1b) does not resemble *'Aj.* Būlāq (III, 255–7, l. 1), because, as in the case of the Dār al-Fāris edition, Beirut, long passages of poetry and prose as well as some passages in the narration of events are deliberately deleted. However, it resembles the Beirut Dār al-Fāris edition (II, 588–91) and Dār al-Kutub al-ʿIlmiyya, Beirut 1997 (II, 410–13), in that it has the fourth paragraph of the French Proclamation distorted. It contains the Wahhābī proclamation of 29 Ṣafar 1218 [/19–20 June 1803] in full, but lacks literary quotations in the biographies of poets and writers. The poetry of al-ʿAṭṭār is also missing while corrections in the margins are few. This is also the case with the manuscripts in Dār al-Kutub al-Qawmiyya, MS *'Aj.* Tārīkh 466/microfilm 34682 (VI. 15. c. above), f. 234; MS *'Aj.* Tārīkh 1425/ microfilm 19286 (VI. 18. c. below), f. 465; MS *'Aj.* Tārīkh 2129/microfilm 36545 (VI. 23. c. below), fascicle (*kurrās*) 50, f. 1b. This fact indicates clearly that one of the copyists who was only interested in the chronicle, not in poetry or prose, made this summary of the work and that all the printed editions of Beirut in three volumes might have been copied from this MS.

Above the colophon the seal is as in the case of MS *'Aj.*, Tarikh 1226 (VI. 19. c.) حسن ظني بالله ('my good trust in God'). On ff. 540b–541a it is stated that the manuscript was copied by Aḥmad b. Muḥammad b. Mūsā al-Shāhid on 18 Shawwāl 1292 (/16/17 November 1875). Al-Shāhid is the copyist of volume IV of MS *'Aj.* Leeds 132 (History), in 1290 (/1873–4) (III. 5. d. above): ...السادة الصوفية وحسن به ختم هذا الجزء الثالث من كتاب عجايب الآثار في التراجم والأخبار لغاية سنة عشرين ومائتين والف من الهجرة النبوية على صاحبها الف تحية وعليه افضل السلام. وسنقيد ان شاء الله سبحانه وتعالى ما يتجدد بعدها من الحوادث من ابتدا سنة احدى وعشرين التي نحن بها الان ان امتد الاجل واسعف الامل ونرجوا [!] من الكريم المتعال صلاح الاحوال وانقشاع الهموم وصلاح العموم انه على كل شيء قدير وبالاجابة جدير. نجز هذا الكتاب في ثمانية عشر من شهر شوال يوم الاحد المبارك سنة اثنين وتسعين ومايتين بعد الالف على يد كاتبه المتوكل على ربه الواحد عبده احمد ابن موسى الشاهد اللهمّ الى الابد آمين بجاه سيد المرسلين ونصر الله سلطاننا ... عبد العزيز خان وايده وابقاه آمين وصلى الله على سيد المرسلين وعلى آله واصحابه اجمعين والحمد لله رب العالمين آمين. The colophon has a mistake in the sentence وحسن به ختم، انتهى، هذا الجزء الثالث من كتاب عجائب الآثار في التراجم والأخبار in which after *khatm* (to end) the word *intahā* (completed) is wrongly added. This corrupted version is the same as in MS *'Aj.* Tārīkh 1426/microfilm 35532 (VI. 19. c. below), and it indicates that VI. 17. c. was copied from VI. 19. c. which is undated.

Moreover, this MS (fascicle 42, f. 5a) resembles MS *'Aj.* Cam., Qq. 171, III, f. 213b in that it does not contain the biographies of those who died in 1216 [/1801–2] which appear in *'Aj.* Būlāq, III, 211–20.

VI. 17. d. MS *'Aj.* Tārīkh 1424/microfilm 15011 (negative), microfilm 37439 (positive, copied twice), vol. IV, in 449 folios with very few corrections in the margins. There is no title page and f. 1a states that it was donated to the Būlāq Press on 6 January 1895 where its shelf mark was: نمره ١ يومية ، خصوصية ١٤٢٤ تاريخ. عمومية ٢٨١٥٩. Under this line there is a stamp of al-Kutubkhāna al-Khudaywiyya al-Miṣriyya. F. 1b starts with the year 1221 (/1806–7): سنة ١٢٢١ احدى وعشرين ومائتين... استهل شهر المحرم بسم الله الرحمن الرحيم الخميس حسابا ويوم السبت هلالا...بيوم والف It ends with the events of 1237 (/1821–2). The colophon on f. 449b states that the manuscript was copied by Aḥmad b. Muḥammad b. Aḥmad b. Mūsā al-Shāhid on 17 Rabīʿ II 1289 (/24 June 1872) from an autograph of al-Jabartī written in 1237 (/1821–2) and that 'after this date the author died and therefore nothing else was written: والبعض باق الى الآن وهي حادثة الاروام. وذلك الى هنا انتهى ما نقل من خط العلامة الشيخ عبد الرحمن بن الشيخ حسن الجبرتي مؤرخ هذه المدة وما قبلها لغاية هذا التاريخ سنة ١٢٣٧ وهذا آخر الجزء الرابع وبعده توفي الشيخ ولم يكتب شيء وصلى الله على سيدنا محمد وعلى آله وصحبه وسلم. غفر الله له، وكان الفراغ من نسخه يوم السبت ١٧ من شهر ربيع الثاني من سنة الف ومايتين [و]تسعة وثمانين من بعد الهجرة النبويه على صاحبها الف تحية على يد كاتبه الفقير الى رحمة ربه القدير احمد بن محمد بن احمد بن موسى الشاهد. م. It ends with the seal of al-Kutubkhāna al-Khudaywiyya al-Miṣriyya. Because of the similarity in formula in the statement that this MS was copied from an autograph of al-Jabartī, it seems that this is either the MS or a copy of the MS which was used for *'Ajā'ib al-Āthār* by al-Jabartī, as printed in the margin of the edition of *Tārīkh al-Kāmil* by Ibn al-Athīr al-Jazarī known as ʿIzz al-Dīn (1160–1234), (Cairo 1301 [/1883–4], vols 1–12). In vol. 12, 236 the colophon reads: وجد بآخر بعض النسخ ما نصه: الى هنا انتهى ما نقل من خط العلامة الشيخ عبد الرحمن بن الشيخ حسن الجبرتي مؤرخ هذه المدة وما قبلها لغاية هذا التاريخ سنة ١٢٣٦ [1821] وهذا آخر الجزء الرابع وبعده توفي الشيخ ولم يكتب شيئا.

VI. 18. a. MS *'Aj.* Tārīkh 1425/microfilm 14352 and microfilm 14200 (negative), vol. I. The manuscript is written in *ruq'a* script in 437 rubricated folios of 25 lines each. It covers the events of the years 1101–89 (/1689–1776). The title page (f. 1a) reads: هذا الجزء الأول من كتاب الآثار [كذا] في التراجم والأخبار للشيخ العالم العلامة الاستاذ عبد الرحمن \ م [!] بن حسن الجبرتي \م تغمدهما الله \ م برحمته \ واسكنّا وايّاهما والمسلمين م م بحبوحة جنته \ م م انه سميع بصير وبالاجابة جدير وصلى الله على سيدنا محمد النبي الامي وعلى آله وصحبه وسلم. After these lines there is a sentence stating that this MS was in the possession of the Būlāq Press and was donated to the Bibliothèque Khédiviale (al-Kutubkhāna al-Khudaywiyya al-Miṣriyya), on 6 January 1895 with the shelf mark: نمره ١ يومية. خصوصية ١٤٢٥ تاريخ. عموميه ٢٨١٦. Under these lines is an oval stamp reading: حسن ظني بالله ('My good trust in God'), and another one reading: al-Kutubkhāna al-Khudaywiyya al-Miṣriyya. On f. 1b the *basmala* is fully vowelled, and consists of the same version as in the Būlāq edition: وعالم الذرات بالحقايق ('who knows even the atoms of reality') and not as in the Cambridge MS, where the version is: ومنزّه عن العلايق ('he is without any cause'): بسم الله الرحمن الرحيم \ الحمد لله القديم الاول الذي لايزول ملكه ولا يتحول خالق الخلايق وعالم الذرات بالحقايق...

The colophon in f. 437a states that the MS was copied by Muḥammad Aḥmad al-Shafiʿī without a date: الى ان حصل ما حصل من الخراب والدمار ونزل بهم

وبالناس ما نزل وسيتلى عليك من ذلك أنبا واخبار وما حلّ بالاقليم بسببهم من الخراب والدمار والله اعلم بالصواب واليه المرجع والمآب، وصلى الله على سيدنا محمد وصحبه \ وسلم.م [= آمين].

بالله إن نظرت عيناك ما كتبت — يد الفقير الى غفران مولاه

فاقرأ له مهديًا أمَ الكتاب وقل — يجعل جنة الخلد مأواه

الله على سيدنا محمد وعلى صحبه وسلم عدد معلوماتك ومداد كلماتك كلما ذكرك الذاكرون وغفل عن ذكره الغافلون، وصلّى على يد كاتبه الفقير الحقير محمد احمد الشافعي.

Under the colophon there is a stamp reading: al-Kutubkhāna al-Khudaywiyya al-Miṣriyya.The end of this volume coincides with the end of volume I of the Būlāq edition.

VI. 18. b. MS *'Aj.* Tārīkh 1425/microfilms 12749 (negative) and 14199, pt. 1–14200, pt. 2, vol. II, is in 365 folios, each of 24 lines, written in a neat *ruq'a* script. It contains the events of the years 1190–1212 (/1776–98). F. 1a states that this MS was in the possession of the Būlāq Press and was donated to the Bibliothèque Khédiviale (al-Kutubkhāna al-Khudaywiyya al-Miṣriyya), on 6 January 1895. Its shelf mark is:.نمره ١ يوميه. خصوصيه ١٤٢٥ تاريخ. عموميه ٢٨١٦

Under these lines, the stamp of the al-Kutubkhāna al-Khudaywiyya al-Miṣriyya is found. F. 1b starts with the text of volume II of the Būlāq edition: سنة تسعين وماية والف كان سلطان العصر فيها السلطان عبد الحميد ابن السلطان احمد خان العثماني ووالي مصر الوزير محمد باشا عزت... The colophon on f. 365a states that the MS was copied by Muḥammad Aḥmad al-Shāfi'ī: الى آخرها وهي طويلة وله غير ذلك سامحه الله تعالى، توفي في منتصف شهر شعبان من السنة وصلّى الله على سيدنا محمد النبي الامي الطاهر الزاكي كلما ذكره الذاكرون وغفل عنه الغافلون . تم هذا الجزء على يد الفقير الحقير المعترف بالذنب والتقصير محمد احمد الشافعي م غفر الله له ولوالديه ولكل المسلمين اجمعين آمين

VI. 18. c. MS *'Aj.* Tārīkh 1425/microfilm 19286, vol. III. F. 1b begins as follows: بسم الله الرحمن الرحيم. سـنـة ثلاثة عشـر ومايتين والف وهي اول سـني الملاحم العظيمة... This manuscript resembles MS *'Aj.* Cam., Qq. 171 (f. 168a) in that it ends with the month Dhu 'l-Ḥijja 1216 (4 April–2 May 1802) and similarly does not give the biographies of men who died that year, but continues directly with the events of 1217 [(/1802–3) (f. 392): وفي خامس عشرينه قبضوا على امراة سرقت امتعة من حمام وشنقوها عند باب زويلة. محرم الحرام ابتدآء[!] سنة الف ومائتين وسبعة عشر هجرية..., ('on the twenty-fifth a woman was caught stealing clothes at a bath and was hanged near Bāb Zuwayla, Muḥarram, the beginning of 1217 [/May

1802]'), while the biographies in the Būlāq edition take up ten pages (III, 210, l. 27–220, l. 10): [1216] وانقضت هذه السنة. ودفن بالاسكندرية. The Wahhābī proclamation of 29 Ṣafar 1218 (/19–20 June 1803) is cited in full: بسم الله الرحمن الرحيم... المارقين المتعصبين. Lines 1–4 in *'Aj.* Būlāq, III, 257 وقد بسط الكلام ... وغير ذلك. انتهى are missing.

The colophon on f. 655a states that the manuscript was copied at the end of Dhu 'l-Qaʿda 1287 (/20 February 1871] by Aḥmad Yūnis, Abu 'l-Taysīr: انه على كل شيء قدير وبالاجابة جدير. بخط الراجي عفو مولاه القدير احمد يونس ابو التيسير سنة ١٢٨٧ غاية القعدة.

The style resembles that of the Būlāq edition and of MS *'Aj.* Tārīkh 1426, vol. III (VI. 19. c.). For instance, on f. 390 we find: شهر الحجة الحرام سنة ١٢١٦ استهل بيوم الاحد. في رابعه حضر خمسة اشخاص ... فقابلوا حضرة والي مصر. This reads as *'Aj.* Būlāq (III, 211), whereas in MS *'Aj.* Cam., III, f. 167a, is found: حضرة الباشا *ḥaḍrat al-Bāshā* instead of حضرة والي مصر *ḥaḍrat wālī Miṣr*. This shows that they were written after 1806, the year in which al-Jabartī finished writing the third volume, one year after the official appointment of Muḥammad ʿAlī as *wālī* (governor) of Egypt.

VI. 18. d. MS *'Aj.* Tārīkh 1425/microfilm 12749 (negative) and 54400 positive, vol. IV. The manuscript is in 393 folios of 16.5 x 23 cm., each of 23 lines, written in a neat *ruq'a* script. F. 1a states that the MS was in the possession of the Būlāq Press and was donated to the Bibliothèque Khédiviale (al-Kutubkhāna al-Khudaywiyya al-Miṣriyya), on 6 January, 1895 and given the shelf mark: نمره ١ يوميه. خصوصية ١٤٢٥ تاريخ. عمومية ٢٨١٦٠. Under these lines, the stamp of the al-Kutubkhāna al-Khudaywiyya al-Miṣriyya is given. F. 1b starts with the text of volume IV of the Būlāq edition: بسم الله الرحمن الرحيم. وبه الاعانة. استهل شهر محرم الحرام الخميس سنة ١٢٢١ حسابا ويوم السبت هلالا... بيوم It starts with the year 1221 (/1806–7).

The colophon on f. 393a states that the manuscript was copied in 7 Rabīʿ II 1289 (/13–14 June 1872): ... والرطل السمن الى خمسين نصفا والى ستين نصفا وقس على ذلك. واما حادثة الاروام التي هي باقية الآن وما وقع منهم من الافساد وقطع الطريق على المسافرين ... وما ينتهى حالهم فسيتلى عليك ان شاء الله تعالي بكماله في الجزء الآتي بعد ذلك والله الموفق للصواب واليه المرجع والمآب .وكان الفراغ من كتابة هذا الجزء يوم الخميس المبارك سبعة ايام خلت من شهر ربيع الثاني سنة ١٢٨٩ من الهجرة النبوية على صاحبها افضل الصلوة والف تحية. تم.

This MS, which was in the possession of the Būlāq Press as mentioned in f. 1a of the MS, is very similar to the Būlāq edition and it seems therefore, that the editor used it in editing volume IV of the book.

VI. 19. c. MS *'Aj.* Tārīkh 1426/microfilm 35532, vol. III (the microfilm catalogue in the DKQ Reading Room states that it is volume I). This manuscript is in an 'ordinary' (*mu'tād*) handwriting, in 174 folios of 25 lines each. It is without a title-page and starts with the year 1213 (/1798–9).F. 1a states that this MS was in the possession of the Būlāq Press and was donated to the Bibliothèque Khédiviale (al-Kutubkhāna al-Khudaywiyya al-Miṣriyya), in Cairo in 1895 with the shelf mark: عدد ١. يوميه. خصوصية ١٤٢٦ تاريخ. عمومية ٢٨١٦١. with the stamp of al-Kutubkhāna al-Khudaywiyya al-Miṣriyya. F. 1b starts after the *basmala* with the events of the year 1213 (/1798–9): بسم الله الرحمن الرحيم. سنة ثلاثة عشر ومايتين والف وهي اول سني الملاحم العظيمة والحوادث الجسيمة ...

Like MS *'Aj.* Cam., Qq. 171, III, f. 141a it ends with the events of 25 Dhu 'l-Ḥijja 1216 (/28 April 1802) concerning the hanging of a woman, who stole from the public baths. There are no biographies of the personalities who died in 1216 (/1801–2). The narration continues directly with the events of the year 1217 (/1802–3). There are various changes to the sequence of events, style and contents. Many additional passages of the Būlāq edition are also found in this MS. Others passages are identical with *Maẓhar al-Taqdīs*. The *tā' marbūṭa* (ـة) is written with two dots, the *hamza* (in a word like *bā'i'* and not *bāyi'* as in al-Jabartī's handwriting.) is not written on *kursī yā'* (بائع). There are many spelling mistakes and missing paragraphs, while other paragraphs are given either in greater detail or are missing in the Būlāq edition and in all other manuscripts. There is no indication who copied this manuscript or why it differs so from all of the others.

In ff. 162b–163a, the month of Rabī' (al-Thānī) 1218 (/20 July–18 August 1803) the following information is added (cf. *'Aj.* Būlāq, III, 260), which does not occur in any other MS: وفيه وصلت مراكب من الديار الحجازية الى السويس وفيهم حجاج ومغاربة ولم يصل منها الا القليل واكثرهم قتله العسكر الذي بقي في مكة بعد موت شريف باشا. This added sentence in a MS, which was in the possession of the Būlāq Press and appears only in the Būlāq edition, is the best proof that the editor of this press used this MS and that MS *'Aj.* Tārīkh 1424/microfilm 14198 (17. c. above) in which the prose and poems were deleted, was based upon it.

It seems that this MS 19. c. was copied from MS *'Aj.* Tārīkh 1424/microfilm 14198 (VI. 17. c.), because they have the same colophon (f. 172b) and both have the words: وحسن به ختم [!] انتهى هذا الجزء الثالث من كتاب عجايب... while in the other MSS the sentence is: وحسن به ختم هذا الجزء الثالث من كتاب عجايب...: The colophon reads:

وبه ختمت دائرة المسلكين في الخلوتية ورجال السادة الصوفية. وحسن به ختم [!] انتهى هذا الجزء الثالث من كتاب عجايب الآثار في التراجم والأخبار لغاية سنة عشرين ومائتين والف من الهجرة النبوية. وسنقيد ان شاء الله سبحانه وتعالى ما تجدد بعدها من الحوادث من ابتدا سنة احدى وعشرين التي نحن بها الان ان امتد الاجل واسعف الامل ونرجوا [!] من الكريم المتعال صلاح الاحوال وانقشاع الهموم وصلاح العموم انه على كل شيء قدير وبالاجابة جدير. وصلى الله على سيدنا محمد النبي الأمي وعلى آله وصحبه وسلم تسليما كثيرا والحمد لله رب العالمين

The collation of this manuscript with other manuscripts of the same volume indicated that it contains passages which are identical to *Maẓhar al-Taqdīs* and that it contains passages not found in the autograph of MS *'Aj.* Cam., Qq. 171,III. This fact might confirm the suggestion that this volume has been revised and that it might well be that this MS was copied from the first draft of volume III before the decision of al-Jabartī to write the *'Ajā'ib al-Āthār* in three volumes in 1805.

VI. 19. d. MS *'Aj.* Tārīkh 1426/microfilm 38301, vol. IV (although the microfilm catalogue in the DKQ Reading Room states that it is volume II. The manuscript is in a neat and clear, 'ordinary' (*mu'tād*) script, in 244 folios. It starts with the year 1221 (/1806–7). There is no title page.

F. 1a reads: من كتبخانه مطبعة بولاق مجانا ومضاف في ٦ يناير سنة ١٨٩٥. عدد ١ يومية. خصوصية ١٤٢٦ تاريخ، عموميه ٢٨١٦١. It was donated to the Khedivial Library (later on Dār al-Kutub al-Qawmiyya) by the Library of the Būlāq Press on 6 January 1895.

The final page (f. 244a) states that the copying was at the end of Shawwāl 1296 (/17 October 1879), one year before it was printed in Būlāq Press. It ends with the events of the month Shawwāl 1236 (/1/2–29 July 1821) and not as in the Berlin MS (III. 9. d.) and the Būlāq edition with the events of Dhu 'l-Qaʿda. Moreover, it gives the year 1237 (/1821–2) as the end of the book, as follows:

وفيه سافر ايضا محمد كتخدا لاظ المنفصل من كتخدائيه [!] الى اسنا ليلقى القادمين ... وفيه وصلت بشاير من جهة قبلي باستيلاء اسمعيل باشا على سنار ... وهي حادثة الاروام وذلك الى هنا

انتهى ما نقل من خط العلامة الشيخ عبد الرحمن بن الشيخ حسن الجبرتي مورخ هذه المدة وما قبلها لغاية هذا التاريخ سنة ١٢٣٧ وهذا آخر / الجزء الرابع وبعده توفي الشيخ ولم يكتب شيء وصلى الله على / سيدنا محمد وعلى آله وصحبه وسلم . وتم كتابة في اواخر شهر شوال سنة ١٢٩٦ اللهم اغفر / لكاتبه ولجميع المسلمين / امين امين / امين

VI. 20. c. MS *'Aj.* Tārīkh 1427/microfilm 14201 (negative), vol. III. (Volumes I and II of this MS are missing). The manuscript is in a neat *ruq'a* script, in 204 unpaginated folios, each of 17 lines. F. 1a reads that it is the third volume: الجزء الثالث من الجبرتي Under the title is a statement that this manuscript was in the possession of the Library of the Būlāq Press and was donated to the Khedivial Library (later on Dār al-Kutub al-Qawmiyya) on 6 January, 1895: من كتبخانه مطبعة بولاق مجانا ومضاف في ٦ يناير سنة ١٨٩٥. نمره ١ يوميه، خصوصيه ١٤٢٧ تاريخ. عموميه ٢٨١٦٢. The stamp under these lines reads: الكتبخانة الخديوية المصرية al-Kutubkhāna al-Khudaywiyya al-Miṣriyya. On f. 1b there is a stamp reading: حسن ظني بالله ('my good trust in God'). The manuscript starts with the year 1221 (/1806–7) and so is the equivalent to volume IV of the Būlāq edition: بسم الله الرحمن الرحيم / سنة احدى وعشرين ومايتين والف،استهل شهرالمحرم بيوم الخميس حسابا... and ends with the year 1225 (/1810–11) (*'Aj.* Būlāq, IV, 126, l. 16). The colophon in f. 204a, after the biography of Muʿallim Jirjis al-Jawharī, reads:

ولازمته الامراض حتى مات وخلى (!) الجو للمعلم غالي وتعين بالتقدم ووافق الباشا في اغراضه ولكل شئ آخروالله اعلم . تم الجزؤ الثالث من الجبرتي ويليه بعون الله وتوفيقه الجزء الرابع والحمد لله وحده وصلى الله على سيدنا محمد وعلى آله وصحبه وسلم .

VI. 20. d. MS *'Aj.* Tārīkh 1427/microfilm 14202 (negative), vol. IV. The manuscript is in a neat *ruq'a* script in 189 paginated folios, each having 17 lines with a few corrections in the margins. F. 1a reads: هذا الجزء الرابع / من تأليف الشيخ عبد الرحمن بن الشيخ حسن الجبرتي غفرله . آمين. The word after الجزء has been crossed out and is unclear. Under the title, the date of the donation of the manuscript to the Khedivial Library (later on Dār al-Kutub al-Qawmiyya) from the Library of the Būlāq Press is given as 6 January 1895: من كتبخانه مطبعة بولاق مجانا ومضاف في ٦ يناير سنة ١٨٩٥. نمره ١ يوميه . خصوصيه ١٤٢٧ تاريخ . عموميه ٢٨١٦٢. There are two stamps under these lines. One reads: الكتبخانه الخديوية المصرية al-Kutubkhāna al-Khudaywiyya al-Miṣriyya. The other reads: حسن ظني بالله ('my good trust in God'). F. 1b starts with the year 1226 (/1811) instead of 1221 (/1806–7) as in *'Aj.* Būlāq, IV, and it reads:

بسم الله الرحمن الرحيم / واستهلت سنة ست وعشرين ومايتين والف فكان اول المحرم يوم السبت . فيها ظهر الباشا الاهتمام بامر الحجاز والتجهيز للسفر وركب في ليلة سابعه الى السويس وسافر صحبته السيد محمد المحروقي وقام باحتياجاته ولوازمه ولما وصل الى السويس حجز الدواب ...

The manuscript ends with the events of the year 1236 (/1820–1). The colophon states that the manuscript was copied on 18 Rabīʿ I 1292 (/25 April 1875) by al-Sayyid Yūsuf:

وانقضت هذه السنة ومابها من الحوادث التي انقضى بعضها والبعض باق الى الآن وهي حادثة الاروام. وهذا آخر ما كتب من خط الشيخ العلامة الشيخ عبد الرحمن بن حسن الجبرتي مؤرخ هذه المدة وما قبلها لغاية هذا التاريخ/ وكان الفراغ من كتابة هذا التاريخ المبارك يوم الجمعة المبارك الموافق لثمانية عشر خلت من شهر ربيع الاول ١٢٩٢ على يد ناسخها الفقير الراج يعفو ربه الكريم عبده السيد يوسف غفرالله له ولوالديه ولجميع المسلين والمسلمات الأحياء منهم والأموات انك سميع قريب مجيب الدعوات . وصلى الله على سيدنا محمد النبي الأمي وعلى آله وصحبه وسلم تسليما كثيرا والحمد لله رب العالمين

At the end of the colophon the stamp reads: الكتبخانة الخديوية المصرية al-Kutubkhāna al-Khudaywiyya al-Miṣriyya.

VI. 21. a. 1. MS *ʿAj.* Tārīkh 1428/microfilm 12748, vol. I, pt. 1, in 184 folios. F. 1a reads: الجزء الاول من تاريخ / الجبرتي رحمه الله / أمين. Under this short title the statement that the MSS was in Library of the Būlāq Press and was donated on 6 January 1895 to the Khedivial Library (later on Dār al-Kutub al-Qawmiyya): من كتبخانه مطبعة بولاق مجانا ومضاف في ٦ يناير سنة ١٨٩٥. عدد 1 يوميه. خصوصية ١٤٢٨ تاريخ . عمومية ٢٨١٦٣. Under these lines the stamp reads: الكتبخانه الخديوية المصرية al-Kutubkhāna al-Khudaywiyya al-Miṣriyya.

F. 1b starts according to the Cambridge autograph: بسم الله الرحمن الرحيم/ الحمد لله القديم الاول الذي لا يزول ملكه ولا يتحول خالق الخلايق وعالم الذرات بالحقايق...

F. 184 ends part 1 of volume I. It contains two seals of al-Kutubkhāna al-Khudaywiyya al-Miṣriyya and *Ḥusn Ẓannī bi ʾl-Lāh*. The end of this part reads: وهو مغطى الرأس فقبضوا عليه ونظروا في وجهه فوجدوه علي قرقاش فعرفوا عنه ابراهيم جاويش فامرالوالي بقتله فقتله والله اعلم بالحقايق والى هنا انتهى نصف الجزء الاول من تاريخ الجبرتي ويليه النصف الثاني وابتداؤه فصل وعود وانعطاف في ذكر حوادث مصر وترجم اعيانها وولاتها من ابتداء سنة ١١٦٢ الى آخرالسياق. والله اعلم بالصواب . تم. It starts with the events of the year 1162 (/1748–9).

VI. 21. a. 2. MS *ʿAj.* Tārīkh 1428/microfilm 12747 (negative), vol. I, pt. 2, in 438 pages of 27 lines each. F. 1a reads: بسم الله الرحمن الرحيم / فصل وعود وانعطاف في

ذكر حوادث مصر وتراجم اعيا[نها] من ابتداء سنة اثنين وستين وماية والف الى أواخر سنة ثلاث وسبعين وماية والف وذلك بحسب التيسيروالامكان وما لا يدرك كله لا يترك كله . فنقول لما عدى الجناب المكرم حضرة محمد باشا راغب في الواقعة التي خرج فيها حسنين بيك الخشاب ... It starts with the events of the year 1162 (/1748–9) and ends with the events of the year 1173 (/1759–60).On page 438 the stamp reads: al-Kutubkhāna al-Khudaywiyya al-Miṣriyya and the colophon states that it was copied on 29 Safar 1290 (/27 April 1873) by Riḍwān al-Damanhūjī b. Muṣṭafā al-Damanhūjī:

وهي طويلة وله غير ذلك سامحه الله . توفي في منتصف شهر شعبان من السنة غفر الله لنا وله ولوالدينا وللمسلمين بمنه وكرمه وكان الفراغ من كتابة هذا الجزء ليلة الثلاث االمبارك عشرين خلت (!) من شهر (!) تسع وعشرين خلت من صفر سنة ١٢٩٠ من الهجرة النبوية على صاحبه افضل الصلاة والسلام على يد الفقير المضطرالى رحمة ربه القدير رضوان الدمنهوجي ابن مصطفى الدمنهوجي عفى عنه والصلاة والسلام على أشرف المرسلين آمين . تم .

VI. 21. a. MS *'Aj.* Tārīkh Taymūr 1562/microfilm 27775, vol. I, in 660 pages of 35 lines each, written in a neat *naskhī*, in 33 *karārīs*. The number of the fascicle is given on the left side. It starts with the contents of volume I. P. 1 of the MS reads: الجزء الاول من تاريخ /الجبرتي رحمه الله / أمين. The oval stamp reads: وقف/ احمد بن اسماعيل/ بن محمد تيمور بمصر 1903/ 1320. P. 2 reads: بسم الله الرحمن الرحيم وبه توفيقي. الحمد لله القديم الاول. The last page (p. 659) gives the colophon which states that the MS was copied on 20 Jumada (sic] 1281 (/20–1 October 1864) without stating the name of the copyist:

حمى الله مرقاها ومعراج قدسها   بكوكبها السامي الذي ليس يلحق

الى آخرها وهي طويلة / وله غير ذلك سامحه الله . توفي في منتصف شهر شعبان من السنة / غفرالله وله ولوالدينا وللمسلمين بمنه وكرمه / وكان الفراغ من كتابة هذاالجزء يوم الاربع / المبارك الموافق لعشرين خلت من شهرجمادى الواقع في شهور سنة / الف ومايتين واحد وثمانين / وصلى الله على / سيدنا / محمد وعلى آله / وصحبه / وسلم .

VI. 21. b. MS *'Aj.* Tārīkh Taymūr 1562/microfilm 27762, vol. II, 716 pages. P. 1 gives the contents (*fihris*) with the number of the page and the year. The title page states that this is volume II of *'Ajā'ib al-Āthār*...known as the Chronicle (*Ta'rīkh*) of al-Jabartī, from Rabīʿ II 1213 (/12 September 1798) until the end of the year 1220 (/21 March 1806): الجزء الثاني / من عجائب الأثار المشهور بتاريخ/ الجبرتي من ربيع الثاني سنة ١٢١٣ الى أخر سنة ١٢٢٠.

There are no biographies of those who died in 1216 (/1801–2); that year ends with the event of the hanging of a woman, who stole clothes from a public bath (p.

في خامس عشرينه قبضوا على امرأة سرقت امتعة من حمام وشنقوها عند باب زويلة. سنة سبع :(433 عشرومائتين والف استهل المحرم بيوم الاثنين فيه تواترت الاخبار بحصول الصلح العمومى بين القرانات جميعا ورفع الحروب في ما بينهم . وفيه ترادفت الاخبار بامر عبد الوهاب وظهورشأنه...

Pp. 717–18 states that it was copied in Ṣafar [12]86 (/12 May–10 June 1869): ورجال السادة الصوفية وحسن به ختم هذا الجزء الثالث من كتاب عجايب الآثار في التراجم والاخبار لغاية سنة عشرين ومائتين والف من الهجرة النبوية على صاحبها...وسنقيد ان شاء الله تعالى ما يتجدد بعدها من الحوادث من ابتداء سنة احدى وعشرين التي / نحن بها الآن ان امتد الاجل... وبالاجابة جدير. قد تم هذا / الجزء في يوم الاثنين / من شهر صفر سنة / ستة وثمانين / ممم.

VI. 21. c. MS *'Aj.* Tārīkh Taymūr 1562/microfilm 28298, vol. III, 776 pages of 25 lines each, written in *naskhī* script.

VI. 21.d. MS *'Aj.* Tārīkh Taymūr 1562/microfilm 282980, vol. IV. The manuscript begins with a page giving the contents of the book arranged chronologically according to the year of the events and biographies. It starts with the year 1221 (/1806–7) بسم الله الرحمن الرحيم / سنة ١٢٢١ احدى وعشرين ومايتان والف / استهل شهر المحرم بيوم الخميس حسابا ويوم السبت هلالا...

The title page states wrongly that this volume is the 'third' and last volume of *'Ajā'ib al-Āthār*:الثالث / وهو الاخير من عجائب الآثار للجبرتي P. 775 ends with the events of Shawwāl 1236 (/1/2–29 July 1821). The colophon gives no date or name of copyist, but states that the manuscript was copied from an autographof the author and that it is the end of volume IV, after which the author died and wrote no more (sic]. It gives the same colophon as the Būlāq edition:

وضربت لذلك مدافع من القلعة وانقضت ...واستهل شهر شوال فيه خرجت عساكرومعهم روساوهم هذه السنة ومابها من الحوادث / التي انقضى بعضها والبعض باق الى الآن / وهي حادثة الاروام وذلك الى هنا انتهى / ما نقل من خط العلامة الشيخ / عبدالرحمن بن الشيخ / حسن الجبرتي مؤرخ هذه المدة وما قبلها / لغاية هذا / التاريخ / وهذا / آخر / الجزءالرابع وبعده توفي الشيخ ولم يكتب شيء.

VI. 22. a. 1. MS *'Aj.* Tārīkh 1872/microfilm 35762 (positive), vol. I, pt. I, in 246 unpaginated folios of 25 lines each, written in *Maghribī naskhī* script, only the fascicles are numbered. Each folio has double frame lines. A few corrections in the margin are in the same hand. The title page on f. 1a is in the shape of a triangle, giving the number of the volume. It starts: الجزء الاول من تاريخ الجبرتي. Under the title: خصوصية ١٨٧٢ تاريخ عمومية ٣٧٨٣٨. Under this line is a stamp reading: الكتبخانة الخديوية المصرية al-Kutubkhāna al-Khudaywiyya al-Miṣriyya. F. 1b starts: بسم الله الرحمن الرحيم / وبه نستعين، الحمد لله القديم الاول

The manuscript covers the events of the years 1101–89 (/1689–1776). The colophon on f. 246a states that it contains the first half of *'Ajā'ib al-Āthār* and was copied in Jumādā II 1295 (/2 June–1 July 1878): فامر الوالي بقتله فقتله والله اعلم بالحقايق و الى هنا انتهى نصف الجزء الاول ويليه النصف الثاني واوله فصل عود وانعطاف في ذكر من سنة الف ومائة واثنين وستين[1162] الى آخر السياق وذلك في يوم الاربعاء من ...حوادث مصر شهر جمادى الآخرة سنة ١٢٩٥ نسأل الله تعالى تمام الباقي في خير وسرور وصلى الله على سيدنا محمد وعلى آله واصحابه / اجمعين امين. تم.

VI. 22. a. 2. MS *'Aj.* Tārīkh 1872/microfilm 40549 (positive), vol. I, pt. II, in 284b ff. In f. 1a in the shape of an inverted triangle: ابتداء النصف الثاني من الجزء الاول من تاريخ الجبرتي Under the triangle the number of the MS is: خصوصية ١٨٧٢ تاريخ عمومية ٣٧٨٣٨. The stamp reads: الكتبخانة الخديوية المصرية al-Kutubkhāna al-Khudaywiyya al-Miṣriyya.

VI. 22. b. MS *'Aj.* Tārīkh 1872/microfilm 35738, and 35824, vol. II, in 328 unpaginated folios, of 25 lines each, written in *Maghribī naskhī* script. Only the fascicles are numbered. Each folio has double frame lines and few corrections in the margin in the same hand. The manuscript covers the events of the years 1190–1212 (/1776–98). The title page on f. 1a is in the shape of a triangle, and starts with: الجزء الثاني من تاريخ الجبرتي Under the title is: خصوصية ١٨٧٢ تاريخ عمومية ٣٧٨٣٨ Under this line is a stamp reading: الكتبخانة الخديوية المصرية al-Kutubkhāna al-Khudaywiyya al-Miṣriyya.

F. 1b starts as follows: بسم الله الرحمن الرحيم وصلى الله على سيدنا محمد وعلى آله وصحبه وسلم تسلما كثيرا دائما سرمدا / سنة تسعين ومائة والف [1190] / كان سلطان العصر فيها السلطان عبد الحميد بن احمد خان العثماني..

F. 328a, like no. 17. b. above and the Būlāq edition, ends without a colophon, but with a long poem in praise of the family of al-Wafā, with the following lines:

بكوكبها السامي الذي لا ليس يلحق   حمى الله مرقاها ومعراج قدسها

توفي في منتصف شهر شعبان من السنة غفر الله لنا وله ولوالدينا ...الى آخرها وهي طويلة وللمسلمين بمنه وكرمه آمين / وصلى الله على سيدنا محمد النبي الامي / وعلى آله وصحبه وسلم آمين تم .

VI. 22. c. MS *ʿAj.* Tārīkh 1872/microfilm 35107, vol. III, in 396 unpaginated folios, of 25 lines each, in a clear *naskhī* script; only the fascicles are numbered. Each folio has double frame lines; a few corrections in the margin are in the same hand. The title page on f. 1a is in the shape of a triangle and stating that it is volume III: الجزء الثالث من تاريخ الجبرتي واوله سنة ثلاثة عشرومائتين والف مخصوصية ١٨٧٢ تاريخ عمومية ٣٧٨٣٨. Under this line, a stamp reads: الكتبخانة الخديوية المصرية al-Kutubkhāna al-Khudaywiyya al-Miṣriyya, with a square stamp giving the date: 12.2.[19]27.

It starts with the events of the year 1213 (/1798–9); F. 1b starts: بسم الله الرحمن الرحيم وبه نستعين / سنة ثلاثة عشر ومائتين والف [1213] وهي اول سنى "المترجم" العظيمة والحوادث الجسيمة وفي يوم الأحد العاشر من شهر محرم الحرام من هذه السنة وردت مكاتبات .

In this MS the copyist admits in the colophon of volume IV that he has changed some expressions. One of these is the conversation between Muḥammad ʿAlī and the common soldier who insulted him, as mentioned above in MS *ʿAj.* Ber., 9489 (III. 9. c.). The realistic original answer of the soldier given in MS *ʿAj.* Cam., Qq. 171,III, reads: فقال له أما تخاف من الباشا؟ فقال الباشا على زبي، فضربه الباشا وقتله. ('He said to him, "Aren't you afraid of the Pasha?" He replied, 'The Pasha is on my penis, [at which point] the Pasha knocked him down, killing him'.) The changed version in MS *ʿAj.* Ber., 9489, III, f. 446 b, reads:

> قال له : أما تخاف من الباشا؟ فقال : الباشا على كين وكيب (!) [= كيت وكيت] فضربه الباشا وقتله.
>
> 'He said to him, "Aren't you afraid of the Pasha?" He replied, 'The Pasha is a so and so, [at which point] the Pasha knocked him down, killing him'. This same version is found in *ʿAjā'ib al-Āthār*in the margin of Ibn al-Athīr's book. The colophon on f. 396a ends with the year 1220 (/1805–6): وحسن به ختم هذا الجزء الثالث ... بعدها من الحوادث من ابتداء سنة احدى وعشرين...وانقشاع الهموم ... وصلى الله على سيدنا محمدا لنبي الكريم والصادق الامين .

VI. 22. d. MS *ʿAj.* Tārīkh 1872/microfilm 41211 (positive), vol. IV, in 352 unpaginated folios, of 25 lines each, in ordinary *naskhī* script rubricated in a doublelined square frame and only the fascicles are numbered. Each folio has double frame lines. There are a few corrections in the margin in the same hand. The title page on f. 1a is in the shape of a triangle, and starts: الجزء الرابع من تاريخ العلامة الشيخ الجبرتي رحمه الله آمين. Under the title:.خصوصية ١٨٧٢ تاريخ عمومية ٣٧٨٣٨ Under this line, there is a stamp reading: الكتبخانة الخديوية المصرية al-Kutubkhāna al-Khudaywiyya al-Miṣriyya.

F. 1b starts with the events of the year 1221 (/1806–7): / بسم الله الرحمن الرحيم / ثم دخلت سنة ١٢٢١ احدى وعشرين ومايتين والف / استهل شهر محرم فيها يوم الخميس حسابا ويوم السبت هلالا... Some words, left unfinished at the ends of lines, have been completed in the margins. A few corrections and omitted sentences have been added in the margins, like in MS *'Aj.* Cam. In fascicle no. 25, f. 1, the accounts of Dhu 'l-Ḥijja (1216) (/4 April–2 May 1802) start.

In f. 2b, as in the case of the Būlāq edition, there are the biographies of those who died in 1216 (/1801–2):

في خامس عشرينه قبضوا على امراة سرقت امتعة من حمام وشنقوها عند باب زويلة . وفي غايته تواترت الاخبار بوقوع الصلح العمومى بين القرانات جميعا ورفع الحروب فيما بينهم. وفيه تواترت الاخبار بظهور عبد الوهاب النجدي واستفحال امره ... وانقضت هذه السنة وما تجدد فيها من الحوادث التي من جملتها ان شريف افندي ... واما من مات في هذه السنة الشيخ ... مصطفى بن احمد المعروف بالصاوي ...

In fascicle 30, f. 3a the Wahhābī proclamation is given in a summarized form. The colophon on f. 352b states that the manuscript was copied on 10 Ṣafar 1296 (/2 February 1879) from an autograph of the author, and that the copyist took the liberty to change some indecent expressions, such as in the events of Rajab 1219 (/6 October–2 November 1804) which deal with Muḥammad ʿAlī and the soldier who insulted him, as mentioned in III. 9. c. MS *'Aj.* Ber., 9489,Or. Qu. 673, vol. III, and MS *'Aj.* Tārīkh 1872 (VI. 22. c.).

As in the case of *'Aj.* Būlāq, I, 387, the copyist of this MS, out of modesty, also changed the rhyming word of the verse where a paronomasia is used in the mosaic rhyme with a rather vulgar double entendre, hinting at her Amharic background as well. In MS *'Aj.* Cam. the verse ends with the rhyme *am ḥirī*:

فطفقت أسأل عن نعومة ما خفا قالت فما تبتغيه جنسي أم حِرى

('Then I asked about the softness of what was hidden. She said: "Are you asking about my race or about my vulva?"'.), while in this MS the rhyme is '*amḥarī*':('who knows even the atoms of reality'

فطفقت أسأل عن نعومة ما خفا قالت فما تبتغيه جنسي **أمحرى**

This joining of the two words, changes the meaning into a decent expression ('Then I asked about the softness of what was hidden. She said: "Why ask? I am of the Amharic race!"'), which was copied by the Būlāq editor. In the colophon the copyist says that this is the end of what he has copied from an autograph by the author, after which the author stopped writing any more. He asks forgiveness from God for changing some expressions of the author:

والى هنا انتهى ...وانقضت هذه السنة وما بها من الحوادث التي انقضى بعضها والبعض باق الى الآن ما نقل من خط العلامة الشيخ عبد الرحمن ابن الشيخ حسن الجبرتي مؤرخ هذه المدة وما قبلها لغاية هذا التاريخ وهذا آخر الجزء الرابع ثم توفي الشيخ ولم يكتب شيء[!] بعد ذلك / غفر الله لمؤلفه ولمن اطلع عليه وغض النظر عما هو مكنون في باطنه والتمس عذرا لمؤلفه / وناسخه وصلى الله على سيدنا محمد النبي الامي وعلى اله وصحبه وسلم تسليما كثيرا والحمد لله رب العالمين ولا حول ولا قوة الا بالله العلي العظيم . اللهم لا تؤاخذنا بما حصل منا في ذلك الكتاب من بعض تغيير لبعض الفاظ المؤلف وعافنا واعف عنا ولا تؤاخذنا بما فعل السفهاء / وكان تمام نسخه في يوم السبت الموافق ستة عشر شهر صفر سنة الف ومايتين وستة وتسعين هجرية / وصلى الله على خاتم النبيين وسيد المرسلين سيدنا محمد النبي الهاشمي وعلى آله واصحابه والتابعين / وارضى [!] عنا بهم يا رب العالمين / تم .

This colophon is significant not only because it is said to have been copied from an autograph, but also because this is the first time a copyist states that he seeks to 'overlook the hidden content of the book' (وغض النظر عما هو مكنون في باطنه) This seems to hint at al-Jabartī's criticism of Muḥammad ʿAlī and the realistic approach of al-Jabartī, quoting vulgar expressions such as the paragraph mentioned above, when he relates the encounter of the soldier and the Pasha. Possibly the copyist feared that he could be punished for copying the fourth volume with its harsh criticism of the Egyptian ruler. Moreover, this is, as far as we know, the first time that a redactor of al-Jabartī's work confessed that he had taken the liberty to change the author's wording. It is clear that he changed not only the content of some indecent expressions, as we have shown above, but also the style and grammatical structure. The redactor's confession is of great importance since it may indicate that the editor of the Būlāq Press possibly based his edition upon this MS which contains edifications of the grammatical and stylistic structure of al-Jabartī's autograph. The MS was in the possession of the Būlāq Press. The fact that it was copied in 1296 (/1878–9), a year before the book was printed, and that its wording is the closest to the Būlāq edition, may indicate that it was a version made especially for the edition of the Būlāq Press.

VI. 23. a. 1. MS *ʿAj.* Tārīkh 2129/microfilm 38169, vol. I, pt. 1, written in 240 folios in ordinary handwriting. The shelf-mark is given as: خصوصية ٢١٢٩ تاريخ عمومية ٤٤٦٩٥. On the side of the manuscript is written: 'this is a section of an unknown chronicle, the first and the last parts [are missing]': قطع من تاريخ مجهول من الاول والآخر

The first folios are missing. The manuscript starts with the following sentence:...وينهبوا البيت ... عسكر تقويه الى ايوب بيك وعليهم سردار وبيرقا وكذلك العزب

VI. 23. a. 2. MS *'Aj.* Tārīkh 2129/microfilm 14676, vol. I, pt. 2, in 240ff.,written in ordinary handwriting. The title page states that 'this is the beginning of the second half of volume I': هذا ابتداء النصف الثاني من الجزء الاول من تاريخ الاستاذ الشيخ عبد الرحمن الجبرتي رحمه الله ورحم اسلافه وابتداؤه كما ترى والحمد لله. Beside this title the following words are written:٢١٢٩ تاريخ . ١٣٢٠ سنة Under these lines there are two oval stamps, the first: ابراهيم محمود Ibrāhīm Maḥmūd and under it: السكة الحديدية 'the Railway', the second stamp: 1340 دار الكتب المصرية Dār al-Kutub al-Miṣriyya, and on the left side of the folio is the number 3280 and under it the date 1934.

F. 1b starts with the events of 1162 (/1748–9) in the following sentence: بسم الله الرحمن الرحيم الحمد لله رب العالمين والصلاة والسلام على اشرف المرسلين سيدنا محمد وعلى آله وصحبه اجمعين . فَصْل وعود وانعطاف في ذكر حوادث مصر وتراجم اعيانها وولاتها ابتداء سنة ١١٦٢ اثنين وستين ومائة والف وذلك حسب التيسير والامكان وما لا يدرك كله لا يترك كله . فنقول لما عزل المكرم حضرة محمد باشا راغب وكان الكاشف بالبحيرة اذ ذاك حسن اغا كتخدا ...

The MS ends on f. 281a with the end of volume I of the Būlāq edition, without colophon: وسيتلى عليك من ذلك أنبا واخبار وما حل بالاقليم بسببهم من الخراب والدمار وصلى الله على سيدنا محمد وعلى آله وصحبه وسلم تسليما كثيرا . تم .

This manuscript resembles MSS nos. 13, 16, 22 of Dār al-Kutub al-Qawmiyya in Cairo.

VI. 23. c. MS *'Aj.* Tārīkh 2129/microfilm 36545, vol. III, paginated 368 folios each of 23 lines, in *naskhī* script. There are very few corrections in the margins. It is important to note that this MS is similar to the Būlāq edition.

F. 1a states that this is 'volume III, of *'Ajā'ib al-Āthār*... to the end of 1216 (/1802)': .الجزء الثالث من كتاب عجايب الآثار في التراجم والاخبار لغاية ١٢١٦ F. 1b reads from the year 1213 (/1798–9): بسم الله الرحمن الرحيم / سنة ١٢١٣ سنة ثلاثة عشر ومائتين والف وهي اول سنى الملاحم العظيمة. Some pages are half-blank (بياض), but there are no lacuna: f. 39a is half blank: على النيل المعروف بتل العقارب بالناصرية ابنية وكرانك

(بياض) وابراج ; f. 39b: ووضعوافيها عدة من الآلات الحرب ; f. 45b: ١٢١٣ شهر شعبان ; f. 68b: ١٢١٣ شهر الحجة.

The colophon on ff. 367b–368a reads as in the case of the Būlāq edition:

السادة الصوفية. وحسن به ختم هذا الجزؤ الثالث من كتاب عجائب الآثار في التراجم والاخبار لغاية سنة عشرين ومائتين والف من الهجرة النبوية على صاحبها افضل الصلاة / والسلام وسنقيد ان شاء الله ما يتجدد بعدها من الحوادث ابتدى سنة احدى وعشرين التي نحن بها الآن ان امتد الاجل واسعف الامل ونرجوا من الكريم المتعال صلاح الاحوال وانقشاع الهموم وصلاح العموم انه على كل شي قدير وبالاجابة جدير وصلى الله على سيدنا محمد وعلى آله وصحبه وسلم .

Words and names that were not clear to the copyist are left blank (e.g. f. 358b).

VI. 24. a. MS *ʿAj.* Tārīkh 2287 badal/microfilm 35946, vol. I, in 350 rubricated folios each of 25 lines, in a thick *Maghribī naskhī* script; only the fascicles are numbered. The title page (f. 1a) states that it is volume I and that it was in the possession of the celebrated poet, soldier and politician Maḥmūd Sāmī al-Bārūdī (1839–1904) in the year 1285 (/1868–9). He established the Khedivial Library and later became the Minister of War, and participated in ʿUrābī Pasha's revolt of 1882, joining ʿUrābī in his resistance to the British invasion of Egypt. In consequence al-Bārūdī was exiled to Ceylon. It reads as follows: / تاريخ ٢٢٨٧ بدل . الاول / هذا كتاب عجائب الآثار في التراجم والاخبار جمع العالم العلامة الشيخ عبد الرحمن ابن حسن الجبرتي الحنفي عفي عنه م وصلى الله علي سيدنا محمد وعلي آله . وصحبه وسلم م / من كتب الفقير الى الله تعالى محمود سامي الشهير بالبارودي سنة ١٢٨٥ . Under this title there is an oval stamp reading: دار الكتب المصرية Dār al-Kutub al-Miṣriyya. F. 1b reads: ... بسم الله الرحمن الرحيم/ الحمد لله القديم الاول

The MS contains the events of the years 1101–89 (/1689–1776), as in the Būlāq edition. In the colophon on f. 350a the name of the copyist is not mentioned; it was copied in 26 Dhu 'l-? [missing] 1261 (/26–7 November or 25 December 1845): ... من الخراب والدمار ... / تم الجزء الاول من تاريخ الجبرتي / ويليه الجزء الثاني / وذلك / في يوم الجمعة ٢٦ من ذي [!] سنة ١٢٦١ / تم . وصلى الله على سيدنا محمد وعلى آله وصحبه وسلم امين تم

VI. 24. b. MS *'Aj.* Tārīkh badal 2287/microfilm 35959, vol. II, in 240 unpaginated folios, of 25 lines each, written in *Maghribī* script. Only the fascicles are numbered. The beginning of each paragraph is indicated by a red line under the last letter of the words. F. 1b starts with the year 1190 (/1776–7) and ends in 1212 (/1798): بسم الله الرحمن الرحيم/ سنة تسعين ومائة والف / كان سلطان العصر فيها السلطان عبد الحميد بن احمد خان العثماني...

F. 1a states that in 1285 (/1868–9) the MS was in the library of Maḥmūd Sāmī al-Bārūdī: جـ ٢ تاريخ ٢٢٨٧ بدل .من كتب الفقيرالى الله تعالى محمود سامي الشهير بالبارودي سنة ١٢٨٥. Under this title there is an oval stamp reading: محمود سامي Maḥmūd Sāmī. Therefore this MS belongs to Maḥmūd Sāmī al-Bārūdī. Under this line there is yet another oval stamp: دار الكتب الخديوية Dār al-Kutub al-Khudaywiyya.

The colophon on f. 245b does not mention the name of the copyist and states that this is the end of volume II and that it will be followed by volume III: في منتصف شعبان من السنة توفي [حسين ... المنزلاوي الشافعي] غفر الله لنا وله بمنه وكرمه . تم الجزء الثاني من تاريخ الجبرتي ويليه الجزء الثالث بحمد الله وعونه / وصلى الله على سيدنا محمد ... وصحبه وسلم آمين/ تم / This colophon is followed by an oval stamp reading دار: الكتب المصرية Dār al-Kutub al-Miṣriyya.

VI. 24. c. 1. MS *'Aj.* Tārīkh 2287 *badal*/microfilm 35385, vol. III, pt. 1, in 346 unpaginated folios, of 25 lines each, in a *Maghribī* script, only the fascicles are numbered. F. 1a states that this is volume III, pt. 1, and that it was in the possession of Maḥmūd Sāmī al-Bārūdī in 1285 (/1868–9): القسم الاول من الجزء الثالث من كتب الفقير الى الله تعالى محمود سامي الشهير بالبارودي سنة ١٢٨٥ [sic]. Under this title there is an oval stamp reading: دار الكتب الخديوية (Dār al-Kutub al-Khudaywiyya). Under the oval stamp the dates سنة ١٦٦٤ ١٩٢٥ [!] appear. F. 1b starts with the events of 1213 (/1798–9): بسم الله الرحمن الرحيم / سنة ثلاثة عشرومايتين والف / وهي اول سنى الملاحم العظيمة... It ends with the events of 1220 (/1805–6).

The colophon of f. 346a corresponds with the end of volume III, 357 of the Būlāq edition and the Beirut Dār al-Fāris edition, III, 110. The manuscript ends with the following sentence:

... السادة الصوفية وحسن به ختم هذا الجزء الثالث من والله اعلم انتهى / تم بحمد الله وعونه كتاب عجائب الآثار في التراجم والأخبار لغاية سنة عشرين ومايتين وألف [1220] من الهجرة النبوية وسنقيد إن شا الله سبحانه وتعالى ما يتجدد بها من الحوادث من ابتدا سنة احدى وعشرين [1221] التي نحن بها الآن ان امتد الاجل واسعف الامل ونرجو من الكريم المتعال صلاح الاحوال ... انه على كل شيء قدير ... توفيقه / آمين/ م.

This MS resembles the Beirut edition of Dār al-Fāris (II, 518) in that it deletes all the poems and literary parts of the biographies, and thus condenses the book into three volumes instead of four. Volume III of this edition contains the last part of volume III and the whole of volume IV of the Būlāq edition. It resembles MS *'Aj.* Ber., III, ff. 315a–326a (III. 9. c.) and *'Aj.* Būlāq, III, 211–20, in that it has (in fascicle 21, f.12b–fascicle 22, f. 6b) the biographies of those who died in the year 1216 (/1801–2), which are lacking in MS *'Aj.* Cam., Qq. 171, III (III. 1. c.)

VI. 24. c. 2. MS *'Aj.* Tārīkh *badal* 2287/microfilm 35547, III, pt. 2, in 283 unpaginated folios, of 25 lines each, in *Maghribī* script. Only the fascicles are numbered. It starts with the events of volume IV dealing with the year 1221 (/1806–7) which is similar to the edition of Dār al-Fāris, Beirut. There are many calligraphic mistakes, such as المقري for المغري (fasc. 12, ff. 2b–3a), الفلقي for القلعي (ibid.) etc.

F. 1a starts with: تاريخ٢٢٨٧ بدل / القسم الثاني من الجزء الثالث .من كتب الفقير الى الله تعالى/ محمود سامي [sic] Maḥmūd Sāmī. الشهيربالباروي سنة ١٢٨٥/١٦٦٤/١٩٢٥. Under this title there is an oval stamp reading: محمود سامي Maḥmūd Sāmī and under it is yet another oval stamp reading: دار الكتب المصرية (Dār al-Kutub al-Miṣriyya). Under the stamps appears the date 1925 سنة. F. 1b starts with the events of the year 1221 (/1806–7): بسم الله الرحمن الرحيم / سنة احدى وعشرين ومايتين والف استهل شهر المحرم بيوم الخميس حسابا ويوم السبت هلالا

The MS ends with the events of the year 1236 (/1820–1) and the colophon states that the continuation of the events of volume IV will be discussed in full in the following volume. The colophon states that it was copied on 25 Dhu 'l-Ḥijja 1262 (/14 December 1846) from an autograph by al-Jabartī without mentioning the name of the copyist: واما حادثة الاروام ... وما وقع معهم من الوقايع وما سينتهي حالهم اليه فسيتلى عليك ان شأ الله بكماله في الجزء الآتي بعد ذلك والله الموفق للصواب واليه المرجع والمآب . تم لسنة ستة وثلاثين [1236] ونقل هذا من نسخة بخط العلامة الفاضل الشيخ عبد الرحمن ابن الشيخ حسن الجبرتي المؤرخ في ٢٥ الحجة تمام ١٢٦٢ وصلى الله على سيدنا محمد وعلى آله وصحبه وسلم آمين تم .

This colophon resembles the end of volume III, 630 of the Beirut, Dār al-Fāris edition which states that it was copied from an autograph by al-Jabartī and that the continuation of the events of volume IV will be discussed in full in the following volume: وأما حادثة الاروام ... وما وقع معهم من الوقايع وما سينتهي حالهم اليه

فسيتلى عليك ان شأ الله بكماله في الجزء الآتي بعد ذلك والله الموفق للصواب واليه المرجع والمآب . الى هنا انتهى [ما] نقل من خط العلامة الشيخ عبد الرحمن ابن الشيخ حسن الجبرتي مؤرخ هذه المدة وما قبلها لغاية هذا التاريخ سنة ١٢٣٦. وهذا آخر الجزء وبعده توفي الشيخ ولم يكتب شيئا .

Although this MS, which resembles the Beirut Dār al-Fāris edition, omits all the poems and literary sections and the obituaries, the editor still claims that it was copied from an autograph of al-Jabartī. The Beirut Dār al-Fāris edition contains three volumes which are equivalent to the Būlāq edition in four volumes, because this MS, volume III consisting of two parts, is equivalent to the complete volume III of the Cambridge autograph, with the second part equivalent to volume IV of the Būlāq edition.

VII. In Dār al-Kutub wa 'l-Wathā'iq al-Qawmiyya, Cairo, there is a collection of manuscripts entitled 'al-Zakiyya'. According to Jurjī Zaydān, al-Khizāna (Library) al-Zakiyya belonged to Aḥmad Zakī Pāshā.[69] The authorities of the Egyptian National Library in Cairo were kind enough to allow the writer of these lines to examine all the MSS of *'Ajā'ib al-Āthār* in this collection after being copied by microfilm at their National Library. Therefore it seems that Aḥmad Zakī Pāshādonated this collection to the Wizārat al-Awqāf (Ministry of Endowments) and from there it was moved to the Egyptian National Library.[70] This collection is of great importance since MSS al-Zakiyya nos. 858 (vol. II) and 859 (vol. III) were copied in 1237 (/1821–2) and read in 1240 (/1824–5) to its author, ʿAbd al-Raḥmān al-Jabartī after he became blind. According to Jurjī Zaydān,[71] there was in Maktabat Muḥammad Bek Āṣaf a copy of *'Ajā'ib al-Āthār* which was copied in 1237 (/1821–2) and read to al-Jabartī in 1240 (/1824–5). In fact, at Dār al-Kutub al-Qawmiyya in Cairo, there are two MSS, in al-Zakiyya collection of *'Ajā'ib al-Āthār*, namely, al-Zakiyya nos. 858 and 859, which were copied inj 1237 (/1821–2) and read to al-Jabartī by Aḥmad Ḥasan al-Rashīdī al-Shāfiʿī known as Ṣawbaʿ.[72] It is most likely that these two

69 On al-Zakiyya (al-Khizāna al-Zakiyya which belonged to Aḥmad Zākī Pāshā the secretary of Majlis al-Nuẓẓār [Council of Ministers]), see Jurjī Zaydān, *Kitāb Tārīkh Ādāb al-Lugha al-'Arabiyya*, Cairo, Maṭbaʿat al-Hilāl, 1937, IV, 107. This Khizāna (Library) has a MS of the *History* of Ibn Khaldūn copied by Ḥasan al-ʿAṭṭār.

70 See Zaydān, *Ādāb*, 1937, IV, 245; cf. the new edition by Shawqī Ḍayf, IV, 256.

71 Zaydān, *Ādāb*, 1937, IV, 108; cf. the new edition by Shawqī Ḍayf, IV, 114.

72 See the last folios of MS *'Aj.* al-Zakiyya, 858 (vol. II), and 859 (vol. III), where the copyist states that he ended the reading and copying the MS in the presence of al-Jabartī on 14 Rabīʿ Awwal 1240 (/6 November 1824).

MSS originally belonged to al-Maktaba al-Āṣafiyya which was owned by Muḥammad Bek Āṣaf Ibn ʿAlī Pāshā Āṣaf who was the nephew of Aḥmad Bek Taymūr.[73] Jurjī Zaydān was informed by Muḥammad Bek Āṣaf that the latter was intending to endow his library to one of the Egyptian scientific institutions. It is possible to presume, according to the seals in these two MSS, that Muḥammad Bek Āṣaf died before endowing them to any Egyptian institution so that they went to the Ministry of Endowments and were later presented to al-Zakiyya Library.[74]

The importance of these two MSS is that the date of reading them in the presence of al-Jabartī in 1240 (/1824–5) indicates clearly that the author was still alive by then and not, as some colophons of other MSS state, that al-Jabartī died soon after he ended writing his fourth volume, i.e. in 1237 (/1821–2). Secondly, it should be noted that these two MSS, which were the last to be copied during the life of the author, are identical with the Cambridge autographs of al-Jabartī, therefore we can be sure that the version of the Būlāq edition was based upon MSS, which have gone through the 'correction' of style, grammatical usage and the misreading of personal names and places as well as several homoeoteleuton by copyists.

VII. 25. b. MS *'Aj.* al-Zakiyya, 852/microfilm 9217 (negative) microfilm56588 (positive), vol. II, in 435 folios of the size 21 x 27 cm. copied by Muḥammad Aḥmad Khalīl. F. 1a reads volume II: جزو ثاني with two seals, the first states that it belonged to the Library of Jibrā'īl Yūsuf Mukhallaʿ in 1877: من بلطف ايداع عبده جبرائيل يوسف مخلع. مكتبة سنة ١٨٧٧ ميلادية and the second seal states that it belongs to 'The Ministry of Endowments, book no. 852 of al-Zakiyya Library': وزارة الاوقاف. رقم الكتاب ٨٥٢ الخزانة الزكية . F. 1b starts with a completely different beginning from all the other MSS. After the *basmala*, praise to God, and a prayer to the Prophet, it gives the usual formula phrase linking the introductory blessings with the actual subject of the book (*ammā ba'du*) 'Now

73 Zaydān, *Ādāb*, 1937, IV, 108; cf. the new edition by Shawqī Ḍayf, IV, 114.

74 See Zaydān, *Ādāb*, IV, 107 where he deals with al-Maktaba al-Āṣafiyya. On the style of al-Jabartī, see Rifʿat al-Faranawānī, 'Lughat al-Jabartī', in Aḥmad ʿIzzat ʿAbd al-Karīm (ed.), *'Abd al-Raḥmān al-Jabartī, Dirāsāt wa-Buḥūth* (Cairo 1976), 255–88. Al-Farnawānī, noticed that the style and diction of al-Jabartī are not even, sometimes they are in a high language and some times they are flawed. In fact, one can attribute this fact to the standard of the writers from whom al-Jabartī in *'Ajā'ib al-Āthār* (volumes I–II) copied his information, such as al-Zabīdī's *Mu'jam Mukhtaṣṣ* and Ibn ʿAbd al-Ghanī's *Awḍaḥ al-Ishārāt.*

to our topic, the eminent Shaykh al-Jabartī, may God have mercy upon him, has said: the year 1190 [/1776–7]': بسم الله الرحمن الرحيم الحمد لله رب العالمين والصلاة والسلام على سيدنا محمد وعلى آله وصحبه اجمعين . اما بعد فقد قال الفاضل الشيخ الجبرتي رحمه الله تعالى / سنة ١١٩٠ تسعين وماية والف . كان سلطان العصر فيها السلطان عبد الحميد بن احمد خان العثماني ...

The MS ends with f. 435 with the Būlāq version but with a different colophon written by Muḥammad b. Aḥmad b. Khalīl, a Shāfiʿī from the village of Ṭanbash, in Rabīʿ I 1287 (/1–28/29 June 1870):

حمى الله مرقاها ومعراج قدسها ... غفر الله لنا وله بمنه وكرمه آمين . وكان الفراغ من تمام هذا الجزء من تاريخ الجبرتي يوم الثلاث المبارك خلت من شهر ربيع الاول الذي من شهور سنة ١٢٨٧ سبعة وثمانين ومايتين والف من الهجرة النبوية على صاحبها افضل الصلاة وازكى السلام وذلك على يد افقر العباد واحوجهم الى ربه الجليل محمد بن احمد بن خليل الطنبشاوي بلدا الشافعي مذهبا . غفر الله له ولوالديه ولاحبائه والمسلمين آمين بجاه سيد المرسلين :

يـا نـاظرا فيه سـل مولاك رحمة — على المصنف واستغفر لكاتبه

واطلب لنفسك من خير تريده[!] — من بعد ذلك اسعادا لصاحبه

Under these two verses there is a seal of Jibrāʾīl Yūsuf Mukhallaʿ, 1877.

VII. 26. c. MS *ʿAj.* al-Zakiyya, 853/microfilm 9215 and its continuation in microfilm 9216 (negative) and microfilm 56631 (positive), vol. III, pt. 2, in 634 folios (32 fascicles) in 21 x 27 cm. of 23 lines each. This MS starts with the contents (*fihris*) of volume III, in 6 pages: فهرس الجزء الثالث من تاريخ مصر المسمى عجائب الآثار في التراجم والاخبار للشيخ عبد الرحمن بن حسن الجبرتي الحنفي . This second part is the continuation of the first and starts with page 565.

This MS, covering up to 1220 (/1805–6), ends with pages 632–3 with the usual ending of the former MSS: ... ورجال السادات الصوفية . وحسن به ختم هذا الجزء الثالث من كتاب عجايب الآثار في التراجم الاخبار لغاية سنة عشرين ومايتين والف من الهجرة على صاحبها افضل الصلاة واتم التسليم وسنقيد ان شاء الله ... ما تجدد بعدها من الحوادث من ابتدا سنة احدى وعشرين التي نحن بها الآن ان امتد الأجل ... واليه المرجع والمآب وحسبنا الله ونعم الوكيل.

About fifty years after the death of al-Jabartī the copyist Muḥammad b. Aḥmad b. Khalīl, express his great admiration to the author. In the colophon on page 633, he praises him as unique in his time, intelligent, skilled, ingenious, and eloquent. He states, in a rhetorical rhymed style, that the MS was copied on 16 Jumādā II 1287 (/12 September 1870) by Muḥammad b.

Aḥmad b. Khalīl by the order of Jibrā'īl Yūsuf Mukhallaʿ: بسم الله الرحمن الرحيم الحمد لله رب العالمين والصلاة والسلام على اشرف المرسلين سيدنا محمد وعلى آله وصحبه اجمعين. وبعد فقد بلغ هذا الجزء المبارك حد التمام واسفر عن لثمه وجه غرة بدر التمام تأليف وحيد عصره وفريد دهره الاريب الماهر ... واللوذعي المناظر الاستاذ الجبرتي عبد الرحمن اسكنه الله فراديس الجنان في ستة عشر خلت من شهر جمادي الآخر وتبيضه في جمادى الاولى سنة ١٢٨٧ سبعة وثمانين ومايتين والف من هجرة من خلقه الله على أجمل وصف وصلى الله عليه وسلم . برسم ذي المآثر والمفاخر سعادة الخواجه جبرائيل مخلع أسعده الله آمين وغفر لكاتبه وقاريه وكتبه الفقير الذليل الراجي عفو ربه الجليل محمد بن احمد بن خليل غفر الله له ولوالديه والمسلمين امين.

The round seal at the end of the colophon reads: من بلطف ايداع عبده جبرائيل يوسف مخلع مكتبة سنة ١٨٧٧ ميلادية .

The importance of this MS is that in the first 33 pages there are footnotes, which give the meaning of some words and terms, which seem to have become unfamiliar to the average reader already in the year 1872. Words such as 'قايق' are explained in the footnotes as قارب (boat), and the word بنديرات is explained as الوية (flags) (p. 2), while on page 29 the same term is explained in length, such as 'a European term which means standard or flag': (لفظة افرنجية معناها اللواء أو البيرق). In other cases the term is explained with details such as the term *ju'aydī* in شيخ الجعيدية where the copyist explains the morphological development of the term: الجعيدي البخيل أو الرئيس وهي عامية قيل أن رجلا من اهل مصر يقال له جعيد كان يطوف على الناس لابسا قلنسوة ذات اجراس وينشد المدائح مستعطيا عليه فتبعه في هذه الصناعة ناس عرفوا بالجعيدية نسبة اليه ثم وسعوا في هذه الكلمة فاطلقوها على سائر سوقة مصر. (The *ju'aydī* is the avaricious, or the chief. It is a colloquial term. It is said that a man from Cairo, who was called Juʿayd used to walk around among people wearing a tall headgear decorated with bells and reciting panegyrical poems in praise [of the Prophet Muḥammad], begging. In this profession, he was followed by some people who became known as *Ju'aydiyya*, as attributed to him. Then this term was expanded in its meaning and was given to all the rabble of Cairo).

Some sentences were corrected grammatically. All these 'improvements' indicate that by the year 1872 the terms used by al-Jabartī were already forgotten, that his style and grammatical usage were considered obsolete and that some copyists felt the need to 'correct' his style, terminology and grammatical usage. Such attempts at simplifying al-Jabartī's style for the general reader have continued up to 1969 by the editors of *Maẓhar al-Taqdīs*. This fact might explain why the Būlāq edition is different from the Cambridge autographs and the other MSS which al-Jabartī had edited by himself after they were copied by his copyists.

The paragraph with the first French proclamation (p. 5 of the MS) is identical to the Cambridge autograph. In the Būlāq version, this proclamation is corrupted and the Wahhābī proclamation (pp. 445–7 of the MS) is given in summary as is the case in the Cambridge autograph. However, the events of 25 Ṣafar 1216 (/7 July 1801) (pp. 366–70) are given in their complete version with the biographies of those who died in the year 1216 (/1801–2) as in the case of MS *'Aj.* Tārīkh 173 (VI. 13. b.) revised by al-Jabartī himself.

VII. 27. d. 1. MS *'Aj.* al-Zakiyya, 854/microfilm 9214 and its continuation in microfilm 9217 (negative) and microfilm 56630 (positive), IV, pt. I in 288b folios in 21 x 27 cm. in size and 23 lines in each with no corrections in the margin. Muḥammad Aḥmad Khalīl copied it in 1287 (/1870–1). The names of months and years are rubricated with bigger letters. F. 1a reads '*'Ajā'ib al-Āthār*... known as al-Jabartī's *Chronicle*': عجائب الآثار في التراجم والاخبار المعروف بتاريخ الجبرتي الجزء ٤ القسم ١ with two stamps, the first is of the Ministry of Endowments: وزارة الاوقاف رقم الكتاب ٨٥٤ الخزانة الزكية and the second is of Jibrā'īl b. Yūsuf Mukhalla', 1877. The first three pages start with the contents volume IV, pt. 1 of the book: فهرست القسم الاول من الجزء الرابع من تاريخ مصر المسمى عجائب الاثار في التراجم والاخبار للشيخ عبد الرحمن بن حسن الجبرتي الحنفي The title page states: جزو رابع 'volume four' only with the seal of the Ministry of Endowments. F. 1b above the *basmala* the seal reads: من بلطف ايداع عبده جبرائيل يوسف مخلع. مكتبة سنة ١٨٧٧ ميلادية. The text starts in the year 1221 (/1806–7) بسم الله الرحمن الرحيم/ سنة ١٢٢١ احدى وعشرون ومايتين والف / استهل المحرم بيوم الخميس حسابا وبيوم السبت / هلالا ووافق ذلك انتقال الشمس لبرج الحمل...

The MS ends with the necrology of Shaykh Muḥammad who died in 1227 (/1812–13), called Abu 'l-Su'ūd, (cf. *'Aj.* Būlāq, IV, 165) while in this MS (p. 289), due to homoeoteleuton, the name is given as Abu 'l-Surūr. The words in square brackets [...] indicate the missing sentence:

ومات ... الشيخ محمد المكنى [ابا السعود ابن الشيخ محمد جلال ابن الشيخ محمد افندي المكنى بابي المكارم ابن السيد عبد المنعم ابن السيد محمد المكنى] بابي السرور صاحب الترجمة ...

This missing sentence indicates clearly that MS *'Aj.* al-Zakiyya, 854 was copied from an autograph of the author, as it is stated in the margin of part 2 of this volume in MS *'Aj.* al-Zakiyya, 857, 541 and 551 (below 30. d. 2.), where the copyist states twice that he is copying from an autograph MS (خط المؤلف). This part of the MS ends with page 289 with the sentence on Muḥammad al-Bakrī ... وان يأخذ له فايظا من بعض الاقطاعات ويعفى من الحلوان وسكن بدار جهة ... The continuation of this volume is in MS *'Aj.* al-Zakiyya, 857/microfilm 17885 (see below VII. 30. d. 2).

The MS ends with two seals of Wizārat al-Awqāf and Jibrā'īl Ibn Yūsuf Mukhallaʿ as in the case of MS *'Aj.* al-Zakiyya, 855 below.

VII. 28. a. 1. MS *'Aj.* al-Zakiyya, 855/microfilm 9214 (negative) and microfilm 56632 (positive), vol. I, pt. 1, in 539 pages of 16 x 22 cm., copied in 1237 (/1821–2). The MS starts with 23 pages of Index: القسم الاول من فهرست الجزو الاول من تاريخ مصر المسمى عجايب الآثار في التراجم والأخبار للشيخ عبد الرحمن بن حسن الجبرتي الحنفي.There is no title page and instead there are two seals, the first of Jibrā'īl Yūsuf Mukhallaʿ, 1877, which reads: من بلطف ايداع عبده جبرائيل بن يوسف مخلع. مكتبة ١٨٧٧ ميلادية, and the second of the Ministry of Endowments: وزارةالاوقاف. رقم الكتاب ٨٥٥ الخزانة الزكية. Between these two seals the sentence of acquisition reads: من كتب الفقير الى مولاه جبرائيل مخلع. Page 1 starts with the *basmala* and the beginning of volume I, according to the version of the Cambridge autograph which states: ومنـزه عن العلائق instead of the Būlāq version: وعالم الذرات بالحقائق بسم الله الرحمن الرحيم وبه نستعين/ الحمد لله القديم الاول الذي لا يزول ملكه ولا يتحول خالق / الخلائق ومنـزه عن العلائق مفني الامم ومحيي الرمم.

In the margin there are a few explanations of terms such as ماه روز (p. 3) and names of historians such as Ibn al-Athīr al-Jazarī (p. 8). The MS ends with page 539 with the sentence:...وقال يمدحه بهذه الابيات الثلاثة ('He said praising him with the following three verses ...')

VII. 29. a. 2. MS *'Aj.* al-Zakiyya, 856/microfilm 9215 (negative) and microfilm 56591 (positive), and microfilm 57422 (positive), vol. I, pt. 2, in 518 folios of 16 x 22 cm. each, written in clear *naskhī* without any corrections in the margin. There is no title-page and in ff. 1a–5b there are 11 pages of the contents of vol. I, pt. 2, under the title: فهرست القسم الثاني من الجزو الاول من تاريخ مصر المسمى بعجايب الآثار في التراجم والأخبار للشيخ عبد الرحمن بن حسن الجبرتي الحنفي . نمره ٥٤٠ الشيخ يوسف الدلجي توفي ١١٧١. After the title there are two seals of the Ministry of Endowments. P. 529 of the MS starts with ff. 6b–8a and contains a summary of the biography of ʿAlī Bek al-Kabīr known as Bulūṭ Qaban from Wāṣif's

History:[75] ملخص ما ذكره واصف في تاريخه المشهور فيما يخص أحوال شيخ البلد علي بيك الكبير المعروف ببلوط قبان أنه وقتا فوقت لم يخلو الحال من ظهور رجل من أمراء المصرية وبواسطة احتشاده الأموال وتكثير الخدم والحشم فيتغلب على رفاقه وبناء على ما هو متداول على السنة الخلق من المثل الساير في حق مصر أنها لمن غلب ... . On ff. 8b–10b there is a firman by Muḥammad ʿAlī to the Egyptian people صدر هذا الفرمان الجليل الشان من ديوان مصر المحروسة العالي دامت له المفاخر والمعالي بأمر من جنابه الكريم المناب على أهل هذا الزمان فاظهر العدل والأمان ... وقد زال من قلوب الناس الحزن والاضطراب وجرى ضرب المدافع من المعسكر علامة للسرور . It ends with p. 1057 and has no colophon: من الخراب والدمار والله اعلم بالصواب واليه المرجع والمعاد (= المآب) تم وسيتلى عليك من ذلك أنباء وأخبار وما حل بالاقليم بسببهم. Under these lines there are two oval seals, one of the Khedivial Library: الخزانة الخديوية المصرية al-Khizāna al-Khudaywiyya al-Miṣriyya and the second is the seal of the Ministry of Endowments: وزارة الاوقاف رقم الكتاب ٨٥٦. الخزانة الزكية.

VII. 30. d. 2. MS *'Aj.* al-Zakiyya, 857/microfilm 17885, vol. IV, pt. 2, in 213 folios pages. The MS is copied from an autograph of the author (see below). F. 1b states that the book belongs to the Wizārat al-Awqāf (Ministry of Endowments) from the Zakiyya Library 857: وزارة الأوقاف . رقم الكتاب ٨٥٧. الخزانة الزكية. The margins contain several notes and a summary of the historical events or the name of the person in the necrologies in the Arabic and Turkish languages. Page 3 contains a copy of a letter sent by Muḥammad ʿAlī to Sharīf Ḥammūda of Mecca written by ʿAbbūd Baḥrī, who is mentioned in page 660 of this MS. The following are part of the beginning and end of the letter (pp. 3–5):

> نسخة كتاب من المرحوم محمد علي باشا الى شريف مكة المكرمة من إنشاء المرحوم عبود بحري المنشئ المذكور ترجمته في صفحة ٦١٦ من هذا الجزء: من أفضل ما تتزين به سطور الطروس وأكمل ما تتحلى مجلاه عواطل النفوس حمد الله الملك القدوس وشكره ... أما بعد فقد ورد كتابكم المرسل و... الأكمل الى ولدنا الوزير الخطير .../(ص 5) وحسن التدبير لإتمام ختام هذه المصلحة الخيرية وبأفضل الصلاة والسلام على أشرف المرسلين الكرام بحسن البدء والختام. في ١٢٢٨.

Only on pages 6–9 is the contents of volume IV, pt. 2 given: فهرست القسم الثاني من الجزء الرابع من تاريخ مصر المسمى عجايب الاثار في التراجم والاخبار للشيخ عبد الرحمن بن حسن الجبرتي الحنفي. On pages 11–14 there is a copy of a letter from Muḥammad ʿAlī to the Imām of the Yemen dated 1 Jumada I 1228 (/2 May 1813) and composed by ʿAbbūd Baḥrī صورة كتاب من المرحوم محمد على باشا إلى إمام اليمن في غرة:

75 MS *'Aj.* al-Zakiyya, 856/microfilm 9215, ff. 6b–8a. A history of Egypt, *Jawāhir al-Buḥūr*, written 606/1209 byIbrāhīm b. Wāṣif Shāh al-Miṣrī.

شهر جـ ١٢٢٨ من إنشاء المرحوم عبود بحري: إن أولى ما يتحلى به جيد الافتتاح، وأعلى ما يتوشح به كشف الكشح والإفصاح، حمد الله الذي بيده مقاليد السموات والأرض .../ (ص١٤) والسلام على اشرف الرسل الكرام، بحسن البدو والختام.

The page which starts the text of part 2 is paginated with no. 422 and contains two stamps, the first is of al-Maktaba al-Zakiyya and the second is of the Ministry of Endowments: وزارة الأوقاف. رقم الكتاب ٨٥٧ المكتبة الزكية. Part 2 starts with page 422 in which the text continues the last sentence of part 1, which deals with al-Shaykh Muḥammad Abu ʾl-Saʿūd b. Muḥammad ... Abi ʾl-Surūr (see MS *ʿAj.* al-Zakiyya, 854 [VII. 27. d. 1]): جهة باب الخرق وراج أمره واشتهر ذكره من جديد ... ومات الأجل المكرم المهذب في نفسه، النادرة في أبناء جنسه، محمد أفندي الودنلي الذي عرف بناظر المهمات. As is stated twice by the copyist, this MS was copied from an autograph of the author. The first time being in the margin of p. 541: منتصف شهر شعبان سنة ١٢[١٢]٢٤ مكتوب هذا في طيارة بخط المؤلف فيها من ابتدى [!] ترجمة الحصاوى [!]لغاية ترجمة الطحطاوي . ا. هـ . ترجمة الطحطاوي الحنفي السيد احمد بن محمد بن اسماعيل (من ذرية محمد الدوقاطي الطهطاوي الحنفي) . ('The events of the middle of Shaʿbān, the year 1224 [/25 September 1809], are written on a slip of paper (*ṭayyāra*) written by the author's hand from the beginning of al-Ḥaṣāwī's biography up to the end of the biography of al-Ṭaḥṭāwī, End...'). The second time in which the copyist mentions that he is copying from the autograph is on p. 551 where there is a lacuna between the name of a person and his nickname: ومات في هذه السنة العمدة الفاضل الفقيه النبيه الشيخ حسب الله المعروف بابن الكاشف ..., and in the margin the copyist's comment is 'lacuna in the autograph' (بياض في خط المؤلف) . On the margin of page 662 opposite the paragraph dealing with a new bridge on the Nile at Qanṭarat al-Laymūn, it is written: على نهر النيل، ومنها أنه انشا جسرا ممتدا من ناحية قنطرة الليمون ... The correction on the margin reads: هذا الجسر ليس فيه أشجار توت بل الأشجار التي فيه لبيخ وجميز . ا. هـ . ('This bridge has no mulberry trees, but the trees there are acacia and sycamore'). There is another comment written in another hand, signed by Muḥammad ʿĀrif which says that: 'Ḥājj ʿAlī Aghā al-Rashīdī informed me that the mulberry trees were not successful and instead acacia and sycamore trees were planted. I have seen in the Canal every tree [?], but it was of no use. End. Muḥammad ʿĀrif (كان غرس فيه توت وما نفع فغرس به اللبيخ وجميز هكذا اخبرني الحاج علي اغا الرشيدي واني رأيت بالقنال كل شجرة كزية (!) ولم تنفع . ا. هـ. محمد عارف.

The last page reads as in the case of MS *ʿAj.* al-Zakiyya, 861 (VII. 33. d.): والبعض باق الى الان وهي حادثة الاروام ., and in the margin the colophon states 'This is the end of what the erudite al-Jabartī, the historian of this period until this date, has written. End. Written by ʿAbd al-Ḥamīd Nāfiʿ in the year 1273 (/1856–7)': هذا آخر ما خطه العلامة الشيخ عبد الرحمن بن حسن الجبرتي مؤرخ هذه المدة وما قبلها لغاية هذا التاريخ . ا. هـ . كتبه عبد الحميد نافع سنة ١٢٧٣. Under this colophon a certain Muḥammad ʿĀrif Sālim wrote that he read this volume in Ṭanṭā: طالعت هذا المجلد بطنطا. محمد عارف سالم ٢٤ [!]

VII. 31. b. MS *'Aj.* al-Zakiyya, 858/microfilm 54237 (positive)/microfilm 17952 (negative),vol. II, in unbound (*mufakkak*) 52 fascicles of 1,009 pages of the size 15.5 x 21 cm. in 19–20 lines, in *naskhī* handwriting with few corrections in the margin. On the last page the photographer of the MS erroneously gives it no. 859.

The importance of this MS is that it was copied by Aḥmad Muḥammad who also copied volume III of MS *'Aj.* al-Zakiyya, 859 (VII. 32. c.) in the year 1237 (/1821–2), while al-Jabartī was alive. Moreover, this MS is identical with the Cambridge autograph. There is no title-page. F. 1b has the year 1099 تسع وتسعونand the word 9 تسع is deleted: الجزؤ الثاني / سنة تسعون وألف [1090]/ كان سلطان العصر فيها عبد الحميد / ابن احمد خان العثماني ووالي مصر الوزير محمد باشا عزت ...

The colophon on page 1009 states that this MS (vol. II) was copied on 18 Rabīʿ I 1237 (/13 December 1821), by Aḥmad Muḥammad :توفي في منتصف شهر شعبان من السنة غفر الله لنا وله ولوالدينا وللمسلمين بمنه وكرمه وكان الفراغ من كتابة هذا الجزء أواخر يوم الخميس المبارك ثامن عشر شهر ربيع الأول سنة ١٢٣٧ من الهجرة على صاحبها الصلاة والسلام على يد الفقير احمد محمد عفى [!] عنهما آمين .

Therefore, this MS also was read and compared with the assistance of its author on 1240 (/1824–5) as it is the case of MS *'Aj.* al-Zakiyya, 859 (VII. 32. c. below).

VII. 32. c. MS *'Aj.* al-Zakiyya, 859/microfilm 54236 (positive) and microfilm 17952 (negative), vol. III, in unbound (*mufakkak*) 1,373 pages of 15.5 x 21 cm. containing 19–20 lines. This MS was copied, as in the case of MS *'Aj.* al-Zakiyya, 858 (VII. 31. b.), by Aḥmad Muḥammad in 1237 (/1821–2). Some of the corrections in the margin are written in a hand similar to that of al-Jabartī. In f. 1a the title is: الجزء الثالث من عجايب الآثار للجبرتي, with a seal which reads: وزارة الأوقاف رقم الكتاب ٨٥٩. الخزانة الزكية رقم 859. ('Ministry of Endowments, book no. 859'.) F. 1b start with the events of the year 1213 (/1798–9) سنة ثلاثة عشر وما يتين وألف، وهي أول سني الملاحم العظيمة والحوادث الجسيمة ...

The French proclamation (ff. 3a–b) is identical with the Cambridge autograph but the events of 25 Dhu 'l-Ḥijja 1216 (/28 April 1802) are complete to the end of the necrology of the year 1216 (/1801–2) as in the case of MS *'Aj.* Tārīkh 174 (see above VI. 14. c). The Wahhābī proclamation is given in a summarized version (p. 948), as it is in the Cambridge autograph. On page 1109 the number of days after which the *fallāḥ*s and servants were to leave Cairo is corrected in the margin, in a hand similar to al-Jabartī, from seven into three days. On the upper side of the right margin of page 1178 (cf. *'Aj.* Būlāq, III, 312) there is a remark indicating the incident between Muḥammad ʿAlī and the soldier: . [؟؟] مطلب قول العسكري للباشا : الباشا على كيزات وكيزات

The end of this MS in page 1373 which is written in the shape of a triangle is identical with the Būlāq edition: وحسن به ختم هذا الجزء الثالث من كتاب عجايب الآثار ... وصلاح العموم انه على كل شيء قدير والله اعلم. On page 1374 the round seal reads: وزارة الاوقاف رقم الكتاب 859 ('Ministry of Endowments, book no. 859'.)

This MS is of special importance because the colophon on p. 1373 reads that its fair copy was made on 22 Rajab 1237 (/14/15 April 1822) by a copyist called Aḥmad Muḥammad and that on Saturday 14 Rabīʿ I 1240 (/6 November 1824) it was compared with the assistance of its author ʿAbd al-Raḥmān al-Jabartī: تم تبيضه في ٢٢ رجب سنة ١٢٣٧ على يد الضعيف أحمد محمد غفر له ولوالديه ومشايخه والمسلمين اجمعين، آمين آمين آمين . On the left side of this colophon an important paragraph is added. It statesthat this MS was read to its author ʿAbd al-Raḥmān al-Jabartī on Saturday 14 Rabīʿ I 1240 (/6 November 1824) by Aḥmad b. Ḥasan al-Rashīdī al-Shāfiʿī known as Ṣawbaʿ: بلغ مقابلة وقراءة على مولفه من أوله إلى آخره في يوم السبت المبارك رابع عشر شهر ربيع الأول سنة ١٢٤٠ بمرأى ومسمع من مولفه متع الله الوجود بطول حياته ولا احرمنا والمسلمين من صالح دعواته وغزير بركاته انه سميع قريب مجيب . رقمه بيده الفانية أحمد ابن حسن الرشيدي الشافعي الشهير بصوبع عفي عنه . ا. هـ.('The collation and reading [of the MS] was executed from the beginning to the end [of the MS] on Rabīʿ I [Saturday, 14], of the year 1240 [/6 November 1824] in the sight and hearing of its author, may God make the universe enjoy his long life ... Written by his ephemeral hand, Aḥmad b. Ḥasan al-Rashīdī al-Shāfiʿī, well-known as Ṣawbaʿ. The end').

It seems that this MS is the last copy of *'Ajā'ib al-Āthār*,which al-Jabartī revised before his death and that this is the copy which Jurjī Zaydān consulted in the Muḥammad Bek Āṣaf Library (al-Maktaba al-Āṣafiyya) and described in his book *Tārīkh Ādāb al-Lugha al-'Arabiyya* to prove that al-Jabartī died in 1240 (/1825)or after this year and not in 1237 (/1821–2) as is generally given.

VII. 33. c. MS *'Aj.* al-Zakiyya, 860/microfilm 9218 and its continuation in microfilm 6219 (negative) and microfilm 56587 (positive), vol. III, in 938 pages in unbound (*mufakkak*) fascicles of 15.5 x 21 cm. containing 21 lines each. Page 1 has an unclear title-page in large letters, which does not belong to al-Jabartī's history:

> ٨٦٠ محمد عبد القادر . هذا الكتاب الملذ بالسمع الأوزان [!] الجليل القدر وانشا[ء] المرحوم عبد القادر احمد بن المرحوم جمعة غابر دوفلي [!] محمد عبد القادر ... It has two seals which read: وزارة الأوقاف رقم الكتاب ٨٦٠ . الخزانة الزكية رقم٨٦٠ ('Ministry of Endowments, book no. 860'.)

The text starts without *basmala* and begins in the year 1213 (/1798–9): سنة ثلاثة عشر ومايتين وألف / وهي أولى سني الملاحم العظيمة ... and the French proclamation (p. 9 of the MS) is identical with al-Jabartī's version as it is in the case of the Cambridge autographs. The text of the trial of Sulaymān al-Ḥalabī (p. 297 of the MS) is complete and the text of the Wahhābī proclamation (pp. 644–7 of the MS) is given in summary as in the case of the Cambridge autograph. However, the events of the month Dhu 'l-Ḥijja 1216 (/4 April–2 May 1802) are given in brief (p. 529) with the complete necrology of the year 1216 (/1801–2) (p. 535) as it is in MS *'Aj.* Tārīkh 174 (VI. 14. c.).

The MS ends with the page 938 with no colophon:

> وحسن به ختم هذا الجزء الثالث من كتاب عجائب الآثار في التراجم والأخبار ... ونرجو من الكريم المتعال صلاح الأحوال وانقشاع الهموم وصلاح العموم ... انه على كل شيئ قدير وبالإجابة جدير. والله اعلم ... تم بحمد الله وعونه وحسن توفيقه امين امين .

Under these lines the same seal of the Ministry of Endowments is given.

VII. 33. d. MS *'Aj.* al-Zakiyya, 861/microfilm 52898 (negative) and microfilm 54238 (positive), vol. IV, in 1153 pages of 21 x 27 cm. of 21 lines each copied in 1287 (/1870–1) by Muḥammad Aḥmad Khalīl. The seal reads: وزارة الأوقاف . رقم الكتاب 861. الخزانة الزكية. ('Ministry of Endowments, book no. 861'.) F. 1b states: هذا الجزء الرابع من تاريخ الأستاذ الشيخ عبد الرحمن ابن الشيخ حسن الجبرتي رحمه الله تعالى ورحم أسلافه امين امين امين .On p. 1153 the end of the events of the year 1236

(/1820–1) is given. The colophon states that it was copied from an autograph and that under the stamp of the Ministry of Endowments: فيه خرجت عساكر ومعهم روساوهم ... مدافع من القلعة . وانقضت هذه السنة وما بها من الحوادث التي انقضى بعضها والبعض باق إلى الآن وهي حادثة الاروام وذلك إلى هنا انتهى ما نقل من خط العلامة الشيخ عبد الرحمن بن الشيخ حسن الجبرتي مؤلف هذه المدة [!] وما قبلها لغاية هذا التاريخ وهذا آخر الجزء الرابع وبعده توفي الشيخ ولم يكتب شيئا . والله اعلم. The order of the events of the last months from Shawwāl to the end are given in the same order as in the Būlāq edition.

VIII. 'Ajā'ib MSS of al-Maktaba al-Azhariyya, Cairo.[76]

VIII. 34. a–d. MS *'Aj.* al-Maktaba al-Azhariyya, (276) Abāẓa 6573 (henceforth **MS *'Aj.* MA**) ‘in four volumes written in ordinary handwriting, [vol. I] in 610 ff.,[vol. II] in 395 ff., [vol. III] in 448 ff. [sic] [the number of folios in vol. IV is not given], in 21 lines each’. According to Maḥmūd al-Sharqāwī, this manuscript was copied from al-Jabartī’s autograph.

VIII. 35. a–c. MS *'Aj.* MA, (584) 8538, in three volumes, written in ordinary handwriting by Khalīl b. Ibrāhīm al-ʿAjūz in 1289 (/1872–3), vol. I, in 419 ff, vol. II in 427 ff., vol. III in 345 ff., with 25 lines each. According to Maḥmūd al-Sharqāwī, this manuscript was copied from al-Jabartī’s autograph.

VIII. 36. a–d. MS *'Aj.* MA, (3065) 21594, ‘in seven volumes, written in ordinary handwriting, [vol. I] in 238 ff., [vol. II] in 363 ff., [vol. III] in 282 ff., [vol. IV] in 249 ff., [vol. V] in 257 ff., [vol. VI] in 275 ff., [vol. VII] in 301 ff., in 25 lines each’.

IX. Additional MSS

IX. 37. The *'Ajā'ib* MS Birmingham, 908–11 (1361–4). In our Arabic edition has the abbreviated symbol بع. Its variant versions are indicated between inclined lines /…/. This MS is in four volumes. In the catalogue of the Selly Oak Colleges Library, Mingana Collection of Manuscripts, History, vol. IV,

76 Seeal-Maktaba al-Azhariyya, *Fihris al-Kutub al-Mawj-da bi 'l-Maktaba al-Azhariyya. Al-Juz' al-Khāmis, wa-Yashtamil 'ala 'l-Funūn al-Ātiya: al-Adab-al-Tārīkh-Taqwīm al-Buldān–(al-Jughrāfiyya)* (Cairo 1949), 493.

Islamic Arabic Manuscripts,[77] there is a very brief description of the MS, which reads as follows: ''Abdarrahman ibn Hassan al-Gabarti (1167/1754–1237/1822), *'Ajā'ib al-Āthār fi t-Tarājim wa 'l-Akhbār'*. *GAL*, II, 480, esp. II, 730–1. Dated 1296/1878–9 written in *Nashki*, red headings, copied from the autograph. Size: 27 x 197mm folio 263, 165, 186, 192; 29 lines'.

On a slip of paper inside volume I, only the nos. of the volumes are mentioned: 1361, 1362, 1363, 1364. The name of the author and the title of the work are as follows: 'Arūb. Ḥ. Al-Jabartī, 1167 [/1754–1237/1822]. *'Ajā'ib al-Āthār fi 'l-Tarājim wa 'l-Akhbār*, *GAL*, II, 480, II, 730/1. Several MSS printed. The present MS, dated Sha'bān 1296 [/21 July–19 August 1879], and copied from the autograph dated 1236 [/1820–1], was written in clear *naskhī*, by Ḥu. Bek Ḥasany. Red headings and rubrics. 23/6/[19]43'.

According to the microfiche from the IDC (Inter Documentation Company AG, Switzerland) Publishers, Leiden, the MS has no title pages. All the volumes are clearly written in neat *naskhī* handwriting without marginal corrections. According to the examination of these four volumes at Birmingham University Library, the volumes are in hard leather cover, the words *Tārīkh al-Jabartī* and the name of the owner Nūr al-Dīn Bayk Muṣṭafā are inscribed in gold.

IX. 38. a. MS *'Aj.* Birmingham, 908 (1361), vol. I, in 263 ff. in 29 lines each, of 27 x 19.50 cm. in 27 fascicles written in the same hand in neat *naskhī*. The MS has no title page and f. 1b starts with the *basmala* and the opening lines of the *Introduction* to volume I, is according to the version in the Būlāq edition and not according to the Cambridge autograph: بسم الله الرحمن الرحيم، الحمد لله القديم الأول الذي لا يزول ملكه ولا يتحول خالق الخلايق وعالم الذرايات [!] بالحقائق...

In this MS there are many missing sentences, misreadings and spelling mistakes. It ends in f. 263a with a short colophon stating the end of volume I of the *History of al-Jabartī*: ... من الخراب والدمار . انتهى الجزء الاول من تاريخ الامام العلامة الشيخ الجبرتي تغمده الله برحمته وضوانه امين يا رب العالمين م. Under the colophon an oval stamp which reads: 'Mingana Collection'.

77 See H.L. Gottschalk, *Catalogue of the Mingana Collection of Manuscripts Now in the Possession of the Trustees of the Woodbrooke Settlement, Selly Oak, Birmingham, and Preserved at the Selly Oak College's Library* (vol. 4. Islamic Arabic Manuscripts, Birmingham 1948), 167.

IX. 38. b. MS *'Aj.* Birmingham, 909 (1362), vol. II, in 17 fascicles of 165 ff. of 27 x 19.50 cm. in 29 lines each. On f. 1a the title page of volume II written in red and black ink, reads: الجزء الثاني من عجايب الآثار في التراجم والاخبار / تأليف العالم العلامة والبحر الفهامة الشيخ عبد الرحمن الجبرتي تغمده الله برحمته امين يا رب العالمين امين . Under this title there is an oval stamp which reads: 'Mingana Collection' and the shelf mark is given in pencil: 'Mingana Arabic 1362'. The MS starts volume II with *basmala* and the events of the year 1190 (/1776–7): بسم الله الرحمن الرحيم / سنة ١١٩٠ تسعين ومائة والف / كان سلطان العصر فيها السلطان عبد الحميد بن احمد خان العثماني ووالى مصر الوزير محمد باشا عزت الكبير ...

F. 165a ends volume II with a short colophon: حمى الله ... بمنه وكرمه امين . انتهى الجزء الثاني من تاريخ العلامة الشيخ عبد الرحمن بن حسن الجبرتي ويليه الجزء الثالث واوله سنة ١٢١٣. م . Under this colophon there is an oval stamp which reads: 'Mingana Collection' and the shelf mark is given in pencil: 'Mingana Arabic 1362'.

IX. 38. c. MS *'Aj.* Birmingham, 910 (1363), vol. III, in 186 ff., is without pagination. This MS starts on f. 1b with no title page. It has a stamp reading: 'Mingana Collection' and the shelf mark is given in pencil: 'Mingana Arabic 1363'. It starts with *basmala* and the events of the year 1213 (/1798–9) as follows: بسم الله الرحمن الرحيم . سنة ١٢١٣ ثلاثة عشر ومائتين وألف وهي أول سني الملاحم العظيمة والحوادث الجسيمة .... Ff. 2b–3a cites the French proclamation in a corrupted way especially the paragraph which asks the Mamluks 'what is there of virtue, and knowledge, which would distinguish them from others'. Many lines are deleted and some words are corrupted: وقولوا ايضا لهم ان جميع الناس متساوين وان الشيء الذي يفرقهم عن بعضهم هو العقل والفضايل تضارب في اذى [!] غيرهم [!] حتى يستوجبوا ان يتملكوا مصر وحدهم ويختصوا بكل شيء حسن فيها من الجواري الحسان والخيل العتاة [!] [= العتاق] والمساكن المفرحة ... While in Napoleon's proclamation this paragraph reads: وقولوا ايضا لهم ان جميع الناس متساووين عند الله . وان الشيء الذي يفرقهم من بعضهم بعضا فهو العقل والفضايل والعلوم فقط. وبين المماليك ما العقل والفضايل والمعرفة التي تميّزهم عن الاخرين وتستوجب ان يتملكوا وحدهم كلما يحلوا [!] به حيات [!] الدنيا * حيثما يوجد ارض مخصبة فهي مختصّة للمماليك والجواري الاجمل والخيل الاحسن والمساكن الاشهى فهذا كله لهم خاصا .

The trial of Sulaymān al-Ḥalabī (ff. 69a–b, 21 Muḥarram 1215 [/14 June 1800]), is given in a different version very similar to the *Maẓhar al-Taqdīs* and identical word for word with volume III of MS *'Aj.* Tārīkh 1426 (VI. 19. c.) (ff. 88b–89a). In this version the author describes the way in which General Kléber was stabbed by al-Ḥalabī, the latter hiding in a well and that a poor Egyptian woman indicated to the French the place where the assassin had hidden himself.

However, the events of the month Dhu 'l-Ḥijja 1216 (/4 April–2 May 1802) ends with the event of 25th of the month with the hanging of the woman who stole clothes from a public bath and the necrologies of the year 1216 (/1801–2) are missing. The text of the Wahhābī proclamation (f. 131a) is copied in its complete form.

The MS ends with the events of the year 1220 (/1805–6) with the biography of Muḥammad b. Sīrīn ... Ibn Jaysh al-Shāfiʿī al-Maqdisī, without mentioning the name of the copyist or the date of the end of the redaction: وبه حسن ختم الجزء الثالث من كتاب عجايب الآثار في التراجم والاخبار لغاية سنة عشرين ومايتين والف من الهجرة النبوية . تم

Under these lines there is an oval stamp which reads: 'Mingana Collection' and the shelf mark is given in pencil: 'Mingana Arabic 1362'.

IX. 38. d. MS *'Aj.* Birmingham, 911 (1364), vol. IV, in 192a ff. starts with the *basmala* and the events of the year 1221 (/1806–7). Unlike the Būlāq edition and all the other MSS of volume IV which end with the events of Dhu 'l-Ḥijja 1236 (/30 August–27 September 1821), this MS states that these same events took place in the month Shawwāl of 1236 (/1/2–29 July 1821). However, there are some abbreviations in the final section, and some information, e.g. that the Nile stopped rising and that the exchange rate of currency rose, has been deleted. The MS ends with the events of Shawwāl 1236 (/1/2–29 July 1821) which correspond to the events of Dhu 'l-Qaʿda in the printed editions, as well as the events following the sentence: 'Thus ended the year and its events ...' (وانقضت هذه السنة). The colophon states that this is the end of volume IV that it is the full text, and that after this al-Jabartī died without writing any more. The copying of the book ended on Shaʿbān 1296 (/21 July–19 August 1879) by the order of the director of the Būlāq Press, Ḥusayn Bek Ḥusnī. Under the colophon is a stamp reading: 'Mingana Collection'.

The last section of the MS with the colophon, as in the case of Khūdā Bakhsh MS, gives the events in the wrong order of the months. In both MSS the events of the month Dhu 'l-Ḥijja 1236 (/30 August–27 September 1821) in the Būlāq edition and other MSS, are attributed to the month of Shawwāl as follows:

واستهل شهر شوال

فيه خرجت عساكر ومعهم رؤساوهم وفيهم محو بيك ... وانقضت هذه السنة وما بها من الحوادث التي انقضى بعضها والبعض باقي الى الآن وهي حادثة الاورام وذلك الى هنا انتهى ما نقل من خط العلامة الشيخ عبد الرحمن بن الشيخ حسن الجبرتي مؤرخ هذه المدة وما قبلها لغاية هذا التاريخ سنة ١٢٣٦ وهو آخر الجزء الرابع من التاريخ وهو تمامه وبعده توفي الشيخ ولم يكتب شيء انزل الله عليه سحائب الرحمة والرضوان واسكنه اعلا فراديس الجنان انه كريم منان ذوا (!) الفضل والاحسان . تم الكتاب بحمد الله الملك الوهاب في شهر شعبان سنة ١٢٩٦ بعد الهجرة النبوية برسم من اخلاقه عليه تثني المكرم حسين بيك حسني ناظر المطبعة الكبرى والكاغدخانه ومديرها أحسن الله عونه وأدام صونه، آمين. م . ('Thus ended this year (1236/1820–1] and its events, except for those events which are ongoing at the present time, [I mean] the Greek incident. With this event ends what the learned Shaykh ʿAbd al-Raḥmān b. Ḥasan al-Jabartī, historian of this era and the preceding period, up to 1236 [/1820–1]. This is the end of volume IV of his history and with this it is complete.

Thereafter, the Shaykh died without having written any more. May God pour on him showers of mercy and grace, and may He make him dwell in the elevated gardens of paradise. He is the Gracious, the Benefactor, and the Benevolent. The book ends with thanks to God, the benevolent King, in the month of Shaʿbān [1296/ 21 July–19 August 1879] of the *Hijra* at the command of the revered Ḥusayn Bey Ḥusnī, of praiseworthy character, director of the Great Press [of Būlāq] and Paper Factory. May God continuously help and sustain him. Amen').

The fact that this MS was copied at the command of the director of the Būlāq Press on 1296 (/1878–9), one year before the Būlāq edition was published,might indicate that it was the copy which served as the final version for the Būlāq edition. It might be also, that the editor noticed the mistake of the copyist and avoided repeating the same mistake, and continued printing the event from another manuscript.

X. Related Problems

I. MS sources, the Būlāq edition and other printed editions of *'Ajā'ib al-Āthār*. A precise comparison of the MSS MS *'Aj.* Cam., MS *'Aj.* BN, MS *'Aj.* BM and MS *'Aj.* al-Zakiyya, 859, with the Būlāq edition (1297/1879–80), showed that on the one hand there are many passages in Būlāq, which are missing in these four manuscripts, while on the other hand there are passages which have been omitted in Būlāq, mainly due to the homoeoteleuton. This indicates that all other MSS were copied from MS *'Aj.* Cam. Since there are great differences in style and grammatical usage between these MSS and the Būlāq edition, it therefore seems likely that the Būlāq editor used several manuscripts of *'Ajā'ib al-Āthār*, but he does not say whether there was an autograph among them. The following MSS probably served as the basis for the Būlāq edition: MSS MS *'Aj.* Tārīkh 466, MS *'Aj.* Tārīkh 1872 in 4 volumes, and MS *'Aj.* Birmingham nos. 908–11 (1360–3).

A few years after writing *'Ajā'ib al-Āthār* and the death of the author al-Jabartī in 1240 (/1824–5), some copyists probably felt that al-Jabartī's style and terminology were obsolete and old. This point can explain why the copyist of MS *'Aj.* al-Zakiyya, 853/microfilm 9215 and its continuation in microfilm 9216 (negative) and microfilm 56631 (positive) copied in 1287 (/1870–1) (26. c. above) made an attempt to provide in the footnotes the meaning of many terms and words contained in the first 33 pages, but it seems that the copyist decided not to continue with this rather difficult task. On the other hand the copyist of the MSS made after the death of the author took the liberty of correcting the style and the grammatical usage of al-Jabartī. The editor of the Būlāq Press, who had in his possession only those MSS which were copied after the author's death, took them as a basis for his edition. This fact might explain why there are many homoeoteleuton, misreadings and lacunae in the Būlāq edition. After examining the *'Ajā'ib al-Āthār* manuscripts kept at Dār al-Kutub al-Qawmiyya, especially those inscribed that 'they were donated by the Library of the Būlāq Press in 1895', it is possible to understand why the Būlāq edition differs so frequently from most of the MSS, including the autograph. Comparison showed that the Būlāq editor preferred the two MSS in which their copyists admitted that they changed the style. These are MSS *'Aj.*, Tārīkh 466 and *'Aj.* Tārīkh 1872 (VI. 22. c. above), in which the copyists took the liberty to 'correct' many passages that they found unclear or were not familiar with. They corrected grammatical mistakes, corrupt style, the author's vocabulary and even the text of the documents, which al-Jabartī emphasized that he had copied carefully. In spite of his assurance that he had followed al-Jabartī's method of adhering faithfully to the text of the documents he cites, the editor of the Būlāq edition adopts all these 'corrections' which change the original style and grammatical usage of al-Jabartī's autograph: نهاية احداث شهر ذي الحجة سنة ١٢١٦ ([4 April–2 May 1802/] Dhu'l-Hijja 1216).

The fuller text of the Būlāq edition and the versions from other manuscripts which the editor sometimes gives in the margins, show that some manuscripts in his possession differed from and often contained more details than the Cambridge autograph. The editor of the Būlāq edition selected and combined elements of the versions according to his opinion.

A good illustration of the editor's attitude is the following passage in al-Jabartī's autograph MS *'Aj.* Cam. and in all the other MSS copied from it and revised by the author, such as MS *'Aj.* BN, MS *'Aj.* Tārīkh 174, and the MSS copied from them such as MS *'Aj.* al-Zakiyya 859 (pp. 10–11), of the proclamation issued by the French Army to the people of Egypt on 2 July 1798:[78] وبين المماليك ما العقل والفضايل والمعرفة التي تميزهم عن الآخرين وتستوجب انهميتملكوا وحدهم كلما يحلوا به حيات الدنيا . حيثما يوجد ارض مخصبه فهي مختصّة للمماليك والجواري الاجمل والخيل الاحسن والمساكن الاشهى ... . ('But amongst the Mamlūks, what is there of reason, virtue and knowledge which would distinguish them from others and qualify them alone to possess everything which sweetens life in this world?

78 The French translation of this proclamation given by Joseph Cuoq, in his translation of *Maẓhar al-Taqdīs: 'Abd al-Raḥmān al-Jabartī*, is identical to the Cambridge group of MSS: 'Or, quelle sagesse, quels talents, quelles vertus, distinguent les Mamlouks, pour qu'ils aient exclusivement tout ce qui rendre la vie aimable et douce?' The French proclamations published in Egypt are to be found in C. de la Jonquière, *L'Expédition d'Égypte (1798–1801)*(5 vols, Paris 1899–1907); Napoleon I, *Correspondance de Napoléon 1er*, Paris, Henri Plon, 1858–70, vols IV–V, and Napoleon I, *Pièces diverses relatives aux opérations militaires et politiques de général Bonaparte*, Paris, Didot l'ainé, year VIII [c.1800], 2 vols. Another copy of this first French proclamation together with many other French proclamations in Arabic and/or French can be found in the Bibliothèque Nationale in Paris, Gr.fol. L h4, 117 (see Bibliothèque nationale de France, *Catalogue général des livres imprimés de la Bibliothèque Nationale: auteurs*, Tom. 122, Paris, Imprimerie Nationale, 1823, nos. 329, 331, 333). A collection in the British Museum (1296.h.12) also contains several French proclamations published in Egypt. Vol. 8 of Saladin Boustany's *The Journals of Bonaparte in Egypt: 1798–1801/Ṣuḥuf Būābart fī Miṣr* (in 10 volumes), including *La Decade Égyptienne* andthe *Courier de l'Égypte*, contains 'Bonaparte's proclamations, as recorded by ʿAbd al-Raḥmān al-Jabartī'. Text in Arabic and the translation in English in 184 pages. Vol. 9, part I, comprises 'Recueil des arrêtés et proclamations d'autorité françaíse en Égypte pendant l'occupation' (translations made by the translators of the French Expedition!) in 182 pages. (My thanks are due to the Library of Congress, Washington, D.C., for allowing me to use its copy). An Arabic study of the proclamations is Aḥmad Ḥusayn al-Ṣāwī's *Fajr al-Ṣiḥāfa fī Miṣr: Dirāsa fī I'lām al-Ḥamla al-Faransiyya* (Cairo 1975). See also Marsden Jones, 'The First French Proclamation and al-Jabartī', in Aḥmad ʿIzzat ʿAbd al-Karīm (ed.), *'Abd al-Raḥmān al-Jabartī, Dirāsāt wa-Buḥūth* (Cairo 1976), 31–42.

Wherever fertile land is found, it is appropriated by the Mamlūks; and the handsomest female slaves, and the best horses, and the most desirable dwelling-places, all these belong to them exclusively').

Comparing al-Jabartī's version with the text of the original Arabic proclamation sent by the French and kept at the British Museum (general catalogue 1296 h. 12 [1]) we find that al-Jabartī copied the text quite accurately, except for some minor differences; e.g. the word *ḥayā* (with *tā' marbūṭa*), appears in al-Jabartī as *ḥayāt* (with *tā' ṭawīla*), and Farānsāwī as Faransāwī. In the Būlāq edition this corrupted paragraph becomes (III, 5, ll. 1–3): وبين المماليك والعقل والفضايل تضارب فماذا يميزهم عن غيرهم حتى يستوجبوا ان يتملكوا مصر وحدهم ويختصوا بكل شيء احسن فيها من الجوارى الحسان والخيل العتاق والمساكن المفرحة ('But amongst the Mamlūks, what is there of reason and virtue which would distinguish them from others that they should deserve to rule over Egypt by themselves, and that they should take exclusive possession of the best of everything: beautiful slave girls, noble horses, and delightful residences?')

Yet not all the corrections are hyper-corrections. The corrupted words which appear in most of the MSS are the phrase ناسور ايات copied by al-Jabartī from another work, and corrected into: ناشر رايات which is an example of a correct reading made by the copyist of the manuscript chosen by the Būlāq editor. Moreover, many missing sentences caused by homoeoteleutons, misreadings and hypercorrections, appear in the Būlāq edition and other printed editions. The following are a few examples:

1. The phrase أهل الحوف (*ahl al-ḥawf*) appears three times in the text of the autograph and in most of the *'Ajā'ib* manuscripts, but in MS *'Aj.* Tārīkh 1426 (VI. 19. c.), and in the Būlāq edition (see *'Aj.* Būlāq, I, 21; III, 197) it appears twice as أهل الحرف and only once as الحوف (*'Aj.* I, 381). The substitution of *waw* for *rā'* changes the meaning completely and the English translators of *'Ajā'ib al-Āthār* (1993) rendered the phrase in *'Aj.* Būlāq, I, 21 (Eng. trans. I, 34) once as 'the people of vulgar expression', the second time in *'Aj.*,I, 381 (Eng. trans., I, 638), as 'beduins or frontier dwellers' and in the third case, *'Aj.*, III, 223 (Eng. trans., III, 340) as the meaningless 'the riffraff of the guilds'. This change of الحوف into الحرف can be easily detected if we remember that the word أهل denotes inhabitants of a place, quarter or city such as أهل مصر (inhabitants of Cairo or Egypt), while for guilds the word أرباب is used, e.g. ارباب الملاعيب ،

ارباب الحرف ، ارباب الملاهي, but never with *ahl*. The region of alḤawf is described in Arabic geographical dictionaries, mainly in Yaqūt, *Mu'jam al-Buldān* where under the word حوف most of the villages to the west, east and south of Cairo are mentioned.[79] Therefore, الحوف denotes a geographical regionand أهل الحوف are the inhabitants of al-Ḥawf, and الحرف (guilds) is a false reading.

2. Other corrupted readings are:

a. *'Aj*. Būlāq, I, 167, بدار عند قبة where the Cambridge autograph reads: بدار عند قبو.

b. *'Aj*. Būlāq, I, 171, تحت مصطبة البوابة في الخرابة where the Cambridge autograph reads: تحت مصطبة البوابة في الخزانة.

c. *'Aj*. Būlāq, I, 182, ولفت وجهه where the Cambridge autograph reads: ولفت جواده.

d. *'Aj*. Būlāq, I, 190, عذارات where the Cambridge autograph reads: غدَارات.

e. *'Aj*. Būlāq, I, 141, ففروا على الخازندار where the Cambridge autograph reads: فعزَوا على الخازندار.

f. *'Aj*. Būlāq, I, 141, كامنوهم where the Cambridge autograph reads: كاونوهم.

g. *'Aj*. Būlāq, I, 150, 152: ابو يوسف، فريد علي where the Cambridge autograph reads: ابو سيف، قرد علي

h. *'Aj*. Būlāq, I, 387: قالت فما تبتغيه جنسي امحري فطفقت أسأل عن نعومة ما خفا.

The Būlāq version misses the paronomasia in the mosaic rhyme and the double entendre. This word is given correctly in the Cambridge autograph, which reads:

قالت فما تبتغيه جنسي أم حري ؟ فطفقت أسأل عن نعومة ما خفا

and it should be translated as, 'Then I asked about the softness of what was hidden. She said, 'Are you asking of my race or of my vulva?' hinting at the same time at her race as Amharic.

Even MS *'Aj*. Ber., IV عجب (III. 9. d.) which is copied from al-Jabartī's autograph of volume IV, as stated by the copyist, has a better reading than the Būlāq edition, e.g.: j. in the Būlāq edition of *'Aj*.,IV, 186, there is the

79 Yāqūt ibn 'Abd Allāh, al-Ḥamawī, *Jacut's Geographisches Wörterbuch: aus den Handschriften zu Berlin, St. Petersburg, Paris, London und Oxford auf kosten der deutschen morgenländischen Gesellschaft*, Ferdinand Wüstenfeld (ed.)(Leipzig1868–70). Cf. the review of S. Moreh of the English translation, 'Abd ar-Raḥmān al-Gabartī: *'Abd al-Raḥmān al-Jabartī's History of Egypt, 'Ajā'ib al-Āthār fi 'l-Tarājim wa 'l-Akhbār* (Stuttgart1994). Edited by Thomas Philipp and Moshe Perlmann, vols I…IV, with *A Guide to 'Abd al-Raḥmān al-Jabartī's History of Egypt: 'Ajā'ib al-Āthār fi 'l-Tarājim wa 'l-Akhbār*, by Thomas Philipp and Guido Schwald…', in *Die Welt des Islams* 35:2 (1997), 235–42.

expression صعلوكا (a penniless pauper), while the right version is found in MS *'Aj.* Ber., IV, f. 173b: مفلوكا (unlucky, ill-starred, and unfortunate).

k. *'Aj.* Būlāq, IV, 230, المكللة بالذهب (adorned with a wreath, crowned with gold), where the MS *'Aj.* Ber., IV, f. 214b, gives the right version المكفتة بالذهب (plated or inlaid with gold).

l. *'Aj.* Būlāq, IV, 151 the word الاوربيون (European), does not fit the context, while the right version is found in the MS *'Aj.* Ber., IV as الربويون (usurer).

m. *'Aj.* Būlāq, IV, 241, the sentence: وسكنى الدور والحزم (living in spacious houses, to steadfastness), while the right version in the MS *'Aj.* Ber., IV, f. 224b reads: وسكنى الدور والخدم. (living in spacious houses with servants). These changes in the Būlāq edition show clearly that although the grammatical and stylistic errors of al-Jabartī are corrected, some words, mainly eloquent ones used by al-Jabartī, were hypercorrected through misreading and misunderstanding the term and words and endured diglossia, which change the actual meaning intended by the author.

n. In MS *'Aj.* Cam., Qq. 171, III, f. 262a: وبقوا بين الشك والرج (they remained (in a state) of turmoil and doubts), while in *'Aj.* Būlāq, III, 306, the version is distorted into: وبقوا بين الشنك والفرح (they stayed celebrating with fireworks and rejoicing). This change was deliberate by the copyist expecting that the Muslim population would welcome the Ottomans.

3. However, the chief defect of the Būlāq edition is the great number of homoeoteleutons, which distort the actual meaning of many paragraphs. Some examples of such homoeoteleutons are in:

a. *'Aj.* Būlāq, IV, 243: عوضا عن السيد محمد المحروقي while in MS *'Aj.* Ber., IV, f. 226b the sentence: عوضا عن السيد محمد/ الدواخلي وقد كان الباشا قبل حضورهم احضر السيد محمد/ المحروقي is missing. Another sentence in MS *'Aj.* Ber., IV, f. 226b of 9 words is missing in *'Aj.* Būlāq, after 8 lines.

b. *'Aj.* Būlāq, IV, 251 (month Dhu 'l-Qaʿda 1231 [/23 September–21 October 1816]): فتهدمت / وتكسرت أخشابها, while in MS *'Aj.* Ber., IV, f. 234a the sentence is: تهدمت /وتشلخت قطعا وقرابيض صارت تتدحرج في التيار/ وتكسرت أخشابها

These defects can be easily corrected by comparing the Cambridge University Library autograph with the Būlāq edition. (For more examples compare our edited Arabic text of *'Ajā'ib al-Āthār* and the footnotes).

There are many homeoteleutons in the Būlāq edition which can be corrected by comparing the text with the Cambridge MS. The following are but a few examples:

a. *'Aj.* Būlāq, I, 203: وتولى السلطان عثمان بن احمد . In the Cambridge autograph the full sentence is: وتولى بعده السلطان عثمان فلم تطل أيامه ومات سنة احدى وسبعين وتولى بعدهالسلطان مصطفى بن احمد

Such an error can be easily detected if the year and the name of the Sultan are checked.

b. *'Aj.* Būlāq, I, 212 gives the following verse:

هذا هوالفضل هذا   مقام من رام يغنم

Comparison with the Cambridge autograph and other manuscripts shows that there are four hemistiches missing as a result of homoeoteleuton in the word *hādhā*:

فامدحه ان كنت تعلم   هذا هو الفضل هذا
االمعلى المعظم   هذا علي ابن تاج
مقام من رام يغنم   الله اكبر هذا

All these changes and misreadings are common to all printed editions of *'Ajā'ib al-Āthār* including the edition printed in the margin of *al-Kāmil* by Ibn al-Athīr (vol. IV, 173). This edition seems to be printed from MS *'Aj.* Tārīkh 1872/microfilm 35107, vol. III (VI. 22. c. above). Some proper names given in MS *'Ajā'ib al-Āthār* of the Bibliothèque Nationale, Paris are vowelled. This manuscript was most probably edited by al-Jabartī himself because the handwriting of the corrections in the margins is very similar to that of al-Jabartī's autograph; in this case the Paris version is preferable.

These proper names are:

1. *'Aj.*, II, 103–5: حسين بيك شفت, is vowelled in Paris (MS *'Aj.* BNII, f. 96b)(III. 7. b.) as *shufut* (شُفُت).

2. *'Aj.*, II, 209: عثمان بيك طبل, is vowelled in Paris (MS *'Aj.* BNII, f. 201b) as *ṭubbal* (طُبّل) .

3. *'Aj.*, III, 227: مقدار, is written in the MS *'Aj.* Cam. (Qq. 171, III, f. 276b) and Paris MSS as *miqdād* (مقداد).

4. *'Aj.*, III, 242: متش القبطان , is vowelled in Paris (MS *'Aj.* BNIII, f. 295a)(III. 7. c.) as *mutsh* مُتْش

It is important to note here that MS *'Aj.* BN is almost identical with MS *'Aj.* Cam., MS *'Aj.* BM and MS *'Aj.* al-Zakiyya 859.

The poetry in al-Jabartī's works shows that his knowledge of the rules of Arabic prosody was weak and that he makes many metrical mistakes, perhaps because he is quoting from memory. The fact that the Būlāq edition, which is based on at least one of the MSS in which metrical and stylistic mistakes have been corrected, proves that the copyist of this MS was well-versed in prosody and literature; however, his lack of knowledge of Arabic history, Egyptian geography and technical terminology, caused many mistakes in these fields.

XI. The relationship between the printed versions of Maẓhar al-Taqdīs and the manuscripts

A comparison between the manuscripts of *Maẓhar al-Taqdīs* and the printed version edited by Muḥammad 'Aṭāshowed that the texts of MSS*Maẓ.* Rampur, Bayazīd and BM correspond word for word, that the printed version corresponds to these three, and that MS*Maẓ.* Cam. does not contain exactly the same text.[80] Some passages are missing in MS*Maẓ.* Cam., such as two passages in which al-Jabartī quoted his friend, Ḥasan al-'Aṭṭār, and the biography of Muṣṭafā Bāshā.[81] Thus the text of MSS *Maẓ.* Ram., Bay., and BM is more correct and complete than that of MS*Maẓ.* Cam. Moreover, the text of these three contains fewer errors of homoeoteleuton, dittography, misreadings, metathesis, and disfigurement of words than occur in 'Aṭā's edition.[82] Another edition of *Maẓhar al-Taqdīs*, by 'Umar al-Dasūqī and Ḥasan Jawhar (Cairo 1967), is based on a corrupted manuscript and is full of misreadings.

80 al-'Aṭṭār's passages in*Maẓhar al-Taqdīs*,'Aṭā's edn., II, 124, 129–31; *Maẓhar al-Taqdīs*,'Abd al-Raḥīm's edn., 241, 245 and *Maẓhar al-Taqdīs*, Aḥmad 'Abduh 'Alī's edn., 206, 210.

81 For Muṣṭafā Bāshā see MS*Maẓ.* Cam. f. 82; *Maẓhar al-Taqdīs*,'Aṭā's edn., II, 77, ll. 2–19, *Maẓhar al-Taqdīs*, 'Abd al-Raḥīm's edn., 205; *Maẓhar al-Taqdīs*,Aḥmad 'Abduh 'Alī's edn., 174.

82 On the MSS used by 'Abd al-Raḥīm and Aḥmad 'Abduh 'Alī, see the introductions to their new editions of *Maẓhar al-Taqdīs*.

The fact that the Būlāq edition of *'Ajā'ib al-Āthār* (which does not correspond with MSS *'Aj.* BM, BN, Cam.) and Muḥammad ʿAṭā's edition of *Maẓhar al-Taqdīs* (which corresponds with MS *Maẓ.* Ram., Bay., and BM) contain more details than the two Cambridge autographs suggests that these Cambridge manuscripts were the drafts for the second versions of these books. Because we know that al-Jabartī spent his last days in selling and copying books in Cairo, he may have made more than one copy of his historical works. Therefore, the possibility exists that besides the MS of *Maẓhar al-Taqdīs* kept in Dār al-Kutub al-Qawmiyya in Cairo and of volumes II and III of *'Ajā'ib al-Āthār*, written in 1237 (/1821–2) and kept in the al-Zakiyya collection of Dār al-Kutub al-Qawmiyya (nos. 858–9), still other autographs of *Maẓhar al-Taqdīs* and *'Ajā'ib al-Āthār* will be found. However, comparison of all the MSS and the Būlāq edition shows that the harsh criticism of Muḥammad ʿAlī Pasha was not omitted from the printed edition. This refutes the accusation made by Jurjī Zaydān and by Anistās al-Karmilī that on account of this criticism, Muḥammad ʿAlī's family had confiscated the existing copies of *'Ajā'ib al-Āthār*, and that the Būlāq edition was censored before it was published.[83]

XII. Comparison between Muddat al-Faransīs, Maẓhar al-Taqdīs, and of 'Ajā'ib al-Āthār and the sequence of their compilation.

Comparison of MS *Tārīkh Muddat al-Faransīs bi-Miṣr* with MS *Maẓhar al-Taqdīs* and MS *'Ajā'ib al-Āthār* of the same period, showed that MS *Mudda* contains 41 passages which give more details of important events that took place during the French occupation. These passages throw light on the context of many vague passages in the other two books.[84] A good illustration of the elaborate and detailed text of MS *Mudda* is the passage dealing with the battle against British naval power at Abū Qīr and with the attempt of the French to strike at British interests in India by occupying Egypt and the Suez region which leads to the Red Sea.[85]

83 See Kūrkīs ʿAwwād, *al-Makhṭūṭāt al-Tārīkhiyya fī Khizānat Kutub al-Matḥaf al-'Irāqī bi-Baghdād* (Baghdad 1957) and *Mudda*, 3.

84 See Bjørneboe, *In Search*, 84–219.

85 Such as the passage about Aḥmad al-Zarw, f. 10b, l. 20 (*Mudda*, Leiden, Eng. tr. 63–4). Cf. Muḥammad Kurayyim (*Mudda*, Leiden, ff. 12a, l. 21–12b, l. 3; cf. *'Aj.*, III, 63, ll. 1–2; *Maẓhar al-Taqdīs*, I, 70, ll. 17–18.

Comparison of these two autographs also shows the various ways of writing certain terms such as الداشاة and الضاشات (Janissary or comrade), غيلونجيةand قلينجية (sailors),الروزنامجي، الرزنامجي and الرزمانجي (controller) (See the Arabic text of MS*Mudda*, n. 15, 87); the meaning of certain terms, colloquial and otherwise, which al-Jabartī uses in the chronicles such as عوقوهم = حاشوهم (to detain) (see n. 9), بطالين = سنادلة (idlers) (see n. 137), قايق = مركب (boat) (see n. 140), قبلي = صعيد (Upper Egypt)(see n. 143), لزقة = لصقة (stick) (see n. 146), شلوار = سروال = شروال (trousers) (see n. 149).

Seven passages in MS *Mudda* have a different context from those in the other two books. Out of 31 passages which are similar to passages in *Maẓhar al-Taqdīs*, but different from *'Ajā'ib al-Āthār*, are imprecations or insults against the French. Only 10 passages in MS *Mudda* are similar to those in *'Ajā'ib al-Āthār*; unlike the *Maẓhar al-Taqdīs* passages these hardly contain insults of the French. Moreover, only 13 short passages are more detailed in *Maẓhar al-Taqdīs* and *'Ajā'ib al-Āthār*. These facts show that there is some similarity between MS *Mudda* and *Maẓhar al-Taqdīs*, while the similarity between *Maẓhar al-Taqdīs* and *'Ajā'ib al-Āthār* is much greater than that of either with MS *Mudda*.

As we have seen before, many passages, which are in the margins of MS *Mudda* appear in the text of MS *Maẓ.* Cam. Additions in the margins of MS*Maẓ.*Cam. are missing in MS *Mudda* while they are found in the text of MS *'Aj.* Cam., and passages in the margin of MS *'Aj.* Cam. are not in MS*Maẓ.* Cam.

All this, combined with the fact that al-Jabartī finished compiling *Maẓhar al-Taqdīs* at the end of Shaʿbān 1216 (/4 January 1802) and that he began to compile the material for *'Ajā'ib al-Āthār* after the expulsion of the French from Egypt,[86] completing the compilation of the first three volumes between 1220 (/1805–6) and 1221 (/1806–7),[87] shows that *'Ajā'ib al-Āthār* was the last

86 See the end of MS *Maẓhar al-Taqdīs* and *'Aj.* Būlāq, I, 6, ll. 17–19.

87 *'Aj.* Būlāq, I, 178, ll. 4–6, 373, l. 33–374, l. 13; II, 7, l. 30; III, 357, ll. 3–7. We are not dealing here with the way in which al-Jabartī collected his material, which we have discussed in 'Al-Jabartī's Method', *JSAI*, 25 (2001), and the contradictory versions which he gave (see Ayalon, 'The Historian', 222–7); however, the fact that in MS *'Aj.* Cam. the second version given in the biography of al-Murādī was written in the margin might shed a new light on the problem. Moreover, our research led us to the conclusion that between 1200/1785–6 and 1206/1791–2 al-Jabartī mainly collected biographies for al-Murādī and not much important chronological

book that he wrote.[88] As MS *Mudda* apparently was written while the events it recorded were happening,[89] probably in 1798, we can say that al-Jabartī's first work on Egyptian history was the MS entitled *Tārīkh Muddat al-Faransīs bi-Miṣr*, composed while under French occupation. The second work, *Maẓhar al-Taqdīs bi-Zawāl Dawlat al-Faransīs*, was completed at the end of Shaʿbān 1216 (/4 January 1802). Following the success of *Maẓhar al-Taqdīs*, he compiled his third and final work, the first three volumes of *'Ajā'ib al-Āthār fī 'l-Tarājim wa 'l-Akhbār*, in 1220–1 (/1805–7), and his fourth volume which he continued to compile until he became blind in 1821 (1236–7).

XII. Cardin's French translation.

Scholars have discussed the French translation (*Journal d'Abdurrahman Gabarti, pendant l'occupation française en Egypte, suivi d'un précis de la même campagne, par Mou'allem Nicolas El-Turki, secrétaire du prince des Druzes: traduits de l'arabe, par Alexandre Cardin, drogman chancelier du consulat général de France en Egypte*, edited by T.X. Bianchi, Paris 1838) held that this translation was of *Maẓhar al-Taqdīs*.[90] Many of these scholars also remarked that the translation was 'imperfect', but it seems that none of them made a careful scrutiny of it. A brief comparison between this translation and *Maẓhar al-Taqdīs* shows immediately that the translation is in fact 'imperfect' and that it is not a precise translation but an abridged version containing many passages mentioned neither in *Maẓhar al-Taqdīs* nor in

data and that between 1207/1792–3 and 1212/1797–8 he did not record anything. This conclusion of ours confirms Ayalon's proposals, 'The Historian', 227–8.

88 *'Aj*. Būlāq, I, 178, ll. 4–6, 373, l. 33–374, l. 13; II, 7, l. 30; III, 357, ll. 3–7.

89 See especially the two places where the author said: في العام الماضي ('in the last year'), *Mudda*, ff. 12b, ll. 10–12; 13a, ll. 19–20. On this topic, see Bjørneboe, *In Search*, 84–134.

90 On Cardin, see *al-Jabartī's Chronicle*, 19, n. 59; cf. *GAL*, II, 480; *GAL*, II, 2nd edn., 632; Yūsuf Ilyān Sarkīs, *Mu'jam al-Maṭbū'āt al-'Arabiyya wa 'l-Mu'arraba* (Cairo 1928), col. 676; Babinger, 340; Shaybūb, *'Abd al-Raḥmān al-Jabartī*, 112; and Jamāl al-Dīn al-Shayyāl, *al-Tārīkh wa 'l-Mu'arrikhūn fī Miṣr: fī 'l-Qarn al-Tāsi''Ashar* (Cairo 1958),26, 243. It seems that von Kremer was the first scholar who expressed this opinion and the others followed him. Macdonald, 'al-Djabartī', *EI*[1], ii, 986 clearly shows this influence in his statement: 'Another detailed diary of the French occupation (*Muẓhir al-Taqdīs*) is still unprinted in Arabic, but has appeared in Turkish, and an imperfect (so Alfred von Kremer, *Aegypten, Forschungen über Land und Volk während eines zehn Jährigen Aufenthalts*, Leipzig, Brockhaus, 1863, II, 326) French version by Cardin'.

Tārīkh Muddat al-Faransīs bi-Miṣr, but only in the third volume of *'Ajā'ib al-Āthār*. The following will be sufficient illustration.

a. Cardin, *Journal*, 6: 'En 1213 de l'hégire (1798–9), commencérent les guerres,les calamités, le bouleversement des affaires, les révolutions, enfin la ruine générale. Le dimanche 10'. This passage is a summary of the beginning of the third volume of *'Ajā'ib al-Āthār* (Būlāq, p. 2, ll. 2-7): سنة ثلاث عشرة ومائتين والف . وهي اوّل سنى الملاحم العظيمة، والحوادث الجسيمة، والوقائع النازلة، والنوازل الهائلة، وتضاعف الشرور، وترادف الامور، وتوالى المحن، واختلال الزمن، وانعكاس المطبوع، وانقلاب الموضوع، وتتابع الاهوال، واختلاف الاحوال، وفساد التدبير، وحصول التدمير، وعموم الخراب، وتواتر الاسباب، وَمَا كَانَ رَبّكَ مُهْلِكَ القُرَى بِظُلْم واأهلُها مُصْلِحُون. (في يوم الاحد العاشر من شهر محرم الحرام من هذه السنة . In *Maẓhar al-Taqdīs* (I, 32, ll. 1–3) the passage reads واول شرح القضية انه في يوم الاحد العاشر: من شهر محرم الحرام افتتاح سنة عشرة ومائتين والف ...

b. Cardin, *Journal*, 8: 'Bakir-Pacha expédia en consequence un Tartare a Constantinople pour apporter de la thériaque du pays de l'Yrak. (Proverbe significant que le remède arrivera après la mort du malade)'. The passage in *'Ajā'ib al-Āthār* (III, 3, ll. 28–30) reads:
فاتفق رأيهم على ان يرسلوا مكاتبة بخبر هذا الحادث الى اسلامبول ... وكتبوا المكاتبة وارسلها بكر باشا مع رسوله على طريق البر ليأتيه بالترياق من العراق ...
In *Maẓhar al-Taqdīs*, which was written in honour of the return of the Ottomans, this insulting remark is absent, and the passage reads (I, 34-35):
فاتفق الرأى على يرسلون مكاتبة للدولة بخبر هذه الحادثة، فأرسلها باشا مصر اذ ذاك وهو بكر باشا على قاصد من جهة البرّ ويجهزون عسكراً ...

c. Cardin, *Journal*, 13–14: 'Les personnes sensées voulaient les engager à se taire: le Prophéte et ses disciples, leur disaient-ils, se battaient avec le sabre et l'épée, et non avec des cris et des aboiements comme des chiens. Ils ne furent ni écoutés ni compris'. In *'Ajā'ib al-Āthār* (III, 8, ll. 14–17), this passage is:
فكان العقلاء من الناس يصرخون عليهم ويامرونهم بترك ذلك ويقولون لهم ان الرسول والصحابة والمجاهدين انما كانوا يقاتلون بالسيف والحراب وضرب الرقاب لا برفع الاصوات والصراخ والنباح فلا يستمعون ولا يرجعون عماهم فيه ومن يقرأ ومن يسمع . In *Maẓhar al-Taqdīs* the passage is missing (cf. I, 51, l. 12)

d. Cardin, *Journal*, 108–12: in these pages Cardin gives a summary of the biographies of 13 Shaykhs. All these biographies are given in detail in

'Ajā'ib al-Āthār, III, 60, ll. 30–67, l. 26, while in *Maẓhar al-Taqdīs* they are not given at all (cf. I, 172, l. 4).

e. While *Maẓhar al-Taqdīs* ends with the events of 5 Shaʿbān 1216 (/11 December 1801), the Cardin translation ends with the events of 10 Shawwāl 1216 (/13 February 1802),[91] i.e. two months later. Only if Cardin had made his abridged translation from *'Ajā'ib al-Āthār*,would he have been able to end on that date.

Cardin's translation is thus an abridged version of the third volume of *'Ajā'ib al-Āthār*, from the beginning of the year 1213 (/1798) to 10 Shawwāl 1216 (/13 February 1802).

It would be interesting to know what gave rise to the assumption that this was a translation of *Maẓhar al-Taqdīs*. Cardin's translation has a title which does not indicate the real name of the book that he translated. Moreover, the preface contains a passage from the introduction of Muṣṭafā Bahjat to his Turkish translation, entitled *Maẓhar al-Taqdīs bi-Khurūj Ṭā'ifat al-Faransīs*, which Cardin translated as 'Déliverance de l'Egypte par la sortie de la nation française'.[92] It seems that those who have written about this French translation

91 Cardin, 256; cf. *'Aj.*, III, 208, l. 22.

92 See Cardin, *Journal d'Abdurrahman Gabarti*, 5. *GAL*, II, 480, and *GAL*, *Suppl.*, II, 371, quoting Ottokar Maria von Schlechta-Wssehrd, *Denkschriften der Kaiserlichen Akademie der Wissenschaften, Philosophisch-historische Klasse* (Vienna 1857), VIII, 13, stated that this Turkish translation was printed in Istanbul in 1217/1802–3. This date is impossible because Muṣṭafā Bahjat translated *Maẓhar al-Taqdīs* (or started translating it) in Muḥarram 1222 (11 March–9 April 1807) and finished the task in Rabīʿ I 1225 (/5 April–4 May 1810). Professor Uriel Heyd looked for the printed version of this translation in the main libraries of Istanbul when he was in Turkey in the summer of 1960, but could not trace it. Babinger does not mention this printed version. The only catalogue that lists this printed translation is the *Catalogue of the Arabic and Persian Manuscripts in the Oriental Public Library at Bankipore* (Calcutta 1929), XV, 159–60, no. 1075. According to this catalogue, the book was translated by Muṣṭafā Bahjat and published in Istanbul in 1281/1864–5. This date is also given by Rieu, *Supplement*, 360, with a reference to Schlechta-Wssehrd, *Denkschriften* (VIII, 13 (but *Denkschriften*, VIII, was published in 1857, and p. 13 contains no mention of a printed translation). With reference to the manuscripts of the Turkish translations, Professor Heyd found five such in the Istanbul Universitesi Kutuphanesi. On three of them the name of the translator is '*Ra'īs al-aṭibbā'* Muṣṭafā Bahjat', while on the other two the name is Aḥmad ʿĀṣim. The date of the termination of all five is Rabīʿ I 1225. Professor Heyd compared some pages of a copy from the first group with one of the second group and found that the texts were the same word for word.

We were able to obtain a microfilm of a MS of Muṣṭafā Bahjat's translation from the Nationalbibliothek in Vienna (see *Die arabischen, persischen und turkischen Handschriften*

were led astray mainly by this passage.[93] Al-Jabartī's *'Ajā'ib al-Āthār* has since, been translated into many languages, amongst which are French and Russian.[94]

Stemma of al-Jabartī's Manuscripts

Muddat Tārīkh al-Faransīs bi-Miṣr

A first draft of the events of 15 June-December 1798.
Muddat Tārīkh al-Faransīs bi-Miṣr, Leiden, autograph, 1799.

---

der Kaiserlich-Koeniglichen Hofbibliothek zu Wien [Vienna 1865–7], II, 316, no. 1144). With the help of Dr Ḥusayn Atay of Ankara University we were able to examine this manuscript and found that it is a summarized version of *Maẓhar al-Taqdīs* written in a very eloquent Turkish style with a preface by the translator on the French Revolution and its development up to the occupation of Egypt (see the French translation by Cardin, *Journal d'Abdurrahman Gabarti*, 5. (It is surprising that the date of the completion of the translation given in the preface is 1222 [/1807–8] [see also Cardin, 5], while in the colophon it is 1225 [/1810–11]).

93 The complete French translation of *'Ajā'ib al-Āthār* is *Merveilles biographiques et historiques, ou chroniques du Cheikh Abd-el-Rahman el-Djabarti, traduites de l'arabe par Chefik Mansour Bey, Abdulaziz Kahil Bey, Gebriel Nicolas Kahil Bey et Iskender Ammoun Effendi* (9 vols, Cairo 1888–96).

94 Russian translations of ʿAbd al-Raḥmān al-Jabartī are:
ʿAbd al-Raḥmān al-Jabartī. *Egipet v kanun ekspeditsii Bonapart (1776–1798)* (Egypt on the Eve of Bonaparte's Expedition). Translation from Arabic into Russian preface and comments by H.I. Kilberg (Moscow 1978) (translation of volume II, *'Ajā'ib al-Āthār fi 'l-Tarājim wa 'l-Akhbār* (al-Qāhira 1297/1879–80).
ʿAbd al-Raḥmān al-Jabartī. *Egipet v period ekspeditsii Bonapart (1776–1798)* (Egypt during the Expedition of Bonaparte). Translation from Arabic into Russian, preface and comments by I.M. Filshtinskiy (Moscow1962) (translation of volume III, Part I, *'Ajā'ib al-Āthār fi 'l-Tarājim wa 'l-Akhbār* (al-Qāhira 1297/1879–80)
ʿAbd al-Raḥmān al-Jabartī. *Egipet pod vlastiy Muhammada Ali (1806–1821)* (Egypt during the Reign of Muḥammad ʿAlī). Translation from Arabic into Russian, preface and comments by H.I. Kilberg (Moscow 1963) (translation of volume IV, *'Ajā'ib al-Āthār fi 'l-Tarājim wa 'l-Akhbār* (al-Qāhira 1297/1879–80)
For a Russian bibliography about al-Jabartī's *Chronicle*, see:
Filshtinsky I.M., 'Kairskie vosstania 1798–1800 gg. I opisanie ih v hronke Abd ar-Rahmana al-Jabarti (Cairo Revolts of 1798–1800 and their Description in the Chronicle of ʿAbd al-Raḥmān al-Jabartī)', *Sovetskoe vostokovedenie* (Soviet Oriental Studies) 3 (1958).
——, 'Egipetskiy istorik al-Jabarti I ego hronika (The Egyptian Historian al-Jabartī and his Chronicle)', *Vestnik istorii mirovoy kulturi* (Bulletin of the History of World Culture) 4 (1960).
——., 'Hronika Abd ar-Rahmana al-Jabarti kak istoritcheskiy istotchnik (The Chronicle of ʿAbd al-Raḥmān al-Jabartī as a Historical Source), *Kratkie soobshenia Instituta narodov Azii* (Brief Reports of the Institute of the Peoples of Asia, Academy of Sciences, USSR) 47, Arabskie strain (Arab Countries), (Moscow 1961).

Maẓhar al-Taqdīs bi-Zawāl Dawlat al-Faransīs

The events of the French occupation of Egypt 1798–1801.

Maẓ. Cambridge, Qq 214, bought by Burckhardt (al-Shaykh Ibrāhīm) in 1232 (/1816–17), autograph.

Maẓ. DKQ, Tarikh M 101, microfilm 29362, revised autograph, 1224 (/1809–10).

Maẓ. Bayezid Library, Istanbul, MS Cevdet Pāshā 76, n.d. copied from an autograph.

Maẓ. Riḍā Library, Rampūr, from an autograph, copied in 1216 (/1801–2).

Maẓ. British Library, London, 561, copied by Aḥmad Rizq in 1263 (/1846–7) owned by Maḥfūẓ, the son ʿAbd al-Raḥmān, 'BT of Baron von Kremer 9 Jan. 1886'.

'Ajā'ib al-Āthār fi 'l-Tarājim wa 'l-Akhbār

A chronicle of Egypt from 1688–1821 recorded by al-Jabartī; biographies collected by al-Zabīdī until 1791 and by other authors.

'Ajā'ib, vol. I (sic) (= vol. III), DKQ, Tārīkh 1426, microfilm 35532, seems to be a rough draft of *'Ajā'ib al-Āthār* based upon *Maẓhar al-Taqdīs*, and continued until the year 1220 (/1805–6), n.d. and no name of the copyist.

'Ajā'ib, the first half of vol. I, Iraq Museum, purports to be an autograph.

'Ajā'ib, vol. I, Munich, Or. Prunneri 259, n.d.

'Ajā'ib, vol. I, Birmingham, 908 (1361) 'Mingana Collection', n.d. and no name of the copyist.

'Ajā'ib, vol. II, Birmingham, 909 (1362) 'Mingana Collection', n.d. and no name of the copyist.

'Ajā'ib, vol. III, Birmingham, 910 (1363) 'Mingana Collection', n.d. and no name of the copyist.

'Ajā'ib, vol. IV, Birmingham, 911 (1364) 'Mingana Collection', copied in 1296/1878–9 by the order of Ḥusayn Bek Ḥusnī, the director of al-Maṭbaʿa al-Kubrā.

Cambridge Group of Manuscripts, vols I–III

'Ajā'ib, vols I–III, Cambridge, Qq. 169–71 (علك), autograph copied in 1806.

'Ajā'ib, vols I–III, Cambridge, Qq. 166–8, in *Maghribī* script, revised and edited by al-Jabartī, marginal remarks by al-ʿAṭṭār.

'Ajā'ib, vols I–III, BN, Paris, Suppl. arabe, 1861–3, revised and edited by al-Jabartī, n.d. (عب).

'Ajā'ib, vols I–III, BN, Paris, Suppl. arabe, 1864–6, copied from Jabartī's autograph, n.d.

'Ajā'ib, vol. III only, DKQ, Tārīkh 174, microfilm 10730, copied in 1220 (/1805–6) (3 نمره).

'Ajā'ib, vol. II–III, al-Zakiyya 858/microfilm 54237 (copied by Aḥmad Muḥammad) and al-Zakiyya 859/54236, copied in 1237 (/1821–2), read to al-Jabartī in 1240 (/1824–5) by Aḥmad b. Ḥasan al-Rashīdī al-Shāfiʿī known as Ṣawbaʿ.

'Ajā'ib, vols I–III, British Library (British Museum), London, Add. 26,042–4, copied by Ṣāliḥ al-'Azab al-Jabalāwī in 1242 (/1826–7), owned by Yaʿqūb (!).

'Ajā'ib, vols I–III, British Library (British Museum), London, Or. 4628–30, copied by ʿAlī Maṭar al-Ghiryānī in 1245 (/1829–30), owned by E.W. Lane.

'Ajā'ib, vols I–III, John Rylands University Library, Manchester, 278–80 (699–701),copied for and ordered by M. Asselin in about 1830, owned by Silvestre de Sacy, acquired by Lord Crawford.

'Ajā'ib, vols I–III, Inst. Or. Stud. Leningrad (St. Petersburg), C 732, Cat. 9420, vol. I, copied 1259 (/1843–4), by the order of Maḥfūẓ the son of al-Jabartī, volumes II–III, copied in 1262 (/1846), by Sulaymān Salāma al-Sunbulāwī and owned by Timaviov, the Dragoman of the Russian Consul.

'Ajā'ib, vols I–II, DKQ, Tārīkh 173, microfilm 10728–9, copied in 1262 (/1845–6), owned by Yaḥyā Ḥakam in 1263 (/1846–7) and read by 'Alī Fahmī, the son of Rifā'a Bek Rāfi' in 1287 (/1870–1).

'Ajā'ib, vols II–III, DKQ, al-Zakiyya, 852–3, microfilms 9215–17, copied in 1287 (/1870–1) by Muḥammad b. Aḥmad b. Khalīl al-Ṭanbashāwī, by the order of Jibrā'īl Yūsuf Mukhalla'.

'Ajā'ib, vol. I, pts. 1–2, al-Zakiyya, 855–6, microfilms 9214–5, n.d., owner: Jibrā'īl Yūsuf Mukhalla', copied in 1237 (/1821–2).

The Būlāq Group of 'Ajā'ib Manuscripts, vols I–IV Copied from an Autograph.

'Ajā'ib, vol. I, Berlin 9487, Or. Qu. 658, copied in 1260 (/1844–5) with no name of copyist.

'Ajā'ib, vol. II, Berlin 9488, Or. Qu. 659, copied in 1264 (/1847–8) by 'Umar al-Khaṭṭāb.

'Ajā'ib, vol. III, Berlin 9489, Or. Qu. 673, copied in 1295 (/1878) by Muṣṭafā al-Shalshamūnī b. Muḥammad al-Shalshamūnī.

'Ajā'ib, vol. IV, Berlin 9490, Or. Qu. 660, copied in 1264 (/1847–8) from an autograph dated (12)36 (/1820–1).

'Ajā'ib, vol. I, DKQ, Būlāq 1895, Tārīkh 466, microfilm 36339, copied by Muḥammad Ḥusayn Aḥmad Miṣbāḥ al-Shāfi'ī in 1272 (/1855–6).

'Ajā'ib, vol. II, DKQ, Būlāq 1895, Tārīkh 466, copied by Muḥammad Ḥusayn Aḥmad Miṣbāḥ al-Shāfi'ī in 1272 (/1855–6).

'Ajā'ib, vol. III, DKQ, Būlāq 1895, Tārīkh 466, microfilm 34682, no name of copyist and n.d.

'Ajā'ib, vol. IV, DKQ, Būlāq 1895, Tārīkh 466, microfilm 35088, copied by Muḥammad Ḥusayn Aḥmad Miṣbāḥ al-Shāfi'ī (?) in 1272 (/1855–6). Part of the events of Ṣafar-Dhu 'l-Ḥijja are attributed to the following months, Rabī' I -Shawwāl 1236 (/1820–1), and it ends with Shawwāl.

'Ajā'ib, vol. I, DKQ, Būlāq 1895, Tārīkh 1425, microfilm 14352 and 14200, copied by Muḥammad Aḥmad al-Shāfi'ī, n.d.

'Ajā'ib, vol. I, part 1, DKQ, Būlāq 1895, Tārīkh 1428, microfilm 12748.

'Ajā'ib, vol. I, part 2, DKQ, Būlāq 1895, Tārīkh 1428, microfilm 12747, copied by Riḍwān al-Damanhūjī b. Muṣṭafā al-Damanhūjī in 1290 (/1873–4).

'Ajā'ib, vol. I, DKQ, Tārīkh Taymūr 1562, microfilm 27775, copied in 1281 (/1864–5), Waqf Aḥmad b. Ismā'īl b. Muḥammad Taymūr 1320 (/1902–3).

'Ajā'ib, vol. II, DKQ, Tārīkh Taymūr 1562, microfilm 27762, copied in 1286 (/1869–70).

'Ajā'ib, vol. III, DKQ, Tārīkh Taymūr 1562, microfilm 28298.

'Ajā'ib, vol. II, DKQ, Tārīkh Taymūr 1562, microfilm 282980, copied from an autograph.

'Ajā'ib, vol. I, part 1, DKQ, Būlāq 1895, Tārīkh 1872, microfilm 35762, copied in 1295 (/1878).

'Ajā'ib, vol. I, part 2, DKQ, Būlāq 1895, Tārīkh 1872, microfilm 40549.

'Ajā'ib, vol. II, DKQ, Būlāq 1895, Tārīkh 1872, microfilm 35738, and 35824, n.d. and no name of the copyist.

'Ajā'ib, vol. III, part 1, DKQ, Būlāq 1895, Tārīkh 1872, microfilm 35107, copied in 1295 (/1878).

'Ajā'ib, vol. IV, part 1, DKQ, Būlāq 1895, Tārīkh 1872, microfilm 41211, copied in 1296 (/1878–9).

'Ajā'ib, vol. II, DKQ, Būlāq 1895, Tārīkh 1425, microfilm 14199 (part I), microfilm 14200 (part II), copied by Muḥammad Aḥmad al-Shāfiʿī, n.d.

'Ajā'ib, vol. III, DKQ, Būlāq 1895, Tārīkh 1425, microfilm 19286, copied by Aḥmad Yūnus, Abu 'l-Taysīr in 1287 (/1870–1).

'Ajā'ib, vol. IV, DKQ, Būlāq 1895, Tārīkh 1425, microfilm 12749, copied in 1289 (/1872–3) probably by the same copyist.

'Ajā'ib, vols III–IV, DKQ, Būlāq 1895, al-Zakiyya 860/microfilm 9218 and al-Zakiyya 861/microfilm 52898, vol. IV copied by Muḥammad Aḥmad Khalīl in 1287 (/1870–1).

'Ajā'ib, vol. IV, pt. I, DKQ, Būlāq 1895, al-Zakiyya 854, microfilm 9214, copied in 1287 (/1870–1), by Muḥammad b. Aḥmad b. Khalīl al-Ṭanbashāwī, and kept in the library of Jibrā'īl Yūsuf Mukhallaʿ from the autograph of volume IV of the author's MSS.

'Ajā'ib, vol. IV, pt. 2, al-Zakiyya 857/microfilm 17885, copied in 1273 (/1856–7) by ʿAbd al-Ḥamīd Nāfiʿ from an autograph of the author's MSS.

'Ajā'ib, vols III–IV, DKQ, Būlāq 1895, Tārīkh 1427, microfilm 14201–2, vol. IV copied in 1292 (/1875–6) by al-Sayyid Yūsuf.

'Ajā'ib, vol. I, Leeds Library, 9, copied by ʿUmar b. Khaṭṭāb in 1266 (/1849–50), by the order of Maḥmūd b. Musṭafā Qāsim, and later in the possession of Muḥammad Ḥasan al-Fākihīnī.

'Ajā'ib, vol. II, Leeds Library, 129, copied by ʿUmar b. Khaṭṭāb in 1266 (/1849–50).

'Ajā'ib, vol. III, Leeds Library, 130, copied by ʿUmar b. Khaṭṭāb in 1267 (/1855–1).

'Ajā'ib, vol. III, Leeds Library, 131, n.d., and there is no name of the copyist.

'Ajā'ib, vol. IV, Leeds Library, 132, copied by Aḥmad b. Muḥammad known as al-Shāhid in 1290 (/1873–4), claimed to be copied from an autograph of al-Jabartī.

'Ajā'ib, vol. III, DKQ, Tārīkh 2129, microfilm 36545 (defective).

'Ajā'ib, vols I–IV, Oriental Public Library, Bankipore, 1076–83; 1076–8, 1081–2, n.d.; 1079, copied by Ḥusayn Ḥasan Idrīs in 1274 (/1857–8); 1083, copied 1301 (/1883–4).

'Ajā'ib, vol. III, DKQ, Cairo, Tārīkh 1226, microfilm 365545.

'Ajā'ib, vol. II (= vol. IV), DKQ, Cairo, Tārīkh 1426, microfilm 38301, copied in 1296 (/1878–9).

Al-Maktaba al-Azhariyya

'Ajā'ib, vols I–IV, (276) Abāẓa 6573, copied from an autograph.

'Ajā'ib, vols I–III, (584) 8538, copied by Khalīl b. Ibrāhīm al-ʿAjūz, in 1289 (/1872–3), from an autograph).

'Ajā'ib, vols I–VII, (3065) 21594.

Dār al-Fāris Group of Manuscripts, vols I–IV.

'Ajā'ib, vol. I, DKQ, Tārīkh 2287 *badal*, microfilm 35946, copied in 1261 (/1845), owner: Maḥmūd Sāmī al-Bārūdī in 1285 (/1868–9).

'Ajā'ib, vol. II, DKQ, Tārīkh 2287 *badal*, microfilm 35959, n.d. no copyist, owner: Maḥmūd Sāmī al-Bārūdī in 1285 (/1868–9).

'Ajā'ib, vol. III, part 1, DKQ, Tārīkh 2287 *badal*, microfilm 35385, copied on 1262 (/1845–6), owner Maḥmūd Sāmī al-Bārūdī in 1285 (/1868–9).

'Ajā'ib, vol. III, part 2, DKQ, Tārīkh 2287 *badal*, microfilm 35547 copied on 1262 (/1845–6), owner: Maḥmūd Sāmī al-Bārūdī in 1285 (/1868–9).

'Ajā'ib, vol. I, part 1, DKQ, Būlāq 1895, Tārīkh 1424, microfilm 14586, copied by Aḥmad b. Mūsā al-Shāhid in 1289 (/1872).

'Ajā'ib, vol. I, part 2, DKQ, Būlāq 1895, Tārīkh 1424, microfilm 14674, copied on 1289 (/1872–3).

'Ajā'ib, vol. I, part 1, DKQ, Tārīkh 2129, microfilm 38169 (defective).

'Ajā'ib, vol. I, part 2, DKQ, Būlāq 1895, Tārīkh 2129, microfilm 14676, owned by Ibrāhīm Maḥmūd.

'Ajā'ib, vol. II, DKQ, Būlāq 1895, Tārīkh 1424, microfilm 14673, copied on 1290 (/1873) by Aḥmad b. Muḥammad al-Shāhid.

'Ajā'ib, vol. II, DKQ, Būlāq 1895, Tārīkh 1872, microfilm 35738.

'Ajā'ib, vols III, DKQ, Būlāq 1895, Tārīkh 1424, microfilm 14198, copied in 1292 (/1875) by Aḥmad b. Muḥammad al-Shāhid from *'Ajā'ib*, vol. III, DKQ, Būlāq 1895, Tārīkh 1426, microfilm 35532, after deleting all literary passages and poems as in the case of Dār al-Fāris.

'Ajā'ib, vols IV, DKQ, Būlāq 1895, Tārīkh 1424, microfilm 15011, copied on 1289 (/1872–3) by Aḥmad b. Muḥammad b. Aḥmad b. Mūsā al-Shāhid (*'Ajā'ib* in the margin of *al-Kāmil* by Ibn al-Athīr).

Chapter Three

Al-Jabartī's Method of Composing his Chronicle *'Ajā'ib al-Āthār fi 'l-Tarājim wa 'l-Akhbār* (The Marvellous Compositions of Biographies and Chronicles)[1]

In his pioneering work on 'The Historian al-Jabartī and his Background', the late Professor David Ayalon indicated that: 'al-Jabartī gives two versions regarding the compilation of his book, which covers the period 1100–1236/1688–1821'.[2] For the beginning of this period, al-Jabartī states that he only had a few poorly written pamphlets by 'common soldiers', the best among these being the work of Aḥmad Shalabī b.ʿAbd al-Ghanī (d. 1737), which starts with the occupation of Egypt by the Ottomans and ends in 1150 (/1737–8). Al-Jabartī claims that this work was lost, and that he had to record information from specific oral or written sources.[3]

The second version is that 'the main cause of the compilation of the chronicle in its existing form was the Damascene historian al-Murādī',[4] who provoked al-Jabartī's historical interest when he was still a student of the

1 Al-Jabartī used the word *āthār* in the sense of 'literary works, compositions, books, news', as in the case of al-Murādī's biography (II, 233–4), where he says وكان رحمه الله مغرما بصيد الشوارد وقيد الأوابد واستعلام الأخبار وجمع الآثار وتراجم العصريين على طريقة المؤرخين...: ('He was, may God have mercy upon him, fond of hunting for (linguistic) irregularities and recording peculiarities, and inquiring about events and collecting compositions and biographies of contemporaries in the manner of historians'). In another place (*'Aj.*, II, 236), al-Jabartī states فتراجمهم وآثارهم مجموعة في مجلد واحد (Their biographies and works are assembled in another volume). However, in *Maẓhar al-Taqdīs* (ʿAbd al-Raḥīm's edition [1998], 9), the author gives with al-ʿAṭṭār the term *akhbār* as a synonym to *āthār*. The English translation is according to the translation of Philipp and Perlmann, II, 392. Other such usages of the term *āthār* as books and compositions see *'Aj.*, I, 209 (al-Shubrāwī); I, 253 (al-Marḥūmī); II, 16 (al-Ḥammāmī); II, 54; II, 85 (al-Bannānī). Jack Crabbs in *The Writing of History in Nineteenth Century Egypt* (Detroit 1984), 43, also noticed that the term *āthār* means 'composition' and translated the title in a rhymed version: '*The Marvellous Compositions of Biographies Wondrous Seeds of Men and Their Deeds*'.

2 Ayalon, 'The Historian', 1960, 22; cf. Reichmuth, 'Notes', 374–83.

3 *'Aj.* Būlāq, I, 6. Cf. also Reichmuth, 'Notes', 374–83.

4 See Ayalon, 'The Historian', 224; cf. *'Aj.*, II, 234. It is important to note here that Ḥasan al-ʿAṭṭār recorded in the margin of his copy of *'Ajā'ib al-Āthār*, equivalent to al-Murādī's biography (*'Aj.*, II, 234), that during his journey to Damascus no one in Syria was interested in this book. He adds that a relative of al-Murādī copied it and omitted some biographies of scholars, who were not on good terms with him.

scholar Murtaḍā al-Zabīdī. As a contribution to his biographical work entitled *Silk al-Durar fī A'yān al-Qarn al-Thānī 'Ashar* (The String of Pearls Concerning Eminent Men of the 12th Century [AH]), the Syrian biographer Muḥammad Khalīl al-Murādī[5] (1760–91) asked Murtaḍā al-Zabīdī, a scholar of Indian origin who settled in the Yemen and then in Cairo, to collect biographies of Egyptian scholars living in Egypt and the surrounding areas during the twelfth century AH. Apparently al-Jabartī assisted his teacher with this work. However, al-Zabīdī in his MS *Hādhā Mu'jam Mukhtaṣṣ bi-Dhikr Man Akhadhtu 'anhu al-'Ulūm wa 'l-Ma'ārif min Shuyūkhī wa-Ābā'ī...* which deals with his *mashāyikh*, gives his own version. On the one hand, he confirms that al-Jabartī had collected data for his own chronicle; on the other hand, al-Zabīdī states that al-Jabartī helped him in collecting some biographies which he needed for his *Great History of the People of the Twelfth Century*, withoutmentioning that he had collected biographies for the work of al-Murādī. Al-Zabīdī's remark confirms al-Jabartī's statement that he collected historical information on the period between the end of the twelfth century and the beginning of the thirteenth century of the *hijra*.[6]

According to al-Jabartī, the deaths of both al-Zabīdī (d. April 1791) andal-Murādī (d. 28 October 1791) put an end to al-Jabartī's work of collecting biographical information and data.[7] Yet the foundation was laid for his later historiographical work, which contains a large number of biographies of eminent scholars and *amīr*s who lived and died in Egypt. In fact the two versions are mentioned by al-Jabartī, and therefore we assumed that they are not contradictory, but most probably complementary. This is also the conclusion of Professor Ayalon on the basis of the printed Būlāq edition of 1297/1879–80 alone.

Only recently with Professor S. Reichmuth's article entitled 'Murtaḍā Al-Zabīdī (d. 1791) in Biographical and Autobiographical Accounts. Glimpses of Islamic Scholarship in the 18th Century' has it become possible to obtain precise information about al-Zabīdī MS of biographies.[8] This article helped us

---

5 See Ayalon, 'The Historian', and *'Aj.*, II, 234.

6 I would like to thank Professor Stefan Reichmuth of Bochum University, for supplying me with a few pages of this MS of the *Mu'jam Mukhtaṣṣ*. The MS is kept in the library of Aḥmad 'Ārif Ḥikmet in Medina (*ṭalab*: 52), and its microfilm (no. 6238) is kept in al-Jāmiʿa al-Islāmiyya bi 'l-Madīna al-Munawwara, in 177ff.

7 See *'Aj.*, II, 234.

8 *Die Welt des Islams* 39 (1999), 64–102.

to arrive at different results in our investigation of the different MSS of al-Jabartī's historical works and of al-Zabīdī's MSS. It not only confirms Ayalon's conclusion, but also sheds more light on the methods used by Arab historians in writing their works. In particular, much information about al-Jabartī's method of compiling his chronicles may be found in the manuscripts collected by J.L. Burckhardt, known as al-Shaykh Ibrāhīm after taking the turban in Aleppo. Burckhardt first arrived in Cairo in 1812; he visited Cairo again in the middle of 1815 and died there in 1817.[9] He acquired the first autograph of *Maẓhar al-Taqdīs* on which he recorded that he bought it in 1232 (/1816–17).

It seems that in this year Burckhardt also bought the autograph of the first three volumes of *'Ajā'ib al-Āthār*. Moreover, during his journey to Syria, the Ḥijāz and Egypt, Burckhardt bought about 300 manuscripts which he ordered to be sent to the Cambridge University Library in England after his death. Among these there is a copy of *'Ajā'ib al-Āthār* with a title page and the last lines of the end of each volume written in al-Jabartī's handwriting, while the text is written in *Maghribī* script. The whole three volumes were revised by al-Jabartī himself, and he added his corrections in the margin of this MS which was in the possession of Ḥasan al-ʿAṭṭār. This MS was bought by Burckhardt, who had acquired it from Ḥasan al-ʿAṭṭār after he returned from his journey outside Egypt. In this MS, the latter recorded his comments on al-Jabartī's biographies and added records of his observations during his travels to Izmir, Istanbul, Damascus, Jerusalem and Jaffa.[10]

9 In *'Ajā'ib al-Āthār* (Būlāq, IV, 284) al-Jabartī recorded his meeting with Burckhardt calling him 'Sīdī al-Shaykh Ibrāhīm al-Mahdī al-Inkilīz'. On Burckhardt see Richard Trench, *Arabian Travellers* (Topsfield, Massachusetts andLondon 1986), 59–72; Beatrice Meyer, '"Shaykh Ibrahim" – Johann Ludwig Burckhardt (1784–1817)', *An Exhibition by Pro Helvetia, Arts Council of Switzerland in Kairo, with Arabic Translation and Layout* (Zürich 1990) and 'Arabic Manuscripts from the Burckhardt Collection' (*Catalogue of an Exhibition in the University Library*, Cambridge, 21 May 1990–21 June 1990 [held in conjunction with the exhibition by Pro Helvetia, the Swiss Arts Council, of posters on 'Shaykh Ibrahim'-Johann Ludwig Burckhardt (1784–1817) on display in the Faculty of Oriental Studies, Sedgwick Avenue, Cambridge, between the same dates]). With thanks to Mrs Jill Butterworth, Under-Librarian, Cambridge University Library (Near Eastern Section), for presenting me with a copy of the booklet *'Sheikh Ibrahim'-Johann Ludwig Burckhardt (1784–1817)* and the catalogue of the exhibition.

10 See E.G. Browne, *A Hand-list of the Muhammadan Manuscripts, Including All Those Written in the Arabic Character, Preserved in the Library of the University of Cambridge* (Cambridge 1900). MS *'Aj.* Cam. 2nd., Qq. 168, III, without pagination, equivalent to *'Aj.* Būlāq, III, 93. See

There are two other MSS of *'Ajā'ib al-Āthār* in which the title page and the last lines of volumes I–III were written and later on edited by al-Jabartī. The first is the MS of Bibliothèque Nationale in Paris.[11] The second MS is kept in Dār al-Kutub al-Qawmiyya in Cairo and contains a copy of volume III only of *'Ajā'ib al-Āthār*.[12] This MS has undergone the same process; al-Jabartī wrote the title page and the last lines of the book and recorded his corrections in the margins.

Moreover, among Burckhardt's collection, there are also two anonymous MSS concerning Muḥammad ʿAlī's invasion of the Ḥijāz, which contain many passages that are identical to passages in al-Jabartī's description of this invasion. The first is entitled *al-Naṣr al-Mumtadd fī Fatḥ Tihāma wa-Najd*.[13] The title of the second MS, which is a copy of the first, was changed from the first title into *al-Washy wa 'l-Ṭirāz fī Fatḥ al-Ḥijāz*, in a handwriting which is very similar to that of Ḥasan al-ʿAṭṭār. Moreover, some information which has

---

plate I in this volume. Cf. ʿAdel Manna, 'Cultural Relations Between Egypt and Jerusalem in the Early Nineteenth Century', *Asian and African Studies, Journal of the Israel Oriental Society*, vol. 17: 1–3 (November 1983), 139–52. This article contains photographs of three letters written by ʿAbd Allāh Sharqāwī, ʿAbd al-Raḥmān al-Jabartī, and Ḥasan al-ʿAṭṭār directed to Ṭāhir Afandī al-Ḥusaynī, the Muftī of Jerusalem, with their English translations. In the second letter, al-Jabartī speaks of his joy at the safe arrival of Shaykh Ḥasan al-ʿAṭṭār in Jerusalem. My thanks are due to Mr Ṣāliḥ ʿAbbāsī and Mrs Lubnā Ṣafadī-ʿAbbāsī for helping in getting copies of these letters from Butrus Abu-Manneh; see Butrus Abu-Manneh, 'Four Letters of Šayḫ Ḥasan al-ʿAṭṭār to Šayḫ Ṭāhir al-Ḥusaynī of Jerusalem', *Arabica*, vol. L: I (2002), 79–95. These letters are reproduced at the end of this book in the Appendix. An account of this journey was given in a lecture by the writer of these lines, entitled 'The Egyptian Scholar Hasan al-ʿAttar (d. 1834) and his Journey from Cairo to Izmir', given in Delphi, November 25–8, 1999, for the 'Colloquium on the Literary Expressions and Representations of the Mediterranean: Islands and Ports, 16th–20th Centuries', arranged by The Greek General and Comparative Literature Association, International Comparative Literature Association, Research Committee, Literary Representation of the Mediterranean. This lecture is published in Siaflekis and Rania Polycandrioti (eds), *Expressions et représentations littéraires de la Méditerranée: Iles et ports, XVIe–XXe siècles, Actes du Colloque, Centre Culturel Européen de Delphes, 5–6 novembre 1999, Z.I.* (Athens 2002), 19–32.

11 *Suppl. arabe*, 1861.

12 MS *'Aj.* Tārīkh 174/microfilm 10730.

13 See Browne, *A Handlist*, 237, no. 1188, shelf mark Add. 2782, where he gives the following description: 'two copies in one volume of an account of the exploits of Muḥammad ʿAlī (from AH 1218–1229 [/1803–14]) entitled *an-Naṣru 'l-mumtadd fī fatḥ Tihāma wa-Najd*, but this title has been subsequently altered (in the first copy only) to that of *al-Washy wa 'ṭ-Ṭirāz fī Fatḥi 'l-Ḥijāz*... [The first copy, which appears to be incomplete, comprises ff. 16, the second, ff. 32 (= ff. 48 in all), of 23.9 x 17.1 cm. and 21 ll; poor but legible *naskh*; rubrications; no date or colophon]'.

no connection with the occupation of the Ḥijāz has been deleted, while in some other places there are additions in the margin dealing with the occupation of the Ḥijāz, also in a handwriting which is very similar to that of Ḥasan al-ʿAṭṭār (plates III–IV, of *al-Naṣr al-Mumtadd*). All these autographs and manuscripts collected by Burckhardt provide valuable information on the traditional method of compiling historical works in the Arab world. Thus, it is important that the additions and corrections in the margins of both these MSS are in a handwriting which is very similar to that of Ḥasan al-ʿAṭṭār, which appears in the margins of the first three volumes of Cambridge MSS of *'Ajā'ib al-Āthār*, Qq. 166, 167, 168 (see plates I–II, al-ʿAṭṭār's comments in the margin of *'Ajā'ib*). Ḥasan al-ʿAṭṭār is known to have been an admirer of Muḥammad ʿAlī, who appointed him as rector of al-Azhar.[14] Therefore it seems likely that Ḥasan al-ʿAṭṭār corrected the MS of *al-Naṣr al-Mumtadd* which depended heavily on the end of the last part of volume III and the beginning of the first part of volume IV of *'Ajā'ib al-Āthār*, after it had been copied by a copyist, intending to present it to this ruler.

Although the autographs of al-Jabartī's works do not have a colophon and are not dated, the sequence in which he wrote his books is proven without any doubt by the fact that al-Jabartī's additions and corrections on the margins of the autograph of *Muddat al-Faransīs* appear in the text of *Maẓhar al-Taqdīs*, and the additions and corrections in the margin of the autograph of *Maẓhar al-Taqdīs* appear in the text of the autograph of *'Ajā'ib al-Āthār*. It is clear that whilst *Muddat al-Faransīs* was written during the first seven months of the French occupation, *Maẓhar al-Taqdīs* was compiled during the time when the French, led by ʿAbdallah Menou, had just started to negotiate with the British in Bilbays, and the Ottoman general Yūsuf Pāshā entered Cairo with the help of the British navy in 1801.[15]

14 On Ḥasan al-ʿAṭṭār, see P. Gran, *Islamic Roots of Capitalism, Egypt, 1760–1840* (Syracuse 1998); J. Crabbs, 'al-ʿAṭṭār, Ḥasan', J.S. Meisami and P. Starkey (eds), *Encyclopedia of Arabic Literature* (London and New York 1998), 1, 111; H.A.R. Gibb, 'al-ʿAṭṭār, Ḥasan b. Muḥammad, *E.I.*^{2} i, 755, and Raymond, *Égyptiens et Français*, 248–9. According to Raymond, the portrait of the astronomer and the poet in the *Description de l'Égypte* may represent ʿAbd al-Raḥmān al-Jabartī and Ḥasan al-ʿAṭṭār, see Raymond, plate 1, 2 and plate 34, 349. On Ḥasan al-ʿAṭṭār's journey to Jerusalem, see also Adel Manna, 'Cultural Relations', 142 and note 10 above.

15 See *Maẓhar al-Taqdīs*, ʿAbd al-Raḥīm (ed.), 232–5; Raymond, *Egyptiens et Français*, 248–9. See also Robert L. Tignor's introduction to Moreh's English translation of al-Jabartī's *Tārīkh*

Under the strong impression of this French invasion, al-Jabartī started to write his chronicle from the first day of the occupation (Thursday, 8 Muḥarram 1213 [/15 June 1798]), an event which he believes was announced by God through the astronomical constellation of the moon and the sun at the beginning of the year 1213/1798. Al-Jabartī considered this occupation as a punishment from God of the unjust Mamluk rulers of Egypt. However, we do not know the reason why he suddenly stopped recording the events after 6 January 1799 in *Tārīkh Muddat al-Faransīs bi-Miṣr*.[16] Our historian was shocked at the cruel destruction of the Mamluk military power by Napoleon's firearms, the new French military tactics and the French occupation which was in constant need of taxes, and this provoked him to record the events from the Egyptian point of view. In both *Muddat al-Faransīs* and *Maẓhar al-Taqdīs* he recorded the events from the point of view of a pro-Ottoman historian. In this period he depended on his eyewitness accounts, on rumours or on information received from Egyptian informants through his contacts with the military and administrative elites and with the French authorities; he extensively quotes their printed proclamations in Arabic. His initial account of this first confrontation between a modern European army and a Muslim military power on Islamic land was a brief pamphlet, which was afterwards entitled *Hādhā Tārīkh Muddat al-Faransīs bi-Miṣr min Sanat 1213 ilā Sanat 1216* by Amīn al-Madanī, the manuscript's owner.[17] This pamphlet dealt with the period of Muḥarram-Rajab 1213 (/15 June 1798–6 January 1799). At this point he was under the impression that the French regime would last for a long time.

The sudden invasion of Egypt by a non-Muslim, French army which destroyed the powerful Mamluk cavalry, and put an end to the cruel extraction of taxes from the poor Egyptian populace, created a tremendous shock among the Muslim population of Egypt. Thus, when the French were forced to leave

---

Muddat al-Faransīs[2], entitled *Napoleon in Egypt* (Princeton and New York 1993), 11; a 3rd expanded edition in honour of al-Jabartī's 250th birthday (Princeton 2004).

16 Browne, *A Hand-list*, 207, no. 1058, Qq. 214. Cf. the title page of *Maẓhar al-Taqdīs*published in *al-Jabartī's Chronicle*, plate VI. Both title pages of al-Jabartī's *Muddat Tārīkh al-Faransīs* (plate no. X) and al-Zabīdī's *al-Murabbā al-Kābulī fīman Rawā 'an al-Shams al-Bābilī* (Leiden Library MS no. OR 244) state that both MSS were acquired by al-Sayyid Muḥammad al-Amīr al-Ḥanafī al-Rashīdī on 6 Jumādā [12] 81 (/6–7 October 1864) (cf. *al-Jabartī's Chronicle*, 1975). Both MSS are kept at Leiden University Library and bought from Amīn al-Madanī. My thanks to Dr Clara Brakel for her help in getting a xerox copy of al-Zabīdī's MS as well as many other works by al-Zabīdī from the library of Leiden University.

17 See *al-Jabartī's Chronicle*, 11, n. 9.

Egypt in 1801, mainly through British intervention on behalf of the Ottomans,[18] al-Jabartī initially rejoiced in the return of the Ottomans and hoped that the suffering of the Egyptian people had come to an end. Al-Jabartī, who had been a member of the third Divan under the French and who had visited French institutions several times with Shaykh al-Bakrī, now wished to clear himself from the accusation that he had collaborated with the French.[19] He hastily collected his data and revised them in such a way as to make a suitable presentation before the new Ottoman General Yūsuf Pāshā. He dedicated his second chronicle to him, giving it a religious title *Maẓhar al-Taqdīs bi-Zawāl Dawlat al-Faransīs* (The Manifestation of Blessing in the Demise of French Authority) and asking him to have mercy on the poor Egyptians, who had suffered greatly under the French occupation.[20]

Johann Ludwig Burckhardt,[21] who visited al-Jabartī in 1816 and bought from him a number of his MSS, including the first autographs of *Maẓhar al-Taqdīs* and of *'Ajā'ib al-Āthār*, explained al-Jabartī's motive for writing *Maẓhar al-Taqdīs* as follows:

> As he used to associate with the French scholars during their stay in Cairo, he was worried about his safety after their evacuation, so he compiled this book in order to relieve his conscience and to demonstrate his allegiance to the Ottoman Empire.[22]

The remark by Burckhardt that al-Jabartī wrote this work in order to clear himself from the accusation of collaboration with the French authorities is supported by al-Jabartī's own remark at the end of *Maẓhar al-Taqdīs*, where he confesses that he wrote this work in Ramaḍān 1216 (/5/6 January–2/3 February 1802) in honour of the Ottoman vizier Yūsuf Ḍiyā Pāshā.[23] This was two years

---

18 See *Maẓhar al-Taqdīs*, ʿAbd al-Raḥīm (ed.), 232–5; Raymond, *Egyptiens et Français*, 248–9. See also Robert L. Tignor, introduction to Moreh, *Napoleon in Egypt*, 11.

19 This note was written by Burckhardt (Shaykh Ibrāhīm) on the title page of the MS of *Maẓhar al-Taqdīs bi-Zawāl Dawlat al-Faransīs*, kept in Cambridge University Library, see Browne, *A Hand-list*, 207, no. 1058, shelf mark Qq. 214. See *al-Jabartī's Chronicle*, plate VI.

20 See *Maẓhar al-Taqdīs*, ʿAbd al-Raḥīm (ed.), 303. Cf. also Marsot, 'A Comparative Study', in Crecelius, *Eighteenth Century Egypt*, 117.

21 See note 9 above. On the Burckhardt Papers, see Browne, *A Hand-list*, 342–5, nos. 1501–9, Add. 273–Add. 282. On Burckhardt's MSS in Cambridge see Browne, *A Hand-List*, 373–80 from no. 348 Qq. 1 (12) a–Qq. 300 (10) a and no. 652, Add. 177.

22 See *al-Jabartī's Chronicle*, 11, n. 39, 12, n. 40, and plate VI.

23 See *al-Jabartī's Chronicle*, 8 and plate VI. On the Egyptians' collaboration with the French, see Raymond, *Egyptiens et Français*, 319–34.

after the date at which ʿAbd Allāh al-Sharqāwī went with some Egyptian *'ulamā'* to meet the Yūsuf Pāshā in the city of Bilbays, during Ramaḍān 1214 (/27 January–25 February 1800) after the first peace agreement with the French. Al-Sharqāwī was advised by one of the companions of the vizier to write the history of the French occupation and present it as a gift.[24] We do not know whether al-Jabartī was among these *'ulamā'*, but he must surely have heard of this suggestion which would clear him from the accusation of collaboration with the Muslims' enemies.

To present a book to a governor was in fact not at all unusual; there is much evidence that it was customary in the Muslim world to compose a literary or historical work in honour of a sultan or an influential personality and to offer it to the (new) ruler in order to obtain his favour. In fact, ʿAbd Allāh al-Sharqāwī, who had served as the head of the French *Dīwān*, also took seriously the hint to write a book. He compiled a book on the history of Egypt, including a brief account of the French occupation of Egypt, entitled *Tuḥfat al-Nāẓirīn fī-man Waliya Miṣr min al-Wulāt wa 'l-Salāṭīn* (The Present of the Spectators concerning the Governors and Sultans Who Ruled Egypt), and presented it to the Vizier.[25] We can assume that the same request was made to al-Jabartī, and consequently he composed *Maẓhar al-Taqdīs*.[26] In this respect al-Jabartī was not different from other *'ulamā'* at the time.

Under the rule of Muḥammad ʿAlī, only five years after the French evacuation, al-Jabartī started as a first step to revise *Maẓhar al-Taqdīs*, adding a few biographies and updating it. At that time he had reached the age of fifty-two, and must have felt secure enough to criticize the corrupt and tyrannical Muslim rulers, the Mamluks. He accused them of bribery (*rashwa*) and oppression (*ẓulm*), considering the unusual event of the French occupation as God's punishment for their failure to promote Islamic military power and to

24 'Abd Allāh b. Ḥijāzī al-Sharqāwī, in the introduction to his *Tuḥfat al-Nāẓirīn* in the margin of Muḥammad b. 'Umar al-Wāqidī, *Kitāb Futūḥ al-Shām* (Cairo 1368 [/1948–9]), 3–4. A new edition was published recently and edited by Riḥāb 'Abd al-Ḥamīd al-Qārī (Cairo 1416/1996).

25 See al-Sharqāwī, *Tuḥfat al-Nāẓirīn*, in the margin of al-Wāqidī, *Futūḥ al-Shām*, margin, 3–4.

26 Cf. P.M. Holt, 'Literary Offerings: a Genre of Courtly Literature', in Philipp and Haarmann (eds), *The Mamlūks*, 3–16. Al-Zabīdī dedicated several pamphlets which he wrote to many amīrs, scholars and friends to win their favour and friendship, cf. his Introduction to his *Mu'jam Mukhtaṣṣ*.

keep the Islamic laws, and for failing to rule their Muslim subjects according to the *sharī'a*.[27]

We were fortunate to find a MS of *'Ajā'ib al-Āthār* at Dār al-Kutub al-Qawmiyya in Cairo, MS *'Aj.* Tārīkh 1426.[28] The manuscript starts with the year 1213 (/1798–9). This MS is unique because it is very similar in content and style to *Maẓhar al-Taqdīs*, therefore it may well be a copy of the first draft of *'Ajā'ib al-Āthār*. It is written in what seems to be a Syrian *naskhī*, and the copyist is not familiar with the names of the quarters of Cairo and of the history of Egypt.[29] Apparently, this MS was copied from the first draft of *'Ajā'ib al-Āthār* when the author had not yet obtained either al-Zabīdī's biographical dictionary (*Mu'jam Mukhtaṣṣ*), or the protocol of the trial of Sulaymān al-Ḥalabī, Kléber's assassin.[30] Instead, he recorded the popular rumours on the incident, which must have been circulating among the citizens, such as that Sulaymān hid himself in a well, that a woman indicated to the French where he was hiding, and that he spat on those who came to arrest him.[31] This story is so similar to Nīqūlā al-Turk's version of the event that it seems to support the suggestion of T. Philipp, who says when discussing Nīqūlā al-Turk's report about the (French) occupation, that 'some long passages of great, almost verbatim, similarity raise the tantalizing question whether they shared the same sources'.[32] This is a serious question which needs to be investigated thoroughly. The autograph of the three volumes in Cambridge University Library seems to be the first final draft written by al-Jabartī himself.

Al-Jabartī discussed the method of compiling his comprehensive history of Egypt *'Ajā'ib al-Āthār*, saying that 'I found only a few booklets written by some common soldiers … However, I succeeded in obtaining one such history written on the whole in a simple and natural style by a person named Aḥmad Chalabī b. 'Abd al-Ghanī. It begins with the capture of Egypt by the Ottomans

27 See *'Aj.* Būlāq, I, 8–10, III, 21.

28 See MS *'Aj.* Tārīkh, 1426/microfilm 35532, vol. III.

29 Cf. MS *'Aj.* Tārīkh 1426, f. 145a, l. 7.

30 See the protocols of Sulaymān al-Ḥalabī's assassination of General Kléber in *'Aj.* Būlāq, III, 116. This protocol is missing in MS *'Aj.* Tārīkh 1426, f. 89a.

31 MS *'Aj.* Tārīkh 1426, f. 89a.

32 T. Philipp, 'The French and the French Revolution in the Works of al-Jabartī', in D. Crecelius, *Eighteenth Century Egypt*, 139.

and ends, like the others which I have mentioned in 1150 [/1737–8]'.[33] Al-Jabartī claims that this copy was lost and that 'from that date to the present 1220 [/1805–6], no one has recorded or written anything in this field. I have therefore had recourse to transmitting the words of elderly people, to documents from the registers of clerks and custodians and to inscriptions on tombstones from the beginning of the century up to the year 1170 [/1756–7]. What follows, up to the year 1190 [/1776–7] are events which we ourselves witnessed but partly forgot and partly remembered. From the latter date [1190/1776–7] to the present there are events which we have considered, evaluated and written down, until we achieved our goal, such as it was, namely, to narrate this in an orderly arrangement from our time to that period'.[34] This statement of al-Jabartī's is confirmed by Murtaḍā al-Zabīdī, who says in his manuscript of *Mu'jam Mukhtaṣṣ*: وقد جمع تاريخا لعصره ذكر فيه أشياء مستجادة أعانه الله على إتمامه وأعانني على بعض تراجم احتجت إليها في كتابى التاريخ الكبير لأهل القرن الثاني عشر، بارك الله فيه. '[Al-Jabartī] was already compiling a history of his epoch in which he mentioned excellent things, may God help him to finish it. He [al-Jabartī] has helped me in [collecting] some biographies which I have needed for my *Great History of the People of the Twelfth Century*, God bless him'.[35]

It is not clear what al-Zabīdī meant by في كتابى التاريخ الكبير لأهل القرن الثاني عشر ('in my book, *Great History of the People of the Twelfth Century* [*al-Ta'rīkh al-Kabīr li-Ahl al-Qarn al-Thānī'Ashar*]'), and whether he was intending to write a comprehensive biography of the Muslim world or to enlarge the same biographical work, which he had completed up to the letter *mīm*.

One can presume that if al-Jabartī contributed to al-Zabīdī's biographical work, it would be very difficult to identify which bibliography among them was written completely by al-Jabartī and used by al-Zabīdī. According to al-Kattānī, al-Zabīdī's greater work on biographies is his great *Mu'jam* (*Mu'jamihi al-Kabīr*) which is kept at Medina in the Library of the Shaykh al-Islām, containing 600 biographies of scholars.[36] However, Reichmuth arrived at the conclusion that this 'Great History'. seemed to have been lost, and that

33 Al-Jabartī repeated his claim that this book was lost in *'Aj.*, I, 6.

34 See *'Aj.*, I, 8, cf. Ayalon, 'The Historian', 222–4, cf. 224–32.

35 See al-Zabīdī, *Mu'jam Mukhtaṣṣ*, f. 60b. In this manuscript, al-Jabartī's biography is in folio 60a–b. See Reichmuth, 'An Annotated Index', 28–9.

36 See Reichmuth, 'Notes', 337–79.

al-Jabartī used a large number of the biographies of the *Mu'jam Mukhtaṣṣ* for his own work. He concludes that 'as far as can be said now, more than 145 of them were incorporated into *'Ajā'ib al-Āthār*, sometimes in full, sometimes in smaller or greater modifications'.[37] Afterwards Reichmuth gives a list of scholars whom al-Jabartī mentioned between the years 1188 (/1774)[38] until 1189 (/1776) including 17 obituaries of scholars to indicate the extent to which al-Jabartī relied on al-Zabīdī's materials, although there are several mistakes and inaccuracies involving names and dates. From this list we can find that only Ḥasan b. Ibrāhīm al-Jabartī, Zayn al-Dīn Qāsim al-ʿIbādī and Aḥmad al-Khalīl al-Shāmī that were mentioned by al-Jabartī are missing in the *Mu'jam Mukhtaṣṣ* of al-Zabīdī.[39]

In compiling the first two volumes of his third and largest work, *'Ajā'ib al-Āthār*, al-Jabartī depended to a great extent on two chronicles: *Awḍaḥ al-Ishārāt* ('The Clearest Indication') (1737), by Aḥmad Shalabī b. ʿAbd al-Ghanī (1675?–1737) and *al-Durra al-Muṣāna* [sic] *fī Akhbār al-Kināna* ('The Well-kept Pearl on the History of Egypt') (1755) by Aḥmad al-Damurdāshī (d. after 1756). A number of biographies were also compiled by al-Jabartī at the request of Murtaḍā al-Zabīdī, and still others were taken from *Mu'jam Mukhtaṣṣ* (Special [Biographical] Dictionary), collected according to the request of al-Murādī (1760–91) by Murtaḍā al-Zabīdī.[40]

After several years of severe oppression by the Ottoman rulers, al-Jabartī apparently changed his attitude towards the Muslim rulers and regretted his former flattery in *Maẓhar al-Taqdīs*, as he wrote in his *Introduction* to his third and largest work *'Ajā'ib al-Āthār*: 'In collecting this work, I did not aim at serving any prominent person of high rank or at obeying any vizier or *amīr*'.[41] So he decided to write this new, comprehensive history as a religious scholar who not merely records events, but also participates actively in making history through his criticism of the Muslim rulers, Muḥammad ʿAlī. He judges the events, rulers and scholars according to the criterion of the Islamic value system, i.e. their tyranny, injustice and exploitation especially, of the common

37 See al-Kattānī, *Fihris al-Fahāris*, I, 537.

38 *'Aj.*, I, 385.

39 See Reichmuth, 'Notes', 337–79.

40 *'Aj.*, II, 233–6. On the contribution of al-Jabartī to al-Zabīdī's biographies, he says: 'When I obtained the papers which the late master had assembled …I gathered what I had jotted down and added to it. These are only biographies without events and occurrences'. (See *'Aj.*, II, 234).

41 *'Aj.* Būlāq, I, 6.

people. This criticism of the Muslim rulers, the corrupt economy and system of administration was no doubt enhanced by his experience of French law and sense of justice. This encouraged him to revive the Muslim principle of: *al-amr bi 'l-ma'rūf wa 'l-nahy 'an al-munkar* ('to enjoin good and forbid evil').[42] This critical attitude contrasts with that of other *'ulamā'*, who were afraid to criticise the rulers and limited themselves to writing biographies, leaving the writing of chronicles to what al-Jabartī indicates as '*ba'ḍ al-'āmma min al-ajnād*' ('soldiers of humble origin').[43]

Several scholars have accused al-Jabartī of plagiarism, inappropriately judging his work from a modern, twentieth century point of view. However, his decision to start the *History of Egypt* from the beginning of the twelfth century AH (1100/1689) forced him to collect material from existing historical writings, including those which were produced by 'common soldiers'. One may infer that al-Jabartī is hinting at the chronicles written by common soldiers such as Ibn ʿAbd al-Ghanī and al-Damurdāshī, whose works he mentions with derision, but used nevertheless. Both Laylā ʿAbd al-Laṭīf Aḥmad,[44] and later on Daniel Crecelius proved that al-Jabartī relied more heavily on Aḥmad Chalabī Ibn ʿAbd al-Ghanī's chronicle than on the al-Damurdāshī account, at least for the period 1688–1737.[45]

But al-Jabartī's critics are not only found among scholars of the twentieth century. In fact, his friend Ḥasan al-ʿAṭṭār, who was frequently quoted with great admiration by al-Jabartī, was the first to criticize him severely. In his private copy of MS *'Aj.* Cam., which was edited by al-Jabartī, al-ʿAṭṭār did not only record the notes about his own journey, but also added at least twenty four remarks, some quite long remarks, with corrections on al-Jabartī's biographies.[46]

In volumes I and II of *'Ajā'ib al-Āthār*, when al-Jabartī was using material borrowed from authors such as Ibn ʿAbd al-Ghanī and al-Damurdāshī, al-

42 See Qur'ān, 3:110, 7: 157, 9:71, 31:17, etc.

43 *'Aj.* Būlāq, I, 6, cf. Ayalon, 'The Historian', 222.

44 Laylā ʿAbd al-Laṭīf Aḥmad and ʿAḥmad al-Damurdāshī Kathkhud'Azabīn, ṣāḥib *al-Durra al-Muṣāna*' in Laylā ʿAbd al-Laṭīf Aḥmad (ed.), *Dirāsāt fī Tārīkh wa-Mu'arrikhī Miṣr wa 'l-Shām ibbān al-'Aṣr al-'Uthmānī* (Cairo 1980), 165–70.

45 Daniel Crecelius, ʿAḥmad Shalabī Ibn ʿAbd al-Ghanī and Aḥmad Katkhudā ʿAzabīn al-Damurdāshī: Two Sources for al-Jabartī's "*Ajā'ib al-Āthār fī 'l-Tarājim wa-'l-Akhbār*"', in Crecelius (ed.), *Eighteenth Century Egypt*, 101.

46 Cf. MS ʿAj. Cam., Qq. 170, II, f. 169a, and f. 170a.

Jabartī did not merely copy the information from earlier historical writings, but he improved their colloquial style and clarified the connection between events. From ʿAbd al-Ghanī there are also some verbatim quotations. Al-Jabartī also apparently summarized descriptions taken from various historical writings and added biographical data from other sources.

Al-Jabartī stated in *'Ajā'ib al-Āthār* that he copied some material from al-Zabīdī's MS *al-Murabbā al-Kābulī fiman Rawā'an al-Shams al-Bābilī*,[47] but he belittled the importance of his *Mu'jam Mukhtaṣṣ*. He says that he had bought the MS of the latter's *Biographical Dictionary* entitled *Hādhā Mu'jam Mukhtaṣṣ bi-Dhikr Man Akhadhtu 'anhu al-'Ulūm wa 'l-Ma'ārif min Shuyūkhi wa-Ābā'ī...* from al-Zabīdī's widow, changing its title into *al-Mu'jam al-Mukhtaṣṣ*: 'When I obtained the papers which the late Sayyid [al-Zabīdī] had assembled, there were about 10 fascicles which he had arranged according to the successive order of the letters of the alphabet and had named *al-Mu'jam al-Mukhtaṣṣ*'.[48] Although al-Jabartī belittled al-Zabīdī's biographical work, yet it seems to have served him not only as a guide to names of important scholars, but al-Jabartī also used most of al-Zabīdī's biographies of thetwelfth century (eighteenth century CE), and integrated them in his work according to their years of death and not according to their alphabetical order. What confirms that al-Jabartī possessed the MS of the *Mu'jam Mukhtaṣṣ* obtained by Professor Stefan Reichmuth is that al-Jabartī added a long passage to the biography of his father in law, ʿAlī b. ʿAbd Allāh al-Rūmī, describing how he married his second wife, the step-daughter of al-Rūmī, after the death of the first.[49] In his unpublished article 'Preliminary List of Scholars, Students,

47 See al-Zabīdī, *Mu'jam Mukhtaṣṣ*, f. 61b.

48 See *'Aj.* Būlāq, II, 234–5. The English translation is quoted from Philipp and Perlmann, *'Abd al-Raḥmān al-Jabarti*, II, 389. Al-Jabartī said that this *Dictionary* is entitled *al-Mu'jam al-Mukhtaṣṣ* but according to the Reichmuth's description, al-Zabīdī did not give a title page to his biographical dictionary, but defined it in his introduction as '*hādhā mu'jam mukhtaṣṣ bi-dhikr man akhadhtu minhu 'l-'ulūm...*'('this is a lexicon specially mentioning those from whom I took the sciences…').

49 See al-Zabīdī, *Mu'jam Mukhtaṣṣ*, in the margin of f. 109b, which begins with the following sentence in which he identified himself: يقول الحقير عبد الرحمن بن حسن الجبرتي إني صاهرت المترجم المذكور وتزوجت بابنة زوجته في سنة 1196 وذلك أن في تلك السنة توفت [كذا] التي كانت عندي أيام المرحوم الوالد. (The humble ʿAbd al-Raḥmān b. Ḥasan al-Jabartī says that I have been related by marriage with the above mentioned person and married his step daughter on 1196 [/1781–2]. It happened that in the same year the [wife that was married to me] during the lifetime of my late father, died).

Visitors and Acquaintances mentioned in Murtaḍā az-Zabīdī's *Mu'jam*', Reichmuth gives a list of 632 biographies mentioned in this *Biographical Dictionary* of 176 folios. This list confirms the statement of the *Maghribī* author ʿAbd al-Ḥayy b. ʿAbd al-Kabīr al-Kattānī in his *Fīhris al-Fahāris wa 'l-Ithbāt* that *al-Mu'jam al-Mukhtaṣṣ*, which he copied from the Library of the Shaykh al-Islām in Medina, terminates with the letter *mīm*.[50]

A vehement attack was made by al-Kattānī on al-Jabartī's use of this *Biographical Dictionary*. He says: 'The most peculiar thing that might be mentioned here is that this *Mu'jam Mukhtaṣṣ* forms the greatest (source for the) material of al-Jabartī in his chronicle. One can even say that all the biographies of the *'ulamā'* of the twelfth century which it contains, are taken verbatim from this *Dictionary*'.[51] Al-Kattānī says that in fact this *Mu'jam Mukhtaṣṣ* contains about thirty fascicles and not ten, as al-Jabartī claimed. He also accused al-Jabartī of being careless in copying al-Zabīdī indiscriminately, and attributing to himself particular statements which were clearly made by Murtaḍā al-Zabīdī. Al-Kattānī adds that such heavy borrowing is similar to what Badr al-Dīn Maḥmūd al-ʿAynī (d. 1451) did with the chronicle of Ibrāhīm Ibn Duqmāq (1349–1406). Sometimes, when Murtaḍā al-Zabīdī did not mention the year of a person's death (because he died before the person described in the biography), al-Kattānī said that al-Jabartī provided an incorrect date. Moreover, he suggested that the reason why al-Jabartī criticized al-Zabīdī's biographies for dealing mainly with unimportant people was that al-Zabīdī had not mentioned his father, Ḥasan al-Jabartī. According to al-Kattānī, al-Jabartī did not contribute many original biographies to those collected by Murtaḍā al-Zabīdī; he argued further that al-Jabartī only added 'some biographies of *amīr*s, generals, officers and some Jews'.[52]

In fact, the biographies of many *amīr*s and generals, such as Hammām b. Yūsuf al-Hawwārī,[53] Amīr Ḥasan Bey Riḍwān,[54] are among the best and most important biographies written by al-Jabartī and cannot be derogated in such a cavalier fashion. By Jews, al-Kattānī means the biographies of some *amīr*s and Beys of Jewish descent, such as *amīr* Aḥmad Bey al-Muslimīn, also known as

50 See al-Kattānī, I, 523, biography no. 300; cf. ibid., I, 102, biography no. 8.

51 See ibid., I, 623.

52 See ibid., II, 623.

53 See *'Aj.*, I, 343–5.

54 See ibid., II, 38–50.

Askī Nāzī (Ashkenazi). Al-Muslimīn was most probably of Polish-Ukrainian Jewish descent and converted after the massacre of 1648.[55] The case of Amīr Yūsuf Bey al-Muslimīn is similar. It is possible to attribute al-Zabīdī's failure to add biographies of both Ḥasan al-Jabartī and al-Murādī, both of which can be considered among the masterpieces of al-Jabartī's biographies, to the fact that al-Jabartī did not include them in his contribution to al-Zabīdī's *Biographical Dictionary*.

Our research on the autograph MS of *'Ajā'ib al-Āthār* kept at Cambridge University Library proves that some evidence may be found in these MSS to confirm the critical remarks made by al-Kattānī. These are several biographies added in the margins next to the biographies which already form part of the text of the Cambridge MS of volumes I and II of *'Ajā'ib al-Āthār*, including the long biography of al-Murādī and many others added with the year of death to which they belong after the first revision of the entire volume in 1806. The fact that the author worked on the text and revised it several times is evident from several instances in the original Cambridge MS, such as the biography which was added in the margin after the composition of the main text of MS *'Aj.* Cam. Qq. 170, II, f. 170a (plate V). The word *al-wakāyil* was added in the margin first, and later encircled with a line, in order to enable al-Jabartī to add the biography of Ḥusayn b. al-Nūr ʿAlī b. ʿAbd al-Shukūr al-Ḥanafī al-Ṭā'ifī. According to Reichmuth, 'al-Jabartī used a large number of the biographies of the *Mu'jam Mukhtaṣṣ* for his own work. As far as can be said now, more than 145 of them were incorporated into *'Ajā'ib al-Āthār*, sometimes in full, sometimes with smaller or greater modifications … most of these biographies are concentrated in the 1180s and 1190s [1760s–1780s]'.[56]

The question raised at this stage of the research was whether al-Jabartī's biographical additions in the margin were copied by al-Jabartī from Murtaḍā al-Zabīdī's *Biographical Dictionary*, and whether those biographies which were written in the text of MS *'Ajā'ib* Cambridge, were written by al-Jabartī alone.To determine the answer to this question I have enlisted the help of Stefan Reichmuth. His comparison of my new edition of *'Ajā'ib al-Āthār*, with al-Zabīdī's *Biographical Dictionary* confirmed that most of al-Jabartī's additions in the margins of the Cambridge autograph, if not all of them, are al-

55 See the English translation of *'Ajā'ib al-Āthār* by Philipp and Perlmann, I, 185, n. 64.

56 Reichmuth, 'Notes', 379.

Jabartī's original work. But most of the biographies in the text of the Cambridge MS 'were taken directly from al-Zabīdī, either verbatim' or adding some information from al-Jabartī's own knowledge. Sometimes he was not even accurate when copying from al-Zabīdī. Therefore, one can say with certainty that al-Murādī's biographical entry added in the margin of the MS *'Aj.* Cam., Qq. 170, II, was composed by al-Jabartī and not copiedfrom al-Zabīdī's *Mu'jam Mukhtaṣṣ* specially, because this biography depends on al-Murādī's correspondence with both al-Jabartī and his teacher al-Zabīdī.

This important observation of both al-Kattānī and Reichmuth, that al-Jabartī used many biographical entries from al-Zabīdī, confirms Crecelius' assumption in his book, *Eighteenth Century Egypt*: 'Further investigation of al-Jabartī's biographies of the *'ulamā'* and saints from the period before the 1770s will reveal other sources which al-Jabartī consulted'.[57] Regarding this accusation that al-Jabartī borrowed his biographies from al-Zabīdī, one should remember that al-Zabīdī admitted in his biography of al-Jabartī that the latter helped him in collecting some biographical material for his work, *The Great History of the People of the Twelfth Century*. Professor Reichmuth arrived at the conclusion that this biographical dictionary of the twelfth century 'is of a more general kind, including scholars and other personalities with whom he had not been in personal contact, but had gathered information about them, and that he was assisted in this by al-Jabartī'. In Reichmuth's opinion, this book has been lost.[58] al-Zabīdī even included 'a laudatory poem written by the poet al-Idkāwī at the occasion of al-Jabartī's marriage', a poem which al-Zabīdī could not have obtained if it had not been supplied to him by al-Jabartī. Moreover, the biography of al-Jabartī's 'father-in-law, ʿAlī b. ʿAbdallah al-Rūmī alias Maḥarram Efendī (d. 1199 [/1784–5])' could not have been included in the *Mu'jam Mukhtaṣṣ* without the help of al-Jabartī. The fact that al-Jabartī added details in his own handwriting, which are not included in *'Ajā'ib al-Āthār* to the margin of this biography in the *Mu'jam Mukhtaṣṣ*, indicates that al-Zabīdī copied first what was supplied to him by al-Jabartī. If this is the case, then al-Zabīdī added the biographies written by al-Jabartī to his *Mu'jam Mukhtaṣṣ*. The question now arises whether the verbatim correspondence between al-Jabartī's and al-Zabīdī's works are due to this

57 See Daniel Crecelius, *Eighteenth Century Egypt*, 102.

58 See Reichmuth, 'Notes', 376.

collaboration. Since there is no way of solving this question, one should be careful of accusing al-Jabartī of borrowing without acknowledgement, especially in such a case of cooperation between a student and his master. This question can be solved only when the manuscript of biographies collected by al-Jabartī to be sent to al-Murādī will be discovered.

In conclusion, the Cambridge autograph[59] and our Arabic new edition of *'Ajā'ib al-Āthār* in which we indicated the paragraphs and biographies added by al-Jabartī in the margin of the autograph MS by curled brackets {...}, give the best indication of which biographies were copied from al-Zabīdī's *Biographical Dictionary* and which were added after compiling the first two volumes of *'Ajā'ib al-Āthār* in 1220 (/1805–6). During this year al-Jabartī finished writing the first three volumes of *'Ajā'ib al-Āthār*, revising them by recording missing words and making a few new corrections in the margin of his Cambridge autograph. It seems most probable that, after acquiring the biographies from al-Zabīdī's widow, al-Jabartī was able to add details to the biographies which he had already written, and to add biographies of people about whom he had forgotten to write. Still, al-Jabartī accused ʿAbd Allāh al-Sharqāwī of copying the biographies of the Shāfiʿīs verbatim from his *'Ajā'ib al-Āthār*: 'The shaykh (i.e. al-Sharqāwī) compiled the biographies of some of the ancient and modern Shāfiʿī jurists, both of his time and from the twelfth century. He took the biographies of the older ones from the works of (ʿAbd al-Wahhāb) al-Subkī and al-Isnawī. As for the contemporary [jurists], he took them word for word from my work'.[60]

Whether one considers al-Jabartī's borrowing from other sources as plagiarism or not, it is not to be expected that al-Jabartī suddenly would have changed the traditional method of composing chronicles by borrowing from other historians without acknowledgement and derogating their achievements. Professor Reichmuth's observation that 'al-Jabartī's history can be seen both as a unique individual and, at the same time, as a collective work incorporating the products of at least a century of intellectual activities',[61] is in fact indulgent. It is possible to say that in compiling volumes I–III of his *'Ajā'ib al-*

59 See Browne, *A Hand-list*, 118. The autograph is nos. 666–71, MSS *'Aj.* Cam., Qq. 169, 170, 171, while Ḥasan al-ʿAṭṭār's copy is MSS *'Aj.* Cam. 2nd., Qq. 166, 167, 168. Cf. Moreh, 'al-Jabartī's Method', 372–3, plates V–VI, and the plates in this book.

60 See *'Aj.*, IV, 163.

61 See Reichmuth, 'Notes', 374.

Āthār, al-Jabartī who possessed his father's library and acquired other books, exploited extensively most of the eighteenth century historical, biographical, literary and poetical works available to him. He either summarizes them or adds new details, or rewrites the colloquial works which he used in the conventional Azharī style of his time, closing the gaps between the events. He adds to these works oral history and legends which he heard from his elders. Collecting biographies for al-Zabīdī and al-Murādī, and his possession of al-Zabīdī's *Biographical Dictionary* enabled him to combine the history with biographies, adding new details or shortening the historical events and biographies which he might have borrowed from al-Zabīdī and others.

This conclusion is confirmed by the following important observation of Jane Hathaway, who distinguishes between different schools of historiography in the Muslim world: 'Al-Jabartī's chronicle is not an anomalous throwback to the glory days of Mamluk historiography but, on the contrary, is entirely consistent with the Ottoman Egyptian historical school, exemplified by *Akhbār al-Nuwwāb* and the chronicles of Ḥallāq and Aḥmad Chelebi. While al-Jabartī breaks out of the classic 'pasha' chronicle mould by abandoning the 'new pasha' rubric and by separating *akhbār/waqāʾiʿ* from *tarājim*, his presentation of *waqāʾiʿ* retains the characteristics of earlier eighteenth century chronicles, although he does embellish his *tarājim* by borrowing from the Mamluk biographical tradition. There is no denying that al-Jabartī was an innovator. Yet his innovations occurred within a living and evolving historical tradition. While harking back to the Mamluks, he remained an Ottoman historian'.[62] It must be noted here that al-Jabartī's innovative separation of *akhbār/waqāʾiʿ* from *tarājim*, must be in fact, attributed to al-Murādī. Al-Jabartī confirms this fact by saying: 'He [al-Murādī] was the greatest motive and cause for the composition of this history in this arrangement'.[63]

Although an autograph of al-Jabartī has been kept in Cambridge University Library since the death of Burckhardt in 1817, none of the printed editions of *ʿAjāʾib al-Āthār* have been based on the autographs or on the copies revised by al-Jabartī himself. Instead other MSS were used which were kept at the Būlāq Press. It is very likely that the Būlāq edition of 1297/1879–80 was based upon these MSS which were donated on 6 January 1895 to the Bibliothèque

62 See Jane Hathaway, 'Sultans, Pashas', in Crecelius, *Eighteenth Century Egypt*, 77–8.

63 See *ʿAj.*, II, 234, according to the translation of Philipp and Perlmann, II, 392.

Khédiviale in Cairo and are marked: من كتبخانه مطبعة بولاق مجانا ومضاف في 6 يناير سنة 1895. ('gratis from the Library of the Būlāq Press, and added [to the Khedivial Library [later on Dār al-Kutub al-Qawmiyya] on January 6, 1895'), as recorded on the title page of many MSS kept in the Egyptian National Library. The results of our research confirm the statement of the editor of the Būlāq edition, who repeated several times in the margin of the book (e.g. vol. IV, 7 and 79) that his edition is based upon a comparison and combination of different MSS of *'Ajā'ib al-Āthār*. The MSS which were in the possession of the Būlāq Press are MS *'Aj.* Tārīkh 1425/microfilm 14352 and 14200) (copied in 1287–9 [/1870–3]) and MS *'Aj.* Tārīkh 1872 (microfilm 35824) (copied in 1296 [/1878–9]), both in 4 volumes and donated to Dār al-Kutub by the Būlāq Press Library. In these MSS the copyists took the liberty of correcting the style and grammar of al-Jabartī's autograph. This is why the editor of the Būlāq edition, who compared several MSS of *'Ajā'ib al-Āthār*, preferred them to other MSS of *'Ajā'ib al-Āthār* which are copied from the Cambridge autograph. It seems that the correct grammatical usage and style were so important to the editor of the Būlāq edition that he chose the MSS of copyists who were not well acquainted with the history of Egypt and made many mistakes even when copying names of persons and places. They even felt free to make changes to some rare words which they did not understand, thereby changing the meaning of the text and distorting al-Jabartī's original intention. There were many homeoeteleutons in copying the author's text.In this case the eyesof the copyist jumped from the end of the first sentence to the end of the second, thus omitting a whole sentence. Such as the full sentence: ورأيناهم وهم راجعون، وانا للهوانا اليه راجعون becomes: ورأيناهم وهم راجعون thus omitting وانا للهوانا اليه راجعون

Another important observation is the question of al-Jabartī's denial of copying from his predecessors and not even from his mentor al-Zabīdī, or what one can call an attempt to hide the sources from which he copied his biographies and historical information. This fact was observed by al-Kattānī, Laylā Aḥmad, Crecelius and Reichmuth. In our opinion al-Jabartī follows a well established method among Arab historians. If we examine al-Murādī's correspondence with al-Jabartī we find that Arab historians and biographers used not only to depend on the works of their predecessors, but also to ask for the help of other scholars in different parts of the Islamic and Arabic speaking regions to collect biographies for them or to write accounts for them on the events of their region.

According to al-Jabartī such requests were sent via merchants, enclosing their letters with presents.[64] After receiving the ordered works, scholars would integrate them in their books without acknowledging the contributor or the original author from whom they copied. This custom of cooperation between Muslim scholars is confirmed by fact that al-Murādī asked al-Zabīdī and later al-Jabartī to send him the biographies collected for him. It seems that these biographies collected by al-Jabartī never reached al-Murādī, since, by collating the 31 biographies of Egyptian scholars in *Silk al-Durar*, with the same scholars mentioned by al-Jabartī of *'Ajā'ib al-Āthār* (copied from al-Zabīdī's *Mu'jam Mukhtaṣṣ*), there were no similarities in contents or style. This fact proves that al-Murādī had asked for the help of other Egyptian scholars beside al-Zabīdī. Moreover, al-Zabīdī integrated many autobiographical details written by his friends at his own request into his *Biographical Dictionary* in which they acclaimed (*qarraẓ*) and enumerated the merits of his *Tāj al-'Arūs* and *Sharḥ Iḥyā' 'Ulūm al-Dīn*. He did not find it necessary to acknowledge their contribution. Al-Murādī also did not acknowledge the help of those scholars who supplied him with these biographies. However, what distinguished al-Jabartī, in this case, is that he not only hides his sources, but instead of acknowledgment, he belittled the authors and the works from which he copied. In our opinion, the reason for this attitude is due to the criterion which al-Jabartī set for his judgment of events and biographies based upon the Islamic value system of justice, Islamic unity and devotion.

Even if one overlooks the fact that al-Jabartī cooperated with al-Zabīdī in collecting biographies, the process of writing a book by depending on previously written historical works, through verbatim copying of passages, summarizing and improving the sequence of events as well as the style, was not unique to al-Jabartī's *'Ajā'ib al-Āthār*, but must have been common practice in traditional Islamic historiography. This point is proven by further research of historical MSS of the period. We will illustrate this by two MSS which are found among the papers, books, pamphlets and some Wahhābī proclamations that Burckhardt bought during his journeys in the Arab world, some of which were bought from al-Jabartī. They are kept in Cambridge University Library and are listed under shelf mark Add. 2782 (9).[65] The first

64 See *'Aj.*, II, 233ff.

65 See note 13.

MS is entitled *al-Naṣr al-Mumtadd fī Fatḥ Tihāma wa-Najd* (The Prolonged Occupation of the Tihāma and Najd) in f. 21b and the second MS, entitled *al-Washy wa 'l-Ṭirāz fī Fatḥ al-Ḥijāz* in 47b folios. These two MSS contain various passages copied from the preface of *'Ajā'ib al-Āthār*, while in the end of volume III and the beginning of volume IV of *'Ajā'ib al-Āthār*, the events seem to be summarized with only a few differences. In the *Introduction* to *al-Naṣr al-Mumtadd* the anonymous writer praises Muḥammad ʿAlī and his great deeds, especially his occupation of the Ḥijāz after defeating the Wahhābīs. It starts in 1218 (/1803–4), introducing Muḥammad ʿAlī's appointment as the ruler of Egypt on Monday 14 Ṣafar 1220 (/14 May 1805) and deals with his preparations for a military campaign against the Wahhābīs in the Ḥijāz until Jumādā I 1229 (/21 April–20 May 1814). This MS, which is to a some extent identical with the Cambridge MS of *'Ajā'ib al-Āthār*, seems to have been compiled by an anonymous author who intended to present it to Muḥammad ʿAlī. The second MS, entitled *al-Washy wa 'l-Ṭirāz fī Fatḥ al-Ḥijāz* (Qq. 170, Add. 2782 [9]) is based on the first MS. The copyist of *al-Washy* deleted the title of the MS (f. 3a) and wrote over the original title, *al-Naṣr al-Mumtadd*, a new title, *al-Washy wa 'l-Ṭirāz fī Fatḥ al-Ḥijāz* (The Ornament and Embroidery Concerning the Occupation of the Ḥijāz) which is more precise than the first one. These folios which deal with events in Egypt are identical with the passages in the Cambridge MS of *'Ajā'ib al-Āthār*, and with *'Aj.* Būlāq, III, 341–2. In its place in the margin of *al-Naṣr al-Mumtadd* (f.12a), these folios have been summarized in three lines, relating that Imperial Orders were given to prepare for the invasion of the Ḥijāz in order to liberate it from the Wahhābīs who occupied the holy city of Medina. This paragraph written in a handwriting similar to al-ʿAṭṭār, which was added in the margin of *al-Naṣr al-Mumtadd*, appears in the text of *al-Washy wa 'l-Ṭirāz*. This shows that *al-Naṣr al-Mumtadd* was an attempt to summarize some passages from the text of *'Ajā'ib al-Āthār* as in the Cambridge MS, and not from the revised version from which the Būlāq edition was prepared. The fact that the corrections in the text of *al-Naṣr al-Mumtadd* and the additions in the margin have been inserted into the text of *al-Washy wa 'l-Ṭirāz*, while the deletions do not appear there, confirms the supposition that *al-Washy* was copied from *al-Naṣr* and that the latter was copied from MS *'Aj.* Cam.[66]

---

66 See *al-Naṣr*, ff. 12a–13a, where three complete folios have been deleted by crossing them

Moreover, the style and grammatical usage have been corrected and improved. For example, in *al-Naṣr*, f. 11b: وقطع الخليج عند خروج المشار اليه مع كبار الدولة والعسكر صبيحة ذلك اليوم على العادة فتكون البلدة خلية [كذا] منهم فيملكوها من غير ممانع. ففعلوا ذلك ووصل فرقة منهم وافرة ومروا خلف الجبل وحضر من أخبر المشار اليه بذلك ليلاً...

In *al-Washy*, f. 8b, the style was improved as follows: وقطع الخليج ويكون الباشا مع كبار الدولة والعسكر صبيحة ذلك اليوم على العادة فتكون البلدة خلية [كذا] منهم فيملكونها من غير ممانع ففعلوا ذلك ووصل فرقة منهم كبيرة ومروا خلف الجبل وحضر من أخبر الباشا بذلك ليلا

It seems that the above paragraph depends upon the following passage from MS *'Aj.* Cam., Qq. 171, III:[67]

> وأشيع في ذلك اليوم وصول فرقة من الأمراء المصريين من خلف الجبل وبات الناس مستعدين للفرجة على موسم الخليج على العادة فأمر الباشا بإخراج الخيام والنظام إلى ناحية الجسر وعمل الحراقة وأمر بكسر السد ليلا فما طلع النهار إلا والماء يجري في الخليج ولم يذهب الباشا ولا القاضي ولا أحد من الناس ولم يشعر بذلك وكان قد بلغه ورود الأمراء فتأخر عن الخروج وهم ظنوا خروجهم مع العسكر خارج المدينة ...

Moreover, folios 7b–10a of *al-Washy* are almost verbatim with the *Introduction* of *'Aj.* Būlāq, I, 7–10.

It seems therefore that the copyist of *al-Naṣr al-Mumtadd* had created an easy task for himself. Intending to write a work in praise of Muḥammad ʿAlī and to present it to him, he copied certain passages from the MS of *'Ajā'ib al-Āthār*, volumes III and IV that dealt with Muḥammad ʿAlī's invasion of the Ḥijāz. It is possible that the writer of this MS died before the work was completed, and that another person acquired this MS, and if the assumption that the handwriting is of al-ʿAṭṭār is correct, then it is possible to presume that al-ʿAṭṭār, or some other writer, changed the title and made some improvements and added about 16 folios in order to attribute the booklet to himself.

It is clear that in a similar way the first two volumes of *'Ajā'ib al-Āthār* must have been composed with the use of historical information taken from some previously written works, such as from Ibn ʿAbd al-Ghanī's and al-Damurdāshī's chronicles. He also added long moral and elegiac poetry as well as material which al-Jabartī heard from his father and in literary salons. al-Jabartī also added information he had learned from Shaykh al-Sādāt, al-Bakrī, ʿAbd Allāh al-Sharqāwī, al-Mahdī, and from correspondence with al-ʿAṭṭār and others, or taken from elderly people, tombstones and from his memories.

---

with vertical and horizontal lines.

67 Cf. *'Aj.* Būlāq, III, 341.

In addition he used al-Zabīdī's biographies, to which he contributed, for the first two volumes.

For more than a century, al-Jabartī's work was the only source available to scholars, who were unaware of or did not want to use poorly written manuscripts in colloquial Arabic. Copying from other historians without acknowledgment, as we have demonstrated, was not only done by al-Jabartī, but also by many other historians, including al-Jabartī's contemporaries, al-Zabīdī, al-Murādī, and others. In fact it was common practice in the Arab world to use historical work without acknowledgment, even when there was cooperation between scholars. On the other hand, if a poet copied from other poets he was accused of plagiarism (*sariqāt shi'riyya*) and many books were written on plagiarism of Arab poets from others. However, it seems that such a strict rule was not applied to Arab historians,[68] following the Arabic saying that *al-'ilmu laysa waqfan 'alā aḥad* (knowledge is not restricted to anybody).

In spite of the criticism that has been made, al-Jabartī remains, as Ayalon wrote: 'a giant among dwarfs'.[69] His status in Arabic historiography is similar to that of Shakespeare in English drama. Shakespeare was also accused of borrowing from Chaucer and from Italian dramatists, yet he still remains 'a giant among dwarfs'. The genius of al-Jabartī has been expressed most clearly in volumes III and IV of *'Ajā'ib al-Āthār,* where he gave an abundance of indispensable information in a highly personal way. His work is still used by scholars and historians all over the world. The fact that he borrowed from earlier works in the first two volumes of *'Ajā'ib al-Āthār* making their information more clear and coherent, evaluating the events, scholars and rulers by strict Islamic values, does not diminish his genius and his great contribution to Arabic historiography.

68 See 'Amr b. Baḥr al-Jāḥiẓ, *Kitāb al-Ḥayawān* (Cairo 1965), 89.

69 See Ayalon, 'The Historian', 218.

Chapter Four

The Egyptian Scholar Ḥasan al-ʿAṭṭār and his Contribution to al-Jabartī's Works[1]

The aim of this chapter is to verify Ḥasan al-ʿAṭṭār's life and activities according to his own recording in the margin of his copy of *'Ajā'ib al-Āthār* written in *Maghribī* script, which accompanied him during his travels outside Egypt, and was bought by Burckhardt and kept at the Cambridge University Library.[2]

Some Egyptian scholars, such as al-Jabartī and Shaykh Ḥasan b. Muḥammad al-ʿAṭṭār (c. 1166–1250 [/1766–1835]), both Khalwatī *Ṣūfī*s who were interested in *ḥadīth* and *kalām*,[3] were zealous adherents of the Islamic theory of time (*dahr* and *zamān*), characterized by the dynamics of regressive development in which the old is superior to the new. They followed a well known theory of stagnation and decline in Muslim civilization reflected in al-ʿAṭṭār's saying '*in'akasa al-zamānu wa-'amma al-jahlu*' (time has inverted and ignorance prevailed),[4] compared to the old time of lore when rulers were men of learning. It is analogous to the moonlike circle: rise, full moon and wane. But while al-Jabartī arrived at this conclusion through writing history and his encounter with the struggles of the Beys' military factions, the French occupation and the Ottoman military power, al-ʿAṭṭār arrived at this conclusion

---

1 This chapter is based upon a lecture given at the Greek General and Comparative Literature Association, International Comparative Literature Association Research Committee, Literary Representations of the Mediterranean, on 'Expressions et representations littéraires de la Méditerranée: Iles et ports, XVIe–XXe siècles' (Colloquium on the Literary Expressions and Representations of the Mediterranean: Islands and Ports, 16th–20th Centuries), held in Delphi on 5–6 November, 1999. My thanks are due to the organizers Professor Jean Bessières, Professor Rania Polycandrioti, and Professor Z.I. Siaflekis. The lecture is published in Z.I. Siaflekis and Rania Polycandrioti (eds), *Expressions et représentations littéraires de la Méditerranée: Iles et ports, XVIe–XXe siècles* (Athènes 2002), 19–32. This research was made by a grant from The German-Israeli Foundation (GIF).

2 MSS *'Aj.* Cam. 2nd., Qq. 166, 167, 168, see Chapter Two of this book.

3 Gran, *Islamic Roots*, 42–75.

4 This comment was expressed when al-ʿAṭṭār compared the scholarly abilities of the old generation of the viziers compared with the new one. See al-ʿAṭṭār's comment in the margin of MS *'Aj.* Cam. 2nd., Qq. 166, I, f. 239a, on al-Jabartī's statement in *'Aj.*, I, 260 dealing with *Safīnat al-Rāghib*; ff. 259b–260a.

after a long journey of frustration and suffering in the northern provinces of the Ottoman Empire in quest of knowledge and in search of a patron. At last he found his pledge in the rising new ruler of Egypt and backed him at the expense of his friendship with his devoted friend and admirer al-Jabartī to the point that, as far as we know, he did not even elegize him with a poem after his death in 1825.

Ḥasan al-ʿAṭṭār was a talented, diligent and ambitious Arab scholar and poet of Maghribī origin. His *Dīwān* written in his thirties, an early age for an Arab poet, included his eulogies and elegies on eminent Shaykhs, as well as his erotic poems on handsome young men whom he was fond of, mainly French scientists. Twice in his comments on al-Jabartī's *'Ajā'ib al-Āthār* he recorded that his *Dīwān* was with him in Izmir when he stayed in Fattāḥ Ughlū School but he later lost it in Damascus.[5]

Unlike other Arab talented poets and learned scholars, such as his predecessors the Egyptian poets ʿAlī al-Qalʿī (d. 1172/1758–9), Ḥasan b. ʿAlī al-Badrī al-ʿAwaḍī (d. 1215/1800), Muḥammad b. Riḍwān al-Suyūṭī known as Ibn al-Ṣalāḥī (d. 1180/1766), and Qāsim b. ʿAṭā' Allāh al-Miṣrī (1204/1789–90),[6] he was unable to find a patron in Egypt. Al-ʿAṭṭār was unsuccessful in finding patronage in the Ottoman centres in Istanbul, Izmir, Ashkodra and Damascus, so he returned to Cairo in 1814 and contented himself with Muḥammad ʿAlī as his patron. He assisted his friend the historian al-Jabartī in writing his chronicles by sending him reports, letters, poems and memoirs which our author integrated into his chronicle.

However, most of al-Jabartī's biographies of poets and writers in his first two volumes of *'Ajā'ib al-Āthār* prior to the French occupation were copied from al-Zabīdī's *Mu'jam Mukhtaṣṣ*. These biographies seem to be written by the poets and the writers themselves at the request of al-Zabīdī or were quoted from their own anthologies by al-Jabartī. In this case, these biographies reflect the collective awareness of their literary life and its ideals. Their main aim was to find a patron. The poet Qāsim b. ʿAṭā' Allāh

---

5 MS *'Aj.* Cam. 2nd., Qq. 167, II, f. 151a, on al-Jabartī's statement in *'Aj.*, I, 164 on Ḥasan al-Jaddāwī and in MS *'Aj.* Cam. 2nd., Qq. 167, II, f. 236b, on al-Jabartī's statement in *'Aj.*, II, 254 on Aḥmad al-ʿArūsī.

6 On al-Qalʿī, see *'Aj.*, I, 211–16; on al-ʿAwaḍī, see *'Aj.*, I, 114–15 and Gran, *Islamic Roots*, 59; on al-Miṣrī, see *'Aj.*, II, 184–98; on Ibn al-Ṣalāḥ' see *'Aj.*, II, 184–98, and Gran, *Islamic Roots*, 60.

whose patron was the Wafāʾī family, can be taken as a criterion for the poetic talents which were admired in these centuries. He was well known for his ability to improvise poetry (*irtijāl*), which was admired by the Arabs, as well as composing strophic verses for singing, such as the literary strophic verses *muwashshaḥāt* and the colloquial *azjāl*. He excelled in composing poems in which the numerical value of the letters (*ḥisāb al-jummal*) of the second hemistich of the last verse denote the date of the occasion on which the poem was composed. This is known in Arabic prosody as *fann al-taʾrīkh*.[7] As is mentioned above, unlike these eighteenth century poets who were patronized mainly by the Wafāʾī family, al-ʿAṭṭār, who was accused of collaboration with the French, was unable to find a patron in Cairo to support him financially and to introduce him to influential officials, so he tried to find one in another part of the Ottoman Empire.

Al-ʿAṭṭār admired the French quest for knowledge, their interest in learning languages, their scientific and cultural activities, their libraries, laboratories and their interest in history, geography, medicine and humanities in general, their military tactics and administration. Yet, as he admitted in his *maqāma* he was careful not to be associated with them in order not to be considered a collaborator with the oppressive non-Muslims occupiers. It seems that, as in the case of his friend al-Jabartī, he also arrived at the conclusion that there was a need to learn even from the *kuffār* (infidels) to bring about a religious, cultural and scientific renaissance among the Muslims. Uncertain of his future after the departure of the French, and horrified by the atrocities committed by the Ottoman soldiers after the French evacuation with the help of the British navy, he decided to seek patronage outside Egypt. So he left for Turkey looking for a patron who would introduce him to influential officials in Istanbul or in other Islamic cities. As a bibliophile who yearned for his books which he had left in Cairo, he took several books with him, including his own copy of *ʿAjāʾib al-Āthār* (vols I–III), written in *Maghribī* handwriting and

7 Cf. Chapter Five below. Gran, *Islamic Roots*, 60, did not understand the term *fann al-taʾrīkh*, (composing verses in which the numerical value of the letters are equivalent to the *hijrī* date of the composition of the poet), and thought it is 'reading history' (Gran, *Islamic Roots*, 60). On the art of poetics during this period, see S. Moreh, 'Arabic Poetics from the Eighteenth to the Twentieth Centuries', in Binyamin Abrahamov (ed.), *Studies in Arabic and Islamic Culture* (Ramat-Gan 2000), vii–lxvii.

edited by his friend al-Jabartī.[8] It is possible to presume that al-Jabartī sent this copy to al-ʿAṭṭār, probably after he failed to interest the North African sultans and scholars in buying it or copying it, possibly due to his criticism of their apathy toward mysticism. This indicates that al-Jabartī sent him this special copy circa 1806 after al-ʿAṭṭār's departure to Turkey in 1803, hoping that the latter would introduce it to influential Ottoman personalities, as in the case of al-Zabīdī's books.[9] The books which al-ʿAṭṭār took with him beside *'Ajā'ib al-Āthār*, helped him not only to write some of his memoirs, comments and impressions on the margins of several pages, but also to secure his living by selling some of them in time of distress and of lack of money. It seems that al-ʿAṭṭār was very busy travelling, earning his living, studying, reading medicine, astronomy, philosophy and logic and copying rare manuscripts and writing his *ḥawāshī* (super-commentaries) on rhetoric, eloquence and grammar.[10] However he never found the time or the desire to collect his observations and reminiscences in a book form. The valuable remarks and reminiscences that he recorded in the margin of many of the manuscripts he took the trouble to carry with him on his journey are still waiting to be collected and evaluated.[11] These observations on the cultural, political, and religious activities in the Ottoman cities he visited are of great importance to understand his views on the

8 This MS is kept at Cambridge University Library, Qq. 166–8, with notes and remarks written by al-ʿAṭṭār and signed by him. See the Appendix at the end of this book. These additions are given also in the footnotes in our Arabic edition of *'Ajā'ib al-Āthār*.

9 See al-Jabartī's comment on al-Zabīdī's *Sharḥ Kitāb Iḥyā' 'Ulūm al-Dīn* (*'Aj.*, II, 201, according to the English Translation of Philip and Perlmann): 'He began a commentary on the book *Iḥyā'*... and completed a fair copy of chapters which he sent to Istanbul, Syria, and the Maghrib so it would become known like the commentary on the *Qāmūs* and causes a desire for demanding it and copying it'. This MS was read also by a certain ʿAbd al-Wahhāb Shakkī (sic) Makkī al-Maqdisī in Jerusalem indicating that it was circulated among some scholars (see the margin of MS *'Aj.* Cam. 2nd., Qq. 168, III, f. 109b, on al-Jabartī's statement in *'Aj.*, III, 115, dealing with al-Sharīf al-Ḥasan b. ʿAlī al-Badrī al-ʿAwaḍī [d. 1799] who was buried Muḥammad al-Budayrī, in the Cemetery of Ma'man Allāh in Jerusalem).

10 See al-ʿAṭṭār's comment in the margin of MS *'Aj.* Cam. 2nd., Qq. 166, I, f. 239a, on al-Jabartī's statement in *'Aj.*, I, 260 dealing with *Safīnat al-Rāghib*; ff. 259b–260a, on *Ta'rīb Risālat Mullā 'Iṣām fī 'l-Majāz*,in *'Aj.*, I, 287; f. 263a, on *Risālat al-'Aḍud li 'l-Sa'd*, in *'Aj.*, I, 289, etc.

11 Mrs Lubna Safadi-ʿAbbasi is preparing her Ph.D. Thesis on 'The Cultural and Literary Activities of al-Azhar Rector Ḥasan al-ʿAṭṭār (1766–1835) in Egypt ...' at the Hebrew University in Jerusalem (2011), with the intention of discussing al-ʿAṭṭār's comments on the margins of his MSS. On al-ʿAṭṭār, see note 51 below, *Maẓhar al-Taqdīs*, Aḥmad ʿAbduh ʿAlī (ed.), 24–8.

Ottoman rulers and scholars, both Turks and Arabs. Although al-ʿAṭṭār kept in constant correspondence with al-Jabartī, served as his agent for selling books from his father's collection and composed elegies on eminent scholars, no elegy by al-ʿAṭṭār lamenting the death of his close friend al-Jabartī in 1241/1825 has yet been discovered. Such an elegy might enable us to know the exact date of the death of his friend, since the custom was to end elegaic poems with the conventional ending verse in which the date of the event can be deduced according to the numerical value of the letters of its last verse (*bayt al-ta'rīkh 'alā ḥisāb al-jummal*). If al-ʿAṭṭār dared to write such a poem in spite of his patron Muḥammad ʿAlī's unfavourable attitude towards al-Jabartī who abstained from flattering rulers and condemned tyranny and oppression,[12] we might know about al-Jabartī's character, achievements, and the impression which his work made in his lifetime.

David Ayalon regards al-ʿAṭṭār and Ismāʿīl al-Khashshāb (d. 1814)[13] as possible sources for al-Jabartī's 'historical work during Muḥammad ʿAlī's reign, when he was in disgrace while they enjoyed the Bāshā's favour' and keeping in touch with the affairs in the ruling circles.[14]

The most interesting, pioneering, stimulating and controversial study that uses al-ʿAṭṭār's manuscripts and remarks in the margins of the many manuscripts which he read to evaluate his cultural, social, economic, intellectual and religious background, has been attempted by Peter Gran in his book on the history of Egypt, entitled *Islamic Roots of Capitalism, Egypt, 1760–1840*. However, this is a controversial work in which the author has focused on the importance of the post classical Muslim literature of commentaries (*ḥawāshī*) which was neglected by orientalists. Peter Gran who, like Reinhard Schulze and others, has attempted to prove that there was an Islamic eighteenth century intellectual movement toward rational thinking in various Arabic commentaries written by Egyptian scholars. In his work Gran tries to convince us that this movement indicates the emergence of modernity and enlightenment in the Ottoman Empire in the seventeenth and eighteenth

12 See *'Aj.*, I, 6, where al-Jabartī says: 'I did not aim at serving any prominent person of high rank or at obeying any vizier or amir…, flatter any regime with hypocrisy, or lavish praise, or blame contrary to good character'.

13 On al-Khashshāb, see Crabb, *The Writing of History*, 45, 58. His short historical account is *Khulāṣat mā Yurīd min Akhbār al-Amīr Murād*, is reprinted in *'Ajā'ib al-Āthār*, ʿAbd al-ʿAzīz Jamāl al-Dīn (ed.), III, 37, 709.

14 Ayalon, 'The Historian', 244. Cf. *'Aj.*, IV, 238–41.

centuries. He argues that this Muslim enlightenment corresponded to, yet was independent of the European era of Enlightenment. Gran fixed the date of the emergence of modern Egypt and his investigation of the *Islamic Roots of Capitalism* at 1760, the year in which ʿAlī Bey al-Kabīr (1727–72) became ruler (*Shaykh al-Balad*). This is because, according to Gran, ʿAlī Bey 'was the first to work through the foreign merchant community and to attempt to reform key institutions, such as the army, by means of European advisers'.[15] This is in spite of the fact the ʿAlī Bey al-Kabīr was a despotic ruler, whose primary interest was in expanding his military campaigns and in building mosques and shops. He had little or no serious interest in building schools for Islamic philosophical, secular and rational sciences which became *farḍ kifāya* (an obligation not incumbent on the community as a whole) in the Muslim world, to the degree that the Ottoman governor of Egypt Aḥmad Pāshā al-Kūr (1748–50) could not find any Egyptian mathematician to discuss with him arithmetical methods, except Ḥasan al-Jabartī.[16] ʿAlī Bey al-Kabīr's revolt against the Ottomans and his independence lasted a very short time (1760–72) with no substantial achievements.[17] Gran emphasized the socio-economic and the global significance of the industrial revolution of the late eighteenth century, as well as the changes in the economic structure of Europe and the development of the world market. He adds 'that modern Egyptian culture has a coherent indigenous basis which is rooted in social and economic changes which took place in the middle and late eighteenth century'.[18] The weak point of Gran's research is that he puts the emphasis upon social and economic relations between Europe and the Arab world only and ignores the crucial importance of Islamic dogma and attitude towards Christian Europe along with the aversion of the Muslims towards any cultural contact with Europe since the Crusaders' invasions which was still alive in their collective memory during the eighteenth century. Both al-Jabartī and al-ʿAṭṭār criticized the Ottoman rulers for their ignorance of basic knowledge of the Qur'ān. This is in contrast to former generations of Sultans and rulers who were scholars as well.[19] Al-

---

15 Gran, *Islamic Roots*, 12.

16 See *'Aj.*, I, 187, and Ayalon, 'Historian', 239.

17 See M. Winter, 'The Re-emergence of the Mamlūks Following the Ottoman Conquest', in Philipp and Haarmann (eds), *The Mamluks in Egyptian Politics and Society*, 87–106.

18 Gran, *Islamic Roots*, 3.

19 See our Arabic Edition of *'Ajā'ib al-Āthār*. (The comment of al-ʿAṭṭār in MS *'Aj.* Cam. 2nd., Qq. 166, I, f. 239a, is in the margin of our new edition, equivalent to *'Ajā'ib*, Būlāq, I, 260),

Jabartī's supernatural explanation judging the rule of ʿAlī Bey al-Kabīr contradicts Gran's conclusion of rational thinking among the rulers and religious scholars. Proof of the *'ulamā"*'s and al-Jabartī's irrational and supernatural thinking is his explanation of the reason why the Islamic world was defeated in its conflict with the technical and scientific superiority of the European imperialists. He argued that it was because the rulers of Egypt did not heed the advice of the *'ulamā'*, especially that of the *Ṣūfī* saint al-Shaykh Muḥammad b. Sālim al-Ḥifnāwī (or al-Ḥifnī). His advice was ignored and he was poisoned:

> ʿAlī Bey came to power; with no one to deter him, he too did as seemed best to him, and as a result affliction descended on Egypt, Syria, and the Ḥijāz, and spread to include the whole world and all countries. This is the open secret, which is an indubitable consequence of the inner (secret), which consists of respect for the inheritors of prophecy, complete conformity (to them), making the foundations firm, setting up the guide posts of the right way and Islam, and strengthening the edifice of piety.[20]

However, Gran's revealing discovery 'that glosses disguised a new body of thought ... that important developments in secular culture were taking place and these were supportive of capitalism',[21] is an important one. In fact this 'introduction of secular cultural matter in the midst of a religious subject', was part of the general orientation in the Ottoman Ḥanafī school of jurisprudence, which was emphasized in the publication of the Turkish secular and rational *Qānūnnāmeh*. However, this 'secular cultural matter', although it is an important point, was not effective enough to initiate among the Egyptian *'ulamā'* a cultural initiative to start an Islamic rational and systematic scientific movement, which could resume the magnificent innovative work of earlier Muslim scholars such as Ibn al-Haytham (d. 430/1039) on optics; Ibn Rushd (Averroes) (d. 1198) in his endeavour to reconcile between Aristotelian thought and Islamic religious thought; Ibn Khaldūn (d. 1406) in his rational materialist philosophy of history in his emphasize on socio-political factors in historical development; Ibn Sīnā (Avicenna) and Ibn al-Nafīs in medicine, Ibn

---

where al-ʿAṭṭār wrote: فهكذا كانت الوزرا، سابقا أكثرهم عُلما، وأما الآن فاكثرهم لا يعرف يقرأ الخطّ ولا يكتب ولا يصحح قراءة الفاتحة' ('thus most ministers previously were *'ulamā'*, but now most of them do not know how to read script, nor write nor correctly read the *fātiḥa*'.)

20 *'Aj.*, I, 303–4.

21 Gran, *Islamic Roots*, liii.

Ḥāzim al-Qarṭājannī on literary criticism, Ibn Ṭufayl on religious thought, and many other Muslim scientists and thinkers on which the European Enlightenment was partly based through their Latin translations.[22] The paradox is that Arab scholars rediscovered their great Muslim scientific and philosophical achievements through European research. In fact, the period of stagnation in Islamic culture, whether it started, according to Ernest Renan, after the death of Ibn Rushd in 1198, or according to the Arab historians, with the destruction of Baghdad by the Mongols in 1258, reveals that after the total withdrawal of the Arabs from their political, cultural and military engagement in determining their future, and after they succumbed to the non-Arab rulers of their countries newly converted to Islam, it is possible to say that the 'dynamic of stagnation' in the Muslim world at that time was in contrast to the European dynamic of Enlightenment in the same period. Only through the impact of the West, did Arab countries start their actual *nahḍa* (renaissance) with the invasion of Napoleon of Egypt in 1798 after a long period of *inḥiṭāṭ* (decadence or decline).[23] Al-Jabartī and al-ʿAṭṭār did not consider the works of al-Zabīdī and al-Murādī as 'dynamic', but rather as the last works of 'glorious' conventional Islamic scholarship.[24] They were described as the last flickers of the candle before its final extinction by Muḥammad ʿAlī's rule. Napoleon tried to restore the Arab scholars' authority to rule Egypt. Some *'ulamā'* informed him that the populace would only obey the cruel and brutal Mamluk rulers.[25]

The successors of al-Jabartī and al-ʿAṭṭār, such as Rifāʿa Rāfiʿ al-Ṭahṭāwī (d. 1870) and Muḥammad ʿAbduh (d. 1904) attempted to revive and reform Islamic culture and the 'might of Islam' (*shawkat al-Islam*) in the hope of

22 See S. Wild, 'Between Ernest Renan and Ernst Bloch: Averroes Remembered, Discovered, and Invented. The European Reception Since the Nineteenth Century', in Mourad Wahba and Mona Abousenna (eds), *Averroes and the Enlightenment* (New York 1996), 155–70.

23 See S. Wild, 'Islamic Enlightenment, and the Paradox of Averroes', *Die Welt des Islams* 36:3 (1996), 386 where he says: '*Inḥiṭāṭ* was first used to denote "decadence" as a self-view of intellectuals of the Ottoman Empire'.

24 See MS *'Aj.* Cam. 2nd., Qq. 167, II, f. 236b, on al-Jabartī's statement in *'Aj.*, II, 254, dealing with *Silk al-Durar* by al-Murādī that no Syrian scholar was interested in copying this book, and no one was at al-Murādī's outstanding standard. Since his death, the country and its people changed and ignorance prevailed.

25 S. Moreh, 'Napoleon and the French Impact on Egyptian Society in the Eyes of al-Jabartī', in Irene A. Bierman (ed.), *Napoleon in Egypt* (Los Angeles 2003), reprinted in ʿAbd al-Raḥmān ibn Ḥasan al-Jabartī, *Napoleon in Egypt, al-Jabartī's Chronicle of the French Occupation, 1798*, trans. S. Moreh (Princeton 2004), 183–204.

challenging Christian Europe. This led fundamentalist Muslims by the end of the twentieth century to a great disappointment in such modernization, and to the rise of the fundamentalist and extremist Muslim movements in several Muslim countries, such as Egypt, Algeria, Iran and the Ṭālibān in Afghanistan and to the emergence of such figures as the Ḥanbalī-Wahhābī Usāma Bin Lādin, who rejected the achievement and superiority of the secular Western scientific and democratic culture and vowed to bring about its destruction.

Gran considered al-ʿAṭṭār a 'link between eighteenth-century Egypt to nineteenth-century Egypt and to the larger Arabic-language Ottoman culture of his time'.[26] He emphasized the spiritual and cultural impact of the *Ṣūfī majlis* al-Wafā'iyya on al-Jabartī, al-ʿAṭṭār and Ismāʿīl al-Khashshāb.[27] He considered al-ʿAṭṭār, who belonged to the Khalwatī mystical order, and to the rational Ḥanafī school of jurisprudence, as an Andalusian in his cultural orientation, and *mutakallim* and Ashʿarī in his Islamic thought. He put the emphasis upon economic and social aspects and links the rise of capitalism to global economic and industrial revolution in Europe to transformations that took place in Egypt. He thinks that 'from the late eighteenth century onward there was a growth of capitalism and of national participation in the world market'.[28] However, his astonishing confidence that 'one need not be a philologist oneself or even try to emulate one; one can be a social scientist and totally ignore language. This does not change anything', is the most deficient point in his arguments.[29] This statement can be true for English and American social studies written by an English speaking scholar, but one needs to be an expert in Arabic philology if one wants to be an orientalist in any Muslim and Arabic discipline. If Gran were such an expert, he would not have mixed between pseudo-classical and neo-classical revival in Arabic literature.[30] He would have distinguished between *saj'* (rhymed prose generally in couplet sentences) and *qāfiya* (rhyme in verses of a serious ode [*qaṣīda*]), and would not have defined the *saj'* used strictly for rhyming prose with confusing,

26 Gran, *Islamic Roots*, lv.

27 Ibid., 76. On the friendship, the literary and cultural activities of these three see ibid., xlv, 76–84. Cf. the biography of al-Khashshāb and the friendship between the three in *'Aj.*,IV, 238–41.

28 Gran, *Islamic Roots*, xlx.

29 Ibid., xxi

30 This subject will be discussed in Chapter Five on poetry, below. See S. Moreh, 'The Neoclassical *Qaṣīda*, Modern Poets and Critics', in S. Moreh, *Studies in Modern Arabic Prose and Poetry* (Leiden 1988), 33–56.

meaningless and irrelevant terms, such as 'insincere rhyme-verse', or 'official *saj'* poetry' [sic].[31] The Arabic terminology in this case is *urjūza*, 'a versification in *rajaz* meter rhyming in couplets.' The Arab prosodists strictly distinguish between *saj'* (rhyming prose), *urjūza* (versified speech in *rajaz* meter [- - u - and its variations u - u -, - u u -, u u u - (rare) and its final foot: u - -]), and the serious Arabic ode (*qaṣīda*), the official form of poetry, in which the verses are divided into two equal hemistiches and composed according to the remaining15 meters.[32]

In fact, the 'two poems cited by al-Jabartī, are not referring to coffee drinking', but the poet Ibn al-Ṣalīḥī in his erotic poem written in the masculine gender, used the word *qahwa* in double-entendre (*tawriya*) of 'wine' in classical Arabic and 'coffee' in post-classical Arabic, asking his beloved to allow him to drink *qahwat al-shifā'* (the wine of healing) from his lips. This double-entendre use is clear from the other verses quoted by al-Jabartī in which the poet once used the term *qahwata bunnin* (coffee) and the Arabic synonym of *qahwa* as wine, i.e. *rāḥ*.[33] Moreover, the poet did not say: '*alqāki wa fī ḥashīshatī al-ashwāq*' ('I meet you and in my *ḥashīsh* [cannabis] there is longing to you') but the word *ḥashīshatī* ('my cannabis'), should be read *ḥushīshatī* ('last breath, last spark of life'). Now the right version is: '*alqāki wa fī ḥushīshatī al-ashwāq*' ('I meet you and still in my last spark of life there is yearning to you'). In this way the explanation that the poet has 'built on the imagery of *ḥashīsh*', as Gran suggested, has nothing to do with the poet's intention.[34] Gran translated these two words, i.e. *qahwa* and *ḥushīsha* as 'coffee' and *ḥashīsh* to fit his absurd argument that 'al-ʿAṭṭār when not writing the official *saj'* poetry [sic], wrote for the coffee shop, a place where poetry and song, wine and *ḥashīsh* united people from different walks of life'.[35] In fact, contrary to Gran's understanding, what the poet Ibn al-Ṣalīḥī said to his beloved boy friend, '*alqāka wa-fī ḥushīshatī al-ashwāq*' ('I meet you, and longing fills what remains of my soul'), has nothing to do, what so ever, with *ḥashīsh*.[36] Another no less astonishing hypothesis is Gran's assumption that

31 Gran, *Islamic Roots*, 89.

32 See Wright, *A Grammar of the Arabic Language*, vol. II, *Prosody*.

33 Gran, *Islamic Roots*, 60.

34 Ibid., 60.

35 Ibid., 60, cf. *'Aj.*, I, 268 and Philipp and Perlmann's English translation, I, 444.

36 Gran, *Islamic Roots*, 61.

Majnūn Laylā (d. 699?) is a pre-Islamic poet and not an Umayyad poet. All this erroneous information on Arabic literature and poetry would have been avoided had Gran's approach to Arabic philology been more serious and his social and economic theories would have helped him arrive at a sound conclusion. Besides, there is no evidence that 'al-Zabīdī's study of al-Ḥarīrī led him to study the pre-Islamic and early Umayyad sources of the Arabic language which al-Ḥarīrī himself had drawn on'.[37] These erroneous conclusions indicate clearly that Gran intended to force his socio-economic theories upon Egyptian cultural life whether it was suitable or not and whether he understood the Arabic text or not. In Gran's research one can realize that we are reading a work of another victim of the 'syndrome of theory',[38] which is observed among some orientalists, who have not mastered the Arabic language, and are not well acquainted with Islamic culture. In this case also, Gran, as a compensation for his limited knowledge of Arabic, looked for a Western theory in his study of Islamic society and culture, forcing the meaning of the text and twisting it to fit his dubious theory.

Our discovery of Ḥasan al-ʿAṭṭār's notes,[39] in the margins of the first three volumes of *'Ajā'ib al-Āthār* kept at Cambridge University Library in England (MS *'Aj.* Cam. 2nd., Qq. 166, 167, 168),[40] and his letters to the muftī of Jerusalem, Appendix II below, are important to understand al-ʿAṭṭār's personality, works, poems and the route of his journey to various cities in the Ottoman Empire between 1803–13, and the impression which this journey left upon him. This is due to the fact that the details about his itinerary and the

37 Ibid., 62, nos. 19–20, which refer the reader to al-Zabīdī's treatise on pre-Islamic gambling *al-maysar wa 'l-qidāḥ*, has nothing to do with al-Zabīdī's elegies to his wife in the fashion of the Umayyad emotional love poetry of the poet Majnūn Layla and bringing out 'the more radical equality of sexes found in tribal contexts than in some urban situations', (ibid., 62), and it is not possible to consider it as 'symptomatic of trends in sexual relations in the later eighteenth century, and the appearance of women in the chronicles'. This is a far fetched conclusion. In fact, talented poetesses and women who endowed institutions for charity are mentioned in many biographical and historical works in Arab history. On Majnūn, see the article Ch. Pellat, 'Maḏjnūn Laylā', *EI*^{2}, V, 1102–3.

38 For a similar case, see my review of Boaz Shoshan's *Popular Culture in Medieval Cairo*, in *JSS* 42:2 (1997), 441–5.

39 See Browne, *A Handlist*, 342–5, nos. 1501–9, Add. 273–Add. 282.

40 See ibid., 118, nos. 663–5, Qq. 166–8.

route mentioned by ʿAlī Mubārak,[41] which were supplied by his son and family are in contrast with the information recorded by al-ʿAṭṭār in the margin of this manuscript. These notes were not known to scholars who have written on al-ʿAṭṭār. They can also shed new light and add new details to Peter Gran's[42] comprehensive but controversial work on this important *'ālim* who served Muḥammad ʿAlī faithfully and helped to establish his educational institutions. One can presume that the reason for this mistake in identifying al-ʿAṭṭār's route of his journey as a land route by his son and not the sea route which is given by al-ʿAṭṭār, is due to the fact that it was dangerous to travel by sea in the Mediterranean at that time.

During the Middle Ages, Arabs were not as skilled as the sailors of the Italian ports such as Venice and Genoa in shipbuilding and navigation in the Mediterranean Sea. Bedouin horsemen performed the main Islamic conquests in Asia and Africa. Sea battles between Muslim and Christian mariners in the Mediterranean often proved fatal to the Muslim fleets. This weakness of Muslim sea power forced the Mamluks to destroy the ports and fortresses of the Holy Land and the Syrian coast. It was necessary to do so in order to prevent the Crusaders from capturing once more the holy cities of Jerusalem, Bethlehem, Nazareth and Tiberias.[43]

As long as the Ottoman Empire expanded at the expense of other states and nations, its main revenue was mainly war-booties (*ghanā'im ḥarb*) from invading (*jihād*) Christian countries in Europe and pagan territories in Asia. However, after the Ottoman occupation of Egypt (1517) and the return of the Ottoman Sultan Sulaymān the Magnificent (1520–66) from the walls of

41 See ʿAlī Mubārak, *al-Khiṭaṭ al-Tawfīqiyya al-Jadīda li-Miṣr al-Qāhira wa-Muduniha wa-Bilādihā al-Qadīma wa 'l-Shahīra* (Būlāq, 1305/1887–8), IV, 38–40 (Cairo 1980), 83, and Gran, *Islamic Roots*, 78.

42 Gran, *Islamic Roots*, 76–110, 123–62, 169–208. Al-ʿAṭṭār's notes can give accurate answers to the dispute and to the question raised by Fred De Jong in his review article on P. Gran's book in 'On Peter Gran, *Islamic Roots of Capitalism: Egypt 1760–1840*, A Review Article with Author's Reply', *International Journal of Middle East Studies*, 14 (1982), 381–99; F. de Jong, 'The Itinerary of Ḥasan al-ʿAṭṭār (1766–1835): A Reconsideration and Its Implication', *JSS* 28:1 (1993), 99–128. See the rejoinder of Gran 'A Note on Critical Reception', in his book, *Islamic Roots*, xliii.

43 See D. Ayalon, *Outsiders in the Lands of Islam: Mamluks, Mongols and Eunuchs* (London 1988), 31–47.

Vienna in 1526,[44] the Ottoman Empire began to lose territories and became a tax collecting state, developing a bureaucracy using a special script (*khaṭṭ al-qurma*) for official bookkeeping. A clear proof of the Ottoman weakness as a marine power in the Mediterranean is their recruiting Muslim corsairs in the service of their maritime power.

According to al-Jabartī, by the end of the eighteenth Century, the welfare of the Arab provinces of the Ottoman Empirehad been neglected and the fortifications of many Arab ports on the Mediterranean coasts had gone to wrack and ruin through lack of maintenance. However, only at the beginning of the nineteenth century were corsairs suppressed and slavery abolished by the European powers. Until then, sailing in the Mediterranean was extremely dangerous for both Muslims and Christians. Muslim corsairs used to attack European and American ships to take Christian captives. One of the favourite subjects of novels in the 'new American state was the encounter of its Navy with the Barbary corsairs to protect American shipping and to stop the local sea-captains in Morocco and the Regencies from taking Christian captives from foreign shipping'.[45]

The Mediterranean sea was the field of battle between Muslims and Christians. Muslim corsairs attacked Christian ships from the coast of North Africa and sold their passengers in the slave markets. The Christians retaliated, mainly through the knights of the Order of St John of Jerusalem who were based in Rhodes until 1522. After their expulsion by the Turks from Rhodes they established themselves in Malta between 1530 and 1798. They organized in the Mediterranean a strong war fleet to attack Ottoman ships, the Barbary pirates and the Levantine boats, and thousands of Muslim captives were imprisoned in Malta.[46] Al-Jabartī quotes the first Arabic proclamation in which Napoleon, in order to win the sympathy of the Muslims, declared proudly that the French had expelled the Knights of Malta 'who claimed that God the Exalted required them to fight the Muslims'.[47] Many Muslim captives were

44 See C. Brockelmann, *History of the Islamic Peoples*, trans. J. Carmichael and M. Perlmann (New York 1947), 290f.

45 See S. Moreh and P.C. Sadgrove, *Jewish Contributions to Nineteenth-Century Arabic Theatre* (Oxford 1996), 47–8.

46 See the article E. Rossi, 'Malta', *E.I.*^{2} VI, 295f.

47 See *al-Jabartī's Chronicle*, 41f.

only able to free themselves after paying a heavy ransom, and when Napoleon captured Malta they were able to return to the Muslim lands.[48]

However, the commercial and cultural contacts between the Mediterranean countries helped to develop a lingua franca among the inhabitants of the Mediterranean shore known as *Sabir*. It is an amalgam of Provencal, Italian, Spanish and Arabic vocabulary.[49] The French invasion of Egypt helped to secure the navigation of Muslim ships in the Mediterranean, especially when the British ships under Nelson's command destroyed the French squadron at Trafalgar and the British cooperated with the Ottomans in driving the French out of Egypt in 1801. According to al-Jabartī, after this naval battle the Mediterranean became a British sea, '[the British] remained in their ships in front of Alexandria, coming and going freely eastwards and westward, lying in wait for the supplies coming to the French or those which they sent to their country and intercepting them'.[50] This fact might help us to understand why al-ʿAṭṭār took the sea route to Turkey and not the land route claimed by al-ʿAṭṭār's relatives after his death. It seems that in spite of the dangers of travel by the Mediterranean, Muslim merchants and scholars used the sea route to the Ottoman ports of the eastern Mediterranean, which had become by now a safe sea dominated by the British, while the land route was dominated by looting Bedouin horsemen.

Al-Jabartī unequivocally admires al-ʿAṭṭār's poetic talent and enjoys his poems composed in praise of some handsome French scholars.[51] In *Maẓhar al-Taqdīs* al-Jabartī mentions al-ʿAṭṭār's contribution towards furnishing the title of the book and includes some of ʿAṭṭar's *maqāma*s and a few poemscomposed about the French and in praise of the Ottoman vizier Yūsuf Ḍiyā Pasha.[52] The improvement in the level of style and grammatical usage in

48 Cf. *'Abd al-Raḥmān al-Jabartī's History*, III, 64, and *'Aj*. Būlāq, III, 40.

49 See Marc Baroli, *La Vie quotidienne des Français en Algérie, 1830–1914* (Paris 1967), 90–1. Cf. Moreh and Sadgrove, *Jewish Contributions*, 46.

50 See *Mudda*, Leiden, Arabic text, ff. 10b–11a/*al-Jabartī's Chronicle,* English tran., 64; *'Aj.*, III, 56, 168, 192; cf. Gran, *Islamic Roots*,17.

51 On al-ʿAṭṭār's life and activities see Gran, *Islamic Roots*,75–110, 123–62, 169–208. On his homosexuality, see ibid., 127 and 237, n. 48.

52 Al-Jabartī, *Maẓhar al-Taqdīs bi-Dhahāb Dawlat al-Faransīs, bi 'l-Ishtirāk ma'a Ṣadīqih ... Ḥasan al-'Aṭṭār*, Aḥmad ʿAbduh ʿAlī (ed.)(Cairo 1419/1998), who claimed that the book is a joint work by both writers. Al-Jabartī states that he had recorded the details of some events on the occupation of Egypt by the French (hinting to *Mudda*) and that 'he added' (*fa-ḍamamtu*)

Maẓhar al-Taqdīs compared with the style of *Tārīkh Muddat al-Faransīs bi-Miṣr* indicates that al-ʿAṭṭār, who was skilled in Arabic grammar and style, had helped al-Jabartī. However, such cooperation does not make him a co-author of *Maẓhar al-Taqdīs* as claimed by some scholars.

Al-Jabartī described the miserable condition of the walls of Alexandria during the events of the French occupation of Egypt. He added that the Mamluk rulers of Egypt neglected the fortifications of the ports in order not to be accused that 'their intention is rebellion against the Sultan':

> News and letters arrived from the ports of Alexandria, Rosetta, and Damanhūr with word that...the people of the port suddenly realized that the French and their ships had reached al-ʿAjamī, and were advancing on the town at daybreak ... Meanwhile the French continuously increased in number. They scaled the ruined parts of the wall surrounding the port and entered it. The people looked about and suddenly found the French behind them, and withdraw in haste seeking their homes only to discover that the French had occupied the new Manshiyya and had surrounded the walls.[53]

The reason for the destruction of the walls, were according to al-Jabartī:

> Since the time of ʿAlī Bey not only did they [the Mamluks] not pay sufficient attention to the port but even removed what weapons and cannons were already there...All this after Alexandria and its towers had once been extremely well built and fortified with an excellent wall surrounding her; a wall which had been maintained by former generations... All these were neglected until nothing remained while the wall and its towers fell into ruin, until in some places the walls became level with the ground.[54]

Moreover, the war ships of Murād Bey which were under the command of the admiral (*ra'īs*) ʿNīqūlā al-Naṣrānī al-Armanīʿ, and his three hundred Greek marines, were not meant for battles at sea, although the largest ship was armed with twenty-four canon, but according to al-Jabartī:

> The seven galleons, three of which were large ones, were in fact, to imitate the Sultan, and had spent enormous sums of money upon them... He [Murad Bey] had them stationed in front of

---

some of al-ʿAṭṭār's poems and prose. Later on, both decided to entitle it *Maẓhar al-Taqdīs* (ibid., 9).

53 See *al-Jabartī's Chronicle*, 36f. English/ff. 1b–2a Arabic text.

54 Ibid., 37 English/f. 2a Arabic.

the palace at Jīza for a long time as decoration to glorify himself before his own people and others.[55]

Al-ʿAṭṭār's remarks and comments in the margin of MS *ʿAj.* Cam. 2[56] are of great importance to our subject. It can help us to get a glimpse about the travels of some Muslim scholars by sea to various Ottoman ports in the Mediterranean at the beginning of the nineteenth century. This MS was found in the archives of Johann Ludwig Burckhardt. It is kept at Cambridge University Library (Near Eastern Section),[57] together with letters collected during his travels in Syria, Egypt and Arabia after his taking the turban under the Muslim name, 'Shaykh Ibrāhām Ibn ʿAbd Allāh'.[58] Besides letters of recommendation written for him by important Muslim scholars to help him buy Arabic manuscripts, we find some letters written by members of well-known indigenous Christian families living in ports of the east Mediterranean. Some of these letters were sent to European consuls informing them about Ottoman and European ships visiting Beirut and other Near Eastern ports.[59]

It was also the custom of some European merchants, who formed colonies in these ports, to send such reports to their governments. Among these were fifty to sixty French merchants in Alexandria headed by Charles Magallon and his wife who resided there for more than thirty years. In 1793 Magallon was appointed Consul General of France in Alexandria. His letters to the French Foreign Office, his work *Mémoire sur l'Égypte* (February 1795), together with the accounts of the French traveller C.F. de Volney (1775–1820), convinced Napoleon Bonaparte to invade Egypt in 1798. Napoleon's intention was to strike at British interests in India on the pretext of protecting the French merchants in Egypt from the Mamluks' malicious treatment and corruption. This pretext for invading Egypt is emphasized in the first printed Arabic

55 Ibid., 38 English/f. 2a Arabic.

56 See Browne, *A Hand-list*, 342–5, nos. 1501–9, Add. 273–Add. 282. For a sample of such comments in al-ʿAṭṭār's hand see Moreh's article 'Al-Jabartī's Method', *JSAI*, plates I–II, 368–9.

57 On Burckhardt, see Trench, *Arabic Travellers*, 59–72.

58 On the Burckhardt papers, see Browne, *A Handlist*, 273–380, from no. 348 Qq. 1 (12) a–Qq. 300 (10) a and no. 652, Add. 177.

59 See Gran, *Islamic Roots*, 9–10; *Maẓhar al-Taqdīs*, ʿAbd al-Raḥīm (ed.), b–3; cf. Tignor's introduction to *al-Jabartī's Chronicle*, 6–7.

proclamation Napoleon sent to the Egyptians.[60] The style and content of the proclamation enumerating the ideals of the French revolution, induced al-Jabartī to criticize it in his books *Tārīkh Muddat al-Faransīs bi-Miṣr*,and *Maẓhar al-Taqdīs bi-Zawāl Dawlat al-Faransīs* ('The Manifestation of Blessing in the Demise of French Authority').[61] Burckhardt, who bought this autograph from al-Jabartī in 1816, wrote on its title page that the author compiled this book to clear himself and his friend Shaykh Ḥasan al-ʿAṭṭār of collaborating with the French. In fact al-ʿAṭṭār contributed to this book not only by helping the author to formulate the rhymed title of *Maẓhar al-Taqdīs*, but also with panegyrics to the Ottomans, defamatory poems on the French, a description of the ruin caused by the French army during the two Cairo revolts (21–22 October, 1798 and 21 March, 1800) and the plague in Upper Egypt (May 1801).[62] Yet this does not mean that he was co-author. In his 'assembly' (*maqāma*) describing his close relations with the French savants who accompanied Napoleon, entitled *Maqāmat Ḥasan al-'Aṭṭār fi 'l-Faransīs*,[63] al-ʿAṭṭār admitted visiting their libraries and laboratories and helping them read some Arabic books. His description about his visit to their library and laboratories, unlike al-Jabartī, was short, vague and written in embellished rhymed style in which the play on words is more important than the precise and actual description. He added only that most of their books were in mathematics and humanities and that they showed him their astronomical and engineering apparatuses. On the other hand al-Jabartī's description was more detailed and precise:

---

60 The original French proclamation in Arabic is published and translated into English in *al-Jabartī's Chronicle*, plate XIII, and pp. 7–10 Arabic text, English translation 40–2.

61 See *al-Jabartī's Chronicle*, Leiden, Arabic text, 10–17, ff. 3b–5b/English translation 41–7. The book is translated into French under the title *Journal d'un notable du Caire; durant l'expédition française 1798–1801*, trad. Joseph Cuoq (Paris 1979).

62 See *al-Jabartī's Chronicle*, 8 and plate VI.

63 See *Maqāmat al-Adīb al-Ra'īs al-Shaykh Ḥasan al-'Aṭṭār fi 'l-Faransīs*, at the end of Jalāl al-Dīn 'Abd al-Raḥmān b. Abī Bakr al-Suyūṭī, *al-Maqāmāt al-Suyūṭiyya, li-.... Jalāl al-Dīn 'Abd al-Raḥmān b. Abī Bakr al-Suyūṭī... Mudhayyala bi-Maqāmat.... al-Shaykh Ḥasan al-'Aṭṭār* (Cairo 1275/1858–9), 91–6. On Ḥasan al-ʿAṭṭār see Gran, *Islamic Roots*, 76ff; the English translation of this *maqāma* by P. Gran is in pp. 189–91. This translation is not accurate, for instance, the words '*ba'ḍ al-ukhwa, min ahl al-khalā'a wa 'l-nashwa*', should be translated into 'One friend known for his dissipation and wine-drinking', and not 'Various profligate wine-drinking people'; '*maskan al-qawm*', is not 'the residence of the wealthy', but should be translated as 'the residence of the people (from whom I have escaped, i.e. the French)'. On al-Jabartī's description of the French scientific activities, see *'Aj.*, III, 35–6.

> The administrators, astronomers and some of the physicians lived in this house in which they placed a great number of their books and with a keeper taking care of them and arranging them. And the students among them would gather two hours before noon every day in an open space opposite the shelves of books, sitting on chairs arranged in parallel rows before a wide long board. Whoever wishes to look up something in a book asks for whatever volumes he wants and the librarian brings them to him… When some Muslims would come to look around they would not prevent them from entering. Indeed they would bring them all kinds of printed books in which there were all sorts of illustrations and maps (*cartes, kartāt*) of the countries and regions, animals, birds, plants, histories of the ancients… tales of the prophets including pictures of them, of their miracles and wondrous deeds, the events of their respective peoples and such things which baffle the mind… They have a great interest in the sciences, mainly in mathematics, and a knowledge of languages…They possess extraordinary astronomical instruments of perfect construction and instruments for measuring altitudes of wondrous amazing and precise construction… In a similar manner they assigned…a place in the house…and built in it neat and well designed stoves and ovens, and instruments of distilling, vaporizing, and extracting liquids andointments belonging to medicine and sublimated simple salts, the salts extracted from burnt herbs, and so forth.[64]

With his heavily embellished style al-ʿAṭṭār was not able to make a realistic and precise description. He ended his *maqāma* by saying that he later realized his fault and cut his relations with the French fearing the accusation of being a collaborator. In *Maqāmat Ḥasan al-'Aṭṭār*, his main aim was to write in a highly rhetorical literary Arabic, embellished with plays on words and alliteration; facts are secondary. It was written in the conventional form and structure of the *maqāmāt*, with a narrator (*rāwī*) who is supposed to be objective, relating an anecdote about a hero representing al-ʿAṭṭār. Imagination and allusion replace reality to the point that the precise description usually used inhistoriographical writing becomes rather difficult to achieve. It is written in both rhymed prose and poetic verse, decorated with synonymous and antithetic parallel sentences, with pun, allusion and double-entendre. The hero tells us that he met by accident a group of French savants, whom the narrator described and addressed as beautiful women using the Arabic feminine gender in plural form with *nūn al-niswa* (ending with the letter *nūn* indicating feminine in the plural). This gender might be used by the author to emphasize the 'other', the invading French which are in contrast to his identity

64 See *Maqāmat Ḥasan al-'Aṭṭār*, 91–6.

as 'self'. It might also reflect the fact that the author intends to insult the French by alluding to them as feminine and women. It might reveal the factthat al-ʿAṭṭār was an active homosexual. The encounter with the other, the foreigner who is different in appearance, culture, religion, customs, mentality and language, was a shock and aroused a curiosity as to whether these foreigners were behaving according to the Islamic criterion of *ḥalāl* (lawful) and *ḥarām* (unlawful) and the taboos of his religion and culture. He asserts that they were *kuffār* (infidels) who reject all divine books, interested in secular knowledge and Islamic languages, religion and history, and that they intended to imbue the Egyptians their revolutionary secular ideology of liberty, equality and fraternity. Their request for his help in translation and instruction, led him to avoid them, so that he wouldnot be considered as a collaborator deserving 'rebukes and hostility ... as well as the scorn of society'.[65]

Both al-Jabartī and al-ʿAṭṭār say that after the liberation of Egypt from the French by the British and Ottoman armies (1801), the Ottoman soldiers, especially the Albanian (*Arnā'ūṭ*) among them, played havoc among the Egyptian population.[66] Some scholars presume that 'his prolonged absence from Egypt, unusual for an *'ālim* of his time, suggests that he may initially have been branded by Muḥammad ʿAlī as a French collaborator'.[67] However, it seems that the real reason for his journey was not only the oppression of the Ottomans, but also his ambition to achieve a high office as an *'ālim* (religious scholar) in Istanbul, Izmir or Albania.[68]

---

65 See *Maqāmat Ḥasan al-'Aṭṭār*, 96, and Gran, *Islamic Roots*, 191.

66 See *'Aj.* Būlāq, III, 93 and the English translation of the passage in *al-Jabartī's History of Egypt*, III, 144–5. The comment of al-ʿAṭṭār is in the margin of his copy of MS *'Aj.* Cam., Qq 168, III, f. 89b, opposite the events of Saturday, 24 Shawwāl 1214/20 March 1800. See also MS *'Aj.* Cam., Qq 168, III, f. 239b, equivalent to the event mentioned in *'Aj.* Būlāq, III, 254, the events of 28 Ṣafar 1218/18–19 June 1803. On the relations between al-Jabartī and al-ʿAṭṭār, see Gran, *Islamic Roots*, 76–80, 87–91.

67 See Gran, *Islamic Roots*, 80 and Crabb's article, 'Al-ʿAṭṭār, Ḥasan', *Encyclopedia of Arabic Literature*, I, 111. Cf. H.A.R. Gibb, *E.I.*^{2}, I, 755.

68 There are some passages in Ḥasan al-ʿAṭṭār, *Inshā' al-'Ālim al-'Allāma al-Ḥabr al-Fahhāma Dhī al-Faḍl al-Midrār al-Muḥaqqiq al-Shaykh Ḥasan al-'Aṭṭār* (Cairo 1315/1897), in which he hinted that he as an Arab felt a stranger in the parks of Constantinople (pp. 71–3) in which he described the cold weather and snow and the suffering of the poor from the cold weather. Muḥammad ʿAbd al-Ghanī Ḥasan, in his book *Ḥasan al-'Aṭṭār*, gives a poem written by al-ʿAṭṭār describing Damascus (Cairo 1968, 93) a panegyric poem dedicated to the *Naqīb al-Ashrāf* (the head of the descendants of Muḥammad) (p. 101) and a poem on the parks of Constantinople (pp. 101–4).

Al-ʿAṭṭār's commentary and remarks in the margin of his personal copy of the first three volumes of *'Ajā'ib al-Āthār*, composed by al-Jabartī in 1806 and which might have been sent to him by al-Jabartī to Turkey, can shed new light on his comments on *'Ajā'ib al-Āthār*, his stylistic, and historical corrections,[69] his superficial literary criticism,[70] his bibliographical additions,[71] his studies, scholarly activities, his evaluation of personalities whom he met, the opening verses of his three elegies on Ḥasan al-Jaddāwī, three on Yūsuf al-Sinbilāwī, and two on Aḥmad al-ʿArūsī,[72] and the manuscripts which he copied and commentaries which he composed.

No less important is his description of his itinerary in Turkey, Albania and Syria from 1803–13. These remarks can put an end to some aspects of the dispute between Gran and Fred De Jong on various points on al-ʿAṭṭār's achievements and journey.[73] We owe the preservation of al-ʿAṭṭār's remarks to J.L. Burckhardt, who bought this copy from al-ʿAṭṭār after the latter's return to Cairo. Burckhardt ordered on his death-bed that all the 300 manuscripts which he had bought in the Arab world should be kept at Cambridge University Library.[74] Among about twenty books which al-ʿAṭṭār took with him are the three first volumes of al-Jabartī's comprehensive history of Egypt *'Ajā'ib al-Āthār fī 'l-Tarājim wa 'l-Akhbār* (The Marvellous Compositions of Biographies and Chronicles) (1688–1806), in which he recorded his comments in the margin during his long travels in Turkey, Albania and Syria. From his

69 See the footnotes in *'Aj.*, I, 10, 13, 14, 15, marked (a), (b), (c), (d), according to the Būlāq pagination in our Arabic edition.

70 See the footnotes in *'Aj.*, I, 352, 535. There are three comments on al-Idkāwī, marked (k), (l), (m), in which his criticism is *laysa fīhimā ṭalāwa walā ḥalāwa* ('there is no grace or charm in his versification'), with no discussion.

71 See the footnotes in *'Aj.*, I, 259, (e) in which he added the works of al-Balīdī and footnote (g) I, 262, adding a remark on *Mukhaddirāt al-Fuhūm* by Khalīl al-Maghribī; (h) I, 278, on *Risālat Mullā 'Iṣām*, and 290, on Muḥammad al-Ḥifnāwī's works, and his comments.

72 See the footnotes in *'Aj.*, II, 164 (b), II, 248 (d), II, 254 (e).

73 See Gran, 'Notes on Critical Reception', in his paperback edition of his book *Islamic Roots of Capitalism, Egypt, 1760–1840*, in response to the articles of De Jong, 'On Peter Gran, Islamic Roots of Capitalism', *International Journal of Middle East Studies*, 381–99 and the 'Itinerary of Ḥasan al-ʿAṭṭār (1766–1835)', 99–128.

74 See our Arabic edition of *'Ajā'ib al-Āthār*, using the Būlāq pagination, I, 287, quoting the margin of MS *'Aj.* Cam. 2nd., Qq. 166, I, f. 260a. In the margin of MS *'Aj.* Cam. 2nd., Qq. 168, III, f. 105a = *'Aj.*, III, 109 dealing with al-ʿAṭṭār's letters sent to al-Jabartī from Asyūṭ, al-ʿAṭṭār gives the same route: Istanbūl, Bilād al-Rūm Iylī (Rumelia), Bilād al-Arnā'ūṭ (Albania), Istanbul and Izmīr.

remarks given in the Appendix at the end of this book, we understand, in contrast to the information supplied by ʿAlī Mubārak, that al-ʿAṭṭār left Cairo in 1803 for Cyprus, Turkey, Albania and Greater Syria, and not from the Ḥijāz. He devoted his journey to his studies, to meeting Muslim scholars and dedicating panegyric poems to them, probably in the hope of getting a job or of finding a patron. He also devoted his time to reading religious and literary books and copying manuscripts, such as the treatise of Khalīl b. Muḥammad al-Maghribī with his comments on Arabic philology *Ḥāshiyat al-Azharī* (footnote [g] in I, 262), and the Arabic translation of the Persian *Risālat al-Mullā 'Iṣām* (footnote [h] I, 287), by Munajjim Pāshā al-Mawlawī. He took with him also several books, some of which he sold in time of need (*'Aj.*, III, 109, footnote [b]).

The Egyptian statesman and man of letters, ʿAlī Pāshā Mubārak (1823–93) says in his geographical dictionary *al-Khiṭaṭ al-Tawfīqiyya*[75] that al-ʿAṭṭār's journey started after his pilgrimage to Mecca and Medina. He then travelled to Maʿan in Jordan and to Hebron in Palestine, then to Jerusalem and Damascus and only after that he travelled to Turkey. This route which does not fit with the places and dates given in some of al-ʿAṭṭār comments in the margin of his manuscript of *'Ajā'ib al-Āthār*, indicates that his journey was by land. In fact, this land route is different from the sea route given by al-ʿAṭṭār himself in these margins. Here he states clearly that he left Cairo (in 1803) for Cyprus. Then he arrived at Istanbul and left for Bilād al-Rūm Iylī (Rumelia), living for a period of time in Bilād al-Arnāwūd (Albania).[76] This remark was written in connection with al-Jabartī attributing the translation of *Risālat al-Mullā 'Iṣām* on metaphors from Persian into Arabic to Aḥmad al-Mujayrī al-Malawī and not to Munajjim Pāshā al-Mawlawī:[77]

ثم سافرت من مصر وقد كتبت منها جملة على الهوامش فاستقرّيت بقبرص وكتبت أولها هناك ثم ذهبت اسلامبول فكتبت بها حصة ، ثم ذهبت بلاد الارناود فكتبت بها قدرا، ثم عدت إلى اسلامبول ولم اكتب بها شيا ثم وصلت لأزمير فكتبت بها شيا يسيرا ثم وصلت للشام فما كتبت بها شيا لأني اشتغلت ثم بحاشية على الولدته [!]. ثم خرجت من الشام ودوّرت في ذلك القطر حتى أقمت بيافا

75 See Mubārak, *al-Khiṭaṭ al-Tawfīqiyya*, IV, 38–40; Gran, *Islamic Roots*, 77–8, *Maẓhar al-Taqdīs*, Aḥmad ʿAbduh ʿAlī (ed.), 25.

76 See al-ʿAṭṭār's comment, note. e, in the margin of MS *'Aj.* Cam. 2nd., Qq. 167, II, f. 236b, describing the same events as *'Aj.* Būlāq, II, 254.

77 See below Appendix I, h. On al-ʿAṭṭār's activities in Istanbūl, see Gran, *Islamic Roots*, 98–100, and in Damascus, see ibid., 100–2.

وأنا وقت تسطير هذه الحروف بها،وكان وصولي الى يافا العشرة الأخيرة من شهر ذي القعدة سنة 1225 ... كتبه الفقير حسن العطار المصري في شهر المحرم سنة 1226 [/ 1811].

If this was his actual route by sea to the Mediterranean coastal ports then we can add with the help of Gran who quotes from *Ḥāshiyat al-'Aṭṭār 'alā Sharḥ al-Azhariyya*,[78] that al-ʿAṭṭār sailed from Damietta to Cyprus, then crossed the Mediterranean to Istanbul. Although al-ʿAṭṭār's speaks of his travel to Albania, he does not mention his marriage in Ashkodra where according to ʿAlī Mubārak, his bad luck followed him to this city, where all his children died. This remark enabled us to correct Gran, who said that this 'Ushkodra' must be 'a part of Istanbul known in English as Skutari and in Arabic as Ashkūdarīʿ'.[79] Ashkodra which al-ʿAṭṭār speaks about is in fact in Albania. This is because al-ʿAṭṭar says later on: 'I was in Bilād al-Arnāwūd [Albania]', then 'I arrived to the city of Magnesia in Bilād al-Rūm (Turkey)' in Anatolia, where he became acquainted with its Muslim scholars.[80] In Ṣafar 1226 (/25 February–26 March 1811), al-ʿAṭṭār wrote that he observed that most of the Muslim viziers at that time were *wuzarā' Arnāwūd*, a fact known to those who saw them and roved this country. 'Nowadays there is no one who can be compared with ʿAlī Pasha al-Tabandalī and the late Ibrāhīm Pasha the governor of Ashkodra... especially ʿAlī Pasha and Ibrāhīm Pasha the governor of Ashkodra, since I witnessed and observed (all these) by myselfʾ.[81]

From Magnesia he returned to Istanbul and later left for Izmir (Smyrna) at the end of Shawwāl 1224 (/8 December 1809), where he lived in poverty and isolation.[82] From Izmir, he left for Syria where he visited Damascus (1809)[83]

78 Gran, *Islamic Roots*, 77–8, 192, 248, n. 1.

79 Ibid., xliv.

80 See *'Aj.*, I, 289, note I (al-ʿAṭṭār's copy), MS *'Aj.* Cam. 2nd., Qq. 166, I, f. 263a.

81 See *'Aj.*, III, 254, note e (al-ʿAṭṭār's copy), MS *'Aj.* Cam. 2nd., Qq. 168, III, f. 239b. Cf. V.H. Aksan, 'Manning a Black Sea Garrison in the Eighteenth Century, Ochakov and Concepts of Mutiny and Rebellion in the Ottoman Context', in Jane Hathaway (ed.), *Mutiny and Rebellion in the Ottoman Empire* (Madison2002), 63–88; A. Anastasopoulos, 'The Mixed Elite of a Balkan Town: Karaferye in the Second Half of the 18th Century', in A. Anastasopoulos (ed.), *Provincial Elites in the Ottoman Empire*, Rethymno (Heraklion 2005), 259–68. My thanks are due to Professor Jane Hathaway for supplying me with a copy of these two chapters.

82 See *'Aj.*, III, 109, n. b (al-ʿAṭṭār's copy) MS *'Aj.* Cam. 2nd., Qq. 168, III, f. 105a. Unlike Gran's statement in *Islamic Roots*, 193, al-ʿAṭṭār did not mention the city of Alexandretta (al-Iskandarūn) in any of his comments.

83 See *'Aj.* Būlāq, III, 254, n. e. Al-ʿAṭṭār tells us with bitterness about his sufferings in Izmir: (1) *'Aj.*, II, 164, n. b (al-ʿAṭṭār's copy), margins of MS *'Aj.* Cam. 2nd., Qq. 167, II, f. 251; (2) *'Aj.*,

and then he made his pilgrimage to Jerusalem where he used the library of Ḥasan Effendi al-Naqīb.[84] From there he left for the port of Jaffa and dwelled there for a year from the end of Dhū 'l-Qaʿda 1225 (/17 December 1810). From Jaffa, he travelled back to Damascus. The last date in al-ʿAṭṭār's remarks, 2 Muḥarram 1226 (/27 January 1811)[85] seems to be the last date in which he stayed in Syria. He said that he wished to return to Egypt to his books and to teach in al-Azhar as he did before he left Egypt. It seems that he returned to Cairo only in 1813, a date that is confirmed also by De Jong, who added that al-ʿAṭṭar ended his wanderings with his pilgrimage to the Holy cities of Mecca and Medina.[86] This likely occurred after his stay in Jaffa. All his attempts to find a rich and influential patron to help him to promote his ambitions and get an important religious post in Turkey, Albania, or Syria were of no success.

Most of the comments written by al-ʿAṭṭar constitute harsh criticism against Izmir and its inhabitants. The greatest disappointment awaited him in Izmir where he endured neglect, cold and hunger. There he prayed God to deliver him from this cruel cosmopolitan port that ignored his talents as a Muslim scholar, and his excellent linguistic and poetic talents in Arabic.[87] He repeated in his comment on his itinerary that he visited Istanbul, Anatolia, Albania (*Bilād al-Arnāwūd*), Istanbul, Izmir, etc., and recorded his shock at the various bad experiences that he suffered in this prosperous, multi-faith,

---

II, 254, n. e, (al-ʿAṭṭār's copy), margins of MS *'Aj.* Cam. 2nd., Qq. 167, II, f. 236b; (3) *'Aj.*, III, 109, n. b (a long comment with a poem on Izmir, see al-ʿAṭṭār's copy), MS *'Aj.* Cam. 2nd., Qq. 168, III, f. 105a; (4). *'Aj.*, III, 254, n. e (al-ʿAṭṭār's copy), margins of MS *'Aj.* Cam. 2nd., Qq. 168, III, f. 239b. It seems that this long note by al-ʿAṭṭār is listed by Gran, *Islamic Roots*, 198 (Appendix III, 'The Writing of Ḥasan al-ʿAṭṭār, no. u'), under the title: *Risāla al-Tadmīr 'alā Izmīr* (The Epistle of the Destruction on Izmir), classifying it as *Kalām* (sic) and added that it was 'un-located'. Gran adds that it is cited by (Aḥmad) al-Ḥusaynī, *Sharḥ al-Umm al-Musammā bi Murshid al-Anām ilā Birr Umm al-Imām* (See Dār al-Kutub, Cairo, 1411 al-Ta'rīkh, Taymūr, p. 38). Al-Ḥusayni 'states that al-ʿAṭṭār wrote this while in Izmīr, Tuesday (probably in 1806/1807). It is mentioned in conjunction with other essays on *kalām* which he was studying at this point'.

84 See *'Aj.*, I, 260 (al-ʿAṭṭār's copy), MS *'Aj.* Cam. 2nd., Qq. 166, I, f. 239a (Appendix I, f.).

85 See n. h, margin of MS *'Aj.* Cam. 2nd., Qq. 166, I, ff. 259b–260a, equivalent to *'Aj.* Būlāq, I, 287.

86 See De Jong, 'The Itinerary of Ḥasan al-ʿAṭṭār (1766–1835)', 99–123. Cf. Gran's 'Introduction' to the second edition of his *Islamic Roots*.

87 See *'Aj.*, III, 254, equivalent to (al-ʿAṭṭār's copy), MS *'Aj.* Cam. 2nd., Qq. 168, III, f. 239b (Appendix III, e.).

Turkish commercial port. What surprised him as a Muslim scholar was the indifference of its citizens to the visit of a well-known Muslim scholar, poet, and writer of his standard, while in Cairo scholars were invited to stay with hospitable and rich Egyptian families with no limit of time. In a poem and several written notes, he complains that in Izmir he felt like a poor stranger and that he sold most of his books to survive. He added that in Izmir learned men perish. Nobody showed them any respect or offered them even a glass of water and they would die of hunger. He prayed to God to rescue him from this terrible city. He added that he had travelled in most countries of the world and never found a city like Izmir whcih suffered from famine (*qaḥaṭ*), a high cost of living (*ghalā'*), and xenophobia (*karāhiyyat al-ghurabā'*) especially towards religious scholars. He ended by quoting, as in the case when a Muslim is in distress, a verse from the Qur'ān, asking God to help him depart safely from this cursed city of Izmir, and prayed God to punish its people with the severe punishment that they deserved.[88] In the same note, he added that there was no security in this city and its governor did not care for its welfare. Its inhabitants were free to commit whatever offenses they liked. They would sell their goods at any price they desired. They killed each other in market places and streets and no one dared arrest the killer. On the contrary, some criminals would kill their victims and sit near the body smoking their pipes, as if they had slaughtered a chicken. For this reason, he suggested that every Muslim religious person, wise man, and scholar should avoid visiting this terrible port because it combined all these despised peculiarities.[89]

It seems that the reason for al-ʿAṭṭar's grudge against Izmir is that although he took with him twenty books that he had composed, for several months he was neglected in the Madrasa (the religious boarding school) of Fattah Oghli Mosque in the city of Izmir. Nobody cared for him. Nobody invited him to be his guest. In Egypt, a visiting scholar and his household would customary be asked to stay indefinitely as a guest of local scholars but he was not invited. Filled with anger, he pours out a torrent of rhymed curses on Izmir: 'May

88 See al-ʿAṭṭār's comment on the margin of MS *'Aj.* Cam. 2nd., Qq. 168, III, f. 239b, equivalent to *'Aj.* Būlāq, III, 254, (note e below, Appendix I).

89 See al-ʿAṭṭār's comment on the margin of MS *'Aj.* Cam. 2nd., Qq. 168, III, f. 105a, equivalent to *'Aj.* Būlāq, III, 109, (note b below, Appendix I).

Godruin it, because it hates strangers, especially religious scholars (*'ulamā'*);[90] it is an ordeal for distinguished men of letters. No eminent or generous men live in it but only a multitude of foolish people'.[91]

Al-ʿAṭṭār left Izmir in 1224 (/1809) complaining that the Ottoman Empire was dominated by ignorant and cruel Albanians (*Arnūwūṭ*) viziers and that even the Ottoman Grand Vizier was of Albanian origin. He accused the Albanian governors of being ignorant and cruel and that they had ruled Egypt tyrannically and without justice, while in the past the Grand Viziers were learned men of letters and sciences.[92] He lamented the low standard of religious education of Ottoman rulers accusing them of being ignorant and unable to read or write. He added that in his day they were unable even to correct others if they read wrongly the *fātiḥa* (the first chapter of the Qur'ān), and that illiteracy prevailed in the Ottoman Empire not only among common people but also among the rulers.[93] One can consider al-ʿAṭṭār and al-Jabartī's testimony of the low cultural and scientific life during the eighteenth and the beginning of the nineteenth centuries in which they lived, as proof of the Gabriel Baer's remark that there was at this time no dynamic renaissance movement in the Ottoman Empire equivalent to but separate from the European renaissance as Gran and other revisionist historians have claimed.[94]

From Izmir, al-ʿAṭṭār went to Damascus. It is the only city that he praised exclaiming, 'What a wonderful city Damascus is'.[95] There, he lived at al-Madrasa al-Badriyya with his friend the poet Shaykh Muḥammad al-Masīrī and composed a long poem in praise of Damascus. There he also composed a commentary on the detailed medical handbook *Tadhkirat Dāwūd al-Anṭākī* (d.

---

90 See al-ʿAṭṭār's comment on the margin of MS *'Aj.* Cam. 2nd., Qq. 167, II, f. 251a, equivalent to *'Aj.* Būlāq, II, 164, (note b below, Appendix I).

91 See al-ʿAṭṭār's comment on the margin of MS *'Aj.* Cam. 2nd., Qq. 168, II, f. 236b, equivalent to *'Aj.* Būlāq, II, 254, (note e below, Appendix I).

92 See al-ʿAṭṭār's comment on MS *'Aj.* Cam. 2nd., Qq. 168, III, f. 239b, equivalent to *'Aj.* Būlāq, III, 254.

93 See al-ʿAṭṭār's comment on MS *'Aj.* Cam. 2nd., Qq. 166, I, f. 239a, equivalent to *'Aj.* Būlāq, II, 260.

94 See G. Baer's review of Gran's book in *Journal of the Economic and Social History of the Orient*,25, 2 (1982), 217–22. Cf. Gran's response in his 'Introduction' to *Islamic Roots* (1998), xxxiv, xlviii–l.

95 Loc. cit.

1599) which he called *Nuzhat Dāwūd.*[96] However, he criticizes the cultural stagnation in Syria, saying that he asked to read the biographies collected by the famous Syrian scholar al-Murādī (1760–91) entitled *Silk al-Durar* (The String of Pearls), dealing with the Muslim scholars of the eighteenth century. He was informed that nobody was interested in this book and that its author was a rare exception in Syria. He adds that ignorance and illiteracy prevailed in Syria and that there was no interest in cultural life, to the degree that there was only one copy left of this book in Damascus. However, a certain relative of the author al-Murādī summarized it, omitted many biographies from the book, for no scholarly reasons, except for whim and personal connection.[97]

From Damascus al-'Aṭṭar travelled to Jerusalem on a pilgrimage to al-Bayt al-Maqdis. He stayed at the house of ʿUmar Afandī al-Naqīb, who was the head of the prophet Muḥammad's descendants. There he read some manuscripts at the library of Ḥasan Afandī al-Naqīb. From Jerusalem he went to Jaffa in 1225 (/1810) intending to travel to Egypt, and, when nostalgia overwhelmed him from time to time he refers to it as, 'my original homeland' (*al-waṭan al-aṣlī*).[98] However, unexpected circumstances forced him to stay there for a long time before he was able to return to Cairo after his *ḥajj* (pilgrimage) to the Ḥijāz. Al-ʿAṭṭar arrived in Jaffa twelve years after Napoleon's destruction of its walls and his massacre of its garrison. He added in a short remark dated Ṣafar 1226 (/25 February–26 March 1811), that he found Jaffa 'one of the most filthy of all the cities of God, and the most contemptible place in the world', praying to God to release him as He had released him from Izmir.[99]

Filled with bitterness for the Muslim world he had visited and with nostalgia for his friends and books in Cairo, he succeeded in returning there, most probably, in 1813.[100] This conclusion of ours, that al-ʿAṭṭar returned to

96 See al-ʿAṭṭār's comment on the margin of *'Aj.* Cam. 2nd., Qq. 167, II, f. 13a, equivalent to *'Aj.* Būlāq, II, 14.

97 See al-ʿAṭṭār's comment on MS *'Aj.* Cam. 2nd., Qq. 167, II, f. 219a, equivalent to *'Aj.* Būlāq, II, 236.

98 *'Aj.* Būlāq, II, 236.

99 See al-ʿAṭṭār's comment on MS *'Aj.* Cam. 2nd., Qq. 168, III, f. 239b, equivalent to *'Aj.* Būlāq, III, 254.

100 See *'Aj.*, I, 262, 287, 289 notes g, h, i (al-ʿAṭṭār's copy), MS *'Aj.* Cam. 2nd., Qq. 166, I, ff. 240b, 259b–260a, 263a, footnote (g) I, 262. Cf. Gran, *Islamic Roots*, xliv where De Jong mentions 1813 as the year of al-ʿAṭṭār's return. See also De Jong, 'The Itinerary of Ḥasan al-ʿAttar', 99–128.

Egypt in 1813, confirms the date given by De Jong, and contradicts Gran's conclusion that it was in 1815. Al-Jabartī in his necrology of al-Khashshāb. who died on 2 Dhu 'l-Ḥijja 1230 (/5 November 1815), relates that 'after the return of al-ʿAṭṭār from his journey, he became the close friend and frequent companion of Sayyid Ismāʿīl [al-Khashshāb], they used to spend time in his home to discuss literature and history, and events they had witnessed'.[101] After the death of the latter, al-ʿAṭṭār 'exchanged eloquence for silence, abandoned the composition of all poetry and prose except in case of necessity or as a means of flattery to the famous people of the time'.[102] All these facts confirm that some time had passed since the return of his friend al-ʿAṭṭar from his journey.

However, in spite of al-ʿAṭṭār and al-Jabartī's hatred for the Ottomans, al-Jabartī remained faithful to his pan-Islamic principles, while al-ʿAṭṭār became an Egyptian patriot. Though al-ʿAṭṭār despised Albanian generals and soldiers, he offered his services to the Ottoman governor Muḥammad ʿAlī, who was of Albanian origin. The latter appointed him to the post of editor of the Egyptian official gazette, *al-Waqā'i' al-Miṣriyya,* and later to the prestigious office of Rector of al-Azhar, an office which he held until his death in 1835.[103]

To conclude, as in the case of al-Jabartī, al-ʿAṭṭar's contacts with French scholars and Ottoman rulersgave him the opportunity to compare the two civilizations. In Cairo, he visited the French libraries and laboratories, and acclaimed their quest for culture and knowledge, making him aware of the low cultural and scientific standards of his country and the weakness of the Ottoman military power and culture.[104] He expressed his hope that a scientific and cultural renaissance would start soon in Egypt. During his long journey to the ports and islands of the eastern Mediterranean, he realized the cultural, scientific, and moral stagnation prevailing in the Ottoman Empire. He understood that as an Arab Egyptian he had no future abroad and that there was no real Islamic solidarity in the Ottoman Empire. He felt that only in his homeland, Egypt, could he take part in its cultural renaissance. He went back to Egypt, became an Egyptian patriot, and backed Muḥammad ʿAlī Pasha in

---

101 See al-Khashshāb's biography in *'Aj.*, IV, 238–42.

102 See *'Aj.*, IV, 239.

103 Gran, *Islamic Roots*, 126.

104 See *Maqāmat al-Adīb al-Ra'īs al-Shaykh Ḥasan al-'Aṭṭār fi 'l-Faransīs.* See its English translation by Gran, *Islamic Roots*, Appendix I, The *Maqāmat* al-ʿAṭṭār, 189–91.

his reforms based upon European methods. His student Rifāʿa Rāfiʿ al-Ṭahṭāwī (1801–73) continued his efforts. The latter wrote during his studies in Paris a book entitled 'The Golden Synopsis Epitomising the Aspects of Paris' (*Takhlīṣ al-Ibrīz fī Talkhīṣ Bārīs*) in which he gave a description of the city, its cultural and social life comparing it with Islamic culture. He criticized the false ideas of the Egyptians about European social values and their attitude towards culture and women as well as giving a description of the important events of his time.[105]

105 Ḥusayn Fawzī al-Najjār, *Rifāʿa al-Ṭahṭāwī, Rāʾid Fikr wa-Imām al-Nahḍa* (Cairo n.d.); cf. 'Rifāʿa Bey al-Ṭahṭāwī', EI^2, 523–4.

Chapter Five

The Islamic Moon-like Cycle of Civilization in Arabic Poetry Arabic Poetics from the 18th Century to the Beginning of the 19th Century

The revelation of the Qur'ān to the Prophet Muḥammad in Arabic as a universal religion was the greatest upheaval in the history of the Arabs. It changed them from idol worshipers with strict morals of hospitality, traditions of blood revenge, unrestrained behaviour and ignorance (*jāhiliyya*) dictated by their hard geographical environment, from rival tribes invading each other's camps, into a united multi-racial and multi-cultural nation in one Islamic *umma* (Muslim community). This new united *umma* now bore a new religious message, 'the light of Islam' (*nūr al-Islām*), rendering them victorious and rich conquerors with booty and poll taxes. It changed them into a united nation bearing a new religious and spiritual message that affected most nations and civilizations, carried by the zealous Arab warriors on horseback. In fact, the Qur'ān, which reflects the collective historical and cultural memory of the Arabs, was a spiritual, cultural and ideological revolution of logical and rational observation[1] of the eternal Creator of the Universe. It expresses deep insight into former religions and beliefs, formulating them into one eternal creed and command for redemption from this ephemeral world and the hereafter. This trend was followed by a vast Muslim quest for *'ilm* (knowledge) using every possible source from other nations, including Greek and Persian, to back the superiority of Islamic thought and creed against other religious beliefs.

The Qur'ān started a new civilization of religious, legislative, political, philosophical, cultural, scientific, economic and literary impact, which had with all its vigour and zeal an effect on world civilization to the present day. The Qur'ān,which was the main miracle of 'the perfect Prophet', is believed to be revealed in a perfect and most poetic and rhetorical language (Arabic), for

1 A trend which al-Mas'ūdī (d. 956), the Shī'ite, violated with his irrational explanations and which was condemned by Ibn Khaldūn (d. 1406) in his *Muqaddima*. On al-Mas'ūdī's Shī'isms seeMichael Cooperson, *Classical Arabic Biography, The Heirs of the Prophets in the Age of al-Ma'mūn* (Cambridge 2000), 23, 72.

the perfect religion (Islam) which Allāh chose for all humanity to replace the older revealed religions (Judaism, Christianity and Zoroastrianism) and to annihilate paganism. This divine revelation is formed ina purified holy language above the dialects of the Arab tribes, considered by Muslims as a miracle beyond the imitation of human beings (*i'jāz*) endowed by God to his last Prophet by the Angel Gabriel.[2]

The new dogmas, teachings and rhetorical style of the revealed book posed a dilemma for the first Muslim Arabs, since their tribal solidarity and sense of tribal collective security was replaced by solidarity between Muslim believers (*umma*) consisting also of new converts from different nations, creeds, cultures, history and languages, creating a victorious nation blessed by Allāh. The individual was now responsible for achieving happiness in this world and the hereafter by observing the obligations of the new religion. In this spiritual and religious revolution, poetry became secondary to the Qur'ān and became mainly a literary, social, political, and aesthetic art in Arab civilization.

In a short time after the revelation of the Qur'ān, the Arabs had achieved their great military triumphs and under Islam conquered a considerable part of the civilized world of that time, assuring the Arabs of their special identity. It was the best proof that God had chosen the Arabic language as His favourite and the Arabs to spread His message for His final accomplished religion. Arabic supplied the Arabs with their national myth, and obscured their cultural backwardness in comparison to the nations they conquered. Consequently, Arabic acquired an aura of sanctity, stability, and eternity. Since the Qur'ān is considered a direct revelation from Allāh in highly rhetorical, rhythmical Quranic verses (*āyāt*) of similar endings (*fāṣila*, pl. *fawāṣil*), its style was neither considered prose (*nathr*) and its similar verse endings were never considered as *saj'*(rhyme in prose). The latter was attributed in the pre-Islamic period to the *kuhhān* (soothsayers) and credited to the *jinn*; it was not considered poetry (*shi'r*) but rhymed prose devoid of metre. Its inspiration was credited to *shayāṭīn* (jinn or devils) dwelling in their valley (*Wadī 'Abqar*). The similar endings in poetry were termed *qāfiya* (prosodic rhyme). To distinguish the Qur'ān from both prose and poetry, its similar endings were given a special term, *āyāt mufaṣṣalāt* (Quranic verses with similar endings),

2 See the articles by T. Fahd and S. Moreh, '*Shā'ir*', *EI*², IX, 225–35, and Alber Arazi and S. Moreh, '*Shi'r*', *EI*², IX, 448–65.

revealed by God and beyond the power of human beings to equal (*i'jāz*). With theirconvention of claimed omnipotence, Arab poets, writers and historians wrote their works, quoting Quranic (*āyāt*) verses to admonish rulers and commoners with the wrath and punishment of God if they disobeyed His commands were to safeguard just rulers and pious and righteous men in this world and in the hereafter. On the other hand, poetic verses that were considered as the Arab registrar of wisdom and history were quoted for secular and moral admonition. The duty of religious scholars and learned men was to command 'to enjoin good and forbid evil' (*al-amr bi 'l-ma'rūf wa 'l-nahy 'an al-munkar*).[3]

With its impact as an invading new and vigorous religion, or an imperialist military power with religious, political, economic and cultural aims, Islam forced the invaded nations into a defensive and apologetic position. Islam induced nations to revive relevant traditional cultural elements in thought, science, literature and customs, in order to stem the tide of the new foreign culture. When the revival of old traditions seemed to be incapable of enabling the conquered nation to revive its glorious past, the new invading culture gave rise to a new pattern of thinking and ways of revival. In the case of Islam also, the impact of the new Islamic civilization upon the old through wars and cultural ties aroused new revolutionary tendencies in the defeated nations. Its impact on the Persians split the Islamic *umma* into two, the Sunnis and the Shiʿa, and various religious and philosophical sects emerged. Some old beliefs and values were preserved and others mutated, receiving new functions and orientations, while in some cases the revival of the old religious and cultural values seemed to be the only way to face the hostile culture. The result was a new Islamic civilization.

In Islam, the belief in a moon-like cycle of civilizations revealed itself already in the universal spiritual message of Islam: its arrival, its zenith and its decline. This cycle revealed itself through successive Arab and the Islamic dynasties, beginning with the first 'righteous' Caliphs, the Umayyads and the consequent split of the Islamic *umma* into Sunni and Shīʿī factions. The Sunni Abbasids and later the Ottoman sultans tried to subdue, through wars and assassinations, the esoteric Shīʿī Persian oriented faction frustrated by its continuous failure to recover the divine right of the ʿAlids for spiritual and

3 Qur'ān, 3:110, 114; 7:157; 9:67, 71, 112; 22:41; 31:17.

political rule. With the rise of the industrial imperialist European powers, Islamic civilization that had reached its zenith through the fruitful adaptation of Greek thought during the Middle Ages was partly replaced, this time in the Sunni world, by esoteric spiritual religious activities through mystical *Ṣūfī* orders opposing the dynamic of Greek-Islamic thought and finally failed to challenge the European cultural dynamics. The successive defeats of the Ottoman armies in their confrontation with the *Dār al-Ḥarb* front in Europe, triggered the dynamics of decline in Islamic civilization. Both Muḥammad ʿAlī and the Ottoman sultans realized that it was possible to stem the decline and to confront Europe only by adopting European, military, administrative and scientific methods.

At the dawn of Islam, the Muslims were easilyable to overcome the surrounding nations and civilizations, which were unable to withstand the swift onslaught of courageous and zealous Arab horsemen. The Qur'ān was the miracle which made the Arabs rise upon the stage of history and develop vast religious communities that continued to grow to the present day. They considered Islam as the light of God and its language holy. They believed that Arabic, due to its uniqueness, rich vocabulary, subtlety, and the logical structure of its syntax, was the fitting vehicle for divine revelation enshrined in the Holy Qur'ān. Consequently, they also considered their own poetry as the most sublime art that ensured eternity to the poet and his tribe or patron, and the Arabic language as the richest language in vocabulary and rhyming words.

The secular pre-Islamic tribal need for collective security and the Jāhiliyya (i.e. pre-Islamic) raids (*ghazw*) against rival tribes were replaced by an Islamic collective unity and an individual responsibility to worship Allāh with devotion and self-sacrifice in a *jihād* (holy war) to spread Allāh's final religion. Thus *jihād* and the strict observance of the five obligations of the new religion (*arkān al-Islām*), i.e. the *shahāda* (to utter the doctrinal formula of the Muslim creed), the five daily prayers (*ṣalāt*), paying *zakāt* (alms tax), fasting (*ṣawm*) during the month of Ramaḍān and pilgrimage to the Kaʿba (*ḥajj*), enabled the believer to achieve happiness and remission of all his sins in this world and eternal bliss in the hereafter.

Islam denounced the role of Arab pagan poetry and 'poets whom the erring follow ... do you not see that they rove distraught in every valley, and say that which they do not do? Save those who believe and do good works, and oft remember God' (Qur'ān, 26:224ff). The divine rhetorical charm of the Qur'ān and its sanctity replaced the ancient status of poetry, which ceased to be the most venerated genre as it was in the Jāhiliyya period.

The rise of Islam as a new religion with its mission for the salvation of humanity and its cultural contacts with former civilizations such as Greece, Byzantium, Persia, and India, culminated in a swift victory and the gradual moulding of a new and triumphant civilization. *Jihād* (holy war) triggered continuous conflicts with *Dār al-Ḥarb* (non-Muslim countries), and enabled Islam to spread in Asia, Africa and Europe and later on to defeat the Crusaders in their religious wars, beginning with Ṣalāḥ al-Dīn (Saladin) in the Battle of Ḥiṭṭīn (1187). The Mamluk system of peaceful conversion and expansion enabled Islam to stem the tide of various nomadic tribes from the Asian prairies, such as that of the Tatars and Mongols, defeated by al-Ẓāhir Baybars in ʿAyn Jālūt (1260). The rise of the Ottomans, led to the occupation of Constantinople (1453) and later on to the occupation of Egypt (1517) and the surrounding countries, thanks to the Ottomans' fire arms, developed by Jewish artisans expelled from Spain to the Ottoman Empire. The Ottoman victories continued until they were stopped at the walls of Vienna (1529). The French occupation of Egypt is the best example of cultural impact. The rise of Muḥammad ʿAlī who adopted the French military, administrative and economic capitalistic system and his efforts to preclude the *'ulamā'* from their former influential position, prompted new trends and convulsions in Arabic culture and literature. The reforms of both Napoleon and Muḥammad ʿAlī were important factors which led to the new revolution in modern Arabic culture, injecting new blood to Arabic literature through French literature.

The tenet concerning the sanctity of the Arabic language and its main literary genres remained dominant among the Arabs until the mid-twentieth century and was strictly observed by conservative writers. The classical period, which extended from pre-Islamic times to the end of the tenth century CE, was characterized by strict uniform genres using canonical Arabic poetical diction maintaining the conventional parts of the *qaṣīda* (Arabic ode) written in classical Arabic style with case-endings (*mu'rab*), and dealing with specified serious subjects. Moreover, classical poetics calls for poetic versification according to the sixteen conventional Arabic meters (*buḥūr*) in the mono-rhymed *qaṣīda*, in which each verse is divided into two hemistiches (*shaṭr*) of equal length. The classical ode deals with the pre-Islamic conventional genres of serious moral, social and political themes stemming from the Bedouin value system of pre- and post- Islamic society, such as *madīḥ* (panegyrics) to their heroes and Caliphs, *fakhr* (vainglory) of the poet's and his tribe's achievements, and *ḥamāsa* (heroic poetry) descriptions of battles and victories against enemies.[4] Odes are used in wars, sung with heroic and ardent melodies. Other poetic genres, including *rithā'* (elegy) to lament the dear departed and dead heroes, *hijā'* (satire, defamatory poetry) of enemies of the tribe or the religion, *adab* (morality), *waṣf* (description), etc., were essential genres of a tribal and military society in which rivalry, animosity, blood revenge, defending heroes and ancestors, heroic battles and generosity all played an important role.Islam endeavoured to keep a harmony between man and nature.

During the Middle Ages the intellectual quest for knowledge and sciences induced Arabs to translate ancient Greek philosophy, which enriched Muslim culture and caused the rise of several philosophical and religious sects. Avicenna (Ibn Sīnā) (980–1037) at the end of his summary of Aristotle's *Poetica* says that his aim was to 'make an inquiry into the sciences, which may be to [the Muslims'] advantage', and to 'stimulate [in Arabic poetry] a scientific and detailed exposition of the general art of … poetry current in our time'. Avicenna expresses his hope that Arabs would write a study of Arabic poetry using Aristotle's methodology by saying: 'This is a summary of the part of the book *Poetics* by Aristotle found in this country, a good part of which we were unable to find. It is not unlikely that we should endeavour to formulate a discussion of great scientific and elaborate exposition from the general art of Poetics and the art of the poetry current in our time. We now have to limit ourselves to this extent.'[5]

Many critics of Arabic poetry and theatre thought that subsequently Averroes (Ibn Rushd) (d. 1198) misunderstood Aristotle's *Poetica*,because he used Arabic poetical terminology, 'panegyric poetry' (*madīḥ*) as equivalent to Aristotle's term 'tragedy' and 'satire' (*hijā'*) for his term 'comedy'.[6] Ibn Rushd used this classical Arabic terminology not because of his ignorance of Greek theatrical performances and their terminology, but because he wished to

4 In *Rasā'il Ikhwān al-Ṣafā* (tenth–eleventh centuries) (I, 132–6, 154–5) some verses which are quoted by Abū Tammām in his *Ḥamāsa* are called *al-mushajji'* (favouring or encouraging poems).

5 See Arisṭūṭīlīs, *Fann al-Shi'r, ma'a al-Tarjama al-'Arabiyya al-Qadīma wa-Shurūḥ al-Fārābī wa-Ibn Sīnā wa-Ibn Rushd, tarjamahu 'an al-Yūnāniyya wa-sharaḥahu wa-ḥaqqaqa nuṣūṣahu 'Abd al-Raḥmān Badawī* (Beirut 1973), 198.

6 Ibid., 201–50.

apply Aristotle's methodology of poetic criticism to Arabic poetry. The Andalusian critic of Arabic poetry, Ḥāzim al-Qarṭājannī (1211–85), provides proof of this. He admitted in his book *Minhāj al-Bulaghā' wa-Sirāj al-Udabā'* (The Programme of Rhetoric and the Lamp of Men of Letters), that he composed his work to fulfil the aspiration Avicenna expressed at the end of his summary of the *Poetics*. In discussing the differences between Greek and Arab poetry, al-Qarṭājannī commented that Greek poetry was limited to certain themes. Each theme was written in a certain meter and deals mainly with invented legends (*khurāfāt*) upon which the poet would set his poetic imagination; Avicenna condemned this kind of poetry and explained that there was 'no need for poetic imagination of the simple fables which are but invented narratives that do not suit all temperaments'.[7]

When Greek philosophy was integrated into Muslim thought, some critics of Arabic poetry such as Qudāma bin Jaʿfar, ʿAbd al-Qāhir al-Jurjānī (976–1078) and al-Qarṭājannī applied Greek logic and thought to Arabic poetry, and other Arab philosophers tried to combine *sharī'a* and Greek philosophy. Such an attempt was made by a group of Ismāʿīlī philosophers who argued that cosmic harmony is echoed in mathematics and hence in music. It seems that al-Jabartī was influenced to a limited extend by their ideas. The Ikhwān al-Ṣafā (The Faithful Brothers) found that the rules of music were similar to the rules of Arabic prosody (*'arūḍ*)[8] and singing (*ghinā'*), and that both had the same spiritual and emotional effects. The four strings of the *'ūd* were equivalent to the four elements of the universe, fire, water, air and earth.[9] Moreover, there was harmony between the universe and the celestial bodies and between music and poetry: 'The plucking of strings is in the position of pens, the sharp tunes are in the position of letters, the tunes are in the position of words and singing is in the position of statements, the air which carries the sound is in the position of papers, while the meaning included in these tunes and melodies are in the position of the souls in the bodies, ... these motions (*ḥarakāt*) and the vowellessness of letters (*sukūnāt*)[10] which are measures of time, are in

7 See Hāzim b. Muḥammadal-Qarṭājannī, *Minhāj al-Bulaghā' wa-Sirāj al-Udabā', aw al-Manāhij al-Adabiyya* (Tunis 1966).

8 See Gotthold Weil, '*'Arūḍ*', *E.I.*^{2}, I, 667ff. and Wright, *A Grammar of Arabic Language*, II, pt. IV, *Prosody*, 355–90. Cf. *Rasā'il*, 144.

9 *Rasā'il*, 157–8.

10 See Wright, *A Grammar of Arabic Language*, II, pt. IV, *Prosody*, 355, B and note.

harmony with the celestial bodies and the stars'.[11] Then the human souls would yearn to unite with the souls of their ancestors and with their bliss in heaven. As for the music of poetry, it enables the body to endure hard work and encourages (*mushajji'a*) warriors during wars and battles, but also incites civil strife among nations, religious factions, and parties. On the other hand, music is used in temples, religious ceremonies and prayers, on both sad (*muḥzin*) and happy occasions, especially when these poems are composed according to melodies accompanied by musical instruments.[12]

Some religions forbid music because some poets use it for entertainment and inciting sexual lust[13]. Nevertheless, the *Ṣūfī*s including the Khalwatīs allowed it and used it in their *dhikr* to help achieving religious and spiritual ecstasy.[14] These philosophers found harmony with the universe in the classical division of the poem (*qaṣīda*). Time (*zamān*) is divided into equal parts, half is daylight and half is darkness, half-hot summer and half-cold winter, revolving alternately. One might apply this analogy to the classical Arabic poem. Generally, every poem starts with an opening line consisting of two rhyming hemistiches, like day and night repeated in the verses of the poem and ending with an end-stop rhyme, which is equivalent to the evening prayer (*ṣalāt al-maghrib*). The four divisions of the poem into *nasīb* (opening with love verses) *waṣf* (description of the journey and the mount), *bayt al-qaṣīd* (the principal verse of the ode), *khitām* (end of the poem) with gnomic verses, consisting in the four parts of the ode which are equivalent to the four seasons of the year.

Already in the tenth century CE, during the Abbasid period (749–1258), *saj'*and highly embellished prose prevailed in literary, official correspondence and historical writing. With the Ottoman conquest of Egypt (1517), the formerly mighty cavalry-based Mamluk Sultanate was defeated and Egypt became a remote province in the Ottoman Empire, serving as a manpower pool and supplying the Holy Cities with grain. Arabic historiography and literature deteriorated under the new non-Arab rulers whose official language was Turkish and who ceased to invade non-Muslim lands (*Dār al-ḥarb*) for the

---

11 *Rasā'il*, I, 150–1.

12 *Rasā'il*, I, 132–5. They used the term *mushajji'a* for verses quoted from the *Ḥamāsa* of Abū Tammām on the Māzin tribe and on al-Basūs, the forty-year war in the *jāhiliyya*between the tribes of Taghlib and Bakr.

13 *Rasā'il*, I, 150–1, 154–5 and Lane, *Manners*, 246–50, 359f. Cf. S. Moreh, *Live Theatre and Dramatic Literature in the Medieval Arab World* (Edinburgh 1992), 21–4.

14 Lane, *Manners*, 359f.

sake of Islam. They contented themselves with the role of Defender of Islam (*ḥāmiyat al-Islām*) and tax collector, and suffered continuous defeat by Christian European powers.

In his history *'Ajā'ib al-Āthār fī 'l-Tarājim wa 'l-Akhbār* ('The Marvellous Compositions of Biographies and Chronicles'), al-Jabartī repented his exaggerated flattery of the Ottoman commanders and soldiers in his work *Maẓhar al-Taqdīs*. Horrified by their vicious atrocities committed against the Muslim Arab Egyptians, his own fellow citizens, al-Jabartī adopts an objective approach in writing his history. He consciously reflects the Islamic value system and conventions with the declared aim of appealing to Quranic justice and equality, and hoping for the restoration of the might of Islam (*shawkat al-Islām*). The non-Arab political and military leaders should pay heed to the advice of the heads of *Ṣūfī* orders, religious leaders and the *'ulamā'* since they are the representatives of the *sharī'a*. Moreover, the *ashrāf* should be at the top of this hierarchy, since they are descendants of the Prophet Muḥammad. The *'ulamā'* are the right advisors to the non-Arab foreign rulers, i.e., the Mamluks, who were destined by God to rule Egypt, following the example of the Biblical Joseph[15] who saved Egypt from famine and destruction. He insisted on the superiority of Muslims over non-Muslims, restoring Islamic morals, justice and solidarity through the revival of Islamic and secular sciences and restoring the status of the *'ulamā'* as advisors and guides to rulers and defenders of the common people. His style wavered between semi-colloquial and canonical, following the style and method of Islamic historiography that reflected the cultural, literary, and scientific stagnation of the period.[16]

The rhetorical usages in poetry as well as in the *maqāma* genre[17] in Arabic were due to the fact that both became written genres, although they were still read and recited orally even after the spread of the paper industry in the

15 Qur'ān, 12:56, 40:24. Cf. Al-Jabartī's Introduction to *Maẓhar al-Taqdīs*, edited byAḥmad 'Abduh 'Alī, (Cairo 1419/1998), 8, and Urlich Haarmann, 'Joseph's Law-the Careers and Activities of Mamluk Descendants before the Ottoman Conquest of Egypt', *The Mamluks*, Philipp and Haarmann, 55–84.

16 On the term *'aṣr al-inḥiṭāṭ* (period of decadence), see R. Allen and D.S. Richards, *Arabic Literature in the Post-classical Period* (Cambridge 2006), 1–2, 5–13, 60–73, and 237–8.

17 On the *maqāma*, see Allen and Richards, *Arabic Literature in the Post-classical Period*, 145–58, 347–68; James Monroe, *The Art of Badī' al-Zamān al-Hamadhānī as Picaresque Narrative* (Beirut 1983); Moreh, *Live Theatre*, 105–10.

Muslim world. Nevertheless, the switch from oral to written literature induced poets and writers to elaborate new rhetorical forms of puns, with plays on letters as well as on the diacritical dots on top of and underneath these letters. Later on, a more elaborated method was developed, the art of denoting the date (*ta'rīkh*) of events celebrated by verses or hemistiches in which the sum of the numerical value of their letters (*ḥisāb al-jummal*) gives the Hijrī date. Our author informs us that poets used to record their poems and to hand them after recitation to the person whom they eulogized or to the family whose dear one had passed away.

Poetry and *belles lettres* became a popular and social art serving both rulers and common people for religious and social occasions, such as happy and tragic occasions, feasts, *Ṣūfī dhikr* circles and *mawlid* festivals, the recitation and singing of the praise of Muḥammad (*madā'iḥ nabawiyya*), saints, their *mawlid*s and the blessing of their shrines. In fact, al-Jabartī did not distinguish between canonic and vernacular poetry considering them all as poetry. The versified Bedouin and urban women's eulogies enumerating the merits of their heroes and grandees, and women and children chanting slogans in demonstrations and protests, were all poetry. Poems, songs, *muwashshaḥāt*[18] (strophic verses), were performed by professional reciters and singers, with or without musical instruments, at funerals, festivals, Ramaḍān and secular celebrations by men, women and children.[19] It is of great significance that our author placed poets and men of letters in the Islamic hierarchy after the *'ulamā'* (where God, the prophets, saints and *'ulamā'*, are at the top),[20] but above rulers, military commanders and government officials, indicating the high esteem in which he held them as defenders of Islamic morals and justice. Our author is a rare example of a courageous intellectual, who was aware of corruption among rulers, military and administrative officials, secular and religious scholars during the Ottoman-Mamluk rule and later on that of Muḥammad ʿAlī in Egypt. Serious poets and writers defended and preserved moral values and criticized the defects of society. This is not only because the

---

18 See Samuel Miklos Stern, *Hispano-Arabic Strophic Poetry*, L.P. Harvey (ed.)(Oxford 1974) and S. Moreh, 'The Meaning of the Term *Kharja* in the Arabic-Andalusian *Muwashshah*', in Isaac Benabu (ed.), *Circa 1492, Proceedings of the Jerusalem Colloquium: Litterae Judaeorum in Terra Hispanica* (Jerusalem 1992), 134–44.

19 See *Moolids* (*Mawlids*), in Lane, *Manners*, 246–8, 448–76.

20 See Chapter Seven, 'The Role of the *'Ulamā'* in Egypt in the Years 1688–1821', in this book.

rulers were evil in his time, but also because poetry in Arabic culture with its meter and rhyme is easily memorized to become an integral part of Arab collective memory. It is the most sublime Arabic art, which enables both poets and patrons to enjoy moral and physical rewards, the poet through presents and wages, and the patron through fame that might enable him to achieve an immortal name. Poetry dealing with historical events served as an admonition to readers and audience and helped memorize sciences and preserve the achievements and date of death of eminent scholars and preserve the occasion for which they composed their poem according to the numerical value (*ḥisāb al-jummal*) of its letters in the last verses.[21]

Al-Jabartī admired poets who composed moral and admonishing poetry and the role they played in literary salons (*majālis adabiyya*) and *mawlid*s frequented by religious scholars, rulers and secular dignitaries, as well as by poets and writers. He quotes several such poems because of their moral value and social criticism to the point that one has the impression that this genre became the vanguard of a moral and ethical revival in a *Ṣūfī* society. Literary salons took place in rulers' palaces, in splendid halls (*qā'āt*) decorated with chandeliers, ponds and fountains. Both rulers and poets needed each other, the former to boast of the distinguished poets who attended their salons, and the latter for the opportunity to be known and have contacts with dignitaries who might become patrons. In these salons panegyric poems (*madīḥ*) and *maqāmāt* were recited in praise of the patron. In addition to stories of lore, details of historical events were related and debated, proverbs, proverbial sayings, anecdotes and jokes were exchanged, riddles (*lughz*) were composed, poems were admired and superficial literary criticism was debated according to al-Sakkakī's (1160–1229) *Miftāḥ al-'Ulūm*, and al-Khaṭīb al-Qazwīnī's (d. 1338) *Talkhīṣ al-Miftāḥ* and its plethora of commentaries by Azhari scholars.

However, al-Jabartī was aware that the profession of the majority of Arab poets was confined to the status of *al-shā'ir al-nadīm* (convivial poet), a person who entertains his patron and earns his living by selling his poetry to the highest bidder. Moreover, popular poets were asked to compose poetry for various social occasions such as births, weddings, funerals and *mawlid*s, encouraging common people by their religious praise-poems (*madā'iḥ*) to visit the shrines of Muslim saints (*walī*, pl. *awliyā'*). Accordingly, when al-Sayyid

21 *'Aj.*, I, 359; II, 184, etc.

(a descendant of the Prophet) ʿAlī the dull-witted one (*ablah*), who was believed to be a saint, died on 16 Rabīʿ I 1214 (/17 September 1799), his brother encouraged poets and reciters of poetry (*shu'arā' wa-munshidūn*) to sing his praise and enumerate his miracles and blessings in order to instigate people to visit his tomb and thereby to offer their donations and offerings to the saint in order to secure the income of the shrine. Moreover, when the beloved wife of Murtaḍā al-Zabīdī died, he mourned her, composed poems imitating (*mu'āraḍa*) the emotional and sentimental style attributed to the ʿUdhrī poet Majnūn Laylā (seventh century). Professional itinerant poets and singers, hired men and women mourners, flocked to offer their condolences and to lament her with elegies in expectation of generous rewards. al-Zabīdī accepted their poems and rewarded them (*fa-yujīzuhum*).[22]

In his chronicle (covering 1100 [/1688] to 1236 [/1821]), al-Jabartī quotes a few poetic verses of the Abbasid period and hundreds of poems and verses by poets who lived during the period covered by his chronicle. His works provide an eyewitness account as to the role of poetry and of Arab poets during the eighteenth century until the first quarter of the nineteenth century, which give the impression that there was a revival of moral poetry. In his first two volumes, he quotes a great number of verses to support his arguments as well as poems from some anthologies of important poets of his time, mainly in the necrologies of volumes I–II of *'Ajā'ib al-Āthār*. Most of these poems were copied from biographies included in various collections mainly that of *Mu'jam Mukhtaṣṣ* of his mentor Murtaḍā al-Zabīdī[23] who was aware of the effect of poetry in Arabic society. In order to get a wide circulation for his important works, such as *Tāj al-'Arūs* and his commentary on al-Ghazālī's *Iḥyā' 'Ulūm al-Dīn*, al-Zabīdī used to invite famous scholars, poets and writers to festive celebrations on the occasion of his works' completion, and they duly provided him with their written praise (*taqrīẓ*, pl. *taqārīẓ*) in poetry and prose.[24] It seems that on these occasions he would also ask these scholars to write for him not only their praise but their biographies also. Although many poems in praise of

---

22 *'Aj.*, II, 201.

23 On al-Zabīdī, see Stefan Reichmuth, 'Murtaḍā az-Zabīdī (d. 1791) in Biographical and Autobiographical Accounts. Glimpses of Islamic Scholarship in the 18th Century', *Die Welt des Islams*39:1 (1999), 64–102 and 'Notes on al-Murtaḍā al-Zabīdī's *Mu'jam* as a Source for al-Jabartī's History', in *JSAI*, 25 (2001), 374–83.

24 *'Aj.*, II, 201.

al-Zabīdī's books were deleted from these biographies, there are many poems and *maqāmāt*s that give a comprehensive picture of cultural life, versification in *rajaz* meter (*urjūza*, pl. *arājīz*) of religious and grammatical sciences and historical events, literary criticism and the ethical and moral values of the period. In this way he was able to preserve them from oblivion.

The examples that our author quotes indicate that poets did not subject themselves to the rules of the neo-classical *qaṣīda* of the golden age of the Abbasid period, which were affected by Greek logic and philosophical ideas. Poets, influenced by *Ṣūfī* ideas and morals, generally tried to deal directly with the subject in their elegy and eulogy poetry without the conventional prologues of the erotic, journey, and transitory verse (*bayt al-qaṣīd*) leading to the main motif of the poem and ending it with an effective proverbial saying (*ḥusn al-khitām*). Their poetry was composed in a rhetorical style, deriving their metaphors derived from nature and various Islamic sciences. The beloved's face is always a shining full moon, his figure is a spear or a fresh bough, he or she is a haughty, a tyrannical gazelle, whose teeth are pearls, whose eyelashes are fascinating and whose eyes send arrows of charm piercing the heart of the lover.[25] The poetry and *maqāma*s of this period reflect urban life and deal with important contemporary historical incidents, which they express in the form of short 'epics' in the *rajaz* or *ṭawīl* meters on the history and battles of Mamluk *amīr*s, as supplements to the historical information.[26] Other poets rebelled against the conventional meters and the mono-rhyming *qaṣīda*, and looked for 'new inventions', using the special form and diacritical dots of Arabic calligraphy to come up with plays on words, unique meanings and metaphors, visual innovations using letters with and without diacritical dots, or extracting verses from tables of letters as in the case of the poet Qāsim b. ʿAṭā Allāh al-Miṣrī. Only in official odes (*qaṣīda*) composed by religious scholars in praise of religious and *Ṣūfī* shaykhs were the conventions of the classical *qaṣīda* upheld, and the motif of battles and places associated with the Prophet Muḥammad's message were mentioned as inspiring spiritual and religious themes of Islam. The popular poets quoted by al-Jabartī, generally used short verses, a popular strophic rhyme-scheme and the lyrical style of the post-

25 See the poems of al-Khashshāb and al-ʿAṭṭār expressing their infatuation with young French men, *'Aj.* IV, 240–1.

26 *'Aj.*, II, 265–7.

classical period for performance with music, singing and *Ṣūfī* dancing during the *dhikr*.[27]

In keeping with the convention of Arabic literary and historical works, al-Jabartī uses poetry for a number of literary purposes. He quotes verses in support of his ideas and conclusions, but rarely mentions the names of their authors. Generally, he precedes these quotations with a very general introductory phrase, in order to avoid mentioning the name of the poet, for example *kamā qīla* (as it has been said), or *qīla al-shā'ir* (the poet said), or he may add the word *shi'r* (poetry) before the verse, in order to alert the reader or the copyist to the fact that these lines are verses of poetry, with meter and rhyme.

Unlike his father Ḥasan who was a skilled composer of didactic poetry, ʿAbd al-Raḥmān al-Jabartī admitted in his *Introduction* that he 'lacks competency in the rules of Arabic rhetoric and the mastery of Arabic prosody'.[28] The only versified lines by ʿAbd al-Raḥmān al-Jabartī that the writer of these lines was able to trace are five couplets of ten verses in *rajaz* meter. This *'urjūza*, which sounds like the didactic *rajaz* poems of a novice, in praise of Muftī Ṭāhir al-Ḥusaynī of Jerusalem, was written in order to convince him to buy one of his father's manuscripts:[29]

مُحَمَّدُ الاسْمِ حَمِيدُ النَّعْتِ   عَلاّمَةُ الوقْتِ، الّرئيسُ المُفْتِى
وطاهِرٌ مُطَهّرٌ مِنْ سُحْتِ   جَمالُ أهْلِ القُدْسِ فِي ذَا الّوَقْتِ
وَكُلَّ مَنْ كانَ السّيِّدُ يَأتِي   يِشْفِى غَليلَ السّايلِ المُسْتَفْتِى
مُحَوَّطًا مِنَ الجِهاتِ السّتِ   يَعودُ بِالجَبْرِ وَطِيبِ الّبَخْتِ
يُهْدِي لَكُمْ مِنَ السَّلامِ الّبَتّ   وَعَبْدُ الرّحْمنِ هُوَ الّجَبْرتِي

The most erudite scholar of his time, the Grand *Muftī*, /
Muḥammad is his name and of praised qualifications.
He is the beauty of Jerusalem's population in this period /
He is virtuous and clean of sins.
He gives the right answers to those who asks for his *fatwā*[30]/
and to everyone who visited this *Sayyid* (of the Prophet's family).[31]

---

27 On popular poetry, see M. Larkin, 'Popular Poetry in the Post-Classical Period, (1150–1850)', in Allen and Richards, *Arabic Literature in the Post-classical Period*, 191–242.

28 *'Aj.*, I, 7.

29 See in the Appendix a letter from Ḥasan al-ʿAṭṭār to the Muftī of Jerusalem Muḥammad Ṭāhir Afandī al-Ḥusaynī. See the English translation of this letter by Manna, 'Cultural Relations', 139–52.

30 *Fatwā*: a legal opinion.

Such a person would be gratified and of good luck /
Protected from all sides.
And ʿAbd al-Raḥmān, I mean al-Jabartī /
Sends you definite greetings.

These simple, denotative, and prosaic versified lines are a clear indication that our author had not mastered Arabic poetry where sense and rhythm add emotional and spiritual dimensions to words. Additionally, some quotations cannot be scanned according to Arabic rules of prosody and need correction in accordance with their particular meters. Only rarely did he add vowel marks to his poetic quotations.

Al-Jabartī followed the medieval classification of the pseudo-neoclassical Arab poetic conventions of his time, as they were defined by the Iraqi post-neoclassical poet and scholar Ṣafī al-Dīn al-Ḥillī (1278–1349) in his *dīwān* of post-classical poetry entitled *al-ʿĀṭil al-Ḥālī wa 'l-Murkhaṣ al-Ghālī* ('The Unadorned Now Bedecked and the Cheapened Made Costly').[32]The following chapters in al-Ḥillī's *Dīwān*, are selections of other *funūn al-shiʿr* (genres of poetry), such as elegy (*rithāʾ*), eulogy (*madīḥ*), the chaste erotic opening line (*nasīb*), morality (*adab*), description (*waṣf*), etc.

These poetic genres were composed mainly for recitation in the presence of sultans, rulers, chiefs of tribes, dignitaries, or patrons, during tribal or literary debates and assemblies or on festive or sad occasions. The poetic rules of the classical period were formulated by Abī ʿAlī Aḥmad al-Marzūqī (d. 421/1030) in his book *Sharḥ al-Ḥamāsa* (Commentary on Heroic Poetry).[33] In his *Introduction* to this book, al-Marzūqī enumerated seven rules for poetry of superior quality.[34] These seven rules he termed *ʿamūd al-shiʿr* (the seven pillars of conventional poetics): the poem must express depth of emotion and thought, be composed in a rhetorical and sonorous tone in which the rhyme is end-stopped, where the sense, the grammatical structure, and the meter end

31 A *sayyid* is a descendant of the Prophet's family.

32 Ṣafī al-Dīn al-Ḥillī, *Die vulgärarabische Poetik al-Kitāb al-ʿĀṭil al-Ḥālī wal-Muraḫḫaṣ al-Ġālī des Ṣafīyaddīn Ḥillī*, W. Hoenerbach (ed.) (Wiesbaden 1956); W.P. Heinrichs, 'Ṣafī al-Dīn al-Ḥillī', *EI*[2], VIII, 801–5; C.E. Bosworth, 'Ṣafī al-Dīn al-Ḥillī', *Encyclopedia of Arabic Literature* 2, 675.

33 See Moreh, *Studies*,32; Ch. Pellat, 'al-Marzūḳī, Abū ʿAlī Aḥmad b. Muḥammad b. al-Ḥasan', *EI*[2], IV, 635–6.

34 See Aḥmad b. Muḥammad al-Marzūqī, *Sharḥ Dīwān al-Ḥamāsa*, Aḥmad Amīn and ʿAbd al-Salīm Hārūn (eds)(Cairo 1951), 9–11.

together, and the rhyme forms an integral part of the sense. The similes, allegory, and metaphors are to be derived from urban or desert nature with verisimilitude between objects. The sonorous poetry of the golden age of the Abbasid period,[35] was rational, sincere and original, represented by Abū Tammām (788–845), al-Buḥturī (820–97), Ibn al-Rūmī (835–96), al-Mutanabbī (915–65) and Abū al-ʿAlā' al-Maʿarrī (979–1058). It is distinguished by deep understanding of human character, morality, sublimity, and vigour of expression, purity of diction, rhetorical talent and embellishment with antithesis and paronomasia. These traits were expressed in harmony with emotion and sense, deep understanding of the human soul and existence, mixed with proverbial philosophy and maxims. They are based upon philosophical and religious standards, admiring the wisdom of God and questioning the meaning of human life, calamities of time and the eternal religious, ethical, and moral values, with unique mastery of the poetic lyric and rhetoric. All these traits distinguished the poetic values of the golden age of medieval Arabic poetry and literature.[36]

In post-classical poetry,[37] when the Arabs were content with religious studies and mystical practices, after they had lost their military and political hegemony and sovereignty in favour of non-Arabic speaking white slave military communities of horsemen who only used Arabic as a religious language, the poetic themes, forms and the dominant genres of Arabic poetry were changed. There is no evidence that al-Jabartī and his friend al-ʿAṭṭār, who excelled in belles lettres, read the famous Arab critics of poetry who were influenced by Greek logic, such as Qudāma bin Jaʿfar, ʿAbd al-Qāhir al-Jurjānī (d. 1078) and al-Qarṭājannī.[38] The critical remarks on literature and poetry by both and al-ʿAṭṭār are superficial and confined to general statements such as 'he was an excellent or good poet' or 'his poems were of sonorous jingling

35 See the articles of Alber Arazi and S. Moreh, *'Shi'r'*, *EI*[2], IX, 448–65.

36 On the similarity between Aristotle's ideas and the proverbial sayings of al-Mutanabbī, see Abū al-Muẓaffar al-Ḥātimī, *al-Risālat al-Ḥātimiyya*, in Anṭūn Būlād (ed.), *Rāshid Sūriyā* (Beirut 1868/1285).

37 On this subject see Allen and Richards, *Arabic Literature in the Post-classical Period*, 25–73.

38 On these critics, see *EI*[2]; on al-Qarṭājannī, see Wolfhart Heinrichs, *Arabische Dichtung und griechische Poetik* (Beirut and Wiesbaden1969).

(*ṭannāna*)' with no attempt at rhetorical, aesthetical and analytical discussion.[39] However, al-Jabartī was interested in poetry of moral, political and social criticism, as well as canonical poetic diction and form, use of which was limited to the rank of the *'ulamā'* and learned scholars including the sons of Mamluk *amīr*s, while the popular poets used colloquial language for their popular poetry and songs using new rhyme schemes and meters. In such a society of illiterates, where *Ṣūfī*s and dervishes performed their rites by dancing and singing, strophic verse such as *tawāshiḥ nabawiyya* (panegyrics to the Prophet), *muwashshaḥ* and *zajal* prevailed in the composition of songs for religious gatherings, circles of *dhikr* and religious feasts and entertainment. Most of the poems of the *qaṣīda* form quoted by al-Jabartī were in the *madīḥ* (panegyric) and *rithā'* (elegy) categories[40] and took the form of the post-neoclassical *qaṣīda*, which is composed in an embellished style for its external aesthetic and decorative values and not for its integral sense. In this post-classical period, exaggerations were preferred to precise expression, fantasy to reality, fancy to creative imagination, flattery to admonition. Al-Jabartī observed that al-ʿAṭṭar's poetry during his later years, was mainly for the social purposes 'of flattery and hypocrisy towards the eminent people of his time' (*fī nifāq ahl al-'aṣr*).[41] This form of neoclassical *qaṣīda* composed for and by *'ulamā'* consists of several parts, including the following:

1. The *nasīb*, chaste erotic opening verses, starting with lines of two rhyming hemistiches (*maṭla' muṣarra'*) expressing a lover's sorrow. This verse calls for highly rhetorical *barā'at al-istihlāl* (excellent exordium of a poem) to attract the attention and admiration of the audience.

2. The second part of a classical poem should describe a journey (*raḥīl*) to the person who is the subject of the panegyric. However, most of the post-classical poems quoted by al-Jabartī omit this journey and continue with a *bayt al-takhalluṣ* (a verse of transition from the erotic opening lines) to the panegyric section (*madīḥ*) or elegy (*rithā*'). The transition should be elegant (*ḥusn al-takhalluṣ*) and without sudden jumps from one subject to another.

39 See al-Jabartī where he refers to such poems as *qaṣā'id ṭannīna* (celebrated poems) and *gharrā'* (magnanimous), in *'Aj.*, I, 205, 370–1, III, 115, and elsewhere. Cf. also Sarkīs, *Mu'jam al-Maṭbū'āt al-'Arabiyya*, cols. 1732–3.

40 See *'Aj.*, I, 121, and elsewhere. Cf. Gran, *Islamic Roots*, xxvi, 1, 61 where he misunderstood the differences between classical, pseudo-classical and neo-classical poetry. On this subject see S. Moreh, 'The Neoclassical Qaṣīda, Modern Poets and Critics', in *Studies in Modern Arabic Prose and Poetry* (Leiden 1988), 32–56.

41 *'Aj.*, I. 270–1; IV, 239.

3. The concluding verses express a maxim or praise or prayers for the person in whose honour the poem is composed. In this case the poem is considered as having an excellent ending (*ḥusn al-khitām*). In the pseudo-neoclassical period, poets invented a new method of ending the poem with a final verse. In such verse the name of the poet is mentioned, adding after the words '*qultu mu'arrikhan*' (I said, denoting the date) in the first hemistich, a second hemistich (*'ajuz al-bayt*) in which the total numerical value of the letters (*ḥisāb al-jummal*) gave the date of the poem's composition, to commemorate the sad or happy event for which the poem was composed. This Arabic post-classical technique was considered a high art, which needed a special poetic talent and a unique genre called by al-Jabartī *fann al-ta'rīkh* (the art of composing verses in which the total numerical value of each letter amounts to the date of the event).[42] This extremely difficult art is classified by our author as one of the three components of *belles-lettres*, *adab* (literature), *ta'rīkh* (composing verses denoting a numerical date) and *shi'r*. Talented poets were able to compose several verses in the same poem denoting the same date. This unique 'craft' should be, according to our author, performed 'with smoothness, harmony and lack of affectation'; the Egyptian poet Qāsim b. ʿAṭā' Allāh al-Miṣrī (d. 1204/1789–90) excelled in this and was able to compose two versified lines, which contain thirty six possibilities of the date in the same year. This rare talent was attributed to a *jinni*, since no human being was capable of such sophisticated poetry. In a typical poem structured in this manner,[43] the poet Muḥammad Ibn al-Ṣalīḥī (d. ca. 1800) pays tribute to Shaykh al-Shams al-Ḥifnī, who was considered one of the great saints in Islam. Our author confirms that all the calamities which befell the Muslim world were caused by God because of the Shaykh's assassination by ʿAlī Bek al-Kabīr (1728–73):

بِـجَـدّكَ طه مَـنْ شَـرُفْتَ بِحَسْـبِهِ[44]   وَطابَ لَـهُ مِنْ جاهِـهِ لَكَ مَحْتِـدُ

42 *'Aj.*, I, 275. See these two verses by Qāsim b. ʿAṭā in *'Aj.*, II, 183–4. In praising his talent in composing such dates, al-Jabarti said (*'Aj.*, II, 184): أما في فن التاريخ فإليه المنتهى مع السلاسة والتناسب وعدم التكلف فيه ; the term *fann al-tārīkh* is translated as 'history' (See Philipp and Perlmann, II, 300), while it should be translated: 'As for the art of composing verses with the numerical value of their letters giving the hijrī year of the event, he reached the highest degree, with smoothness and harmony and lack of affectation'.

43 Arab scholars admired poetic talents. Al-Jabartī admired such talent and praised poets who were able to improvise verses with ease in any meter and with any rhyme. Cf. *'Aj.*, I, 403 on Ibrāhīm Ibn Abi 'l-Barakāt al-ʿAbbāsī al-Baghdādī.

44 In the text of the Būlāq edition the version *bi-ḥubbihi* seems incorrect. This word was emended here to *bi-ḥasabihi* based on synonymy between *ḥasab* (noble descent) and *maḥtid* (descent) at the end of this verse. Gran in his book *Islamic Roots of Capitalism*, 60 misunderstood the sentence *fa 'shtahara bi-fann al-adab… wa-fann al-ta'rīkh* (*'Aj.*, II, 184) in which the poet Qāsim b. ʿAṭā' Allāh excelled. Gran translated it 'was widely read in literature and history', while it should be translated into, 'He excelled in the genre of literature … and

عليه مع الآل الكرام تحيةً   تنالك منه رحمة ليس تنفذُ
مدى الدهر ما قال الصلاحي مؤرخًا: 'هو العزّ ها من أجله دُحِضَ العدو'

In the final verse, the numerical values of the letters of the second hemistich add up to the year 1177 (1763–4). Upon the death of ʿAbd Allāh al-Baṣrī's the following hemistich was written, which gives the year of his death 1134 (/1721–2):[45]

علم الحديث ماتا

Here the numerical value of the word علم is 140, the word الحديث is 552 and ماتا is 442, and the total gives the year 1134 (/1721–2).

Since the *'ulamā'* formed the bulk of educated society, most of the elegies and eulogy poems quoted were composed in praise of Arab religious scholars, renowned descendants of the Prophet Muḥammad (*sādāt* or *ashrāf*), *Ṣūfī* saints, chiefs of Bedouin tribes, friends, and sometimes even Mamluk *amīr*s, as well as Ottoman Pashas, some of whom were also capable of composing poetry in Arabic.

Some poets, such as Shaykh Ḥasan al-Badrī al-Ḥijāzī (d. 1131 [/1718–19])composed critical and satirical poems on political, religious, superstitious, and social topics,[46] while others were fond of homosexual and pornographic poetry, which gave the audience special delight and catharsis in their literary *majālis*. In such salons, there were occasional competitions between Turkish and Arab poets. For further documentation and illustration al-Jabartī quotes several of al-Ḥijāzī's poems, which illustrate certain historical and socio-religious events related in the biographies. He praises the poet's achievements, his fluency of style, his successful moulding of end-stop rhyme, meaning, meter, and grammatical structure into an integral whole 'with no padding of words and sense'.[47] He admires al-Ḥijāzī's perceptive critiques of contemporary social, religious, and political events in Egypt. He also praises his skill in composing long poems on scholarly subjects such as his *urjūza* (poem in *rajaz* meter) on *taṣawwuf* (mysticism) containing 1500 verses, in imitation of the long poem *al-Ṣādiḥ wa 'l-Bāghim* ('The Singing Bird and the Groaning Gazelle') by Abu 'l-

---

the genre of composing verses indicating the year of its composition or the year of death of a certain person'.

45 See, *'Aj.*, I, 84, see also 165, 233, 263, 274–7, 281 and elsewhere.

46 Ibid., I, 54–5, 58, 90, 94, 140–54, 174, 182–3, 186, 190–5 (al-Ḥijāzī's biography).

47 Ibid., I, 140.

ʿAlā' al-Maʿarrī (973–1057) which included proverbs (*amthāl*), anecdotes (*nawādir*) and tales (*ḥikāyāt*). Al-Ḥijāzī arranged his anthology (*dīwān*) in alphabetical order according to the rhyming letters (*rawiyy*) of the verse-lines. The *dīwān* bears the didactic twin title *Tanbīh al-Afkār li 'l-Nāfi' wa 'l-Ḍārr/Ijmā' al-Iyās 'an al-Wuthūq bi 'l-Nās* ('Awakening the Mind to Useful and Harmful Matters/Total Despair in Trusting People') in accordance with his belief that man is evil by nature and essence. It offers advice, warns against evil persons, since al-Ḥijāzī believes in the motto, *homo homini lupus* (man to man is a wolf), and ends with several elegant poems in *rajaz* meter (pl. *arājīz*) including anecdotes, proverbs, entreaties for succour (*istighāthāt*) and fervent pleas (*tawassulāt*) to God and His Prophet for pardon and relief from calamities. Al-Jabartī inserts several monorhyme poems from this anthology into his necrologies of the years 1100–1142 (/1688–1730). These poems provide practical advice on the kind of persons and objects one has to avoid, such as bad neighbours, narrow houses, rides on vicious animals, tight-fitting shoes, big turbans, hot food, evil men and women, envious relatives, belief in the sanctity of man, *Ṣūfī* saints, etc.[48] He also mentions other works by al-Ḥijāzī: a couplet (*muzdawija*), a versification of *Risālat al-Waḍ'*, by ʿAḍud al-Dīn al-ʿĪjī (d. 765/1363–4) and three more scientific treatises in verse.[49]

Al-Jabartī also quotes an anthology by 'the distinguished poet of his own time' (*shā'ir waqtih*) Aḥmad al-Dilinjāwī who is not included in al-Zabīdī's *Mu'jam Mukhtaṣṣ*. One of the strophic verse forms presented is a *tawjīh* (lit. 'guidance'),[50] in which the poet hints at the personage referred to by the poem. Another is the *takhmīs* (lit. 'quintuple') in which al-Dilinjāwī added three hemistiches to each verse of two hemistiches in a *qaṣīda* by the poet Ibn Manjak, to demonstrate his ability in such poetic techniques. The *mukhammis* (the poet who adds three new hemistiches), must add new ideas or expand the meaning of the original verses. These additional hemistiches help to illustrate the meaning and to elaborate the intention of the poet. Al-Jabartī also quotes a *mawāliyā* (a poem in colloquial language, often sung to the accompaniment of a reed pipe).[51]

48 Ibid., I, 141–50.

49 *'Aj.*, I, 140; on al-ʿĪjī, see Sarkīs, *Mu'jam al-Maṭbū'āt*, cols. 1331–3.

50 *'Aj.*, I, 360.

51 Ibid., 133.

By contrast, the poems of the post-neoclassical period were composed not only for social purposes, as was the case in the conventional ode (*shi'r* proper), but rather more for entertainment, mainly in songs, praises for the Prophets and saints, *dhikr* sessions with musical accompaniment. Such poems could be written in colloquial Arabic (*malḥūn*) with unconventional meters and strophic rhyme scheme. The post-neoclassical genres, or the seven 'arts' of medieval Arabic poetics, are known in Arabic as *al-funūn al-sab'a.* The following description of these 'arts' is given by al-Ḥillī. The first three genres composed in classical Arabic (*mu'rab*) which al-Ḥillī included in his *dīwān*, are *al-shi'r*, *muwashshaḥ* and *dubayt.*[52]

1. *Al-shi'r*, the conventional classical ode, also known as *al-shi'r al-qarīḍ*[53] or *nasīb.*[54] The latter term is used in quoting a *maqāma* by Shaykh Ḥasan Shamma (d. 1176), which discusses the seven post-neoclassical genres of poetry (*al-funūn al-shi'riyya*) and is entitled *Fayḍ al-Mughnībi-Madḥ al-Ḥifnī* in praise of Shaykh Muḥammad b. Sālim al-Ḥifnāwī. Most of the poems quoted fit the *madīḥ* and *rithā'* classifications and employ the *al-kāmil* or *al-sarī'* meters, where the verses are divided into two hemistiches with monorhyme ending.[55]

As in the classical genres, the opening verses (*maṭla'*) of these neoclassical poems start with a line of two rhyming hemistiches (*maṭla' muṣarra'*). These form the beginning of the *nasīb* (erotic verses), which should be of an impressive and rhetorical character (*barā'at al-istihlāl*). These poems were dedicated to Muslim scholars, mainly Arabic speaking *'ulamā'*, sultans, Mamluk *amīr*s, Bedouin tribal chiefs, and friends.

2. The second post-neoclassical genre listed in al-Ḥillī's *Dīwān* is the *muwashshaḥ.*[56] Like *al-shi'r*, and in accordance with Andalusian strophic poetry, it is composed in classical Arabic (*mu'rab*), with a *kharja*[57]in various dialects. This form became restricted to strophic verses in praise of the Prophet Muḥammad (*madā'iḥ* or *muwashshaḥāt nabawiyya*) intended to be sung ('by singers' *ahl al-maghānī*) with instrumental accompaniment ('by players' *ālātiyya.*)[58]

52 Al-Ḥillī, 2–3.
53 Ibid., 3.
54 *'Aj.*, I, 462.
55 Elegies on Ismā'īl Bey b. Iywāḍ Bey al-Qāsimī in ibid., I, 212–13.
56 See G. Schoeler, 'Muwashshaḥ', *EI*[2], VII, 809–12, and L. Alvarez, 'Muwashshaḥ', *Encyclopedia of Arabic Literature*, 2, 563–6.
57 A parting segment in vernacular Arabic or romance. Moreh, 'Meaning', 134–44.
58 *'Aj.*, II, 50, l. 8.

3. The third genre is the *dūbayt* rhyme scheme using quatrains of the form [a b a b] or [a a b a]. It is constructed of couplets in a special neo-classical meter: - - u u -/ u – u - / - u u - where the last two feet may be replaced by other variations of the foot in *rajaz* meter.[59]

The second group of genres includes the five 'arts' numbered 4 through 8, which are composed in the colloquial (*'mm*).

4. *Zajal*, colloquial quatrains to be sung, in local Arabic dialects, following the rhyme scheme [a a b b b a, c c c a], etc.[60]

5. *Mawāliyā*. This genre may use either canonical language or colloquial dialect. It may employ various meters, mainly *al-basīṭ* (- - u - / - u -), repeated twice in each hemistich of a verse, or else unfixed rhyme schemes of quatrain form.[61] Al-Jabartī notes that Shamma distinguishes between three sub-genres of *mawāliyā*, viz. *al-qaraqyā*, used for frivolous bantering (= *hazl*, or joking) themes; *al-bullayq*, for erotic (*ghazal*) themes; and *al-mukaffir*, a gnomic poem for religious exhortation (*mawā'iẓ*).[62]

6. The *kān wa-kān*. This genre uses the *mujtathth* meter (- - u - / u - -), repeated four times in each verse of two hemistiches, with rhyme schemes in quatrain form of [a a a a, b c d a], etc.[63]

7. *Al-Ḥammāq*, in colloquial quatrains, used for satire and frivolous subjects.[64]

8. *Al-Qūmā*. Its meter is (- - u - / u - o) or (- - u - - / - u - -) and its rhyme scheme is a quatrain of the form [a a x a].[65]

Other types of post-classical poetry quoted are:

59 See Aḥmad al-Hāshimī, *Mīzān al-Dhahab fī Ṣinā'at Shi'r al-'Arab* (Cairo 1418 /1998), 140–1.

60 Al-Ḥillī, 5–104; L. Alvarez, 'zajal, medieval', *Encyclopedia of Arabic Literature* 2, 818–19.

61 P. Cachia, 'Mawāliyā', *EI*², VI, 867–9, and D. Semah, 'zajal, modern', *Encyclopedia of Arabic Literature* 2, 819–20.

62 *'Aj*., I, 462, 466.

63 G. Schoeler, 'Muwashshaḥ', *EI*², IV, 809–12 and W. Stoetzer, 'kān wa-kān', *Encyclopedia of Arabic Literature* 2, 425–6.

64 On these genres, see the relevant terms in *EI*² and the *Encyclopedia of Arabic Literature*.

65 M. Bencheneb, revised Charles Pellat, 'al-Ḳūmā or al-Ḳawmā', *EI*², V, 372–3; *Ma'rūf al-Ruṣāfī, al-Adab al-Rafī' fī Mīzān al-Shi'r wa-Qawāfīh*² (Baghdad 1969), 124–6; for definitions of the terms see Salma Khadra Jayyusi, *Trends and Movements in Modern Arabic Poetry* (Leiden 1977), I, 25 and S. Moreh, *Modern Arabic Poetry, 1800–1970* (Leiden 1976), 319–25.

9. The *badīʿiyyāt* (metaphorical odes), referring to embellished odes in praise of the Prophet Muḥammad, in verses of two hemistiches in *basīṭ* meter containing one figure of speech or more.[66]

10. The *urjūza muzdawija*, couplets in *rajaz* meter (- - u -), in which the hemistich is equal to a verse in a conventional *qaṣīda*. This meter was used for versifying scientific subjects, such as mathematics, astronomy, history, and grammar, etc. It may use one of two rhyme schemes, either couplets of the form [a a b b], etc. or else strophes of five hemistiches each of [a a a a b] rhyme scheme.[67]

11. Another poetic 'art' which the poets of the eighteenth century admired is *tashṭīr*. In this genre, the poet pads a well-known poem by adding a second hemistich to the first hemistich of each verse, and adding a first hemistich to the second one, thus lengthening the original poem and stretching its meaning.[68]

12. The concluding verses of poems commemorating happy or tragic social and historical events, such as births, marriages, the dedication of a new building or mosque, usually indicated the year of the event commemorated (*bayt al-taʾrīkh*) by the numerical value of the letters (*ḥisāb al-jummal*) of the last hemistich or verse.[69] By such devices the poets of this period tried to display their wit and their command of classical literary techniques.

13. A number of terms were applied to the interchange of poems between friends, such as *ikhwāniyyāt* (congratulating friends), *tarāsul* (exchanging poems of praise between friends), *musājalāt* (argumentative poetry), *muḥāwarāt* (dialogues), *mudāʿabāt* (jesting or pleasantries), *mujūniyyāt* (frivolous and erotic poems dealing with homosexual and pornographic subjects),[70] and *muṭāraḥāt* (friendly interchange).[71] Such poetry was important in the society described by al-Jabartī, in which courtesy, flattery and what he terms *nifāq ahl al-ʿaṣr* (hypocrisy towards the important personalities of the time) were standard forms of social intercourse.[72]

---

66 For the different types of *badīʿiyyāt*, see *ʿAj.*, I, 211–15, and Jayyusi, *Trends*, 25.

67 See the *muzdawija* in 56 quintets by Qāsim ʿAṭāʾ Allāh in praise of Amīr Riḍwān Katkhudā al-Jalfī, in *ʿAj.*, I, 193–8, 230–3. See also the *urjūza* in couplets on medicine (*ʿAj.*, I, 333–4) and on Arabic grammar (ibid., I, 210).

68 *ʿAj.*, I, 263, 284; cf. Jayyusi, *Trends*, 25, 43, 283.

69 *ʿAj.*, I, 263, 284; cf. Jayyusi, *Trends*, 25, 35.

70 *ʿAj.*, I, 200, 396. Such poems still form subjects for discussion and humour in oriental societies.

71 Ibid., I, 352; II, 16.

72 Ibid., I, 239. See the *muʿāraḍa* of al-Zabīdī to Majnūn Laylā, ibid., II, 201–2; IV, 239.

14. *Muʿāraḍa* (imitation). The post-classical poets used to imitate a successful poem of an earlier period by copying its theme, meter, and rhyme scheme in an attempt to surpass it. Al-Jabartī quoted many poems and *muwashshahāt* that were composed as imitations of the works of classical poets, such as the Andalusian poet Lisān al-Dīn al-Khaṭīb (d. 1374). The poet Qāsim b. ʿAṭāʾ Allāh composed a *muʿāraḍa* in praise of the Amīr Riḍwān Katkhudā al-Jalfī.[73]

The following post-classical categories of poetic genres (*al-funūn al-shiʿriyya*) placed emphasis upon form: play on words with or without diacritical dots upon the letters or under the letters, or letters and words with diacritical dots changing alternatively,[74] spurious embellishment, paronomasia (*al-tajnīs* or *al-jinās*),[75] plagiarism, alliteration, antithesis and different types of parallelism and puns. They were called *al-muḥassināt al-badīʿiyya* (forms of metaphorical embellishments, plays on words and their diacritical dots) by Ḥasan Shamma.[76]

15. *Al-Muʿaṭṭalāt* poems and *maqāmāt* employing only words without diacritical marks on or under the letters.[77]

16. *Al-Ḥayya al-raqṭāʾ* (or *al-arqaṭ*, the speckled serpent), where one letter is dotted and the next un-dotted; such a verse by ʿAbd Allāh al-Idkāwī is quoted admiringly:[78]

جميل بديع جلّ ذاتـا بَهِيّةً   بِـهِ زدت حباً فاتك بمجاله

17. *Wusʿ al-iṭṭilāʾ* : this is a newer technique invented by ʿAbd Allāh al-Idkāwī. Al-Jabartī quotes two examples, one in which each word in a verse starts with the same letter, and another one in which each word starts with the final letter of the preceding word.[79]

18. *Al-ʿAwd* (the return or repeat). This is a poem in which each verse of two hemistiches is followed by a shortened version of itself, as in the following example in *al-basīṭ* meter: [80]

دلاله بولاة الحبّ زاد فلو   قد عاد بالقرب يا صحبي شفى سقمي

73 Ibid., I, 198–9; cf. also 248–9, 378 and elsewhere; Jayyusi, *Trends*, 48, 197, 283.

74 *ʿAj*., I, 357.

75 See W. P. Heinrichs, 'rhetorical figures', *Encyclopedia of Arabic Literature*, 2, 660, col. 2.

76 *ʿAj*., I, 290.

77 Ḥaqqī, 154.

78 *ʿAj*., I, 35.

79 Ibid., I, 353. There are two examples of such a technique.

80 On al-ʿawd, see *ʿAj*., I, 353, a technique which was condemned by al-ʿAṭṭār, (I, 413, no. m of our new Arabic edition) as a weak style and trite in content, see Appendix I below. (MS *ʿAj*. Cam., Qq. 169, I, f. 354).

دلاله زاد حبي　　　　بالقرب زاد دلاله

In his comment in the margin of his own copy of MS *'Aj.* Cam., I, f. 354 al-ʿAṭṭār, condemned this invention as senseless and superficial.

19. *Al-Mushajjar*: composed in the form of a tree. The refrain is written on the trunk, the variations of the theme are on vines branching out from it.[81] Al-Jabartī quotes four types of metaphors of this genre by ʿAlī b. Muḥammad al-Qalʿī.[82]

20. *Al-Lughz* and *al-Mu'ammā*: verses with riddles in which the poet hints at the answers.[83]

21. *Al-Muṣaḥḥaf*:[84] Al-Jabartī quotes verses and *maqāmāt* in which the letters in each pair of consecutive words are graphically similar but differ in the placement of the diacritical dots:

قاتل فاتك أغرّ أعزّ　　　　حسنه جيشه كثير كبير

22. Two types of *iqtibās* or *taḍmīn*: The poet quotes from the Qur'ān, verses by other poets, or proverbs. Sometimes the quotation is in a different language, such as Turkish or Persian.[85]

The genres of post-classical Arabic poetics described above in which play on words and diacritical dots were the main technique, remained in vogue from 1517–1798, during the Ottoman-Mamluk period and the French occupation of Egypt. After the military and administrative reforms of Muḥammad ʿAlī (d. 1849) who massacred the Mamluks in 1811, when non-Arab rulers dominated Egypt, Greater Syria and Iraq, poetry passed through a stage which modern Arab critics call *'aṣr al-jumūd wa 'l-inḥiṭāṭ* (the period of stagnation). As illustrated above in the categories of poems numbered 15 through 22 poetry became preoccupied with metaphorical and rhetorical forms, plays on words, embellishment, pun, alliteration, antithesis and different types of parallelism and paronomasia (*tajnīs*). These rhetorical practices prevailed until the

81 ʿAdnān Ḥaqqī, *al-Mufaṣṣal fī 'l-'Arūḍ wa-'l-Qāfiya wa-Funūn al-Shi'r*, 160.

82 *'Aj.*, I, 213–14.

83 Ibid., I, 322.

84 Ibid., I, 341; cf. Ibid., I, 322.

85 Ibid., I, 357, 358–9; cf. Louis Cheikho, *Kitāb 'Ilm al-Adab* (Beirut 1908), I, 181–2. In the margin of his copy of *'Ajā'ib al-Āthār* (kept in Cambridge University Library), Ḥasan al-ʿAṭṭār criticized this type of invention, saying that it has no beauty or sense. For a quotation of a Persian hemistich, see *'Aj.*, I, 357, and for a borrowing of the meaning of a Persian verse, see *'Aj.*, I, 361.

philosophical, humanitarian and cultural revival in Europe began to exert its influence upon the Arab Middle East.

When the military power of the Ottoman empire became exhausted after its occupation of Egypt in 1517 and its invasions in Europe and Asia, it turned from an invading (*ghāzī*) power into a tax collector state.[86] As the non-Arabic speaking rulers of the Ottoman provinces, Egyptian scholars claimed, that they had no educational or cultural interests, being merely concerned with intrigues to secure their survival, and with the collection of the taxes assigned for the Ottoman Sultan, education became limited to religious institutions, especially in *madrasa*s (religious schools) affiliated to mosques. The Mamluk factions were engaged in continuous plots to exterminate each other, and the Ottoman authorities were too weak to interfere. Under such cultural, political, and economic conditions, one might not expect to find much interest in Arabic poetry. However, the opposite appears to be the case. As illustrated in al-Jabartī's chronicle, poetry still played an important role in the daily life of the Arabs during the eighteenth and the first part of the nineteenth century.

The role of Arab poets in our author's chronicles range from composing a verse to be engraved upon a seal in a finger-ring up to elegies. Verses and poems were ordered to be engraved on marble and plated with gold upon the vault of reception rooms (*majlis*) or upon the entrance of the mosques, on the walls of the bedroom, on tomb stones with blessings for a good omen, or engravings on the stone of sundials, or the *miḥrāb* (prayer niche), with the name of the artist and the date all in metric versification. Generally, the last verses denote the date of the building and the name of the owner. In al-Jabartī's *Chronicle,* there is a distinction between the poor poets who earned their living by composing panegyrical poetry and the high-ranking scholars who wrote poetry to honour rulers and friends as well as for social purposes and entertainment.

The main aim of Arab poets, whether they wrote in canonical Arabic or in the vernacular, was to earn their living by entertaining and glorifying dignitaries (*akābir*, *a'yān*) who were their patrons. Many celebrated Arab

86 Cf. Doris Behrens-Abouseif, 'Pattern of Urban Patronage in Cairo; a Comparison between the Mamluk and the Ottoman Periods', in T. Philipp and U. Haarmann, *The Mamluksin Egyptian Politics and Society* (Cambridge 1998), 230–1. A different view on cultural life in Egypt under the Ottomans is expressed by N. Hanna, 'Cultural Life in Mamluk Households (Late Ottoman Period)', in Philipp and Haarmann, *The Mamluks*, 194–204.

poets were court poet laureates or convivial boon-companion poets (*shā'ir nadīm*), and table companions (*jalīs*) to their patrons. They would compose poems praising the generosity and 'noble' character of their patron. Many a poet who was retained (*lāzama*) by a certain patron received his entire livelihood from him. The *Naqīb al-Ashrāf*, ʿAlī Burhān Zādah, expressed praise for the poet Shaykh ʿAlī al-Qalʿī,[87] whose patron, the vizier ʿAlī Pāshā al-Ḥakīm 'showered him with indescribable largesse … and he began to ride about with a large retinue in imitation of the vizier'. In Istanbul, he grew even further in grandeur under his patron's aegis, until he became one of the grandees of the Sublime Porte. He shared his patron's good and bad fortunes and 'when the vizier was dismissed and exiled ... he [al-Qalʿī] was stripped of all his properties and exiled to Alexandria, where he remained until his death in 1172 [/1758–9], a victim, and a stranger'.[88]

The poet Ḥammāda al-Sadīdī al-Maḥallāwī (1163/1749–50), a talented writer of poetry and prose, dedicated many panegyric poems and *maqāmāt* to his patron.[89] One well-known panegyric *maqāma* is *al-Mudāma al-Urjuwāniyya fi 'l-Maqāma al-Riḍwāniyya* by the poet and writer Muṣṭafā Asʿad al-Luqaymī (1693–1765)[90] in praise of Amīr Riḍwān Katkhudā ʿAzabīn al-Jalfī, whose favourite boon companion (*nadīm wa-jalīs wa-anīs*) was the physician ʿAlī b. Jibrīl.[91] His patron was so pleased with him that he presented him with a house situated on the shore of the lake of al-Azbakiyya.[92]

The companion poets would recite their poem in their patron's assembly (*majlis* or *dīwān*), praise them with panegyrics (*madīḥ*), or satirize their rivals, and also congratulate them at celebrations on the birthday (*mawlid*) of the Prophet Muḥammad or of popular *Ṣūfī* saints (*awliyā'*, singular *waliyy*), where poets and men of letters used to compete with their poems in both *fuṣḥā* and colloquial. Such *madā'iḥ nabawiyya* (strophic verses in praise of the Prophet) were recited or sung in public (*tunshad fi 'l-jumū'*), with, or without

87 On al-Qalʿī, see *'Aj.*, I, 211–16.

88 Ibid., I, 213.

89 Ibid., I, 205 ff. On the *maqāma*, see James Monroe, *The Art of Badī' al-Zamān al-Hamadhānī as Picaresque Narrative* (Beirut 1983), and Charles Pellat and Carl Brockelmann 'Maḳāma', *EI*², VI, 107–15.

90 *'Aj.*, I, 221–9; *GAL*, II, 363.

91 *'Aj.*, I, 205.

92 Ibid., I, 216.

instrumental accompaniment.[93] These seasonal festivities of celebrating the birthdays of saints' *mawlid*s, mainly those of Aḥmad al-Badawī at Tanta and Ibrāhīm al-Dasūqī at Dasuq, were the best occasions for the poets to meet rich and influential scholars and officials, to recite their poems in their presence, and to give out written copies of their verses. It seems that these *mawālid* gatherings replaced the old seasonal trading markets, such as ʿUkāẓ and the caliphs' courts as venues for poetic competitions and recitations. Not only notables, such as *amīr*s or rich merchants in urban centres, were interested in poetry, but also chiefs of Bedouin tribes. ʿAbd al-Qādir b. Khalīl b. ʿAbd Allāh al-Rūmī (d. 1773) who was a talented poet, used to visit the Shaykhs of the Hawwāra tribe, who paid him generously for his highly rhetorical poems (*qaṣā'id ṭannīna*).[94]

Poorer poets would frequent the literary salons *majālis* and often the dining tables of famous religious personalities such as al-Shaykh Shams al-Dīn Muḥammad Abu 'l-Anwār ʿAbd al-Raḥmān, known as Ibn ʿĀrifīn Sibṭ Banī 'l-Wafā, and Shaykh al-Sādāt, standing before their patron and flattering him with their exaggerated eloquent eulogies, in the hope of getting his miserly gifts, hoping that they would acquire fame and become well known among the *amīr*s and the grandees who frequented his salon.[95] According to al-Jabartī, special ceremonies were called for when poetry and *maqāmāt* were recited in the presence of the patron. The writers would kiss their patron's hand, or the edge of his trouser-band (*tikka*) or his garments, and wait humbly for their reward. They would hand over a written copy of their compositions after the recitation, bestowing a profusion of good wishes upon the patron.[96] If the patron were pleased with the recited work, he would kiss the paper on which it was written[97] and present, or promise a gift (*jā'iza*), to the author. In cases when the patron forgot to fulfil such a promise, a new poem would be composed requesting fulfilment (*istinjāz*).[98] Ḥasan, the father of our historian,

93 Ibid., II, 16.

94 Ibid., I, 379. On the gathering at *mawlid*s between poets, scholars and rulers, see ibid.,II, 264 dealing with Shams al-Dīn al-Sabarbā'ī who was a poet and a judge. See also ibid., II, 260 on Aḥmad al-Samālijī who al-Jabartī met during the pilgrimage to the shrine of Aḥmad al-Badawī.

95 See the comment on al-Shaykh Shams al-Dīn Muḥammad Abū al-Anwār, *'Aj.*, IV, 187.

96 Ibid., I, 228.

97 Ibid., I, 215.

98 Ibid., I, 229; Hanna, 'Cultural Life', 196–204.

was a pious scholar who used to accept the poem dedicated to him, reward the poet, and burn the poem out of modesty.[99] Needy poets used to arrange these visits to the patron 'near the lunch hour' in order to receive a double award, 'a good lunch and a gift', in cash, sometimes in gold coin. This custom continued until the time of Aḥmad Shawqī (1868–1932) among conventional poets in Arab royal courts.[100] At funerals, poems were recited from the pulpit (*mimbar*) or from the bench (*dikka*) of the mosque at the time of the funeral prayer. The recitations were either given by the poets themselves, or by special reciters (*munshidūn*) of the Qur'ān endowed with 'loud and tender voices'.[101]

A renowned scholar like Ḥasan al-ʿAṭṭār composed elegies to honour his deceased friends, scholars, or rulers, and at the funeral, his poems were recited after the prayer by a special reciter (*munshid*). In his old age, he composed poetry to honour influential people, 'only when necessary, and in order to show dissimulation [to carry favour] towards the people of (his) age' (إلا بقدر الضرورة ونفاق أهل العصر).[102] Still, a poet capable of extemporaneous recitals on subjects under discussion, or in praise of his patron, and who was able to answer his patron or his friends in debate by improvised verses, was held in even greater esteem, and considered of greater poetic talent.[103] These poets served as an effective herald for the rulers, rich patrons, merchants, and religious scholars mainly the heads of *Ṣūfī* orders (*Shaykh al-Sajama*) and particularly descendants of the Prophet (*ashrāf*).

Eventually, the descendents of the Mamluks, known as *awlād al-nās*, and even some of the Ottoman governors who mastered the three Islamic languages (*al-lughāt al-thalāth*), Turkish, Arabic and Persian, appear to have developed a taste for Arabic literature, poetry and prose.[104] ʿUthmān Chelebi (d. 1130/1717–18), the son of Amīr Sulaymān Bey al-Armanī, was fond of reading, reciting and memorizing poetry.[105] Al-Jabartī writes that the Indian scholar Murtaḍā al-Zabīdī, who had come to Egypt after first settling in Zabīd

---

99 *'Aj.*, I, 302.

100 See the article T. Fahd, S. Moreh, et al, 'Shāʿir', *EI*², ix.

101 *'Aj.*, I, 189, 405.

102 Ibid., IV, 239.

103 Ibid., I, 403–4; Abū al-Faraj al-Iṣfahānī, *'Alī b. Ḥusayn, The Book of Strangers: Mediaeval Arabic Graffiti on the Theme of Nostalgia, Attributed to Abu 'l-Faraj Al-Iṣfahānī*, trans. Patricia Crone and Shmuel Moreh (Princeton, NJ 2000), 159.

104 Haarmann, 'Joseph's Law', 77–84.

105 *'Aj.*, I, 93.

in the Yemen, buried his wife in a tomb. 'People assembled there with him as did reciters and chanters [of the Qur'ān and prayers (*al-qurrā' wa 'l-munshidūn*)]'. Poets came to recite their elegies, which he accepted from them gratefully and 'he rewarded them' (*yujīzuhum*) for their poems.[106] Al-Zabīdī himself composed several elegies lamenting his wife's death 'in the fashion of the poet Majnūn Laylā'.

There were men of letters who were eloquent writers of poetry and prose, especially *maqāmāt*, such as Ismāʿīl Effendi al-Zuhūrī al-Miṣrī (d. 1211/1796–7). He was a talented musician, singer, and poet, and like other popular poets, both male and female, who composed songs for social gatherings, celebrations commemorating happy or tragic events, demonstrations, funerary gatherings or processions, he dedicated his poems to friends and patrons for different occasions (*ikhwāniyyāt*) and also composed 'longing poetry' (*ḥanīn*), satires to ridicule his rivals, or panegyric *maqāmāt* and strophic verses in imitation of Andalusian *muwashshaḥ*s. al-Zuhūrī composed odes and congratulatory poems for his patron Amīr Ḥasan Bey Riḍwān, such as his *tahānī* (congratulation) upon his patron's return to Cairo from exile. The closing verse of that poem contained a chronogram for the year in which it was written (1177/1763–4]). Because of his reputation, other poets who wished to gain recognition would ask Ismāʿīl Effendi to compose odes praising their work.[107] Accomplished poets were those who were able, such as Shams al-Dīn al-Sabarbāʿī (d. 1210/1795–6), to excel in various poetic genres. They excelled in eulogy, especially in praise of the Prophet Muḥammad (*madā'iḥ nabawiyya*), elegy, erotic poetry directed to women and young men (*al-tashbīb wa 'l-ghazal*), heroic poetry (*ḥamāsa*), earnest and jesting (*jidd wa-hazl*) poetry, especially poems containing all varieties of the art of metaphors.

Both patrons and poets were in need of each other: the patron for enhancing his prestige and esteem and the poet for sustenance, social connections and for contacts with the ruling class. The generous Mamluk *Amīr* Murād Bey Muḥammad (d. 1215/1801) used to encourage poets to join his *majlis* and lavished presents on poets for composing poems in his honour and increase his notability. When he died, poetesses and female singers composed elegies and sang them accompanied by music to lament his death. Poetry was

106 Ibid., II, 201.

107 Ibid., II, 268–9.

also employed to express social protest during revolts against excessive taxes, oppressive Ottoman pashas and other officials. Poets composed critical poems and versified slogans and taught them to children, women and blind 'holy men' in order for them to chant these lines in the streets and in front of the ruler's palace.[108]

In a society of foreign military factions engaged in continuous clashes, slaughtering and exterminating each other and extracting taxes from the poor populace, the gap between rich and poor increased. Spiritual, scientific, cultural activities, when the quest of knowledge (*ṭalab al-'ilm*) had reached the point of stagnation. In *maqāmāt* and poetry, innovations were limited to using the terminology of the Islamic sciences to entertain and to fill spare time; writers, poets and poetry provided means of entertainment and continued to serve as an effective means of communication for the rulers, rich patrons, merchants and religious scholars.[109] Beside riddles (*lughz*) and puzzles (*mu'ammā*) for intellectual entertainment in literary and social salons, poets tried to vie with former poets and versifiers in inventing new visual techniques of plays on words. Poets during this period developed techniques that no poet had been able to invent before them. Some such plays on words, especially with versification exploiting the diacritical dots of the Arabic script, became a mere game of play on words with absurd meanings.

However, to prove their unique talent in versification some poets invented impressive ways of playing with words, in which the letters of their poem were arranged in squares and in a special order to enable the reader to reconstruct these verses by reading the letters according to a fixed pattern of sequence in these squares. The following verses were composed by the distinguished and talented poet Qāsim b. 'Aṭā Allāh al-Miṣrī (d. 1204/1789–90),[110] who used mathematical computing squares of a crossword puzzle like system. It is possible to reconstruct these verses in *majzū' al-kāmil* (with the foot u u – u – repeated twice in every hemistich). Each verse contains 24 letters written in 12 perpendicular squares and 12 horizontal small squares, for 144 squares. The first verse can be reconstructed by putting the finger on the first square (line 1) on the left side with the letter '*mīm*', then counting to column 7 in the

108 Ibid., I, 209.

109 Lane, *Manners*, 371, gives another interpretation of the term *shā'ir*: 'The reciter of this romance [Abū Zayd al-Hilālī] is called a '*shá'er*' or 'poet'.

110 *'Aj.*, II, 184–6.

perpendicular squares where the letter ‘*wāw*’ is installed, thus getting the letters مو. Then the finger is moved to the first letter in line 2: لا, and add the letter in column 7 with the letter ي and gets the word: مولاي. By continuing to read the first letter in line 3 with the letter in column 7 in the same line, one gets the letters حز. With the first letter in line 4, one gets the word حزت. By continuing to read the first letter in line 3 with the letter in column 7 of the same line to the end, the verse will be completed by its twelfth letter. The second verse is constructed by moving the finger from line 1, col. 2, and adding the letter in column 8, and so on. The following verses and squares will illustrate this new technique:[111]

مَوْلاَيَ حُزْتَ مَهَابَةً
أَلسَّعْدُ جَاءَكَ مُقْبِلاً
دَامَتْ لِعِزِّكَ بَهْجَةٌ
لاَ تَخْشَ كَيْدَ حَوَاسِدٍ
كُنْ فِي سُرُورٍ آمِنًا
قَدْ لاَحَ عِزَّكَ آهِلاً

وَبَلَغْتَ خَيْرَ مَآثِرِ
صَفْوًا بِحُسْنِ سَرَائِرِ
بِجَمَالِ وَقْتٍ بَاهِرِ
مَوْلاَكَ أَكْرَمُ نَاصِرِ
وَكُفِيتَ شَرَّ مُنَاظِرِ
بِعُلاَكَ عَبْدَ الْقَادِرِ

Line	Col. 1	Col. 2	Col. 3	Col. 4	Col. 5	Col. 6	Col. 7	Col. 8	Col. 9	Col. 10	Col. 11	Col. 12
1	م	ا	د	لا	كـ	ق	و	ل	ا	ت	ن	د
2	لا	س	م	خ	ف	لا	ي	ع	ت	ش	ي	ح
3	ح	د	ل	كـ	س	ع	ز	ج	ع	ي	ر	ز
4	ت	ا	ز	د	و	كـ	م	كـ	ك	ح	ر	ا
5	هـ	م	ب	و	ا	هـ	ا	ق	هـ	ا	م	لا
6	ب	ب	ج	س	ن	ب	ت	لا	ت	د	ا	ع
7	و	ص	ب	م	و	لا	ب	ف	ج	و	كـ	كـ
8	ل	و	م	لا	ف	ع	غ	ب	ا	كـ	ي	ب
9	ت	ح	ل	ا	ت	د	خ	س	و	كـ	ش	ا
10	ي	ن	ق	ر	ر	ل	ر	س	ت	م	م	ق
11	م	ر	ب	ن	ن	ا	ا	ا	ا	ا	ا	د
12	ث	ي	هـ	ص	ظ	ر	ر	ر	ر	ر	ر	عبد القادر

In a society which considered poetry as a craft (*ṣinā'a*) in the sense of *fann* (art), other talented poets had to compete with them. The poet al-Idkāwī

---

111 My thanks to Dr Fu'ād Kanʿānī for preparing the two squares.

accepted the challenge. He also composed a poem of six verses with 24 letters each and distributed the letters in the same order to get the following verses:

يَـا سَــيِّدًا بِجَمَالِهِ   وَبِحُسْنِهِ وَكَمَالِهِ
بزَّ الْبَرِيَّةَ جُمْلَةً   قَسْرًا بِـفَرْطِ دَلاَلِهِ
لاَ أَنْثَنِي عَنْ حُسْنِهِ   أَنْ مَـنّ لِي بِوِصَالِهِ
غُصْنٌ تَـثَنَّى مُعْجَبًا   وَأَمَـضَّـنِي بِنِبَالِهِ
نَادَيْتُهُ صِـلْ آيِسًا   قَدْ مَـلَّ مِنْ بِلْبَالِهِ
فَأَجَـابَ مَهْلاً إِنّـنِي   أُنْــجِيكَ مِنْ عُذَّالِهِ

Line	Col. 1	Col. 2	Col. 3	Col. 4	Col. 5	Col. 6	Col. 7	Col. 8	Col. 9	Col. 10	Col. 11	Col. 12
1	ي	ب	لا	غ	ن	ف	ا	ذ	ا	ص	ا	ا
2	س	ا	ن	ن	د	ج	ي	ل	ث	ت	ي	ا
3	د	ب	ن	ث	ت	ب	ا	ر	ي	ن	هـ	م
4	ب	ي	ع	ي	ص	هـ	ج	هـ	ن	م	ل	لا
5	م	ج	ح	ع	ا	ا	ا	م	س	ج	ي	ن
6	ل	ل	ن	ب	س	ن	هـ	ت	هـ	ا	ا	ي
7	و	ق	ا	و	ق	ا	ب	س	ن	ا	د	ن
8	ح	ر	م	م	م	ج	س	ا	ن	ض	ل	ي
9	ن	ب	ل	ن	م	ك	هـ	ف	ي	ي	ن	م
10	و	ر	ب	ب	ب	ن	كـ	ط	و	ن	ل	ع
11	م	د	ص	ب	ب	ذ	ا	لا	ا	ا	ا	ا
12	ل	ل	ل	ل	ل	ل	هـ	هـ	هـ	هـ	هـ	هـ

As we can see from the above discussion, poets of talent were considered an important and influential religious, political, and social support for distinguished personalities and households that sought their company and used them to decorate their literary and religious salons. The poets themselves sought the protection of patrons not only in order to acquire wealth and distinction but also to secure their safety, welfare, living and future. The kind of poetry which was considered to be the best medium for prestige and fame was divided into several genres (*funūn*, sing. *fann* = arts), both in canonical and vernacular Arabic. Panegyrics and elegies dominated poetry in conventional literary style, as well as the strophic verse of the *muwashshaḥāt*, the most important of which was the *muwashshaḥāt nabawiyya* in praise of the

Prophet, whom the *Ṣūfī*s considered as the source of their spiritual esoteric knowledge. They praised their saints, religious and *Ṣūfī* leaders. Others composed love poetry for singing and entertainment.

The *azjāl* in Egyptian Arabic colloquial dominated the vernacular poetry composed by talented literary poets as well as popular poets and shaykhs, who composed songs in colloquial Arabic to be sung by singers and reciters (*munshidūn*) of praise poems and women dancers (*ghawāzī*) accompanied by music in praise of popular saints. During the French occupation *azjāl* were composed even in praise of the French soldiers.

Al-Jabartī presents the Cairene poet Qāsim b. Aṭā' Allāh al-Miṣrī al-Adīb,[112] who enjoyed the protection of many rich and influential religious and military patrons, as an example of an outstanding contemporary poet and a talented man of letters who excelled in most of the post-classical poetic genres,. In addition to plays with words and rhetorical forms, his main skill was in inventing new and useful formal techniques for denoting the date of the occasion for which he composed his verses. To improve his style in literature, Qāsim memorized *Mulḥat al-I'rāb* by al-Ḥarīrī (1056–1122) and *al-Alfiyya* by Ibn Mālik (d. 1274), both didactic poems on grammar.[113] He excelled in letters, in both canonical and colloquial idioms. As a poet he was known first as a *zajjāl* (a composer of *zajal*, strophic colloquial verse composed to be set mainly to music and singing). Later he became master in the art of the melodious Andalusian strophic verse (*muwashshaḥāt*). This genre was composed in post-Andalusian poetry without the famous *kharja* (the parting segment in vernacular Arabic or romance), a kind of lyrical poetry, which required much sensitivity and expertise; it was sung to the accompaniment of music. He was bestowed with a special gift of improvisation (*irtijāl*), a talent admired by the Arabs since the pre-Islamic period; it was considered such a unique poetical talent that al-Shaykh ʿAbd al-Raḥmān al-ʿAydarūs attributed Qāsim's poetic talent to the supernatural power of a jinn,[114] as was customary in pre-Islamic society. When Qāsim Ibn ʿAṭā' Allāh attended al-Zabīdī's *Tāj*

112 *'Aj.*, II, 184–8; J. Heyworth-Dunne, 'Arabic Literature in Egypt in the Eighteenth Century', *BSOAS* 9:3 (1938), 683–5.

113 *GAL*, I, 277.

114 See al-Zabīdī, *Mu'jam Mukhtaṣṣ*, ff. 126b–130b and *'Aj.*, II, 184–8. Among other poets who were talented with *irtijāl* is Ḥasan b. ʿAlī b. Dhiyāb Shamma. See al-Zabīdī, *Mu'jam Mukhtaṣṣ*, MS Princeton, 63, f. 30b, and *'Aj.*, II, 126.

al-'Arūs celebration he improvised two verses in praise of the author with a hemistich denoting the date of the celebration.

Another rare talent which Qāsim possessed was the *fann al-ta'rīkh* (the art of denoting the date), where the numerical value of the Arabic letters of the last hemistich comes after the words *qultu mu'arrikhan* (I say denoting the date [of the occasion]) or the word *arrikhuhu* (I give the date [of the occasion]). Another proof of his rare talent is his two verses containing 36 dates of the *hijrī* year 1165 (/1751–2). According to al-Jabartī, he achieved in this art 'the highest degree, with smoothness and harmony and lack of affectation'. Qāsim was among the Egyptian poets who devoted most of their panegyrics to important personalities, especially Amīr Riḍwān, Katkhudā of the ʿAzabīn of al-Jalfī whose palace was a *majlis adabī* (salon or meeting place) for talented poets and writers. He favoured the *Ṣūfī* family of Banū Wafā and al-Wafā'ī *Ṣūfī ṭarīqa*, especially al-Sayyid Majd al-Dīn Muḥammad Ab- Hādī al-Wafā'ī[115] and Sayyid Abu 'l-Anwār Muḥammad b. Wafā.[116] Both al-Qāsim and Ḥasan al-Badrī al-ʿAwaḍī were poets of the Banū Wafā. The latter collected a *dīwān* entitled *al-Lawā'iḥ al-Inwāriyya wa 'l-Madā'iḥ al-Anwāriyya* (Signs of Illuminations Concerning the Anwāriyya Panegyrics). Our author gives an impressive description of such *majālis adabiyya* (literary salons), where famous poets competed with each other in the presence of their patrons to show who could improvise the most impressive verses.[117]

Another talented poet was ʿAbd Allāh b. Salāma al-Idkāwī al-Miṣrī al-Shāfiʿī, known as al-Mu'adhdhin (d. 1184 [/1770–1]),[118] who had several influential patrons. At first his patron was Sayyid ʿAlī Afandī Burhān Zādeh, the *Naqīb al-Sāda al-Ashrāf*, whose deeds he praised; in 1147 (/1734–5) he joined him on in his pilgrimage to Mecca and visited the Prophet's tomb with him. Through his patron he was able to meet and praise many notables. He lent some of his books to al-Zabīdī and encouraged him to continue composing his *Tāj al-'Arūs*. After the death of his first patron he became a close boon-companion to al-Shaykh al-Shubrāwī, and composed many eulogies in his praise. After the latter's death he joined the famous *Ṣūfī quṭb*, al-Shaykh al-

115 *'Aj.*, I, 260.

116 Ibid., IV, 185–96.

117 Ibid., II, 184ff.

118 See al-Zabīdī, *Mu'jam Mukhtaṣṣ*, biography no. 291, ff. 46a–52b, and MS Princeton, 98–109, and *'Aj.*, I, 352ff.; *GAL*, II, 283; *GAL*, *Suppl.*,II, 392.

Shams al-Ḥifnī. He accompanied him on his travels and devoted many of his panegyrics to him. Many of al-Mu'adhdhin's books dealt with poetry and praise. He wrote *al-Qaṣīda al-Fardiyya fī Madḥ Khayr al-Bariyya* in praise of the Prophet Muḥammad, composed in honour of ʿAlī Bāshā al-Ḥakīm, who had written a compendium (*mukhtaṣar*) of al-Suyūṭī's commentary on the poem *Bānat Su'ād* by Zuhayr in praise of Muḥammad. In his *al-Fawā'iḥ al-Jināniyya fī 'l-Madā'iḥ al-Riḍwāniyya* he collected all the panegyric poems he had composed in praise of Riḍwān Katkhudā, followed by his own panegyrics in poetry and prose. In his poem *al-Nuzha al-Dhahabiyya bi-Taḍmīn al-Raḥbiyya* he turned the subject of *Raḥbiyya* dealing with inheritance (*farā'iḍ*) into an erotic poem.[119] Some of his works were didactic in nature, such as his *'Uqūd al-Durar fī Awzān al-Abḥur al-Sitat 'Ashar* on Arabic prosody dealing with the 16 meters of Arabic poetry, in which he provided examples of verses composed according to the Arabic meters. Another didactic work was his *al-Durr al-Thamīn fī Maḥāsin al-Taḍmīn* on the beauty of the art of *taḍmīn* (enjambment or quotations of verses from other poets). In his *takhmīs* of *Bānat Su'ād*, also known as the *Burda*, by Kaʿb b. Zuhayr (d. 627?), al-Idkāwī added three hemstitches between the first and second hemistich of every verse by Zuhayr with its opening verse 'Bānat Suʿād' ('Suʿād has departed [me]'). He wrote two very artificial *maqāmāt*, in which form and diacritical dots are more important than meaning and emotion. Thus, in *al-Maqāma al-Taṣḥīfiyya* the diacritical dots of every two similar words in the shape of their letters are changed to give a different meaning, while *al-Maqāma al-Qummudhiyya* (The Assembly on the Long and Thick One [the male organ]) deals with impudent (*mujūn*) poetry and homosexual anecdotes,[120] a favourite subject in literary salons.

All these innovations were restricted to plays on words and the forms of the Arabic letters and these letters' diacritical dots that were developed when poetry and *maqāma* became written texts following the introduction of paper in the Middle Ages. In these centuries, there was no real reform or revolution in thought, spiritual creativity, philosophy and rhetoric. Earlier the great poets

119 *Al-Raḥbiyya* here is the *urjūza* by al-Raḥbī, in 180 lines in *rajaz* meter on the *farā'iḍ* (law of division of inheritances according to all four legal schools), known as *al-Urjūza al-Raḥbiyya* (see Thomas Philipp and Guido Schwald, *A Guide to al-Jabarti's History of Egypt* [Stuttgart 1994], 252, no. 599.)

120 See al-Zabīdī, *Mu'jam Mukhtaṣṣ*, ff. 46b–47b, and *'Aj.*, II, 184–8.

and writers of medieval Arabic–Islamic culture influenced by Greek thought of the calibre of al-Mutanabbī (d. 965), al-Maʿarrī (d. 1057), Ibn al-Fāriḍ (d. 1235), Ibn al-ʿArabī (d. 1240) and other great Arab poets had ventured into new vistas of thought, metaphysics and sublime spiritual values and aspirations. During the Ottoman-Mamluk period, poetry was confined to social and religious festive occasions, with motifs such as elegies, eulogies, erotic homosexual songs accompanied by music, *Ṣūfī* poems and songs praising the Prophet and giving moral and social advice. These were mostly repetitive in content and the play on words was the main technique. This period is considered by Arab scholars as one of stagnation, in which the lunar cycle of poetic creativity passed once more into decline. The first poets and writers who came into close contact with European literature felt the need for a revolution.

Rifāʿa Rāfiʿ al-Ṭahṭāwī (1800–70),[121] a scholar and poet who joined Muḥammad ʿAlī's educational mission to Paris, revived the neoclassical style and themes to serve the aims of Muḥammad ʿAlī's secular reforms and European-oriented administrative and cultural system. He used strophic verse forms and the *qaṣīda* for new themes, such as martial songs and didactic poems about science. He used his pure diction and serious thought to promote the kind of reform in thought, customs, social practices and the economy, which he believed were needed to replace the old and corrupt social and political system that oppressed the common people of Egypt. This was also true in the case of al-Jabartī, who became convinced that Europe and its civilization could offer Muslims a chance to revive Islamic values of justice and modernity, and so restore Islamic civilization to its former glory. The Egyptian Aḥmad Shawqī, crowned by Arabs as 'the Prince of Poets', represented the wavering between neoclassicism and modernity, expressed in his writings through the borrowing of European poetic ideas, forms, metaphors, and similes. The conservative Shawqī, who opposed women's liberation, also wrote school songs, versified plays, epics, and historical poems. He is an interesting example of the cultural and literary impact of Western literature on the Arab world. He called for the revival of Islamic values, but also for the adoption of useful European sciences, as did al-ʿAṭṭār and al-Ṭahṭāwī.

121 On al-Ṭahṭāwī's poetry see Moreh, *Modern Arabic Poetry*, 11–21.

Chapter Six

Theatrical Performances in Egypt According to *'Ajā'ib al-Āthār*

Egypt is the cradle of one of the most ancient and unique civilizations which originated in connection with its eternal river, the Nile, with its natural flood and fall, and was controlled by a central and strong government of various indigenous Pharaonic dynasties and conquerors.[1] Therefore, Egyptian festivities even under Islam were connected to the solar not to the lunar calendar, since its agriculture and economy were husbandry inseparable from the annual inundation and fall of the Nile to which Egypt owed its immense fertility. The Nile was regulated by an elaborate system of dams and canals. The flood occurred year after year at the same season and was celebrated with its special festivities and ceremonies which retained elements of pagan ceremonies concerning the cutting of the dams.[2] Since Pharaonic times, festive celebrations based upon myth, legends and religious practices connected to rites of fertility and renewal of nature, dominated its religious, agricultural, cultural and social life. These celebrations were accompanied by theatrical performances, which symbolized the eternal cycle of nature. With the rise of a new religion these ancient rites were adapted to serve the needs of the new creed, 'skilfully contrived to plant the seeds of the new faith on the old stock of paganism'[3] as in the case of 'the Christian and the heathen festivals of the divine death and resurrection solemnized at the same season and at the same places'.[4]

After Pharaonic Egypt came under Roman dominion, and the rise of the three monotheistic religions, Egypt became a meeting point of these religions and hostile to all other 'pagan' rites and religions, as well as the battlefield of great and decisive battles. However, under Christianity the Copts continued to practice many Pharaonic rituals connected with the Nile festivities under the

1 Etienne Drioton, 'Le Théâtre dans l'ancienne Egypte', *Revue de la Société d'Histoiredu Théâtre* (1954), I–II.

2 J.G. Frazer, *The Golden Bough, a Study in Magic and Religion*, abridged edition in one volume (London 1960), 485–507.

3 Ibid., 455.

4 Ibid., 474.

'mantel of Christianity'; 'the Church may have consciously adapted [the festivals] to its heathen predecessor for the sake of winning souls to Christ'.[5]

Rites that were connected with nature and fertility remained firmly observed since it was believed that in sympathetic or imitative magic it was possible 'to regulate the course of nature quite independently of human will'.[6] On the other hand, in monotheistic religions God is placed outside nature, dominating it by His omnipotent powers and directing it by His divine principle of reward and punishment. Verses of the Holy Scriptures and evoking God's name and its derivations, enabled the believers, by God's will, to change the course of nature and to prevent calamities through repentance and prayers for the benefit of the pious community of believers.

Since the rise of Islam, the observations of some pagan rites concerning the inundation of the Nile by the Copts were looked upon by Muslim authorities with exasperation; although these rites were adopted by the majority, they lost their original significance and became an occasion among the populace of merry making and dissipation. Such festivals were condemned by religious and political authorities, who prohibited such ancient 'pagan celebrations'. Many rulers and scholars such as Ibn al-Ḥājj (d. 1336 in Cairo) who compiled his *Madkhal* in 732/1331, decreed that the Islamized carnivals of the 'Prince of Nawruz' during the New Year celebrations in Egypt, 'are censured by the law of Islam'.[7] The same process can be observed when the Persian pre-Islamic Siyavush's ceremony rooted in Persian culture lamenting and venerating deceased heroes was transformed into the Muḥarram processions in memory of the massacre of Ḥusayn and his family in Karbala on 10 Muḥarram 60/10 September 680.[8] This ʿĀshūrā' day of mourning sacred to the Shīʿites was also prohibited from time to time by Sunni rulers up to the present day.

The *Midrash* gives a hint of theatrical performances connected with the Nile's fertility. It relates that Joseph 'went into the house to cast up his master's accounts' where Zulayka, the wife of his master Potiphar, took the opportunity to seduce him 'when all flocked to see the day of the Nile Festival,

5 Ibid., 473.

6 Ibid., 25.

7 Ibn al-Ḥājj al-Fāsī al-ʿAbdarī (d. 737/1336), *al-Madkhal aw Madkhal al-Shar' al-Sharīf* (Cairo 1929), II, 52ff. Cf. also 146.

8 See Ehsan Yarshater, '*Ta'ziyeh* and Pre-Islamic Mourning Rites in Iran', in Peter J. Chelkowski (ed.), *Ta'ziyeh Ritual and Drama in Iran* (New York 1979), 90–3.

a day of theatrical performances'.[9] The importance of the Nile festival and its continuity, which was connected with nature and economic and social life in Egypt, was so great for the daily life of the Egyptians; according to the medieval Arab writers[10] the festival, considered a direct continuation of Pharaonic celebrations by the Copts, was perpetuated by the Muslim population until the nineteenth century.[11] These festivals and customs which exerted an osmotic influence upon each other were carried over from both Byzantine and Persian civilizations to the Muslim world.[12] The Persian Nawrūz was transformed in Judaism to the Purim festival; the righteous Mordecai, Esther's uncle, defeated the plot of the evil Haman to massacre the Jewish people, symbolizing the victory of good against evil and celebrated it in a victorious procession, after the hanging of Haman. These Jewish tales seem to play the same role as the Amīr al-Nawrūz procession in expelling the old year with its evils to receive the new one with its hoped-for blessing.

This festival was celebrated annually and was closely tied to the flooding cycle of the Nile. A special significance can be attributed to the legend concerning ʿAmr b. al-ʿĀṣ (d. 663), the Muslim conqueror of Egypt and its governor, who forbade the pagan rite of sacrificing a virgin bride to the Nile. When he asked the second caliph ʿUmar b. al-Khaṭṭāb (634–44) how he should deal with the fall of the Nile, the caliph ordered him to cast a paper in the Nile, with the words 'Allāh alone can cause the Nile water to flow', and behold, 'on the day of the Ṣalīb [17th of the autumn month of Tout, the first month of the Coptic calendar] festival, Allāh, the Almighty, caused the Nile to flow,

9 Rabbi Dr H. Freedman and Maurice Simon, *Midrash Rabba* (London 1939), vol. I, chapter 87, 187, no. 7.

10 See for example Ibn al-Ḥājj, *al-Madkhal*, II, 49–51.

11 See B. Shoshan, *Popular Culture in Medieval Cairo* (Cambridge 1993), 50–1.

12 Cf. Zakariyya ibn Muḥammad al-Qazwīnī, *Zakarija ben Muhammed ben Mahmud el-Cazwini's Kosmographie/ Kitāb 'Ajā'ib al-Makhl-qāt wa-Gharā'ib al-Mawjūdāt*, Ferdinand Wüstenfeld (ed.)(Göttingen1848), vol. II, 82 (on the Persian *yawm Hurmuz*); Ibn Iyās, *Badā'i' al-Zuhūrfi Waqā'i' al-Duhūr*, Muḥammad Muṣṭafā (ed.)(Wiesbaden and Cairo 1960), vol. I, pt. ii, 363ff describing Shaʿbān, year 787/7 September–6 October 1385; E.W. Lane, *An Arabic-English Lexicon* (London 1869–93), s.v. 'ksj' (on the *kawsaj* [Persian *kawsa*, a thin-bearded man], and his procession, known as *rukūb al-kawsaj* which was practiced in Egypt as Amīr al-Nayrūz). See also Aḥmad b. ʿAlī al-Maqrīzī, *al-Mawā'iẓ wa 'l-I'tibār bi-Dhikr al-Khiṭaṭ wa 'l-Āthār*, Gaston Wiet (ed.)(Cairo 1911–27), vol. IV, 245f; Aḥmad b. ʿAlī al-Maqrīzī, *al-Sulūk*, vol. I, pt. 1, 136f. and Ibn al-Ḥājj, *al-Madkhal*, II, 51–2.

reaching 16 cubits in one night'.[13] This incident signifies the first step in the process of imposing the strict rules of Islamic monotheism by the small army of the conquerors to dominate and defeat the Coptic majority and their culture, in accordance with Allāh's promise that Islam will dominate all other civilizations and 'replace the darkness of all former religions with its Light'.[14] From the beginning of the conquest Muslim rulers and scholars realized the necessity of continuing the pagan Pharaonic practices revealed in the various Coptic Nile festivals celebrating the eternal natural power of the annual inundation of the Nile.

All Coptic festivals coincided with the seasonal undulation of the Nile's rise and fall and the sowing of the seasonal crops. These festivals, *'Īd al-Ghiṭās* (the festival of submersion into the Nile on 11 Tūbah/18 January) and *'Īd al-Shahīd* (the festival of the Martyr, held on 8 Bashnas = the ninth month of the Coptic calendar falling during the spring season) were abolished during the reign of the Baḥrī Mamluks by al-Malik al-Ṣāliḥ Ismāʿīl (ruled 1342–5), who ordered that the finger of a Copt be burnt. This Coptic martyr, after conversion to Islam, had dared to apostate. The Copts used to throw a representation of the Coptic martyr's fingerinto the Nile, supposedly to bring about its inundation.[15] By 1836 the year in which Lane's *An Account of the Manners and Customs of the Modern Egyptians* was published after his two visits to Egypt (1825–8 and 1833–5), the Coptic Christian festivities, then seven in number, were confined to churches and private houses and that 'On *leylet al-Gheeṭās* (in commemoration of the baptism of Christ) ... is now observed by a few of those residing in the metropolis'. To emphasize the

13 Aḥmad b. 'Alī al-Maqrīzī, *al-Mawā'iẓ wa 'l-I'tibār bi-Dhikr al-Khiṭaṭ wa 'l-Āthār* (Būlāq 1270/1853), I, 58. See also Lane, *Manners*, 500; Huda Lutfi, 'Coptic Festivals of the Nile: Aberrations of the Past?' in Philipp and Haarmann (eds), *The Mamluks*, 256–7. A similar advice is said to have been given by the Caliph 'Umar to 'Amr concerning the Library of Alexandria and the alleged order to destroy it, since 'if what is written in them agrees with the Book of God, they are not required: if it disagrees, they are not desired. Destroy them therefore'. See A.J. Butler, *The Arab Conquest of Egypt and the Last Thirty Years of the Roman Domination* (Oxford 1902), 401–26. See also S. Moreh, 'Napoleon and the French Impact on Egyptian Society in the Eyes of al-Jabartī', in Irene A. Bierman (ed.), *Napoleon in Egypt* (Los Angeles 2003), 88, 97, notes 51–2.

14 Lutfi, 'Coptic Festivals', 254–5. See also Lane, *Manners, Supplement, I.-The Copts*,535–58, and J.H. Kramer, 'al-Nīl', *EI*², VIII, 37–43.

15 Al-Maqrīzī, *al-Mawā'iẓ*, Gaston Wiet (ed.) (Cairo 1911–23), I, 70, discussed by Lutfi, 'Coptic Festivals', 263–8.

hostility between Copts and the Muslim majority, Muslims informed Lane that with every plunge into the Nile's water, the Copts exclaimed to each other 'Plunge, as thy father and grandfather plunged; and remove El-Islám from thy heart'.[16]

Muslim scholars and rulers considered the Coptic festivals of the Nile as *bida'* (sing. *bid'a*) (heretical practice), a pagan continuation of Pharaonic rituals which should be abolished by Islam. Medieval Muslim historians, before al-Jabartī, portrayed the history of the Coptic festivals in Egypt in humiliating and hostile terms, as a continuous Islamic struggle to free Egypt of 'Coptic pagan rites' as a means to emphasize the domination of victorious Islam over the indigenous Coptic population to the point that the Copts preferred to convert to Islam in great numbers.[17] While those festivals which became Christianized such as *'Īd al-Ghiṭās*, *'Īd al-Shahīd* and *'Īd al-Ṣalīb*, were gradually abolished by the Mamluk authorities, the pagan festivals of the Nile which became Islamized, such as the feast of *Wafā' al-Nīl* and its ceremony of *Kasr al-Sadd* or *al-Khalīj*, and the feast of al-Nawrūz (1 Tout) with its dramatic performance of Amīr al-Nawrūz, continued to be observed. Yet, the condemned dissolute, impudent behaviour and public revelry of drinking, dancing, music, mockery and theatrical performance, were practiced by Muslims during these Islamized Coptic festivals and the occasions of the Prophet Muḥammad's and Muslim saints' birthdays (*mawlid*s).

Al-Jabartī and his Reports on the Nile Festivals

In al-Jabartī's *Chronicle*, several Coptic festivals of the Nile that he mentioned give the impression that their practices were revived, especially during ʿAlī Bey al-Kabīr's reign, the French occupation and later during Muḥammad ʿAlī's rule. These rulers favoured Copts and other Christian minorities as well as Jews in their administrations and restricted the influence of the *mashāyikh* (religious scholars). On the *'Īd al-Ṣalīb*, the Coptic New Year celebrations were renewed, while the festival of *Wafā' al-Nīl* and *Kasr al-Sadd* (the dam piercing) or *al-Khalīj* (canal) became an important official Islamic festival celebrated with the Pashas, the Katkhudā (his deputy), Beys and the judges in

16 Lane, *Manners*, 546.

17 Lutfi, 'Coptic Festivals', 266–7.

attendance. These events were recorded annually by the historians. By 9 August 1820 (the third day of the Coptic month Misrā), the information given by our author was short, with no details: 'the Nile reached its crest. The dam was pierced on Wednesday morning and the water flowed in the Canal in the presence of Katkhuda Bey and *qāḍī*'.[18]

Most of the ceremonies of the Nile inundation mentioned by al-Jabartī, took place during the Coptic month of Misrā, but those in Babah were rarely reported, being formulated in a short, laconic phrase:[19] 'The high Nile was proclaimed. The pasha came down at dawn on [that] day, and the dam was pierced in accordance with custom. The water rushed into the Canal and the pasha returned to the Citadel'. Only when extraordinary incidents happened would al-Jabartī reveal more details of the celebration, adding that these festivals were celebrated according to the customs of the old days. From the 30 cases in which the *wafā'* is mentioned in his chronicle, the following picture of a marriage ceremony between the Nile (the male) and the thirsty land of Egypt (the female) is witnessed by the ruler, his entourage and the people:[20]

> When the Nile reaches the high level of at least 16 cubits, its inundation is proclaimed at that night by criers (*munādī*)[or according to Lane *munādī al-Nīl*] accompanied by boys, who commence their daily announcement of the Nile's rise. They make their rounds with red banners in markets and streets announcing the cresting of the river with a dialogue between the crier and the boy accompanying him [which seems to be, according to Lane's description, a long dramatic dialogue of evocation calling on God to bless the Nile to pour abundantly over the country].[21] Great crowds of people and soldiers set off to view the ceremony of piercing the dam in a manner resembling a wedding night. Many of the riffraff congregated to go to Rawḍa and the dam. As in grandiose weddings, they join parties and receptions in the houses overlooking the Canal whose owners supply them with food at their own expense to take part in the collective festival and celebration by fireworks and processions.[22] The next morning, the pasha comes down riding on horseback or in a carriage, followed by the *qāḍī*, the katkhuda,

18 *'Aj.*, IV, 310–11. The day of the cutting of the dam of the Canal is called by various terms, *Wafā' al-Nīl* (the completion or abundance of the Nile), or *Yawm Wafā' al-Baḥr*, or *Yawm Jabr al-Baḥr* (the day of the breaking of the river).

19 See ibid., II, 12. On Friday, August 8, 1777; Misrā is the 12th month of the Coptic calander.

20 See ibid., I, 30; II, 12, 24, 82, 93, 116, 145, 163, 179, 183, 196, 250; III, 14, 78, 191, 226, 262, 309, 341; IV, 16, 63, 98, 119, 146, 178, 224, 250, 289, 304, 310. For a detailed description of the celebration of *Wafā' al-Nīl*, see Lane, *Manners*, 495–505.

21 See Lane, *Manners*, 496–9.

22 See *'Aj.*, IV, 81, 98.

> *amīrs*, and notables being present with army officers and soldiers. They arrive to the mouth of the Canal amidst the customary pomp with the people promenading and sailing on skiffs, boats, and ships, which were permitted to enter the Canal, firing their rifles together with those who were standing in their houses. The custom was that governors would bestow garments of honour, and scattered gold and silver coins.[23]

Lane's description is in more detail and emphasizes the traces of pre-Islamic customs in this festival. The first 'a round pillar of earth ...' was called the '*'arooseh*' (= *'arūsa*) (doll or bride), representing the 'young virgin', whom the ancient Egyptians used to throw into the river as a sacrifice to obtain a plentiful inundation. The second is the very large decorated boat called the ''Aḳabeh', believed to represent the vessel in which the virgin of the Nile is carried to be thrown into the river.[24]

On the other hand the performance of *Jabr al-Khalīj* or *Kasr al-Sadd* (the Piercing of the Dam), bears significant features of a wedding night with sexual symbols. It was attended by dancing-girls, singers, musicians, and reciters of romances amid an exhibition of fire-works with firing from guns and gun-boats. When the Governor of the metropolis arrives, the *qāḍī* writes a document, as in the wedding ceremony, to be sent to Constantinople to attest to the fact of the river's having risen to a height sufficient for the opening of the canal and of this operation having been performed. Lane goes on to describe theclear significance of the sexual act celebrated in the ceremony by the collective unconsciousness of the crowd,[25] where the boat represents a phallic symbol, by saying: 'When the dam has been cut away to the degree above mentioned, and all the great officers whose presence is required have arrived, ... A boat, on board of which is an officer ... is propelled against the narrow ridge of earth, and, breaking the slight barrier, passes through it, and descends with the cataract thus formed'.[26]

During the French occupation, there are more details, which reveal the old custom of celebration with actors performing farces and theatrical plays to ridicule their Mamluk oppressors: 'The commander in chief [Napoleon]

23 See *'Aj.*, III, 191, 226.

24 Lane, *Manners*, 500–3.

25 See Wilyam Naẓīr, *al-'Ādāt al-Miṣriyya bayn al-Ams wa 'l-Yawm* (Cairo 1967), 50, who also thinks that the Nile symbolizes the male entering, as in a wedding, his virgin wife, the Land of Egypt.

26 Lane, *Manners*, 503.

ordered the preparation and decoration of the boat called al-ʿAqaba as usual. The *amīr*s also decorated several ships and galleons and called upon the people to go out for their promenades along the Nile and the Nilometer and al-Rawḍa, as was their habit. The commander in chief sent orders to (Muṣṭafā Bey), the *katkhuda* of Bakr Pasha, the *qāḍī*, the members of the *Dīwān*, and the members of the council, the office holders, and others to present themselves in the morning. He rode with them in a pageant with full decorations, with his army, drums, and horns to the palace at the bridge of the dam (*Qaṣr Qanṭarat al-Sadd*). The dam was pierced in their presence while they celebrated with cannon shots and fireworks (*shannik madāfi' wa-nufūṭ*), until the water flowed in the canal (*khalīj*). Then he rode back with the same escort to his residence. Nevertheless, none of the inhabitants went out that night for pleasure trips in boats, as was the custom — nobody, that is, except the Syrian Christians, the Copts, the Greek Orthodox, the local foreigners, and their wives. Only a few idle people were present in the morning'.[27]

However, because of the decisive importance of the annual inundation of the Nile on the economy of Egypt, the increase and decrease of the water level during the season of the *Wafā'* caused either rejoicing or panic among the inhabitants. Whenever there were signs of the Nile overflowing, the price of corn stabilised to the general rejoicing of the people, but when the crest of the Nile was delayed, people were greatly disturbed and merchants removed grain from the markets causing theprices to rise. In such cases, the Pasha would order prayers for water (*'amal al-istisqā'*) and to beseech God to raise the Nile level to its regular height. For this reason the rulers asked those people whom God answers their prayers, the descendants of the Prophet (*sādāt* and *ashrāf*), the shaykhs, and the scholars of al-Azhar and the people, mainly the children, the sick and the weak among them, to go out into the desert to be nearer to God or to go to the holy places, such as the Mosque of ʿAmr b. al-ʿĀṣ, where it was believed that prayers made would be responded to by God. The brave *'ulamā'* would dare to ask the rulers to repent, to be kind to people and stop their oppression, so that God might have mercy upon his creatures.[28] In case that there was a need for support to the Muslim prayers, Christians would also be invited to join in the prayers. 'That night, Monday (Jumādā II 1223 [/25

27 See *'Aj.*, III, 14–15, according to the English translationof *'Ajā'ib.* edited by Philipp and Perlmann.

28 See *'Aj.*, IV, 80–1.

July–23 August 1808]), the water rose and the cresting [of the dam] was proclaimed. The people rejoiced, and the Christians began to say, "It would not have risen if we had not come out"'.[29] However, two years later, Shaʿbān 1225 (/31 August–29 September 1810), when the Nile stopped rising, the Copts and Christians were also asked to pray for water and boasted that 'when the Nile stopped rising the year before last the people went to pray for water in the mosque of ʿAmr b. al-ʿĀṣ. The Christians went out the next day, and that night the waters rose'. Al-Jabartī, who was sure of the superiority of Islam and hostile to Christians,[30] commented, revealing the general aversion of the *'ulamā'* to non-Muslims: 'That is groundless. It was no surprise that the Nile rose at that time, because those days were the end of Misrā and the five or six days of the twelfth Coptic month of Nasī and Nawrūz when the Nile usually rises'.[31]

The celebrations during the *Wafā' al-Nīl* day, which had been Islamized for a long time, as well as the wedding and circumcision celebrations, were similar to Ramaḍān festivities. When the crescent moon was seen, and the customary festivities were announced by cannon fire, the procession of the *muḥtasib* and guild chiefs rode out.[32] They participated in the pageantry of coaches or floats depicting the shops of various guilds engaged in their profession, such as carpenters, bakers, blacksmiths, weavers and confectioners to the accompaniment of the drums and pipes.[33] Numerous other groups would join this celebration such as the heads of the guilds, entertainers, corporations, groups of Upper Egyptians, and some of the residents of Būlāq and other places.[34] Another occasion with similar parades was the Maḥmal[35] with the pomp of its processions of dervishes, the Rifāʿiyyees among them some bearing spikes which they thrust violently into their eyes, men armed with swords and shields enacting a mock battle, a horseman with a 'grotesque false beard with moustaches formed of two long brown feathers' playing the part of a Muftī pretending to write 'fetwās'. The Maḥmal followed after these groups

29 See ibid., IV, 80.

30 See ibid., IV, 49.

31 See ibid., IV, 122.

32 On *muḥtasib*, the supervisor of bazaars and trade, see Lane, *Manners*, 125.

33 See ibid., IV,198–9, 224. Cf. Moreh, *Live Theatre*, 58, figure 5, 64–83.

34 See *'Aj.*, IV, 91, in the procession of the circumcision of ʿUmar Makram's grandson on 1224 [/1809–10]. Cf. also, *'Aj.*, II, 224.

35 On the Maḥmal litter carried the *kiswa* in procession to Mecca, see Lane, *Manners*, 443–4.

of performers with the procession of the *kisweh*. After two or three weeks, the great caravan of pilgrims followed.

Amīr al-Nawrūz

Muslim *'ulamā'*, following the saying (*ḥadīth*) of the Prophet Muḥammad that life should be dedicated to prayers, *jihād* and the hereafter, did not encourage entertainment. Pious Christian dignitaries, Muslim rulers and scholars would from time to time prohibit the celebration of Nawrūz and other Coptic feasts.[36] Yet, the gap between the religious scholars and common people was so great that prohibition did not stop its development among the masses. These customs were sometimes secretly practiced in the metropolis, in its taverns of wine and *ḥashīsh*, while in distant villages to which such decrees of prohibitions rarely arrived, the pagan customs of Nawrūz and the performance of its Amīr al-Nawrūz procession and the Nile festivals continued. The festival of Nawrūz or Nayrūz (New Year's day) was considered by Muslim scholars as pagan of Pharaonic origin. In fact it is a Persian term, which the Egyptians adopted when Egypt was under Persian rule. It was celebrated on March 21 every year (in the Coptic month of Tūt [Coptic: Thout]),[37] and is still celebrated in Iran. This Islamized celebration was condemned by Muslim scholars as a heretical (*bid'a*) Pharaonic custom, because of the folly and revelry of Amīr al-Nawrūz, who rules for one day in a world set upside down with the rabble ruling and imposing taxes.[38]

Only in rare cases were these events recorded. European travellers, curious to witness ancient fertility festivals and carnivals, recorded them as in the case of the traveller J.J. Rifaud, who engraved pictures of the procession of Amīr

36 On Nawrūz, see Lutfi, 'Coptic Festivals', 254–82.

37 See I. Lassy, *The Muharram Mysteries among the Azarbeijan Turks of Caucasia* (Helsingfors, printed by Lilius and Hertsberg, 1916); Mary Boyce, *A History of Zoroastrianism* (Leiden 1975), vol. I, 224, 245; vol. II, 108–10; J. Patel, 'The Navroz, its History and its Significance', *Journal of the K.R. Cama Institute* (Bombay), XXXI (1937), 1–51.

38 Ibn al-Ḥājj, *al-Madkhal*, II, 49–51. Cf. Moreh, *Live Theatre*, 47–51. There is a striking similarity between the pagan festivals such as the Greek spring festival and the orgiastic nocturnal festival, the *Maiumas*, which recurred every three years and that of later Coptic festivals. In both, people kindled large numbers of lamps along the river banks, in the main streets, in public and private buildings and in markets during these two feasts. Both festivals were celebrated for seven days 'with singing and shouting and lewd behaviours' (see Moreh, *Live Theatre*, 8–11).

al-Nawrūz in detail during his work in Egypt between the years 1805–27.[39] The details of these engravings illustrate precisely the descriptions of the medieval Egyptian historians such as Ibn Zūlāq (d. 997), al-Qazwīnī (1203–1338), Ibn al-Ḥājj al-Fāsī (d. 1336), al-Maqrīzī (1364–1442), Ibn Iyās (d. 1524), and others. This festival procession resembles the 'Feast of Fools' in which a play of a 'temporary king' or 'false *amīr*' is enacted to symbolize the expulsion of winter or the driving out of the old year. According to Ibn al-Ḥājj, the Amīr al-Nawrūz would change his countenance with lime and flour and stick a beard of fur or the like on his face, dressed in a red or yellow garment, with a long conical cap (*ṭurṭūr*) on his head and ride an ugly donkey. Moreover, he would be surrounded with green palm branches and bunches of dates, holding a ledger in his hand and imposing taxes[40] on shop keepers and houses, and knocking on doors as if imposing taxes, but instead asking payment for their performance.[41] During this festival Egyptian historians describe the immoral behaviour of people drinking wine, frolicking with water and wine, splashing it on their friends, throwing each others' turbans around and slapping each other with leather mats and slippers, lighting fires, roving the streets carrying statues, with comical figures, music and singing accompanied by entertainers with comic masks and costumes.[42]

Profane Performances

Beside these ancient festivals of religious background, there were various types of profane performances of merrymaking, festive celebrations of weddings and circumcision with mimicry to ridicule enemies or performed for didactic purposes. Such theatrical performances and mimicry are mentioned in Egyptian historical works more than they are in other Arabic speaking lands. Among the first such performances in Egypt known to us is connected with the Abbasid governor, Aḥmad Ibn Ṭūlūn (835–84) the founder of the Ṭūlūnid dynasty, who wasridiculously mimed by al-Ḥusayn b. Abī Shaʿra the comedian (*muḍḥik*) of al-Mutawakkil. The latter dressed in the same turban and attire as Ibn Ṭūlūn and imitated his way of sitting and speaking, an act

39 Shoshan, *Popular Culture*, 50–1.

40 Ibn al-Ḥājj, *al-Madkhal*, II, 52.

41 See ibid., II, 51–2. Cf. Moreh, *Live Theatre*, 50–1, 94.

42 See Moreh, *Live Theatre*, 48–51; Lutfi, 'Coptic Festivals', 265–6.

which led to him being flogged and his house being demolished.[43] The princess Qaṭr al-Nadā also paid an enormous sum of money for both masked performers (*samājāt*) and servant girls to play with the *ṣafā'ina* (slapstick comedians) to celebrate Nawrūz.[44] In another Egyptian festival, the historian al-Musabbiḥī (d. 1029), described the procession of entertainers during the pilgrimage to the prison of Joseph including statues, comic figures, mimers and masked actors.[45]

Ibn al-Ḥājj (d. 1336), gives an explicit description of the *mukhāyilūn* (live actors) performing a play (*khayāl*) called *Bābat al-Qāḍī* (the Scene of the Judge). The actor wore the complete attire of a Muslim judge with a large turban, long wide sleeves and a long garment (*ṭaylasīn*). The play was performed with the actor dancing in the attire, voicing rude remarks, amid the mockery and applause of the audience expressing their disapproval of the judges' biased judgments.[46]

The term *khayāl* (plays performed by live actors) is used by al-Jabartī only when quoting al-Damurdāshī (d. after 1755), dealing with the great feast held after the plague given by Amīr ʿAbd al-Raḥmān Bey (d. 1113/1701–2) to celebrate the circumcision of his son. ʿAbu 'l-Yusr, the dancer (*al-jink*), performed his dances day and night at the celebration held at the *dīwān* of al-Ghawrī; Jewish male dancers (*jink al-Yahūd*) performed at the celebration held at the *dīwān* of Qā'itbāy, while other entertainers (*arbāb al-malā'ib* = snake charmers and monkey trainers), acrobats (*bahālawīn*) and performers of live plays (*al-khayāl*), performed in the courtyards.[47] Both rulers and subjects,

---

43 Aḥmad b. Yūsuf Ibn al-Dāya, *Kitāb al-Mukāfa'a wa-Ḥusn al-'Uqbā*, Maḥmūd Muḥammad Shākir (ed.)(Cairo 1940), 86 and ʿAbd Allāh al-Madanī al-Balawī, *Sīrat Aḥmad b. Ṭūlūn*, Muḥammad Kurd ʿAlī (ed.)(Damascus 1358/1939), 148f.

44 Ibn al-Dāya, *Kitāb al-Mukāfa'a*, 38.

45 Muḥammad b. ʿUbayd Allāh al-Musabbiḥī, *Akhbār Miṣr*, Ayman Fu'ād Sayyid and Thierry Bianquis (eds)(Cairo 1978), 39, 41–3; note 13 above, al-Maqrīzī, *al-Khiṭaṭ* (Būlāq 1270/1854), IV, 245. See Shmuel Moreh, 'acting and actors, medieval', *Encyclopedia of Arabic Literature*, 1, 52–4.

46 Ibn al-Ḥājj, *al-Madkhal*, 146.

47 *'Aj.*, I, 100. Cf. Aḥmad al-Damurdāshī, *Kitāb al-Durra al-Muṣāna fī Akhbār al-Kināna*, ʿAbd al-Raḥīm ʿAbd al-Raḥmān ʿAbd al-Raḥīm (ed.)(Cairo 1989), 31 and its translation into English by Daniel Crecelius and ʿAbd al-Wahhab Bakr, *al-Damurdashi's Chronicle of Egypt 1688–1755* (Leiden 1991), 65 and the book review by Shmuel Moreh, in *Die Welt des Islams*, 237–8. Al-Damurdāshī's version has more details, distinguishing between *khayāl* and *muḥabbaẓīn*, considering the former a 'shadow play': وأتى أبو اليسر الجنكي ديوان الغوري بمماليكه وجنك اليهود في ديوان قايتباي والحواة والقريداتية والخيال والأدبا والمحنبزين في حوش الديوان. While al-Jabartī (*'Aj.*,I,

Muslims and non-Muslims, especially the Copts, were keen to join the ceremonies and festivals. These entertainments would serve as an outlet for their hardships from the calamities of nature connected with the Nile, like famine, drought, plagues, and poverty, which were attributed to both God's punishment due to the rulers' injustice and cruelty.[48]

Wafā' al-Nīl

During the French occupation, the Copts felt free to celebrate the Nile day according to their old customs as an upside down festival with theatrical performances. Indeed, the Copts who were fond of merry making to ease their feeling a persecuted minority were always under pressure of exploitation and taxes. They used every opportunity arising during the French occupation to exercise their relative freedom to rejoice with the French their victories, an act that aroused the anger and the disdain of the Muslims. When the French conquered the fortress at al-ʿArīsh (25 Ramaḍān 1213 [/2 March 1799]), the Christians surrendered and joined the French celebrations. They 'showed their happiness and joy in the streets and at home. They gave banquets in their houses, changed their clothes and headgear, gathered for pleasure and merrymaking'. Al-Jabartī expressed his wrath against this, accusing such celebrations as being 'accompanied by much abominable licentiousness', because they did not confine themselves to the *dhimma* restrictions in order to avoid offending Muslim feelings.[49]

Al-Jabartī's description of the Nile celebration by Christians of Eastern Mediterranean origin is of great significance, because traces of the resurrection of ancient fertility gods were dominant in their popular heritage, festivals and carnivals.[50] Their festivities included theatrical performances 'in the manner of the previous *amīrs*'. During the French occupation these theatrical

100) summarized the sentence by giving *arbāb al-malā'īb* as synonyms for *al-ḥuwāt wa 'l-quraydātiyya*, he used the term *al-khayāl* as a synonym for *al-muḥabbazīn*: وأبو اليسر الجنكي ملازم بديوان الغوري ليلا ونهارا وجنك اليهود بديوان قايتباي وأرباب الملاعيب والبهالوين والخيال بالحيشان... On 'Jink' or 'Gink' as male dancers 'generally Jews, Armenians, Greeks, and Turks', see Lane, *Manners*, 389, 464. On *arbāb al-malāhī* and *arbāb al-malā'īb*, see *'Aj.*, I, 100, 146, 220, 252, II, 100, 224, 227.

48 See *istisqā'*, p. 288, above, and Shoshan, *Popular Culture*, 4–7.

49 *'Aj.*, III, 46. It seems that they changed clothes and headgear to perform farces and comedies, cf. ibid., III, 78.

50 Ibid., III, 78.

performances were performed in public 'miming and mocking Muslims'. Our author frequently mentioned such performances:

> Monday, 24 Rabīʿ I 1214 [/26 August 1799/ 9 Mesra], was the day of the inundation of the blessed Nile (*wafā' al-Nīl*). The local Christians, Copts, Syrians, and Greeks went out and made ready for dissipation, revelry, merrymaking, amusement, and entertainment. That night they went to Būlāq, Old Cairo, and Rawḍa. They rented barges and boarded them, taking along musical instruments and singers. During this night, they lost all self-control, discarded all decency, and behaved in the manner of the previous *amīr*s, going on boats with many oars in the company of their women and whores, drinking and displaying publicly the vilest laughter and mockery (*sukhriyya*), blaspheming and ridiculous imitation (*muḥākāt*) of the Muslims. One of them dressed up like an Egyptian *amīr*, wearing armour, imitating them and their expressions (*ḥākā alfāẓahum*) by way of mockery and satire (*istihzā' wa 'l-sukhriyya*)'.[51]

What al-Jabartī termed as *ḥākī* and *muḥakāt* should be understood as theatrical performance by live actors in the manner of the *muḥabbaẓīn* described by Lane.[52] The information given by the *Courier de l'Egypte*, about an Arabic play given by General Yaʿqūb al-Qubṭī in 1798 confirms that the Copts had troupes of actors of a high standard that Yaʿqūb found it appropriate to invite a troupe of them to perform for Bonaparte and his generals: 'Muʿallem Yaʿcoub, commandant general des legions qobtes', put on a 'representation d'un comédie arabe' after a magnificent dinner to Bonaparte and his generals.[53] This fact of a comedy given by Coptic actors, confirms al-Jabartī's information above that the mockery and satire of the Copts during the Nile celebrations were comedies and farces as in the case of the farce described by Lane.

During the *Wafā' al-Nīl* of 1215 (/1800–1), filling the *Khalīj* (Canal), Egyptian women mingled with the French in a dissolute manner on boats. The Egyptian sailors who were reported by European travellers as performing

51 Ibid., III, 78, 162 (where *muḥākāt* and *taqlīd* [mimicry and imitation] are used as synonyms).

52 On *ḥikāya* as impersonation and plays, see Moreh, *Live Theatre*, 87–105. On the *muḥabbaẓīn*, see Lane, *Manners*, 172, 395.

53 *Courier de l'Égypte*, no. 102, 24 pluviouse, IXᵉ année de la République. On the French theatre in Cairo during the French occupation, see the *Courier de l'Égypte*, nos. 95, 98, 102. For the French text of the *Courier* with an Arabic translation, see Ṣalāḥ al-Dīn al-Bustānī, *Ṣuḥuf Būnabārt fī Miṣr, 1798–1801* (Cairo 1971).

farces,[54] would joke and clown (*hazl wa-mujūn*) imitating French expressions in their songs and their conversations.[55]

Not only did the Copts mock their rivals and enemies in a vengeful fashion by performing farces and plays, but Muslims actors's mockery included religious scholars. When Muḥammad al-Dawākhilī, was dismissed from his office and banished to Dasūq (1231 [/1815–16]), many of his jealous colleagues among those who pretended to be knowledgeable in *fiqh* (*mutafaqqihūn*), rejoiced at his fall and celebrated the occasion with parties, banquets and comedies (*walā'im wa-'azā'im wa-muḍḥikāt*)[56] most probably ridiculing him and rejoicing at his mishaps and fall.

Our author recorded the opening of the French theatre, *Comédie Française*, in al-Azbakiyya, in Cairo on 11 Shaʿbān 1215 (/29 December 1800), to which he gave the French term *al-Kumidī* (Comedy) with the relevant Arabic performing term *malā'īb*. He defined the theatre as 'a place in which they gather every ten nights to watch plays (*malā'īb*) which they performed (*yal'abuhā*) for the purpose of amusement and entertainment (*tasallī wa 'l-malāhī*) for four hours each night in their language'.[57]

Muḥammad ʿAlī, who took power in 1805, and his family were more liberal towards European officials and towards the customs of non-Muslim subjects. His son Ibrāhīm Pasha is accused by al-Jabartī of being a heretic, 'an ignorant youth … of no knowledge of the law (*sharī'a*) or of what is good or evil'.[58] The new ruling family's attitude towards the Copts in particular, Christians and Jews was more tolerant than the Ottomans or the Mamluks. Al-Jabartī gives a lot of information concerning entertainments and theatrical performances during the French occupation and Muḥammad ʿAlī's reign. However, while the French were tolerant towards the *'ulamā'* and keen to acquire their cooperation, Muḥammad ʿAlī, who was able to assend to power

54 See C.D. Warner, *My Winter on the Nile* (Hartford 1904), 314f.

55 *'Aj.*, IV, 162. Cf. *'Aj.*, IV, 69.

56 Ibid., IV, 244–5, 294.

57 On the French theatre 'Kumidī' (Comédie), see *'Aj.*, III, 142. On the awareness of some Egyptians of theatrical comedy in London, see Lane, *Manners*, 232, dealing with the 'kumedyeh' (or comedy), described to an Egyptian by an 'Algerine', who gave 'an account of a spectacle of this kind which he had seen in London'. On Napoleon's theatre in Egypt, see P.C. Sadgrove, *The Egyptian Theatre in the Nineteenth Century, 1799–1882* (Reading 1996), 27–31.

58 *'Aj.*, IV, 184–5.

with their help, rewarded themby restricting their influence and limiting their economic concessions.[59] The ruling family is portrayed by our author, as in the case of the Abbasid historian who slandered the Umayyad dynasty, by putting the emphasis upon their interest in secular life and entertainment rather than on religion. According to al-Jabartī Albanian soldiers were accused of arriving, in Ramaḍān 1224/November 1809, with a group of effeminate men (*mukhannathūn*) known as *khawal* who spoke like women and played on tambourine (*duff*) and drum (*ṭunbūr*).[60] Aḥmad Pasha Ṭūsūn, the son of Muḥammad ʿAlī, 'took with him to Istanbul singers and musicians such as al-Warrāq, al-Ḥabbābī, Qashwa' and others, while from Turkey came a troupe of dancers (*raqqāṣūn*) who joined him in his palace in Barnibāl'.[61]To prove that the ruler and his family deviated from the venerated custom of respecting the religious scholars, our author related how Ibrāhīm Pasha ignored and by doing this humiliated the *'ulamā'* who came to congratulate him after his safe arrival from Quṣayr (17 Ṣafar 1235 [/5 December 1819]). He did not stand up for them, and did not answer their greetings. Instead he pretended to speak with a comedian (*shakhṣ sukhriyya*) until they left ashamed and humiliated.[62] When Ibrāhīm Pasha defeated the Wahhābī forces, a pompous festival and celebrations took place with sham fortresses (*qilāʿ*).[63]

Lane gave us a long description of a long 'low and ridiculous farce', performed in the presence of the Pasha by about ten *muḥabbaẓīn* (live male actors), dressed and equipped with props suitable for the various *dramatis personae* of men and women. This comedy was played during a festival in honour of the circumcision of one of Muḥammad ʿAlī Pasha's sons, 'with the view of opening his eyes to the conduct of those persons to whom was committed the office of collecting the taxes' and to attract his attention to their corruption and bribery.[64]

The actors were not always safe to perform farces ridiculing religious scholars and Muslim judges, as in the case of medieval Arab theatre of which Ibn al-Ḥājj warned. When Shaykh Shams al-Dīn Abu 'l-Anwār the *khalīfa* of

59 Ibid., IV, 32–3, 191–3.

60 Ibid., IV, 101.

61 Ibid., IV, 264.

62 Ibid., IV, 306.

63 Ibid., IV, 297–8.

64 Lane, *Manners*, 395–7.

the noble Sādāt al-Wafā'iyya (d. 1228/1813) was informed 'that several citizens of Cairo (*awlād al-balad*) [= comedians] and notables, gathered one night ... began to satirize and imitate (*yaskhar wa-yuqallid*) the manners of important personages... and that they included him in their farces and comedies (*sukhriyyatihim*), he had them summoned one by one in order to reprimand and humble them with a flogging'.[65]

The Amīr Muḥammad Agha al-Bārūdī (d. 1205/1790–1), who was fond of amusement and joking with his boon companions whom al-Jabartī described as *nudamā' wa-julasā' min al-luṭafā' wa-awlād al-balad*, should be understood as, 'boon companions and local entertainers performing comedies and farces'.[66] The term *laṭīf* (pl. *luṭafā'*) seems to be used as a common expression in Arab theatrical terminology. Both al-Jabartī and Ya'qūb Ṣanūa' use the well-established terms of *awlād al-balad* and sometimes they add the adjective *liṭāf* (witty) and *ẓirāf* (graceful) for popular local actors and comedians.[67] Ṣanūa' in his play *Mulyīr Miṣr wa-Mā Yuqāsīhi* (The Molière of Egypt and What He Suffers) attempts to depict actual trouble with his actors who demanded to be paid the same high payment received by the actors at the Opera and the *Comédie*. Isṭifān, a loyal actor of Ṣanūa''s, observes that 'these people think there are no actors in all Egypt except them', but that he has found 'twenty nice local actors (*'ishrīn li''ib min awlād al-balad al-liṭāf*), so we are not afraid of their intimidation'.[68] Already, a play composed by 'Alī Ibn Mawlāhum al-Khayālī's (a contemporary of Ibn Dāniyāl (d. 710/1310–11) *al-Maqāma al-Mukhtaṣara fi 'l-Khamsīn Marra*, refers to professional women as *ẓirāf* (witty entertainers), a synonym of *liṭāf*.[69]

It seems that these dramatic activities, as described by al-Jabartī and as recorded by many travellers to Egypt, gave a new impetus to theatrical performance. Among these European travellers who gave important

---

65 *'Aj.*, IV, 191. Our translation differs from the English translation in Philipp and Perlmann, II, 369.

66 *'Aj.*, II, 223. On *Awlād al-Balad*, see *Owlád el-Beled* in Lane, *Manners*, 27.

67 See *'Aj.*, I, 219, II, 223 (*wa 'ttakhadha lahu nudamā' wa-julasā' min al-liṭāf wa-awlād al-balad*); IV, 191. See Moreh, *Live Theatre*, 134.

68 See Y. Ṣanūa', *Mulyīr Miṣr*, in Muḥammad Yūsuf Najm, *al-Masraḥ al-'Arabī, Dirāsāt wa-Nuṣūṣ, 3, Ya'qūb Ṣannū' (Abū Naḍḍāra)*(Beirut 1963), 189; Moreh, *Live Theatre*, 161–2; Sadgrove, *The Egyptian Theatre*, 111–15.

69 See 'Alī Ibn Mawlāhum al-Khayālī, in his play, *al-Maqāma al-Mukhtaṣara fi 'l-Khamsīn Marra*, British Library MS., shelf mark: Add. 29411; cf. Moreh, *Live Theatre*, 134.

descriptions of live actors and troupes mainly in Egypt are the Danish C. Niebuhr (1733–1815), the Italian Giovanni Belzoni (before 1815), James Saint-John (1833), John Bowring (1839), the Prussian G. Wetzstein in Damascus (1857), the Briton Edward Lane (*c.* 1857), C.D. Warner (1874–5), R.L.N. Michell (1877) and A.J. Butler (1881). Their descriptions of Egyptian actors performing farces and plays in popular Egyptian theatre prove with no doubt the existence of indigenous live drama in Arabic, which reveals clearly its connection with Arab medieval theatre.[70]

Al-Jabartī's wealth of terms and descriptions of daily life in Cairo in his *'Ajā'ib al-Āthār* can shed new light on many forgotten and obscure Shamanic cultural and religious activities and performing art, during the historic span of his chronicle (1100–1221/1688–1807). There are a few dramatic terms and customs which al-Jabartī took the trouble to define and describe in his book.[71] On the other hand, he neglected to define some important terms of religious customs, entertainments and performing arts, which he might have considered to be clear to his contemporary readers. Other terms show that he considered some guilds and low professions as unworthy of description and discussion. Our author condemned the common people, especially the Egyptian fellahs, since he considered their manners and practices as indecent, against sober religious behaviour. He accused actors of dealing with obscenities and vulgar mocking intending to insult respectable people such as *'ulamā'* and Mamluk *amīr*s, whom the actors ridiculed in their entertainments. The British scholar and engraver, Edward William Lane (1801–76), was al-Jabartī's contemporary and possessed a copy of his first three volumes of *'Ajā'ib al-Āthār.* While he used al-Zabīdī's *Tāj al-'Arūs* for his Arabic-English Lexicon, he used al-Jabartī's work as a guide for his thorough research in his *Manners and Customs of the Modern Egyptians*, taking the trouble to illustrate and deal in length with many terms and aspects of Egyptian religious and cultural popular manners and customs. In this way, he fills most of the gaps left by al-Jabartī, who as a historian did not consider it his duty to define and explain to the Egyptians aspects of their religion and daily life.

---

70 See Moreh, *Live Theatre*, 154–8 and Sadgrove, *The Egyptian Theatre*, 1–26.

71 See the Arabic Index and Glossary of *'Ajā'ib al-Āthār* dealing with *muḥabbaẓūn*, *hazl*, *masākhir*, etc. in our Arabic edition of *'Ajā'ib al-Āthār*.

When Lane arrived in Cairo in 1825 or 1826, it was soon after the death of ʿAbd al-Raḥmān al-Jabartī.[72] This date was as close to al-Jabartī's death in May 1825 as was possible to detect according to the *Waqf* documents explored by the Egyptian scholar Dr Muḥammad Anīs.[73] It is most fortunate for students of Egypt that Lane, although he did not have the chance of meeting al-Jabartī, was able to add his descriptions and illustrations from the point of view of a European scholar and artist with sharp observation and intellectual curiosity. He was able to describe many contemporary manners, customs, culture, arts, architecture, popular religion, folklore, superstitions, and literary aspects in Cairo from the point of view of a European, who was curious about the special features of Islamic and Egyptian culture which were unknown in the West. Thus, Lane's book can serve, certainly, as an important supplementary source to al-Jabartī's descriptions of religious practices, customs, manners, social structure, education, men and women, and high and low society, using terminology which help us to verify obscure terms the exact meaning of which both modern indigenous scholars and orientalists were uncertain.[74]

Both al-Jabartī and Lane have enabled historians to solve one of the enigmas of Arab culture and to reveal the fact that there was a live theatrical tradition of mimics, and itinerant actors in Egypt, along with other popular entertainments such as shadow theatre performers, farce-players, dancers, musicians, storytellers, acrobats, rope-dancers, monkey trainers, and pageants.[75] These entertainers used to perform in public places such as coffee houses, markets, parks and town squares, as well as in the palaces of local rulers. These performances were given during religious or secular rituals and

72 Lane, *Manners*, 222.

73 See Chapter One above.

74 See Chapter Two above. It seems that during this visit Lane acquired his copy of the *'Ajā'ib* MS now held in the British Library in London (see above Chapter Two, III. 4. 2 a–c, shelf no. Or. 4628–4630, 'Bought of Dr. N.I.L. Tisrud [representing the heirs of Mr. E.W. Lane']).

75 See Lane, *Manners*, *'ālima* pl. *'awālim* (female singer), 172, 195, 361–2, 506; *bahluwān* (rope-dancer), 394; *ghawázee* (dancing-girls), 180, 196, 384–5, 434, 506, 509, or *barámikeh* (dancing men and girls), 386, 393; *ḥāwī* (performer of sleight of hand tricks with serpents), 391; *qurayḍātī* (Lane: *ḳureydátee*)(monkey handler), 395; *khawal* (dancing men), 180, 398, 509; *moḥabbazoon* (*muḥabbaẓūn*)(itinerant actors or farce-players), Lane, *Manners*, 172, 395–6; *khalbooṣ*, 507 (a dancer's servant for collecting *nuquṭ* (largesse) or a farce player, live actor), or as ʿAbd al-Wahhāb al-Shaʿrānī (1565), called them in his *Laṭā'if al-Minan* (Cairo 1321/1903), II, 172 '*khalbūṣ al-maghānī*' (buffoon), see C. Brakel and S. Moreh, 'Reflections on the Term *Bāba*: From Medieval Arabic Plays to Contemporary Javanese Masked Theatre', *Edebiyāt* 7, 21–39.

private occasions as well as religious and seasonal public celebrations, such as during Ramaḍān, *mawlid*s, the New Year Festival (Nayrūz), and at the celebration of events such as births, circumcisions, and weddings. Lane transcribed the term *muḥabbaẓūn* as *moḥabbaẓeen* to indicate actors of live theatre,[76] who perform with dialogues, gestures, clothes, head gear, a staff, to represent an incident which happened in the past or present, giving the audience the allusion that it is happening in the present. This term, among many terms for entertainments used by al-Jabartī, was familiar to earlier historians and playwrights such as the writer and actor, Muḥammad Ibn Dāniyāl (d. 1310), author of three shadow plays. In his shadow play *Bābat Ṭayf al-Khayāl*, one of the characters, the Amīr Wiṣāl, introduces himself as *anā muḥabbaẓ al-Shayṭān* ('I am the live actor of Satan').[77] Lane described them as men and boys who perform the parts of women in female attire, with vulgar jests and indecent actions. Al-Jabartī mentions them among the lowest guilds such as *arbāb al-malā'ib wa 'l-mughazlikīn,*[78] *wa 'l-junbādhiyya wa 'l-ḥaqqababẓiyya wa 'l-ḥababẓiyya, wa 'l-ḥuwāt wa 'l-qirdātiyya wa 'l-raqqāṣīn wa 'l-barāmika* (entertainers, itinerant singers, acrobats, jugglers (performer of tricks with cups), live actors, snake charmers, monkey handlers, male dancers and unveiled women dancers called *ghawāzī* or *barāmika*).[79] In another place, he used the verbs *yaskhar wa-yuqallid* for playing farce and imitating personalities including Abu 'l-Wafā al-Sādāt using the term *sukhriyya* for comedy.[80]

Both al-Jabartī and Lane described *Ṣūfī* orders and their practices and gave us important descriptions of their popular religious culture, performed by common people who were condemned by al-Jabartī pointing to the Shamanic roots of *mawlid*s, the Nile festivals, the Nawrūz festive processions, and Coptic celebrations. Some Muslim scholars, such as Ibn al-Ḥājj al-ʿAbdarī[81] attribute these to Egypt's Pharaonic festivals.

---

76 Lane, *Manners*, 395–7. Lane, *Manners*, terms it 'Nórooz', 504. *'Aj.*,III, 108.

77 Ibn Dāniyāl in Ibrāhīm Ḥamāda, *Khayāl al-Ẓill: wa-Tamthīliyyāt Ibn Dāniyāl* (Cairo 1963), 154.

78 For *mughazlikūn* as 'itinerant singers' (*chanteur ambulant*), see E. Fagnan, *Additions aux dictionnaires arabes* (Alger 1923), 126. My thanks are due to Dr P.C. Sadgrove for pointing out this dictionary to me.

79 *'Aj.*, IV, 198. In *'Aj.*, III, 70, the entertainers called *khalābīṣ* (sing. *khalbūṣ*) are added. On *khalbūṣ* see the article by Brakel and Moreh, in note 75 above. Lane, *Manners*, 386–7, 393.

80 *'Aj.*, IV, 191.

81 See Ibn al-Ḥājj, *al-Madkhal*, II, 49–52.

Live Actors (muḥabbaẓūn)

One of the main enigmas in studying medieval Arabic culture is whether the Arabs were aware of performances of drama prior to their contact with Europe during the French invasion of Egypt. Lane's description of the entertainers of the performing arts called *Moḥabbaẓeen* as 'players of low and ridiculous farces ... chiefly by vulgar jests, and indecent actions, that they amuse, and obtain applause', who 'perform ... at the houses of the great; and sometimes attract rings of auditors and spectators in the public places in Cairo'. Lane's detailed descriptions can fill the gaps, which are left by al-Jabartī's undefined terminology of the same term. Lane's description of these players is from the point of view of a puritan Victorian English intellectual who is used to highbrow Shakespearian drama and a high standard of dramatic and theatrical performance. From Lane's description of al-Jabartī's terminology, it is clear that these players were performing an indigenous theatrical play deeply rooted in Islamic culture. The play that he witnessed *c.* 1834 was performed in order to reconstruct an imaginary or real event. 'The *dramatis personae* were a Náẓir (or governor of a district), a Sheykh Beled (or chief of a village), a servant of the latter, a Copt clerk, a Felláḥ indebted to the government, his wife, and five other persons, of whom two made their appearance first in the character of drummers, one as a hautboy-player, and the two others as dancers'. The play deals with corruption and sexual extortion committed by government officials during their tax collection 'with the view of opening the eyes [of the Báshà].[82]

The term *muḥabbaẓīn* (sing. *muḥabbaẓ*) with its synonym *ḥababẓiyya*,[83] is defined by Lane as farce players or live actors.[84] On the last Friday of

82 Lane, *Manners*, 172, 395–7. On the *muḥabbaẓūn*, see Moreh, *Live Theatre*, 152–60. On live theatre see the *Encyclopedia of Arabic Literature*, articles by Moreh: 'acting and actors, medieval'; 'Shadow-play'; 'Masks and Masqueraders'; '*Khayāl*'; '*Mukhannath*'; the actor 'Abū al-'Ibar'. See ibid., C.E. Bosworth's article, 'Abū al-Muṭahhar al-Azdī', *Encyclopedia of Arabic Literature*, I, 39–40.

83 *'Aj.*, III, 107. See also ibid., III, 346: 'during Sha'bān 1220 [/November 1805], Muḥammad 'Alī married his retainer Ḥasan al-Shamāshirjī to the daughter of Salīm Kāshif al-Asyūṭī. Muḥammad 'Alī ordered that her nuptial procession be celebrated with as much splendour as those of the amīrs of old. The master craftsmen were invited to construct wagons and clever or amusing devices at their own expense'. For drawings of a pageant with coaches shaped as the shops of members of different guilds, see Moreh, *Live Theatre*, 58, figure 5 and Metin And, *Osmanli Senliklerinde Turk Sanatlari* (Ankara 1982), plate no. 131.

84 On *arbāb* or *ahl al-malā'īb*, see *'Aj.*, I, 220, 252, II, 224, 227, IV, 200 and its synonym *muḥabbazūn*, see *'Aj.*, III, 107; and *ḥababẓiyya*, IV, 198. Cf. S. Moreh, 'The Arabic Theatre in

Ramaḍān in about 1212 (/16 March 1798) 'entertainers used to meet such as snake charmers (*ḥuwāt*),[85] monkey trainers (*qirdātiyya*),[86] *ahl al-malāʿīb* (live actors), and unveiled female dancers know as *ghawāzī'* in the courtyard of the mosque of ʿAmr b. al-ʿĀṣ'.[87] In another paragraph, our author uses the term *muḥabbaẓūn*: 'The [French] distributed [the taxes] among tax contractors (*multazimīn*), members of guilds (*arbāb al-ḥiraf*), and even among snake charmers (*ḥuwāt*), monkey-keepers (*qirdātiyya*) and live actors (*muḥabbaẓūn*).[88] All sorts of entertainers performed during feasts in palaces, gardens, market places, and recreation grounds such as al-Azbakiyya. On the occasion of the wedding of Ismāʿīl Pasha in 1813 a long list of performers gathered in al-Azbakiyya among them the *mughazlikīn*, who are not mentioned by Lane.[89]

Other players used to act upon rafts on the water of the Nile using them as a platform or stage, while the audience sat on the slope of the bank. At the wedding celebrations of Ismāʿīl Bey in 1174 (/1760–1) a stage of wood was constructed upon the surface of al-Fīl pond in Cairo, on which *arbāb al-malāhī wa 'l-malāʿib wa-bahluwān al-ḥabl* performed.[90] Such a stage on the surface of a pond during the eighteenth century is preserved in a drawing depicting Turkish itinerant actors (*Orta ayunu*, and in Arabic *muḥabbaẓūn*) performing according to the music of the *naqqāra* (a small drum with a hemispheric body of wood), *duff* (tambourine) and *mizmār* (flute or single-pipe) during the rule of Sultan Aḥmed III (1703–30).[91]

Egypt in the Eighteenth and Nineteenth Centuries', in *Etudes Arabes et Islamiques, II – langue et literature, vol. 3, Actes du XXIXe Congres international des Orientalistes, Section organisée, par Charles Pellat* (Paris 1975), 109–13, see in particular p. 111.

85 *'Aj.*, III, 70, 107, 108, 170, IV, 198, 309. On this kind of performers, see according to Lane, *Manners*, 391: '*ḥöwáh*' (sing. *ḥāwī*); in note 2 he defines the term 'so called from his feats with serpents'.

86 According to Lane, *Manners*, 395, those who perform with 'a monkey, an ass, a dog, with a kid' are called *quraydātī*.

87 Ibid., 180, 196, 384–9, 434–5, 506–9, termed by Lane '*gháwázee*' (sing. *gházeeyeh*), dancing-girls.

88 *'Aj.*, III, 107.

89 Ibid., III, 198.

90 See ibid., I, 252.

91 See And, *Osmanli Senlikerine Turk Sanatlari*. Cf. Moreh, *Live Theatre*, 153, figure 7, where an illustration of such a play in Turkey is given.

Ibn Rābiya

The term Ibn Rābiya, which was given to a performer of 'low' farces, replaced the term *muḥabbaẓīn* used by al-Jabartī and Lane. As far as it is possible to tell, this term was first mentioned by 'Alī Mubārak (1823–93), when comparing historical and didactic European theatre with the vulgar language, indecent behaviour, and crude jokes of Egyptian entertainers (Awlād Rābiya), in his novel *'Alam al-Dīn*, published in 1882.[92] Moreover, C. Prūfer, in his article on 'Drama (Arabic)' gave the name of the Egyptian comedian Aḥmad Fahīm al-Fār known as Ibn Rābiya as an example of such low farces in Egypt.[93] Texts of these farces were discovered and published by Manfred Woidisch and Jacob M. Landau in 1993. In these farces, al-Fār performs the role of the *khalbūṣ* (the comedian or the buffoon) or *khawal* (effeminate dancer), who performs at weddings, circumcision and other celebrations after the prelude of dance and music.[94]

Al-Sāmir

Another puzzling term used by Arab historians in dealing with performing arts in medieval Egypt, is the term *al-sāmir*;[95] Dr Nadia Ra'ūf Farag in her research on the popular Egyptian farce known as *faṣl muḍḥik* (*commedia del arte*), defines *masraḥ al-sāmir* as an ancient Egyptian rural theatre mostly performed in villages during feasts, weddings, circumcisions, births of male children and peasants' entertainment during 'warm summer nights'. The troupes contained musicians, dancers (*ghāziye*, pl. *ghawāzī*), and actors (*mukhāyilūn*, or *muḥabbaẓīn*), who wore attire appropriate to the character they represented,painting their faces with flour or lime and donning a beard, as

92 'Alī Mubārak, *'Alam al-Dīn* (Alexandria 1882), 397–440. On *Awlād Rābiya*, see also Aḥmad Amīn, *Qāmūs al-'Ādāt wa 'l-Taqālīd wa 'l-Ta'ābīr al-Miṣriyya* (Cairo 1953), 9.

93 C. Prüfer, 'Drama (Arabic)', *Encyclopaedia of Religion and Ethics*, James Hastings (ed.) (New York 1914), vol. IV, 872–8.

94 See J.M. Landau and M. Woidisch trans. and eds, *Arabisches Volkstheater in Kairo, im Jahre 1909, Ahmad il-Far und seine Schwanke* (Beirut1993).

95 On the *sāmir*, see Rushdī Ṣāliḥ, *al-Masraḥ al-Miṣrī* (Cairo 1972), 40–1; Samīr Sarḥān and I'tidāl 'Uthmān (eds), *Yūsuf Idrīs (1927–1991)*(Cairo 1991), 331–46. Cf. Yūsuf 'Ādil al-'Ulaymī, *al-Drāma al-Sha'biyya al-Miṣriyya* (Cairo 1992); Yūsuf Idrīs, 'Naḥwa Masraḥ Miṣrī', *al-Kātib* (Cairo, January-February and March, 1964); Nadia R. Farag, 'Yussef Idris and Modern Egyptian Drama', Ph.D. dissertation (Columbia University 1975) and its Arabic version (Cairo 1976), 59–60.

was the case with the Amīr al-Nawrūz.[96] One of the rare descriptions of a *sāmir* performance is give by Ibn Iyās (d. ca. 1524) concerning the distinguished and accomplished singer Khadīja al-Raḥābiyya, whose beauty and excellent singing enamoured many men of high society and who achieved great fame among the ruling class. She was also a *mukhāyila* (live actor), who performed with women Arab singers (*maghānī al-'Arab*) frequent participants in theatrical performances. It is derived from the verb *samura* (to chat at night around the campfire), and consequently the *sāmir* acquired the meaning of 'performing plays under moon light during summer nights'. According to two verses composed by some poets cited by Ibn Iyās, praising the singer and actress Khadīja al-Raḥābiyya's talents and beauty, the poet distinguishes between her *inshād* (recitation or singing) and her *maqāl* (speech) which embellished her performance. These two terms are two aspects of theatrical performances denoting the songs and dialogues of her repertoire. The poet adds that she used to perform during the full moon light (*wa-qad khāyalat bi 'l-badri laylata tammih*) in an unforgettable performance, which haunted the poet's eyes and heart. Her influence upon notable people was so great that she was considered a distinguished personality (*ṣīrat min jumlat al-a'yān*). Al-Raḥābiyya was accused by the governor of Cairo of corrupting eminent people, so he arrested her, bastinadoed her, an act that caused her death at the prime of her youth at the age of thirty.

Al-Jabartī vehemently criticizes the impudent behaviour of some of his contemporary religious scholars for participating in *sāmir*'s plays and other popular theatrical performances and becoming interested in the farming of taxes, thereby neglecting their religious duties. He argued that from a religious point of view, if the *'ulamā'* took part in dissipated and indecent entertainments with music and singing, they would forfeit the right to judge other people in court and disqualify themselves from dealing with religious matters. Our author accused them of joining a theatrical performance termed *al-sāmir* in which the *khalbūṣ*[97] (servant of the singers [*'awālim*, sing. *'ālima*]) participated. Al-Shaʿrānī (d. 1565) speaks of a *khalbūṣ al-maghānī* (buffoon) who accompanies female singers and dancers, and performed a scene from a

96 Farag, *Yussef Idris*, 59.

97 See Lane, *Manners*, 507.

play (*idhā kharaja fī bābat al-khayāl*) representing a judge or scholars'.[98] There is a strong similarity between the descriptions of Lane and al-Jabartī of such performances.[99] Both authors describe the *khalbūṣ* as a servant who collect largesse (*nuqūṭ*) from the audience[100] for the *'awālim* (women singers) 'and who often acts the part of a buffoon', playing some roles in farces and plays. While Lane states that the buffoon calls out, at each contribution, '*Shobash 'aleyk y' ṣaḥib al-faraḥ*!' that is, 'A present is due from thee, O giver of the entertainment', and adds, 'such one has given so many '*maḥboob* ', or '*kheyreeyehs* '; 'turning a few piasters into a much larger number of gold coins of considerably greater value, or, if gold be given, exaggerating the sum in the same manner'. It is important to note here that Lane's last sentence is an exact translation of al-Jabartī's Arabic sentence: من النصفيات الذهب قدر مسماه كثير وجرمهقليل. On the other hand al-Jabartī, in order to emphasize the low moral standard of the shaykhs, attributes such calls to the *'ulamā'*, who direct the *ra'īsat al-maghānī* (the chief singer) in a loud voice: 'O my lady, his highness, the Shaykh of Islam and Muslims, ..., the most learned shaykh so and so has given so much in gold coins, he would name a large or small samount. The sum would sound like a lot but would be actually small.'

Al-Jabartī decrees that the *'ulamā'*in this case had 'involved themselves in immoral matter to the extent they could no longer be the arbiters of justice since they gathered in places of amusement to listen to singers and music'.[101] He added that those scholars used to attend comic performances which he called *al-hazliyyāt wa 'l-muḍḥikāt* (comedies and satiric plays) as synonyms of *istihzā' wa 'l-sukhriyya*. The only two performers of *hazl* and *ḥusn al-musāmara*[102] mentioned by al-Jabartī are the *ra'īs* (maestro) Ḥasan Afandī b. Muḥammad Afandī known as al-Zāmik who is defined by al-Jabartī as *ra'īs* (maestro 'of a troupe of actors'), calling him '*'anīs al-jalīs wa-'l-nādira al-ra'īs*' (entertaining companion and the excellent chief actor) who surpassed his

98 Al-Sha'rānī, *Laṭā'if al-Minan*, II, 172; cf. Brakel and Moreh, 'Reflections on the Term *Bāba*', 28–9.

99 *'Aj.*, IV, 69, cf. Lane, *Manners*, 506–7.

100 Lane, *Manners*, 506.

101 *'Aj.*, IV, 69:... وارتكابهم للأمور المخلة بالمروءة المسقطة للعدالة كالاجتماع في سماع الملاهي والأغاني, see Philipp and Perlmann (eds), IV, 98 of the English translation.

102 See page 297 above where the terms *luṭafā'* and *musāmara* are used.

father in *hazl* (jest) and *jidd* (ernestness) and was in on intimate terms with eminent and comedians (*luṭafā'*) with *ḥusn al-musāmara.*[103]

Moreover, in his last two volumes of *'Ajā'ib al-Āthār*, al-Jabartī emphasizes the deviation of Muḥammad ʿAlī from the Islamic value system of justice and the principle of equality among Muslims, by ruling with tyranny. Among his vices, he enumerates extracting taxes, ignoring the advice of the religious scholars, employing non-Muslims with authority over Muslims, replacing Muslim scholars by secular officials as his advisers and eliminating the political influence of the *'ulamā'*. He also violated the venerated custom of generous Arab hospitality by the abolition of the tax-exempt *maḍāfa* (guests' houses) administered by the heads of villages, advising that the guest should buy their own food.

Al-Jabartī, Lane and Ottoman Drawings

The historian Jonathan P. Berkey,[104] made an important observation 'the Mamluks may still appear on the surface as culturally alien, Turkish rather than Arabic in speech, in some cases only superficial Islamicized, participants in culture which had its root in the nomadic, even shamanistic world of Central Asia'. Shamanic dances which affected popular *Ṣūfī* practices in Egypt attracted not only al-Jabartīand Lane, but Muslim artists as well. One of al-Jabartī's descriptions deals with Ṭāhir Pasha, an Albanian, who was devoted to popular Sufism, 'drawn to the feeble-minded, the possessed and dervishes (*yamīlu li 'l-maslūbīn wa 'l-majādhīb wa 'l-darāwīsh*), and fond of *dhikr* recitation.... The rabble exploited his belief, dressed themselves up in fantastic dresses, decking themselves with tall conical dervish hats (*ṭarṭūr*), patched robes (*dilq*), and long cloaks, hanging bells and all sorts of trumpery on themselves, and taking painted staffs to which they attached rattles and tassels, and drums which they would beat, as they shrieked and jerked from side to side and spoke in unseemly language and fantastic locutions to the effect that

103 *'Aj.*, II, 170.

104 See Jonathan P. Berkey, 'The Mamluks as Muslims: the Military Elite and the Construction of Islam in Medieval Egypt', in Philipp and Haarmann, *The Mamluks*, 163, and the bibliography in note 1 of Berkey's article. See also Haarmann, 'Arabic in Speech, Turkish in Lineage', *JSS* 33 (1988), 81–114.

they were possessors of supernatural powers'.[105] Al-Jabartī's description can shed light on drawings and paintings from the thirteenth century onwards which have puzzled many Western scholars, such as R. Ettinghausen. In a painting from the sixteenth century by Muḥammad-I Haravi (d. *c.* 1590) described by Ettinghausen, the latter admitted that he could not find any written description of such dancing.[106] In this drawing Ettinghausen noticed three figures performing within a landscape, dressed up as goats, gambolling in animal fashion with three other figures performing very exaggerated steps accompanied by equally exaggerated gestures. It seems significant that one of the high conical caps worn by these dancers is decorated with bells, which are also applied to the cap of a third type of dancer. The latter's headgear is also adorned with the tail of an animal which is meant to flutter by means of bizarre gestures... The music for these performers is provided by four men in the lower right foreground who play the tambourines, a panpipe, and two types of drums.

In fact, al-Jabartī's description of cultural life and entertainment are very similar to those described by the earlier Mamluk and Ottoman historians, mainly al-Maqrīzī (1364–1441), Ibn Taghrībirdī (c. 1410–70), and Ibn Iyās (1448–1524). Their works, which constitute the main historical works of the Mamluk period, can help to shed better light on the Ottoman historiographical works. Al-Jabartī's work revived the Mamluk historiographical method, which 'was annalistic in form', in which the author records history chronologically and combines it, on the other hand, with the Ottoman method of 'sequences of biographies'. These Mamluk works can help us to understand the terminology of entertainment and theatrical activities during the Ottoman period. Most probably, these cultural activities did not change to a great extent during Muḥammad 'Alī's epoch and continued even after the traditional popular entertainment had dwindled with the extensive westernization by the Khedive Ismā'īl Pasha (ruled 1863–79).

As in the case of the Mamluk historians, al-Jabartī also described in detail many aspects of political, administrative, social, and cultural life not only in the courts of rulers and grandees. However, as a pious religious scholar his detailed description was intended to criticize the *bida'* (heretical innovations)

105 On Ṭāhir Pasha and the *darāwīsh*, see *'Aj.*, III, 248.

106 See R. Ettinghausen, 'The Dance with Zoomorphic Masks', in G. Maqdisi (ed.), *Arabic Studies in Honor of Hamilton A.R. Gibb* (Leiden 1965), 212–19.

of the lower classes at *Ṣūfī mawlid*s, feasts, and religious festivals in mosques, graveyards, special places of entertainment (*muftarajāt*) and on board boats sailing on the Nile. As an intellectual, fond of literature and poetry, his interest was devoted to the scientific and literary salons (*majlis* pl. *majālis*) of the *amīr*s, *'ulamā'* and men of letters. Al-Jabartī's description of the luxurious buildings where salons were held was meant to emphasis the wealth and prosperity of the *amīr*s and rich merchants. His accounts of the topics of discussions, which took place in these salons, were meant either to praise the high standard of some of these meetings or to slander those who encouraged flattery, hypocrisy, defamation, and gossip. Such descriptions were given in details in the necrology of religious scholars, *amīr*s, poets, writers, and *awlād al-nās* who became interested in literary and cultural fields.[107]

When scholars deal with cultural life in Egypt, they treat the subject as if the courts of the Ottoman Pashas and Mamluk *amīr*s in Egypt were different from cultural life in the Ottoman Sultans' palaces. Jane Hathaway remarks on how 'the tension developed among competing loci of power' in the Ottoman Sultans' palaces, 'in the Ottoman provinces... the governors' households imitated the sultan's palace on a smaller scale. But any governor's household was itself liable to face competition from the households of local elites'.[108] This remark is relevant also to cultural life throughout the Ottoman Empire and especially in Egypt. The paintings of Ottoman artists illustrating entertainment and cultural activities in the Ottoman palaces reflect perfectly such activities as described by Egyptian historians.[109] These miniatures, paintings of entertainers, actors, mimers, dancers, musicians, jesters, comedians playing on rafts, clowns, acrobats, monkey trainers, snake charmers in *mawlid*s, feasts, festivals, carnivals of Amīr al-Nayrūz, wedding ceremonies, pageants and parades of craftsmen on floats, can shed better light

---

107 See Otfried Weintritt, 'Concepts of History as Reflected in Arabic Historiographical Writing in Ottoman Syria and Egypt (1517–1700)', in Philipp and Haarmann, *The Mamluks*, 189–90.

108 See Jane Hathaway's article '"Mamluk Households" and "Mamluk Factions" in Ottoman Egypt: a Reconsideration', in Philipp and Haarmann, *The Mamluks*, 108.

109 The best illustrations of Ottoman cultural life are in Metin And's works on entertainments and theatre in Ottoman Turkey, such as: 1. *Osmanli Şenliklerinde Türk Sanatlari* (Ankara 1982), *Culture, Performance and Communication in Turkey* (Tokyo 1987) and *Drama at the Crossroads, Turkish Performing Arts Link Past and Present, East and West* (Istanbul 1991). See also Moreh, *Live Theatre*, figures nos. 3, 5, 7 illustrating live actors, hobbyhorse players, dancers and musicians.

on and illustrate precisely the same activities described by al-Jabartī in his *'Ajā'ib al-Āthār*.

The achievements of the great thinkers in Islam, the zenith of Muslim sciences, were translated by European scholars into Latin enabling European scholars to continue the dynamic of the human sciences. Lane was able to use the last works of two great scholars of the Muslim world of the eighteenth-nineteenth centuries, i.e. al-Zabīdī's *Tāj al-'Arūs*, for his *Arab-English Lexicon*, and al-Jabartī's *'Ajā'ib al-Āthār* for his master piece *Manners and Customs of the Modern Egyptians* for the benefit of British and European orientalism. Thus, he made use of the intellectual achievements of Islam, dedicated to Islamic *jihād* and spreading Muslim domination.

Chapter Seven

The Role of the *'Ulamā'* in Egypt in the Years 1688–1821

ʿAbd al-Raḥmān al-Jabartī, scion of an eminent family of Egyptian *'ulamā'*, originally from the Jabart region, was among the few Arab historians who was interested in the status of the *'ulamā'*. He describes their interests and duties in Egyptian society, their function, and relations with the Mamluk and Ottomans as advisors to the rulers and defenders of the Islamic *umma*.[1] He was a pious and scrupulous scholar, who took the obligation to observe the Islamic, mainly Ashʿarī dictum of *al-amr bi 'l-ma'rūf wa 'l-nahy 'an al-munkar* ('to enjoin good and forbid evil')[2] so seriously in his third chronicle that he aroused the anger of rulers and religious scholars alike, especially during the reign of Muḥammad ʿAlī. Pious *'ulamā'* observe the Islamic principle that any order that contradicts the *sharī'a* (Islamic law) should be disobeyed: 'The ruler or his deputy should not be obeyed in a matter contrary to the sacred law'.[3] *'Ulamā'* 'should avoid acquiring morally corrupting political authority and wealth, follow in the footsteps of the *salaf* (venerable forefathers) in not meddling in worldly affairs, not take pride in (sumptuous) garments, not ride a horse or enter the house of an *amīr*, and should devote themselves only to learning and to scholarship'.[4] al-Jabartī found only a few scholars of his time who were worthy of the title of *'ulamā'*; in this group he included his father, the great *Ṣūfī* scholars of the Khalwatiyya order, in particular the saintly Shams al-Dīn Muḥammad b. Sālim al-Ḥifnī or al-Ḥifnāwī (1689–1767), ʿAbd al-Ra'ūf al-Bashbāshī (d. 1731) and Maḥmūd al-Kurdī al-Khalwatī (d. 1780), and many scholars of the twelfth/eighteenth century. He ordered the various clerics in a descending hierarchy of *'ālim* (a theologian-jurist or a man of science and

---

1 On the *'ulamā'* in Egyptian society, see M. Winter, *Egyptian Society under Ottoman Rule 1517–1798* (London 1992) and *Society and Religion in Early Ottoman Egypt* (New Brunswick 1982).

2 Qur'ān, 3:104, 110, 114; 7:157; 9:67, 71, 112; 22:41; 31:17. See *'Aj.* Būlāq, I, 163, 260, 289–300, 303–4, where he praised the scholars who followed this injunction during the period, which he covered in his chronicle. Cf. Cooperson, *Classical Arabic Biography*, 189.

3 *'Aj.*, I, 148.

4 Ibid., II, 100 on Muḥammad al-ʿAzīzī, known as Ibn al-Sitt. Cf. also ibid., III, 165.

learning), *shaykh* (a scholar of traditional sciences; the *mashāyikh al-'ulamā'* were the scholars of al-Azhar, of whom the *Shaykh al-Azhar* held the highest rank), and *muta'ammim*, pl. *muta'ammimūn* (a turbaned cleric).[5] In the biographies of the *'ulamā'* he gives the titles *imām* (prayer leader of the five prayers, and also used formerly to describe the head of the Muslim Sunnī state), and its superlative *imām 'allāma*; *faqīh* (a scholar versed in religion and law); *muqri'* (a reciter of the Qur'ān), *muftī* (an official expounder of Islamic law), and *'allāma* (a most erudite scholar). If the Shaykh is a great *Ṣūfī* and performer of miracles, he is called *al-shaykh al-quṭb* (supreme *Ṣūfī* master) and *waliy* (pl. *awliyā'*, ally or affiliate of God).

We are indebted to the numerous volumes of the *Cambridge Studies in Islamic Civilization* and to a long list of scholars who over the last two decades have devoted their research to study and clarify the role of the *'ulamā'*in Muslim society.[6] Michael Cooperson proved that classical Arabic biography rose not only ,in conjunction with the study of *ḥadīth* and *ḥadīth* transmitters', but also in the form of biographical collections on poets, singers, Qur'ān readers, jurists and even the biographies of the Prophet which were older than the biographies of the transmitters.[7] In addition, Cooperson clarified important terms of classical Arabic biographical literature. These pioneering studies shed a great deal of light on historical and biographical writings, and have enabled us to understand the structure, developments and changes in the status of the *'ulamā'* during the eighteenth and nineteenth centuries, as reflected in the works of al-Jabartī, the last great conventional chronicle writer of Muslim historiography. Other Western scholars have studied the social and political position of the *'ulamā'* in Egypt during the eighteenth century, among them Stanford Shaw, Andre Raymond, G. Baer, Afaf Marsot, M. Winter, D. Crecelius, P.M. Holt, J. Hathaway, A. Levanoni and others who have dealt with the *'ulamā'*'sreaction to reform and modernization.[8] The Danish scholar

---

5 See Bjørneboe, *In Search*, 144: 'a derogatory term. They are not distinguished by their learnedness (*'ālim*), but by the outer sign of their position, the turban'.

6 Among them Cooperson's painstaking study, *Classical Arabic Biography*, 31, 38, 45, 58, 60, 115–16, valuable especially for understanding the role of the *'ulamā'* in classical Islamic civilization.

7 Cooperson, *Classical Arabic Biography*, 1–2.

8 Afaf Lutfi al-Sayyid Marsot, because of her Egyptian origin, deals with the *'ulamā'*from a nationalist point of view, as a struggle between a 'native religious elite' and the Ottoman dignitaries dispatched from Istanbul. F. De Jong's studies of the *Ṣūfī* orders, are important

Lars Bjørneboe discussed the writings of *'ulamā'* and analysed their political positions in the light of al-Jabartī's three chronicles, *Mudda*, *Maẓhar* and *'Ajā'ib*.[9]

Because of the many available studies on the role of the *'ulamā'* in Islamic society, the present chapter will focus on al-Jabartī's concept of their role in the Islamic hierarchy based upon the Qur'ān and the *sunna* i.e. *'ulūm naqliyya*, or *al-manqūl* (transmitted sciences), as opposed to *ma'qūl* (secular sciences supplementing religious studies, such as logic, rhetoric, grammar, metrics and calligraphy). In his necrologies he listed first members of the former hierarchy: the *quṭb* (the supreme head of saints), the *waliy* (the saint), *shaykh al-sajjāda* (the leader of a *Ṣūfī* order), *Ṣūfī* (pl. *mutaṣawwifa* = a member of a mystic order), *'ālim* (pl. *ulamā'* = a religious scholar, especially of *ḥadīth*), *qāḍī* (pl. *quḍāt* = a jurist), *muḥaddith* (pl. *muḥaddithūn* = *ḥadīth*-a scholar), *muqri'* or *qāri'* (pl. *qurrā'* = Qur'ān readers), *imām* (pl. *a'imma* = prayer leaders), *shaykh* (pl. *shuyūkh* = a cleric or scholar) of various types, such as *Shaykh al-Azhar* or *Shaykhal-Mashāyikh* (a leading *shaykh* of al-Azhar), *mufassir* (pl. *mufassirūn* = exegetes), *mu'adhdhin* (an announcer of the hour of prayer), and even *ḥāfiẓ al-ni'āl* (a keeper of the shoes at a mosque). Among scholars of the secular *'ulūm 'aqliyya* or *al-ma'qūl* we find *naḥwī* (pl. *nuḥāt* = philologists), *'arūḍī* (a prosodist), *ḥaysūb* (an expert in computation), *farḍī* (an expert in the law of descent and distribution); some of the scholars are experts in both *al-manqūl* and *ma'qūl*.[10]

Al-Jabartī's *'Ajā'ib al-Āthār* is written from the point of view of an *'ālim* who is devoted to the class of religious scholars, and to the integrity of his colleagues, who were supposed, according to the *sharī'a*, to devote their lives to religious studies and serve as advisors to the rulers to curb their tyranny. Our author was unable to stem the tide of their corruption and the tyranny of Muḥammad ʿAlī, whom he saw as the instrument of God's punishment of a religious establishment which had given legitimacy and backing to his unjust

contributions to the subject, see *Ṭuruq and Ṭuruq-Linked Institutions in Nineteenth-Century Egypt* (Leiden 1978).

9 Bjoerneboe, *In Search*, 33–85.

10 Such as Shaykh Aḥmad al-Mūsawī known as al-Khalīfī (see *'Aj.*, I, 73), who was *muḥaddith, faqīh, uṣūlī, naḥwī, bayānī* (an expert in rhetoric), *mutakallim, 'arūḍī,* and *manṭiqī* (an expert in logic), while ʿAbd al-Ḥayy al-Shurnbulālī (see *'Aj.*, I, 68) was, in addition to his expertise in *fiqh* and *ḥadīth*, also an expert in *ma'qūl*, such as *naḥw, uṣūl, ma'ānī, ṣarf and farā'iḍ.* Cf. Cooperson, *Classical Arabic Biography*, 161.

exploitation of the populace. The conspiracy of the scholars to dismiss Sayyid Aḥmad al-Taḥṭāwī from the position of *muftī* of the Ḥanafīs in 1224 (/1809–10), because he refused to obey Muḥammad ʿAlī by giving false testimony against ʿUmar Makram al-Naqīb (c. 1755–1822), reveals two types of God's revenge: one, that the *'ulamā'* helped the tyrant to be appointed as the ruler of Egypt, and the other, that the plotting of these *'ulamā'* deprived honest scholars and the people of Egypt of a defender and a pleader for their cause, and thus the *'ulamā'*'s position and influence continued to diminish.[11] Our author realized that his epoch was the swan-song of traditional Islamic military, administrative, economic, cultural and historiographical writing.

During the first centuries of the Abbasid caliphate, the *imāms* and caliphs were the rulers (*ūlū 'l-amr*) of the Muslim *umma*, i.e. the heirs of the Prophet Muḥammad. With the abolition of the Abbasid caliphate the *'ulamā'* (religious scholars), especially the descendants of Muḥammad and the heads of the *Ṣūfī*orders, became the *ūlū 'l-amr*, the legitimate authority of *sharī'a* interpretation and enforcement, in fact, the heirs of the Prophet.[12] In the late eighteenth and the nineteenth centuries they came to consider the doctrine of mystical association with the person of the Prophet as important as the association with God.[13] Although the saying *Inna 'l-'ulamā'a warathatu 'l-anbiyā'* ('The bearers of knowledge are the heirs of the Prophets'),[14] ascribed to the Prophet, was disputed among the *ṭā'ifas* (a group entrusted with an exclusive body of knowledge)[15] in the early Abbasid period, because they were unable to agree on who these 'heirs' were. Al-Jabartī took it for granted that the intended 'heirs' were the religious scholars and used this interpretation in order to define and bolster the status of the *'ulamā'* in his time. During a debate between the Ottoman governor Ṭāhir Pasha and ʿUmar Effendi al-Naqīb, the latter presented the argument that the *ūlū 'l-amr* (those in authority), 'are the *'ulamā'*, the bearers of the religious law and the just sultan', and that 'it has been customary from time immemorial that the people

11 *'Aj.*, IV, 100–1. Cf. Bernd Radtke, 'Sufism in the 18th Century: An Attempt at a Provisional Appraisal', *Die Welt des Islams* 36:3 (November 1996), 337–8.

12 Cf. Cooperson, *Classical Arabic Biography*, xii, 1–23.

13 Radtke, 'Sufism', 360–1. Cf. *'Aj.*, I, 72.

14 See Arend Jan Wensinck, *Concordance et indicesde la tradition musulmane/al-Mu'jam al-Mufahras li-Alfāẓ al-Ḥadīth al-Nabawī* (Leiden 1936–43), IV, 321, quoted by Cooperson, *Classical Arabic Biography*, xii, n. 5.

15 Cooperson, *Classical Arabic Biography*, 15 and glossary, xxi.

should depose rulers, even the caliph or the sultan, if the latter act tyrannically towards the people'.[16]

The chronicle distinguishes between *ta'rīkh* (annalistic histories) and *tarājim* (biographical collections that mention death dates) of men who died in a certain year or years between 1100–1236/1688–1821 after the annals of these years. It thus constitutes in a sense a compound of the major works of *akhbār* or *tārīkh* and *tarājim* of the eighteenth century. This is a combination which the author arrived at by accident, having been initially interested in the history of events, and only later did he come upon the wealth of biographies written by his mentor al-Zabīdī (d. 1791) and initiated by the Syrian scholar al-Murādī (d. 1791), or collected by other contemporary scholars. Al-Jabartī's work enables us to understand the important role played by the *'ulamā'*in Islamic society after the destruction of the Abbasid caliphate and its capital Baghdad in 1258 by the Mongols. The calamities which befell the descendants of the house of Muḥammad, especially the ʻAlids (the descendants of ʻAlī b. Abī Ṭālib), during the Abbasid period, were partly due to the fear that if the ʻAlids came to rule they would transfer power to the Sassanid rulers of Persia.[17] These calamities induced the Shīʻa to resort to esoteric hope for salvation through various supernatural aspirations, such as the return of twelfth Imam, Muḥammad al-Mahdī from his occultation (329/940) to restore justice to the world. The same esoteric resolution occurred after the destruction of Baghdad; a strong wave of Sunni mystical belief in spiritual salvation continued with greater zeal.

A long time before the Ottoman Sultan ʻAbd 'l-Ḥamīd I used in 1774 the title of *Khalīfa*, the *ashrāf* and the *'ulamā'*continued to renounce political and military power and contented themselves with the duty of being interpreters and developers of the *sharī'a*.[18] The Ottomans, who conquered Egypt in 1517, deprived the descendants of Muḥammad, the *ashrāf* and *sādāt*, and the Arabs in general of all political and military authority, except in the far parts of the Ottoman Empire.[19] To compensate themselves for this loss the *ashrāf* and the *'ulamā'* secluded themselves from political power and contented themselves,

16 *'Aj.*, III, 331–2, cf. ibid, III, 148.

17 Cooperson, *Classical Arabic Biography*, 193.

18 Bjørneboe, *In Search*, 24.

19 See M. Winter, 'The Ashraf and Niqabat al-Ashraf in Egypt in Ottoman and Modern Times', *Journal of the Israel Oriental Society* 19: 1 (1985), 17–41.

like the Shīʿī Imāms, with the role of spiritual leaders, kings of the heart; the *Ṣūfī* orders thus became a favourite refuge for the Arab *'ulamā'*, especially the *ashrāf* who claimed to be heirs of the Prophet and defenders of the *sharī'a* against the tyranny of foreign rulers, who were generally ignorant of Muslim law. Among the last descendants of the Abbasids was Shaykh Ibrāhīm b. Abī al-Barakāt al-Baghdādī, known as Ibn al-Suwaydī. When he arrived in Cairo in 1175/1761–2, he was deprived of any authority and ended his life as a virtuous and eloquent *imām*, able to improvise verses with ease (*irtijāl*) in any meter and with any rhyme, a talent said to have been bestowed by God on the descendants of the Abbasid *imāms*. Having no wealth of his own, he enjoyed the hospitality of our author's father Ḥasan al-Jabartī and lived out his life in peace with no political aspirations.[20] The decline of the status of the *'ulamā'* continued under the Ottoman Mamluks and the French occupation, culminating under Muḥammad ʿAlī.[21] The latter replaced them with secular officials who had received a European education, both administrative and military, mainly in France.[22]

Al-Jabartī was aware that he was witnessing the last generation of pious Muslim scholars and rulers, and the end of the conventional Islamic administration and the traditional economic and military system, customs, and moral values, as well as religious attitudes towards the *dhimmī*s (non-Muslims under Muslim protection)[23] and *ḥarbī*s (non-Muslims resident outside the *dār al-Islām* [the Muslim abode]) in continuous war with Islam. The changes he witnessed were taking place under the impact of continuous defeats of Ottoman armies in their *jihād* against the 'infidel' European powers and Shīʿī Persia.[24] European aggression culminated with the French occupation of Egypt in 1798, which was perceived as a continuation of the Crusaders' attempts to recapture the Christian holy sites in the Holy Land (1096–1291). The obituariesin the first two volumes of *'Ajā'ib al-Āthār* were copied mainly from his mentor al-Zabīdī's *Mu'jam Mukhtaṣṣ*. These adopted a new socio-religious hierarchy in accordance with the Quranic injunction of 'obey God, His

20 See *'Aj.*, IV, 403–44.

21 See ibid., IV, 68–9, 122, 125, 152, 244–5, cf. 295.

22 See Afaf Lutfi al-Sayyid Marsot, *Egypt in the Reign of Muhammad 'Ali* (Cambridge 1984); Bjørneboe, *In Search*, 81.

23 *'Aj.*, III, 44, 51, 93, 109, 112–13, 135, IV, 104 (Shaykh ʿAbd al-Munʿim al-ʿAmmāwī).

24 See B. Lewis, *What Went Wrong? Western Impact and Middle Eastern Response* (London 2002).

messenger and your rulers' (*aṭā'ū Allāha, wa-rasūlahu wa-ūlū al-amri minkum*) (Qur'ān, 59/4 and 92/4).[25] The Quranic verse quoted indicates that the third authority in Islam is the ruler, the Prophet's successor, i.e. the Caliph. As in the case of the first Abbasid period, al-Jabartī's chronicle showed that '[t]he history of *akhbār* after *c*. 200/800 becomes the history of the diffuse fields of specialization that emerged from it. These include not only *ḥadīth* but also the various branches of *adab*'.

The *sādāt* and *ashrāf*, who were descendants of the Prophet Muḥammad, both ʿAlids and descendants of Abū Bakr, became heads of the *Ṣūfī* orders, at least in Ottoman Egypt after Sulayman the Magnificent (1494–1566), the representative of *ūlū 'l-amr minkum* (the authorized Muslim authorities). The new Ottoman military and political rulers, despotic non-Arabs not well versed in the Islamic *sharī'a*, were expected to obey and respect the *'ulamā'*, especially the *ashrāf*. The latter added to their religious status their legitimate claim of authority as descendants of Muḥammad, as representing the *sharī'a* and the Prophet's family, the possessor of ultimate authority in Islamic society.[26]

Al-Jabartī argued that there were two epochs in Islamic history during which the rulers were just and followed the *sharī'a*. These epochs waxed and waned like the cycles of the moon. According to al-Jabartī the first epoch was that of the four righteous caliphs (632–60) who ruled after the death of the Prophet, and the second was during the reigns of the sultans Salīm I (1516–20) and Sulaymān, when the Ottomans were at the height of their accomplishments in the sciences, the arts, the system of justice and their military expansion: 'At the outset of their reign, the Ottomans were among the best to rule the (Islamic) community since the Rightly-Guided Caliphs. They were the strongest defenders of religion and opposers of the unbelievers, and for this reason, their dominions expanded through the conquest, which God gave to them and to their deputies. They upheld the performance of Islamic rites and the *sunna* of Muḥammad. They honoured the *'ulamā'* and religious leaders, supported the maintenance of the Two Holy Cities, Mecca and Medina, and

25 On this order during the first Abbasid rule, see Cooperson, *Classical Arabic Biography*, 3, 6–23.

26 On these rulers see Haarmann, 'Joseph's Law', 55–84 and the articles of Amalia Levanoni (17–31) and D.S. Richards (32–54) in the same book.

upheld the rules and principles of justice by observing Islamic laws and practices'.[27]

Al-Jabartī accused later Ottoman rulers of corruption, oppression, bribery, and injustice. The Ottomans and the Mamluks of al-Jabartī's time were accused of ignorance of the fundamentals of Islam.[28] He called them tyrants whose main aim was to invent means to extract taxes with brutality from poor fellaheen, and denounced the Mamluks for their vicious brutal factional struggles and for exploiting their subjects, both the urban populace and the peasants. He praised the French for their justice, their love of knowledge and order, and their respect for the *'ulamā'*, who were the main advisors to the French in the *Dīwān* which they established. Nevertheless, the French were also criticized for their cruelty in collecting taxes to maintain their army, and in suppressing the two revolts of the Egyptians in Cairo. Al-Jabartī believed that the heads of the *Ṣūfī* orders, in particular the pious descendants of the Prophet Muḥammad's family, were the ideal advisors, if not the legitimate rulers, of Egypt. The descendants of the prophet were considered the natural candidates for *al-khilāfa al-bāṭina* or the *imāmat al-qulūb* but not the *imāmat al-jusūm or imāma ẓāhira*.[29] There was at least one occasion on which the Egyptian soldiers, who were disatisfied with the tyrannical rule of the Sultan al-Ghawrī (1501–16) offered Shaykh Jalāl al-Dīn al-Bakrī, a descendant of Abū Bakr, the post of Caliph of Egypt, an offer which the latter rejected, because he maintained that power leads to corruption. Moreover, when a few religious scholars, mainly the *ashrāf*, did achieve political and religious authority through *awqāf* revenues, the rulers of Egypt feared that they might lose their political and military power.[30] The belief among the defenders of the *ashrāf* was that God honoured the descendants of the Prophet with the *quṭbāniyya* (title of supreme head of the *Ṣūfī*s), and that the reformer of Islam at the beginning of every century should be among them.[31]

Indeed, during what is considered 'the golden age' of the *'ulamā'*in Egypt, religious scholars servedthe rulers, by giving legitimacy to their rule and their

27 See *'Aj.*, I, 20–1.

28 Cf. ibid., IV, 213, 215, 227.

29 ʿAbd Allāh b. Muḥammad b. ʿĀmir al-Shubrāwī al-Shāfiʿī, *Kitāb al-Itḥāf bi-Ḥubb al-Ashrāf* (Cairo 1318/1900–1), 47, cf. 6.

30 According to ʿAbd al-Ghanī al-Nābulsī, printed in the margin of *'Ajā'ib al-Āthār*, ʿAbd al-ʿAzīz (ed.), vol. 2, 37, 416.

31 Al-Shubrāwī, *al-Itḥāf*, 6.

policies, as well as by reminding them of their obligation to treat the populace with justice. The *'ulamā'*'s wealth was acquired through supervision of *waqf* properties, tax farming (*iltizām*) income and private business, and used for the maintenance of *madrasas*, *zāwiyas* and mosques, as well as financing *mawlids* and religious festivals, which gave them immense social and religious power.[32]

This period lasted from the poisoning of Muḥammad Bey al-Kabīr by his Mamluks in Syria (1775) to the expulsion of the *sharīf* ʿUmar Makram, who was betrayed by Muḥammad ʿAlī in 1224/1809 after ʿUmar had backed him in 1805 to be appointed the ruler of Egypt. The most daring among the *'ulamā'* was Shaykh Shams al-Dīn Muḥammad Abu 'l-Anwār, who obtained his authority and self-confidence thanks to his being a respected descendant of *ashrāf* and head of a *Ṣūfī* order. He confronted and scolded many Ottoman officials, among them Ḥusayn Pasha al-Jazāyrlī,[33] when the latter violated the *sharī'a* and humiliated his Muslim subjects. Shaykh al-Sādāt openly accused al-Jazāyirlī of having confiscated the Egyptian *amīrs*' money. He 'seized their women and children, and had them sold at public auction', claiming they were slaves of the public treasury. Shaykh al-Sādāt asked him: 'Did the sultan send you to this city to establish justice and to eliminate oppression as you say, or to sell freemen and mothers of children and to dishonour women?'[34] During the second Cairo revolt of April 1800, al-Sādāt scolded 'Uthmān, the Katkhudā, in writing, on the authority of his ancestor the Prophet Muḥammad, for having 'violated his covenant and forsaken the friendship of the family of the house of my grandfather' for cooperating with the rebel riffraff among the populace of Cairo and causing severe damage to the Muslims.[35]

In fact, showing opposition to unjust rulers depended upon the personality of the *sharīf*. Thus Sayyid al-Bakrī, who was of a weak character, handed Murād Bey's deposits to Ḥasan Pasha, while Shams al-Dīn Ibn Wafā al-Sādāt refused to hand him Ibrāhīm Bey al-Kabīr's.[36]

In the biographies of the *'ulamā'* one finds long lists of books which they read, the names of their teachers and their compositions, as well as posts which they held. Eminent scholars in the fields of Qur'ān and *ḥadīth* are given the

---

32 Bjørneboe, *In Search*, 81–5.

33 *'Aj.*, IV, 186–8, cf. also IV, 192, 196.

34 *'Aj.*, IV, 188.

35 Ibid., III, 103.

36 Ibid.

honorific title of *wārith ʿulūm Sayyid al-Mursalīn* (heir of the sciences of the Master of the Messengers [of God]) while the *Ṣūfī* scholars, mainly those of the al-Sādāt and the Bakrī families, are called by the honorific title *sīdī* ... *Shaykh al-sajjāda* (my master ... the head of the *Ṣūfī* order). However, such standard honorific titles at the beginnings of biographies should be read with caution, because the author at the end of such a biography often revealed the deceased's notorious character and the deceitful way in which he behaved at the end of his life.[37] He mentions only a few biographies of secular scholars, mainly those who were in power after the rise of Muḥammad ʿAlī; the scholars he mentions were students of mathematics and philosophy.

The biographies adhere to a certain framework of presentation: the most important who died in a certain year is generally given the title of *Imām*. An exceptionally profound and pious scholar will be called *al-Imām al-ʿālim*; the highest honorific is *al-Imām al-ʿālim al-ʿallāma*. The title *al-ḥabr al-fahhāma* is added to *Shaykh al-Islām wa ʾl-Muslimīn*. The *shuhra* (renown or surname) is sometimes added. Then the scholar's school of jurisprudence (*madhhab*) and the *nisba* of his city or village are mentioned. This is followed by a list of his teachers, the books which he read and composed, his classes and the name of the mosques in which he lectured, the names of his teachers and students, the scholars who gave him licences to teach their works or to whom he gave such license, and whether the scholar studied rational subjects (*ʿulūm ʿaqliyya*) or transmitted sciences (*ʿulūm naqliyya*).[38] In a society, which attached importance to learning by rote, it is understandable that one would also mention the fact that a person had memorized the Qur'ān, possessed a good memory and wrote verses to help students in their learning. This was followed by the names of men of letters (*adīb*, pl. *udabāʾ*) and poets who composed poems dealing with Islamic faith and morals and criticism of corrupt scholars, popular *Ṣūfī*s and dervishes.[39] A biography ended with the date and place of the scholar's death. The longest biographies of scholars were those of the

37 See for instance the biographies of Abū al-Anwār al-Sādāt (*ʿAj.*, IV, 185–96), Muḥammad Murtaḍā al-Zabīdī (*ʿAj.*, II, 196–215, especially, 200–1.), etc., a method which was also applied by al-Sakhāwī in his biography of al-Maqrīzī, see Muḥammad ʿAbd Allāh ʿInān, *Muʾarrikhū Miṣr al-Islāmiyya wa-Maṣādir al-Tārīkh al-Miṣrī* (Cairo) 1991, 97–104.

38 *ʿAj.*, I, 73.

39 Cf. Radtke, 'Sufism', 341.

author's relatives and ancestors, especially his father, his *Ṣūfī* teachers, and close friends.

In the first two volumes by al-Jabartī the necrologies contain lengthy elegies composed for the deceased, which were read over his grave either by the poet himself or by a professional orator. Equipped with his profound knowledge of Islamic *fiqh* (jurisprudence) and its rules of composition, al-Jabartī set out to write his final chronicle, evaluating events and judging rulers, personalities and scholars according to the Islamic value system and Khalwatī *Ṣūfī* dogma, as shown in the following hierarchical system:

God (Allāh)

As a Khalwatī *Ṣūfī*, al-Jabartī's concept of the universe is purely Quranic and based upon the *sunna*, with an emphasis on justice and truth, which God provided for the welfare of His creatures. His conception of the universal hierarchy is based upon the Quranic verse according to which God created human beings weak, so that 'they should collaborate and cooperate in securing and providing their needs. God created in mankind both justice and injustice' and mankind is in need of a just and wise ruler who will establish rules of justice and law of government to control their relations with each other. Therefore 'He sent down His Book to bring the truth and His Balance to bring justice' (Qur'ān, 42:16), references to knowledge and justice, respectively. He appointed certain knowledgeable and just persons as His successors based upon the lawful religion and chose a successor (caliph), so that he may rule people with truth and justice'. Moreover, 'God created people according to ranks (*darajāt*) and raised some of you in rank above others' (Qur'ān, 6:65). The author cites this source for the Islamic system of universal authority no less than three occasions.[40] This system stems from God, who sends His Prophets (*anbiyā'*) to deliver His creatures from Hell and to guide them to Paradise. Only by 'conformity to the rules of the Book and Justice' can equity be maintained in a God-created society of the weak and the strong, to protect the weak. Therefore God sent down the Book (*al-Kitāb*) with the truth, and the balance (*al-mīzān*) (Qur'ān, 42:16), i.e. knowledge of the content of the *sharī'a*so that the rulers chosen by God will be able to rule justly.

40 See *'Aj*. Būlāq, I, 7ff.

There are five categories of human beings who dispense justice in this hierarchal system. These are His successors (*khalā'if Allāh*), who carry out His orders and prohibitions, as follows:

The Prophets (al-Anbiyā')

Prophets are the highest of the five ranks of human beings created by God. They 'are the guides of the community, the pillars, and repositories of the Book and God's faithful custodians over his creature ... to guide humanity aright' for its salvation now and in the hereafter. They are commissioned by God to be messengers to their people; God 'provided them with the Book and the Balance to enable people to act with justice and truth to deliver them from infidelity and tyranny to the light of wakefulness and faith'.[41] Like other prophets who were sent by God with their religions, His Messenger Muḥammad can intercede (*shafā'a*) to save his followers from Hell and to guide them towards Paradise. While only Moses was *kalām Allāh*,[42] able to converse face-to-face with God, Muḥammad was allowed to receive His divine revelation through the angel Gabriel, who served as an intermediary between God, his *Lawḥ Maḥfūẓ* (the well-kept slab on which God inscribed the history of humanity) and His Messenger. It is the belief of the followers of the Khalwatī order that the angels Gabriel and Isrāfīl communicated with the Prophet Muḥammad. The saints among the *'ulamā'* are privileged to see the Prophet in their dreams and can evocate his spirit as well as those of his companions during their prayer sessions; one of these was Muḥammad al-Kurdī, an eminent *Ṣūfī* Khalwatī. During the eighteenth century, Egyptian and Turkish *'ulamā'* debated the question of whether it was possible for saints or even prophets to see *al-Lawḥ al-Maḥfūẓ*.[43]

The saints (*awliyā'*, sing. *waliy*), or the *abdāl*, according to al-Jabartī, are also 'immune to temptation, and live in austerity. Their faith can perform miracles and cause their prayers to be answered. They are a minority whose number is constant and for whose sake God increases nations, causes the rain to fall, and prevents catastrophe'.[44] Such a saint was al-Saqqāf Bā ʿAlawī, who

41 See *'Aj.*, I, 8.

42 Cf. *'Aj.*, I, 402.

43 Ibid., II, 62 (al-Khiṣr).

44 Cooperson, *Classical Arabic Biography*, 165. Cf. *'Aj.*, II, 303. On the *abdāls*, see Ghālib Anābsī, 'Ḥadīth Abdāl al-Shām', in *Dirāsāt* (Amman 2008).

was thought to have been in intimate spiritual relations with the Prophet Muḥammad. Bā ʿAlawī was an admired scholar, performer of miracles (*karāmāt*) and recipient of inspired knowledge. He studied the Naqshabandī path with prominent *Ṣūfī*s and applied himself to it until its light shone upon him. He believed that 'There is no veil remaining between him and the Prophet!' in fact, he would not initiate anyone into the Naqshabandī order except with the permission of the Messenger of God. He also claimed to have been given the sword of Abū Bakr Ibn al-ʿAydarūs al-Akbar.[45] Such beliefs would seem to be the reason why Lane, who dealt with saints and dervishes among the Egyptians in two chapters, referred to them as 'Superstitions'.[46]

The 'Ulamā'

The second category is the saints (*awliyā'*) and religious scholars (*'ulamā'*).[47] They are the heirs of the prophets but below them in rank. They take the prophets, God's favourites, as their example and follow their path in order to preserve justice and truth. As servants of God they know the Qur'ān or *al-Kitāb* and the *sunna* (binding precedent in the form of Muḥammad's sayings and behaviour), in order to keep His divine law. They will inherit Paradise and dwell in it forever.[48] Al-Jabartī criticized the deterioration of the moral standard of some scholars in his time, who instead of being devoted to God and His rules were afflicted with the love of 'worldly honour and riches, leadership and position, and who show envy and malice'. As an example of the latter, he mentions Shaykh Shams al-Dīn Muḥammad Abu 'l-Anwār ʿAbd al-Raḥmān, Shaykh al-Sādāt.[49] The latter was the opposite of what an ideal good Muslim and decent scholar should be, according to the standards of our author. 'His family home was like that of the *amīr*s in its spaciousness and elegance, its ornamented salons and palatial halls …', for in those days the greater part of prestige and standing lay in grand houses, fancy clothes, a large income and

45 See *'Aj.*, I, 72.

46 Lane, *Manners*, 228–53.

47 See N.R. Keddie (ed.), *Scholars, Saints and Sufis* (Berkeley1972). Cf. also Bjørneboe, 'Al-Jabarti and the *'Ulamā'* of Cairo', *In Search*, 143–55.

48 Qur'an, 23:10–11. Cf. *'Aj.*, I, 8. Women could also be saints, see *'Aj.*, II, 106–7. Both al-Jabartī and Lane, *Manners*, 228, agree that 'The Arabs are a very superstitious people; and none of them are more so than those of Egypt'.

49 *'Aj.*, I, 8, IV, 189f.

many servants and retainers.[50] Al-Jabartī distinguished between the *'ulamā'* and the *Ṣūfī* leaders who were mainly descendants of the Prophet Muḥammad and considered their duty to be to defend the faith.

As we have seen above, the *'ulamā'*and *Ṣūfī* scholars of Arab descent in the Sunni world were able to survive by waiving their right to rule the Muslim world as Caliphs of the believers. The roots of this policy go back to the 'Alids' conflict with the Umayyad rulers in a series of cruel and bloody incidents and battles. This began with the assassination of ʿAlī b. Abī Ṭālib (661), then the poisoning of his son Ḥasan (d. 669?) by the Umayyad caliph Yazīd b. Muʿawiya (d. 683), followed by the brutal massacre of his brother Ḥusayn and his family in Karbala (d. 680). With the rise of the Abbasids, the attitude of the Caliphs towards the ʿAlid dynasty and the Shīʿī imams was ambivalent. Shīʿite historians attribute this to the jealousy, which the Caliphs felt at the Shīʿī imams' pious behaviour, esoteric knowledge, and insight, vast mastery of the *sharī'a* and high intelligence on the one hand, and the admiration in which they were held by the populace and the latter's belief that they deserved the *imāma*, on the other hand. The Abbasid rulers saw to it that no descendants of Muḥammad's cousin ʿAlī b. Abī Ṭālib rose to religious, military and political power. According to tradition this policy was established with the brutal crushing of the claim to leadership of Ḥusayn and his family, so that when the ʿAbbasid caliph al-Rashīd (d. 809) asked the Shīʿī Imām Mūsā al-Kaẓim (d. 799) at the Ka'ba, 'are you the person to whom people are pledging allegiance in secret?', Mūsā answered him with pride: 'I am the Imam of the hearts, and you are the Imam of the bodies [of the Muslims]!' The author adds that in fact the Shīʿī Imams and their descendants are kings who rule spiritually, free of the sufferings of political kings, whose sins and tyranny expose them to punishment in the hereafter.[51] Although Mūsā al-Kaẓim, like his son ʿAlī b. Mūsā al-Riḍā (d. 818) and other ʿAlid *imāms*, possessed 'privileged insight' or ' *'ilm* (knowledge) of everything, including the past, the future, and the secret thoughts of men',[52] not given to other men, they did not demonstrate any desire to rule or to revolt against al-Rashīd and his successor

50 Ibid., IV, 186. On the prohibition on wearing luxurious clothes in Islam, see *thawb*, pl. *thiyāb shuhra*, in Shmuel Moreh, *Live Theatre*, 75–6.

51 See al-Shubrāwī, *al-Itḥāf*, 6. Cf. Mu'min b. Ḥasan Mu'min al-Shiblanjī, *Nūr al-Abṣār fī Manāqib Āl Bayt al-Nabī al-Mukhtār* (Cairo 1367/1948), 164–8.

52 Cooperson, *Classical Arabic Biography*, 105.

al-Ma'mūn (786–833). The former 'was allegedly poisonedby the order of the caliph al-Rashīd'[53] while the latter by al-Ma'mūn'.[54] In fact, eleven out of twelve Shīʿī imams were murdered.[55] Since then most of the ʿAlids and other *ashrāf* abstained from political involvement wherever powerful non-Arab rulers reigned in Muslim lands, following the example of al-Riḍā, and were content to serve as advisors to the ruler.[56]

The destruction of the Abbasid dynasty by the Mongols in 1258 was considered by Imami Shīʿism as divine punishment for Abbasid atrocities against the ʿAlids in particular. However, the ʿAlids and other descendants of the Prophet, as well as Arab scholars in general, were reluctant to acquire political power. They preferred to indulge in religious studies and Sufism, and to be 'the kings of the hearts'. By the eighteenth century, the *Ṣūfī* movement in Egypt was headed by descendants of Muḥammad, the Bakriyya, the descendants of Abū Bakr through the line of Muḥammad's young wife ʿĀ'isha, and the *sādāt,* who traced their descent from ʿAlī. Those *ashrāf* preferred to be heads of *Ṣūfī* orders; they were respected and had religious authority over the sinful political and military rulers of the Ottoman and Mamluk periods. According to al-Jabartī, the palaces of the heads of the Bakriyya and al-Sādāt were like royal courts with their masters crowned with special turbans called *tāj* (crown, a special turban), and with an entourage and servants; they were respected by the authorities who acceded to requests in their own favour and in favour of the people. Their reluctance to acquire political and military power was due to their conviction that serving political authorities led to *ẓulm* (oppression) and unjust deeds, which in turn would attract God's wrath in this world and in the hereafter. Even during the French occupation, when the French asked the members of the *dīwān* why they did not control the mobs, they affirmed that the 'Cairo mob did not fear anybody except the Turks, and that nobody else could control the people',[57] since authority was divided into *a'immat al-qulūb* and *a'immat al-jusūm* (spiritual authority and political authority).

53 Ibid., 73–4, 79, n. 45. Cf. E. Kohlberg, 'Mūsā al-Kāẓim', *EI*², I, 272–7; al-Shubrāwī, *al-Itḥāf,* 55–6.

54 Cooperson, *Classical Arabic Biography*, 73–4.

55 Ibid., 28–31, 73–4, 88–98, 193–6.

56 Ibid., 93.

57 *'Aj.*, III, 11.

Al-Zabīdī in his *Mu'jam Mukhtaṣṣ* added that a good *'ālim* should respect the *Ṣūfī*s, and the *ashrāf*, put his trust in the *awliyā'* (saints) praise them in his poetry and frequent their graves. The *imām*, *faqīh* and poet ʿAbd Allāh b. Muḥammad al-Shubrāwī al-Shāfiʿī, who was appointed rector of al-Azhar, possessed a strong personality. The Ottoman authorities and the Mamluk *amīr*s respected him when he intervened on behalf of both poor and rich, asking that they be treated justly. The rulers accepted his recommendations and thanks to his strong and effective personality the *'ulamā'*were respected among high and low.[58] The Ottoman Sultan, the Mamluk rulers and the Sultan of al-Maghrib, respected al-Zabīdī, who was a *muḥaddith*, a *faqīh*, a *Ṣūfī* and a lexicographer. An *'ālim* who supported the Sādāt al-Wafā'iyya gained prestige and would become well-known and favoured by rulers.[59] In his *Tāj al-'Arūs*, al-Zabīdī confirmed that *'ulamā'* who were also interested in secular sciences, such as medicine, astronomy, and history, suffered a diminution of their reputation among both the authorities and the common people.[60]

Poets and writers who excelled in the Arabic language and in Islamic ethics, and thus enabled Muslims to understand the Qur'ān and the *ḥadīth* were next in rank to religious scholars. The scholar Michael Cooperson noted that '[t]he history of *akhbār* after *c.* 200/800 becomes the history of the diffuse fields of specialization that emerged from it. These include not only *ḥadīth* but also the various branches of *adab* (the literary and linguistic sciences) and of *ta'rīkh* (history)'.[61]

Kings and Rulers (al-Mulūk wa Wulāt al-Umūr)

The third category after religious and ethical scholars is that of Muslim kings (*al-mulūk*) and rulers (*wulāt al-umūr*) who 'are the guardians of justice and equity among people and subjects'. They are expected to 'maintain order and authority to secure their subjects' life and property, for their prosperity, for justice and generosity',[62] for otherwise tyranny and injustice will lead to their

58 Al-Zabīdī, *Mu'jam Mukhtaṣṣ*, biog. no. 298, f. 53a, and MS Princeton, f. 117.

59 Al-Zabīdī, *Mu'jam Mukhtaṣṣ*, biog. no. 340, f. 64b, and MS Princeton, f. 134, see the biography of ʿAbd al-Raḥmān al-ʿArīshī.

60 Al-Zabīdī, *Mu'jam Mukhtaṣṣ*, biog. no. 339, f. 64b, and MS Princeton, f. 133, see the biography of ʿAbd al-Raḥmān al-Bishbīshī.

61 Cooperson, *Classical Arabic Biography*, 7.

62 Qur'ān, 16:92. Cf. *'Aj.*, I, 9.

destruction and they will perish. Scholars, who wrote a petition to the Sublime Porte to install Muḥammad ʿAlī as pasha, enumerated the duties of the ruler: 'You are God's Caliph, ruler of His creatures and trustee of His creation. We (the *'ulamā'*) shall comply with the authorities carrying out your commands in everything which accords with the Muḥammadan *sharī'a*, according to the command of the Lord of Creation... who says: "O Believers, obey the Messenger, and those in authority among you"'(Qur'ān, 4:62), arguing that they could not oppose the rulers, but should entrust the matter to God.[63]

Al-Jabartī defines the just king (*malik* or *imām 'ādil*) as 'one who deals justly with God's people and keeps himself from oppression and corruption'. If he does not do so, God will consider him His enemy, since God rules according to reward and punishment (*thawāb wa-'iqāb*). Oppression and injustice are the qualities which God hates the most. The duty of kings and rulers is to act in accordance with the Book and the *sunna*, to achieve justice. Justice and equity will preserve a king's realm. In his *Introduction*, our author was courageous enough to criticize the Ottoman Sultans, their governors (*wulāt*, sing. *wālī*) in Egypt, the Mamluk rulers, and high secular officials in their service. The ruling classes were generally corrupt and very few indeed earned our author's praise; one who did was the Ottoman general who expelled the French, Yūsuf Ḍiyā Pasha.[64]

The Middle Classes (Awsāṭ al-Nās)

This is the fourth category of the Muslim hierarchy, consisting of people who 'observe justice in their dealings and settle their crimes with equity. They return good for good and evil for evil'.[65] One such personality was Shaykh al-ʿArab Hammām bin Yūsuf.[66]

People Who Exercise Governance over Themselves (al-Qā'imūna bi-Siyāsat Nufūsihim)

The fifth category consists of those just people who maintain control over themselves, their limbs and faculties, moderating their behaviour and bodily

63 *'Aj.*, IV, 12–13.

64 See *'Aj.*, IV, 268, especially in his introduction to *Maẓhar al-Taqdīs*.

65 See *'Aj.*, I, 10.

66 Ibid., I, 343–5.

movements in order to be an example for others to follow.[67] Good examples of such people are pious porters and shoe-keepers at mosques, like the porter Shaykh Rabīʿ al-Shayyāl of the Aḥmadiyya order, who always engaged in acts of piety. Whenever he readied himself to pray his face became pale and he would tremble. When he pronounced the words 'God is great', it appeared as if his heart was being rent asunder, while his 'entire body and all his limbs were devoted to the purpose for which he was created',[68] as in the case of a *Ṣūfī*absorbed in the contemplation of the *ṭarīqa muḥammadiyya*,which entails conformity between a physical and a spiritual imitation of the Prophet.[69]

Al-Jabartī's hierarchy differs from the one adopted by previous historians, who considered *ūlū 'l-amr* as secular rulers, although they were of non-Arab origin. Al-Jabartī used his new hierarchy especially when arranging his biographical necrology at the end of each year. Already in his *Introduction* to *'Ajā'ib al-Āthār*,[70] which he wrote as an essay on justice and as advice to rulers and religious scholars 'who are the shadow of God on earth'. He preached that God made a 'just man his successor on earth, so that he might rule people with truth and justice'[71] and that the *'ulamā'* as bearers of knowledge were the heirs of the prophets.[72] In defining the science (or art) of history, al-Jabartī states the order in which men of lore should be classified in historical works: prophets (*anbiyā'*) who are the representatives of God; saints (*awliyā'*); religious scholars (*'ulamā'*) who should represent the prophets; wise men or secular scholars (*ḥukamā'*); and poets (*shu'arā'*) who should preach living in accordance with moral values.[73] Kings, sultans and others who should obey the religious law follow this moral and God-fearing hierarchy. Poets, it should be noted, are mentioned in the Qur'ān among the tempters who will end in Hell, due to the fact that Muḥammad suffered from the attacks of poets who were hostile to his mission. Nevertheless, in later Islamic times ascetic and *Ṣūfī*

67 See ibid., I, 10.

68 See ibid., I, 84; his duty was to guard visitors' shoes in al-Ḥusaynī mosque (*ḥāfiẓ ni'āl al-masjid al-Ḥusaynī*).

69 Cf. Radtke, 'Sufism', 355–6.

70 *'Aj.*, I, 3–13. On this Introduction see P.M. Holt, 'Al-Jabartī's Introduction to the History of Ottoman Egypt', *BSOAS* 25 (1962), 38–51.

71 See *'Aj.*, I, 7–8.

72 Ibid., I, 8. Cf. Cooperson, *Classical Arabic Biography*, xii.

73 Cooperson, *Classical Arabic Biography*, 13: the biographers of poets and grammarians sought to justify their subjects' privileged position by invoking the connection between language and revelation.

poets composed poems reflecting high moral values.[74] One promoter of moral values in Islam was the poet Ḥasan al-Ḥijāzī, whom our author admired.[75]

It is likely that the reason why kings and sultans were classified after scholars and learned Muslims, most of whom were Arabs, is due to the author's conviction, as a pious Khalwatī *Ṣūfī*, that authority leads to corruption and tyranny. This is due to the fact that al-Jabartī lived in an epoch when soldiers and Mamluk factions were engaged in exterminating each other and the Ottoman *wālī*s (Turkish governors) together with the Mamluks used the most brutal means to extort taxes from the populace. From time to time our author hints that the Mamluks and their servants were new converts to Islam. He argues that they were originally Christians or heathens who had been kidnapped or bought during their childhood and converted to Islam, and brought up in the corrupt Mamluk military system. This obsolete system no longer provided a good military training or the kind of Islamic education, which would encourage loyalty and obedience; in fact, young Mamluks were no longer well versed in the Islamic *sharī'a*.[76]

These are the main reasons why al-Jabartī classified the military class below the *'ulamā'* and the poets. The role of the *'ulamā'* in the Mamluk period, according to our author, was to be guardians and advisors to the rulers in matters pertaining to the *sharī'a*. The *'ulamā'* advocated knowledge (*'ilm*) and justice (*ḥaqq*, *inṣāf* and *'adl*), as against the ignorance (*jahl*) of the secular rulers and their injustice (*ẓulm*, *jawr*). Thus al-Jabartī distinguished between the *imām 'ādil* (just ruler), who obeys God and follows his law and the advice of the *'ulamā'*, who would be rewarded in this world and the hereafter, and the *imām jā'ir* (tyrant ruler), who would be hated by his subjects and punished by God in this world and in the hereafter. The just ruler should work towards equality (*musāwāt*) among all his Muslim subjects with respect to their rights and duties, preach piety and modesty, treat his subjects with kindness, and renounce the wealth of this world in favour of eternal reward in Heaven. According to al-Jabartī, these traits became 'customary and meaningless clichés' during Muḥammad 'Alī's reign.[77] Among the severe sins that rulers and officials committed was bribery (*rashwa*), which our author criticized and

74 Cf. Cooperson, *Classical Arabic Biography*, 9–13.

75 See *'Aj.*, I, 78–80.

76 Ibid, III, 310. Cf. Haarmann, 'Joseph's Law', 55–84.

77 *'Aj.*, III, 339.

pinpointed as a cause of the destruction of states and rulers.[78] Bribery is among his criteria for evaluating Muslim rulers as sinful.[79] A good Muslim is one who, when offered the advantages of this world (*'uriḍat 'alayhi al-dunya fa-lam yaqbalhā*), does not accept them, but rather prefers a secluded life.[80] A scholar, who accepted the post of *muftī* of the Ḥanafī sect, was helped by one of the *amīr*s to build a costly house,[81] and al-Jabartī gave Shaykh al-Sādāt as an example of a scholar who acquired the advantages of this world. Only a few had to be compelled to accept the position of *muftī*.[82]

Al-Jabartī divided rulers into two categories. There were those who heeded the advice of the *'ulamā'*, ruled justly, and refused to receive bribes,[83] among them the Mamluk Sultan Baybars (1223–77) and the Ottoman Sultans Salīm I (1512–20) and his successor Sulaymān the Magnificent (1520–66). They were just, ruled according to Islamic law, and expanded the territory under Muslim rule at the expense of the European infidels. On the other hand, he condemned rulers who were tyrants, oppressed Muslim subjects, and refused to heed the advice of the *'ulamā'*. The latter also were divided into two categories: those who refused to serve the rulers as judges and other religious posts out of piety since authority led to tyranny, oppression and corruption, and those among the *'ulamā'* who agreed to serve the rulers and exploited their jobs to acquire quick wealth through bribery and oppression.

The Ideal Muslim Scholar

As a pious Muslim al-Jabartī aspired to revive the Islamic system of justice, solidarity and zeal for *jihād* against the 'infidels' (*kuffār*), that is the European powers. He called for treating non-Muslim subjects (*ahl al-dhimma*) according to the *dhimma* rules as stated in the Islamic *sharī'a*. This meant not allowing non-Muslims to rule Muslims, carry weapons or ride horses, forbidding Christian pilgrimage to Jerusalem, the banning of the construction of new

78 Ibid., I, 21, 381, III, 299.

79 Such as Amīr Muḥammad Aghā al-Bārūdī, ibid.,II, 224.

80 Ibid., II, 77, l. 15. See also al-Zabīdī, *Mu'jam Mukhtaṣṣ* MS Madīna, biography no. 49, f. 12b, and MS Princeton, f. 23, biography of Aḥmad bin ʿAlī al-Jaʿfarī al-Jazūlī, عرضت عليه الدنيا فلم يقبلها والغالب عليه إخفاء الحال ('he refused the wealth of this world').

81 Al-Zabīdī, *Mu'jam Mukhtaṣṣ* (biography of Ḥasan bin Nūr al-Dīn al-Ḥanafī al-Maqdisī al-Azharī), MS Madīna, biography no. 181, f. 29b, and MS Princeton, ff. 64–5, and *'Aj*., I, 312.

82 *'Aj*., II, 244.

83 Ibid., I, 18.

churches, the renovation of old sites and the construction of new houses higher than those of neighbouring Muslims.[84] al-Jabartī admired the pious and zealous Wahhābī movement that enabled a woman to defeat the corrupt Ottoman soldiers in the Ḥijāz, but lamented their rejection of the *Ṣūfī* orders and the belief in Muslim saints and their miracles, and their refusal to permit pilgrims to visit their tombs.[85] For the Wahhābīs, the *ṭarīqa muḥammadiyya*, which entails conformity between a physical and a spiritual imitation of the Prophet, is an absurdity although it is a rational procedure.[86]

According to al-Jabartī, the ideal Muslim scholar (*'ālim*) should behave with humility and good manner, provide help to the poor, and be modest in clothing and food. He should refuse to allow others to kiss his hands, abstain from visiting grandees, and refuse to take any presents offered to them during their visits to rulers.[87] Such a scholar should be gentle, humble, and self-effacing; he should not meddle in worldly affairs, wear valuable garments, ride a horse, or enter the house of an *amīr*; he should devote himself to learning and scholarship.[88] Some scholars added to the religious studies of *fiqh* and *ḥadīth* also secular sciences such as mathematics, geometry, constructing sundials (*mizwala*), *zāyirja* (the science of divination with concentric circles), astronomy (*falak*), astrology (*tanjīm*), and the evocation of spirits (*istiḥḍār al-arwāḥ*).[89] Some shaykhs were accused by the *amīr*s of being charlatans and frauds.

Not only should *'ulamā'* be modest and observant of religious duties, but so should every Muslim, especially Mamluk rulers. Some Mamluks who observed their religious duties and behaved accordingly are said by our author to have behaved flawlessly. Riḍwān Jurbajī al-Razzāz was a good Muslim, so much so that there was 'nothing to mar his character, either touching worldly

84 Ibid., II, 103, 154–5, III, 91, 93, 191, IV, 2.

85 Ibid., I, 89, III, 253, IV, 85–6, 136, 137, 229, 288–302; Lane, *Manners*, 112–13.

86 See Radtke, 'Sufism', 353–61.

87 Such as Muṣṭafā al-'Azīzī al-Shāfi'ī, *'Aj.*, I, 162. On rich clothing and riding swift animals by Copts during the French occupation see ibid., III, 18.

88 Such as Shaykh Muḥammad al-Buhūtī, ibid.,II, 99–100. On Muḥammad al-Masīrī as an ideal *'ālim*, see ibid., III, 266, 276, IV, 51, 65 and Bjørneboe, 143–55, especially 145–8.

89 Such as Shaykh Ḥasan b. Manṣūr b. Dāwūd al-Ḥasanī al-Maḥallī, see al-Zabīdī, *Mu'jam Mukhtaṣṣ*, MS Madina, biography no. 149, f. 32a–b, and MS Princeton, f. 69.

affairs or matters of religion' *(wa-mā 'alimnā 'alayhi mā yushīnuh fī dīnihi wa-lā dunyāhu)*.[90]

Al-Jabartī collected and wrote down hundreds of biographies. Almost no scholar is spared his critical scrutiny. The most comprehensive necrologies in *'Ajā'ib al-Āthār* are devoted to three eminent scholars of the eighteenth century. The first is a model Muslim scholar, the author's own father, Ḥasan (1697–1790).[91] The second is his mentor al-Murtaḍā al-Zabīdī, who is depicted as an average pious scholar.[92] The third is Shaykh al-Sādāt, the embodiment of an evil, greedy, and conceited scholar craving for the wealth of this ephemeral world, whose house, previously the cradle of piety and charity, became devoted to the extraction of taxes from poor people.[93] These three biographies constitute masterful depictions of the three categories of religious scholars. The necrology of al-Zabīdī is an excellent example of subtle double-entendre; it is one of the author's shrewdest pieces of writing, in which his praises are veiled criticism. It seems that al-Jabartī's main grudge against his mentor was that al-Zabīdī overlooked the biography of his father in the *Mu'jam Mukhtaṣṣ*, a fact at which he hinted when he wrote that 'he neglected those who were worthy of being written about from among the greatest scholars and important men and the like'.[94]

His father, the first among these three scholars, is depicted as a paragon of Muslim modesty, seclusion, and detachment, as enumerated in his *Introduction* and his comments on the characters of various Muslim scholars. His father's character is described as follows:[95] 'his nature gathered together excellences and virtues, so it was free of faults and vices. He was dignified and modest, inspiring awe in the eyes of the beholder, veneration in the mind, and love in the heart ... Nobility of character, self-control, forbearance, modesty, contentment, an honest spirit, suppression of anger, and an openness to men great and small — such was his temperament and nature. He was without pretence and was never conceited about his rank, never affected, never laying claim to learning, knowledge, or the dignity of a Shaykh in front of his

90 See *'Aj.*, I, 305.

91 Ibid., I, 385–413.

92 Ibid., II,234–46.

93 Ibid., I, 192, 204, 385, II, 197, IV, 186, 333.

94 Ibid., II, 234. Cf. al-Kattānī, *Fihris al-Fahāris*, IV, 260, where he deals with al-Jabartī.

95 *'Aj.*, II, 395.

students. He eschewed expressions of deference or hand-kissing ... It was his habit to sit at the back of the assembly without much regard for making a fine figure- with his turban, or without it; wearing anything that came to hand; using for a waistband a piece of broadcloth salvage, an old piece of cloth, a cashmere shawl, or an apron'.[96]

In contrast to these admirable features of a good Muslim, al-Zabīdī is 'praised' with subtle irony as possessing the contrary traits, those which pious Muslims scholars should avoid: 'He wore splendid clothing and rode purebred (*musawwama*) horses', and '[h]e was luxuriously dressed and wore a turban ... with white muslin. It had ends which dropped down to his nape, and they had fabric and tassels of silk about a span long', in short the turban of a dandy. Al-Jabartī wrote that pious scholars should refrain from such dress, and especially condemned the use of silk, which is denounced by the Prophet as well. Wherever he went, so our author wrote, '[e]very one honoured him and he met all the important people of the areas, the leading men of learning and manners',[97] while a pious scholar should avoid honour and refrain from seeking the friendship of rulers. Al-Zabīdī is depicted as conceited and laying claim to learning and knowledge. When he completed his *Tāj al-'Arūs*'he prepared a festive banquet at which he assembled the scholars and the shaykhs of that era ... He showed it to them and they were pleased with it ... wrote their panegyrics about him in prose and verse. He used to exchange gifts and drew near to them by useful lessons and amulets, and incantations'. He impressed the gullible people of the Maghrib thanks to his unusually good memory, pretending that he was endowed with clear divine revelation and mystic illumination (*min bāb al-kashf al-ṣarīḥ*), and therefore received all manner of presents from these simple pilgrims.[98] The way he flattered rulers can be seen in his letter to the tyrant, the ruler of Acre, Aḥmad Pasha al-Jazzār, in which he wrote that the Pasha was the *Mahdī al-muntaẓar* (the awaited rightly guided one) and that he would attain great importance.[99] While Ḥasan al-Jabartī lost more than forty children and a number of wives without uttering a complaint, since he believed that whatever happened was decreed by God, al-Zabīdī lamented his wife Zubayda, grieved for her greatly, and elegized her

96 Ibid., I, 404.
97 Ibid., II, 196.
98 Ibid., II, 201.
99 Ibid., II, 203.

in the lyrical style of Majnūn Laylā (Qays Ibn al-Mulawwaḥ) in several poems, remaining near her grave for many days.[100] But al-Jabartī, the anti-feminist who criticized the firing of canons in celebration of the birth of the Sultan's daughter and commented that such a thing was unheard of and that 'such innovations, I believe, are fearful (signs) of the Day of Resurrection',[101] mocked his mentor's grief for the death of his wife, but soon remarried after her death.

In contrast, Ḥasan al-Jabartī was a learned scholar who did not neglect his religious duties, whether individual (*farḍ 'ayn*) or collective (*fard kifāya*). He looked after the welfare of the Islamic community, and was well-versed in both traditional or religious (*'ulūm naqliyya*) and rational secular sciences (*'ulūm 'aqliyya*) such as grammar, mathematics, the Hijri calendar, astronomy, astrology, mechanics, inheritance laws, fixing prayer times (*tawqīt*), and philosophy (*ḥikma*). He was righteous and humble, a jurist and *muftī* of the Ḥanafī school of *fiqh*, modest in his behaviour and clothing, generous, maintaining an open house for any needy scholars and students, avoiding flattery and the friendship of grandees. In contrast to al-Jabartī's father, al-Zabīdī was an emigrant to Egypt, a philologist and a *ḥadīth* scholar who gained his fame by the ancient and venerated method of teaching *ḥadīth*, his dictionary *Tāj al-'Arūs*, his commentary on *Iḥyā' 'Ulūm al-Dīn*, and his pompous method of publicity and dissemination. He courted friends by composing verses in praise of their pedigrees as *sharīfs*, gave special licences (*ijāza*) and authorizations to teach various sciences, and pretended to know hidden secrets and to be able to see the future. He flattered rulers, was eager to acquire wealth, and gladly received presents from *amīrs* and from both rich and poor people, a habit that he abandoned at the end of his life.

False 'Ulamā' and Popular Ṣūfī Leaders

A secular person of worthy character, such as the poet Ḥasan al-Badrī al-Ḥijāzī, is one who secludes himself from human society, devoting himself entirely to his own affairs and content with his condition, because in society men behave as predators towards each other.[102] Ḥijāzī was one of the most

100 Ibid., II, 201–2.

101 Ibid., III, 354.

102 Ibid., I, 74–5.

gifted poets, a social and political critic, an eloquent writer of originality and insight, who scolded the scholars of the al-Azhar mosque and the popular *Ṣūfī* orders who permitted indecent gatherings of men and women where *mawlid*s (saints' birthdays) were celebrated. No one escaped his criticism and rebuke, in particular scholars who exploited the belief of Egyptians in saints and encouraged the common people to visit and present offerings at the tombs of idiots and fools after their death. In these festivals, especially those of the Aḥmadiyya, the Saʿdiyya and the Shuʿaybiyya[103] 'a motley multitude of people, high and low, peasants from the country side (entertainers, performers of artifice and farces) [*arbāb al-malāhī wa 'l-malā'ib*] and idle rogues, dancers, prostitutes, monkey trainers, and mountebanks all assembled, filling the plains and gardens, trampling the graves and kindling fires over them, tossing rubbish on them, urinating, defecating, fornicating and sodomizing, sporting and dancing ... day and night'.[104]

His versified criticism of corrupt scholars, such as *'ulamā'*, *Ṣūfī*s, or dervishes, was praised by our author, who quoted his lengthy poems in which their faults and the pagan rites surrounding them are criticized. One example is the case of ʿUthmān of Fayyūm, who came to Cairo in 1699 and claimed to be a saint. Men and women who believed in his sainthood committed fornication in public, provoking the anger of the soldiers, who then killed him. Ḥijāzī described this incident in a long poem as follows:[105] 'the ignorant people consider every mad man among these *Ṣūfī*s. Even their scholars venerate such a man and take them for their lords in place of the Almighty. They forget God; they say that a certain human being grants relief from trouble. When such a man dies, they make his tomb a shrine and throng to visit his tomb, Arabs and non-Arabs alike. Some kiss the gravestone; others kiss the threshold of the door or the dust. Thus, pagans treat their idols, seeking to draw near them!

103 Ibid., IV, 190.

104 Ibid., I, 147, 220–1 (the *mawlid* of Shaykh ʿAbd al-Wahhāb al-ʿAfīfī and the atrocities and fornication committed then), II, 106–7, 248, III, 39, 43–4, 78, 80–1, IV, 190. Lane, *Manners*, discusses Muslim saints under the chapter 'Superstitions', 228–53. Cf. Radtke, 'Sufism', 341, notes 161–4.

105 *'Aj.*, I, 28–9. On indecent behaviour between men and women in *mawlids*, see IV, 6 (fornication in a mosque), IV, 227. On al-Shaykh Ṣādūma, who was believed to be 'one of the saints, a man gifted with mystical states and contemplative knowledge ... an unmatched master of all (spiritual arts)', and was executed because he was deceived by the *amīr*'s concubine, see ibid., II, 17–18.

They are infected with fornication, perjury, and tyranny, with oppression, stealing, and looting. All of this is the result of blindness — woe to the man whose heart God has blinded!'[106]

Very few scholars and poets dared to criticize the popular *Ṣūfī* orders and their holy people in the manner of Ḥijāzī, who exposed what he saw as the fraudulent behaviour of these coarse and rude people.[107] They had defiled the high morals and values of Islam, and cared only for their outward appearance, enlarging their turbans, and broadening their sleeves to look like masters walking with books in their fraudulent attempts at seeking money. Ḥijāzī says that their false and pretentious behaviour was clear to all and in fact, they were like wolves, attempting to prey on people for their money. They boasted of their knowledge in order to hide their ignorance. Our poet encourages people to beware of them and those who pretend to devote themselves to praising God. Such persons fingered the rosary (*misbaḥa*), wore (the *Ṣūfī*'s) wool, carried a staff, wore a hair shirt, and held gourds and pitchers. Those who did this were the hairy shaykhs of the devil (dervishes). 'They hide as many devils as the number of their hairs, yea, even beyond counting. They are cunning; the devil has become their follower, and pleads for their help and support. Their goal is money, not the Muslim saints whom they call ... they have taken beardless boys as objects of desire. They are head-over-heels in love with them. Moreover, they openly call the youths their novices (*bidāyāt*), in grace, passion, and shame'.[108] He condemned the French for giving reign to the *Ṣūfī* orders such as the followers of al-ʿAfīfī, al-Sammān, Ibn al-ʿArabī, and the ʿĪsawiyya and their heretic practices, while the commoners 'would observe the handsome lads who had come to watch, running after them and tempting them'.[109]

However, as a Khalwatī *Ṣūfī*, al-Jabartī denounced false scholars and criticized the Wahhābīs for their rejection of spiritual (*'ilm bāṭin*) and miraculous deeds performed by true *Ṣūfī* saints during their lives and even after their deaths. He censured the Wahhābīs' adherence only to the formal Muslim practices of prayers, fast, alms, pilgrimage, their hostility towards the veneration of Muslim shrines, and their destruction of tombs with domes

106 Ibid., I, 78–81.

107 Ibid., I, 81.

108 Ibid., I, 79–81, III, 81. Cf. the biography of Sayyid ʿAlī al-Bakrī, ibid., II, 248.

109 Ibid., III, 39–40.

(*qubba*, pl. *qibbāb*) which they considered heterodox. They even looted the treasures kept at the Prophet's tomb, claiming that these treasures should be used for *jihād* and to help poor and needy Muslims.[110]

In Ottoman Egypt, the *'ulamā'* were at the mercy of despotic Mamluk rulers. Whenever they stood in a ruler's way by opposing the latter's tyranny and ambitions,[111] he did not hesitate to have them assassinated. Al-Jabartī expresses great reverence for the *awliyā'* and heads of the *Ṣūfī* orders. He explains that they are among the *abdāl*s who are gifted with the special power of *shafā'a* (intercession). Such saints protect Islamic lands from calamities, as happened in Egypt in the case of al-Saqqāf (lit. the Roof-builder [over a country]),[112] Any harm which befell them will be avenged by God on the basis of His rule through 'reward and punishment'. al-Jabartī explains the calamities which befell the Muslim world and the Ottoman defeats at the hand of the European powers as due to the assassination in 1181/1767 of the Khalwatī saint (*walī*) Muḥammad b. Sālim Ḥifnāwī (or al-Ḥifnī) al-Shāfi'ī al-Khalwatī, who was the Grand Master (*khalīfat al-waqt*) and the 'pole' (*quṭb*) of the age.[113] He was assassinated by the Mamluks of 'Alī Bey Abu 'l-Dhahab.[114] *Ṣūfī* scholars of this kind, mainly saints (*walī*, *quṭb*), are given special attention by our author. Ḥifnāwī's long biography was copied by our author from Shamma al-Fawwī and ended with the author's statement of faith in his holiness and in God's punishment of all rulers who do not heed their advice and dare to harm such people:

> Indeed, it is a clearly perceived that if there is no one among men to speak the truth openly, enjoin the right, forbid the wrong, and establish guidance, the order of the world becomes corrupt and men's hearts are filled with dissension. When dissension fills men's heart, afflictions follow. It is a known and established matter that the soundness of the community depends on its scholars and kings. The soundness of kings depends on the soundness of scholars, and the corruption of the effect follows from the corruption of the cause. How much more so when the cause (of soundness) was lost... When the *amīr*s living in Cairo began to

110 Ibid., I, 89, III, 253, IV, 85–6, 136, 137, 229, 288–302; Lane, *Manners*, 112–13. Cf. Samer Traboulsi, 'An Early Refutation of Muhammad Ibn 'Abd Al-Wahhāb's Reformist Views', in *Die Welt des Islams* 49:3 (2002), 373–415.

111 *'Aj.*, I, 419.

112 Ibid., I, 303.

113 Ibid., I, 300–1. On them see *ḳuṭb*, in Lane, *Manners*, 236.

114 *'Aj.*, I, 303–4.

> raise an army against ʿAlī Bey and Ṣāliḥ Bey and asked (al-Ḥifnāwī for his) consent, he denounced them and would not give permission … Knowing that their intention could not be realized while the master stood in the way, they diverted his attention and poisoned him. Afterwards, finding no one to forbid or deter them, they sent out their armies, and the result was their defeat and destruction in an exemplary punishment. ʿAlī Bey came to power, with no one to deter him, he too did as seemed best to him, and as a result affliction descended on Egypt, Syria, and the Ḥijāz, and spread to include the whole world and all countries. This is the open secret, which is an indubitable consequence of the inner (secret)- which consists of respect for the inheritors of prophecy, complete conformity (to them), making the foundations firm, setting up the guideposts of the right way and Islam, and strengthening the edifice of piety. For such men are God's trusted ones in the world, the choicest of the sons of Adam. 'Those are the inheritors who shall inherit Paradise, therein dwelling forever' (Qur'ān, 23:10–11).[115]

Al-Jabartī's narrative upholds an idealistic vision of Muslim scholars who, as representatives of the divine law, maintain their authority over political rulers and seek justice and welfare for the Muslim community. This vision served our author as a mirror in which to examine the moral and religious deviations of the *'ulamā'* of his time, which he believed to be the main reason for Muslim societies having become an easy prey for European civilization.

Like the poet Ḥijāzī, our author looked down on the popular *Ṣūfī* orders such as the 'al-Rifāʿeeyeh', 'Saadeeyeh', 'Shinnāweeyeh' and Aḥmadiyya[116] and the dervishes called *arbāb al-ashāyir*.[117] However, he openly expressed his admiration for sheikhs of this type who were pious in his estimation.[118] Al-Jabartī's main criticism was directed against Muḥammad ʿAlī, who used his monopoly on land, his agrarian reforms, and the heavy taxes he levied to deprive the *'ulamā'*of their farming duty (*iltizām*), concessions which were their main income. Instead of these scholars, he employed non-Muslims, especially Copts, Armenians, Christian Syrians, and Jews. He also employed young Muslim administrators who had received a secular education in his military schools and were sent by his government to be trained in Europe. With the return of Rifāʿa Rāfiʿ al-Ṭahṭāwī (1801–73) from France to Egypt the

115 His necrology is in ibid., I, 289–304.

116 *'Aj.*, I, 80, Cf. Lane, *Manners*, 247–50.

117 Lane, *Manners*, 449–50, 464.

118 *'Aj.*, I, 84.

role and special status of the traditionally educated *'ulamā'* ended. This is in contrast to the status at the end of the seventeenth century of the supervisors of *waqfs*, the *'ulamā'* and the students of al-Azhar, when they were respected by the Pashas. ʿAlī Pasha (1106/1694–5) ordered the Mamluk tax contractors, the *multazims* who had held back the revenues, to pay what ever was due without delay [119] Whenever the military factions clashed to the point of arousing unrest or civil strife among Muslims, the *mashāyikh* and the *'ulamā'* were needed to solve the problem peacefully.[120] In the case of a dispute among military factions (such as between the Sepahis and Janissaries) a *fatwā* by the *Naqībal-Ashrāf*, the *'ulamā'*, the *qāḍī 'askar* (the Chief Turkish Judge of the army in Egypt) and the heads of the popular *Ṣūfī* orders (*arbāb al-ashāyir*, or the dervishes) would put an end to the strife.[121] Among Egyptian scholars, there was solidarity against Turkish scholars. In cases of disputes between a puritan Turkish *'ālim* and Egyptian scholars about whether pilgrimage to saints' tombs and the belief in their miracles were permissible, the Egyptian scholars backed the local popular custom.[122] Such solidarity prevailed among the *sharīfs*, too. Once a Turkish soldier killed a *sharīf*, the *ashrāf* then gathered and declared a strike in the markets, forcing the shopkeepers to shut their shops, fought with the *daftardār's* guards, and defeated them. Regiments set out to restore peace and order, some of the *ashrāfs* were sentenced to deportation, but at the intercession of the *'ulamā'*, they were released out of respect for their status.[123]

At the end of the eighteenth and the beginning of the nineteenth century, the status of Muslim scholars was at its zenith. They maintained their authority over political rulers as the representatives of the divine law, while the *Ṣūfīs* represented the spiritual ties with God Almighty. They advocated 'neutrality, humility, seclusion, and restraint' for rulers who wanted to safeguard their interests. They never attempted to acquire political power for themselves in order to replace the Ottomans or the Mamluks, but tried to mediate between the rulers and their subjects through the divine authority of the *sharī'a*, and sought justice and the welfare of the Muslim community. They were satisfied

119 Ibid., I, 26; on the *Mishaykhat al-Azhar* as the highest rank among the *'ulamā'*, see *'Aj.*, II, 53, 252. Cf. Lane, *Manners*, 217–18, 222.

120 *'Aj.*, I, 32.

121 Ibid., I, 32.

122 Ibid., I, 48–50. Cf. Lane, *Manners*, 55, 243–7, 330, 438.

123 *'Aj.*, I, 50.

with being able to influence in matters of 'taxation and protection of friends, clients' and oppressed people.

In his systematic and careful study of 'the true political position of the *'ulamā'*' during the eighteenth and nineteenth centuries, Lars Bjørneboe arrived at the conclusion that 'the *'ulamā'* were important to the Ottoman government and the *amīr*s. In the decentralized Ottoman Empire, the influence of the central government was maintained by a policy of divide and rule, supporting groups to counterbalance other groups, creating ties of clientage and patronage while weakening or breaking the alliances favoured by local *a'yān* and their households. The *amīr*s of Ottoman Egypt, especially, the masters of what remained of the Qazdaghli household, operated along the same lines, sometimes as in the turbulent 1780s in fierce competition with the central government, at other times in uneasy cooperation'.[124] In fact, the *'ulamā'* were important for Ottomans and Mamluks alike; both lavished presents, offices, and revenues on them, in order to secure their loyalty. Both felt the need to legitimize their rule over Egypt. The Ottomans' policy was to stir factional conflicts to weaken their rivals among the Mamluks and the grandees of Egypt.

Muḥammad ʿAlī decided to implement reforms based on European military and administrative models, and was eager to get rid of his dangerous rivals the Mamluks. This he did in 1811 in the Citadel massacres. Through his agrarian and *waqf* reforms, he was easily able to reduce the status ofthe religious scholars and dervishes who were conservative Egyptian Arabs, including the *ashrāf*, the heads of the *Ṣūfī* orders. They agreed to be the guardians of the *sharī'a* and shun political power, preferring submission and accommodation to Muḥammad ʿAlī's rule after helping him ascend to power. They expected to increase their influence, wealth, privileges, and sources of income. When he consolidated his power, he realized that these scholars were an obstacle to his modernizing reforms, since they insisted on solving all problems through spiritual and esoteric practices; he therefore decided to curb their influence. He dismissed the more powerful religious scholars and sought the loyalty of those *'ulamā'* who backed his reforms, such as Ḥasan al-ʿAṭṭār. Those who opposed him he replaced with secular officials who had received a European

124 Bjørneboe, *In Search*, 321–2.

education.[125] In this way, he was able to end the long period during which the *'ulamā'* dominated the scientific, cultural, literary, and social life in Egypt and introduced reforms of European orientation in Egypt.

The deterioration of the religious scholars' status was enhanced by the victorious general Ibrāhīm Pasha (1789–1848), Muḥammad ʿAlī's son, who deliberately ignored them, whether they were leading *shaykh*s, *qāḍī*s, the *Shaykh al-Sādāt*, al-Bakrī the *Naqīb al-Ashrāf*, or *muftī*s: 'he rose for none of them, nor did he respond by civil word or gesture to their greetings'.[126] When they visited him to congratulate him for his safe return after a victorious campaign, he did not bother to return their greetings but pretended to be busy in conversation with a comedian and made them leave in shame.[127] According of our author, making the acquaintance of entertainers is an act, which from a religious point of view makes *'ulamā'* and rulers unfit to judge other people in court or to deal with religious matters. Muḥammad ʿAlī abolished 'the privileges of the shaykhs and jurists who held the concessions for towns which were exempted from paying taxes'.[128] As a result, they were impoverished and lost the influence which had hindered Muḥammad ʿAlī's ambitions and reforms. However, the shaykhs and judges showed no desire either to unite and rebel against him, or to cooperate with him in secular reforms, which curbed their political influence. Their restraint and detachment was due to the long venerated Khalwatī *Ṣūfī* principle expressed by al-Jabartī, that Muḥammad ʿAlī was God's revenge against the religious establishment that backed his tyranny.[129] This is in conformity with the principle that 'the pious man is also obliged to obey the wicked government authorities that God has imposed as a punishment, and he should not rebel against them',[130] since it is God's will.

125 Ibid., 81–5 arguing against the claims of Afaf Marsot, *Egypt in the Reign of Muhammad 'Ali* (Cambridge 1984), and Marsot's articles on the *'ulamā'* of Egypt, in P.M. Holt (ed.), *Political and Social Changes in Modern Egypt* (London 1968), 264–80; in Andre Assabgui et al. (eds), *Colloque internationale sur l'histoire du Caire* (Cairo 1972), 313–20; in Nikki R. Keddie (ed.), *Scholars, Saints and Sufis* (Los Angeles and Berkeley 1972), 149–65; in T. Naff and R. Owen (eds), *Studies in Eighteenth Century Islamic History* (Carbondale and Edwardsville, IL 1977), 205–16; D. Crecelius, 'Nonideological Responses of the Egyptian Ulama to Modernization', in Keddie, *Scholars*, 167–210.

126 *'Aj.*, IV, 310.

127 Ibid., IV, 306.

128 Ibid., IV, 68.

129 Ibid., IV, 100–1.

130 Cf. Radtke, 'Sufism', 337–8.

Conclusion

The *'ulamā'* played an active role during the history of the Muslim people. The strife in the Muslim world over the question of who should be the caliph and heirs of the Prophet Muḥammad began at an early stage. Disagreement over this question brought about the split between the Sunnis and the Shiʿa, and later between the *Ṣūfīs* and the *'ulamā'* in the Sunni world. It enables us to understand the main reason for the weakness and the great decline that the Muslim world has endured in religious, political, and cultural spheres. Within the limited scope of the present study, there is room for only a simplified overview of the undercurrents of the Islamic factors of decline.

Conclusion

There are few Muslim historians who wrote their works based upon an original and well-defined theory of history. One outstanding exception is ʿAbd al-Raḥmān Ibn Khaldūn (1332–1406), in his *Muqaddima* (Introduction to Universal History). He is a giant amongst Muslim historians, a theorist of history and sociology and a philosopher of socio-political history. Based upon a strict logic of hypotheses and conclusions he discusses certain topics of world history from a new scientific perspective. He wrote his *Muqaddima*, at a time when Greek logic and philosophy were going into a rapid decline in the Islamic world and were ceasing to have any real influence on Islamic thinking, mainly after the burning of the books of the theologian and Aristotelian philosopher Ibn Rushd (Averroes, 1126–98).

On the other hand, ʿAbd al-Raḥmān al-Jabartī (1753–1825) who admired Ibn Khaldūn's unique work, lived in times when al-Ghazālī's (1059–1111) mystical dogma was in vogue and had defeated Averroes' Greek logic of separation between the domain of faith and reason. Sufism was also very important for him, especially the Khalwatiyya sect, based upon the Qur'ān and *sunna* according to al-Ghazālī's teachings in *Iḥyā' 'Ulūm al-Dīn* and the commentary on it by Murtaḍā al-Zabīdī. In his chronicle of Egypt *'Ajā'ib al-Āthār fi'l-Tarājim wa'l-Akhbār* (1688–1821), al-Jabartī recorded daily events and biographies of eminent personalities, with the intention of writing a fifth volume. Al-Jabartī's method enabled him to express his conventional world views in his comments on current events and human psychological behaviour and the traits of the character of the personalities whom he analysed in his necrologies. In his important Introduction to his History of Egypt *'Ajā'ib al-Āthār*, he discussed in detail his Islamic historical philosophy and value system, including the importance of the *sharī'a*, the role of the *'ulamā'* as its guardians and as guides who fearing God and believing in the unity of the Muslim people would show rulers how to adhere to their religious rules and apply the Islamic rules of justice.[1] His observations show a psychological depth of understanding of events and human character. His analysis springs from his

1 See S. Moreh, 'Al-Jabarti's Attitude towards the *'Ulama'* of His Time', in Meir Hatina (ed.), *Guardians of Faith in Modern Times: 'Ulama' in the Middle East* (Leiden 2009), 47–64.

religious logic (*manṭiq*) and Sufi views which he expressed on all aspects of life: religious, social, economic, philosophical, literary, cultural and so on.

For the study of this unique historian it is important to conclude here our findings from his scattered observations in both his chronicles and biographies. Like his father, the scholar and *'ālim*, Ḥasan al-Jabartī (d. 1744), he paid great attention to sciences such as mathematics, geometry, algebra, medicine, astronomy and astrology, which were a *farḍ kifāya* (collective duty) to serve the religious needs of the Muslim community in dividing inheritance and fixing the time of prayer and feasts. But as a Khalwatī, who with the help of his sheikh has to endure seven spiritual stations until achieving the state of *al-nafs al-kāmila* (the perfect soul),[2] he defined himself in the title pages of his autographs as *al-faqīr* (the poor man), distinguishing himself from the *darwishs*, since he was an elitist scornful of popular Sufism or of what he called with disdain, *arbāb al-ishāyir*.[3] However, like them he adhered to the veneration of saints, interpretation of dreams and visions, esoteric sciences and practices. Al-Jabartī placed divine revelation and spiritual Sufi sensitivity above reason, an aspect that made him critical of the Wahhābīs who opposed Sufism, in spite of his sympathy for their zeal and strict observance of Islamic principles (*arkān*). He considered the Wahhābīs as a zealous and militant movement of reform within Islam, a revolt against orthodox Islam. The Sunni Arabs, descendants of the Prophet, aspired for generations to retain their spiritual hegemony in the Islamic world through heading Sufi orders. The heads of these Sufi orders were reluctant to accept worldly authority, since political and military authority leads to tyranny and oppression which are against the principle of the justice and tolerance of Islam.

He was a historian typical of the Muslim East (*Mashriq*) who wrote his work with a defined worldview and a value system based upon Islamic logic (*manṭiq*) based upon religious concepts of predestination, God's determination of the path of world history and the destiny of each person. It is impossible to change God's pre-determination, but prayers, alms and repentance might ease

---

2 *'Aj.*, I, 296–7.

3 See *'Aj.*, IV, 120: فنادى على أهل الطرق الشيطانية المعروفين بالاشاير وهم السوقة وأرباب الحرف المرذولة الذين ينسبون أنفسهم لأرباب الضرائح المشهورين كالأحمدية والرفاعية والقادرية والبرهامية وغير ذلك. (Then he sent for the people of the devilish orders, known as the standard bearers (*al-ishāyir*). They are a rabble, members of the base professions who attach themselves to the tomb of the great saints like al-Aḥmadiyya, al-Rifāʿiyya, al-Qādiriyya, al-Birhāmiyya, and the like.) (The translation is according to Philipp and Perlmann, IV, 169–70).

calamities. God's justice in ruling the world is through reward (*thawāb*) and punishment (*'iqāb*) in this world and the hereafter. He expressed his opinion that the conflict between Muslims and non-Muslims is a religious, cultural and eternal *jihād* which should transfer this world from the darkness of infidelity (*kufr*) to the light (*nūr*) of Islam. Still, he was able to change his mind and admit that justice can be also applied by the French and that God had sent infidels to support Muslims, as in the case of the British who supported the Ottomans against the French occupation.

The history of Egypt was al-Jabartī's main concern. He lived in a period which he himself, his friend Ḥasan al-ʿAṭṭār and other Arab scholars considered to be in serious decline and a low point in Arab and Islamic culture and religious education and one of military impotence against Europe as *dār al-ḥarb*. He argued that the situation was one in which the Mamluk military system, education and morals had deteriorated to a deplorable level, and Ottoman corruption, ignorance and tyranny were responsible for the situation to which Muslim civilization found itself during the 'Islamic eighteenth century'.

In contrast to some European scholars who defended the theory of cultural dynamics,[4] one gets the impression from al-Jabartī's writings based upon Ibn Khaldūn's theory that the Muslim world had plunged into the 'dynamics' of stagnation and deterioration in a moon like cycle from crescent, full moon and wane, and that then another nation or dynasty would take over. This cycle is observed through the first righteous caliphate, the Umayyad and the Abbasid caliphates, and finally the Ottoman Empire. The zenith of Islamic scientific activities had been reached with the giants of Islamic sciences, such as Ibn al-Haytham (Alhazem, 965–1039) in optics, Ibn Sīnā (Avicenna, 980–1037) in medicine, Ibn Rushd (Averroes, 1126–98) in philosophy, Ibn al-Nafīs (1210–88) in discovering blood circulation and others. One can say that Ibn Khaldūn (1332–1406) was on the scene in the wane. The European renaissance started with the translation of their works into Latin, forming a new cultural and scientific cycle in Europe. However, according to al-Jabartī, this decline was God's punishment because the Muslims had neglected their religious duties and zeal for *jihād*.

4 Stefan Wild, 'To Our Reader', *Die Welt des Islams* 36:3 (1996), 271–5 and 'Islamic Enlightenment and the Paradox of Averroes', 379–90.

Al-Jabartī's chronicles and biographies reflect two main periods of religious, political and intellectual trends in Egyptian society. The first two volumes of *'Ajā'ib al-Āthār* (1688–1797) deals with the period in which some Sufi orders, headed by the Sunni branches of the Wafā'iyya and al-Bakriyya, opposed the popular branches of Sufism with their orientation towards magic, superstitions, saint worship, shamanic practices brought to Egypt by various Mamluk races. The popular branches had succeeded in dominating the religious, military, political and economic aspects of Egyptian society. The Wafā'iyya and al-Bakriyya aspired to salvation through spiritual assimilation in the Almighty's spiritual power, seeking knowledge of God through his prophet, angels and saints.

Al-Jabartī's chronicles reflect the collective consciousness of the *'ulamā'*in Egypt and their ambivalent attitude towards the rise and fall of the Ottomans, the Mamluk emirs, and the French invaders. The French occupation confronted the Muslims and our author in particular with an enigma. They assumed that this invasion by a European power was a new religious Crusade. Realizing that Napoleon's occupation of Egypt with his 36,000 men on 19 May 1798 was not religious but military and cultural, al-Jabartī considered it as the first clash between two civilizations, the superior Islamic religious value system and morals and the philosophical French secular culture based upon reason and political power. The Muslim army defeats were considered as punishment from Allāh for the tyranny of the Mamluk rulers and the Ottomans' corruption, tyranny and oppression of their Muslim subjects. Al-Jabartī could not understand Napoleon's cultural zeal recruiting a group of scientists and artists with the intention of fusing Muslim culture with the new humanitarian, philosophic, scientific and secular French culture with its quest for knowledge, modern administration, sophisticated military equipment, tactics, journals and the printing press. Our author can be considered the first Muslim Arab thinker to be aware of the modern spirit of the French revolution and the Napoleonic era. The new French secular morals, social and political aims, especially their trinity of freedom (*ḥurriyya*), justice (*'adāla*) and equality (*musāwāt*), were in complete opposition to the values revealed by Allāh in the Qur'ān and his Prophet's *sunna.* Al-Jabartī argued that their new trinity was invented by their wise men while the Muslim value system is based upon divine revelation according to the Qur'ān. He wondered how man could be free when the Qur'ān determines man's duties and thinking for his salvation. The only justice is according to Allāh's commands in his Holy Book and equality is impossible since Allāh created people with different talents and abilities as is stated in the Qur'ān (6:165).

Al-Jabartī also accused the French as in the case of some of the philosophers of being 'materialists who deny all God's attributes, the Hereafter and the Resurrection, and who reject Prophethood'.[5] He defined the French as 'infidels', who do not believe in any religion, with no divine book, but adhere to reason and logic. Their state, its territories, law, and the administration of their affairs wasin the hands of the intelligent and wise men among them, not according to the Divine Book. 'Abd al-Raḥmān al-Jabartī preached the strict application of the Quranic commands in the treatment of women who should be obedient, modest and veiled and the *dhimmī*s who should observe strictly the rules on their status and pay their pole tax, while the *'ulamā'* should adhere to their duties as advisors to the rulers. He praised the act of forbidding Christians from making the pilgrimage to Jerusalem. He expressed his rage at the relative freedom given to the *dhimmī*s and others under French rule and Muḥammad 'Alī's new administration. However, all the calamities which befell the Egyptians were attributed to God's punishment for their negligence of their religious duties, since Allāh rules the universe by predestination according to reward and punishment.

During the French occupation some Egyptian women who were supposed to veil themselves, behave modestly and be confined to their harem imitated French ladies in their clothing, and indulgedin 'debauchery' and free contacts with men. After their departure, women who were accused of having intimate relations with the French were punished and some were executed with the consent of their fathers. However, after the expulsion of the French from Egypt and the return of the Ottomans with their cruelty and the calamities this caused to the Egyptians, he changed his mind and expressed his appreciation of French justice, their scientific, moral, technical achievements and their quest for knowledge of languages and secular sciences. He admitted, after attending chemical and physical experiments conducted by French scientists, that 'these are things that the minds of people like us cannot grasp.'[6] While the Ottoman

5 See his comment on the first French Proclamation to the Egyptians in S. Moreh (ed. and trans), *al-Jabartī's Chronicle of the First Seven Months of the French Occupation of Egypt*, (Leiden 1975), Arabic text, 9–17 and its English translation in pp. 40–2.

6 See *'Aj*. Būlāq, III, 36, ll. 6–7.

soldiers were accused of having no respect for human life and being ignorant of Islamic morals, he praised the French for their fair trial of the assassin of General Kléber.

In his few biographies on women, there are some notable females who were taught to read and write, like Sitt Nafīsa the wife of Murād Bey[7] and al-Jabartī's second wife Amān. Others were allowed to attend classes of Qur'ān and *ḥadīth*. He describes how wealthy women were used to living prosperous lives, put on precious jewellery and be served by white and black slaves and entertain themselves on the banks of the Nile with music and belly-dancers. Bedouin women were entitled to give refuge to fugitive men in their tents; peasant women were able to sell their products in market places. However, whenever the Mamluk factions clashed or pilgrim caravans were attacked and looted, women and female children suffered most,being enslaved and sold among the soldiers and bedouin. His comments on women ranged from exclamations of surprise that even a Wahhābī woman fought and defeated the Ottoman soldiers to expressing his aversion to the fact that the Sultan proclaimed a celebration for the birth of his baby girl. The poor prostitutes who were homeless used to take men to sleep with them in a small ditch in the fields, in contrast to the *a'yān al-qiḥāb* (the first rank prostitutes) who were invited to the palaces of the grandees. Later the middle class prostitutes took part in the resistance movement of the Egyptians against the French by taking French soldiers to their rooms and murdering them.

Our author confirms that Muḥammad ʿAlī, the Albanian mercenary ruler, is not the benevolent tyrant needed for ruling Egypt with justice. He accused him of being a tyrant who betrayed the *'ulamā'* who supported him in his rise to power by writing a petition to the Sublime Porte to appoint him the ruler of Egypt. Labelled as greedy and an atheist he is said to have exhausted the populace with duties and taxes. After he achieved his economical, agrarian and military aims, he deprived the *'ulamā'* of their former status as advisors to the ruler with special privileges in land holdings and customs' rights. The *'ulamā'* had come to prefer the wealth and delights of this world, attended dinner and

7 Lady Khātūn, first the slave-girl, and then the concubine of ʿAlī Bey Buluṭ Qabān al-Kabīr, who after his death became the wife of the Amīr Murād Bey. See *'Aj.*, IV, 264 (obituary of Lady Khātūn). See also *'Aj.*, I, 379 and II, 106; Afaf al-Sayyid Marsot, *Women and Men in Late Eighteenth-Century Egypt* (Austin 1995), 6–7; also Raymond, *Egyptiens et Français au Caire* (Cairo 1998), 57.

entertainment parties held by grandees, while dervishes and popular Sufi sects chased young and handsome boys during the *mawlids*. As a result of their immoral behaviour, the *'ulamā'* were punished by God and were deprived by the ruler of all their former privileges. Instead the new ruler had transgressed the custom of Muslim superiority over non-Muslims and employed them as his officials in his financial, agrarian, military and economic reforms with vast authorities over Muslims. The appointment of Copts and Jews to high financial offices by the French and then by Muḥammad ʿAlī was opposed and condemned by Muslim religious scholars such as al-Jabartī as violating the will of Allāh clearly expressed in the Qur'ān and *sunna*. Our author confirmed that all these deteriorations in the status of the *'ulamā'* were due to them neglecting their religious duties.

Our author may be considered as representing the historical memory of Egyptian intellectuals and others in the Arabic-speaking world during the eighteenth and the first two decades of the nineteenth century. In writing his chronicle he made use of his knowledge of traditional (*naqliyya*) and rational (*'aqliyya*) Islamic sciences, mainly *ḥadīth*, *fiqh*, astronomy, astrology, the Islamic calendar and medicine according to al-Anṭākī's school, paying attention to recording epidemics and diseasesand describing their symptoms. In the first two volumes of his chronicle, he depended heavily on available chronicles and biographies of his time mainly those of Ibn ʿAbd al-Ghanī and al-Damurdāshī. The fate of the Muslim people and their religious duties, as well as that of the *'ulamā'*, were his main concern in his historical writings. The similarity between the Sultan's letter asking the Muslim Mediterranean ports to oppose the French and the comments of al-Jabartī on Napoleon's first Arabic proclamation to the Egyptians suggest that the Ottomans were aware that al-Jabartī was attempting to write the history of Egypt and had supplied him, as their agent, with their proclamations, correspondence and information. He depended in recording his data upon officials and friends in the Ottoman, Mamluk, French and Muḥammad ʿAlī's administrations. Informants such as al-Khashshāb, al-ʿAṭṭār, travellers, pilgrims, merchants as well as letters sent to him by friends were the main source of his information. He assured his readers that he only recorded information after cross-examination. However, what distinguished him morally from other historians is his critical approach based upon the main principles of the Khalwatiyya. The first is the duty of: '*al-*

amr bi'l-ma'rūf wa'l-nahy 'an al-munkar' (Enjoining to do what is proper and prohibiting doing what is reprehensible), as well as the duty to stand firm in his religious duty of just advice of *'lā ta'khuduhuh fī ḥaqq lawmatu lā'im'* (no censure should deter him from saying the truth).

There is similarity between al-Jabartī's *Chronicle* on the French occupation of Egypt and that of the Lebanese Niqūlā al-Turk, a Christian agent of Bashīr al-Shihābī (1767–1850), governor of Mount Lebanon. Both were contemporary chroniclers who wrote their books from different perspectives. They have been compared by a number of recent scholars. Whereas al-Jabartī was a member of the Muslim Egyptian religious elite, the Christian chronicler Niqūlā al-Turk, who lived in Egypt from 1798–1804, was in fact the spy of Amīr Bashīr al-Shihābī[8] and was a highly respected poet in his court. After the French occupation of Egypt, the latter sent him to Damietta, an excellent observation post between Egypt and Syria, asking him to find out whether the French were planning to expand their activities to his territory.[9] It seems that the similarities in both chronicles are due to their depending on the same sources, and writing on the same subject and the same period.

Al-Jabartī, was one of last eminent Muslim scholars and historians who were able to echo in a traditional method of history writing the swan song of conventional Muslim traditional culture, administration, military lore, and the collective conscience of his time and society. Unlike many other historians, we know very little about the details of ʿAbd al-Raḥmān al-Jabartī's life: we are in the dark even about crucial events in his life, who his mother was, the assassination of his son, the precise date of his death, did his intimate friend Ḥasan al-ʿAṭṭār compose an elegy on him? Did he date the poem, if he composed one, with the date of the year of his friend's death? In such a case it

8 Thomas Philipp observed that al-Turk seemed rather more interested in events outside the Muslim world, especially concerning the French and in particular Bonaparte's activities, and concluded that: 'Niqula shows the beginnings of a world history concept, while al-Jabarti's frame of reference is still firmly rooted in the traditional Muslim world view.' (Philipp, 'The French and the French Revolution', [1990], 139). While this statement seems somewhat exaggerated, it is definitely true that al-Turk who studied the French language was more receptive to European ideas than al-Jabartī could be.

9 Desgranges, *Histoire de l'expédition des Français en Egypte par Nakoula el-Turk* (Paris 1839), publiée et traduite par M. Desgranges Ainée, Cf. Wiet (1954), VI, French Introduction; p. 6, Arabic Introduction.

would be easy to gain more facts about his relations with the rulers of Egypt and the *'ulamā'* of his time?

Unlike al-Zabīdī who was in close connection with and admired the Ottoman rulers and was convinced 'that their rule will last even beyond the coming Mahdī',[10] his student al-Jabarti considered their rule as tyrannical and the French occupation as a punishment for the 'successive sufferings' from their tyranny.[11] His chronicle attests to a certain dynamic within Muslim culture, a period of considerable wealth and cultural efflorescence in jurisprudence, commentaries and literature,[12] which was limited to a few eminent scholars such as Ḥasan al-ʿAṭṭār, al-Zabīdī, and al-Murādī, yet both he and al-ʿAṭṭār considered it to be a period of stagnation, with a continuous dynamic of deterioration. One also gets the impression that his incredible precision and his art of critical biography (for example, the biographies of Shaykh Abu'l-Anwār Ibn Wafā, Shaykh al-Sādāt and al-Zabīdī) represent a step beyond mere traditional writing. Most probably, this approach was due to his strong ties with European travellers whom he met before E.W. Lane's visit to Cairo during 1825–6, such as Burckhardt, and Belzoni[13] and his contacts with French scholars during the French occupation.

He represents the collective consciousness of a pious Muslim with an Azhari education. In this capacity, he might be the first Arab-Muslim historian in the Ottoman period to have revived the connection between Islamic historiography, religion, culture and science. He was willing to change his mind about people and events in accordance with his experience in life and a re-examination of his conclusions. He may be regarded as the first herald of the Arab renaissance, opposing popular Sufism and superstitions, and also the

10 See S. Reichmuth, *The World of Murtaḍā al-Zabīdī (1732–91), Life, Networks and Writings* (Exeter 2009), 120, no. 119.

11 See al-Jabartī, *Maẓhar al-Taqdīs* (Cairo 1419/1998), 1–5.

12 Nelly Hanna, *In Praise of Books: A Cultural History of Cairo's Middle Class, Sixteenth through the Eighteenth Century* (Middle East Studies beyond Dominant Paradigms, Syracuse, NY2003).

13 On Belzoni's friendship with Johann Ludwig Burckhardt (al-Shaykh Ibrāhīm) and the description of tranporting the head of Memnon and Burckhardt's death, see Stanley Mayes, *The Great Belzoni* (London and New York 2006), 115–18. For Burckhardt's death in spite of Dr Richardson's attention, see ibid, 189–90, on al-Jabartī's description of his visit to inspect the statue's head with Burckhardt, see *'Aj.*, IV, 238–84, and the English translation by Philipp and Perlmann, IV, 399, note 33.

first Muslim Arab thinker who was aware of the spirit of the French Revolution which had such a profound effect on European thought and society.

It is true that in vols. I–II the necrologies were sometimes copied word by word from his mentor Murtaḍā al-Zabīdī (1732–90), Shamma al-Fuwwī and some other writers, and that much historical information was copied from al-Damurdāshī's *al-Durra al-Muṣāna* (1668–1755), Ibn ʿAbd al-Ghanī's *Awḍaḥ al-Ishārāt* (1715–55), and others, yet he edited and arranged it in in a clear sequence. His last two volumes, i.e. volumes III–IV were original works. The necrologies were based upon personal acquaintance and friendship, with poignant remarks and criticism. The description of the historical events was precise, with details and deep insight, based upon his own observations, full of criticism of all aspects of life, in a period when life was difficult for him as his financial conditions deteriorated. He remarks that information recorded by him was from informants such as elderly people, officials, travellers, letters and information from reliable friends such as Ḥasan al-ʿAṭṭār and Ismāʿīl al-Khashshāb.

It seems that the invitation of the Damascene biographer and historian al-Murādī (1780–91) to Murtaḍā al-Zabīdī, who was aware of al-Jabartī's interest in recording the historical events of Egypt, to cooperate with him in collecting biographical data provided him with the primary impulse to record the unusual events, as did the traumas of the French occupation and their expulsion from Egypt, events which he recorded in his history of the first seven months of the French occupation, known as *Tārīkh Muddat al-Faransīs bi-Miṣr* (1213/1798). The second chronicle *Maẓhar al-Taqdīs* he wrote at the request of the entourage of the Ottoman General Yūsuf Ḍiyāʾ. Our author responded to this request hoping that it might serve him to clear himself of the accusation of cooperation with the French, since he had been a member of the third Dīwān the French formed to enable Egyptian citizens, *'ulamā'* and merchants rather than the Mamluks, to help them govern Egypt. The success of *Maẓhar* and its translation into Turkish gave him the final impulse to write the three first volumes of *'Ajā'ib al-Āthār* in 1221/1805–6. He continued recording his historical data until the events of the month of Dhu'l-Ḥijja 1230 (/30 August–27 September 1821). It seems that after this date he became blind, but still ordered his copyists to copy his works, to read them to him and dictated his corrections. This fact reveals his great interest in calligraphy, calligraphers and why he devoted some biographies to them.[14]

The method applied in our new Arabic edition of *'Ajā'ib al-Āthār* is one that may be termed 'manuscript archaeology', i.e. to try to establish the text which the author himself left (his 'autograph') in manuscript form. The second stage is to collate the autograph or autographs with other manuscripts copied by various copyists. The autograph(s) enable us to use a detective-like method of 'interrogating' the text of the manuscript, and the deletions and additions of the author in the text and in the margins, and later on to detect the historical and biographical and (other) sources from which the author collected his biographical and other information. This method, although time-consuming, has proven to be the best for arriving at valid conclusions, in a way, which printed editions of al-Jabartī's chronicle cannot offer. By 'interrogating' the autographs and collating them with previous sources it is possible to understand the religious, political and economic factors and trends behind his writings, in particular the additions, deletions and corrections of words and sentences in the margins and within the text of both autographs and printed editions. Moreover, it enables us not only to see the changes in his attitude towards the rulers of Egypt, but also to reveal the actual religious, political and social trends which influenced the author, as Dr Lars Bjørneboe did with my edition of al-Jabartī's *Tārīkh Muddat al-Faransīs bi-Miṣr.*

In the case of al-Jabartī's autographs, this method enables us to reveal the sequence and the dates of composition of his three chronicles of the history of Egypt, viz., *Tārīkh Muddat al-Faransīs bi-Miṣr*, *Maẓhar al-Taqdīs* and *'Ajā'ib al-Āthār*. His manuscript *Muddat al-Faransīs* is his first attempt to write the history of the traumatic events of the first seven months of the French occupation in 1798. The second work is *Maẓhar al-Taqdīs*, composed in honour of the Ottoman General who expelled the French with the help of the British army in 1801. While *'Ajā'ib al-Āthār* is the fulfilment of his dream to write a comprehensive history of Egypt.

This process helped us to arrive at the conclusion that the Būlāq edition of *'Ajā'ib al-Āthār* of 1297/1879–80 is not reliable since it is based upon a copy

14 See al-Jabartī's letter to the Muftī of Jerusalem, al-Sayyid Muḥammad Ṭāhir Afandī al-Ḥusaynī, in the Appendices, no. I below, where he enumerates the merits of his father's manuscripts.

of the text made by the order of the director of the Būlāq Press in 1296/1879. The colophon of MS *'Aj.* Birmingham (MS. IX. 38. d. above) kept at the University of Birmingham Library (MS. no. 911 [1364], vol. IV), states that the copying of this manuscript by the order of the director of the Būlāq Press, Ḥusayn Bek Ḥusnī, ended on Shaʿbān 1296/21 July–18 August 1879. The date of the copying of the Birmingham manuscript and its similarity to the Būlāq edition convinced us that this MS is the one on which the Būlāq edition was based. This fact can explain why in this MS many ranks of officials are changed. It is due to the fact that during the time in which the Cambridge MS was written by the author (1806) and the time of preparing the Birmingham MS (1296/1879) these personalities were promoted to higher ranks. The same might be said of the names of provinces and villages which were changed by Muḥammad ʿAlī's administration, or were unknown to the 1879 copyist, so he distorted the versions of Jabarti's autograph.

Another important result of our new research is the conclusion that the reason for the absence of the *basmala* (Muslim invocation at the beginning of a speech or book) in *Muddat al-Faransīs* and the autographs of *'Ajā'ib al-Āthār*, is not due to the tendency of al-Jabartī to save paper and space in his books, and does not indicate that the MS is considered a continuation of missing parts, but is rather due to a well established custom among the *'ulamā'*. According to Ḥasan al-ʿAṭṭār's marginal gloss (*ḥāshiya*) on the Commentary of Zakariyyā al-Anṣārī on the *Isagoge* (Introduction) to Logic (*Ḥāshiyat al-Shaykh Ḥasan al-'Aṭṭār 'alā Sharḥ Zakariyyā al-Anṣārī 'alā Matn Īsāghūjī fi'l-Manṭiq*,[15] the *basmala* used in didactic literature and compositions is to invoke blessing. However, such an invocation is not necessary in logical *(ḥikmiyya)* sciences, such as medicine, geometry, astronomy, prosody, poetry, historical works and treatises.

In fact al-Jabartī surpassed other historians of the eighteenth century by his at times humoristic and emotional style, his universal view of history, his sound evaluation of events and of the causes of the rise and decline of rival factions, dynasties and states, his vast knowledge of Islamic religious and secular sciences for judging events and personalities. He distinguished himself by his insight, his verification of events, his undertaking to reform the Muslim

15 Ḥasan al-ʿAṭṭār, *Ḥāshiyat al-Shaykh Ḥasan al-'Aṭṭār 'alā Sharḥ Zakariyyā al-Anṣārī 'alā Matn Īsāghūjī fi'l-Manṭiq* (Cairo 1321/1903–4), 3.

world according to Islamic ethics and justice, the absolute divine rules and truth which he believed in. His courage in criticizing fearlessly vicious and unjust rulers and corrupt scholars of his time was based upon the Islamic religious duty of the *'ulamā'* to advise the rulers to keep to *sharī'a* justice. These and his ability to reflect the collective historical memory of his class of Muslim scholars, make him the last outstanding historian of the Arab medieval world.

His awareness of the shortcomings of the Muslim nations of his time predates the call of later generations of reformers for a return to the original, sublime, Islamic religious laws, morals, customs, and beliefs, in order to achieve God's promised rewards, leading to the scientific revival of the Arab world. Al-Jabartī's comments confirm that the renaissance of the Arab intelligentsia in the nineteenth century cannot be attributed only to the internal dynamics of the Arab world and did not commence only with Ottoman reforms. It really began with the French occupation of Egypt, despite the short time this occupation lasted. Al-Jabartī was well aware of the merits of the French society of his days and its superiority over pre-industrial Muslim society.[16]

Both al-Zabīdī and al-Jabartī were the last scholars in the Middle East to use the traditional Islamic method of writing history and dictionaries. Their works provided a link between Arab scholarly works and European scholarship. The celebrated orientalist E.W. Lane used *'Ajā'ib al-Āthār* for his two monumental works, the *Manners and Customs of the Modern Egyptians* and his translation of *Alf Layla wa-Layla.*[17] Moreover, Lane used al-Zabīdī's *Tāj al-'Arūs* for his celebrated dictionary *Arabic-English Lexicon*, an excellent and exhaustive work which is still indispensable to scholars of Arabic language and culture. In fact, Lane arrived in Cairo a few months after the death of al-Jabartī' in 1825, or 1826, soon after my first arrival in Cairo.'[18] He acquired a MS of *'Ajā'ib al-Āthār* copied in 1829 now kept at the British Library in London (formerly, The British Museum Library). It seems to us that Lane may well have used al-Jabartī's book as his guide line to writing his

16 See P. Crone, *Pre-Industrial Societies* (Oxford 1995). On the decline of states in Arab civilization see the English Introduction to the Arabic Edition, note 5; cf. *Rasā'il Ikhwān al-Ṣafā* (Cairo 1928), 130.

17 See D. Ayalon, 'The Historian al-Jabartī and his Background', *BSOAS* 23 (1960), 222, note 6.

18 Lane, *Manners*, 222.

Manners and Customs to explain many aspects of Egyptian life, popular Muslim customs, popular literature, proverbs and other terms. Lane's works help us to understand many terms and descriptions of manners and customs, both religious and cultural, given in *'Ajā'ib al-Āthār*.

With these scholars, the conventional scientific studies in Arabic ended and a new approach based upon European sciences started with Egyptian scholars sent by Muḥammad ʿAlī to study in Europe headed by Rifāʿa Rāfiʿ al-Ṭahṭāwī (1801–73).The moon cycle advocated by Ibn Khaldūn and al-Jabartī had started afresh now in Europe, with the demise of traditional Islamic culture being symbolized by Rifāʿa's discovery of modern Europe in his *Takhlīṣ al-Ibrīz fī Talkhīṣ Bārīs*. Al-Ṭahṭāwī and other graduates of the educational missions to Europe like ʿAlī Mubārak (1823–93) started a new phase of writing history replacing the fantastic exaggerations about European customs and culture in previous Arabic scholarship. The new historical approach was characterized by realty and precise documentations.

No wonder then if we describe al-Jabartī, the author of *'Ajā'ib al-Āthār fī'l-Tarājim wa'l-Akhbār* (Marvellous Compositions of Biographies and Chronicles), as a giant historian of the eighteenth century, although he in fact representsthe swan song of medieval Arabic culture.

Appendices

Appendix I

Ḥasan al-ʿAṭṭār's comments in the margin of MS *'Ajā'ib al-Āthār*, Cambridge University Library, Qq. 166, written in *Maghribī* handwriting, on some of al-Jabartī's information published in volume I, *'Ajā'ib al-Āthār,* Būlāq, 1297/1879–80:

a) In the margin of MS *'Aj.* Cam. 2nd., Qq. 166, I, f. 11a, equivalent to *'Aj.* Būlāq, I,10 where al-Jabartī wrote: قال تعالى: أتأمرون الناس بالبرّ وتنسون أنفسكم، مرفوع خبر محذوف، أي هو دليل، والخبر دليل على ذلك, the comment of al-ʿAṭṭār is: يعود للقول المفهوم من قال. ولو

أنه قال أولا: وقول الله تعالى بصيغة المصدر، لاستقام نظام الكلام وسبق إلى الافهام. انتهى.

b) *'Aj.* Būlāq, I, 13: الخلافة بعدي ثلثون سنة ثم تكون ملكا عضودا (كذا والصواب: عضوضا), the comment of al-ʿAṭṭār, MS *'Aj.* Cam. 2nd., Qq. 166, I, is: قوله وبموت علي تمت مدة الخلافة، إذ كأنه لم يلتفت للأشهر التي تولاها الحسن بن علي رضوان الله عليهما، فان الثلاثين سنة تمت بهذه الأشهر لقلتها، وقوله: 'عضوضا'، بضادين وكتب بالدال، ولكنه كما قلنا . لكاتبه الفقير حسن بن محمد العطار

المترجم في بعض مواضع هذا الكتاب. رحم الله من نظره ودعا له بالمغفرة.

c) *'Aj.* Būlāq, I, 14: افتتحت الديار المصرية والبلاد الشامية على يد عمر بن العاص, the comment of al-ʿAṭṭār, MS *'Aj.* Cam. 2nd., Qq. 166, I, f. 15a, is: قوله على يد عمرو بن العاص ، هذا ظاهر بالنظر لفتح مصر فانه كان أمير جيشها وأما الشام فثم أمرا اخر من الصحابة، وقد

يجاب بان المعنى على يد عمرو وغيره، حذفه اتكالا على ظهور: انتهى.

d) *'Aj.* Būlāq, I, 15:من السواحل وبيت المقدس بعد ما أقام بيد الفرنج نيفا واحدى وتسعين سنة, the comment of al-ʿAṭṭār, MS *'Aj.* Cam. 2nd., Qq. 166, I, f. 16a, is: الأولى بل الصواب حذف قوله "وإحدى'، لاغيا قوله: "نيفا، عنها كما لا يخفى، كاتبه الفقير حسن العطار.

e) *'Aj.* Būlāq, I, 259: مات الشيخ ... الشريف السيد محمد بن محمد البليدي ... حتى توفي ليلة التاسع والعشرين من رمضان سنة ست وسبعين وماية والف, the comment of al-ʿAṭṭār, MS *'Aj.* Cam. 2nd., Qq. 166, I, f. 238a, is: أقول، لم يذكر المؤرخ مولفات السيد البليدي المترجم، فان له حاشية جليلة على الاشموني على الألفية وحاشية على شرح رسالة الوضع وله

شرح على المقولات وهو وان اشتهر بين الطلبة بالدقة والغموض فذلك لعدم معرفة طلاب مصر بالعلوم الحكمية، فاني اطلعت على الشرح المذكور وملكته ولكن رأيت كلامه من فن الحكمة ليس بشي سيما في الفلكيات، فانه في آخر الشرح المذكور تكلم في الفلكيات بكلام غير منظوم أصلا بحيث يضحك منه من مارس تلك العلوم. لكن طلبة زماننا لجهلهم بهذه العلوم يبالغون في وصف هذا الشرح بالدقة والغموض وانه لا يفهمه إلا الفحول وهم معزورون[!] لأنهم ما رأوا غيره. انتهى، كتبه الفقير حسن العطار.

f) *ʿAj.* Būlāq, I, 260: وسفينة الراغب المشهورة, the comment of al-ʿAṭṭār, MS *ʿAj.* Cam. 2nd., Qq. 166, I, f. 239a, is: أقول سفينة الراغب المذكورة مجلد ضخم اعتنى به غالب موالي الروم ولها شهرة كبيرة جدا بين الموالي من أهل اسلامبول وهي كثيرة الوجود في الأوقاف وغيرها، اطلعت عليها عندما كنت مقيما باسلامبول واطلعت لي على مجموعة أخرى من حجمها لكن أكثرها بالفارسي والتركي. ورأيت السفينة المذكورة أيضا في القدس الشريف من وقف حسن أفندي النقيب عندما كنت مقيما بالقدس. فهكذا كانت الوزرا سابقا أكثرهم علما وأما الآن فأكثرهم لا يعرف يقرأ الخط ولا يكتب ولا يصحح قراة[!] الفاتحة. فقد انعكس الزمان وعمّ الجهل الريس والمروس، وإنّا إليه راجعون. انتهى، كتبه الفقير حسن العطار.

g) *ʿAj.* Būlāq, I, 262: الشيخ خليل بن محمد المغربي الأصل المالكي المصري ... وله مولفات منها شرح المقولات العشر, the comment of al-ʿAṭṭār, MS *ʿAj.* Cam. 2nd., Qq. 166, I, f. 240b, is: أقول للمترجم المذكور، رسالة سماها مخدّرات الفهوم في اسما التراجم والفنون، تدل على رسوخه في المعقولات، اطلعت عليها قبل ارتحالي من مصر ولخصت اشيا في رسالة لي على حاشية الازهري، اسأل الله سبحانه أن يجمعني بكتبي بمصر ويمنّ عليّ بالوصول لوطن، انتهى، حسن العطار.

h) *ʿAj.* Būlāq, I, 287: الشيخ أحمد بن عبد الفتاح بن يوسف بن عمر المُجَيْري الملوي الشافعي الأزهري ... وتعريب رسالة ملا عصام في المجاز، the comment of al-ʿAṭṭār, MS *ʿAj.* Cam. 2nd., Qq. 166, I, ff. 259b–260a, is: قوله تعريب رسالة العصام، الخ، هذا غلط من المؤرخ فان تعريب الرسالة الفارسية إنما هو لمنجم باشا الشهير بالمولوي، بواوين، والرسالة أصلها باللسان الفارسي، فعربها المذكور ونقلها للغة العربية، ومعلوم أن الشيخ الملوي المترجم المذكور من علما مصر ابنا العرب وهم لا يعرفون اللغة التركية فضلا عن الفارسية، وللفقير حاشية على التعريب المذكور، فإني كنت قراته بمصر وشرعت في الحاشية ثم سافرت من مصر وقد كتبت منها جملة على الهوامش فاستقرّيت بقبرص وكتبت أولها هناك ثم ذهبت اسلامبول فكتبت بها حصة ، ثم ذهبت بلاد الارناود فكتبت بها قدرا، ثم عدت إلى اسلامبول ولم اكتب بها شيا ثم وصلت لأزمير فكتبت بها شيا يسيرا ثم وصلت للشام فما كتبت بها شيا لأني اشتغلت ثم بحاشية على الولدته [!]. ثم خرجت من الشام ودوّرت في ذلك القطر حتى أقمت بيافا وأنا وقت تسطير هذه الحروف بها، أسال الله سبحانه أن يسهل لي الوصول لمصر التي هي الوطن الأصلي على أحسن حال، وكان وصولي إلى يافا العشرة الأخيرة من شهر ذي القعدة سنة ١٢٢٥. أقول تحقق لي في

حاشية التعريب المذكور قول التفتزاني في شرح التلخيص [التتمة في ورقة 259 ب] وأحرر كل شطر منه في شطر من الغبرا[ء]، وأنا أسال الله سبحانه أن يمن علي بإكمالها وليكن ذلك بموطني الأصلي وهو مصر انه على ذلك قدير وبالإجابة جدير. كتبه الفقير حسن بن محمد العطار المصري في شهر المحرم سنة ١٢٢٦ [/1811].

i) *'Aj.* Būlāq, I, 289: عن محمد بن سالم الحفناوي الشافعي الخلوتي: فمن تاليفه المشهورة حاشية على رسالة العضد للسعد, the comment of al-ʿAṭṭār, MS *'Aj.* Cam. 2nd., Qq. 166, I, ff. 263a, is: أقول الحاشية المذكورة على شرح المنلا علي القوشجي على رسالة الوضع للسعد، وهي رسالة صغيرة شرحها الأفاضل. ومن أجل شروحها شرح الفاضل للعصام. وللفقير عليها حاشية لم تخرج من المسودة لوقت تاريخه بسبب الاشتغال بالأسفار والتنقل بالبلدان. ونظمت المتن أيضا وشرعت في شرح عليه مدة إقامتي باسلامبول فكتبت فيه أوراقا ثم عاقت العوايق، أسال الله إتمامه. والحاشية المذكورة للمترجم على الشرح القوشجي لكن المشهور بمصر على السنة الطلبة شرح السمرقندي، والأتراك يسمونه علي قوشجي. وعلى الشرح المذكور حواشي كثيرة اجلّها حاشية الهروي وقد اعتني بها الفضلا ووضعوا عليها حواشيا[!] لدقتها وعليه حاشية ابي البقا وحاشية المنلا الساسي [!] وكنت رأيت عليه وأنا ببلاد الارناوت حواشيا اخر غير المشهورة، ولما وردت بلدة مغنيسا من بلاد الروم واجتمعت ببعض علمايها المشاهير وكان إذ ذاك يقرأ في الكشافة وحضرت درسه وناقشته في بعض كلمات، اطلعت له على حاشيته للشرح المذكور جليلة فأحببت نقلها ثم أعرضت عنه لعدم قبول الوقت، أسال الله حسن الختام [التتمة في ورقة 262 ب] وأن يمنّ علي بالرجوع لبلدي مصر التي هي الوطن الأصلي، ويهلك كل من سعي في دمارها وخرابها إنه على ذلك قدير. وحرر بيافا سنة ١٢٢٦ [/1811] بتاريخ العشرة الوسط من الشهر [المحرم] كتبه الفقير حسن العطار.

j) *'Aj.* Būlāq, I, 290: عن محمد بن سالم الحفناوي الشافعي الخلوتي، 'وعلى شرح السمرقندي للياسمينية في الجبر والمقابلة'، , the comment of al-ʿAṭṭār, MS *'Aj.* Cam. 2nd., Qq. 166, I, f. 263b, is: ليس للسمرقندي شرح على الياسمينة وإنما هو شرح السبط الصغير فان له عليها شرحان أصغرها هو الذي على الحاشية المذكورة وقد كنت قراته على شيخنا المدقق احمد بن يونس ولشيخنا المذكور على الياسمينة شرح ممزوج لطيف جدا اطلعت عليه وقت القراة[!] انتهى.

k) *'Aj.* Būlāq, I, 310: 'حاشية على عبد السلام' , the comment of al-ʿAṭṭār, MS *'Aj.* Cam. 2nd., Qq. 166, I, f. 282a, is: اقول ليس للمذكور حاشية على الشيخ عبد السلام وإنما هي حاشية على شرح السنوسي لمتن صغراه[!] ولعل له حاشية على الشيخ عبد السلام ولم تشتهر. انتهى.

l) *'Aj.* Būlāq, I, 352: عن "الشيخ عبد الله بن عبد الله بن سلامة الادكاوي المصري الشافعي الشهير بالمؤذن' , the comment of al-ʿAṭṭār, MS *'Aj.* Cam. 2nd., Qq. 166, I, f. 320, is: 'المترجم المذكور نظم كثيرا وكتب الأدب كثيرا ونظم ونثر وله دواوين عديدة ومع ذلك

فنثره ونظمه ليس فيهما طلاوة ولا حلاوة ابدا، يعرف ذلك من ذاق حلاوة الأدب، رحمه الله، انتهى، كاتبه الفقير حسن العطار.

m) *'Aj.* Būlāq, I, 354:'وله في النوع المسمى بالعود:' عن الادكاوي , the comment of al-ʿAṭṭār, MS *'Aj.* Cam. 2nd., Qq. 166, I, f. 322a, is: "أقول هذا النوع المسمى بالعود ما فهمت له معنى سوى ركة اللفظ وابتذال المعنى وعدم الانسجام وحسن الانتظام، ورحم الله المترجم فانه وان كان مكثارا في الشعر إلا أن كلامه ليس عليه طلاوة ولا حلاوة، انتهى، حسن العطار.

Ḥasan al-ʿAṭṭār's comments in the margin of MS *'Aj.* Cam. 2, Qq. 167, written in *Maghribī* handwriting, on some of al-Jabartī's information published in volume II, *'Ajā'ib al-Āthār*, Būlāq, 1297/1879–80:

الجزء الثاني من عجائب الآثار في التراجم والأخبار للجبرتي من طبعة بولاق، 1279هـ/1880:

a) In the margin of MS *'Aj.* Cam. 2nd., Qq. 167, II, f. 13a, equivalent to *'Aj.* Būlāq, II, 14, where al-Jabartī wrote: وفي منتصف شهر رمضان ولدت امرأة مولودا يشبه خلقة الفيل , the comment of al-ʿAṭṭār is: قد ذكر الطبايعيون ان الرجل أو المرأة إذا تخيل واحد منهما وقت المجامعة هيئة إنسان ما، واتفق العلوق في ذلك الوقت خرج المولود شبيها به وكذلك إذا وقعت عين المرأة في ذلك الوقت على صورة ما، ظهر في المولود شبه بها، ولذلك علة مسَطّرة في الكتب الفلسفية. كتبه حسن العطار المترجم في هذا الكتاب، وكتب بمدينة أزمير حين كنت مغتربا بها، ردني الله لوطني مصر واهلك من شرّد أهلها وبددهم عن قريب، انتهى. [ثم أضيفت الملاحظة التالية]: 'ليست العلة هذه بل العلة تخيل صورة الفيل عند الجماع كما بّينا ذلك في شرحنا لنزهة داود الذي ألفناه ونحن بمدينة دمشق الشام

بتاريخ ١٢٢٧[/1812]، كتبه الفقير حسن العطار.

b) *'Aj.* Būlāq, II, 164:الشيخ حسن بن غالي الجداوي المالكي , the comment of al-ʿAṭṭār, MS *'Aj.* Cam. 2nd., Qq. 167, II, f. 152a, is: 'قلت وقد رثيت المذكور بقصيدة أولها [الخفيف]:

وكفى المرء عبرة ما يلاقي — مـا لهذا الـزمان من ميثاق
كَ فبؤنا بلوعـة واحتراق — حسن الاسـم والصفات فقدنا
صابه للأنام طرّا سـاقي — إن يكن فيك اساءنا دهرشوم
يذهب الناس وَهْوَ دوما باقي — فلك الـنـفع بيننا مسـتديم

الخ، وهي مسطرة بديوان شعري، كتبه الفقير حسن العطار، وكتبته بمدينة أزمير وأنا بها في عيش خطير متغرب وللفقير هي بلدة تضيع الفضلا فيها فيموتون جوعا ولا احد يسال عنهم ولا يعتني بهم، خلصنا الله منها سالمين فإنها شرّ البلاد. لقد طوفت أكثر بلاد الله فما وجدت بلدة تشابهها في

القحط والغلا وكراهية الأغراب خصوصا العلما، بحيث لو فرض ان قدم عليها الفخر الرازي لما سقاه احد شربة ما[ء] ولا عَظمه احد لعلمه بل تكون اسوته باسوة أحقر إنسان غريب، ولا حول ولا قوة إلا بالله، أسال الله العظيم أن يخرجني

مها سالما وان يقابل أهلها بما يستحقون، أمين.

c) *'Aj.* Būlāq, II, 236: وتاريخه في أواخر ربيع الثاني سنة مايتين والف, the comment of al-ʿAṭṭār, MS *'Aj.* Cam. 2nd., Qq. 167, II, f. 219a, is: أقول لما سافرت من أزمير إلى دمشق الشام سألت عن تاريخ المذكور فأخبرني بعض الثقاة ممن كان يباشر من النقل والكتابة فيه انه بعد موته اختصره بعض أقاربه وحذف فيه أشيا كثيرة لأغراض نفسانية ولم يرغب احد في نقله بل الموجود نسخة واحدة، وكنت سعيت في الاطلاع على تلك النسخة ففجأني السفر وفي ظني انه لا ينقله احد من أهل الشام لأنهم كما تفرست فيهم ليسوا ممن يرغب في أمثال هذه الأمور وإنما المؤلف كان نادرة منهم وساعدته الدنيا وخدمه الإقبال والان ليس احد بلغ عشر ما بلغه فقد تغيرت البلاد ومن عليها وقلّت الرغبة وفشا الجهل. لكاتبه الفقير حسن العطار المصري الأزهري وكتب بمدينة يافا في اليوم الثاني من شهر محرم سنة ١٢٢٦ [٢٧/ كانون الثاني، 1811]، وكان قدومي إليها في أواخر شهر ذي القعدة سنة ١٢٢٥ [١٧/ كانون أول، 1810]، ردني

الله للأوطان سالما والسلام.

d) *'Aj.* Būlāq, II, 248: مات الإمام العلامة ... الشيخ يوسف بن عبدا لله بن منصور السنبلاويني الشهير برزه الشافعي , the comment of al-ʿAṭṭār in MS *'Aj.* Cam. 2nd., Qq. 167, II, f. 230a is: أقول رثيت المذكور بثلاث قصائد، الأولى منها مطلعها [الطويل]:

بعينيك حاكى الغيث سفحا وكفكف فما شحّها في ذا الزمانِ بمُنصِف

منها قولي [الطويل]:

ألا لا تَلوماني على سَفْحِ أدمُعِي فلي حزنُ يعقوبٍ على فَقْدِ يوسف

الثانية مطلعها [البسيط]:

ما للزمانِ بسهمِ البَيْنِ يَرمينا ومن كووسِ المَنايا الحُزنَ يَسْقينا

والثالثة مطلعها [الطويل]:

إلى مثلِ هذا الخَطْبِ يُدّخرُ الدمعُ فهذا نهارٌ في الخُطوبِ لَهُ وَقْعُ

e) *'Aj.* Būlāq, II, 254: ... وأخيه النبيه ... شهاب الدين السيد احمد , the comment of al-ʿAṭṭār in MS *'Aj.* Cam. 2nd., Qq. 167, II, f. 236b is:

قلت ورثيت المذكور بقصيدتين مطولتين لأنه احد أشياخي، الأولى منهما مطلعها [الكامل]:

قِف بالديارِ وربعِها المأنوسِ واندب معي الأطلال بعد دُروس
وابكي خُطوبا قد صَدَعن جوانحا وفتكن ما أزرى فواتك شوسِ
وانظر إلى عبر الزمان وسلبه لِحُلاه مبتديا بكلّ نفيس

لكَ في تصاريف الزمان تفكرٌ   أنساك وقعة جُرهم وجَديس
قد مُزّقوا أيدي سَبا وتصرمت   اساد بيشة عند شوم بسوس
أتروم سعدا وهو مجبول على   غدر يسوء بطبعه المنحوس
ما للزمان منابذاً لأولى النها[!]   ما زال يرميهم بكل بئيس
فكأنهم ساقٍ أدار عليهمُ   خمر المنايا في أمرّ كووس
وكأنهن أزاهر يجنوا[!] الذي   يلقاه اينع من تعيس نفوس
بين الفتى يختالُ فوق الأرض إذ   في جوفها قد حلّ مع مرموس
أين الملوك وأين من شادوا العلا   وجلوا ظلام الدهر بعد عبوس
وذوو المعارف من بِفَهْم نظموا   دُرَرَ العوارف في سطور طروس
الكلّ بادوا ثم لَمْ يبقى سوى   خبر يجدد دارس القدموس
يا عين جودي بالدمع فإنّما   هذا المصاب يجل عن تجنيس
وابكي إماما قالت العليا لنا   من بعده لا عطر بعد عروس
العالم النحرير قطبَ الوقتِ مَنْ   حازَ الرّياسةَ فوقَ كلُّ رَئيسِ

وهي طويلة، الثانية [الطويل]:

سطور دموع في طروس خدود   أتت لخفيات الشجا بحدود
وَخَطّ شجون في دواير أنفس   على مركز الأحشا يمرّ فيودي
وأحرف شَجْو جرّت القلب للأسى   فقام لنصب الحزن غير جليد
ألا أيّها الدهر الخوون إلى متى   بكف المنايا أخذت بوريد[!]

وهي أيضا طويلة، والثنتان مذكوران[!]، بديواني، لكاتبه الفقير حسن العطار، بمدرسة جامع فتاح[!] أوغلو بمدينة أزمير، خصت بتدمير، فإنها ليست البلدة للغريب، والمنصة للأديب الأريب، ليس بها مفضال، ولا

صاحب نوال، إلا جماهير الجهال ، انتهى

Ḥasan al-ʿAṭṭār's comments in the margin of MS *'Aj.* Cam. 2nd., Qq. 168, written in *Maghribī* handwriting, on some of al-Jabartī's information published in vol. III, *'Ajā'ib al-Āthār* (Būlāq 1297/1879–80):

a) In the margin of MS *'Aj.* Cam. 2nd., Qq. 168, III, f. 89b, equivalent to *'Aj.* Būlāq, III, 92–3 where al-Jabartī wrote: والبعض خلف المتاريس وأحذو عدة مدافع زيادة عن الثلاثة المتقدمة, the comment of al-ʿAṭṭār is: ومن أغرب شي يسمع أن معظم العساكر التي قدمت مع الوزير لاستخلاص إقليم مصر من يد الفرنساوية مع ما انضم إليهم من أهل البلاد والمماليك المصرية حاصروا بيت الألفي الذي بالأزبكية وكان به نحو ماتين من الفرنسيس نحو ثلاثين يوما، فما قدروا على أخذه. وأخذت النصارى الفرنسيس منهم متراسا على كوم الريش ببركة الرطلي فتزاحم عليه بعد ذلك معظم العساكر فما قدروا على استخلاصه، فكيف جا[ء] هولا[ء] لاستخلاص ذلك الإقليم العظيم، هذا غاية العجز والوهن والضعف، ورحم الله القايل [<بحر الكامل> صدر البيت هذا لغزالة الخارجية، عن زوجها، تخاطب الحجاج]:

أسدٌ عَلَيّ وفِي الحروبِ نَعامَةٌ

وهؤلاء الطائفة صار حالهم هكذا من زمان متطاول ضعفا عند ملاقاة الكفار ذوو شدة وبأس على ضعفا المسلمين، فهم على العكس مما وصف الله أصحاب النبي بقوله: أشداء على الكفار رحما[ء] بينهم. ثم بعد أن تمكن هؤلا[ء] الجماعة من مصر على يد الانكليز الذين أخرجوا الفرنسيس منها صلحا فعلوا من الغلظة وتعدي الحدود واستحداث المظالم وايذا[ء] المسلمين وإظهار أنواع الفجور والفسوق ما لا يمكن وصفه.

دمرهم الله تدميرا. انتهى

b) In the margin of MS *'Aj.* Cam. 2nd., Qq. 168, III, f. 105a, equivalent to *'Aj.* Būlāq, III, 109 where al-Jabartī wrote: وكان ممن خرج من مصر صاحبنا النبيه العلامة الشيخ حسن العطار ... ومن جملة رسايله وقد كنت أرسلت له كتابا فأجاب بقوله , the comment of al-ʿAṭṭār is: صاحب الرسالة المذكورة أكثر الترحال والتنقل في البلدان فذهب إلى اسلامبول ثم إلى بلاد الروم ايلي وأقام مدة ببلاد الارناوت ثم عطف على اسلامبول ثم سافر إلى أزمير ولم ير في جميع البلاد التي تنقل بها اسْأم ولا أشأم ولا اشد كراهية للعلما والفضلا، واجمع للخصال الذميمة التي لا تكاد تجتمع بإقليم فضلا عن بلدة غير هذه البلدة، ولم يقاس المذكور شدة مثل ما قاساه من هذه البلدة، ومن كلامه: انه لو أفتى بعد [كذا=بعض] العلماء بحرمة الإقامة بها لذي العلم والدين لأصاب، وأدلة ذلك تظهر للعاقل الذي رآها وشاهدها [الطويل]:

لعمرك ما أزمير إلا بليدةٌ — عليها عذاب الله ينصبّ للأبد
تجمّع فيها كل خزي لو أنه — تَفَرّقَ في الدنيا لما مُدِحَتْ بلد
يموت بها جوعا أولوا[!] الفضل والتقى — وللفاسقِ المَلعونِ عيش بها رغد
أقمت بها في القهر سبعة أشهر — أكابد الأحزان والهم والكمد
فلم أرَ فيها ما يسرّ لقاؤه — ولم أرَ إكراما ولا المونَ من أحد
أكلت بها كتبي فلا قدّس الله أرضها — وأنسيت فيها العلم، دَمّرَها الصَمَد
وها أنا عنها قد ترحّلت ساخطا — عليها رماها الله بالسخط والنكد (انتهى)

وهذه البلدة المذكورة ليس فيها حاكم ضابط بل الناس متروكون هملا يهلك القوي الضعيف ويقتل بعضهم بعضا في الأسواق والشوارع ولا احد يجسر على كفّ القاتل أو مسكه، بل يقتل ويجلس يشرب الدخان والناس ينظرونه فلا يقدر أحد عليه بشي وكأنه قتل طيرا أو دجاجة ومن أمثال هذه المخازي بها كثير ولا يحصر وقد رماها الله بشدة القحط والغلا وتسلط بعضهم على دما بعض وأعراضهم وأحوالهم ولا ناصر ولا مجير ولا منفّذ للأحكام الشرعية، بل تركت أهلها فوضى يفعلون ما يريدون بدون معارض ولا زاجر، ويبيعون كيفما هذه يشتهون بدون ضابط ولا مسعر، وبالجملة ليس في الدنيا أجمع للخصال الذميمة من هذه البلدة فمن الحيثية حرم سكناها لكل عالم وكل متدين ووجب المهاجرة.

c) In the margin of MS *'Aj.* Cam. 2nd., Qq. 168, III, f. 109b, equivalent to *'Aj.* Būlāq, III, 114 where al-Jabartī wrote: العلامة الشريف الحسن بن علي البدري العوضي, the comment of al-ʿAṭṭār is: وقد دفن رحمه الله تعالى في دايرة إحاطة سيدنا

أبي عبد الله القرشي المشهور في الجبانة المسماة بمَأمَن الله غربي بيت المقدس وقد تولى تجهيزه شيخنا جناب الشيخ محمد البديري رحمهما الله تعالى وحشرني في زمرتهما تحت لواي[!] سيدنا محمد صلى الله عليه وسلم آمين. كتبه عبد الوهاب شكي[!] مكي

المقدسي عفى الله عنه، آمين.

d) In the margin of MS *ʿAj.* Cam. 2nd., Qq. 168, III,f. 239b, equivalent to *ʿAj.* Būlāq, III, 254 where al-Jabartī wrote:
والسرّ في تقليد أحمد باشا قايم مقام دون طاهر باشا، أن طاهر باشا أرنوطي وليس له إلا طوخين، ومن قواعدهم القديمة أنهم لا يقلدون الارنوط ثلاثة اطواخ ابدا، the comment of al-ʿAṭṭār is: أقول قد انخرمت هذه القواعد في هذه المدة فان اكبر الوزرا الإسلاميين في هذا الوقت وزرا الارناوط. يعرف ذلك كل من رآهم وساح في البلاد، فانه ليس الان من يضاهي علي باشا التبدنلى ولا المرحوم إبراهيم باشا متولي اشكودرة وكذلك إبراهيم باشا متولي باراط وولد[!] على باشا متولي الموره، فان كل هولا ارناوط ولكل ثلاثة اطواخ وتحت أيديهم بشوات متعددة بطوخين. وليس الان في دولة العثمانية من هو أقوى مالا وعسكرا من المذكورين خصوصا علي باشا وإبراهيم باشا صاحب اشكودرة، فاني شاهدت ذلك وعاينته بل تولى الوزارة العظمى باسلامبول والصدارة يميش باشا وهو ارناوطي من أهل اشكودرة ثم عزل بعد أيام، انتهى. قال ذلك وكتبه الفقير حسن بن محمد العطار المترجم في هذا الكتاب وكتبته وأنا بمدينة أزمير في آخر شهر شوال من شهور سنة ١٢٢٤ [1809/] أسال الله سبحانه أن يرد غربتي وأعود لمصر كما كنت بالجامع الأزهر وأساله سبحانه أن يشتت شمل هؤلا الطاغية الباغية الذين تجاوزوا الحدود، وفعلوا بمصر من المظالم ما لم يفعله المجوس واليهود، أهلكهم الله هلكة عاد وثمود، آمين آمين آمين. أقول قد يسّر لي الله الخلاص من أزمير فسافرت منها إلى دمشق الشام ونعم هي البلدة،فمكثت بها مدة ثم توجهت لزيارة البيت المقدس وذهبت ليافا بغية التوجه لموطني الأصلي مصر فعوقت بها وحصل جبر وإكراه على الإقامة بها فوجدتها أقذر بلاد الله وأسفلهم بقعة. أسال الله الخلاص منها كما خلصني من أزمير عاجلا سريعا. حرر في شهر صفر سنة ١٢٢٦ [1811/].

Appendix II

Six Letters by Ḥasan al-ʿAṭṭārand ʿAbd al-Raḥmān al-Jabartī kept in the Department of the Revival of Islamic Heritage in the Directorate of the *Awqāf* Archive in East Jerusalem and from a collection of documents in the possession of the Ḥusaynī family in Jerusalem[1]

I

A letter from ʿAbd al-Raḥmān al-Jabartī to the Muftī of Jerusalem, al-Sayyid Muḥammad Ṭāhir Afandī al-Ḥusaynī (d. 1866),[2] informing him of Ḥasan al-ʿAṭṭār's safe arrival at Cairo, dated 21 Rabīʿ II 1229 (/12 April 1814).From a collection of documents in the Archive of the Department of the Revival of Islamic Heritage in the Directorate of the Awqāf, in East Jerusalem.[3]

سلام تزفه جنايب القبول، وتحفه نجايب الاقبال، وتنضم معه شمايل الشمول، ونسيم الشمال، الى حضرة حاوي انواع الكمالات والمفاخر، وحايز قصبات السبق على كل مضمر وظاهر. شعر، [الرجز]

علاّمةُ الوقتِ الرّئيسُ المُفتيِ　　　مُحمّدُ الاسْمِ حَميدُ النّعْتِ
جَمالُ أهْلِ القُدْسِ فِي ذا الوَقْتِ　　　وَطاهِرٌ مُطَهّرٌ مِنْ سَحْتِ
يَشْفِى غليلَ السّايلِ المُسْتفتِى　　　وَكلّ مَنْ كانَ إليهِ يَأتِي
يَعُودُ بالجَبْرِ وَطِيبِ البْختِ　　　مُحَوّطـًا مِنَ الجهَاتِ السّتّ
وَعِبْدُ رّحْمنِ هُوَ الجَبَرْتِي　　　يُهْدِي لَكُمْ مِنَ السّلامِ البْتّ

لا زال بكل خير ظافر، ولحساده قاهر، وعلى اعدآئه ظاهر، ولهفوات مخاطبيه غافر، هذا وحيث تلمح الخاطر، بالسوال عن من لم يزل بعد اليوم الى الاخر، لمحاسن اوصافكم ذاكر، فهو بحمد الله، شاكرا لأنعم الله، ويرجو لكم دوام الصحة والسلامه، وصحة المزاج والعافية المستدامه، وقد ورد علينا في أشرف الأوقات، واسعد الساعات، كتابكم المستطاب، المشحون بلذيذ الخطاب، بما يسر الاحباب، وينعش الالباب، فابتهجنا بقدومه، وانتعشنا بوروده، وتشوقنا الي منشيه ومبديه، ومبتدينا قبل ان نبتديه،

1 See the description of these letters and their English translation by Adel Manna, 'Cultural Relations between Egyptian and Jerusalem *'Ulamā'* in the Early Nineteenth Century', in *Asian and African Studies*, 17: 1–3 (November 1983), 139–52. A photo of the original letter is published by Manna on p. 151, and its English translation is given in pp. 142–4.

2 On Ṭāhir al-Ḥusaynī, see Adel Manna, 'Cultural Relations', 141 and Mannāʿ, *A'lām Falasṭīn fī Awākhir al-'Ahd al-'Uthmānī* (Beirut 1995), 111–12.

3 See Adel Manna, 'Cultural Relations', 139–52.

وهي لا شك جاذبة مغناطسيه، وعلامة على خلوص النية، وقد تعشق الاذن قبل العين، وتتصل المودة بين المتباعدين، فربّ كتاب كان اشهى من اللقا، وابرد على كبد المشوق من الزلال المروقا، وخصوصا حيث انبأ عن وصول أعز الخلان، ونادرة الزمان، الاستاذ العلامه، والمدقق الفهامه، الشيخ حسن العطار، ذو الأرج المعطار، الى سدتكم السنيه، وساحتكم القدسيه، بعد طول انتظارنا لاخباره، وتطلعنا لمراسلاته ونظمه ونثاره، فبورود الكتابين، انجلا عن القلب الرين، وقرّت العينين، باجتماع الإلفين، واما قضية البحر الرايق، شرح كنز الدقايق[4]، وما اشترطوه من كونها تكون مكمله، وبتكملة الطوري مُزيّله [كذا = مُذيّلة]، فهي ليست الا تاليف الاصل، من غير ذيل ولا وصل، وكان الوالد لا يعبأ بهذه التكملة ولا يعتنيها، فلذلك لم يقتنيها[!]، ومعلومكم ليس كل من الـّـف الـّف، ولا كل من صنـّف أنصف، ولا يقاس الطورى[5] ولو طار مع الف طاير، بابن نجيم صاحب الفتاوى والاشباه والنظاير، وتأملوا فيمن ذيّل تذكرة داود، حيث لم يات بشئ من المقصود، ولكلٍ مشرب ومزيّه لا توجد في سواه بالكليه.

وملخص المسئلة بالاختصار والحاصل، ان النسخة ثلاثة أسفار في محير الكامل[6]، كل سفر يحتوى على نحو الاربعين من الكراريس، بخط منسوب نفيس، مقروة من اولها الى اخرها ومصححة، ومقابلة على المعتمد ومنقحه، وهي في الاصل نسخة العلامه الدلجى، من اعاظم الحنفيه الخواص لا الخرجي، ثم انتقلت الي الشيخ الوالد، وكان يعتمد عليها في المسايل والمقاصد، وما ذكرتوه من ارسالها، لتروها وتشاهدوها، فان وافقت الغرض تبقوها او تردوها. ولا يخفاكم ان هذا شي مستعصى، لاننا بمصر وانتم بالاقصى، فان كنتم من خُطابها فابعثوا بمهرها، فعند ذلك تحظوا بوصولها، والتملى بجمالها، والا فالراي ما تروه، والمناسب ما تستحسنوه. وان كان ولا بد من التكملة، فهي موجودة متحصله، نستنسخها ونرسلها اليكم، ان كانت معدومة بناديكم، وهذا امر متيسر، غير متعسر، وموجود، لا مفقود. ونرجوا [!] من شيمكم، ومحاسن اوصافكم، تعجيل إياب مولانا الشيخ حسن، ورجوعه مسرورا الي الوطن، فاننا له مشتاقين، ولحضوره منتظرين، وكذلك اهل داره واحبابه، ومن يلوذ بجنابه، وخصوصا طلبة العلم الازهريه، الملازمين للحضور عليه فى البكرة والعشيه، وفي كل وقت وحين، ياتون الينا مستخبرين، وكذلك كل من اجتمع بنا، من علما وقتنا، واكابر الدولة واعيان الزمان، مثل السيد المحروقي وبكتاش وعلى الترجمان، والجميع مثل الوز، حنانه بلا بِز،[7] ويشهدون بفضله وادابه، ويستمطرون من ودق سحابه، وهو كما قال الزمخشري: "غنى من الاداب، لكننى اذا نظرت فما في الكف غير الانامل"، (فالله الله في تعجيل سراحه، مقرونا بسروره وانشراحه، مشمولا بحسن انظاركم البهيه، ملحوظا منكم بالمنى وللامن والامنيه، والمامول منكم العفو عن السقطات، وتكرار العبارات، والالفاظ الشارده، والقوافى البارده، فانتم اهلا للعفو عن الجاني، وكشف العنت عن العانى، وقبول عذر المعذور، لا سيما الممنوع المحصور، الذي تلازمت همومه بقواه النفسيه، تلازم الهيولى للصورة الجنسيه، فالله يزيل الخطوب، ويفرج الكروب، ومنا مزيد التحيه، والتسليمات الزكيه،

---

4 It is a commentary on *al-Nasafī's Kanz al-Daqāyiq*, by Zayn al-Dīn b. Nujaym (d. 970/1563), see Manna's article, p. 142, note 10.

5 Al-Ṭūrī is ʿAbd al-Qādir b. ʿUthmān (d. 1030/1620–1); he was the muftī of the Ḥanafīs in Egypt, see Manna's article, p. 142, note 10.

6 The size of the folio is about fullscap.

7 An Egyptian proverb denoting compassion, see El-Said Badawi and Martin Hinds, *Dictionary of Egyptian Arabic* (Beirut 1986), 935, col. b: 'Like a mother goose, who loves her goslings, yet does not breast-feed them = you say you love, but do nothing to prove it'.

والدعوات المقبولة المرضيه، لحضرة الجناب الأعز الاكرم، والملاذ الأفخر الأفخم، الحسيب النسيب، والمبجل المفضل الاريب، من هو بكل جميل ومعروف مسدي، مولانا السيد عمر افندي، نقيب السادة الاشراف، وطراز عصابة آل عبد مناف، ادام الله سعادته، وأبّد سيادته، ولا زال رحابه ملجا للقاصدين، ومحطّا لرحال الواردين، وحفظ جنابكما من الاكدار، ومن حوادث الليل والنهار، ويهدي اليكما جزيل السلام السامى، حاضر تسطيره السيد محمد التهّامى، وهو على الدوام يدعو لكما، ويكثر من الثنآ عنكما، وعلى الله القبول، وبلوغ المأمول)،

المحب الداعي

عبد الرحمن الجبرتي

في 21 ربيع آخر سنة ١٢٢٩ [/ 12 ابريل 1814]

II

A letter from Ḥasan al-ʿAṭṭār from Cairo, before his marriage in Jumādā I 1229/May 1814, sent to the Muftī of Jerusalem, al-Sayyid Muḥammad Ṭāhir Afandī al-Ḥusaynī, on 21 Rabīʿ II 1229 (/12 April 1814), from a collection of documents in the possession of the Ḥusaynī family in Jerusalem, published by Dr Adel Manna, in *Asian and African Studies*, Jerusalem, vol. 17, nos. 1–3, November 1983, 139–52:[8]

أهدي الى جناب حضرة أخي في الله تعالى سيدي الامام الهمام الفاضل النحرير والعلم الشهير السيد طاهر أبقاه الله آمين،

عاطر تحيات تشرح القلوب بلطف ما حملته من خالص المودة التي هي دايمه الاتصال إن شا الله تعالى بيننا حتى نلتقي على أحسن الأحوال وأجملها، وأتعشم بتلك المودة والإخا والولا[ء] انتظامي في سلك آلِ البيت يوم القيامة فأحشر في زمرتهم وتحت لوآ جدهم عليه أفضل الصلاة وأزكى السلام، فإن المر[ء] يحشر مع من أحب، وإني لأرجو الله تعالى أن ينفعني بمحبة آل بيت نبيه ويزيدني حبا فيهم بمنه وكرمه، وقد وصل للفقير كتابك وبصحبته حاشية التحفة، وأخبرتمونا أنكم تستكتبون حاشية السيالكوتي على البيضاوي، لقد أصبتم في ذلك، وإذا أمكنكم استكتاب جميع [ما] له من التأليفات فافعلوا فإنها من النوادر، وإني أملك حاشية على الخيالي[9] وحاشية على المُطَوَّل[10] والقُطْب[11]، إلا أن الأخيرتين ناقصتان، أرجو من الله تمامها وأقصى أمانيّ أن أقرا البيضاوي بحاشيته، أسأل الله تيسير ذلك قبل الموت، فبعد فراغ نقل حاشية البيضاوي تتفضلون بإرسالها، وإني قد كنت في العام الماضي أختتمت قراة القطب

8 See Manna, 'Cultural Relations', 139–52. A photo of the original letter is published by Manna on p. 152, and its English translation is given on pp. 144–7. The names of authors and books mentionned by al-ʿAṭṭār are provided by Manna in his footnotes in this important article.

9 He is Aḥmad b. Mūsā al-Khayālī (d. 866/1481), a Ḥanafī *faqīh*, see GAL, II, 318; *ʿAj*. Būlāq, I, 263; cf. Manna, p. 145.

10 Cf. *ʿAj*. Būlāq, V, 237. The *Muṭawwal* is by Saʿd al-Dīn al-Taftāzānī.

11 Cf. *ʿAj*. Būlāq, II, 58 by Muḥammad b. ʿUbadā al-ʿAdwā, al-Mālikī.

على الشمسية والتزمت حل حاشية السيالكوتي عليه مع مزجها بحاشية السيد وبعض الحواشي فكتبت من ذلك الى انتها[ء] المقدمة، ثم حصلت عوايق وموانع أسأل الله رفعها حتى أعود للعزيمة الأولى، فإن هذه الحاشية لو تمت على الوجه الذي أردته كانت حسنة.

واخبركم أنني في جمادى الأولي أدخل إنشا الله على الزوجة وهي من قرى ريف مصر، فانى لا يسعني أن أتزوج من أهل الحضر لإحتياجهم الى مزيد نفقه، وذلك ليس في وسعي، تطلبون من الله لي الاعانة وتيسير الرزق، وتبلغون سلامي لحضرة منلا أفندي أدام الله عزه، وتخبرونه بكمال شوقي اليه، ولولا ما أخبرتكم عنه من الزواج لأسرعت القدوم الى حضرته، لأتملى بمشاهدة طلعته الغرا واستجلاب فوايده، وحصول عوايده، وامتع ناظري بما حواه من نفايس الكتب، واشرح خاطري باجتنا ما تضمنه مجلسه السعيد من لطاييف الأدب، وكان اقصى مرادي أن يشرفني بكتاب من عنده، وأن لم تجر العادة بمكاتبة الأسياد للعبيد، لكن وفور محبتي فيه وطمعي في عظيم علمه ورقة سجيته، يطمعني في ذلك. فأنا أرجوه أن يشرفني بالمراسلة أطال الله عمره، وان حاشية الچلنبوي على شرح الدواني على العقايد العضدية وشرح وحيي زاده على المُغْنِي إذا كانا لديه بالقدس يمن علينا بارسالهما. أما شرح وحيي زاده فانه معدوم عندنا بمصر وفي نيتي بعد ختم القطب أقرا المغني فان تيسر لي هذا الشرح تمّ المراد، وأماحاشية الجلنبوي فهي معدومة أيضا لكن الرجل محقق جدا وهذه أجل حاشيه، فالمرجو منه إرسالها أما على طريق العادة حتى نكتبها ونرسلها أو (بعضها للإنتفاع بها، ويكون ذلك في صحايف أعماله ومن جملة خيراته، فإن هذا شي سهل بالنسبة له وثوابه جليل كما لا يخفاه وتخبرونه بذلك وتكونون خير المساعدين، فبما هنالك فأن الدال على الخير كفاعله.

ويا سيدي قد أرسلتم لنا سابقا قدرا من الصابون فبقي عندنا الي الآن وقد شارف الفراغ وتحصيله عندنا بمصر عسير جدا مع غلو سعره، فأنا ارجو من مكارم أخلاقكم وتفضلاتكم علينا إرسال قدر يسير، فإن هذا من عوايد إحسانكم علينا لا زلتم أهلا للإحسان، ويا سيدي أرجو تفضلكم في العفو عن تقصيري بعدم تواصل المراسلات، أما أولا، فإنكم تعتقدون أني كثير الحب لكم، فأنا أعوّل على هذه الصورة، وأما ثانيا فإن حال الفقير لا يخفاكم من التكاسل والذهول ووالله ياسيدي فيتفق أني اذهل عن أمور لازمة لي وأتكاسل عنها وحال الوقت عموما غير خفي على كل عاقل، والعذر مقبول عند خيار الناس، هذا ومني كثير السلام لحضرة نقيب أفندي وبقية من يلوذ بكم وراغب وشاكر وكامل الأحباب، وبلغنا سلامكم وسلام حضرة الملا أفندي لمحبنا الشيخ عبد الرحمن الجبرتي، فهو يخصكما بمزيد السلام والمحبة وكذلك جميع من يلوذ بكم ويسألكم

الدعا بالمكان المقدس أن الله بيسر لنا الامور ويشرح منا الصدور ودمتم بخير، صح)

الفقير حسن العطار غفر الله له

III

A Letter, 1230/1814–15, by Ḥasan al-ʿAṭṭār after the death of his second wife in Cairo, to the Muftī of Jerusalem, al-Sayyid Muḥammad Ṭāhir Afandī al-Ḥusaynī kept at the Archive of the Department of the Revival of the Islamic Heritage in the Directorate of the *Awqaf* in East Jerusalem **(ارشيف دائرة احياء التراث الاسلامي في مديرية الاوقاف في القدس)**

بسم الله الرحمن الرحيم

من العبد الفقير حسن العطار الى حضرة الامام الهمام العلامة المفتي، محبنا وقرة عيننا السيد طاهر افندي، جمعني الله واياه بالديار المقدسه، وادام محبتنا التي هي على صفا القلوب مؤسسه.

اما بعد السلام عليكم ورحمة الله وبركاته، فان العبد الفقير يجب عليه المواصلة بالكتب دائما وعتبكم عليه في كتبكم في محله وغاية الاعتذار يا سيدي اني مقصر فليسعني حلمكم وصدق حبكم، وهناك امور ابدى بعضها تقوم لي بحجة الاعتذار، اني لما توجهت لمصر اشتغلت بقراة بعض الكتب واخذت جاريته بجميع ما تملكه يدي من الدراهم مع بيع اشيا كثيرة ولما حصلت عندي، ولا يخفاك حالي وحال الوقت، احتجت للسعي في المعيشة ولا سبب لي ادلي به الا العلم، وهو بضاعة كاسده لا سيما اذا انضم اليه الخمول وعدم التردد على الناس، فان طبعي لا يخفاكم يميل الى الانفراد، فكان يحصل لي مشقات، ثم مكثنت معي سنة وماتت مطعونة من الطلق، فحصل لي بعض جزع علي فراقها وبقيت بعد ذلك مدة لا استقر بمكان كالهايم، ثم من اول السنة، اعنى ابتدا القراة بالازهر شرعت في قرا[ء]ة الخطيب[12] صباحا، وتكمله شرح العقائد[13] بعد العصر وبعد اتمامها شرعت في قراة القطب علي الشمسية،[14] وهي كتب معضله صعبه تحتاج لمزيد تفرغ، فبنا[ء] على ذلك ضاق علي الوقت بسبب المطالعة واشتغلت بذلك حتى والله عن امور لازمة لي كحلق راسى ودخول حمام للتنظيف، ولكن هذه الامور شانها عدم العاقة عن المكاتبة، الا ان الفقير لضيق نفسه لا يتحمل القليل فضلا عن الكثير من الشواغل، فعدم ارسال المكاتبات لكم ليس والله لملل او تناسي صحبه او جفوة وانما اعتمادي في ذلك علي حسن حبكم وسعة عفوكم وعظيم حلمكم، وقد وصل للفقير منكم كتب، وصحيحًا ما ارسلت بعض الاجوبة وذلك والله لتراخ في طبيعتي او نسيان او اشتغال او غير ذلك مما يعوق، فالقصد عدم المواخذه كما هو المامول، وقد ارسلت اليكم شرح التحفة[15] وحاشيتها، اما شرح التحفة فهو لكم هدية واما الحاشية فانكم تنقلونها وترسلونها بعد النقل فانها لم تنقل بمصر واما حاشية السمرقندية[16] فنرسلها لكم بعد، فاني بعد ان اتممتها وقفتها وحين قدم رسولكم اردت ارسالها فمنعها الطلبة، ان شا الله عند فراغى اكتب لكم نسخه اخرى وارسلها، ولنا حاشية المنار[17] فمن حين استقراري بمصر ما وجدتها تباع ابدا فان حصلت اخذتها لكم، وحاشية الدر[18] هذه لا وجود لها الا بالاستنساخ ويحتاج ذلك لزمن طويل فان النساخ {قليلو الوجود وان وجدوا كلهم محرفون، على انكم في غنية عما بالكتب التي عندكم فان مولفها لم يشرح من عنده شيا، غايته انه نقل عن البحر وغيره والاصول عندكم، وكنت اعطيته كتابكم وقلت له يكتب على الفتوى ويرسل الجواب، فتعلل بان هذا يحتاج لفراغ ان يكن بعد ثلاثة اشهر وقد عرفناكم، وتالله يا سيدي

12 It may be *Sharḥ Abī Shujā'* by al-Khaṭīb al-Shirbīnī.

13 It may be *Takmilat Sharḥ al-'Aqā'id al-Nasafiyya* by al-Sa'd, cf. *'Aj*. Būlāq, II, 28.

14 It may be *Ḥāshiya 'alā Sharḥ al-Shamsiyya fi'l-Manṭiq* by Aḥmad b. Yūnis al-Khalīfī. See GAL, I, 466; GAL, Suppl., I, 845; *'Aj*., I, 390; II, 58, 100, 228, 259.

15 It is called *al-Tuḥfa* or *Nukhbat al-Fikar fī Muṣṭalaḥ Ahl al-Athar* by al-Ḥāfiẓ Ibn Ḥajar al-'Asqalānī. See cf. GAL, II, 68, *'Aj*., I, 390; II, 58.

16 *Sharḥ Zakariyya al-Anṣārī 'alā al-Samarqandiyya fī Ādāb al-Baḥth*, in *'Aj*., I, 310, 368, 390, 398; II, 259 which is known as *Sharḥ al-Risāla al-Samarqandiyya*, see GAL, II,571.

17 *Al-Manār* by 'Abd Allāh b. Aḥmad al-Nasafī. See *'Aj*., I, 165, 288, 390 and GAL, II, 196.

18 *Ḥāshiyat al-Durr or Ḥāshiyat li-Kitāb 'al-Durr al-Mukhtār Sharḥ Tanwīr al-Abṣār'* on Ḥanafī *fiqh*, by Ibrāhīm al-Ḥalabī al-Ḥanafī, see *'Aj*. Būlāq, I, 395.

اني لأتمنى كل ساعة الحصول لديكم ولكن الامور تعوّق فلعل الله ييسّر، فهذا ما عندي، والقصد أنكم بعد كتابة حاشية التحفة ترسلونها على يد السيد مصطفى عبد النبي، وان الصابون قد وصل، جزاكم الله خيرا، واني بعد توجهي لمصر كتبت حاشية على شرح ايساغوجي[19] لكنها تنقص من الاخر، فبعد اتمامها ان شا الله ارسلها لكم هي وحاشية السمرقندية والان أنا اكتب على شرح القطب[20]، نطلب منكم الدعا بالاعانة ولا تقطعوا عنا اخباركم السارة وتفيصل حالنا يخبركم عنه حامل الكتاب.

منا السلام)

IV

An Undated Letter of Ḥasan al-ʿAṭṭār to the Muftī of Jerusalem, al-Sayyid Muḥammad Ṭāhir Afandī al-Ḥusaynī kept by the Husayni Family in Jerusalem:[21]

سلام الله تعالي ورحمته وبركاته وأنر لي بحياته، نخص بذلك حضرة الجناب الاعز الاكرم الفاضل العلامة

حضرة طاهر افندي ابقاه الله امين.

اما بعد فقد ارسلنا لكم قبل هذا مكتوبا نعرفكم فيه انه قد وصل الينا مكتوبكم واخبرناكم ايضا انه قد ارسلنا لكم قبله مكتوبين ان شا الله يكونان قد وصلا اليكما والذي نترجاه منكم يا سيدي ان عندنا بعض كتب نحب ان نرسلها اليكم تكون عندكم امانة لنا وليكن ذلك سرا بيني وبينك لا يطلع عليه احد وتكون عندكم في بيتكم، فاذا انشرح خاطركم لذلك ترسلون من طرفكم رجلا كرجيا امينا توصوه علي في ذلك، وتكتبون لنا مكتوبا بتسليم الكتب له، هذا ما نرجوه من همتكم العليه، وان رايتم في ذلك ثقلة او استربتم في شى ترسلون تعرفونا نلتفت لوجه اخر، فالله الله يا سيدي تبادرون لي بارسال مكتوب مفصل وتشرحون لنا فيه كامل الاحوال على سبيل الفور والعجله والسلام علي كافة الاحباب ودمتم .

الفقير حسن العطار

V

Letter of Ḥasan al-ʿAṭṭār from Cairo to the Muftī of Jerusalem, al-Sayyid Muḥammad Ṭāhir Afandī al-Ḥusaynī, dated 3 Rajab 1229 (/ 21 June 1814)

ارشيف دائرة احياء التراث الاسلامي في مديرية الاوقاف في القدس.

بسم الله الرحمن الرحيم

من العبد الفقير حسن العطار الى حضرة ذي المفاخر والمآثر والفضل الباهر والمجد المتكاثر، العالم

19 *Sharḥ Iysāghūjī* by Zakariyya al-Anṣārī, see *ʿAj*. Būlāq, IV, 185.

20 Cf. *ʿAj*. Būlāq, II, 58. By Muhammad b. ʿUbadā al-ʿAdwā, al-Mālikī.

21 See the English translation of this letter in Butrus Abu-Manneh, 'Four Letters of Šayḫ Ḥasan al-ʿAṭṭār to Šayḫ Ṭāhir al-Ḥusaynī of Jerusalem', *Arabica* L:I (2002), letter no. II, 90.

الفاضل الكامل العامل التقى الوفى، حضرة محبنا العزيز طاهر افندي أطال الله عمره ونفّع به ونفعه وجمعنا واياه في أشرف مكان واسرّ زمان، امين.

اما بعد، السلام عليكم ورحمة الله وبركاته، فانه قد ورد علينا كتابكم علي يد السيد مصطفى فاسفر لنا عن صباح المسرة سفوره، وطالعنا فن فنونه وابتهجنا به ابتهاجا عظيما وبضمنه كتابان احدهما كان ارسله لنا الشيخ عبد الرحمن والثاني من طرفكم للمذكور، اما ما عرّفتمونا عنه من أننا لم نرسل لكم بعد توجهنا من القدس كتابا، فاني يا سيدي قد ارسلت لكم حين استقراري بالسويس كتابا على يد بعض العرب فلعله تهاون، فانا ارسلناه طيّ كتاب للشيخ اسماعيل المحتسب وارسلناه للخليل مع العرب ثم لكم المعذرة في عدم ارسال المكاتبة من مصر والمبادرة بها، فاني يا سيدي وصلت لمصر ضئيلا[!] من المشقات التي حصلت لي، لاسيما من حين ورودي للسويس الى استقراري بمصر، وشرح ذلك يطول، ولما وصلت لمصر مكثت أيامًا مشغولا بمقابلة الأحباب وشيوخ اهل العلم كما هو عادة القادمين من الأسفار، ثم اشتغلت بعدها بقراة شرح ايساغوجي لشيخ الاسلام، فحضر جماعة كثيرون اقتضى الحال شدّة الاهتمام بالكتابة، حتى شرعت في كتابة حاشية عليه أحرّرها درسا درسا، ان شاء الله تتم بخير، وأيضا كان حضرة النقيب اخبرنا عن حاجة شفاها متعلقة بالشيخ عبد الرحمن الجبرتي، فاخبرناه بها وطلبنا الجواب ونلحّ عليه كل يوم في ذلك، وهو الى الآن ما اجابنا عن المطلوب، معتذرا بغوائل الوقت، ويا سيدي حال طرفنا لا نخفاكم، فما رآءٍ كمن سمعا، فقبلنا عذره، وهو يمهلنا كل يوم حتى يجد فراغا من الوقت، فلم يتيسر له ذلك لما هو فيه وغيره من الخطوب المدلهمة، لطف الله بنا وبالمسلمين، فكان في نيتي اني بعد اجابة الشيخ عبد الرحمن عن السوال احرر لكم جوابا ليكون محتويا على الفائدة، فحين وصل الى كتابكم بادرت بارسال هذه المكاتبة لتفيدكم سلامتي وهي تنضمن شرح حالي على الجمله، فاني سافرت من الخليل الى السويس في اثنى عشر يوما، ومكثت بالسويس سبعة ايام، ثم سافرت لمصر فوصلتها في اليوم الثالث من السويس واجتمعت بحمد الله بعد ذلك بسائر الاحباب والكل طيبون بخير ولكن لزمني حال الوقت اني ملازم لبيتي لا ابرح منه الا للذهاب لقراة الدرس بالجامع الازهر وارجع بعد فراغه على اثري لبيتي ألازمه وهكذا حالي، فان الراحة الان في العزلة، وذكركم دائما يدور على لساني ومثالكم متمثل بجناني، ولو استطعت توارد المراسلات عليكم بكرة وعشيا لفعلت ولكن يعوقني عن ذلك امران، الأول عدم وجود السفّار كل وقت، الثاني وهو الأصعب، حال الوقت، فان شرحه يطول وغاية ما نقول لا حول ولا قوة الا بالله العليّ العظيم، واما ما ذكرتم من قضية البحر والمحيط والثمن الذي دفعتموه فان الشيخ عبد الرحمن لم يرض بذلك {حتى انني جعلت له سبعماة، فقال الا اقل من الف، فان جملة الكتابين سبعة أجزا ضخمة، الجلي الخط والضبط، فهو على صحته وحسن خطه وما كتب بهامشه من خطوط الفضلا وتحريراتهم، ان وجد راغبا، دفع فيه خمسماة قرش لكن الرغبة قلّت بل فقدت، ونحن الي الان نعالج الشيخ عبد الرحمن عساه يسمح بسبعماة وسيرسل لكم هو مكتوبا بخطه بعد تاريخه ان شاء الله عن شرح حال الكتب وغيرها، واحرر لكم ولحضرة النقيب كتابا مطولا اذكر له فيه جواب سواله حين ياتي به الشيخ عبد الرحمن، وانما كتبت هذا الكتاب على عجلة لان حامله اخبرني إنه متوجه على الفور وطلب مني التوصية عليه وجنابكم لا يحتاج ذلك، فان بيتكم مفتوح لكل غريب عمّر الله دياركم، واما مكتوب الشيخ ثعيلب فاوصلته اياه وأوعدني بارسال جوابه، وبلّغت سلامكم لكل من ذكرتم والكل يسلمون عليكم لا سيما الشيخ عبد الرحمن، فان له اليكم من الشوق اضعاف ما لي عندكم لما نجده معه كل وقت من حسن الثنا عليكم ويعتذر لكم غاية العذر من

جهة الكتب، فانه لولا ضيق الوقت وحال العالم الان لارسلها لكم بغير ثمن، وليس بينه وبينكم فرق، وان شاء الله بعد تاريخه يصلكم منا ومنه جواب شافي على يد السيد مصطفى، وانما هذا الكتاب اشبه بالملحق وهو مفيد في الجملة، فانه ربما ينزعج خاطركم علينا لعدم المكاتبة خصوصا في امثال هذا الوقت الذي اشتعلت ارجاؤه بالوبا والفساد وغيرهما مما يضيق عنه النطاق والخناق والله يفرج ويلطف، هذا والسلام منا كثيرا لحضرة نقيب افندي وراغب افندي وشاكر افندي والشيخ حسن ابو الهدي وجاد الله والشيخ عبد الوهاب وولده سيدي خليل وولد الشيخ بدير وكل من يسأل عنا وكل من يحتوي عليه مكانكم السعيد، والشيخ عبد الرحيم الموصلى ان كان باقيا، وان السيد محمد التهامي بعد وصولنا لمصر بنحو عشرين يوما انتقل الى رحمة الله مطعونا رحمه الله، ولقد فتّت منا القوي وهدّ الجلد خبر موت السيد حسن كمال رحمه الله، فانه كان من اعز الاحباب لنا ولكم وكان سيد المهذبين واللطفا وهو من نوادر القدس وبقية الناس، قل ان يخلف مثله رحمه الله ثم رحمه الله، فلقد ساءني خبر موته، إنا لله وانا اليه راجعون، عوضكم الله خيرا واحسن عزاكم والهمكم الصبر على فقده، والشيخ عبد الرحمن يسلم عليكم كثيرا وعلى حضرة النقيب والشيخ عبد الوهاب وكل من ارسل اليه سلامه يخصّه باكمل التحية وان المذكور من المخلصين الحب كله والمودة علي البعاد لما يسمعه من حسن ثنا منا عليكم، ادام الله وجودكم وعمر دياركم، أمين. ٣ شهر رجب سنة١٢٢٩[/ 1814].)

On the back of the letter:

يصل انشا الله الى القدس الشريف،يسلم لحضرة العالم العلامة الفهامة طاهر افندي المفتي،سلّمه الله تعالى،آمين

VI

Letter of Ḥasan al-ʿAṭṭār to the Muftī of Jerusalem, al-Sayyid Muḥammad Ṭāhir Afandī al-Ḥusaynī, dated Dhu'l-Ḥijja 1235/9 September–8 October 1820:

بسم الله الرحمن الرحيم، الحمد لله وحده وصلى الله على من لا نبي بعده،

اما بعد اهدا مزيد التحية والتسليم، الي حضرة اخينا في الله تعالى العالم العامل، الفاضل الكامل، فريد الزمان، ووحيد الاوان، طاهر افندي جمع الله شملي به في أسرّ الاوقات واشرف الاماكن، فانه يا سيدي قد وصلني كتابكم المسفر عن صبح المودة، الذي يشفى بمطالعة رقومه غليل الافئدة، جزاكم الله عنا خيرا، وما ذكرتموه من كمال الشوق الينا فنحن يا سيدي عندنا اضعاف ذلك والقلوب شاهد عدل علي المحبة، وانه قد كان من الحزم اني اتعوق بالقدس واتروي في امري حتى ييسر الله لي ما تبرره القدرة، ولكن لما كانت الامور مقدرة لا بد من انفاذها، لا ينفع حذر من قدر، والامر لله، وقد وصلنا من نابلس بعض امتعة وبقي بعض بالشام، وصل الينا مكتوب من الشام بانها باقية ثَمّ، حتى نرسل من يتسلمها فحصل لنا الطمانينة حينئذ، واتفق انه ابرم علينا واكد والح في القضية التي لكم بها شعور، ونحن نغالط ونماطل فلما راينا الامر سماويا، وامتثال القضا بالرضا، خير من مزاحمة الاقدار، رضينا بما اراد الله واجبنا، فتم يوم الجمعة سبب القضية ومقدمتها واظن بعد ايام قليلة تظهر نتيجة القياس، ولكن الامر فيه التباس وحال المكان، معلوم لكم يا سيدي، لقد حصل لي كمال الاسف والحزن علي مفارقتكم ورجعت

على نفسي بالملامه ثم رحبت للاستسلام ولانفاذ لازمة القضا والقدر، والله سبحانه يحسن العاقبة، واما قضية الرسائل فبعد اطمئناننا واستقرارنا بالقدس، واما حاشية الازهرية فسنرسل للشام من ياتي بالكتب ونرسلها لكم تنسخونها، وما دام الفقير بيافا ان شا الله لا تنقطع اخباره عنكم، ولله القايل:

انا على البعاد والتفرق لنلتقي بالذكر ان لم نلتق

ثم ان لنا غرض الفرضه عليكم وهو ان الفقير ليس معه من كتب الشافعية شي، ولا يخفاكم انه قد يسال عن بعض المسائل فيحتاج للمراجعة والمطالعة ليستحضر بعض المسائل، وكنا راينا عند المكرم الشيخ محمود المهتدي شرح المنهج واستحيينا ان نساله في بيعه لنا، وكان اخبرنا انه اشتراه بثمانية عشر قرشا، يا سيدي ان كان تستحبون انكم تسالون المذكور في انه يبيعنا اياه لننتفع به وندعو له لاننا نحتاج اليه، فان اجاب الي ذلك ترسلون تعرفونا عن الثمن الذي يطلبه ونحن نرسله له، ثم يرسل الكتاب وتمضونه على ذلك ولو انه يوقفه علينا ونحن نعطيه ثمنه في مقابلة الهدية، وانه يعيره الينا الى ان يحضر لنا بعض كتبنا من مصر، والحاصل اننا فوضنا لكم النظر في هذه القضية بما ترونه حسنا، والذي حملنا على ذلك خلو يدنا عن كتب مذهبنا راسا، ولا يخفاكم ان حالتنا اليوم تقتضى المراجعة والتفتيش وحسبنا الله ونعم الوكيل، وتسلمون لنا على حضرة السيد حسن الحبي [!] والسيد حسن كمال والسيد محمد العطار وكل من يلوذ بكم والسلام على حضرة الامام الأمجد الهمام الشيخ اليعقوبي وتطلبون لنا منه الدعا وإننا إن شاء الله نكتب له الرسايل أيضا بعد اطمئناننا واستقرارنا ولا تنسونا من الدعا والمراسلة فإنها نصف المواصلة {ويسلم عليكما السيد عبد الله المفتي وهو إلى الآن بيافا، ويا سيدي إنه حين ذكرتكم تتلطفون لنا في أخذ شرح المنهج من الشيخ محمود المهتدي على اي حالة كانت وتواصلون دائما بالكتب والمراسلات)

ودمتم بخير.

الفقير حسن العطار. في سنة ١٢٣٥ ذي الحجة [/ 9 سبتمبر-8 اكتوبر 1820]

Bibliography

Butrus Abu-Manneh, 'Four Letters of Šayḫ Ḥasan al-'Aṭṭār to Šayḫ Ṭāhir al-Ḥusaynī of Jerusalem', *Arabica* L: I (2002), 79–95

Wilhelm Ahlwart, *Verzeichniss der arabischen Handschriften der Königlichen Bibliothek zu Berlin* (Berlin, A. Ascher and Co., 1897)

Laylā ʿAbd al-Laṭīf Aḥmad, ʿAḥmad al-Damurdāshī Kathkhud ʿAzabīn, Ṣāḥib *al-Durra al-Muṣāna*' in Laylā ʿAbd al-Laṭīf Aḥmad (ed.), *Dirāsāt fī Tārīkh wa-Mu'arrikhī Miṣr wa'l-Shām ibbān al-'Aṣr al-'Uthmānī* (Cairo, Maktabat al-Khānjī, 1980), 165–170

V.H. Aksan, 'Manning a Black Sea Garrison in the Eighteenth Century, Ochakov and Concepts of Mutiny and Rebellion in the Ottoman Context', in Jane Hathaway (ed.), *Mutiny and Rebellion in the Ottoman Empire* (Madison, University of Wisconsin, 2002), 63–88

R. Allen and D.S. Richards, *Arabic Literature in the Post-classical Period* (Cambridge, CUP, 2006)

Aḥmad Amīn, *Qāmūs al-'Ādāt wa'l-Taqālīd wa'l-Ta'ābīr al-Miṣriyya* (Cairo, Maṭbaʿat Lajnat al-Ta'līf wa'l-Tarjama wa'l-Nashr, 1953)

A. Anastasopoulos, 'The Mixed Elite of a Balkan Town: Karaferye in the Second Half of the 18th Century', in A. Anastasopoulos (ed.), *Provincial Elites in the Ottoman Empire* (Rethymno, Crete University Press, 2005), 259–69

Metin And, *Osmanli Şenliklerinde Türk Sanatlari* (Ankara, Kültür ve Turizm Bakanlığı,1982)

——*Culture, Performance and Communication in Turkey* (Tokyo, Institute for the Study of Languages and Cultures of Asia and Africa, 1987)

—— *Drama at the Crossroads, Turkish Performing Arts Link Past and Present, East and West* (Istanbul, Beylerbeyi,1991)

Muḥammad Anīs, 'Ḥaqā'iq ʿan ʿAbd al-Raḥmān Mustamadda min Wathā'iq al-Maḥkama al-Sharʿiyya', *al-Majalla al-Tārīkhiyya al-Miṣriyya* IX–X (1960–2), 80

Anon, *Rasā'il Ikhwān al-Ṣafā*, Khayr al-Dīn al-Ziriklī (ed.)(Cairo, Maktabat al-Tijāriyya al-Kubrā, 1347/1928–9)

Anon, MS, *al-Naṣr al-Mumtadd fī Fatḥ Tihāma wa-Najd* (Cambridge University Library, Add. 2782 [9])

Anon, MS, *al-Washy wa'l-Ṭirāz fī Fatḥ al-Ḥijāz* (Cambridge University Library, Qq. 170, Add. 2782 [9])

'Arabic Manuscripts from the Burckhardt Collection' (Catalogue of an exhibition in the University Library, Cambridge, 21 May 1990–21 June 1990)

Arthur J. Arberry, *The Chester Beatty Library: A Handlist of the Arabic Manuscripts* (Dublin, Hodges, Figgis,1962)

Arisṭūṭīlīs, *Fann al-Shi'r, ma'a al-Tarjama al-'Arabiyya al-Qadīma wa-Shurūḥ al-Fārābī wa-Ibn Sīnā wa-Ibn Rushd, Tarjamahu 'an al-Yūnāniyya wa-Sharaḥahu wa-Ḥaqqaqa Nuṣūṣahu 'Abd al-Raḥmān Badawī* (Beirut, Dār al-Thaqāfa, 1973)

Andre Assabgui et al. (eds), *Colloque internationale sur l'histoire du Caire* (Cairo 1972), 313–20

Ḥasan al-ʿAṭṭār, *Maqāmat al-Adīb al-Ra'īs al-Shaykh Ḥasan al-'Aṭṭār fī'l-Faransīs*, at the end of Jalāl al-Dīn ʿAbd al-Raḥmān b. Abī Bakr al-Suyūṭī, *al-Maqāmāt al-Suyūṭiyya, li Jalāl al-Dīn 'Abd al-Raḥmān b. Abī Bakr al-Suyūṭī, Mudhayyala bi-Maqāmat al-Adīb al-Ra'īs al-Shaykh Ḥasan al-'Aṭṭār fī'l-Faransīs* (Būlāq 1275/1858–9)

Ḥasan al-ʿAṭṭār, *Ḥāshiyat al-Shaykh Ḥasan al-ʿAṭṭār ʿalā Sharḥ Zakariyyā al-Anṣārī ʿalā Matn Īsāghūjī fī ʾl-Manṭiq* (Cairo, al-Bābī al-Ḥalabī, 1321/1903–4)

Joseph Aumer, *Die arabischen Handschriften der K. Hofū und Staatsbibliothek in München* (Munich, in Kommission der Palm'schen Hofbuchhandlung, 1866)

Kurkīs ʿAwwād, *al-Makhṭūṭāt al-Tārīkhiyya fī Khizānat Kutub al-Matḥaf al-ʿIrāqī bi-Baghdād* (Baghdad 1957), reprinted from *Sumer* 13 (1957)

David Ayalon, 'The Historian al-Jabartī and his Background', *BSOAS*23:2 (1960), 217–49

—— *Outsiders in the Lands of Islam: Mamluks, Mongols and Eunuchs* (London, Variorum Repr., 1988)

—— ʿal-Djabartī, ʿAbd al-Raḥmān b. Ḥasan', *EI*², 354.

Franz Babinger, *Die Geschichtsschreiber der Osmanen und ihre Werke* (Leipzig, O. Harrassowitz, 1927)

Ismāʿīl Bāshā al-Baghdādī, *Hadiyyat al-ʿĀrifīn bi-Asmāʾ al-Muʾallifīn wa-Āthār al-Muṣannifīn* (Istanbul, Millī Eğitim Basımevi 1951)

ʿAbd Allah al-Madanī al-Balawī, *Sīrat Aḥmad b. Ṭūlūn*, Muḥammad Kurd ʿAlī (ed.) (Damascus 1358/1939)

Ernst Bannerth, 'La Khalwatiyya en Egypte', *Mélanges de l'Institut dominicain d'études orientales* 8 (1964–6), 1–74

Karl K. Barbir, 'From Pasha to Efendi: The Assimilation of Ottomans into Damascene Society, 1516–1783', *International Journal of Turkish Studies*2(1979–80), 61–93

—— *Ottoman Rule in Damascus, 1708–1758* (Princeton, Princeton University Press, 1980)

Marc Baroli, *La Vie quotidienne des Français en Algérie, 1830–1914* (Paris, Hachette, 1967)

Gustav Bayerle, *Pashas, Begs, and Effendis: A Historical Dictionary of Titles and Terms in the Ottoman Empire* (Istanbul, Isis, 1997)

Doris Behrens-Abouseif, 'Pattern of Urban Patronage in Cairo; a Comparison between the Mamluk and the Ottoman Periods', in T. Philipp and U. Haarmann (eds), *The Mamluks in Egyptian Politics and Society* (Cambridge, CUP, 1998), 224–34

Avner Ben-Zaken, 'Political Economy and Scientific Activity in the Ottoman Empire', in Hasan Celâl Güzel, Cem Oğuz and Osman Karatay (eds), *The Turks*, vol. 3 (*The Ottomans*) (Ankara, Yeni Türkiye, 2002), 776–94

—— 'Recent Currents in the Study of Ottoman-Egypt Historiography, with Remarks about the Role of the History of Natural Philosophy and Science', *JSS* 49:2 (2004), 303–28

Jonathan P. Berkey, 'The Mamluks as Muslims: the Military Elite and the Construction of Islam in Medieval Egypt', in T. Philipp and U. Haarmann, *The Mamluks in Egyptian Politics and Society* (Cambridge, CUP,1998), 163–73

Annie Berthier (ed.), *Manuscrits, xylographes, estampages: les collections orientales du Département des manuscrits: guide* (Paris Bibliothèque Nationale, 2002)

Bibliothèque nationale de France, *Catalogue général des livres imprimés de la Bibliothèque Nationale: auteurs,* tom. 122 (Paris, Imprimerie Nationale, 1823)

Mustafa L. Bilge, 'Ârif Hikmet Bey, Şeyhülislâm', *Islâm Ansiklopedesi* (Istanbul 1991), 3, 365–6

C.E. Bosworth, 'Ṣafī al-Dīn al-Ḥillī', *Encyclopedia of Arabic Literature* (1998), 2, 675

—— 'Abū al-Muṭahhar al-Azdī', *Encyclopedia of Arabic Literature* 1, 39–40

Saladin Boustany, *The Journals of Bonaparte in Egypt: 1798–1801 Ṣuḥuf Būnābart fī Miṣr* (Cairo, Al-Arab Bookshop, 1971),10 vols

Mary Boyce, *A History of Zoroastrianism* (Leiden, Brill, 1975), vol. I

Ernle Bradford, The *Sultan's Admiral Barbarossa – Pirate and Empire-Builder* (New York, Tauris Parke, 1969); new edition, 2008

C. Brakel and Shmuel Moreh, 'Reflections on the Term *Bāba*: from Medieval Arabic Plays to Contemporary Javanese Masked Theatre', *Edebiyāt* 7:1 (Amsterdam 1996), 21–39

British Museum. Department of Oriental Printed Books and Manuscripts, *Catalogus codicum manuscriptorum orientalium qui in Museo Britannico asservantur. Pars secunda, Codices Arabicos amplectens. Appendix*, William Cureton and Charles Rieu,Sir Frederic Madden (eds) (London, Impensis Curatorum Musei Britannici, 1871)

G. Brocchi, *Giornale delle osservazioni fatte ne' viaggi in Egitto, nella Siria e nella Nubia* (Basano, A. Roberti, 1841–3), 5 vols

Carl Brockelmann, *Geschichte der arabischen Litteratur* (Leiden, Brill, 1943–4), 2 vols

—— *Geschichte der arabischen Litteratur*, Supplement (Leiden, Brill, 1937–42), 3 vols

—— *History of the Islamic Peoples*, trans. J. Carmichael and M. Perlmann (New York, G.P. Putnam's Sons, 1947)

—— *Tārīkh al-Adab al-'Arabī* (Cairo, Dār al-Maʿārif, pt. 8, 1960–77)

E.G. Browne, *A Hand-list of the Muhammadan Manuscripts Including All Those Written in the Arabic Character, Preserved in the Library of the University of Cambridge* (Cambridge, CUP, 1980)

Anṭūn Būlād (ed.), *Rāshid Sūriyā* (Beirut 1868/1285)

John Lewis Burckhardt, 'Travels in Egypt and Nubia', from the *Calcutta Journal*, in Sir Richard Phillips (ed.), *New Voyages and Travels: Consisting of Originals, Translations and Abridgements* (London, printed for Sir Richard Phillips and Co., 1819)

—— *Travels in Arabia, Comprehending an Account of those Territories in Hedjaz, Which the Mohammadans Regard as Sacred* (London, Henry Colburn, 1829)

A.J. Butler, *The Arab Conquest of Egypt and the Last Thirty Years of the Roman Domination* (Oxford, The Clarendon Press, 1902)

P. Cachia, 'Mawāliyā', *EI*², VI, 867–9

Michael Cooperson, *Classical Arabic Biography, The Heirs of the Prophets in the Age of al-Ma'mūn* (Cambridge, CUP, 2000)

Jack Crabbs, *The Writing of History in Nineteenth Century Egypt* (Detroit, Wayne State University Press, 1984)

—— 'al-ʿAṭṭār, Ḥasan', in J.S. Meisami and P. Starkey (eds), *Encyclopedia of Arabic Literature* (London, Routledge, 1998), i: 111

Daniel Crecelius, 'Nonideological Responses of the Egyptian Ulama to Modernization', in N. Keddie (ed.), *Scholars, Saints and Sufis* (Berkeley, University of California Press 1972), 167–210

—— 'Egypt in the Eighteenth Century', in M.W. Daly (ed.), *The Cambridge History of Egypt, vol. 2, Modern Egypt, from 1517 to the End of the Twentieth Century* (Cambridge, CUP, 1998), 59–86

——*Eighteenth Century Egypt: the Arabic Manuscript Sources* (Claremont, CA, Regina Books, 1990)

—— 'Aḥmad Shalabī Ibn ʿAbd al-Ghanī and Aḥmad Katkhudā ʿAzabīn al-Damurdāshī: Two Sources for al-Jabartī's *'Ajā'ib al-Āthār fī'l-Tarājim wa'l-Akhbār*', in Daniel Crecelius (ed.), *Eighteenth Century Egypt* (1990), 89–102

P. Crone, *Pre-Industrial Societies*: *Anatomy of the Pre-modern World* (Oxford, Basil Blackwell, 1995)

Andrew Dalby, *A Dictionary of Oriental Collections in Cambridge University Library* (Transactions of the Cambridge Bibliographical Society 9: 3, 1988)

M.W. Daly (ed.), *The Cambridge History of Egypt. Vol. 2, Modern Egypt, from 1517 to the End of the Twentieth Century* (Cambridge, CUP, 1998)

Aḥmad al-Damurdāshī, *Kitāb al-Durra al-Muṣāna fī Akhbār al-Kināna*, ʿAbd al-Raḥīm ʿAbd al-Raḥmānʿ Abd al-Raḥīm (ed.) (Cairo, al-Maʿhad al-ʿIlmī al-Faransī li'l-Āthār al-Sharqiyya, 1989)

—— *al-Damurdashi's Chronicle of Egypt 1688–1755*, trans. Daniel Crecelius and ʿAbd al-Wahhab Bakr (Leiden, Brill, 1991)

Dār al-Kutub al-Miṣriyya, Qism al-Fahāris al-ʿArabiyya, *Fihris al-Kutub al-'Arabiyya al-Mawjūda bi'l-Dār li-Ghāyat Shahr Disimbir 1928 m. al-Juz' al-Khāmis wa-Yashtamil 'alā Fihris al-Ta'rīkh* (Cairo, Dār al-Kutub al-Miṣriyya, 1348/1930)

M.J. De Goeje and Th.W. Juynboll, *Catalogus codicum arabicorum bibliothecae academiae Lugduno-Batavae* (Leiden, E.J. Brill, 1907)

Fred De Jong, 'Khalwatiyya', *EI*², IV, 991–3

—— *Ṭuruq* and *Ṭuruq-Linked Institutions in Nineteenth-Century Egypt* (Leiden, Brill, 1978)

—— 'On Peter Gran, *Islamic Roots of Capitalism: Egypt 1760–1840*, A Review Article with Author's Reply', *International Journal of Middle East Studies* 14 (1982), 381–99

—— 'The Itinerary of Ḥasan al-ʿAṭṭār (1766–1835): A Reconsideration and Its Implication', *JSS* 28:1 (1993), 99–128

C. de la Jonquière, *L'Expédition d'Égypte (1798–1801)* (Paris, H. Charles-Lavauzelle, 1899–1907), 5 vols

W.M. le Baron de Slane, *Catalogue des manuscrits arabes de la Bibliothèque Nationale* (Paris, Imprimerie Nationale, 1883–95)

Gilbert Delanou, *Moralistes et politiques musulmans dans l'Égypte du XIXème siècle (1798–1882)* (Le Caire, Institut français d'archéologie orientale du Caire, 1982)

Abd El-Rahman el-Djabarti, *Merveilles biographiques et historiques, ou chroniques du Cheikh Abd-el-Rahman el-Djabarti*, Chefik Mansour Bey, Abdulaziz Kahil Bey, Gebriel Nicolas Kahil Bey and Iskender Ammoun Effendi (trans.) (Cairo, Imprimerie Nationale, 1888–96), 9 vols

R. Dozy, *Supplément aux dictionnaires arabes* (Leiden, E.J. Brill, 1927)

Etienne Drioton, 'Le Théâtre dans l'ancienne Égypte', *Revue de la Société d'Histoire du Théâtre* (1954), 7–45

R. Ettinghausen, 'The Dance with Zoomorphic Masks', in G. Maqdisi (ed.), *Arabic Studies in Honor of Hamilton A.R. Gibb* (Leiden, E.J. Brill, 1965), 211–24

E. Fagnan, *Additions aux dictionnaires arabes* (Alger, Ancienne Maison Bastide-Jourdan, 1923)

Nadia R. Farag, 'Yussef Idris and Modern Egyptian Drama', Ph.D. thesis (Columbia University, New York 1975) and its Arabic version (Cairo, Dār al-Maʿārif, 1976)

Rifʿat al-Faranawānī, 'Lughat al-Jabartī', in Aḥmad ʿIzzat ʿAbd al-Karīm (ed.), *'Abd al-Raḥmān al-Jabartī, Dirāsāt wa-Buḥūth* (Cairo, al-Hay'a al-Miṣriyya al-ʿĀmma li'l-Kitāb, 1976), 255–88

Suraiya Faroqhi, 'Crisis and Change 1590–1699', in Suraiya Faroqhi, Şevket Pamuk, Bruce McGowan and Donald Quataert(eds), *An Economic and Social History of the Ottoman Empire, Volume Two, 1600–1914* (Cambridge, CUP, 1994), 411–622

I.M. Filshtinsky, 'Kairskie vosstania 1798–1800 gg. I opisanie ih v hronke Abd ar-Rahmana al-Jabarti (Cairo Revolts of 1798–1800 and their Description in the Chronicle of ʿAbd al-Raḥmān al-Jabartī)', *Sovetskoe vostokovedenie* (Soviet Oriental Studies), 3 (1958)

—— 'Egipetskiy istorik al-Jabarti I ego hronika (The Egyptian Historian al-Jabartī and his Chronicle)', *Vestnik istorii mirovoy kulturi* (Bulletin of the History of World Culture), 4 (1960)

—— 'Hronika Abd ar-Rahmana al-Jabarti kak istoritcheskiy istotchnik (The Chronicle of ʿAbd al-Raḥmān al-Jabartī as a Historical Source'), *Kratkie soobshenia Instituta narodov Azii* (Brief

Reports of the Institute of the Peoples of Asia, Academy of Sciences, USSR), *no. 47, Arabskie strain* (Arab Countries) (Moscow 1961)

Gustav Leberecht Fluegel, *Die arabischen, persischen und türkischen Handschriften der Kaiserlich-Königlichen Hofbibliothek zu Wien* (Vienna, K.K. Hof- und Staatsdruckerei, 1865–7), 3 vols

J.G. Frazer, *The Golden Bough, A Study in Magic and Religion* (London, Macmillan and Co., 1960)

Rabbi Dr H. Freedman and Maurice Simon, *Midrash Rabbah* (London, Soncino Press, 1960), vol. I

Abdurrahman Gabarti, *Journal d'Abdurrahman Gabarti, pendant l'occupation française en Égypte: suivi d'un précis de la même campagne, par Mou'allem Nicolas el-Turki, traduits de l'arabe par A. Cardin,*T.X. Bianchi (ed.) (Paris, Dondey-Dupré, 1838)

A. Galotta, 'Khayr al-Dīn (Khiḍir) Pasha, Barbarossa', *EI*², IV, 1155–8

H.A.R. Gibb, 'al-ʿAṭṭār, Ḥasan b. Muḥammad', *EI*², I, 755

H.L. Gottschalk, *Catalogue of the Mingana Collection of Manuscripts Now in the Possession of the Trustees of the Woodbrooke Settlement, Selly Oak, Birmingham, and Preserved at the Selly Oak College's Library. vol. 4. Islamic Arabic Manuscripts* (Birmingham, Heffers, 1948)

Peter Gran, *Islamic Roots of Capitalism, Egypt, 1760–1840* (Syracuse, Syracuse University Press, 1998)

Urlich Haarmann, 'Arabic in Speech, Turkish in Lineage', *JSS* 33 (1988), 81–114

—— 'Joseph's Law-the Careers and Activities of Mamluk Descendants before the Ottoman Conquest of Egypt', in T. Philipp and U. Haarmann (eds), *The Mamluks in Egyptian Politics and Society* (Cambridge, CUP, 1998), 55–84

Shaykh Aḥmad b. Muḥammad al-Ḥaḍrāwī al-Makkī al-Hāshimī, *Nuzhat al-Fikar fīmā Maḍā min al-Ḥawādith wa 'l-'Ibar min Awā'il al-Mawjūdāt ilā Ākhir al-Qarn al-Thālith 'Ashar* (Cairo, Dār al-Kutub al-Qawmiyya MS Tārīkh Taymūr 1970/microfilm 29516)

Ibrāhīm Ḥamāda, *Khayāl al-Ẓill: wa-Tamthīliyyāt Ibn Dāniyāl* (Cairo, al-Mu'assasa al-Miṣriyya al-ʿĀmma li'l-Ta'līf wa'l-Tarjama wa'l-Ṭibāʿa wa'l-Nashr, 1963)

Jaakko Hämeen-Antitila, *Maqama, A History of a Genre* (Wiesbaden, Harrassowitz Verlag, 2002)

Nelly Hanna, 'Cultural Life in Mamluk Households (Late Ottoman Period)', in T. Philipp and U. Haarmann (eds), *The Mamluks in Egyptian Politics and Society* (Cambridge, CUP, 1998), 196–204

—— *In Praise of Books: A Cultural History of Cairo's Middle Class, Sixteenth through the Eighteenth Century* (Middle East Studies beyond Dominant Paradigms) (Syracuse, NY, Syracuse University Press, 2003)

Muḥammad ʿAbd al-Ghanī Ḥasan, *Ḥasan al-'Aṭṭār* (Cairo, Dār al-Maʿārif, 1968)

Jane Hathaway, 'Sultans, Pashas, *Taqwīms*, and *Mühimmes:* A Reconsideration of Chronicle Writing in Eighteenth Ottoman Egypt', in Daniel Crecelius (ed.), *Eighteenth Century Egypt: The Arabic Manuscript Sources* (Claremont, CA., 1990), 51–78

—— '"Mamluk Households" and "Mamluk Factions" in Ottoman Egypt: a Reconsideration', in T. Philipp and U. Haarmann (eds), *The Mamluks in Egyptian Politics and Society* (Cambridge, CUP, 1998),107–17

Muḥammad ibn Ḥasan Abu 'l-Muẓaffar al-Ḥātimī, 'al-Risāla al-Ḥātimiyya', Anṭūn Būlād (ed.), *Rāshid Sūriyyā* (Beirut 1868/1285)

W.P. Heinrichs, 'Safī al-Dīn al-Ḥillī', *EI*², VIII, 801–5

Wolfhart Heinrichs, *Arabische Dichtung und griechische Poetik* (Beirut, Franz Steiner, Wiesbaden, i komm, 1969)

J. Heyworth-Dunne, 'Arabic Literature in Egypt in the Eighteenth Century', *BSOAS* 9:3 (1938), 675–89

Ṣafī al-Dīn al-Ḥillī, *Die vulgärarabische Poetik al-Kitāb al-'Āṭil al-Ḥālī wal-muraḫḫaṣ al-Ġālī des Ṣafīyaddīn Ḥillī,* Wilhelm Hoenerbach (ed.) (Veröffentlichungen der Orientalischen Kommission/Akademie der Wissenschaften und der Literatur, Bd. 10) (Wiesbaden, F. Steiner, 1956)

P.M. Holt, 'Al-Jabartī's Introduction to the History of Ottoman Egypt', *BSOAS* 25 (1962), 38–51.

—— 'Literary Offerings: a Genre of Courtly Literature', in T. Philipp and U. Haarmann, *The Mamluks in Egyptian Politics and Society* (Cambridge, CUP, 1998), 3–16.

Clément Huart, *Littérature arabe* (Paris, A. Colin, 1902)

Aḥmad Shalabī Ibn 'Abd al-Ghanī, *Awḍaḥ al-Ishārāt fī-Man Tawallā Miṣr al-Qāhira min al-Wuzarā' wa'l-Bāshāt,* 'Abd al-Raḥīm 'Abd al-Raḥmān 'Abd al-Raḥīm (ed.) (Cairo, Tawzī' Maktabat al-Khānjī, 1978); 2nd edn., 1994; Fu'ād Muḥammad al-Māwī (ed.) (Cairo, Tawzī' Dār al-Anṣār, 1977)

Aḥmad b. Yūsuf Ibn al-Dāya, *Kitāb al-Mukāfa'a wa-Ḥusn al-'Uqbā,* Maḥmūd Muḥammad Shākir (ed.) (Cairo, Maṭba'at al-Istiqāma, 1940)

Ibn al-Ḥājj al-Fāsī al-Mālikī al-'Abdarī, Abū 'Abd Allāh Muḥammad Ibn Muḥammad, *al-Madkhal aw Madkhal al-Shar' al-Sharīf* (Cairo, al-Maṭba'a al-Miṣriyya bi'l-Azhar, 1929)

Ibn Iyās, *Badā'i' al-Zuhūr fi Waqā'i' al-Duhūr,* Muḥammad Muṣṭafā (ed.) (Wiesbaden, Franz Steiner and Cairo, Dār Iḥyā' al-Kutub al-'Arabīya, 1960)

Yūsuf Idrīs, 'Naḥwa Masraḥ Miṣrī', *al-Kātib* (Cairo, January–February and March, 1964)

Muḥammad 'Abd Allāh 'Inān, *Mu'arrikhū Miṣr al-Islāmiyya wa-Maṣādir al-Tārīkh al-Miṣrī* (Cairo, Mu'assasat Mukhtār, 1991)

Abu'l-Faraj al-Iṣfahānī, 'Alī b. Ḥusayn, *The Book of Strangers: Mediaeval Arabic Graffiti on the Theme of Nostalgia, Attributed to Abu 'l-Faraj al- Iṣfahānī, trans. Patricia Crone and Shmuel Moreh* (Princeton, NJ., Markus Wiener, 2000)

al-Isḥāqī al-Manūfī, Muḥammad 'Abd al-Mu'ṭī b. Abi 'l-Fatḥ b. Aḥmad b. 'Abd al-Mughnī b. 'Alī, *Laṭā'if Akhbār al-Uwal fī-Man Taṣarraf fī Miṣr min Arbāb al-Duwal* (Cairo, al-Maṭba'a al-Azhariyya, 1311/1893–4)

'Abd al-Raḥmān al-Jabartī, *Yawmiyyāt al-Jabartī: Maẓhar al-Taqdīs bi-Zawāl Dawlat al-Faransīs,* Ikhtarnā Laka nos. 59–60, Muḥammad 'Aṭā (ed.)) ((Cairo, Dār al-Ma'ārif, 1958), 2 vols

—— *Maẓhar al-Taqdīs bi-Zawāl Dawlat al-Faransīs,* M.F. 'Abd al-Laṭīf, 'A.M. 'Āmir and A.Z. 'Aṭiyya (eds) (Cairo, al-Hay'a al-'Āmma li-Shu'ūn al-Maṭābi' al-Amīriyya, 1961), 2 vols

—— *Maẓhar al-Taqdīs bi-Dhahāb Dawlat al-Faransīs,* Ḥasan Muḥammad Jawhar and 'Umar al-Dasūqī (eds) (Cairo, Lajnat al-Bayān al-'Arabī, 1969)

—— *Maẓhar al-Taqdīs bi-Dhahāb Dawlat al-Faransīs bi'l-Ishtirāk ma'a Ṣadīqih Ḥasan al-'Aṭṭār,* Aḥmad 'Abduh 'Alī (ed.)(Cairo, Maktabat al-Ādāb, 1419/1998)

'Abd al-Raḥmān ibn Ḥasan al-Jabartī, *Maẓhar al-Taqdīs bi-Dhahāb Dawlat al-Faransīs,* 'Abd al-Rāziq 'Īsā and 'Imād Aḥmad Hilāl (eds) (Cairo, al-'Arabī li'l-Nashr wa'l-Tawzī', 1998), 2 vols

—— *Maẓhar al-Taqdīs bi-Zawāl Dawlat al-Faransīs,* 'Abd al-Raḥīm 'Abd al-Raḥmān 'Abd al-Raḥīm (ed.) (Cairo, Maṭba'at Dār al-Kutub al-Miṣriyya, 1998)

—— *Maẓhar al-Taqdīs bi-Zawāl Dawlat al-Faransīs,* Muḥammad Ibn Ḥasan Ibn 'Aqīl Mūsā al-Sharīf (ed.) (Jeddah, Dār al-Andalus al-Khaḍrā', 1999)

'Abd al-Raḥmān al-Jabartī al-Ḥanafī, *al-Tārīkh al-Musammā 'Ajā'ib al-Āthār fi'l-Tarājim wa'l-Akhbār* (Būlāq, 1297/1879–80), 4 vols in 2

—— *al-Tārīkh al-Musammā 'Ajā'ib al-Āthār* in the margin of the tenth part of *Tārīkh al-Kāmil* of 'Izz al-Dīn Ibn al-Athīr al-Jazarī (Cairo, al-Maṭba'a al-Azhariyya al-Miṣriyya, 1301/1883–4)

Abd el-Rahman el-Djabarti, *Merveilles biographiques et historiques, ou chroniques du Cheikh Abd-el-Rahman el-Djabarti*, Chefik Mansour Bey, Abdulaziz Kahil Bey, Gebriel Nicolas Kahil Bey and Iskender Ammoun Effendi (trans.) (Cairo, Imprimerie Nationale, 1888–96), 9 vols

ʿAbd al-Raḥmān al-Jabartī, *al-Tārīkh al-Musammā 'Ajā'ib al-Āthār fi'l-Tarājim wa'l-Akhbār* (Cairo, al-Maṭbaʿa al-ʿĀmira al-Sharafiyya 1322/1904–5), 4 vols

—— *'Ajā'ib al-Āthār fi'l-Tarājim wa'l-Akhbār*, Ḥasan Muḥammad Jawhar, ʿAbd al-Fattāḥ al-Siranjāwī, and al-Sayyid Ibrāhīm Sālim (eds) (Cairo, Lajnat al-Bayān al-ʿArabī, 1958–67), 7 vols; vols 3–7 Ḥasan Muḥammad Jawhar, ʿUmar al-Dasūqī, and al-Sayyid Ibrāhīm Sālim (eds)

—— *Egipet v period ekspeditsii Bonaparta (1776–1798)*, (Egypt during the Expedition of Bonaparte), I.M. Filshtinskiy (trans.) (Moscow, Izdatelstvo vostotchnoy literaturi [Oriental Literature], 1962) (translation of volume III, Part I, *'Ajā'ib al-Āthār fi'l-Tarājim wa'l-Akhbār*, Būlāq, 1297/1879–80)

—— *Egipet pod vlastiy Muhammada Ali (1806–1821)* (Egypt during the Reign of Muḥammad ʿAlī), H.I. Kilberg (trans.) (Moscow, Izdatelstvo vostotchnoy literaturi [Oriental Literature], 1963) (translation of volume IV, *'Ajā'ib al-Āthār fi'l-Tarājim wa'l-Akhbār*, Būlāq, 1297/1879–80)

—— *Tārīkh 'Ajā'ib al-Āthār fi'l-Tarājim wa'l-Akhbār* (Beirut, Dār al-Fāris, 1970), 3 vols

—— *Egipet v kanun ekspeditsii Bonapart (1776–1798)*, (Egypt on the Eve of Bonaparte's Expedition). H.I. Kilberg (trans.)(Moscow, Nauka, 1978) (translation of volume II, *'Ajā'ib al-Āthār fi'l-Tarājim wa'l-Akhbār*, Būlāq, 1297/1879–80)

—— *Tārīkh 'Ajā'ib al-Āthār fi'l-Tarājim wa'l-Akhbār* (Beirut, Dār al-Jīl, 1978), 3 vols

—— *Kitāb Tārīkh al-Faransawiyyīn fī Miṣr: wa-Huwa al-Juz' al-Thālith min Kitāb 'Ājā'ib al-Āthār fī 'l-Tarājim wa'l-Akhbār* (Alexandria, Maṭbaʿat Jarīdat Miṣr, 1978)

—— *Journal d'un notable du Caire; durant l'expédition française, 1798–1801, traduit et annoté par Joseph Cuoq, préface de Jean Tulard* (Paris, Albin Michael, 1979)

—— *'Ajā'ib al-Āthār fi'l-Tarājim wa'l-Akhbār* (Beirut, Dār al-Jīl, 1422/1992)

—— *'Abd al-Raḥmān al-Jabartī's History of Egypt, 'Ajā'ib al-Āthār fī'l-Tarājim wa'l-Akhbār*, Thomas Philipp, Guido Schwald and Moshe Perlmann (eds), translated by D. Crecelius…[et al.](Stuttgart, F. Steiner Verlag, 1994), 5 vols in 3

—— *'Ajā'ib al-Āthār fī'l-Tarājim wa'l-Akhbār, Ṣafaḥāt min Tārīkh Miṣr*, 5/37, ʿAbd al-ʿAzīz Jamāl al-Dīn (ed.) (Cairo, Maktabat Madbūlī, 1997)

—— *'Ajā'ib al-Āthār fi'l-Tarājim wa'l-Akhbār*, Ibrāhīm Shams al-Dīn (ed.) (Beirut, Dār al-Kutub al-ʿIlmiyya, 1997)

—— *'Ajā'ib al-Āthār fi'l-Tarājim wa'l-Akhbār*, ʿAbd al-Raḥīm ʿAbd al-Raḥmān ʿAbd al-Raḥīm (ed.) (Cairo, Maṭbaʿat Dār al-Kutub al-Miṣriyya, 1997–8), 4 vols

ʿAbd al-Raḥmān al-Jabartī, *al-Jabartī's History of Egypt*, Jane Hathaway (ed.) (Princeton Series on the Middle East,Princeton, NJ., Markus Wiener Publishers, 2009)

—— *'Ajā'ib al-Āthār fi'l-Tarājim wa'l-Akhbār*, Shmuel Moreh (ed.) (The Institute of Asian and African Studies, The Max Schloessinger Memorial Foundation, The Hebrew University of Jerusalem, The Faculty of Humanities, Jerusalem)

—— *al-Jabartī's Chronicle of the First Seven Months of the French Occupation of Egypt, Muḥarram-Rajab 1213/15 June-December, 1798, Tārīkh Muddat al-Faransīs bi-Miṣr*, S. Moreh (ed. and trans.) (Leiden, E.J. Brill, 1975)

ʿAbd al-Raḥmān ibn Ḥasan al-Jabartī, *Napoleon in Egypt: al-Jabartī's Chronicle of the French Occupation, 1798*, Shmuel Moreh (trans.) (Princeton, Markus Wiener Publishers, 1993; Princeton, Markus Winner Publishing, Inc., 2004)

Ḥasan al-Jabartī, *Majmū'a Mushtamila 'alā Thalāth Rasā'il* (Cairo, Sharikat al-Maṭbūʿāt al-ʿIlmiyya, 1327/1909)

ʿAmr b. Baḥr al-Jāḥiẓ, *Kitāb al-Ḥayawān* (Cairo, Maṭbaʿat Muṣṭafā al-Bābī, 1965)

Salma Khadra Jayyusi, *Trends and Movements in Modern Arabic Poetry* (Leiden, Brill, 1977)

Marsden Jones, 'The First French Proclamation and al-Jabartī', in Aḥmad ʿIzzat ʿAbd al-Karīm (ed.), *ʿAbd al-Raḥmān al-Jabartī, Dirāsāt wa-Buḥūth* (Cairo, al-Hay'a al-Miṣriyya al-ʿĀmma li'l-Kitāb, 1976), 31–42

J. Kabrda, *Quelques firmans, concernant les relations franco-turques lors de l'expedition de Bonaparte en Égypte (1798–1799)* (Paris, Imprimerie nationale, 1947)

Fu'ād Kanʿānī, 'al-Ḥayāt al-Adabiyya fī Miṣr' (*Literary and Cultural Life during 1688–1821 in Egypt According to 'Ajā'ib al-Āthār ...*), unpublished Ph.D. Thesis (The Hebrew University, Jerusalem 2007)

ʿAbd al-Ḥayy b. ʿAbd al-Kabīr al-Kattānī, *Fihris al-Fahāris wa'l-Ithbāt wa-Mu'jam al-Ma'ājim wa'l-Mashaykhāt wa'l-Musalsalāt*[2], Iḥsān ʿAbbās (ed.) (Beirut, Dār al-Gharb al-Islāmī, 1402/1982)

Nikki R. Keddie (ed.), *Scholars, Saints and Sufis* (Berkeley, University of California Press, 1972)

David A. King, *A Survey of the Scientific Manuscripts in the Egyptian National Library* (Cairo, General Egyptian Book Organization, 1981–4)

—— *Islamic Mathematical Astronomy* (London, Variorum Reprints, 1986; London, Variorum Reprints, 2nd edn. 1993)

—— 'Mamluk Astronomy and the Institution of the *Muwaqqit*', in T. Philipp and U. Haarmann (eds), *The Mamluks in Egyptian Politics and Society* (Cambridge, CUP, 1998),153–62

Willibald Kirfel, *Die Kosmographie der Inder* (Hildesheim, Gg. Olms, 1967)

E. Kohlberg, 'Mūsā al-Kāẓim', *EI*[2], I, 272–7

J.H. Kramer, 'al-Nīl', *EI*[2], VIII, 37–43

Kutubkhāne-i Weli el-Dīn, *Defter-i Kutubkhāne-i Weli el-Dīn* (Istanbul, 1304/1886–7)

Jacob M. Landau, 'The Decline of the Jewish Community in Eighteenth-Century Cairo: A New Interpretation in the Light of Two Iberian Chronicles', in Shimon Shamir (ed.), *The Jews of Egypt, A Mediterranean Society in Modern Times* (Boulder and London, Westview Press, 1987), 15–29

—— *Toldot Yehudei Mitsrayim be-Tkufa ha-Ottomanit (1517–1914)* (in Hebrew) (Jerusalem, Misgav Yerushalayim, 1988)

Jacob M. Landau and Manfred Woidisch (trans. and eds), *Arabisches Volkstheater in Kairo, im Jahre 1909, Ahmad il-Far und seine Schwanke* (Beirut, In Kommission bei Franz Steiner Verlag, 1993)

E.W. Lane, *An Arabic-English Lexicon* (London, Williams and Norgate, 1863–93)

—— *The Manners and Customs of the Modern Egyptians* (Everyman's Library, no. 315, Travel and Topography, London, J.M. Dent and Sons Ltd, 1963)

Edward William Lane and Stanley Lane-Poole, *The Thousand and One Nights: Commonly Called in England, The Arabian Nights Entertainments; a New Tr. from the Arabic with Copious Notes* (London, Chatto and Windus, 1883)

M. Larkin, 'Popular Poetry in the Post-Classical Period, 1150–1850', in R.M.A. Allen and D.S. Richards, *Arabic Literature in the Post-classical Period* (Cambridge, CUP, 2006), 191–242

I. Lassy, *The Muharram Mysteries among the Azarbeijan Turks of Caucasia* (Helsingfors: printed by Lilius and Hertsberg, 1916)

B. Lewis, *What Went Wrong? Western Impact and Middle Eastern Response* (London, Phoenix, 2003)

Huda Lutfi, 'Coptic Festivals of the Nile: Aberrations of the Past', in T. Philipp and U. Haarmann (eds), *The Mamluks in Egyptian Politics and Society* (Cambridge, CUP, 1998), 258–9

D.B. Macdonald, 'al-Djabartī', *EI*[1], II, 986.

John Macdonald, *Catalogue of Oriental Manuscripts* (Leeds, University of Leeds, 1958)

R.J.A. McGregor, *Sanctity and Mysticism in Medieval Egypt, The Wafa' Sufi Order and the Legacy of Ibn 'Arabi* (New York, SUNY, 2004)

D.J. McKitterick, *Cambridge University Library, a History* (Cambridge, CUP,1986)

ʿAbd Allah al-Madanī al-Balawī, *Sīrat Aḥmad b. Ṭūlūn* (Damascus, 1358/1939)

G. Makdisi (ed.), *Arabic and Islamic Studies in Honor of Hamilton A.R. Gibb* (Leiden, E.J. Brill, 1965)

al-Maktaba al-Azhariyya, *Fihris al-Kutub al-Mawjūda bi'l-Maktaba al-Azhariyya. Al-Juz' al-Khāmis, wa-Yashtamil 'ala'l-Funūn al-Ātiya: al-Adab - al-Tārīkh - Taqwīm al-Buldān - al-Jughrāfiyya* (Cairo, Maṭbaʿat al-Azhar, 1949)

Adel Manna, 'Cultural Relations between Egyptian and Jerusalem ʿUlamā' in the Early Nineteenth Century', *Asian and African Studies*, Journal of the Israel Oriental Society 17: 1–3 (November 1983), 139–52

Muḥammad b. ʿAbd al-Hādī al-Manūfī; al-Khizāna al-Ḥasaniyya (al-Ribāṭ), *Fahāris Makhṭūṭāt al-Khizāna al-Ḥasaniyya Ḥasab Arqāmihā 'alā'l-Rufūf* (Rabat, al-Maṭbaʿa al-Malakiyya, 1403–/1983–)

Aḥmad b. ʿAlī al-Maqrīzī, *al-Mawā'iẓ wa'l-I'tibār bi-Dhikr al-Khiṭaṭ wa'l-Āthār* (Būlāq, Dār al-Ṭibāʿa al-Miṣriyya, 1270/1853–4)

—— *al-Mawā'iẓ wa'l-I'tibār bi-Dhikr al-Khiṭaṭ wa'l-Āthār*, Gaston Wiet (ed.) (Cairo, Imprimerie de l'Institut Français, 1911–27)

Afaf Lutfi al-Sayyid Marsot, *Egypt in the Reign of Muhammad 'Ali* (Cambridge, CUP, 1984)

—— 'A Comparative Study of Abd al-Rahman al-Jabarti and Niqula Turk', Crecelius, *Eighteenth Century Egypt* (1990), 115–26

P.D. Martin, *Histoire de l'expédition française en Egypte pendant les années 1798–1801* (Paris, J.-M. Eberhart, 1815)

Aḥmad b. Muḥammad al-Marzūqī, *Sharḥ Dīwān al-Ḥamāsa*, Aḥmad Amīn and ʿAbd al-Salīm Hārūn (eds) (Cairo, Lajnat al-Ta'līf, 1951), 4 vols

Stanley Mayes, *The Great Belzoni, The Circus Strongman Who Discovered Egypt's Treasures* (New York, Tauris Parke, 1959; Tauris Parke, 2003)

Beatrice Meyer and Chahine Nemr, *'Shaykh Ibrahim' – Johann Ludwig Burckhardt (1784–1817), An Exhibition by Pro Helvetia*, Arts Council of Switzerland in Kairo, with Arabic Translation and Layout (Zürich, Pro Helvetia, 1990)

A. Mingana, *Catalogue of the Arabic Manuscripts in the John Rylands Library Manchester* (Manchester, The Manchester University Press, 1934)

James Monroe, *The Art of Badīʿ al-Zamān al-Hamadhānī as Picaresque Narrative* (Beirut, American University of Beirut, 1983)

Shmuel Moreh, 'The Arabic Theatre in Egypt in the Eighteenth and Nineteenth Centuries', *Etudes Arabes et Islamiques, II – langue et literature, vol. 3, Actes du XXIXe Congres international des Orientalistes, Section organisée, par Charles Pellat* (Paris, L'Asiatique, 1975), 109–13

—— *Modern Arabic Poetry, 1800–1970* (Leiden, Brill, 1976)

—— 'The Neoclassical *Qaṣīda*, Modern Poets and Critics', in S. Moreh, *Studies in Modern Arabic Prose and Poetry* (Leiden, E.J. Brill, 1988), 33–56

—— 'The Meaning of the Term *Kharja* in the Arabic-Andalusian *Muwashshah*', in Isaac Benabu (ed.), *Circa 1492, Proceedings of the Jerusalem Colloquium: Litterae Judaeorum in Terra Hispanica* (Jerusalem, The Hebrew University of Jerusalem, 1992), 134–44

—— *Live Theatre and Dramatic Literature in the Medieval Arab World* (Edinburgh, Edinburgh University Press, 1992)

Shmuel Moreh, review article, 'Muhammad Ibn Daniyal: *Three Shadow Plays*, Paul Kahle ed., with a critical apparatus by Derek Hopwood, prepared for publication by Derek Hopwood and Mustafa Badawi, Cambridge, The Trustees of the "E.J.W. Gibb Memorial"', *Die Welt des Islams* 34 (1994), 126–9

Shmuel Moreh, review article, ''Abd ar-Raḥmān al-Gabartī: *'Abd al-Raḥmān al-Jabartī's History of Egypt, 'Ajā'ib al-Āthār fi 'l-Tarājim wa 'l-Akhbār.* Stuttgart: Steiner, 1994. Edited by Thomas Philipp and Moshe Perlmann, vols I...IV, with *A Guide to 'Abd al-Raḥmān al-Jabartī's History of Egypt: 'Ajā'ib al-Āthār fi 'l-Tarājim wa 'l-Akhbār,* by Thomas Philipp and Guido Schwald....', *Die Welt des Islams* 37:2 (1997), 235–42

—— 'Arabic Poetics from the Eighteenth to the Twentieth Centuries', in Binyamin Abrahamov (ed.), *Studies in Arabic and Islamic Culture* (Ramat Gan, Bar-Ilan University, 2000), vii–lxvii

—— 'al-Jabartī's Method of Composing his Chronicle', *Jerusalem Studies in Arabic and Islam*, 25 (2001), 346–73

—— 'The Egyptian Scholar Hasan al-'Attar (d. 1834) and his Journey from Cairo to Izmir', in Z.I. Siaflekis and Rania Polycandrioti (eds), *Expressions et représentations littéraires de la Méditerranée: Iles et ports, XVIe–XXe siècles*, Actes du Colloque, Centre Culturel Européen de Delphes, 5–6 novembre 1999 (Athens, Ekdoseis Patakē, 2002), 19–32

—— 'Napoleon and the French Impact on Egyptian Society in the Eyes of al-Jabartī', in Irene A. Bierman (ed.), *Napoleon in Egypt* (Los Angeles, E. von Grunebaum Center for Near Eastern Studies, 2003), reprinted in 'Abd al-Raḥmān ibn Ḥasan al-Jabartī, *Napoleon in Egypt, al-Jabartī's Chronicle of the French Occupation, 1798*, trans. S. Moreh (Princeton, Markus Wiener Publishers, 2004), 183–204

—— 'Al-Jabarti's Attitude towards the 'Ulama' of His Time', in Meir Hatina (ed.), *Guardians of Faith in Modern Times: 'Ulama' in the Middle East* (Leiden, E.J. Brill, 2009), 47–64

Shmuel Moreh and P.C. Sadgrove, *Jewish Contributions to Nineteenth-Century Arabic Theatre* (Oxford, OUP, 1996)

'Alī Mubārak, *al-Khiṭaṭ al-Tawfīqiyya al-Jadīda li-Miṣr al-Qāhira wa-Mudunihā wa-Bilādihā al-Qadīma wa'l-Shahīra* (Būlāq, 1888–9), 20 vols in 4.

—— *'Alam al-Dīn* (Alexandria, Maṭba'at Jarīdat al-Maḥrūsa, 1882)

Muḥammad b. 'Ubayd Allāh al-Musabbiḥī, *Akhbār Miṣr*, Ayman Fu'ād Sayyid and Thierry Bianquis (eds) (Cairo, Institut Français d'Archéologie Orientale, 1978)

Mawlavi Muinuddin Nadwi, J.A. Chapman, Khuda Bakhsh Oriental Public Library (Patna, Inde), *Catalogue of the Arabic and Persian Manuscripts in the Oriental Public Library at Bankipore, Vol. XV, Arabic Mss., History* (Calcutta, The Baptist Mission Press; Patna, Superintendent of Bihar and Orissa, 1929)

T. Naff and R. Owen (eds), *Studies in Eighteenth Century Islamic History* (Carbondale and Edwardsville, IL, Southern Illinois University Press, 1977), 205–16

Ḥusayn Fawzī al-Najjār, *Rifā'a al-Ṭahṭāwī, Rā'id Fikr wa-Imām Nahḍa* (Cairo, al-Dār al-Miṣriyya li'l-Ta'līf wa'l-Tarjama, n.d.)

Muḥammad Yūsuf Najm, *al-Masraḥ al-'Arabī, Dirāsāt wa-Nuṣūṣ, 3, Ya'qūb Ṣannū' (Abū Naḍḍāra) (*Beirut, Dār al-Thaqāfa, 1963)

Wilyam Naẓīr, *al-'Ādāt al-Miṣriyya bayn al-Ams wa'l-Yawm* (Cairo, Dār al-Kitāb al-'Arabī li'l-Ṭibā'a wa'l-Nashr, 1967)

J. Patel, 'The Navroz, its History and its Significance', *Journal of the K.R. Cama Institute* (Bombay), XXXI (1937), 1–51

Charles Pellat, 'Madjnūn Laylā', *EI*², V, 1102–3.

—— 'al-Marzūḳī, Abū'Alī Aḥmad b. Muḥammad b. al-Ḥasan', *EI*², IV, 635–6

Charles Pellat and Carl Brockelmann 'Maḳāma', *EI*², VI, 107–15

Thomas Philipp, 'The French and the French Revolution in the Works of al-Jabartī', in D. Crecelius (ed.), *Eighteenth Century Egypt: The Arabic Manuscript Sources* (Claremont, CA., Regina Books,1990), 127–40

Thomas Philipp and Ulrich Haarmann, *The Mamluks in Egyptian Politics and Society* (Cambridge, CUP, 1998)

Thomas Philipp and Guido Schwald, *A Guide to 'Abd al-Rahmān al-Jabartī's History of Egypt: 'Ajā'ib al-Āthār fī'l-Tarājim wa'l-Akhbār* (Stuttgart, Franz Steiner Verlag, 1994)

T. Preston, Cambridge University Library, *Catalogus Bibliothecae Burckhardtianae cum appendice Librorum aliorum orientalium in Bibliotheca Academiae Cantabrigiensis asservatorum* (Cambridge 1853)

C. Prüfer, 'Drama (Arabic)', *Encyclopaedia of Religion and Ethics*, James Hastings (ed.) (New York, T. & T. Clark, 1914), IV: 872–8

Ḥāzim b. Muḥammad al-Qarṭājannī, *Minhāj al-Bulaghā' wa-Sirāj al-Udabā', aw al-Manāhij al-Adabiyya* (Tunis, Dār al-Kutub al-Sharqīya, 1966)

Bernd Radtke, 'Sufism in the 18th Century: An Attempt at a Provisional Appraisal', *Die Welt des Islams* 36:3 (November 1996), 326–64

Rāmpūr Raẓā Lāibreri, *Fihrist-i kutub-i 'Arabī mawjūda-i kutubkhāna-i riyāsat-i Rampūr* (Rampūr 1928), 2 vols

André Raymond, 'A propos de deux portraits dans la *Description de l'Egypte*, "l'astronome" et "le poète"', *Annales islamologiques* 35 (Cairo, Institut français d'archéologie orientale, 2001), 385–92

—— *Le Caire des Janissaires: l'apogée de la ville ottomane sous 'Abd al-Rahmân Katkhudâ* (Paris, CNRS éditions, 1995)

—— *Egyptiens et Français au Caire, 1798–1801* (Cairo, Institut français d'archéologie orientale, 1998)

Stefan Reichmuth, 'Murtaḍā az-Zabīdī (d. 1791) in Biographical and Autobiographical Accounts. Glimpses of Islamic Scholarship in the 18th Century', *Die Welt des Islams* 39:1 (1999), 64–102

—— 'Notes on Murtaḍā al-Zabīdī's *Mu'jam* as a Source for al-Jabartī's History', *Jerusalem Studies in Arabic and Islam* 25 (2001), 374–83

—— *The World of Murtada al-Zabidi (1732–91). Life, Networks and Writing* (Exeter, Gibb Memorial Trust, 2009)

—— 'Preliminary List of Scholars, Students, Visitors and Acquaintances Mentioned in Murtaḍā az-Zabīdī's *Mu'jam*', unpublished article

Charles Rieu, *Supplement to the Catalogue of the Arabic Manuscripts in the British Museum* (London, Longmans & Co., 1894)

E. Rossi, 'Malta', *EI*², VI, 295f.

Ḥusayn Afandī al-Ruznāmjī, 'Tartīb al-Diyār al-Miṣriyya fī'l-ʿAṣr al-'Uthmānī', Muḥammad Shafīq Ghurbāl (ed.), *Majallat Kulliyyat al-Ādāb* IV: 1 (Cairo, Jāmiʿat Fu'ād, May 1936)

P.C. Sadgrove, *The Egyptian Theatre in the Nineteenth Century, 1799–1882* (Reading, Ithaca, 1996)

Rushdī Ṣāliḥ, *al-Masraḥ al-Miṣrī* (Cairo, Maṭābiʿ al-Hay'a al-Miṣrīya al-ʿĀmma li'l-Kitāb, 1972)

Muḥammad b. ʿAlī al-Sanūsī, *al-Salsabīl al-Ma'ān fī'l-Ṭuruq al-Arba'īn*, Muḥammad Ibn Ghalbūn (ed.) (Manchester 1990)

Samīr Sarḥān (ed.), *Yūsuf Idrīs, (1927–1991)* (Cairo, al-Hay'a al-Miṣriyya al-ʿĀmma li'l-Kitāb, 1991)

Yūsuf Ilyān Sarkīs, *Mu'jam al-Maṭbū'āt al-'Arabiyya wa'l-Mu'arraba* (Cairo, Maṭbaʿat Sarkīs, 1928)

Yvette Sauvan and Georges Vajda, *Catalogue des manuscrits arabes, deuxième partie, Bibliothèque Nationale, Département des manuscrits* (Paris, Bibliothèque nationale, 1978)

Aḥmad Ḥusayn al-Ṣāwī, *Fajr al-Ṣiḥāfa fī Miṣr: Dirāsa fī I'lām al-Ḥamla al-Faransiyya* (Cairo, al-Hay'a al-Miṣriyya al-'Āmma li'l-Kitāb, 1975)

Fu'ād Sayyid et al, *Fihris al-Makhṭūṭāt al-Muṣawwara* (Cairo, Institut des Manuscrits Arabes, Ligue des États Arabes, 1959)

G. Schoeler, 'Muwashshaḥ', *EI*[2], VII, 809–12

'Abd al-Wahhāb al-Sha'rānī, *Laṭā'if al-Minan* (Cairo, al-Maṭba'a al-Maymaniyya, 1321/1903)

'Abd Allāh b. Ḥijāzī al-Sharqāwī, *Tuḥfat al-Nāẓirīn fī-man Waliya Miṣr min al-Wulāt wa'l-Salāṭīn*, in the margin of Muḥammad b. 'Umar al-Wāqidī, *Kitāb Futūḥ al-Shām* (Cairo, 'Abd al-Ḥamīd Aḥmad Ḥanafī, 1368 /1948–9)

—— *Tuḥfat al-Nāẓirīn fī-man Waliya Miṣr min al-Wulāt wa'l-Salāṭīn*, Riḥāb 'Abd al-Ḥamīd al-Qārī (ed.) (Cairo, Maktabat Madbūlī, 1416/1996)

Maḥmūd al-Sharqāwī, *Dirāsāt fī Tārīkh al-Jabartī: Miṣr fī'l-Qarn al-Thāmin 'Ashara* (Cairo, Maktabat al-Anjlū al-Miṣrīya, 1957)

Stanford J. Shaw, *Between Old and New, The Ottoman Empire under Sultan Selim III, 1789–1807* (Harvard Middle Eastern Studies 15, Cambridge, MA, Harvard University Press, 1971)

Muḥammad b. 'Alīal-Shawkānī, *al-Badr al-Ṭāli' bi-Maḥāsin mā ba'd al-Qarn al-Sābi'* (Cairo, 1332/1914)

Khalīl Shaybūb, *'Abd al-Raḥmān al-Jabartī*, Iqra', no. 70 (Cairo, Dār al-Ma'ārif, 1948)

Jamāl al-Dīn al-Shayyāl, *al-Tārīkh wa'l-Mu'arrikhūn fī Miṣr fī'l-Qarn al-Tāsi''Ashar* (Cairo, Maktabat al-Thaqāfa al-Dīniyya, 2000)

Mu'min b. Ḥasan Mu'min al-Shiblanjī, *Nūr al-Abṣār fī Manāqib Āl Bayt al-Nabī al-Mukhtār* (Cairo, Bābī al-Ḥalabī, 1367/1948)

Ḥaydar Aḥmad al-Shihābī, *Tārīkh Aḥmad Bāshā al-Jazzār* (Beirut, Maktabat Anṭūn, 1955)

B. Shoshan, *Popular Culture in Medieval Cairo* (Cambridge, CUP, 1993)

'Abd Allah b. Muḥammad b. 'Āmir al-Shubrāwī al-Shāfi'ī, *Kitāb al-Itḥāf bi-Ḥubb al-Ashrāf* (Cairo, Bābī al-Ḥalabī, 1318/1900–1)

Samuel Miklos Stern, *Hispano-Arabic Strophic Poetry*, L.P. Harvey (ed.) (Oxford, The Clarendon Press, 1974)

Aḥmad al-Sa'īd Sulaymān, *Ta'ṣīl Mā-Warad fī Tārīkh al-Jabartī min al-Dakhīl* (Cairo, Dār al-Ma'ārif, 1979)

Robert L. Tignor's introduction to Moreh's English translation of al-Jabartī's *Tārīkh Muddat al-Faransīs*, entitled *Napoleon in Egypt* (Princeton, Markus Wiener, 1993); 3rd expanded edition in honour of al-Jabartī's 250th birthday in Princeton, M. Wiener Publishers, 2004

Richard Trench, *Arabian Travellers* (London, Macmillan, 1986)

Nakoula el-Turk, *Histoire de l'expédition des français en Egypte*, trad. M. Desgranges (Paris, 1839)

Yūsuf 'Ādil al-'Ulaymī, *al-Drāma al-Sha'biyya al-Miṣriyya* (Cairo, al-Hay'a al-Miṣrīya al-'Āmma li'l-Kitāb, 1992)

Alfred von Kremer, *Aegypten, Forschungen über Land und Volk während eines zehn Jährigen Aufenthalts* (Leipzig, Brockhaus, 1863), 2 v in 1

Carlo von Landberg, *Catalogue de manuscrits arabes provenant d'une bibliothèque privée à El-Medîna, et appartenant à la maison E.J. Brill* (Leiden, E.J. Brill, 1883)

Ottokar Maria von Schlechta-Wssehrd, *Denkschriften der Kaiserlichen Akademie der Wissenschaften, Philosophisch-historische Klasse* (Wien 1857, Kaiserl.-Königl. Hof- und Staatsdruckerei, VIII)

Petrus Voorhoeve (ed.), *Handlist of Arabic Manuscripts in the Library of the University of Leiden and the Collections in the Netherlands* (Leiden, Leiden University Press, 1980)

C.D. Warner, *My Winter on the Nile* (Hartford, American Publ. Comp., 1904)

Otfried Weintritt, 'Concepts of History as Reflected in Arabic Historiographical Writing in Ottoman Syria and Egypt (1517–1700)', in T. Philipp and U. Haarmann, *The Mamluks in Egyptian Politics and Society* (Cambridge, CUP, 1998), 188–95

Arent Jan Wensinck, *Concordance et indices de la tradition musulmane/al-Mu'jam al-Mufahras li-Alfāẓ al-Ḥadīth al-Nabawī* (Leiden, E.J. Brill, 1936–43), 4 vols

Gaston Wiet, *Index de Djabarti, Merveilles biographiques et historiques/Fihrist 'Ajā'ib al-Āthār fī al-Tarājim wa-al-Akhbār: 'an al-Nuskha al-Maṭbū'a fī 4 Ajzā' fī Maṭba'at Būlāq Sanat 1297 H. 'Abd al-Raḥmān al-Jabartī* (Cairo, Dār al-Maʿārif, 1954)

S. Wild, 'Between Ernest Renan and Ernst Bloch: Averroes Remembered, Discovered, and Invented. The European Reception since the Nineteenth Century', in Mourad Wahba and Mona Abousenna (eds), *Averroes and the Enlightenment* (New York, Prometheus Books, 1996), 155–70

—— 'To Our Reader', *Die Welt des Islams* 36:3 (1996), 271–5

—— 'Islamic Enlightenment, and the Paradox of Averroes', *Die Welt des Islams* 36:3 (1996), 379–90

M. Winter, *Society and Religion in Early Ottoman Egypt* (New Brunswick, Transaction Books, 1982)

—— 'The Ashraf and Niqabat al-Ashraf in Egypt in Ottoman and Modern Times', *Journal of the Israel Oriental Society* 19: 1 (1985), 17–41

—— *Egyptian Society under Ottoman Rule 1517–1798* (London, Routledge, 1992)

—— 'The Re-emergence of the Mamlūks Following the Ottoman Conquest', in T. Philipp and U. Haarmann (eds), *The Mamluks in Egyptian Politics and Society* (Cambridge, CUP, 1998), 87–106

W. Wright, *A Grammar of the Arabic Language* (Cambridge, CUP, 1955)

Yāqūt ibn ʿAbd Allāh, al-Ḥamawī, *Jacut's Geographisches Wörterbuch: aus den Handschriften zu Berlin, St. Petersburg, Paris, London und Oxford auf kosten der deutschen morgenländischen Gesellschaft*, Ferdinand Wüstenfeld (ed.) (Leipzig, F.A. Brockhaus, 1868–70)

Ehsan Yarshater, 'Ta'ziyeh and Pre-Islamic Mourning Rites in Iran', in Peter J. Chelkowski (ed.), *Ta'ziyeh Ritual and Drama in Iran* (New York, NYU Press, 1979), 88–94

Murtaḍā al-Zabīdī, *al-Murabbā al-Kābulī fī-man Rawā'an al-Shams al-Bābilī*, Leiden Library, MS no. OR 244

Murtaḍa al-Zabīdī, *Mu'jam Mukhtaṣṣ bi-Dhikr Man Akhadhtu 'anhu al-'Ulūm wa'l-Ma'ārif min Shuyūkhī wa-Ābā'ī*, MS Princeton, 126–7

Murtaḍā al-Zabīdī, Muḥammad ibn Muḥammad, *Mu'jam al-Mukhtaṣṣ, Yaḥtawī 'alā Tarājim Akthar min Sitti Mi'a min A'yān al-Qarn al-Thānī 'Ashar al-Hijrī, wa-Yalīhi Mu'jam Shuyūkhihi al-Ṣaghīr wa-Ijāzātuhu li'l-'Allāmah Muḥammad Sa'īd al-Suwaydī. I'tanā bi-hi wa-Qābala Uṣūlahu Niẓām Muḥammad Ṣāliḥ Ya'qūbī [wa] Muḥammad ibn Nāṣr al-'Ajamī* (Series: Silsilat al-Ithbāt wa'l-Mashyakhāt wa'l-Ijāzāt wa'l-Musalsalāt, Maktabat Niẓām Yaʿqūbī al-Khāṣṣa, al-Baḥrayn 5, Bayrūt, Dār al-Bashā'ir al-Islāmiyya li'l-Ṭibāʿa wa'l-Nashr wa'l-Tawzīʿ, 2006)

Jurjī Zaydān, *Tārīkh Ādāb al-Lugha al-'Arabiyya* (Cairo, Dār al-Hilāl, 1911–22)

—— *Kitāb Tārīkh Ādāb al-Lugha al-'Arabiyya* (Cairo, Maṭbaʿat al-Hilāl, 1937)

—— *Tārīkh Ādāb al-Lugha al-'Arabiyya*, Shawqī Ḍayf (ed.) (Cairo, Dār al-Hilāl, 1957)

Khayr al-Dīn al-Ziriklī, *al-A'lām* (Beirut, Dār al-ʿIlm li'l-Malāyīn, 1984)

Index

Abbasid, 3, 225, 230, 234, 235, 238, 271, 276, 304–5, 325
ʿAbbūd Baḥrī, 143
ʿAbd al-ʿAzīz Jamāl al-Dīn, xiv, 11, 23, 39, 77, 361
ʿAbd al-ʿAzīz bin Saʾūd al-Wahhābī, 361
ʿAbd al-Fattāḥ al-Siranjāwī, 77, 361
ʿAbd al-Ḥamīd Bek, 105
ʿAbd al-Ḥamīd Nāfiʿ, copyist, 145, 168
ʿAbd al-Ḥaqq, 69
ʿAbd al-Ḥayy b. ʿAbd al-Kabīr al-Kattānī; al-Kattānī, xv, 45, 184, 186, 362
ʿAbd Allāh al-Baṣrī, 241
ʿAbd Allāh al-Idkāwī; ʿAbd Allāh b. Salāma al-Idkāwī al-Miṣrī al-Shāfiʿī, al-Muʾadhdhin, 98, 246
ʿAbd al-Laṭīf al-Baghdadī, 46
ʿAbd al-Qādir b. Khalīl b. ʿAbd Allāh al-Rūmī, 250
ʿAbd al-Qāhir al-Jurjānī, 229, 238
ʿAbd al-Raḥīm ʿAbd al-Raḥmān ʿAbd al-Raḥīm, xiv, 77, 272
ʿAbd al-Raḥmān al-ʿAydarūs; Sayyid ʿAbd al-Raḥmān al-ʿAydarūs, 14, 256
ʿAbd al-Raḥmān Ibn Khaldūn, 1, 323
ʿAbd al-Raḥmān b. ʿUmar al-ʿArīshī, 12, 20
ʿAbd al-Raʾūf al-Bashbāshī, 291
ʿAbd al-Wahhāb al-Subkī, 187
Abū ʿAbd Allāh Muḥammad al-Murrī al-Fāsī al-Tāwūdī Ibn Sūda, 12
Abu ʾl-ʿAlāʾ al-Maʿarrī, 241–2
ʿAbū ʿAlī Aḥmad al-Marzūqī, 363
Abu ʾl-Anwār ibn Wafā; Sayyid Abu ʾl-Anwār Muḥammad b. Wafā, 4, 257
Abu ʾl-ʿAzm, 11
Abū Bakr, 13, 27, 297, 298, 305
Abū Bakr Ibn al-ʿAydarūs al-Akbar, 303
Abu ʾl-Imdād Aḥmad b. Ismāʿīl al-Ḥusaynī, 11
Abū Qīr, 160
Aghā, 39, 62, 73
ahl al-dhimma, 10, 310
Laylā ʿAbd al-Laṭīf Aḥmad; Laylā Aḥmad, 182, 355
Aḥmad b. ʿAbd Allāh, 114
Aḥmad ʿĀrif Ḥikmet, 17, 172
Aḥmad al-ʿArūsī, 12, 14, 196, 214
Aḥmad al-Damanhūrī, 12
Aḥmad al-Dardīr, 113
al-Dilinjāwī; Aḥmad al-Dilinjāwī, 242
Aḥmad b. Ḥasan al-Rashīdī/Ṣawbaʿ; Aḥmad Ḥasan al-Rashīdī al-Shāfiʿī, Ṣawbaʿ, xiii, 35, 51, 137, 146, 166
Aḥmad al-Khalīl al-Shāmī, 181

Aḥmad Pāshā al-Kūr, 200
Aḥmad Muḥammad, copyist, 99, 145–6, 166
Aḥmad b. Muḥammad al-Ṣāwī, 114
Aḥmad Bey al-Muslimīn, Askī Nāzī, 184–5
Aḥmad Rizq, copyist, 71–2, 166
Aḥmad al-Saḥīmī, 113
Aḥmad, al-Shāhid; Aḥmad Muḥammad al-Shāhid; Aḥmad b. Mūsā al-Shāhid; Aḥmad b. Muḥammad b. Mūsā al-Shāhid; Aḥmad b. Muḥammad b. Aḥmad b. Mūsā al-Shāhid; Aḥmad Muḥammad; Aḥmad b. Muḥammad, al-Shāhid, copyist, 88, 99, 115, 117, 119, 145–6, 166, 168–9
Aḥmad al-Sūsī, 12
Aḥmad Ibn Wafī Abū al-Imdād, 14
Aḥmad Shawqī, 251, 259
Sayyid Aḥmad al-Taḥṭāwī, 294
Aḥmad Yūnis, Abu 'l-Taysīr; copyist, 122, 168
Aḥmad Zakī Pāshā, 35, 42, 137
ʿĀ'isha, 27
ʿAj. Būlāq, vi, 20, 27, 38–9, 41, 43, 44, 48, 61, 63, 73–5, 77–8, 97–8, 100, 111–12, 115–19, 122–3, 125, 131, 136, 141, 146, 155–8, 161–2, 171, 173, 179, 181–3, 191–2, 208, 213, 215–20, 291, 301, 327, 337–9, 340–4, 347, 349, 350
ʿAjā'ib al-Āthār; ʿAjā'ib al-Āthār fi 'l-Tarājim wa 'l-Akhbār, vi–vii, xi, xiii–xix, 5, 9–11, 14–17, 19–21, 23–4, 26, 28, 31–2, 34–45, 47, 49–53, 58–62, 67, 73, 77, 79, 80–2, 85, 89, 90–1, 95, 97, 102, 104, 106–10, 112, 120, 124, 127–31, 133, 137–8, 141, 146, 149, 152–3, 155–6, 158, 160–6, 171, 173–5, 177, 179, 181–3, 185–200, 205, 214–15, 231, 234, 247, 278, 286, 289, 293, 296, 298, 308, 312, 323, 326, 332–7, 340, 342, 356, 359–60, 362–3, 365
Akhbār, 29, 171, 188, 295, 297, 306
Akhbār al-Nuwwābi, 27, 188
Albania; Bilād al-Arnāwūd, 214–17
Albanian mercenary ruler, 3, 328
Albanian soldiers, 276
Albanians; *Arnūwūṭ*, 219
Alexandria, 29, 66, 208–10, 249, 264
al-Alfī; Muḥammad Bey al-Alfī, 26, 47, 54, 75
ʿAlī b. Abī Ṭālib, 295, 304
ʿAlī Bey Abu 'l-Dhahab, 317
ʿAlī al-ʿAdawī, 6
ʿAlī Burhān Zādah; Sayyid ʿAlī Afandī Burhān Zādeh, 249, 257
ʿAlī Fahmī, 108–9
ʿAlī Bāshā al-Ḥakīm, 258
ʿAlī b. Jibrīl, 249
ʿAlī Bey al-Kabīr, 200–1, 265
ʿAlī Ibn Mawlāhum al-Khayālī, 277
ʿAlī Pāshā Mubārak; ʿAlī Mubārak, 206, 215–16, 283, 336, 363
ʿAlī b. Muḥammad al-Jurjānī, 20
ʿAlī b. Muḥammad al-Qalʿī; ʿAlī al-Qalʿī, 196, 247
ʿAlī al-Qināwī, 14
ʿAlī Aghā al-Rashīdī; Ḥājj ʿAlī Aghā al-Rashīdī, 144
ʿAlī al-Ṣaʿīdī, 14, 20

ʿAlī Pasha al-Tabandalī, 216
ʿālim, 206, 213, 284, 291–3, 300, 306, 311, 319, 324
Amīn al-Madanī; Amīn Afandī al-Ḥulwānī al-Madanī; Amīn Afandī b. Ḥasan al-Ḥulwānī al-Madanī; Shaykh ʿEmin el-Madanī', 20–1, 28, 58, 60, 176
*Amīr*s, xviii, 3, 8, 20, 47, 56, 64, 172, 178, 184, 235, 239, 241, 243, 250, 267–8, 273–4, 278, 281, 288, 299, 303, 306, 310–11, 314, 317, 320
ʿAmr b. al-ʿĀṣ, 263, 268, 269, 282
al-amr bi 'l-ma'rūf wa 'l-nahy 'an al-munkar, 31, 53, 182, 225, 291, 330
'Aqliyya, 'ulūm 'aqliyya, 3, 23, 293, 300, 314, 329
Arab renaissance, 4, 46, 48, 197, 202, 221, 331
Arab scholars, xii, xiii, 3, 26, 202, 259, 305, 325
Arabic-speaking, 3, 189, 271, 329
Arab world, 4, 48, 175, 190, 193, 200, 214, 259, 335
Arabic, xv, xvi, xvii, 29, 37, 57, 65, 66, 70, 79, 87, 88, 90, 96, 101, 155, 156, 159, 176, 193, 197, 199, 203, 204, 207, 208, 215, 223, 224, 231, 233, 235, 238, 243, 286, 329
Arabic edition, xi, xvi, xvii, xix, 24, 28, 30, 34, 39, 85, 97, 148, 333
Arabic language, 20, 205, 224, 226, 227, 306, 335
Arabic literature, 9, 205, 227, 251
Arabic proclamation, 88, 155, 207, 329
arbāb al-malā'ib, 272, 280, 282, 315
arbāb al-malāhī wa 'l-malā'ib, 282, 315
Arnūwūṭ, 219
Ashʿarī, 203, 291
Ashkodra, 'Ushkodra', 196, 216
Ashrāf, 27, 231, 241, 249, 251, 257, 268, 295–9, 305–6, 319, 320, 321
Asselin; Asselin de Cherville, 35, 68, 89, 92, 95–6, 166
Astrology, 3, 311, 314, 324, 339
Astronomy, 3, 6, 10–13, 24–5, 65–6, 80, 198, 245, 306, 311, 314, 324, 329, 335
autograph; autographs, xii, xiv–xv, xvii, xx, 4–5, 15–18, 21, 33–43, 55, 57, 59–60, 62–7, 69–70, 73, 76–7, 79–80, 88, 90, 93, 95, 99, 101–3, 106–7, 110, 119–20, 124, 126, 128, 131–2, 136–8, 141–9, 152–6, 158, 160–1, 165–9, 173, 175, 177, 179, 185, 187–9, 231, 324, 333–4
Averroes, 1, 201, 208, 323, 325
Avicenna, 201, 228–9, 325
'awālim, sing. *'ālima*, 284–5
Awḍaḥ al-Ishārāt, 43, 181, 332
Awlād Rābiya, sing. Ibn Rābiya, 283
Awqāf, 22, 298, 345, 348
Kūrkīs ʿAwwād, 107
David Ayalon, xi, xviii–xix, 5, 20, 171, 199
al-ʿAynī; Badr al-Dīn Maḥmūd al-ʿAynī, xii, 184
al-Azbakiyya, 41, 249, 275, 282
Azhar Mosque; al-Azhar; Azharī, xviii, 4, 6–7, 10, 12, 14, 20–1, 49, 52, 56, 105, 110, 114, 148, 168, 175, 188, 215–17, 221, 233, 268, 292–3, 306, 315, 319, 331
Azjāl, 197, 256
Bāb Zuwayla', 78, 95, 100, 121
Badr al-Dīn Maḥmūd al-ʿAynī, 184
Gabriel Baer, 219

Bakriyya, 27, 32, 305, 326
Bānat Suʿād, 258
al-Bannānī, 20–1, 51
basmala, 58, 63, 69, 74–5, 80, 82, 84–8, 90, 92, 95–8, 106, 110, 115–18, 120, 123, 138, 141–2, 147, 149–51, 334
Baybars, 227, 310
Bayerische Staatsbibliothek, Munich, 97
Bayezid Library, Istanbul, 70, 166
Belzoni; Giovanni Belzoni, 4, 35, 66, 68, 278, 331
Beys, xiii, 27, 184, 195, 265
Bibliothèque Nationale, Paris, xiv–xv, xix, 15, 37, 73, 91–2, 95, 158, 174
bid'a, pl. *bida'*, 265, 270
Bilbays, 44, 175, 178
Biographical Dictionary, 17–19, 34, 57, 179, 181, 183–8, 190
biographies; biography, xi, xv–xvi, 1, 3–4, 10, 12, 15, 17–20, 22–3, 31–4, 42, 44–5, 47, 49, 53–4, 57–8, 74–6, 78–80, 83, 90–1, 95, 98, 100, 102, 110–11, 118–19, 121–3, 125, 127–8, 131, 136, 141–2, 144, 151, 159, 161, 163, 166, 171–3, 178, 180–90, 193, 196, 220, 234–5, 241, 287, 292, 295, 299–300, 312, 317, 323–4, 326, 328–9, 331, 333, 336
Birmingham University Library, xiv, xix, 149, 166, 334
Lars Bjørneboe, 5, 55–6, 64, 293, 320, 333
Bonaparte, 41, 210, 274
book dealer, 14, 16–17, 35, 59–60, 63, 103
British, 9, 26, 58, 66, 134, 160, 175, 177, 197, 208, 210, 213, 309, 325, 333
British Library, London; British Museum, xiv, xix, 23, 35, 66, 72, 81, 84, 155, 166, 335
Brockelmann, 70, 72
Būlāq edition, vii, xii, xiv, xvii, xx, 19, 34, 39, 40–3, 49, 61–2, 67, 73, 76–9, 82–3, 85, 86–92, 95–6, 98, 100, 106–8, 111–13, 117, 120–5, 128–9, 131–8, 140, 146, 148–9, 151–60, 172, 188–9, 191, 333–4
Būlāq group, Būlāq MSS, 39, 40, 62, 89–90, 166
Būlāq Press, 40, 42, 77, 79, 115–26, 132, 151–3, 188–9
J. L. Burckhardt; Johann Ludwig Burckhardt; al-Shaykh Ibrāhīm, 4, 16, 31, 33, 35–6, 44, 59, 65–8, 73, 76, 79, 92–3, 107, 166, 173–5, 177, 188, 190, 195, 210–11, 214, 331
Cairo, xiii, xiv–xv, xviii–xx, 4–5, 7, 15, 17, 20–4, 27, 32, 34, 36, 40, 42–3, 51–2, 59, 61, 65–70, 73, 77, 84, 89, 97, 99, 111, 123, 133, 137, 140, 146, 148, 155–6, 159–60, 165, 168, 172–5, 177, 179, 189, 196–7, 211, 214–15, 217–18, 220–1, 252, 262, 274–5, 277–9, 281–2, 284, 296, 298–9, 305, 315, 317, 331, 335, 345, 347–8, 350
Cairo University, xiv, xviii, 39, 77
Cambridge autograph, vii, xii, xv, xvii, 34,39-40, 43, 59, 60, 62, 95, 110, 126, 137–8, 141–2, 145–7, 149, 154, 156, 158, 160, 185, 187, 189
Cambridge group of MSS, vii, 39, 60–1, 76, 78, 97, 107, 166
Cambridge University Library, viii, xii, xiv, xv, xx, 15, 33, 36, 43, 59, 65, 67, 73, 80, 158, 173, 179, 185, 188, 190, 195, 205, 210, 214, 337
canonical & colloquial Arabic, xii, xvi, 3, 45, 161, 183, 188, 193, 197, 227, 231, 239, 242–4, 248–9, 255–6
Cardin; Alexandre Cardin, 21, 51, 162–5
Center of Documents and Contemporary History of Egypt (al-Hay'a al-ʿĀmma li-Dār al-Kutub wa 'l-Wathā'iq al-Qawmiyya-Markaz Wathā'iq wa-Tārīkh Miṣr al-Muʿāṣir), Egyptian National Library, 77

Chester Beatty Library, Dublin, Ireland, xx, 17
Christian; Christianity, 25, 46–7, 200, 203, 206–7, 210, 224, 231, 261–2, 264–5, 268–70, 273–5, 296, 309–10, 318, 327, 330
chronicle; chronicles; al-Jabartī's *Chronicle*, xi–xii, xiv–xv, xvii, 3, 5, 9, 13, 20, 23–8, 31–4, 37, 42–5, 47, 49–51, 55, 58, 60, 76, 98, 102–3, 113, 115, 118, 127, 133, 141, 161, 165–6, 171–3, 176–7, 181–2, 184, 187–8, 192, 196, 214, 231, 234, 248, 265–6, 278, 291–3, 295, 297, 301, 323–4, 326, 329–33, 336
Constantinople, 9, 29, 46, 163, 227, 267
Copts; Coptic calendar; Coptic festivals, xviii, 24, 45, 261–2, 268–70, 273–5, 280–1, 318, 329
copyists; copyist, xii, xvii, 1, 4, 15–17, 21, 33, 35–6, 41, 59–60, 67, 73–4, 77, 80, 92–3, 103, 118, 138, 140–1, 153, 189, 332–3
Crusaders, 28, 200, 206, 227, 296
Daniel Crecelius, 5, 45, 182, 186, 189, 292
al-Dalajī, 36
Damascus, 36–7, 49, 67, 81, 173, 196, 215–17, 219–20, 278
al-Damurdāshī; Aḥmad al-Damurdāshī, xii, xv, 44, 181–2, 192, 272, 329, 332
Dār al-Fāris, 61, 76, 78, 100, 116–18, 135–37, 168–9
dār al-Ḥarb, 226–7, 230, 325
dār al-Islām, 296
Dār al-Kutub al-ʿIlmiyya, 61, 76, 78, 118
Dār al-Kutub al-Qawmiyya, Cairo; DKQ; Egyptian National Library, xiii, xix, 15, 17, 23–4, 32, 34, 37, 40, 59, 61, 69–70, 73, 77, 94, 108, 110–11, 113, 115, 118, 123–6, 133, 137, 153, 160, 166–9, 174, 179, 189
Dār al-Kutub al-Miṣriyya, 40, 116, 125–6, 133–6
al-Ḍaw' al-Lāmiʿ li-Ahl al-Qarn al-Tāsiʿ, 19
Dāwūd b. ʿUmar al-Anṭākī; al-Anṭākī, 23–4, 60, 219, 329
Fred De Jong, 214, 217, 221
Defter-i Kutubkhāne-i Weli el-Dīn, 70
G. Delanoue, 48
Description de l'Egypte, 53, 92
Dhikr, 33, 230, 232, 236, 239, 243, 286
*Dhimmī*s, 53, 296, 327
Dīwān, 14, 27, 30, 44, 53, 65, 68, 178, 196, 237, 242–3, 249, 257, 268, 272, 298, 305, 332
al-Durra al-Muṣāna fī Akhbār al-Kināna, 181
Dustūr Taqwīm al-Kawākib al-Sabʿa wa 'l-Jawāhir wa 'l-Ahilla wa 'l-Tawārīkh al-Thalātha wa-Mawāsimihā wa-Tawāqītihā fī Sanat 1209 H. (Ḥisāb) al-Shaykh ʿAbd al-Raḥmān al-Jabartī, 24
Egypt; Egyptian history; Egyptian society; Egyptians, xi–xv, xviii, 3, 7, 9, 11, 23–9, 32, 41, 44, 46–8, 53, 57–8, 66, 79, 81, 134, 171, 176–9, 200–3, 205–6, 208–11, 213, 221–2, 227, 230, 247–8, 261–5, 267–71, 279–80, 295–6, 315
Egyptian script, 81
Emin el-Madanī qv Amīn al-Madanī, Amīn al-Ḥulwānī al-Madanī and Amīn Afandī b. Ḥasan al-Ḥulwānī al-Madanī, 21, 28, 58, 60, 63, 176
England, 26, 47, 173, 205
European consuls, 15, 17, 35–6, 59, 210
fann al-ta'rīkh, 197, 240, 257
faqīh, 292, 306
farḍ kifāya, 7, 200, 314, 324

fātiḥa, 219
Fīhris al-Fahāris, 184
Fiqh, 6, 12, 20, 275, 301, 311, 314, 329
Firmān, 29, 143
Folio, xii, 16, 23–5, 64, 68–70, 72–6, 80, 82–95, 97–100, 102–6, 108–12, 115–26, 128–30, 132–6, 138–9, 141–3, 148–9, 184, 191–2
Fred De Jong, 214, 217, 221
French; French invaders; French occupation, xiii–xiv, 3–5, 9, 14–15, 21, 24–33, 41–2, 44, 46–8, 50, 53, 55, 58–60, 62–3, 65, 68, 79, 87, 89, 92, 94, 96, 118, 141, 146–7, 150–1, 154–5, 160–2, 164–6, 175–9, 182, 195–7, 207–13, 221, 227, 247, 256, 265, 267, 273–5, 281–2, 296, 298, 305, 307, 316, 325–33, 335
French Revolution, 4, 29, 47, 211, 326, 331
Sultan al-Ghawrī, 298
al-Ghazālī, xvi, 234, 323
ʿAlī Maṭar al-Ghiryānī, copyist, 84–5, 166
Ghulām ʿAlī Azad, 46
God (Allāh), xvi, 2, 8, 13, 18–19, 22, 25–7, 30, 38, 40, 46, 48, 62–4, 69, 72, 75, 77, 81–3, 91, 94, 97–8, 102–3, 116–17, 119–20, 125, 132, 138–9, 146, 152, 176, 178, 180, 207, 217–20, 224–6, 231–2, 238, 240, 242, 262–6, 268, 273, 292–4, 296–8, 300–3, 305, 307–9, 313, 315–19, 321, 323–7, 329, 335
Grammar, 20, 30, 37, 66, 189, 198, 209, 245, 256, 293, 314
Peter Gran, 199, 206, 214
Grand Vizier, 30, 32, 44, 64, 219, 249
The Great History of the People of the Twelfth Century, 18, 172, 180, 186
Greek logic; Greek, xviii, 1, 25, 223, 226, 229, 235, 238, 323
ḥadīth, xiii, 13, 25, 32–3, 195, 270, 292–3, 297, 299, 306, 311, 314, 328–9
al-Ḥaḍrāwī; Aḥmad b. Muḥammad al-Ḥaḍrāwī al-Makkī al-Hāshimī; Aḥmad b. Muḥammad al-Ḥaḍrāwī al-Makkī al-Hāshimī, 20–1, 51
Ḥallāq, 27, 188
Hammām b. Yūsuf al-Hawwārī, 184
Ḥammāda Rajab, 23
Ḥanafī, 6, 12, 49, 84
  Ḥanafī jurist, 16, 310, 314
  Ḥanafī law, 10, 20, 201, 203
  Ḥanafī scholars, 115, 294
al-Ḥarīrī, 205, 256
Ḥasan b. ʿAbd al-Rahmān... al-Manzalāwī al-Shāfiʿī, 90
Ḥasan b. ʿAlī al-Badrī al-ʿAwaḍī; Ḥasan al-Badrī al-ʿAwaḍī, 196, 257
Ḥasan b. ʿAlī Shamma al-Fuwwī; Ḥasan Shamma, xix, 44, 243–4, 246, 317, 332
Ḥasan al-ʿAṭṭār; Ḥasan b. Muḥammad al-ʿAṭṭār, xv, 3, 15–16, 19, 26, 30–1, 36–7, 41, 48–50, 53, 58, 65–7, 71, 80–1, 114, 118, 159, 166, 173–5, 182, 191–2, 195–200, 202–6, 208–17, 219, 221, 238–9, 247, 251, 259, 320, 325, 329–32, 334, 337–43, 345, 347–8, 350, 352
Ḥasan al-Badrī al-Ḥijāzī, 33, 241, 314
Ḥasan al-Jabartī; Ḥasan b. Ibrāhīm al-Jabartī; Ḥasan Afandī b. Ibrāhīm b. Ḥasan, Abu ʾl-Tadānī, 6, 7, 9, 10–11, 16–17, 19, 52, 79, 102, 152, 184–5, 296, 313–4, 324
Ḥasan al-Jaddāwī, 214
Ḥasan Muḥammad Jawhar, 77, 159
Ḥasan Afandī b. Muḥammad Afandī, al-Zāmik, 285

Amīr Ḥasan Bey Riḍwān, 184, 252
Ḥasan al-Yūsī, 46
Ḥāshiya, 50, 114–15, 215–16, 334
Jane Hathaway, xix, 27, 188, 288
ḥawāshī, 198–9
Ḥijāz, 66, 173–5, 191–2, 201, 215, 220, 311, 318
al-Ḥijāzī; Ḥasan al-Badrī al-Ḥijāzī, 33, 241–2, 309, 314–16, 318
Hijra, 102, 152, 172
Hijrī, 45, 232, 257, 314
ḥisāb al-jummal, 197, 199, 232–3, 240, 245
historians; Arab historians, xii, xv, 1–3, 9, 29, 46, 55, 77, 142, 173, 187, 189, 193, 202, 219, 225, 265–6, 271, 279–80, 283, 288, 291, 304, 308, 323, 329–30, 334
historical memory, 3–4, 46, 223, 329, 335
historical writings, 1, 3, 182–3, 292, 329
history, xi, xiii–xiv, xvi, xviii, 1–3, 18–19, 25, 28–30, 32, 44–5, 57–8, 62, 89, 159, 162, 178–82, 188–91, 197, 199, 213–14, 221, 223–6, 235, 245, 287, 295, 297, 306, 323–5, 329–30, 332–4
history of Egypt, xi, xiii–xiv, xviii, 1, 3, 5, 15, 19–20, 25, 28–9, 32, 44–5, 58, 62, 89, 97, 162, 178–9, 189, 199, 325, 329, 333
The History of Egypt, 182
Homoeoteleuton, 37, 40, 59, 62, 76–7, 92, 99, 111–12, 138, 141, 153, 155, 157–9
Ḥusayn b. ʿAbd al-Raḥmān al-Manzalāwī, 99
al-Ḥusayn b. Abī Shaʿra, 271
Ḥusayn Ḥasan Idrīs; Ḥusayn Ḥasan Idrīs al-Shāfiʿī al-Damanhūrī al-Khalwatī; Ḥusayn Ḥasan Idrīs al-Shāfiʿī al-Damanhūrī al-Khalwatī, copyist, 105, 168
Ḥusayn Bek Ḥusnī, 151, 166, 334
Ḥusayn b. al-Nūr ʿAlī b. ʿAbd al-Shukūr al-Ḥanafī al-Ṭāʾifī, 185
Ibn ʿAbd al-Ghanī's *Chronicles*, xii, xv, 182, 192
Ibn ʿAbd al-Ghanī; Aḥmad Shalabī Ibn ʿAbd al-Ghanī; Aḥmad Chelebi, xii, xv, 27, 43, 181–3, 188, 192, 329, 332
Ibn al-ʿArabī, 259, 316
Ibn al-Athīr; Ibn al-Athīr al-Jazarī, ʿIzz al-Dīn, 77, 120, 142, 158, 169
Ibn Dāniyāl, Muḥammad, 277, 280
Ibn al-Ḥājj; Ibn al-Ḥājj al-ʿAbdarī, 262, 280
Ibn al-Ḥājj al-Fāsī, 262, 271
Ibn al-Haytham, 201
Ibn Ḥāzim al-Qarṭājannī, 202
Ibn Iyās, xii, 271, 284, 287
Ibn Khaldūn; ʿAbd al-Raḥmān Ibn Khaldūn, 1, 25, 201, 323, 325, 336
Ibn Manjak, 242
Ibn al-Nafīs, 201, 325
Ibn Nujaym, 16
Ibn al-Qayyim, 78
Ibn Rābiya, 283
Ibn Rushd (Averroes), 1, 201–2, 228, 323, 325
Ibn al-Ṣalīḥī; Muḥammad Ibn al-Ṣalīḥī, 204, 240
Ibn Shamma, xix, 317
Ibn Sīnā (Avicenna), 201, 228–9, 325

Ibn Taghrī Birdī, xii, 287
Ibn Ṭufayl, 202
Ibn Zunbul al-Rammāl, xii
Ibrāhīm Pasha, 216, 275–6, 321
Shaykh Ibrāhīm b. Abī al-Barakāt al-Baghdādī, Ibn al-Suwaydī, 296
Ibrāhām Ibn ʿAbd Allāh; Burckhardt, 4, 16, 31, 33, 35–6, 44, 59, 65–8, 73, 76, 79, 92–3, 107, 166, 173–5, 177, 188, 190, 195, 210–11, 214, 311
Ibrāhīm Ibn Duqmāq, 184
Ibrāhīm b. ʿĪsā al-Ḥasan, 98
al-Amīr Ibrāhīm Afandī Katkhudā al-ʿAzab, 93
al-Sayyid Ibrāhīm Sālim, 77
ijāza, 314
iltizām, 9, 299, 318
Imām of the Yemen, 143
Indian, 172, 251
Institute of Arabic Manuscripts, Cairo Maʿhad Iḥyāʾ al-Makhṭūṭāt al-ʿArabiyya, 70
Institute of Oriental Studies, St. Petersburg (Leningrad), Russia, 23, 102
Introduction, 8, 10, 14, 19, 26, 32, 50, 57–8, 62, 69, 149, 181, 191–2, 236–7, 307–8, 312
Iraq Museum, Baghdad, xx, 106–7
Irtijāl, 197, 256, 296
Islam, xiii, 1–2, 20, 30, 48, 59, 66, 201–2, 223–8, 231, 235, 240, 261–2, 264–5, 269, 285, 289, 296–8, 309, 316, 318, 324–5
Islamic calendar (*taqwīm*), 3, 13, 24, 329
Islamic culture, xi, 3, 11, 202–3, 205, 222, 225, 228, 259, 279, 281, 325, 331, 336
Islamic laws, 2, 26, 48, 53, 179, 298, 314, 335
Islamic principles (*arkān*), 2, 26, 221, 226, 228, 324
Islamic Roots of Capitalism, Egypt, 1760–1840, 199
Ismāʿīl; Khedive Ismāʿīl Pasha, 287
Ismāʿīl Bey, 41, 282
Ismāʿīl al-Khashshāb, 50, 114, 199, 203, 221, 332
Ismāʿīl Effendi al-Zuhūrī al-Miṣrī, 252
ʿIwaḍ Sanbāwī, 114
Izmir, 36–7, 67, 81, 173, 196, 213, 216–20
al-Jabartī; ʿAbd al-Raḥmān; ʿAbd al-Raḥmān; ʿAbd al-Raḥmān b. Ḥasan al-Jabartī, xi, xiii–xiv, xvi–xviii, xx, 1–2, 4–7, 10–14, 16–24, 28, 30–2, 34, 36, 38, 40–4, 46, 48–56, 58, 60, 62–6, 68, 70, 72, 74, 76–8, 80, 82, 88, 90–2, 94, 96, 99, 101–3, 106, 108, 110, 1145, 120, 122, 124, 132, 136–8, 140, 146, 1248, 152, 154, 156, 158, 160, 162, 165–6, 168, 172, 174–6, 178, 180, 182–4, 186, 188, 190, 192, 196, 198, 200, 202, 204, 208, 211, 214, 232, 234, 236–8, 240, 242, 244, 246, 250, 256, 266, 272, 274, 276, 278–80, 282, 284, 286, 288, 291–2, 294, 296, 298, 302–4, 308, 310, 312, 314, 316, 318, 323–4, 326–7, 330, 332, 334, 336, 340, 342, 344–5
al-Jabartī's chronicle; al-Jabartī's *Chronicle*, xi, xvii, 3, 5, 13, 23–6, 28, 32–3, 37, 45, 47, 49–51, 55, 58, 60, 76, 98, 102, 113, 115, 127, 141, 165–6, 171–3, 176–7, 184, 187–8, 196, 214, 231, 234, 248, 265–6, 278, 291, 293, 295, 297, 301, 323–4, 326, 329–33, 336
al-Jabartī's handwriting, xv, 22, 33–4, 36, 59, 63–4, 79, 92–4, 107, 109–10, 123, 173, 186
al-Jabartī's autograph, autographs, xii, xvii, xx, 5, 21, 33–6, 41, 55, 59–60, 62, 65, 73, 76, 79, 88, 90, 106–7, 119–20, 132, 136–8, 148, 154, 156, 158, 175, 179, 185, 188–9, 333–4
al-Jabartī's son Maḥfūẓ, 1, 21, 23, 72, 102–3, 166–7
al-Jabartī's son Khalīl, 21–3, 49–50, 106, 167

al-Jabartī's daughter Amīn, 11, 22
al-Jabartī's wife Shawq, 23
jāhiliyya, 223, 226–7
al-Jāmi'a al-Islāmiyya, 12, 18, 172
Jane Hathaway, xix, 27, 188, 288
Janissaries, 27, 319
Jirjis al-Jawharī, 125
al-Jazāyirlī; Ḥusayn Pasha al-Jazāyirlī, 299
Jerusalem, 10, 15–16, 36–7, 49, 64, 67, 80, 173, 205–7, 215, 217, 220, 236, 310, 327, 345, 347–8, 350, 352
Jews, xiv, 45, 184, 265, 275, 318, 329
Jibrā'īl Yūsuf Mukhalla', 138–42, 167–8
Jihad, 8–9, 206, 226–7, 270, 289, 296, 310, 317, 325
John Rylands University Library, University of Manchester, xx, 89, 166
Kalām, 33, 195, 302
al-Kāmil; Tārīkh al-Kāmil, 77, 120, 158, 169
Kasr al-Sadd, 265, 267
khalbūṣ, 283–5
khalīfa, 19, 276, 295, 317
Khalīl b. Ibrāhīm al-'Ajūz, copyist, 148, 168
Khalīl b. Muḥammad al-Maghribī, 215
Khalīl Rif'at Pāshā, 69
Khalīl Shaybūb, 21, 50
Khalwatiyya; Khalwatī, xiii, xviii, 2, 7, 13–14, 32, 53, 60, 63, 94, 102, 105, 111, 195, 203, 230, 291, 301–2, 309, 316–17, 321, 323–4, 329
Ismā'īl al-Khashshāb, 50, 114, 199, 203, 221, 332
Khawal, 276, 283
khayāl, 272
al-Khiṭaṭ al-Tawfīqiyya, 215
al-Khizāna al-Khudaywiyya al-Miṣriyya, Cairo qv Khedivial Library, 42, 124–6, 134, 143, 189
al-Khizāna al-Zakiyya qv al-Maktaba al-Zakiyya, 137–8, 144
Khuda Bakhsh Bankipore Oriental Public Library, Patna, India; Khūdā Bakhsh MS, xx, 39–40, 76, 104, 151
Kuffār, 30, 197, 213, 310
Kurrāsa, 64
al-Kutubkhāna al-Miṣriyya; al-Kutubkhāna al-Khudaywiyya al-Miṣriyya; Bibliothèque Khédiviale; al-Khizāna al-Khudaywiyya al-Miṣriyya; al-Maktaba al-Khudaywiyya al-Miṣriyya, 40, 69, 108–9, 116–23, 125–7, 129–30, 143
Anistās al-Karmilī; Anastase-Marie al-Kirmili, 49, 107, 160
Kléber, 26, 42, 47, 94, 96, 150, 179, 328
Lane; E.W. Lane, 4, 52, 68, 83-5, 166, 264–7, 274, 276, 278–86, 289, 303, 331, 335–6
Stanley Lane-Poole, 52
lectio difficilior, 38–9
lectio facilior, 38–9
Leeds University Library, xiv, xx, 85
Leiden University Library, Netherlands, xx, 15, 17, 19, 25, 59, 62
Lisān al-Dīn al-Khaṭīb, 246

literary circle, 3
logic, 1, 25, 198, 223, 226, 229, 235, 238, 293, 323–4, 327, 334
madā'iḥ nabawiyya, 232, 243, 249, 252
madīḥ, 228, 233, 237, 239, 243, 249
Maghribī script; *Maghribī* hand, xv, 31, 34, 36, 57, 67, 80, 128–9, 134–6, 166, 173, 195
Maḥmūd al-Kurdī; Maḥmūd al-Kurdī al-Khalwatī, 13, 291
Maḥmūd Qāsim; Maḥmūd b. Muṣṭafā Qāsim, 86, 168
Majd al-Dīn Muḥammad Abū Hādī al-Wafā'ī, 257
Majlis, 29, 203, 248–9, 252, 257, 288
Main Library, University of Birmingham, xiv, xix, 149, 334
al-Maktaba al-Āṣafiyya; Maktabat Muḥammad Bek Āṣaf qv al-Maktaba al-Āṣafiyya, 137–8, 147
al-Maktaba al-Azhariyya, 148, 168
al-Maktaba al-Zakiyya, 137–8, 144, 147
Maktabat Aḥmad ʿĀrif Ḥikmat, 12, 18
Maktabat Madbūlī, 39
Mālikī, 49, 114–15
Mālikīs, 115
Mamluk *amīr*s, xviii, 3, 8, 47, 64, 235, 239, 241, 243, 278, 288, 306
Mamluk leader, 26
Mamluk rule, xii, xviii, 3, 26, 32, 55, 64, 176, 178, 202, 209, 231–2, 264, 291, 306–7, 309, 311, 317, 326
Mamluk sultans, xii, 310
Mamluks, xiii, 8, 11, 32, 39, 46, 68, 87, 91, 150, 154–5, 178, 188, 206, 209–10, 231, 247, 251, 264, 275, 286, 296, 298–9, 309, 311, 317, 319–20, 332
manuscript, xiv–xv, xix–xx, 4, 7, 16, 18–19, 25, 31, 34, 37–8, 42, 49, 51, 58, 61–3, 65–6, 69–74, 76–83, 85–93, 95, 97–9, 101–11, 113, 115–26, 128–9, 131–3, 135, 148, 152, 155, 158–9, 165, 179–80, 206, 215, 333–4
manuscripts, xi–xv, xvii, xx, 4, 16–17, 23, 33–4, 40–2, 59, 62, 65, 67–8, 70–1, 73, 78–81, 87, 89, 102, 106–8, 117–18, 124, 137, 153–4, 158–60, 165, 173, 175, 193, 198–9, 214, 220, 333
maqāmāt, 3, 9, 61, 212, 233, 235, 246–7, 249–50, 252–3, 258
Maqāmat Ḥasan al-ʿAṭṭār, 211–12
al-Maqrīzī, xii, 23, 271, 287
Maṭbaʿat Dār al-Kutub al-Miṣriyya, 358–61, 363
al-Maṭbaʿa al-Kubrā, 77, 166
mawlid, 232, 249
*mawlid*s, 33, 232–3, 250, 265, 280, 288, 299, 315, 329
Maẓhar al-Taqdīs; Maẓhar al-Taqdīs bi-Zawāl Dawlat al-Faransīs; Maẓhar al-Taqdīs bi-Dhahāb Dawlat al-Faransīs, xiii, 5, 16, 23, 30, 32, 34–7, 42–4, 56–9, 61, 63, 65–7, 69–72, 76, 79, 123–4, 140, 150, 159–66, 173, 175–9, 181, 208–9, 211, 231, 332–3
Medicine, xviii, 6, 11, 23, 61, 66, 197–8, 201, 212, 306, 324–5, 329, 334
ʿAbdallah Menou, 175
Merveilles biographiques et historiques ou chroniques du Cheikh Abd-el-Rahman el Djabartī, 50, 165
Meters, 204, 227, 235, 237, 239, 243–4, 258
Mingana Collection; Mingana, 89, 148–51, 166
Ministry of Awqāf, 42, 137, 142–3
Mohammed Bey el Defterdar, 51

MS, 15, 19, 23, 37, 39–44, 49, 58, 62–3, 67, 69–70, 73, 75–7, 79, 82–7, 90–4, 96, 98–102, 104–7, 110–12, 119–25, 132–6, 139–52, 158–62, 166, 172–5, 179, 183, 185–7, 191–2, 210, 334–5
MS *'Aj.* Bankipore, 39, 104–6
MS *'Aj.* Ber., 39, 78, 97–100, 111, 130–1, 136, 156–7
MS عجب [Berlin] , 97
MS *'Aj.* Birmingham, 77, 112, 148–51, 153, 334
MS *'Aj.* BM, 81–5, 152, 159–60
MS *'Aj.* BN, 34, 59, 78, 91–6, 109, 154, 158–60
MS *'Aj.* Cam. , xii, 34, 37–9, 41, 44, 57, 59, 64, 68, 73–6, 78–80, 82, 84, 86–8, 90–2, 94–6, 100, 106, 110–11, 115, 119, 121–4, 130–1, 136, 152–4, 157, 161, 182, 185–6, 191–2, 210, 247, 337, 339
MS *'Aj.* Cam. 2nd, 34, 36, 41, 67, 80, 109, 205, 337–44
MS *'Aj.* DKQ. , 34, 94, 113
MS *'Aj.* Iraq, 106, 108
MS *'Aj.* Leeds, 85–8, 99, 119
MS *'Aj.* Len., 102–4
MS *'Aj.* MA, 148
MS *'Aj.* Manchester, 89–91
MS *'Aj.* ML, 97
MS *'Aj.* Tārīkh, 32, 34, 37–8, 41–3, 49, 59, 62, 78–9, 93, 100, 104, 108–13, 115–26, 128–36, 141, 146–7, 150, 153–5, 158, 160, 179, 189
MS *'Aj.* Tārīkh Taymūr, 38, 127–8
MS Cevdet Pāshā, 76; 70, 166
MS *Maẓ.* Bay. , 70–1, 159–60, 166
MS *Maẓ.* Cam. , 64–5, 68–9, 110, 159–61
MS *Maẓ.* DKQ. , 69
MS *Maẓ.* Ram. , 70–2, 159–60
MS *Maẓ.* Tārīkh, xiii, 70
MS *Mudda; Mudda; Hādhā Tārīkh Dukhūl Muddat al-Faransīs bi-Miṣr; Muddat Dukhūl al-Faransīs bi-Miṣr*, 28, 56, 58–9, 62, 64, 79, 110, 160–2
MS Princeton, 18, 22, 28, 257, 306, 310
MSS, xiv, 15, 17, 23, 33, 36–7, 39–42, 49, 53, 55, 59–62, 67, 70–3, 76–9, 89–91, 97, 99–101, 106–8, 110, 112, 124, 126, 133, 137–9, 141, 148–9, 151–5, 159–60, 168, 173–5, 177, 185, 188–91
Mu'āraḍa, 234, 246
muḥabbaẓūn, 280–2
Mu'jam Mukhtaṣṣ; Mu'jam mukhtaṣṣ bi-dhikr man akhadhtu 'anhu al-'ulūm wa'l-ma'ārif min shuyūkhī wa- ābā'ī, xvi, 15, 17–19, 22, 28, 44, 57, 61–2, 64, 80, 172, 179–81, 183–6, 190, 196, 234, 242, 296, 306, 312
Muḥammad, 2, 8, 25, 27, 33, 82, 140, 220, 223, 231–2, 235–6, 241, 243, 245, 249, 252, 258, 265, 270, 294–5, 297–9, 302–5, 322
Muḥammad b. 'Abd al-Wahhāb, 78, 100
Muḥammad 'Abduh, 202
Muḥammad Bek Abu 'l-Dhahab, 28
al-Sayyid Muḥammad Abu 'l-Iqbāl; Muḥammad Abu 'l-Iqbāl b. Wafī Shaykh al-Sādāt 19
Muḥammad Abu 'l-Sa'ūd b. Muḥammad ... Abi 'l-Surūr, 144

Muḥammad Aḥmad Khalīl; Muḥammad b. Aḥmad Khalīl; Muḥammad b. Aḥmad b. Khalīl; Muḥammad b. Aḥmad b. Khalīl, Muḥammad b. Aḥmad b. Khalīl al-Ṭanbashāwī, copyist, 138–41, 147, 167–8
Muḥammad ʿAlī; Muḥammad Bāshā ʿAlī, xiv, 3, 14–16, 21, 23–4, 26–7, 31–3, 39, 49–51, 55, 62, 66, 75, 100, 122, 130–2, 143, 146, 160, 165, 174–5, 178, 181, 191–2, 196, 199, 202, 206, 213, 221, 226–7, 232, 247, 259, 265, 275–6, 286–7, 291, 293–4, 296, 299–300, 307, 309, 318, 320–1, 327–9, 334, 336
Muḥammad ʿAṭā's edition, 159–60
Muḥammad Aḥmad al-Shafiʿī, 120–1, 167–8
Muḥammad al-Amīr al-Ḥanafī al-Rashīdī, 58, 63
Muḥammad Anīs, 22–3, 51–2, 279
Amīr Muḥammad Agha al-Bārūdī, 277
Muḥammad ʿĀrif Ḥilmī, 69
Muḥammad ʿĀrif Sālim, 145
Muḥammad Bey Āṣaf; Muḥammad Bek Āṣaf Ibn ʿAlī Pāshā Āṣaf, 42, 52, 138
Muḥammad al-Busṭī b. Ibrāhīm b. Khalīl Afandī, 114
Muḥammad al-Dūqāṭī al-Taḥṭāwī, 12
Muḥammad al-Fāsī al-Tāwūdī, 12
Muḥammad al-Ghamrī, 41
Muḥammad al-Halbāwī, 34
Muḥammad Ḥasan al-Fākihānī, 86
Muḥammad b. Ḥubaysh al-Maqdisī, 76
Muḥammad Ḥusayn b. Aḥmad Miṣbāḥ al-Shāfiʿī al-Azharī; Muḥammad Ḥusayn Aḥmad Miṣbāḥ al-Shāfiʿī; Muḥammad Aḥmad al-Shāfiʿī, copyist, 49, 110, 120–1, 167–8
Muḥammad al-Kattānī, 45
Muḥammad Khalīl al-Murādī, 75, 172
Muḥammad b. Muḥammad al-Bāsāṭī, 114
Muḥammad al-Muḥibbī, 46
Muḥammad b. Mūsā al-Janājī al-Shāfiʿī, 12
Muḥammad al-Nashartī, 98
Muḥammad b. Riḍwān al-Suyūṭī, Ibn al-Ṣalāḥī, 196, 258
Muḥammad al-Ṣabbāgh al-Dimyāṭī, 105
Muḥammad b. Sālim al-Ḥifnāwī (or al-Ḥifnī), 201, 243, 291, 317
Muḥammad b. Sālim b. Nāṣir, Thuʿaylib al-Ṣaghīr, 114
Muḥammad b. Sīrīn ... Ibn Jaysh al-Shāfiʿī al-Maqdisī; Muḥammad b. Sīrīn ... Ibn Jaysh al-Shāfiʿī al-Maqdisī, 112, 151
al-Mujāwirīn cemetery; Bustān al-Mujāwirīn, 21, 52
Mukhtaṣar Tadhkirat Ūlī al-Albāb wa 'l-Jāmiʿ li 'l-ʿAjab al-ʿUjāb, al-Maʿr-fa bi-Tadhkirat Dāwūd, 23
Munajjim Pāshā al-Mawlawī, 215
Munshid, 234, 251–2, 256
muʿrab, 227, 243
al-Murabbā al-Kābulī fīman Rawā ʿan al-Shams al-Bābilī, 19, 183
Amīr Murād Bey Muḥammad; Murād Bey, 252, 328
al-Murādī; Muḥammad Khalīl al-Murādī, xv, 3, 15, 28–30, 44, 46, 54, 57, 75, 171–2, 181, 185–90, 193, 202, 220, 295, 331–2
al-Musabbiḥī, 272

Muslim; Muslims, xii, 3–4, 7, 25–6, 30, 44–5, 47–8, 52–3, 56–7, 157, 176, 178–9, 182, 197, 199, 200, 203, 206–8, 212, 218, 223–4, 226, 229, 231, 259, 265, 273–4, 286, 289, 294, 296, 306–7, 310–11, 313, 322–4, 326, 334–5
Muslim East (*Mashriq*), 2, 25, 324, 335
Muslim historians, 1–3, 9, 46, 202, 265, 323, 329–30
Muslim historiography, 1, 4, 188, 190, 231, 292, 331
Muslim nations, 48, 335
Muslim rulers, 25–6, 31, 178, 181–2, 264–5, 270, 294, 296, 310–11
Muslim scholars, xviii, 3, 18, 20, 25, 35, 46, 49, 190, 201, 210, 215–16, 218, 220, 243, 264–5, 270, 280, 286, 289, 296, 311–13, 318–19, 330, 335
Muslim traditional culture Muslim world, 1, 3–4, 18, 25, 36, 46, 57, 178, 180, 188, 200, 202, 220, 232, 240, 263, 289, 317, 322, 325, 330–1, 335–6
Muṣṭafā Bahjat Afandī, 31
Muṣṭafā b. Muḥammad al-Dasūqī, 114
Muṣṭafā al-Shalsham-nī b. Muḥammad al-Shalshamūnī, copyist, 99, 167
Muṣṭafā al-Ṭā'ī, 20
muwashshaḥāt, 197, 232, 243, 255–6
mystical dogma, 2, 323
mysticism, 1, 198, 241
nahḍa, 202
Napoleon, xiii, 78, 87–8, 91, 150, 176, 202, 207–8, 210–11, 220, 227, 267, 326, 329
Napoleonic era, 47, 326
Naqīb al-Ashrāf, 249, 257, 319, 321
Naqliyya, *'ulūm naqliyya*, 3, 23, 293, 300, 314, 329
Naqshbandiyya, 7
Naskhī, 69–70, 86–91, 97, 104–6, 109, 112, 127–30, 133–4, 142, 145, 149, 179
al-Naṣr al-Mumtadd; al-Naṣr al-Mumtadd fī Fatḥ Tihāma wa-Najd, 174–5, 191–2
nasta'līq, 64, 68, 70, 73, 108, 110
Nawrūz, 262–5, 269–72, 280, 284
Necrologies, 33–4, 40–1, 143, 151, 234, 242, 293, 301, 312, 323, 332
Nile; Nilometer, xviii, 24, 35, 144, 151, 261–70, 273–5, 280, 282, 288, 328
Nīqūla al-Turk, 31, 42, 47–8, 179, 330
non-Muslim minorities, xviii, 3
Nuzhat al-Fikar fīmā Maḍā min al-Ḥawādith wa 'l-'Ibar min Awā'il al-Mawjūdāt ilā Ākhir al-Qarn al-Thālith 'Ashar, 20
Obituaries, 85, 87–8, 115, 137, 181, 296
Oriental Public Library, Patna, India, xx, 104
Ottomans, 2–3, 8–9, 14, 27–32, 37, 39, 46–7, 57–9, 75, 157, 163, 171, 177, 179, 200, 208, 211, 213, 221, 227, 275, 291, 295, 297–8, 319–20, 325–7, 329
Ottoman armies, 8, 58–9, 213, 226, 296
Ottoman culture, 203, 221, 288
Ottoman Empire, xv, 2, 9, 25, 49, 64–5, 177, 196–7, 199, 205–7, 219, 221, 227, 230, 248, 288, 295, 320, 325
Ottoman sultans, xii, 25, 225–6, 288, 297, 307, 310
Ottoman soldiers, 31, 47–8, 197, 213, 221, 231, 311, 328
Qubba, 86, 88, 317

Pasha, 8, 30–1, 39, 42, 44, 58, 62, 64, 67, 69–70, 100–1, 130, 132, 134 , 137–8, 160, 166, 175, 177–8, 188, 200, 208, 215–16, 221, 241, 248, 253, 265–6, 268, 275–6, 282, 286–8, 294, 307, 313, 319, 321
Pharmacology, 23
T. Philipp, xvi–xvii, xix, 179
Philosophy, xiv, 1, 6, 10, 32, 198, 201, 228–9, 238, 258, 300, 314, 323, 325
Poet, 33, 43, 50, 53, 61, 134, 186, 193, 196–7, 204–5, 218–9, 226, 228–9. 233–8, 240, 242, 245–7, 249, 251–4, 256–7, 259, 284, 301, 306, 309, 314, 316, 318, 330
Poets, 3, 32–3, 55, 118, 193, 196–7, 225–6, 230, 232–5, 239–41, 245–59, 284, 288, 292, 300, 306, 308–9, 315–16
Poetry, xv, xviii, 25, 30, 92, 114, 118, 159, 192, 197, 204–5, 221, 224–41, 243–5, 247–56, 258–9, 288, 306, 334
Princeton University Library, Princeton, USA, 18
Prophets, 2, 26, 40, 64, 212, 232, 243, 294, 301–3, 308
Prosody, 66, 159, 197, 229, 236–7, 258, 334
al-Qarāfa cemetery, 12
al-Qarṭājannī, 202, 229, 238
qaṣīda, 203–4, 227, 230, 235, 239, 242, 245, 258–9
Qāsim b. ʿAṭā' Allāh al-Miṣrī; Qāsim b. ʿAṭā' Allāh, 196–7, 235, 240, 246, 253, 256
al-Qīnālī, xii, xv
qirsh, 16, 58, 63
Qudāma bin Jaʿfar, 229, 238
Qur'ān; Qur'ānic verse, xvi, 2, 22, 25, 66, 200, 218–19, 223–4, 226, 247, 251–2, 292–3, 297, 299–301, 303, 306–8, 318, 323, 326–9
quṭb, 257, 292–3, 298, 317
rajaz, 204, 235–6, 241–2, 244–5, 258
Ramaḍān, 13, 21, 23, 50–2, 71–2, 105, 113, 177–8, 226, 232, 269, 273, 276, 280, 282
Rampur Raza Library, Rampur, India, 70
André Raymond, 45, 53, 292
Professor Stefan Reichmuth, xix, 17–18, 22, 172, 183, 186–7
Ernest Renan, 202
Amīr Riḍwān Aghā al-Faqārī, 34
Riḍwān Katkhudā; Riḍwān Katkhudā al-Jalfī; Amīr Riḍwān Katkhudā Ibrāhīm, 3, 14, 27, 246, 249, 257–8
Riḍwān al-Damanhūjī b. Muṣṭafā al-Damanhūjī copyist, 127, 167
Rifāʿa Rāfiʿ al-Ṭahṭāwī, 109, 202, 222, 259, 318, 336
Risāla bi-Khaṭṭ al-Jabartī fī 'l-'Amal bi 'l-Rub'; *Risāla fī 'l-'Amal bi 'l-Rub'*, 13
Risālat al-Mullā 'Iṣām, 215
rithā', 228, 237, 239, 243
riwāq al-Jabart, 6–7, 14
Riwāq al-Shawām, 12, 20
al-Rūmī; ʿAlī b. ʿAbd Allāh al-Rūmī; ʿAlī b. ʿAbdallah al-Rūmī, Maḥarram Efendī; ʿAbd Allāh Darwīsh al-Rūmī, 22, 80, 183, 250
al-Sādāt al-Wafā'iyya; al-Sādāt, 19, 56, 277, 306
Ṣaḥīḥ al-Bukhārī, 13
Saʿīd, 48
Saints, xviii, 32–3, 186, 232–3, 240–3, 249–50, 256, 265, 293, 302–3, 306, 308, 311, 315–17, 319, 324, 326

saj', 203–4, 224, 230
Ṣāliḥ 'Azab al-Jabalāwī, 83, 166
al-Malik al-Ṣāliḥ Ismā'īl, 264
Sāmir, 283-4
Shāfi'ī, 12, 47, 49-50, 114–15, 139, 187
Sultan Salīm I, 57, 297, 310
Sultan Salīm III, 32, 35, 37
Sālim al-Qayrawānī, 12
Sayyid Aḥmad, 12, 294
Sayyid al-Bakrī, 299
Fu'ād Sayyid, xviii, xix, 70
al-Sayyid Yūsuf, copyist, 126
scholars, xii–xiv, 3–4, 7, 11–12, 14, 18–20, 25–7, 30, 33, 35, 44, 46, 49–50, 53, 58, 62, 67, 92, 105, 108, 113–15, 162, 172, 177, 180–3, 186, 189–90, 193, 195–6, 198–202, 206, 208–10, 213, 215–16, 218–21, 225, 323–5, 239, 241, 243, 248, 250–1, 253, 259, 264–5, 268, 270, 275–6, 279–80, 284–9, 291–6, 298–301, 303–9, 311–21, 325, 329–31, 335–6
Reinhard Schulze, 199
Selly Oak College's Library, xix, 148
Shafi'ī, 12
Shāfi'ī b. Yūnis al-Fayyūmī, 114
Shams al-Dīn Muḥammad b. 'Abd al-Raḥmān al-Sakhāwī; al-Sakhāwī, 19, 300
Shams al-Dīn Muḥammad b. Sālim al-Ḥifnī or al-Ḥifnāwī, 201, 243, 291, 317–18
Shams al-Dīn Muḥammad Abu 'l-Anwār 'Abd al-Raḥmān, Ibn 'Ārifīn Sibṭ Banī 'l-Wafā, 250, 276, 303
Sharḥ Iḥyā' al-'Ulūm, 36, 114, 190
Sharḥ al-Qāmūs, xvi, 20, 114
sharī'a, xiii, 7, 10, 25–7, 30, 32, 51, 53, 179, 229, 231, 275, 291, 293–7, 299, 301, 304, 307, 309–10, 319–20, 323, 335
sharīf, 31, 143, 299, 314, 319
'Abd Allāh al-Sharqāwī, 30, 44, 114, 178, 187, 192
Maḥmūd al-Sharqāwī, 50, 70–1, 148
Shaykh al-Sharqāwī, 56, 114, 187
Shaykh al-Azhar, 6–7, 12, 20, 56, 268, 292–3
Shaykh al-Bakrī, 56, 177, 192, 228, 321
Shaykh al-Balad, 200
Shaykh al-sajjāda, 11, 293, 300
Shaykh al-Sajjāda al-Wafā'iyya Abu 'l-Imdād Aḥmad b. Ismā'īl al-Ḥusaynī, 11
shi'a, 225, 295, 322
shi'r, 224, 236–7, 240, 243, 246
Shubrā, 50
Sidī Abū Bakr, 13
Silk al-Durar, 172, 190, 220
Staatsbibliothek, Berlin, xx, 97
subjects, xiii, xviii, 10, 12–13, 24–7, 179, 207, 227, 241, 244–5, 251, 272, 275, 298–300, 306, 309–10, 319, 326
Ṣūfī, xiii, xviii, 2, 7, 13, 27, 32–3, 46, 53, 60, 102, 111, 195, 226, 230–3, 235–6, 239, 251, 256–7, 259, 280, 286, 288, 291–4, 296–306, 308–9, 311, 315–22

Ṣūfī leaders, xiii, 33, 231, 256, 293, 304, 314
Ṣūfī saints, xviii, 32, 232, 241–2, 249, 256, 306, 315–17
Sufīsm, 2–4, 46, 286, 305, 323–4, 326, 331
Sulaymān the Magnificent, 206, 297, 310
Amīr Sulaymān Bey al-Armanī, 251
Sulaymān al-Ḥalabī, 26, 34, 42, 47, 94, 109, 147, 150, 179
Sulaymān al-Jamal, 20
Sulaymān Salāma al-Sunbulāwī, copyist, 103, 167
Sulaymān b. ʿUmar al-Bajīrmī, 115
sunna, xiii, xvi, 2, 25, 293, 297, 301, 303, 307, 323, 326, 329
Sunni, 27, 32, 225-6, 262, 295, 304, 322, 324, 326
Supplement (*takmila*), 16–17
surriyya, 10–11
Syria; Syrian script, xviii, 31, 36, 64–5, 67, 79–80, 107–8, 173, 179, 201, 206, 210, 214–17, 220, 247, 299, 318, 330
Tadhkirat Dāwūd al-Anṭākī, 23, 219
Ṭāhir; Ṭāhir al-Ḥusayni; Ṭāhir Afandī al-Ḥusaynī; Muḥammad Ṭāhir Afandī, 15–16, 64, 80, 236, 345, 347–8, 350, 352
Ṭāhir Pasha, 286, 294
Tāj al-'Arūs, xvi, 18, 23, 36, 190, 234, 257, 278, 289, 306, 313–14, 335
Takhlīṣ al-Ibrīz fī Talkhīṣ Bārīs, 222, 336
taqwīm, 3, 24
tarājim, 188, 295
Tārīkh Ādāb al-Lugha al-'Arabiyya, 52, 147
Tārīkh al-Jabartī, 149
al-Tārīkh al-Kabīr li-Ahl al-Qarn al-Thānī 'Ashar; al-Tārīkh al-Kabīr, 18–19, 240
Tārīkhī Miṣr, Tarjama-'i Bahjat Afandī Ra'īs al-Aṭibbā', 31, 67
Tārīkh Muddat al-Faransīs bi-Miṣr, xiii, 5, 21, 28, 58, 60, 62, 79, 160, 162–3, 165, 176, 209, 211, 332–3
ṭarīq or *ṭarīqa*, 7, 13, 308, 311
Khedive Tawfīq, 26
Tawqīt, 10–11, 13, 314
Taymūr, 38, 127–8, 138, 167
ṭayyāra, 144
theatre, 228, 275–83
Thuʿaylib b. Sālim b. Tāmir, 114–15
Tuḥfat al-Nāẓirīn fī-man Waliya Miṣr min al-Wulāt wa 'l-Salāṭīn, 178
Turbat al-Ṣaḥrā', 52
'ulamā', xii–xiv, xvi, 2–6, 25–7, 29, 31–3, 35, 45, 55–6, 65, 114, 178, 182, 184, 186, 201–2, 219, 227, 231–2, 239, 241, 243, 268–70, 275–6, 278, 284–6, 288, 291–9, 302–4, 306–11, 314–15, 317–23, 326–9, 331–2, 334–5
ūlū 'l-amr (leaders [of the Muslim community]), 294, 297, 308
'Ulūm 'aqliyya, 3, 23, 293, 300, 314, 329
'Ulūm naqliyya, 3, 23, 293, 300, 314, 329
ʿUmar ; ʿUmar Makram; ʿUmar Makram al-Naqīb; ʿUmar Effendi al-Naqīb, 31, 220, 294, 299
ʿUmar al-Dasūqī, 77, 159
ʿUmar b. Khaṭṭāb; ʿUmar al-Khaṭṭāb copyist, 86–7, 99, 167–8, 263
Umayyad, 205, 225, 276, 304, 325

umma, 223–5, 294
Main Library, University of Birmingham, Birmingham, England, xiv, xix, 149, 334
University Library, University of Leeds, Leeds, England, xiv, xx, 85
urjūza, 204, 235–6, 241, 245
ʿUthmān Chelebi, 251
ʿUthmān b. Salīm al-Wardānī, 12
P. Sj. van Koningsveld, 64
verses, 25, 72, 93–4, 96, 139, 142, 197, 203–4, 214, 224–5, 230, 232–6, 239–43, 245, 247–58, 262, 284, 296, 300, 314
Von Landberg, 62
wafā' al-Nīl, 265–6, 268–9, 273–4, 280
Wafā'iyya, 11, 14, 19, 32, 56, 203, 277, 306, 326
Wahhābī proclamation, 34, 40–1, 78, 83, 85, 87–8, 91, 109, 111, 115, 118, 122, 131, 141, 146–7, 151, 190
Wahhābīs, 2, 53, 66, 111, 191, 311, 316, 324
waliy, pl. *awliyā'*, 249, 292–3, 302
waqf, xiv, 17, 51, 167, 279, 299, 319–20
waṣf, 228, 230, 237
al-Washy wa 'l-Ṭirāz fī Fatḥ al-Ḥijāz, 174, 191
Western reforms, 31–2, 259
Wizārat al-Awqāf, 42, 137, 142–3
Writers, 3, 9, 55, 118, 196, 225, 227, 232–4, 250, 252–3, 257, 259, 263, 288, 306
General Yaʿqūb al-Qubṭī, 274
Yemen, 143, 172, 252
Yūsuf, 30, 58
Amīr Yūsuf Bey al-Muslimīn, 184–5
Yūsuf Pasha qv Yūsuf Ḍiyā Pasha, 30–1, 44, 58, 67, 177, 208, 307
Yūsuf al-Ḥifnī, 13
Yūsuf al-Malwānī, xii
Yūsuf Ṣalāḥ al-Dīn, 30, 58
Yūsuf al-Sinbilāwī, 214
al-Zabīdī; Murtaḍā al-Zabīdī; Murtaḍā al-Zabīdī al-Ḥanafī; Muḥammad b. Muḥammad ʿAbd al-Razzāq, Murtaḍā al-Ḥusaynī al-Zabīdī; Muḥammad Murtaḍā al-Zabīdī, xvi, 3–4, 12–20, 23–4, 28–31, 33–4, 36–7, 44–6, 53–4, 57, 61–2, 64, 80, 114, 166, 172–3, 176, 179, 180–1, 183–90, 193, 196, 198, 202, 205, 234–5, 242, 251–2, 256–7, 278, 289, 295–6, 306, 312–14, 323, 331–2, 335
al-Ẓāhir Baybars, 227, 310
zajal, 239, 256
al-Zakiyya, xii, 17, 42, 52, 137–9, 141–5, 147, 152–4, 159–60, 166–8
al-Zakiyya Library, 42, 138, 143
Jurjī Zaydān, 42, 49, 52, 137–8, 146, 160
Zayn al-Dīn Qāsim al-ʿIbādī, 181
ẓulm, 27, 178, 305, 309

Plates

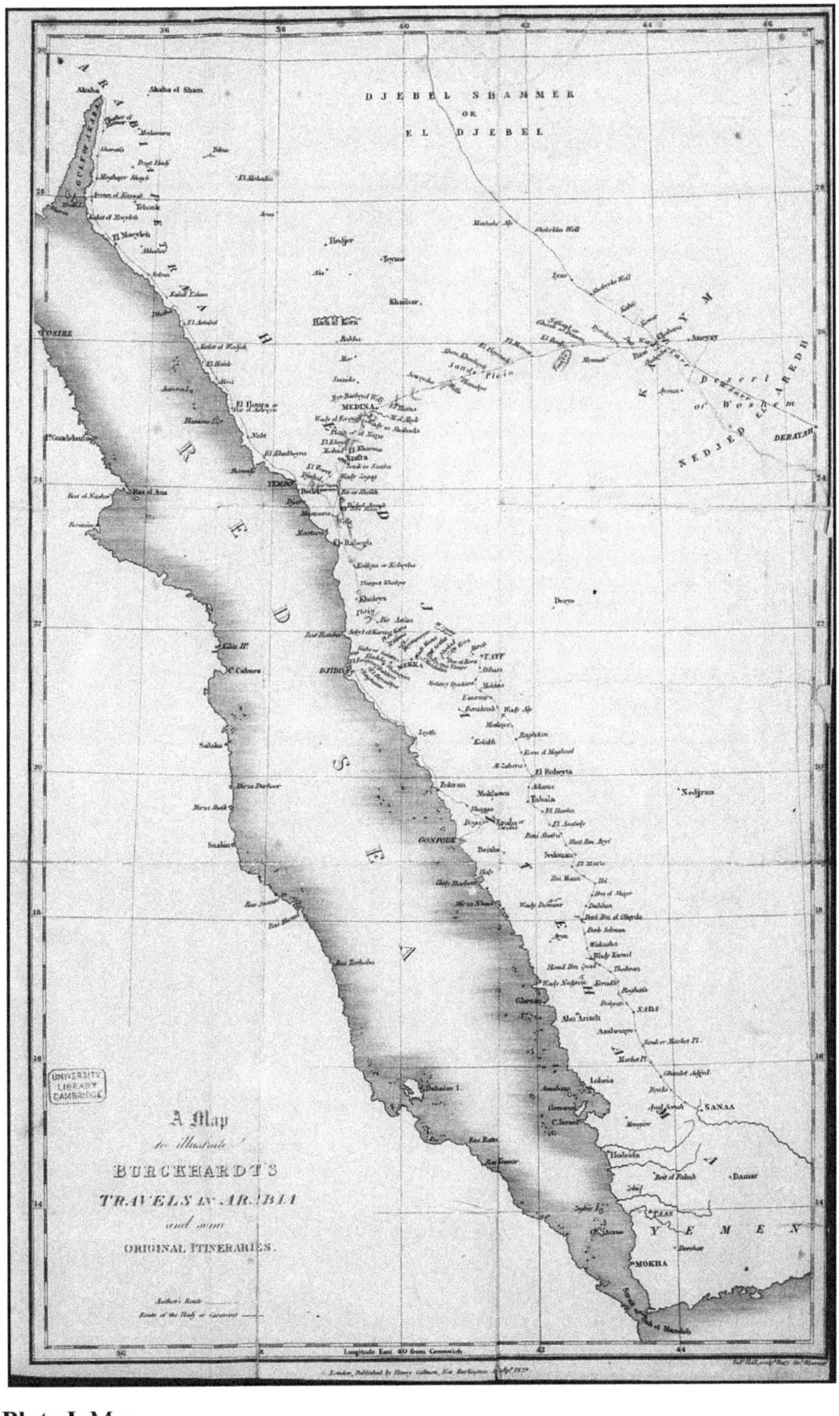

Plate I. Map

al-Jabarti, autograph of Mudda, Leiden MS. no. 61, ff. 1b-2a with the author's additions in the margins.

Plate II. Mudda Leiden 1b-2a

al-Jabarti, autograph of Mudda, Leiden MS. no. 61, f. 26b, with the autho additions in the margins.

Plate III. Mudda Leiden 26b

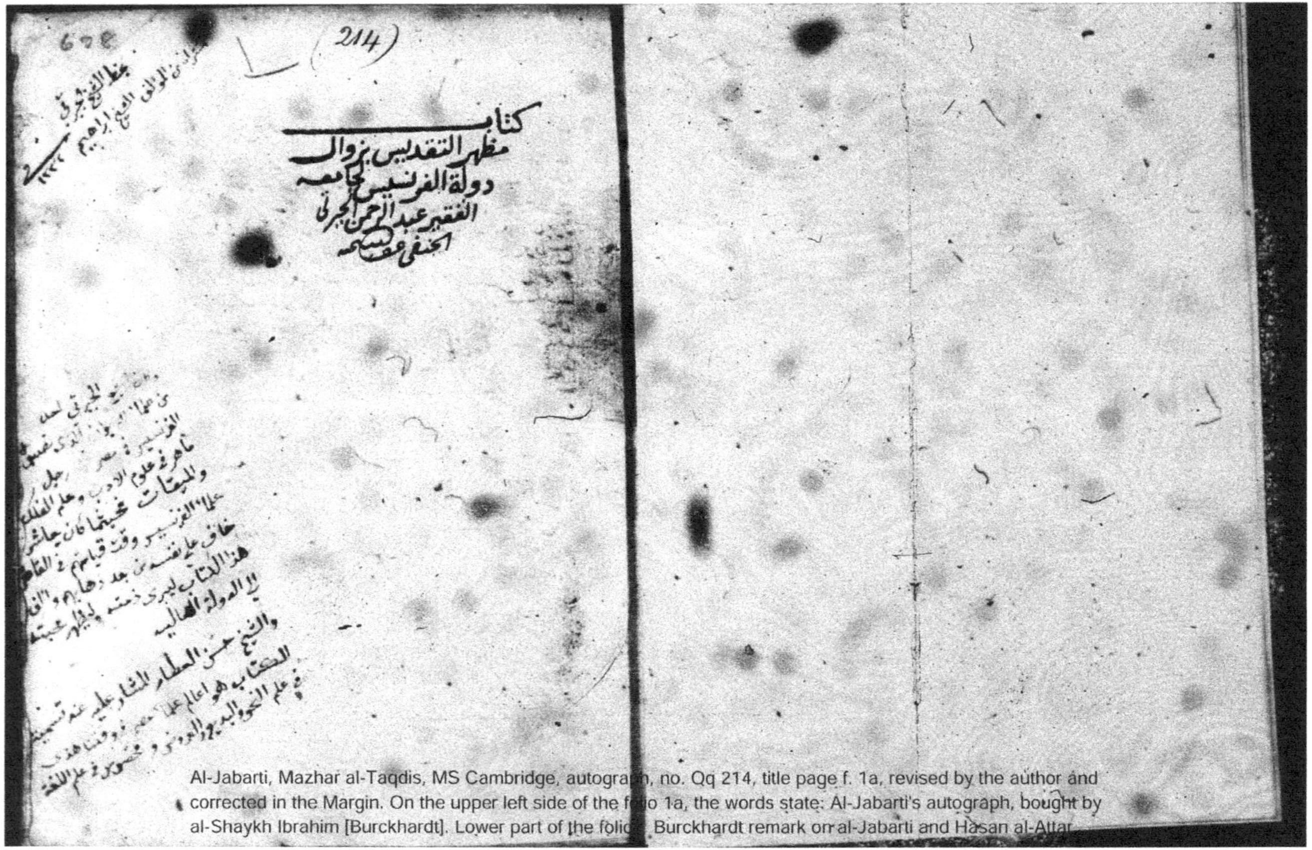

Al-Jabarti, Mazhar al-Taqdis, MS Cambridge, autograph, no. Qq 214, title page f. 1a, revised by the author and corrected in the Margin. On the upper left side of the folio 1a, the words state: Al-Jabarti's autograph, bought by al-Shaykh Ibrahim [Burckhardt]. Lower part of the folio Burckhardt remark on al-Jabarti and Hasan al-Attar.

Plate IV. Mazhar Cam Title

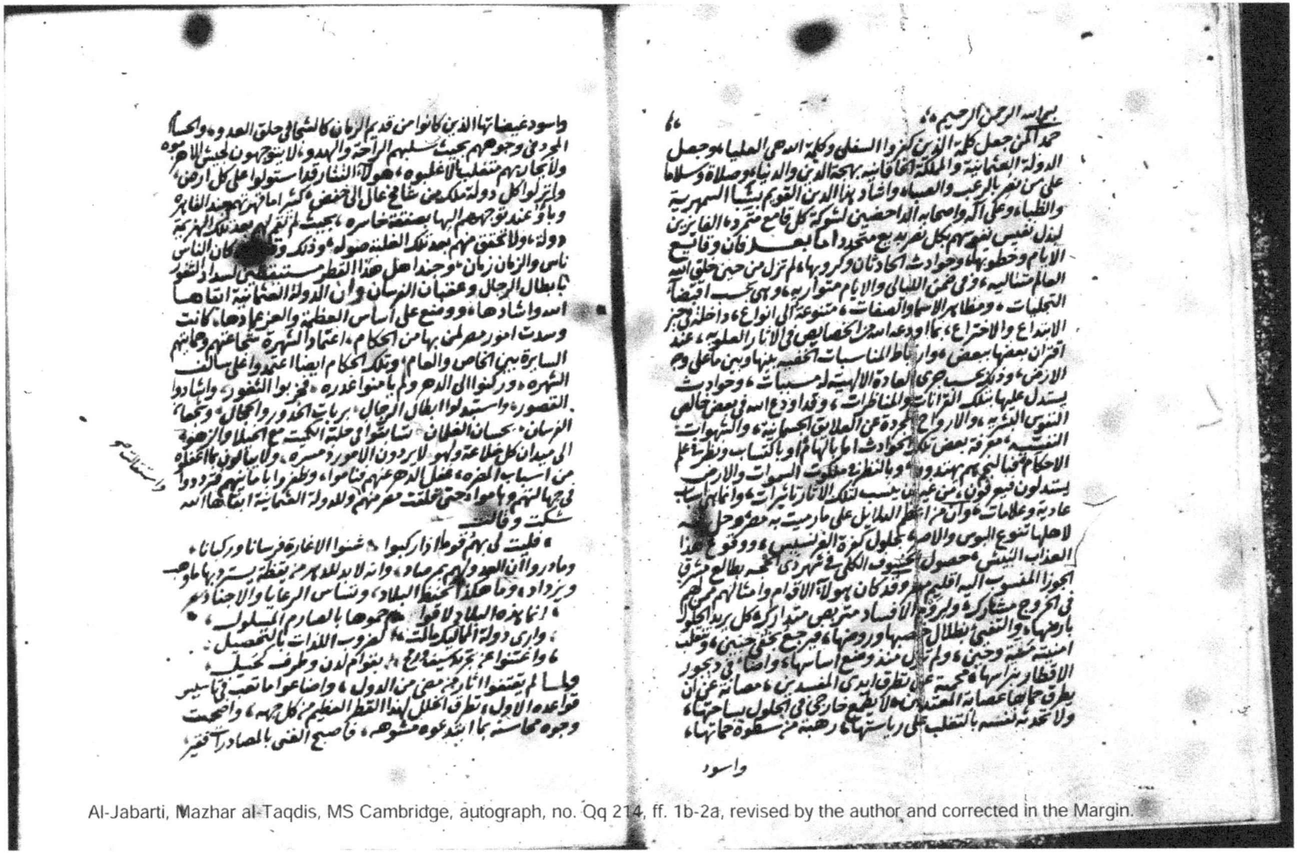

Al-Jabarti, Mazhar al-Taqdis, MS Cambridge, autograph, no. Qq 214, ff. 1b-2a, revised by the author and corrected in the Margin.

Plate V. Mazhar Cam 1b-2a

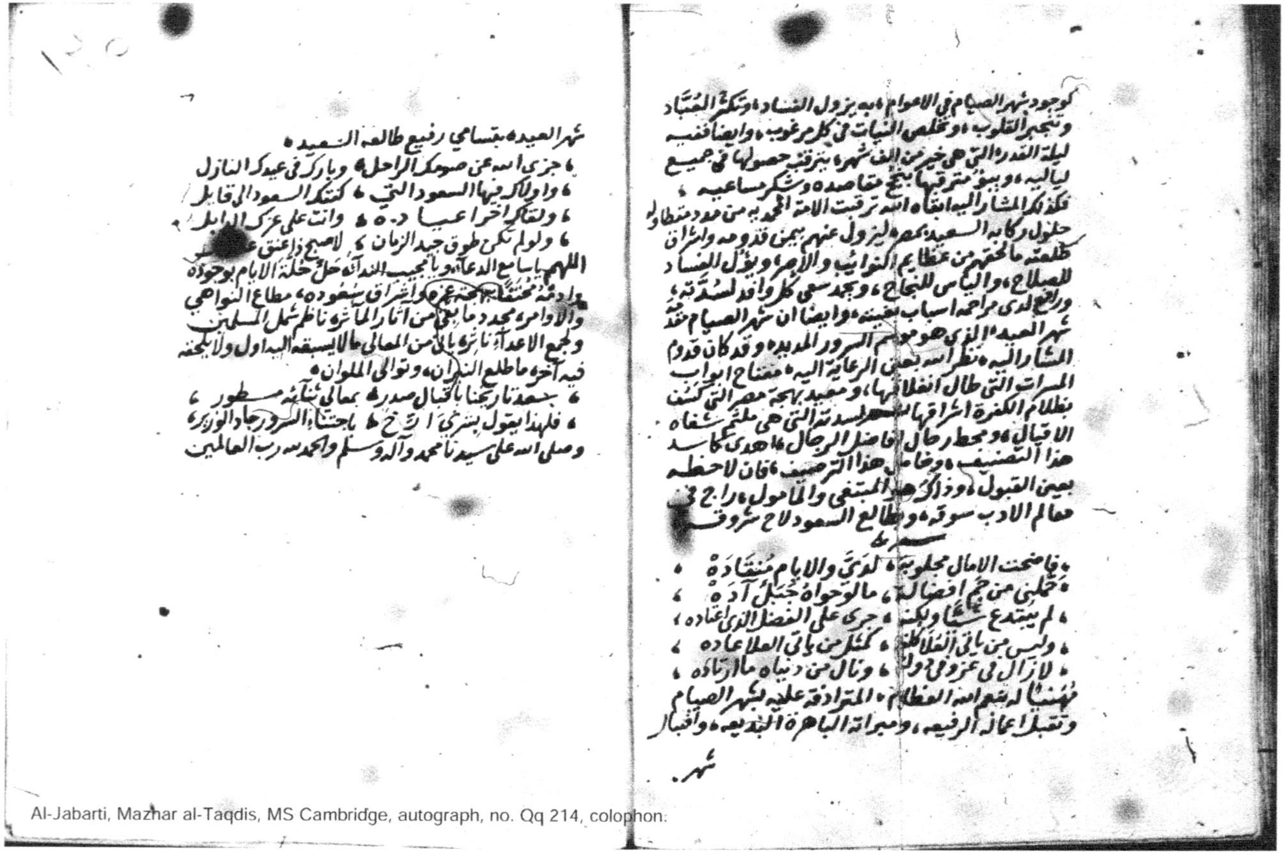

Al-Jabarti, Mazhar al-Taqdis, MS Cambridge, autograph, no. Qq 214, colophon.

Plate VI. Mazhar Cam colophon

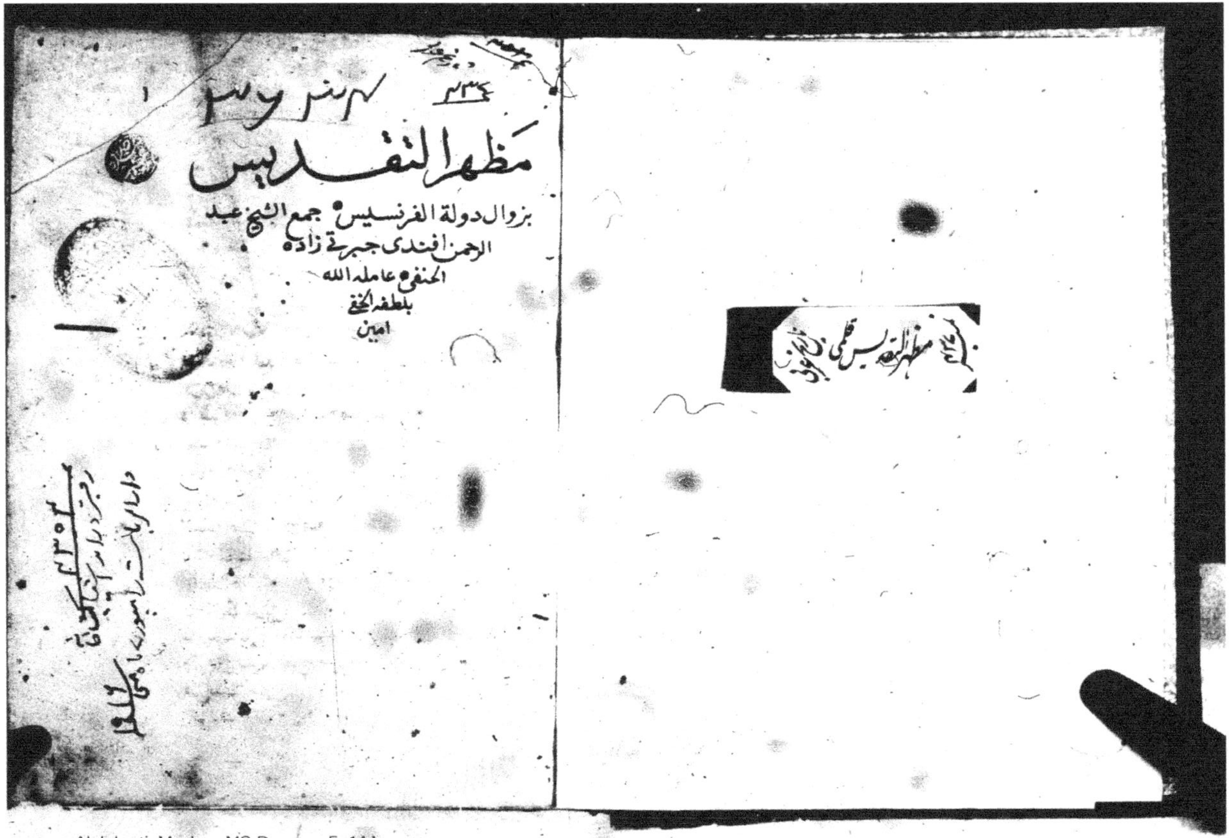

Al-Jabarti, Mazhar, MS Rampur, F. 1A

Plate VII. Mazhar Ram title la

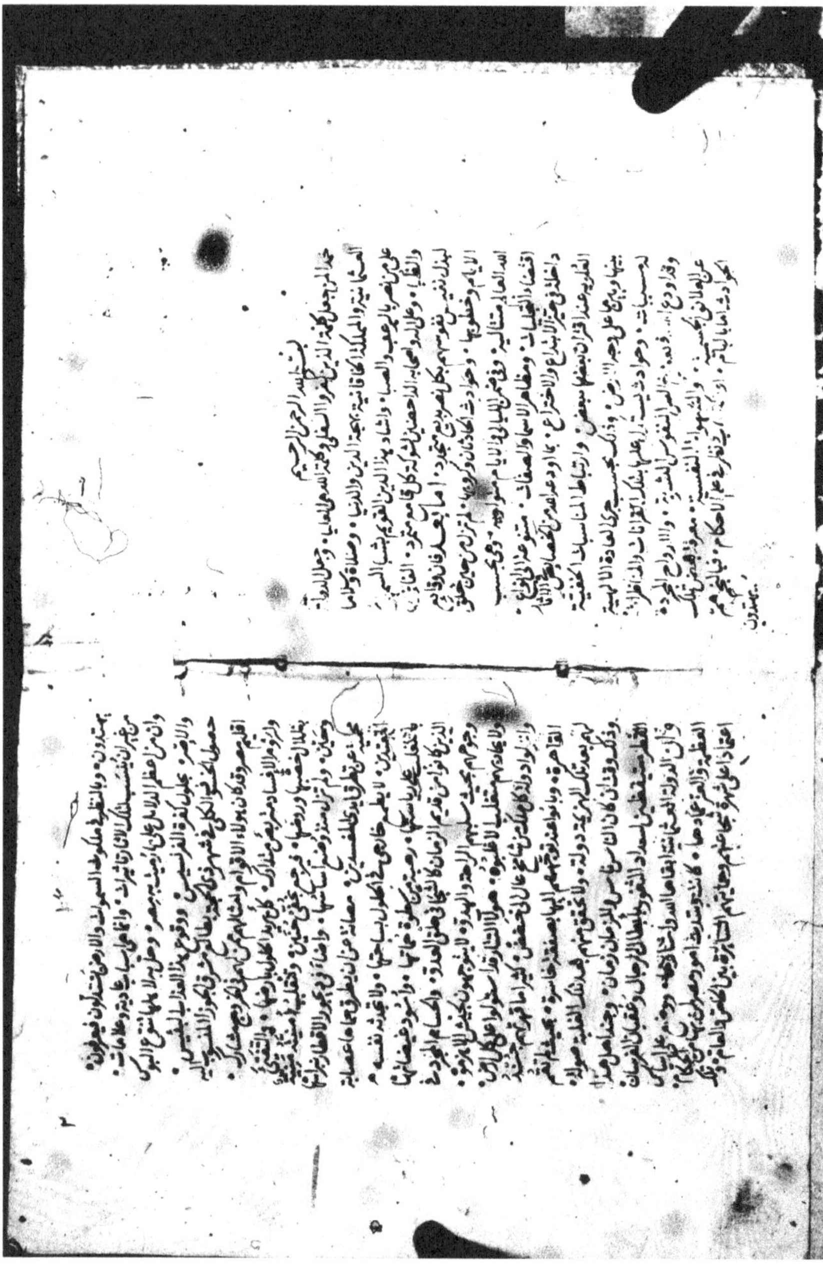

Plate VIII. Mazhar Ram title lb-2[a]

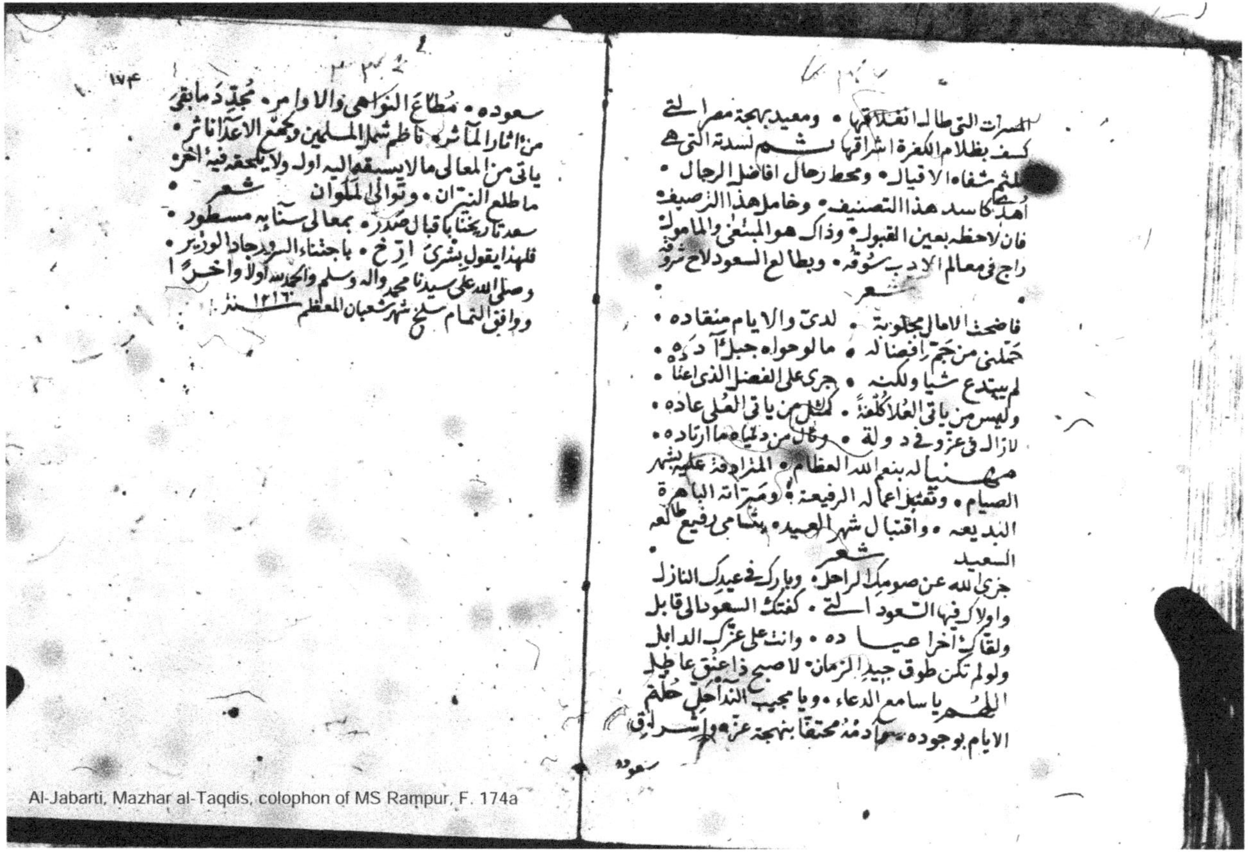

Al-Jabarti, Mazhar al-Taqdis, colophon of MS Rampur, F. 174a

Plate IX. Mazhar Ram title colophon

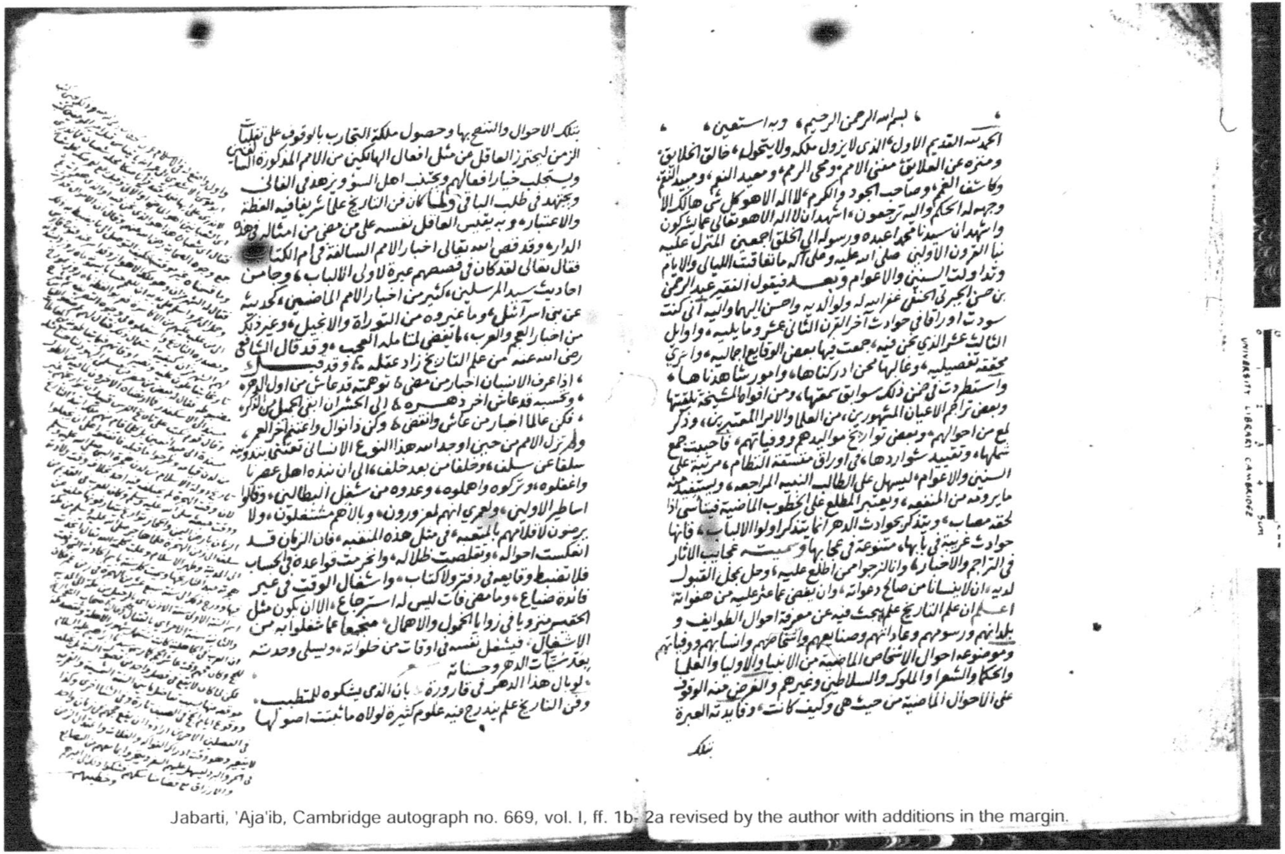

Plate X. ʿAja'ib Cam vol. I 1b-2a

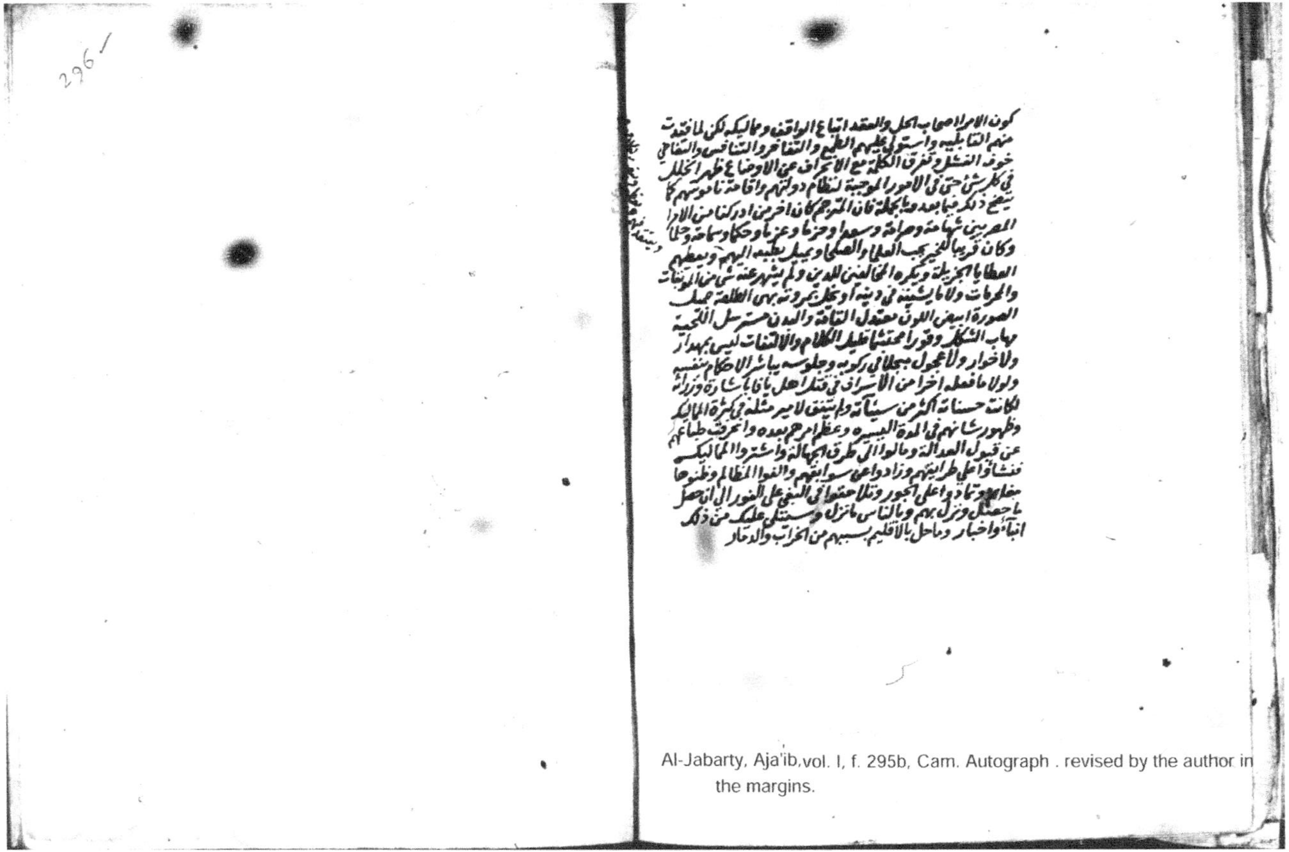

كون الامرا اصحاب الحل والعقد اتباع الواقف ومماليكه لكن لما فقدت
منهم القابليه واستولى عليهم الطمع والتفاخر والتنافس والتفاخي
خوف التشتل وتفرق الكلمة مع الانحراف عن الاوضاع ظهر الخلل
في كل شي حتى في الامور الموجبة لنظام دولتهم واقامة ناموسهم كما
نبين ذلك فيما بعد وبالجملة فان المترجم كان اخر من ادركناه من الامرا
المصريين شهامة وصرامة وسعدا وحزما وعزما وحكما وسماحة وحلما
وكان قريبا للخير يحب العلما والصلحا ويميل بطبعه اليهم ويعطيهم
العطايا الجزيلة ويكره المخالفين للدين ولم يشتهر عنه شي من الموبقات
والمحرمات ولا ما يشينه في دينه او يخل بمروته بهي الطلعة جميل
الصورة ابيض اللون معتدل القامة والبدن مسترسل اللحية
مهاب الشكل وقورا محتشما قليل الكلام والالتفات ليس بمهذار
ولا خوار ولا عجول مبجلا في ركوبه وجلوسه يباشر الاحكام بنفسه
ولولا ما فعله اخرا من الاسراف في قتل اهل يافا باشارة وزرائه
لكانت حسناته اكثر من سيئاته ولم يتفق لامير مثله في كثرة المماليك
وظهور شانهم في المدة اليسيرة وعظم امرهم بعده وانحرفت طباعهم
عن قبول العدالة ومالوا الى طرق الجهالة واشتروا المماليك
فنشاوا على طرايقهم وزادوا عن سوابقهم والفوا المظالم وظنوها
مغانم وتمادوا على الجور وتلاحقوا في البغي على الفور الى ان حصل
ما حصل ونزل بهم وبالناس ما نزل وسيتلى عليك من ذلك
انباء واخبار وما حل بالاقليم بسببهم من الخراب والدمار

Al-Jabarty, Aja'ib, vol. I, f. 295b, Cam. Autograph . revised by the author in the margins.

Plate XI. ʿAja'ib Cam vol. I, 295b

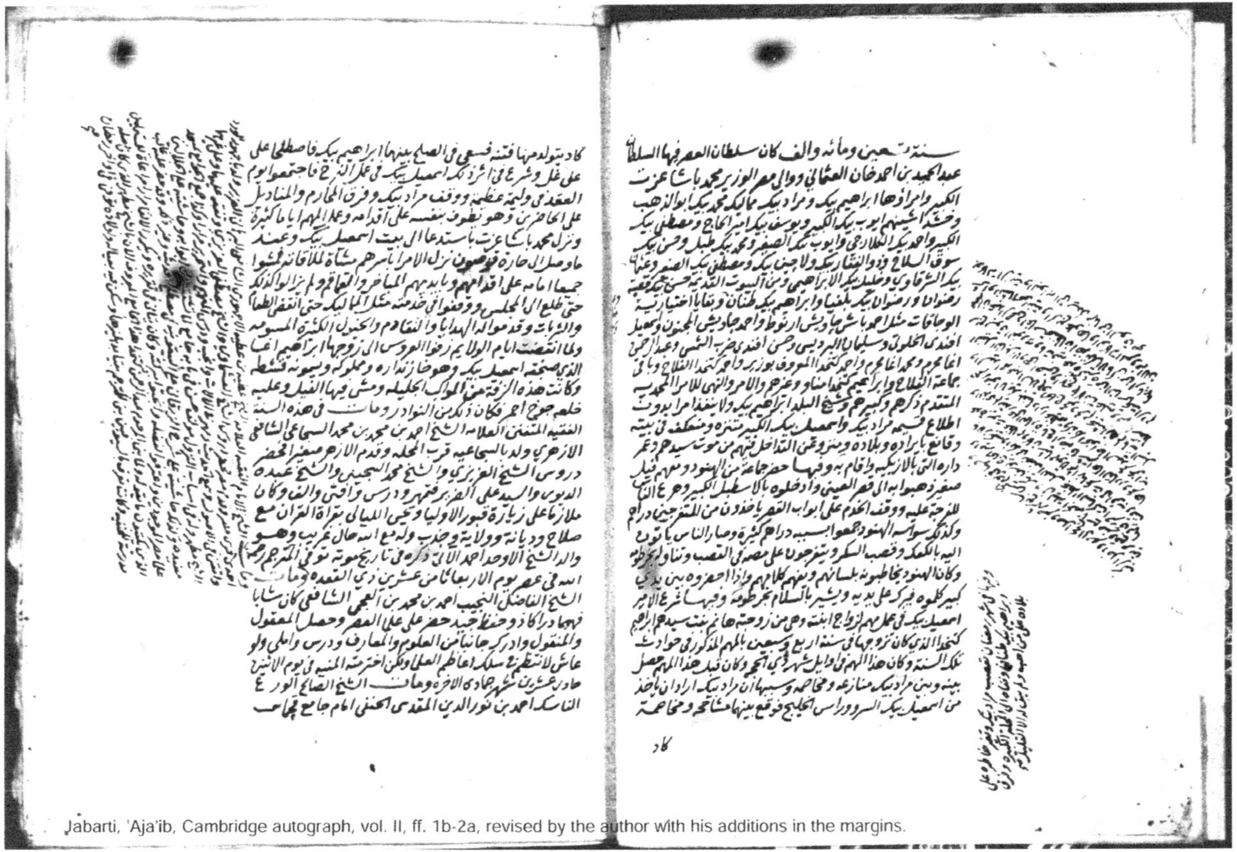

Jabarti, 'Aja'ib, Cambridge autograph, vol. II, ff. 1b-2a, revised by the author with his additions in the margins.

Plate XII. ʿAja'ib Cam vol. II, 1b-2ª

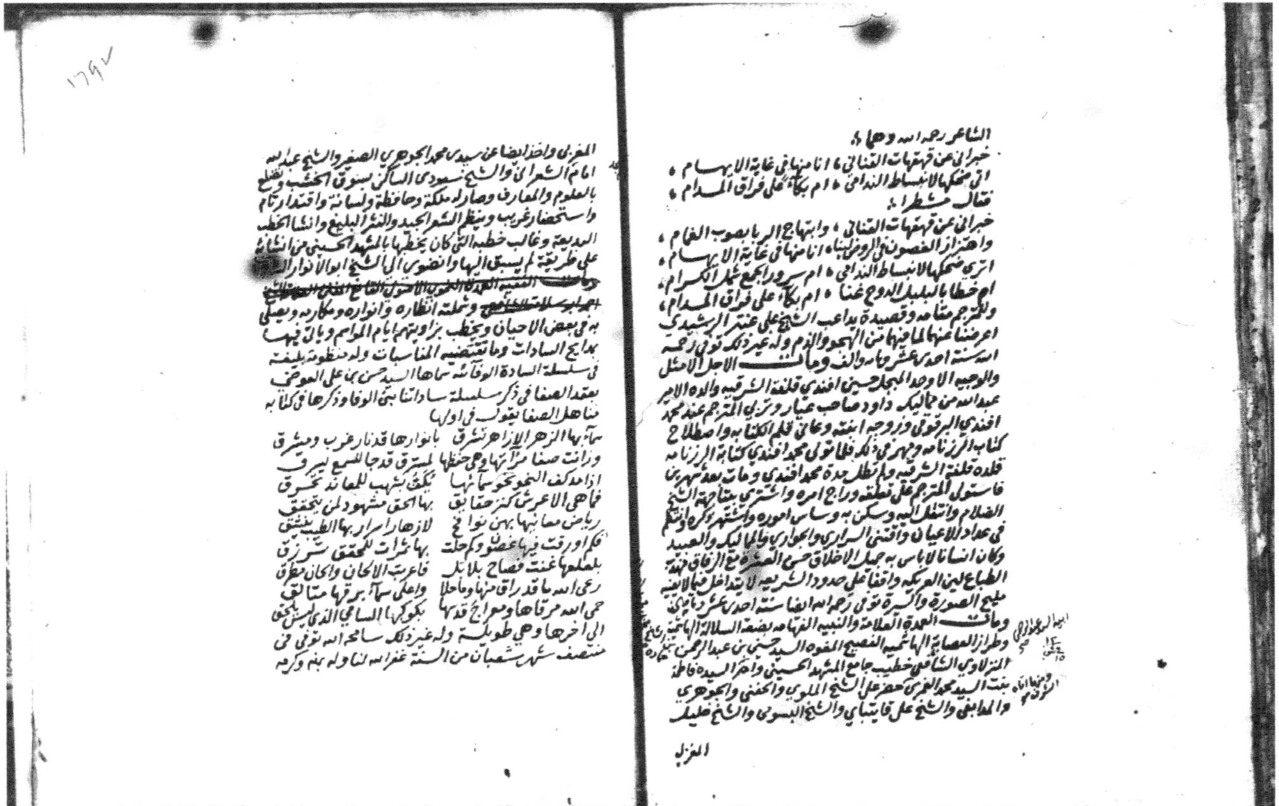

Jabarti, 'Aja'ib, Cambridge autograph, the end of vol. II, f. 179a, = Bulaq, p. 275 , with the author's additions in the margins.

Plate XIII. ʿAja'ib Cam vol. II, 179[a]

Plate XIV. ʻAja'ib Cam vol. III, 1b-2[a]

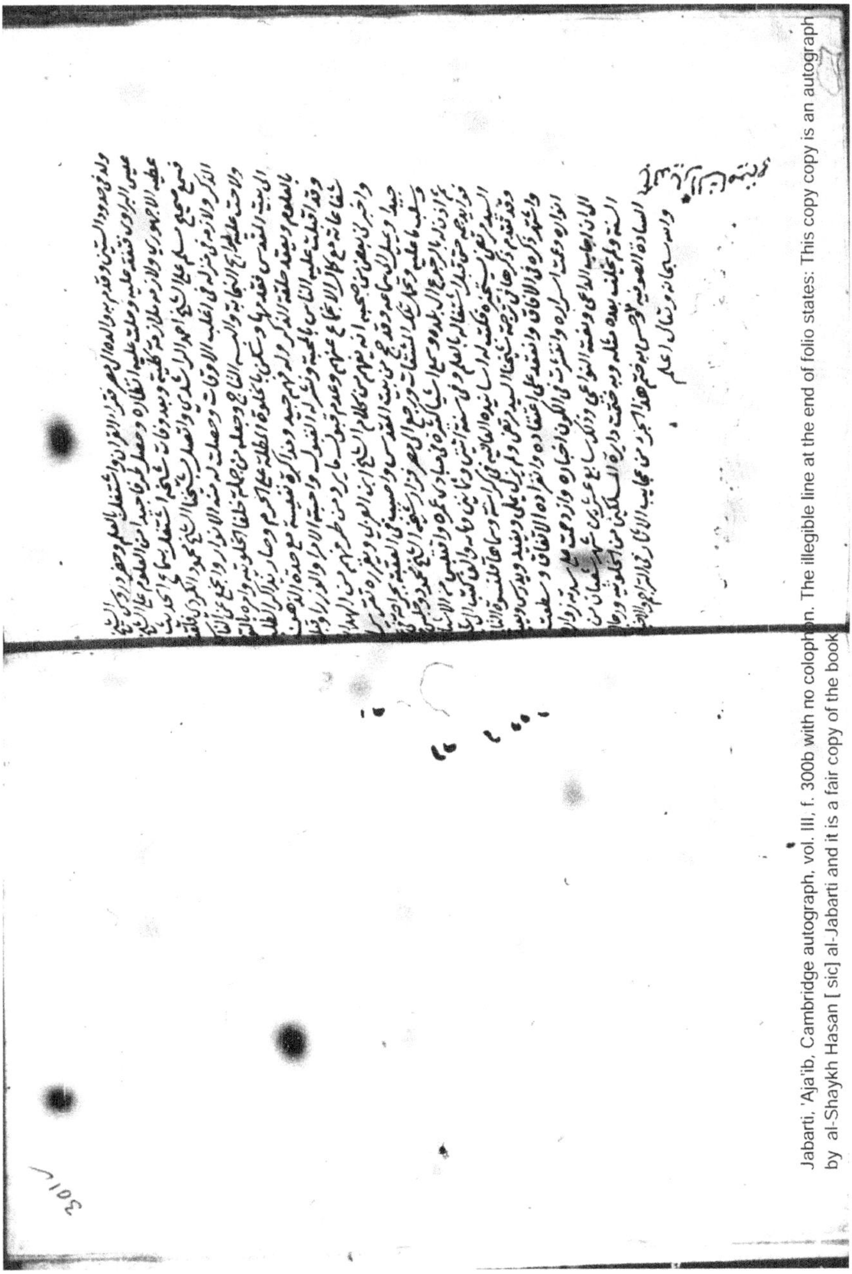

Jabarti, 'Aja'ib, Cambridge autograph, vol. III, f. 300b with no colophon. The illegible line at the end of folio states: This copy copy is an autograph by al-Shaykh Hasan [sic] al-Jabarti and it is a fair copy of the book

Plate XV. 'Aja'ib Cam vol. III, 300b

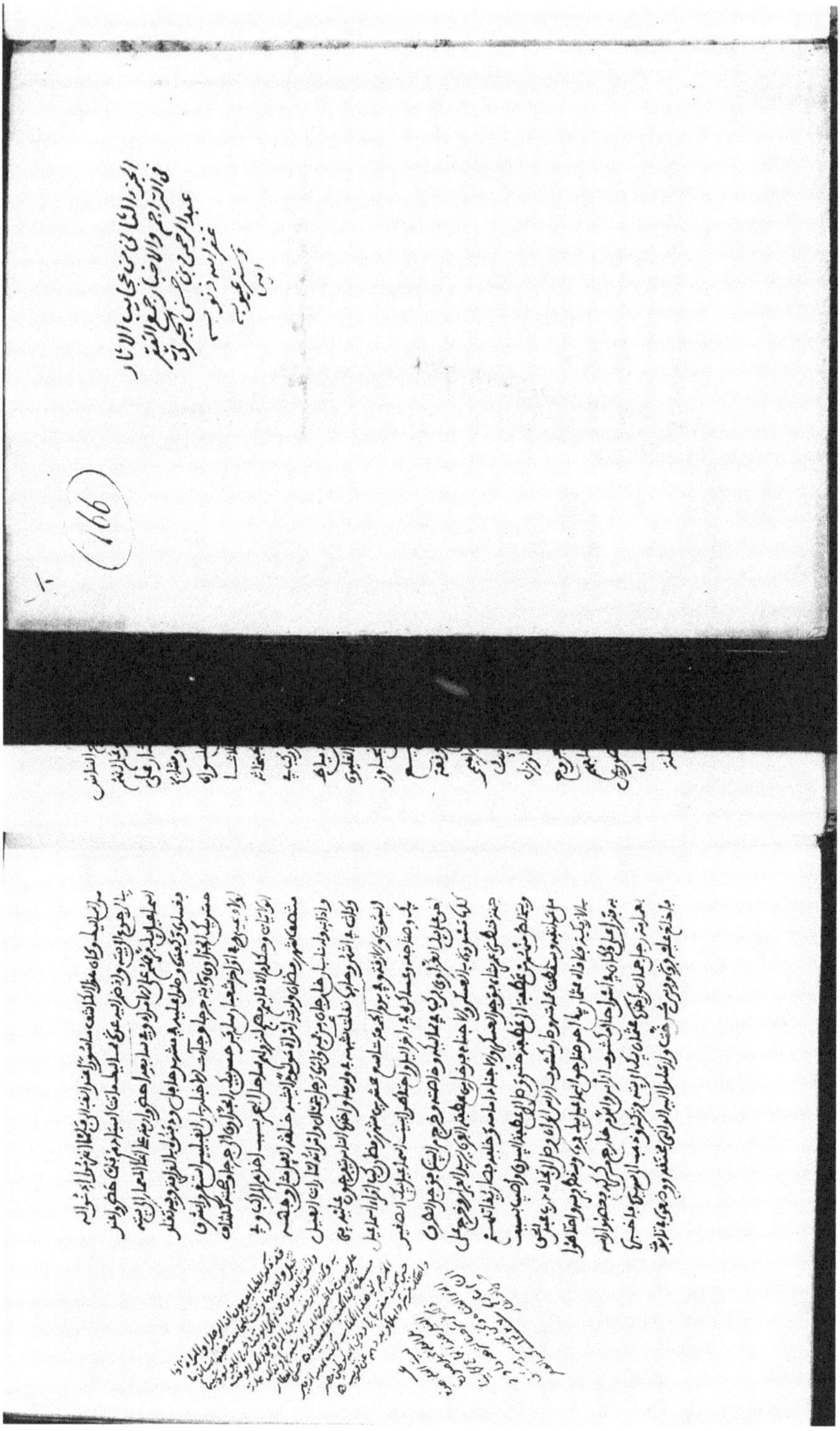

Plate XVI. ʻAjaʼib Sell vol. IV, 1b-2a

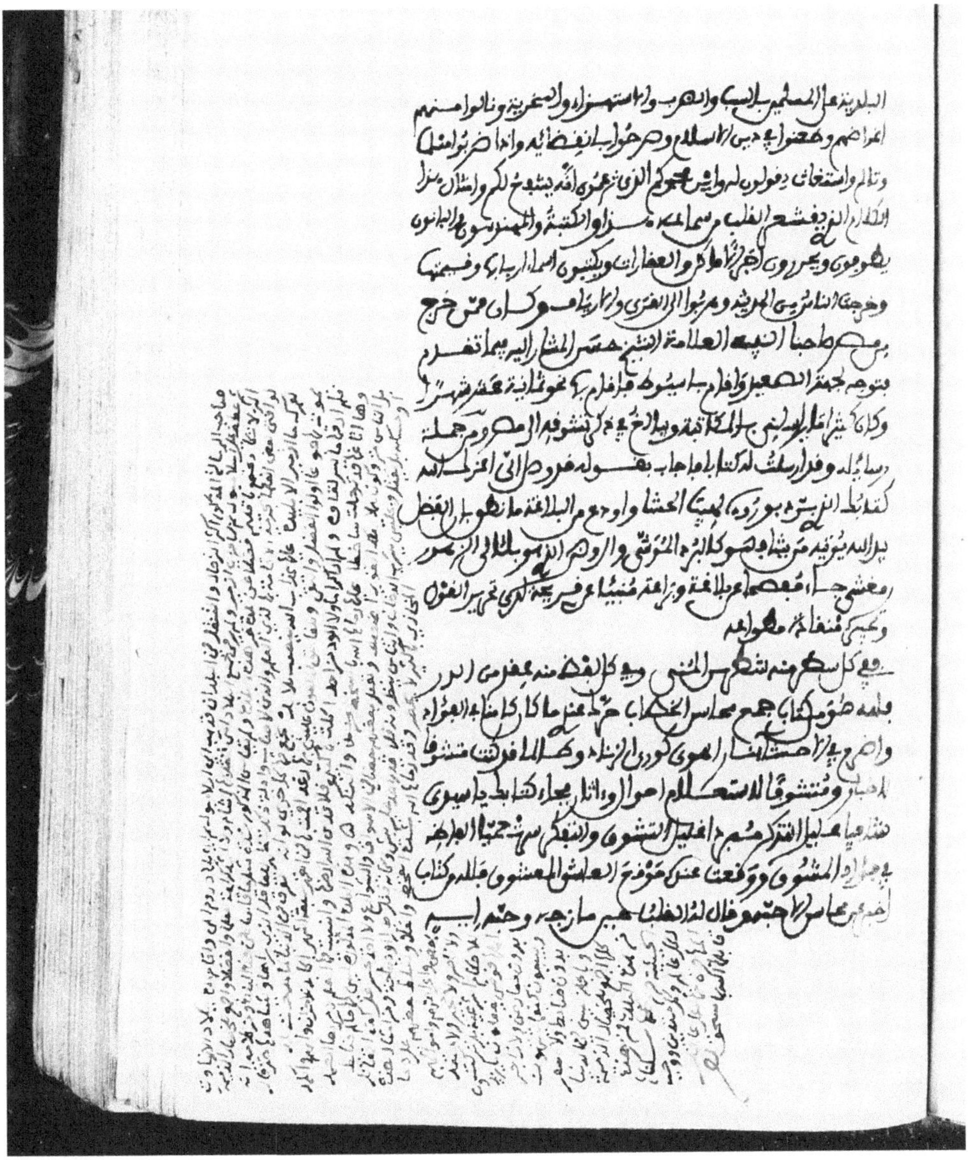

Plate XVII. ʿAja'ib Sell vol. IV, colophon

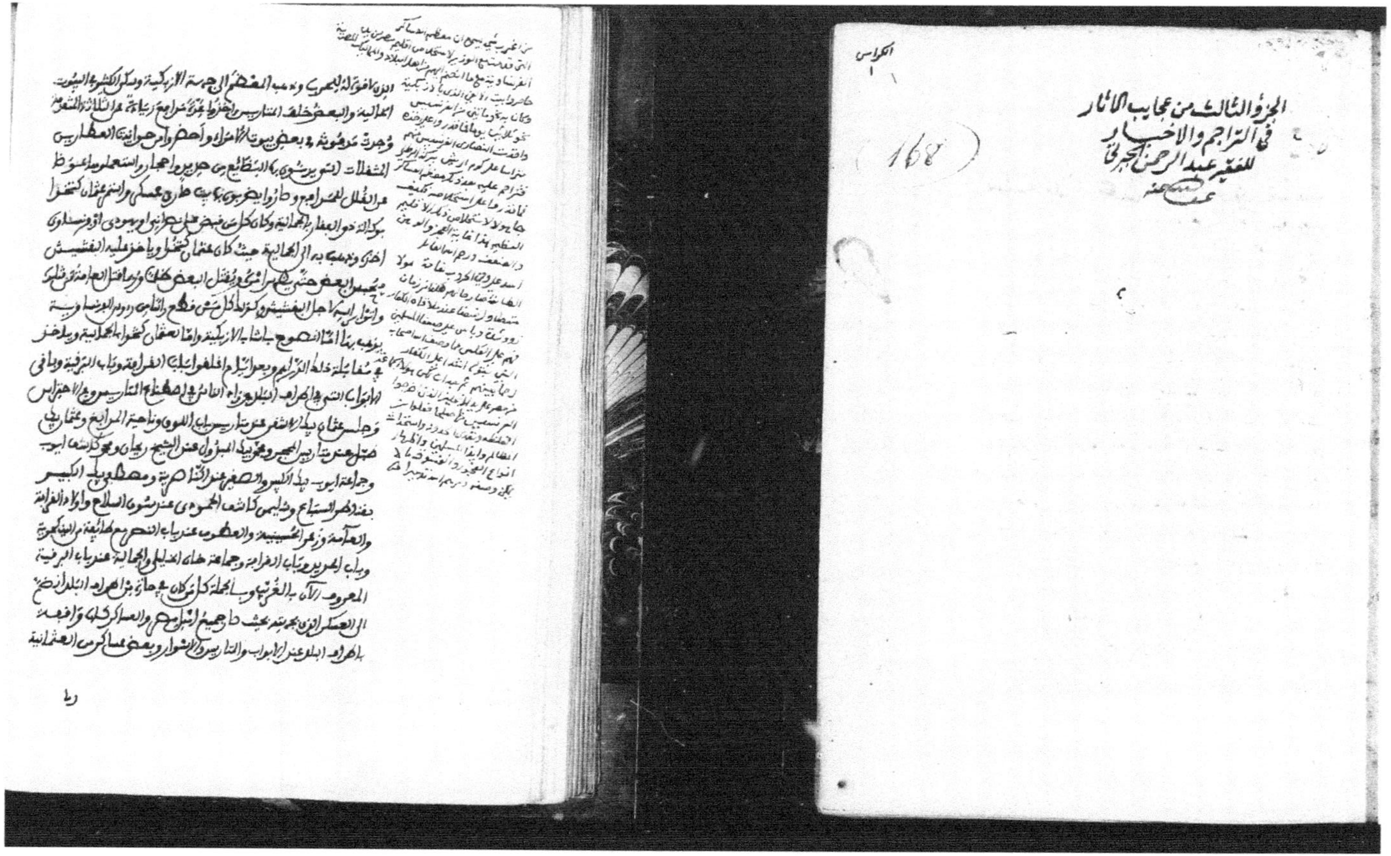

Plate XVIII. 'Aja'ib Cam vol. III, Magh, 1a

Plate XIX. ‘Aja’ib Ber vol. I , 1b-2a

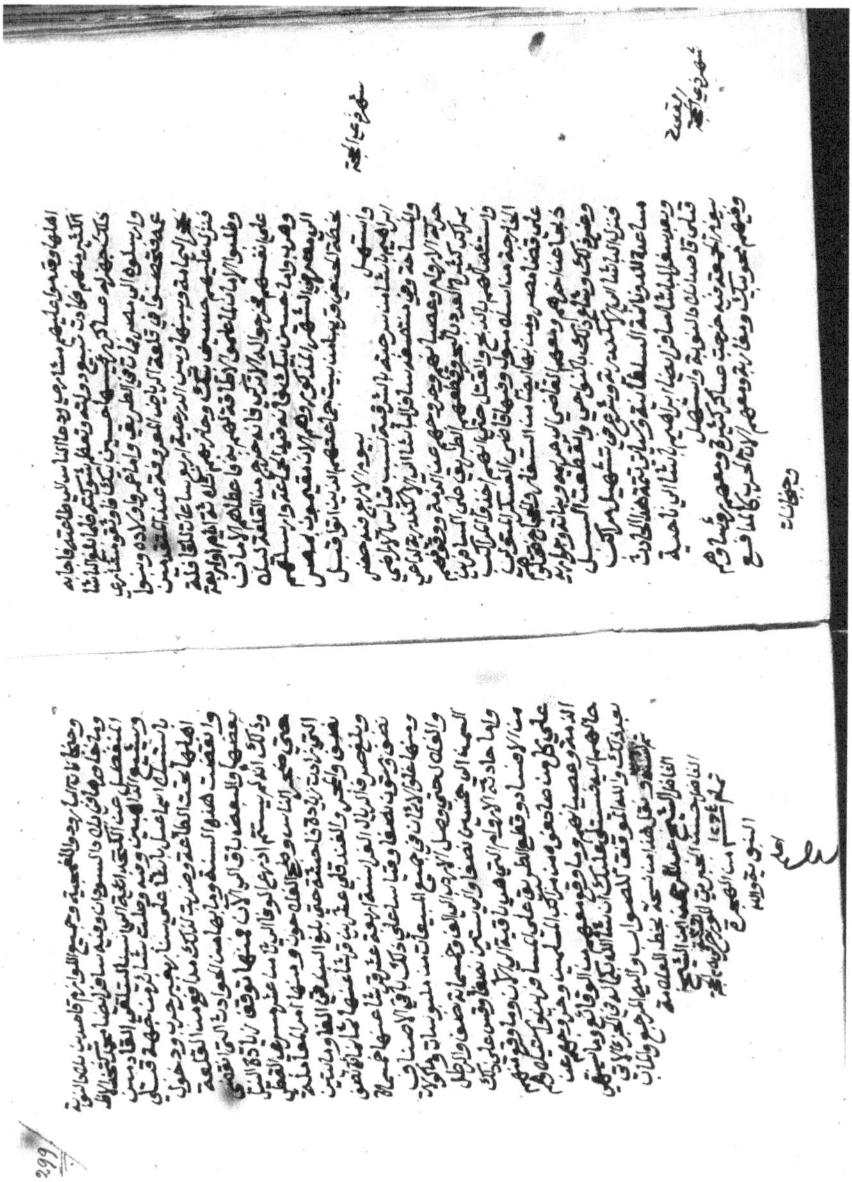

Plate XX. ʻAjaʼib Ber vol. I, 299a

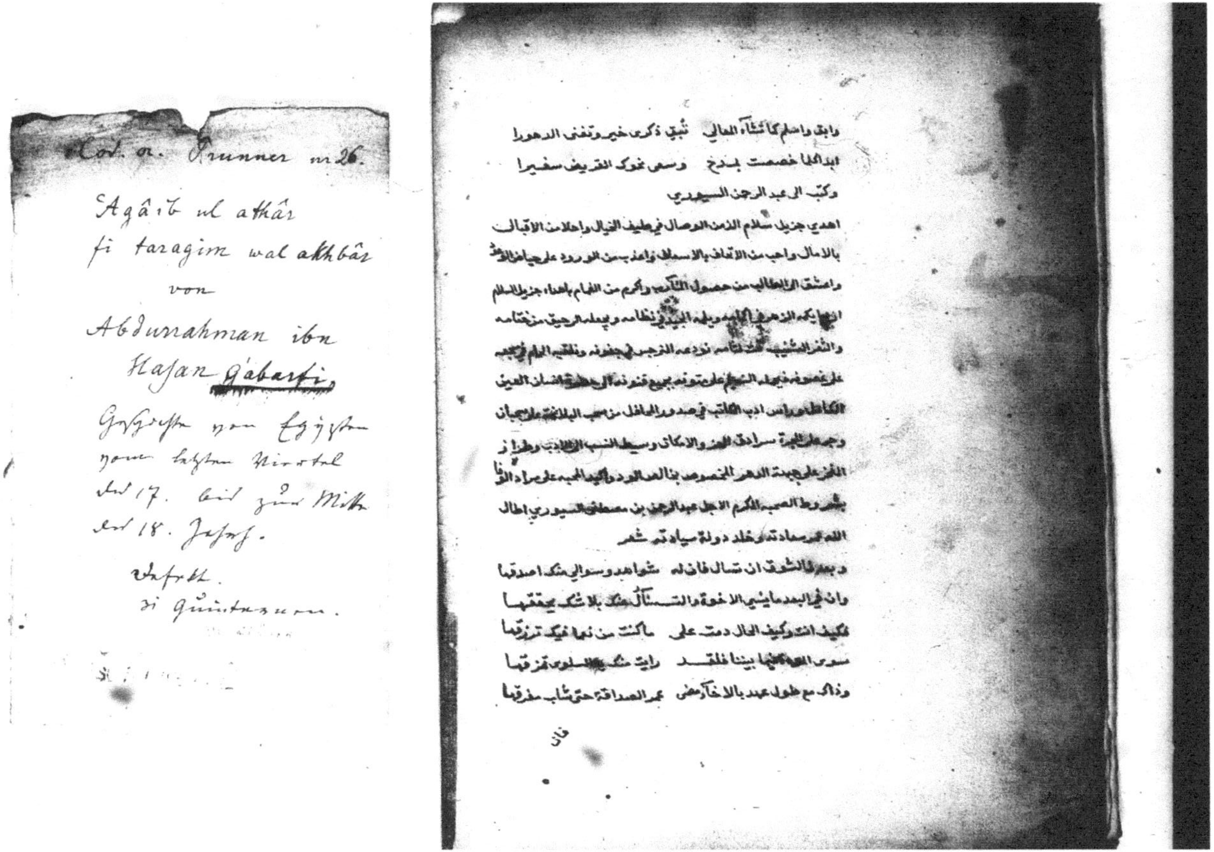

Plate XXI. ʿAja'ib Ber? vol. I, missing folios

Al-Jabarti, 'Aja'ib, vol: IV, ff. 1a, Berlin Or. qu.660: The MS was bought from a book-shop owner in Cairo, 16 Sha'ban, 1292 H.

Plate XXII. ʿAja'ib Ber vol. IV, 1a

Al-Jabarti, 'Aja'ib, vol. IV, ff. 1b - 2a, Berlin Or. qu.660

Plate XXIIII. 'Aja'ib Ber vol. IV, 1b-2a

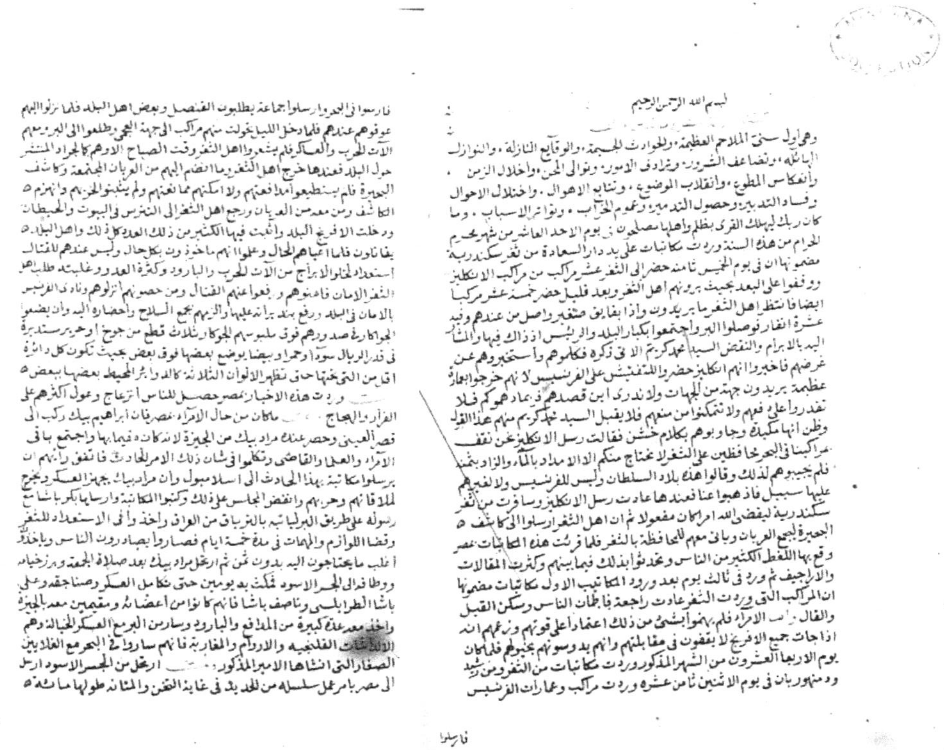

Al-Jabarti, 'Aja'ib, vol. III, ff.1b-2a Mingana Manuscript Collection, Selly Oak Colleges Library, Birmingham, no. 910 .

Plate XXIV. ʿAja'ib Sell vol. III, 1b-2a

بالحوم وصار يذاكر الطلبة بالعلوم ويعقد حلقة الذكر وله فهم جيد مع حدة الذهن
واقبلت عليه الناس بالمحبة ونيل اليه القلوب عند الامراء والوزراء وقبلت شفاعته
مع عدم الانجماع عنهم وعدم قبول هداياهم [illegible] بعض من صحبه انه يفهم من
كلام الشيخ ابن العربي ويقرره تقريرا جيدا ويميل الى سماعه وحج من بيت المقدس
واصيب في العقبة بجراحة في عضده وسلب ما عليه وتحمل تلك المشقات ورجع
الى مصر فزار شيخه الشيخ محمود وجلس معه ثم اذن له في الرجوع الى بلده وسمع
اشيا كثيرة في مبادي عمره واقتبس من الاشياخ فوائد جمة حتى قبل اشتغاله
بالعلم في ١١٨٢ اثنين وثمانين ومائة والف كتب الى الشيخ السيد مرتضى
يستجيزه فكتب له اسانيده العالية في كراسة وسماها تلنسوه التاج وقد
تقدم ذكرها في ترجمة السيد مرتضى ولم يزل يملي ويفيد ويدرس ويعيد
واشتهر في الافاق وانعقد على اعتقاده الاتفاق وسطعت انواره وعمت
اسراره وانتشرت اخباره وازدحمت على سدته زواره الى ان اجاب الداعي
ونعته النواعي وذلك سابع عشرين شهر شعبان من السنة ولم يخلف
بعده مثله وبه ختمت دائرة المسلكين من الخلوتية
ورجال السادة الصوفية وبه حسن ختم
الجزء الثالث من كتاب عجائب
الآثار في التراجم والأخبار
لغاية سنة عشرين
ومائتين وألف
من الهجرة
النبوية
م

Al-Jabarti, 'Aja'ib, the colophon of vol. III, Mingana Manuscript Collection, Selly C Colleges Library, Birmingham, no. 910 .

Plate XXV. ʿAja'ib Sell vol. III, colophon

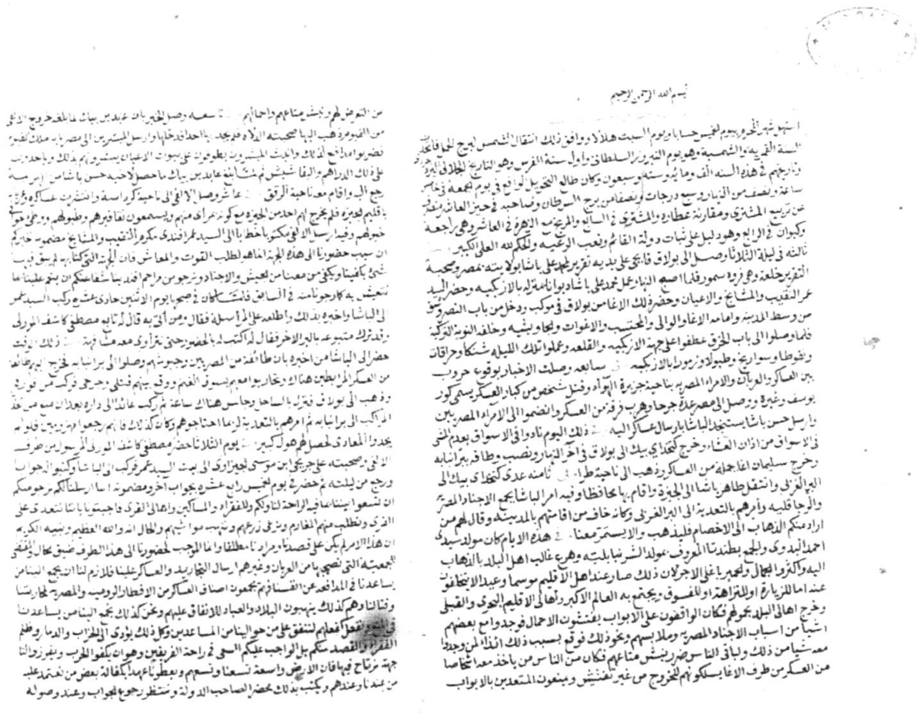

Al-Jabarti, 'Aja'ib, vol. IV, ff.1b-2a Mingana Manuscript Collection, Selly Oak Colleges Library, Birmingham, no. 911 .

Plate XXVI. ʿAja'ib Sell vol. IV, 1b-2**a**

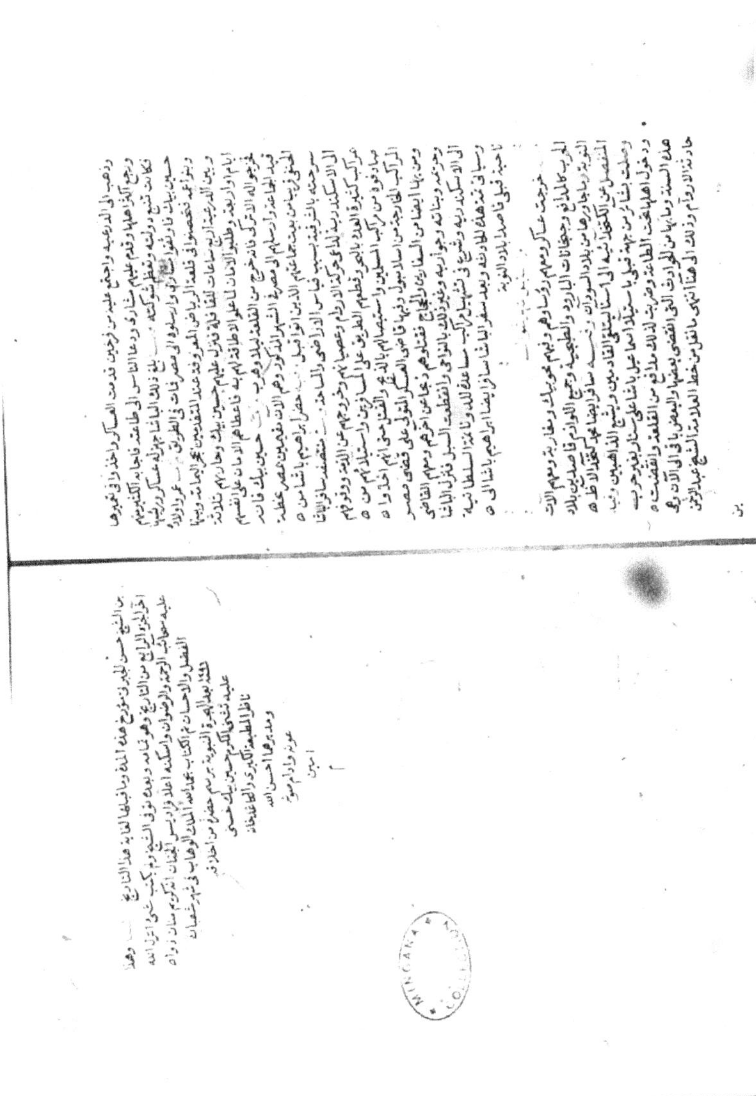

Al-Jabarti, 'Aja'ib, the colophon of vol. IV, Mingana Manuscript Collection, Selly Oak Colleges Library, Birmingham, no. 911

Plate XXVII. ‘Aja’ib Sell vol. IV, colophon

al-Jabari, 'Aja'ib al-Athar, the title page of vol. IV,f. 1a. Khuda Bakhsh Library Patna, no. 1082-1083.

Plate XXVIII. ʿAja'ib Khud vol. IV, 1a

al-Jabarti: 'Aja'ib al-Athar, vol. IV, ff. 11b-2a , Khuda Bakhsh Library Patna, no. 1082-1083.

Plate XXIX. ʿAja'ib Khud vol. IV, 1b-2a

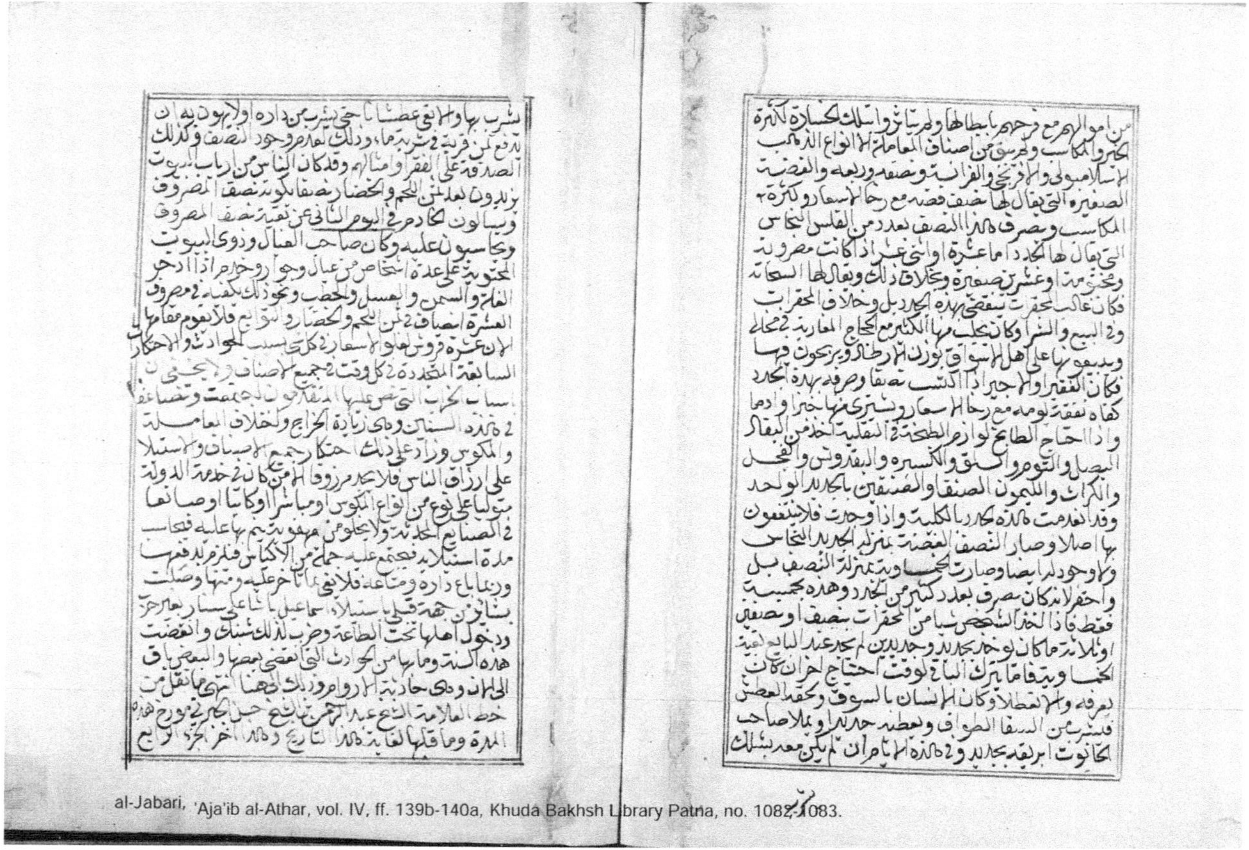

Plate XXX. ʿAja'ib Khud vol. IV, 139b-140a

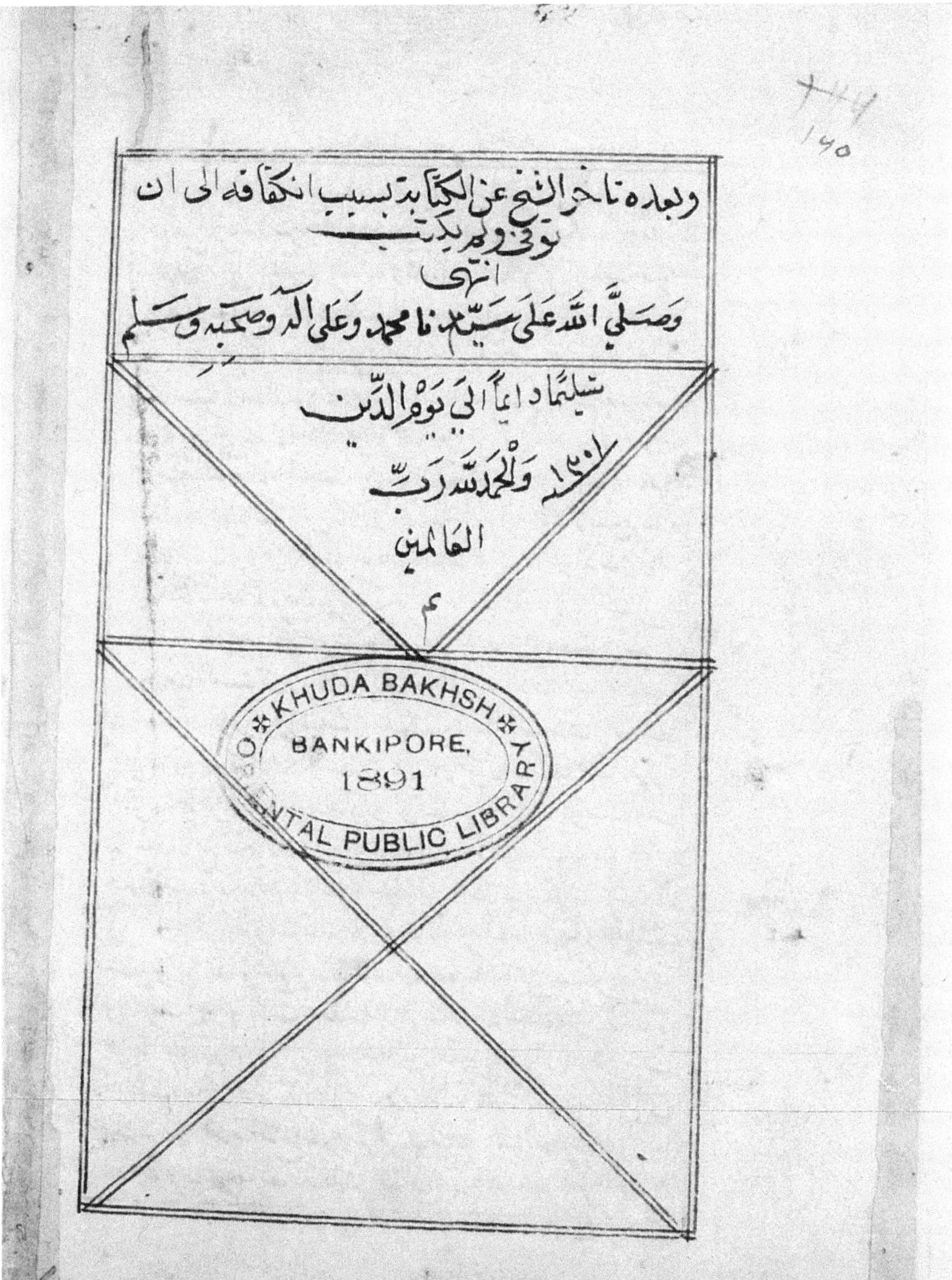

al-Jabari, 'Aja'ib al-Athar, colophon of vol. IV, Khuda Bakhsh Library Patna, no. 1082-1083.

Plate XXXI. ʻAja'ib Khud vol. IV, colophon